D1068495

THE PAPERS OF ULYSSES S. GRANT

THE PAPERS OF

ULYSSES S. GRANT

Volume 7:

December 9, 1862 – March 31, 1863

Edited by John Y. Simon

SOUTHERN ILLINOIS UNIVERSITY PRESS

CARBONDALE AND EDWARDSVILLE

FEFFER & SIMONS, INC.

LONDON AND AMSTERDAM

Library of Congress Cataloging in Publication Data (*Revised*)

Grant, Ulysses Simpson, Pres. U.S., 1822–1885.
   The papers of Ulysses S. Grant.

   Prepared under the auspices of the Ulysses S. Grant Association.
   Bibliographical footnotes.
   CONTENTS—v. 1. 1837–1861.—v. 2. April–September 1861.
—v. 3. October 1, 1861–January 7, 1862.—v. 4. January 8–March 31,
1862.—v. 5. April 1–August 31, 1862.—v. 6. September 1–December 8, 1862.—v. 7. December 9, 1862–March 31, 1863.

   1. Grant, Ulysses Simpson, Pres. U.S., 1822–1885. 2. United
States—History—Civil War, 1861–1865—Campaigns and battles—
Sources. 3. United States—Politics and government—1869–1877—
Sources. I. Simon, John Y., ed. II. Ulysses S. Grant Association.
E660.G756 1967   973.8′2′0924   67–10725
ISBN 0-8093-0880-0 (v. 7)

To George Roberts Jones (1883–1975)

Contents

Maps and Illustrations

Introduction

===

ON DECEMBER 9, 1862, Major General Ulysses S. Grant, with headquarters at Oxford, Mississippi, had advanced in the previous five weeks from his base in Tennessee halfway toward Vicksburg. He planned to establish a major supply base at Grenada for a continued advance down the Mississippi Central Railroad to Jackson, while Major General William T. Sherman embarked at Memphis for a direct assault on Vicksburg. Later that month, Confederate cavalry raids destroyed the U.S. base at Holly Springs and cut supply and communication lines; then Sherman's expedition met a bloody repulse at Chickasaw Bayou. In response to the raids, Grant withdrew most of his troops from northern Mississippi and went to Memphis. Reconsidering later his abandonment of the overland campaign against Vicksburg, Grant concluded that if he had then known the demoralized condition of his opponents and the abundance of supplies in Mississippi, he would have continued to advance despite the raids.

If December, 1862, had been a bad month for Grant, it was even worse for Major General Ambrose E. Burnside and the Army of the Potomac, disastrously repulsed at Fredericksburg. At the end of the month in middle Tennessee the battle of Murfreesboro or Stone's River brought the Army of the Cumberland under Major General William S. Rosecrans heavy casualties and no conclusive results. Stung by Democratic resurgence in the fall elections of 1862, the administration desperately needed to turn the tide of war. New government policy implemented by the Emancipation Proclamation on January 1, 1863, and beginning efforts to recruit Negro troops divided public opinion through the North, and the controversy extended into Grant's army.

Early in 1863, Grant joined the river expedition against Vicksburg. Armed with special authority from President Lincoln, Major General John A. McClernand had assumed command on January 4. Unless Grant personally commanded the army before Vicksburg, he would leave it in the hands of a subordinate whose ability he distrusted and whose ambition he detested. Before leaving Memphis, Grant denounced McClernand's expedition to Arkansas Post as a "wild goose chase," but later learned that it had been planned by Sherman and had produced a notable victory. After assuming command in late January, Grant tried a variety of approaches to the Confederate bastion of Vicksburg.

All in all, it was a winter of frustration. Protected by the Mississippi River on the west and by a delta network of swollen rivers on the north, Vicksburg could only be approached feasibly from the south or east, and Grant's downriver expedition could not reach this ground without passing Vicksburg. To gain position, U.S. forces tried to enlarge a canal across the tongue of land opposite Vicksburg, begun and abandoned the previous summer by an earlier expedition, and also to construct another bypass canal leading through Lake Providence, Louisiana. Two expeditions sought to reach the Yazoo River, one through the Yazoo Pass, the other through Steele's Bayou. All failed to achieve their objectives, and the only bright spot was provided by the success of a few naval vessels in running the Vicksburg batteries, an experiment which foreshadowed the eventual success of the campaign.

Grant was no closer to capturing Vicksburg at the end of the winter, and his position had worsened. Although his troops had seen little military action, camping in the Mississippi River lowlands had decimated the army through disease. Inactivity weakened morale throughout the ranks and made Grant the target of criticism. Politicians, some of them encouraged by Grant's subordinates, began to doubt Grant's ability to capture Vicksburg. Aware of dissatisfaction, Grant had no apparent reaction, but calmly continued to plan his campaign.

By January, 1863, Grant and his staff were receiving an increasing flow of reports and correspondence, forwarding much of it according to established military procedures. Staff officers often prepared formal letters and endorsements for Grant's signature on days when he was away from his headquarters. Grant endorsed many items himself, but so briefly and formally as to contribute little to the documentary record of his career. Such endorsements and equally perfunctory endorsements addressed to Grant will henceforth be omitted from these volumes. Many covering letters from Grant to the War Department, periodically transmitting official papers and updating files, and signatures on returns will also be omitted. These omissions reduce the number of miscellaneous, unrelated items in the Calendar of each volume without eliminating important, revealing, or unusual documents.

We are indebted to W. Neil Franklin, Karl L. Trever, and Richard E. Wood for searching the National Archives; to Barbara Long for maps; to Anita Anderson, Frances Child, and Deborah Pittman for typing; to Harriet Simon for proofreading; to L. Kay Allen, Richard T. Boss, Kathy Heggemeier, and Karen Kendall, graduate students at Southern Illinois University, for research assistance; and to John M. Hoffmann and David L. Wilson, Ulysses S. Grant Association, for research and editorial assistance.

Financial support for the Ulysses S. Grant Association for the period during which this volume was prepared came from Southern Illinois University and the National Historical Publications and Records Commission.

JOHN Y. SIMON

December 29, 1977

Editorial Procedure

1. Editorial Insertions

A. Words or letters in roman type within brackets represent editorial reconstruction of parts of manuscripts torn, mutilated, or illegible.

B. [. . .] or [— — —] within brackets represent lost material which cannot be reconstructed. The number of dots represents the approximate number of lost letters; dashes represent lost words.

C. Words in *italic* type within brackets represent material such as dates which were not part of the original manuscript.

D. Other material crossed out is indicated by ~~cancelled type~~.

E. Material raised in manuscript, as "4th," has been brought in line, as "4th."

2. Symbols Used to Describe Manuscripts

AD	Autograph Document
ADS	Autograph Document Signed
ADf	Autograph Draft
ADfS	Autograph Draft Signed
AES	Autograph Endorsement Signed
AL	Autograph Letter
ALS	Autograph Letter Signed
ANS	Autograph Note Signed
D	Document
DS	Document Signed

Df	Draft
DfS	Draft Signed
ES	Endorsement Signed
LS	Letter Signed

3. *Military Terms and Abbreviations*

Act.	Acting
Adjt.	Adjutant
AG	Adjutant General
AGO	Adjutant General's Office
Art.	Artillery
Asst.	Assistant
Bvt.	Brevet
Brig.	Brigadier
Capt.	Captain
Cav.	Cavalry
Col.	Colonel
Co.	Company
C.S.A.	Confederate States of America
Dept.	Department
Div.	Division
Gen.	General
Hd. Qrs.	Headquarters
Inf.	Infantry
Lt.	Lieutenant
Maj.	Major
Q. M.	Quartermaster
Regt.	Regiment or regimental
Sgt.	Sergeant
USMA	United States Military Academy, West Point, N.Y.
Vols.	Volunteers

4. *Short Titles and Abbreviations*

| ABPC | *American Book-Prices Current* (New York, 1895–) |
| CG | *Congressional Globe* Numbers following represent the Congress, session, and page. |

J. G. Cramer   Jesse Grant Cramer, ed., *Letters of Ulysses S. Grant to his Father and his Youngest Sister, 1857–78* (New York and London, 1912)

DAB   *Dictionary of American Biography* (New York, 1928–36)

Garland   Hamlin Garland, *Ulysses S. Grant: His Life and Character* (New York, 1898)

HED   *House Executive Documents*

HMD   *House Miscellaneous Documents*

HRC   *House Reports of Committees* Numbers following *HED, HMD,* or *HRC* represent the number of the Congress, the session, and the document.

Ill. AG Report   J. N. Reece, ed., *Report of the Adjutant General of the State of Illinois* (Springfield, 1900)

Lewis   Lloyd Lewis, *Captain Sam Grant* (Boston, 1950)

Lincoln, Works   Roy P. Basler, Marion Dolores Pratt, and Lloyd A. Dunlap, eds., *The Collected Works of Abraham Lincoln* (New Brunswick, 1953–55)

Memoirs   *Personal Memoirs of U. S. Grant* (New York, 1885–86)

O.R.   *The War of the Rebellion: A Compilation of the Official Records of the Union and Confederate Armies* (Washington, 1880–1901)

O.R. (Navy)   *Official Records of the Union and Confederate Navies in the War of the Rebellion* (Washington, 1894–1927) Roman numerals following *O.R.* or *O.R.* (Navy) represent the series and the volume.

PUSG   John Y. Simon, ed., *The Papers of Ulysses S. Grant* (Carbondale and Edwardsville, 1967–)

Richardson   Albert D. Richardson, *A Personal History of Ulysses S. Grant* (Hartford, Conn., 1868)

SED   *Senate Executive Documents*

SMD   *Senate Miscellaneous Documents*

SRC   *Senate Reports of Committees* Numbers following *SED, SMD,* or *SRC* represent the number of the Congress, the session, and the document.

USGA Newsletter   *Ulysses S. Grant Association Newsletter*

Young   John Russell Young, *Around the World with General Grant* (New York, 1879)

5. Location Symbols

CLU	University of California at Los Angeles, Los Angeles, Calif.
CoHi	Colorado State Historical Society, Denver, Colo.
CSmH	Henry E. Huntington Library, San Marino, Calif.
CtY	Yale University, New Haven, Conn.
CU-B	Bancroft Library, University of California, Berkeley, Calif.
DLC	Library of Congress, Washington, D.C. Numbers following DLC-USG represent the series and volume of military records in the USG papers.
DNA	National Archives, Washington, D.C. Additional numbers identify record groups.
IaHA	Iowa State Department of History and Archives, Des Moines, Iowa.
I-ar	Illinois State Archives, Springfield, Ill.
IC	Chicago Public Library, Chicago, Ill.
ICarbS	Southern Illinois University, Carbondale, Ill.
ICHi	Chicago Historical Society, Chicago, Ill.
ICN	Newberry Library, Chicago, Ill.
ICU	University of Chicago, Chicago, Ill.
IHi	Illinois State Historical Library, Springfield, Ill.
In	Indiana State Library, Indianapolis, Ind.
InHi	Indiana Historical Society, Indianapolis, Ind.
InNd	University of Notre Dame, Notre Dame, Ind.
InU	Indiana University, Bloomington, Ind.
KHi	Kansas State Historical Society, Topeka, Kan.
MdAN	United States Naval Academy Museum, Annapolis, Md.
MH	Harvard University, Cambridge, Mass.
MHi	Massachusetts Historical Society, Boston, Mass.
MiD	Detroit Public Library, Detroit, Mich.
MiU-C	William L. Clements Library, University of Michigan, Ann Arbor, Mich.
MoSHi	Missouri Historical Society, St. Louis, Mo.
NHi	New-York Historical Society, New York, N.Y.
NIC	Cornell University, Ithaca, N.Y.
NjP	Princeton University, Princeton, N.J.

NjR	Rutgers University, New Brunswick, N.J.
NN	New York Public Library, New York, N.Y.
NNP	Pierpont Morgan Library, New York, N.Y.
OClWHi	Western Reserve Historical Society, Cleveland, Ohio.
OFH	Rutherford B. Hayes Library, Fremont, Ohio.
OHi	Ohio Historical Society, Columbus, Ohio.
OrHi	Oregon Historical Society, Portland, Ore.
PHi	Historical Society of Pennsylvania, Philadelphia, Pa.
PPRF	Rosenbach Foundation, Philadelphia, Pa.
RPB	Brown University, Providence, R.I.
TxHR	Rice University, Houston, Tex.
USG 3	Maj. Gen. Ulysses S. Grant 3rd, Clinton, N.Y.
USMA	United States Military Academy Library, West Point, N.Y.
ViU	University of Virginia, Charlottesville, Va.
WHi	State Historical Society of Wisconsin, Madison, Wis.
Wy-Ar	Wyoming State Archives and Historical Department, Cheyenne, Wyo.
WyU	University of Wyoming, Laramie, Wyo.

Chronology

DECEMBER 9, 1862–MARCH 31, 1863

Dec. 9. USG prepared to send cav. under Col. T. Lyle Dickey to cut the Mobile and Ohio Railroad.

Dec. 13. Maj. Gen. Ambrose E. Burnside suffered a major defeat in the battle of Fredericksburg, Va.

Dec. 15. C.S.A. Brig. Gen. Nathan B. Forrest crossed the Tennessee River on an expedition into west Tenn. to cut USG's lines.

Dec. 16. At New Orleans, Maj. Gen. Nathaniel P. Banks assumed command of the Dept. of the Gulf, replacing Maj. Gen. Benjamin F. Butler.

Dec. 17. USG issued General Orders No. 11 expelling all Jews from the Dept. of the Tenn. On Jan. 4, 1863, Maj. Gen. Henry W. Halleck ordered USG to revoke these orders.

Dec. 18. USG received orders to reorganize troops in the Dept. of the Tenn. into the 13th Army Corps, commanded by Maj. Gen. John A. McClernand; the 15th Army Corps, commanded by Maj. Gen. William T. Sherman; the 16th Army Corps, commanded by Maj. Gen. Stephen A. Hurlbut; and the 17th Army Corps, commanded by Maj. Gen. James B. McPherson.

Dec. 18. Forrest defeated U.S. cav. at Lexington, Tenn.

Dec. 19. Dickey returned from his cav. expedition with word that C.S.A. Maj. Gen. Earl Van Dorn's cav. was advancing on Holly Springs, Miss.

Dec. 20. Van Dorn captured Holly Springs and destroyed USG's supplies. USG began to withdraw his army northward.

DEC. 20. Forrest captured Humboldt and Trenton, Tenn.

DEC. 29. Sherman's army was repulsed at Chickasaw Bayou, Miss.

DEC. 31. Brig. Gen. Jeremiah C. Sullivan engaged Forrest at Parker's Cross-Roads, Tenn.

DEC. 31. Maj. Gen. William S. Rosecrans and C.S.A. Gen. Braxton Bragg fought indecisively at Murfreesboro, or Stone's River, Tenn. The battle continued intermittently through Jan. 2, 1863.

1863

JAN. 1. President Abraham Lincoln issued the Emancipation Proclamation.

JAN. 4. McClernand superseded Sherman in command of the army near Vicksburg and began to move toward Arkansas Post or Fort Hindman on the Arkansas River.

JAN. 4. USG ordered McPherson to withdraw from the Tallahatchie River.

JAN. 9. USG left Holly Springs for Memphis, arriving the next day.

JAN. 10. McClernand attacked Arkansas Post, capturing it the next day.

JAN. 11. Learning of the Arkansas Post expedition, USG telegraphed to Halleck that it was a "wild goose chase."

JAN. 12. Halleck authorized USG to relieve McClernand.

JAN. 13. USG ordered McClernand to return to Vicksburg and decided to take personal command of the expedition.

JAN. 16. USG left Memphis for Vicksburg.

JAN. 17. USG was at Helena, Ark.

JAN. 18. At Napoleon, Ark., USG conferred with McClernand, Sherman, and Act. Rear Admiral David D. Porter about plans for the Vicksburg expedition.

JAN. 19. USG returned to Memphis.

JAN. 21. Halleck authorized USG to command troops in Ark. who could cooperate in the Mississippi River campaign.

JAN. 25. Lincoln appointed Maj. Gen. Joseph Hooker to command the Army of the Potomac.

JAN. 28. USG arrived at Young's Point, La.

JAN. 29. USG ordered the levee cut leading to Yazoo Pass, planning an expedition to approach Vicksburg from the north. The levee was cut on Feb. 3.

JAN. 30. USG organized an expedition to Lake Providence, La., in an effort to get below Vicksburg.

JAN. 30. USG assumed command of the Vicksburg expedition, returning McClernand to the 13th Army Corps.

FEB. 2. U.S.S. *Queen of the West*, commanded by Col. Charles R. Ellet, ran the Vicksburg batteries, damaging but not sinking the steamboat *City of Vicksburg*.

FEB. 5. USG visited Lake Providence.

FEB. 12–13. USG again visited Lake Providence.

FEB. 13. USG revoked orders issued by Hurlbut prohibiting circulation of the *Chicago Times*.

FEB. 13. U.S.S. *Indianola* successfully passed the Vicksburg batteries.

FEB. 14. The *Queen of the West* ran aground in the Red River and was captured by C.S.A. forces.

FEB. 24. The *Queen of the West* sank the *Indianola*.

FEB. 25. Light draft U.S. gunboats entered Yazoo Pass.

MAR. 3. Lincoln signed a bill providing an effective draft.

MAR. 11. U.S. gunboats of the Yazoo Pass expedition attacked Fort Pemberton on the Yazoo River. Further unsuccessful attacks occurred on March 13 and 16.

MAR. 14. Porter began the Steele's Bayou expedition in another effort to reach Vicksburg from the north.

MAR. 15. USG accompanied Porter on a reconnaissance of Steele's Bayou.

MAR. 16. USG sent troops under Sherman to support the Steele's Bayou expedition.

MAR. 19. U.S.S. *Hartford* and U.S.S. *Albatross*, commanded by Rear Admiral David G. Farragut, proceeding up the Mississippi River, passed C.S.A. batteries at Grand Gulf, Miss., and anchored near Warrenton, Miss.

MAR. 22. USG decided to abandon the Yazoo Pass expedition. On the same day, Porter abandoned the Steele's Bayou expedition.

MAR. 25. U.S. rams *Lancaster* and *Switzerland* ran the Vicksburg batteries. The *Lancaster* was sunk and the *Switzerland* disabled.

MAR. 29. USG decided to send troops under McClernand to New Carthage, La., preparatory to crossing the Mississippi River south of Vicksburg.

MAR. 29. Frederick Dent Grant, age twelve, joined his father for the Vicksburg campaign.

The Papers of Ulysses S. Grant
December 9, 1862 – March 31, 1863

Proclamation

————

> Head-Quarters, 13th Army Corps,
> Department of the Tennessee,
> Oxford, Mississippi, Dec. 9th., 1862.

To the People of West Tennessee:

To enable the people of West Tennessee to send Representatives to Congress, and re-establish civil government among them, under the Constitution and laws of the United States, notice is hereby given, that an election will be held in the Eighth Ninth, and Tenth Congressional Districts of the State of Tennessee, on Wednesday, the twenty-fourth day of December,[1] A. D., 1862, for the election of Representatives to the Congress of the United States of America, and such County and State Officers, as, under the laws of the State of Tennessee, the people were entitled to elect at the time of the breaking out of the rebellion.

The election will be conducted, as nearly as may be, in conformity with the laws in force regulating the same, in the year of our Lord eighteen hundred and sixty. Judges and Clerks of election, will be chosen by the legal voters in each Election Precinct, one of which Judges will administer to the other Judges and Clerks so chosen, the oath required to be administered to Judges and Clerks of Election, before entering upon their duties as such, by the laws in force at the time aforesaid, and will, in turn, have the same oath administered to him by one of the said Judges.

The Polls will be opened at ten o'clock a. m., and close at four o'clock p. m., and when Judges and Clerks of Election are not chosen by the qualified voters, District and local Millitary Commanders will appoint them, and cause the Polls to be opened and votes received.

No person will be permitted to be a candidate for any office at said election who would not be qualified to fill the same under the laws of the United States.

The Election returns will be duly certified in accordance with the laws of the State of Tennessee, as they existed at the time aforesaid, and sent to the commanding officer at Memphis, or Jackson, Tenn., as may be most convenient, who will forward them to his excellency, Andrew Johnson, Governor of the State of Tennessee, at Nashville, giving at the same time the result of said Election, so far as may come to their knowledge, to the Press.

Should His Excellency, Andrew Johnson, Governor of the State of Tennessee, issue a call for an Election, the foregoing will be null and void, and in any event is subject to his approval.[2]

(Signed.)   U. S. GRANT,
Major General.

Printed, DLC-Robert T. Lincoln.

On Oct. 31, 1862, Emerson Etheridge, clerk of the U.S. House of Representatives, wrote to USG. "I have the Presidents approval in sending you the accompanying letter. The signature is the Presidents, and the body of the letter is an exact copy of one recently forwarded to Govr. Johnson. I feel assured that so soon as Govr. Johnson shall, by proclaimation, fix a day for the election of members of Congress, you will give him your co-operation: And I send you the letter of the President, in advance of Govr. Johnson's proclamation, that you may have the authority of the President for informing the people that they will soon have an opportunity to be again represented in Congress." ALS, DNA, RG 393, Dept. of the Tenn., Letters Received. On Oct. 21, President Abraham Lincoln wrote to USG, Governor Andrew Johnson, and "all having military, naval, and civil authority under the United States within the State of Tennessee." "The bearer of this, Thomas R. Smith, a citizen of Tennessee, goes to that state, seeking to have such of the people thereof as desire to avoid the unsatisfactory prospect before them, and to have peace, again upon the old terms under the Constitution of the United States, to manifest such desire by elections of members to the Congress of the United States particularly, and perhaps a legislature, State officers, and a United States' Senator, friendly to their object. I shall be glad for you and each of you to aid him, & all others acting for this object, as much as possible. In all available ways give the people a chance to express their wishes at these elections. Follow law, and forms of law as far as convenient; but at all events get the expression of the largest number of the people possible. All see how such action will connect with, and affect the proclamation of Sept. 22nd. Of course the men elected should be gentlemen of character, willing to swear support to the constitution as of old, & known to be above reasonable suspicion of duplicity." ALS, NNP. *O.R.*, III, ii, 675–76. The letter in NNP, fully in Lincoln's hand, is not the actual letter received by USG. The wording of the letter was apparently developed as a form for introducing Unionists to U.S. authorities in the South. See Lincoln, *Works*, V, 462–63, 500.

On Nov. 3, Col. James J. Dollins, Humboldt, Tenn., telegraphed to Lt. Col. John A. Rawlins. "many prominent citizens of this vicinity have applied to me for permission to hold a meeting at this place preparatory to holding a convention for the purpose of nominating a man to represent them in the federal congress from this congressional district they seem to be in good faith & say they are tired of war & want to quit & comply with the Presidents proclamation shall I grant them the privelege—They also desire to communicate by letter to their friends at different points upon this subject open to my surveillance & approval shall I permit them thus to communicate. please answer immediately as they are urging the move strongly" Telegram received, DNA, RG 393, Dept. of the Tenn., Telegrams Received. For a similar telegram of Nov. 6 from Col. William W. Lowe to Lincoln and the reply, see Lincoln, *Works*, V, 489–90. On Dec. 12, Maj. Gen. Stephen A. Hurlbut, Memphis, telegraphed to Maj. Gen. Henry W. Halleck. "I am strongly urged by the Citizens in this District to order an election for Member of Congress. I have declined to do so as not within my authority I think it should be ordered by Congress. I submit the question & ask instructions. It is so difficult to reach Genl Grants Head Quarters that I report this matter direct" Telegram received, DNA, RG 107, Telegrams Collected (Bound). On Dec. 17, Halleck telegraphed to Hurlbut. "The ordering of elections in Tenn properly belongs to the Governor. Please consult him." Telegram received, *ibid.*

1. On Dec. 10, Rawlins telegraphed to Brig. Gen. Mason Brayman, Bolivar, that the original proclamation calling an election for Thursday, Dec. 26, should be corrected to Wednesday, Dec. 24. Telegram received, Brayman Papers, ICHi.

2. On Dec. 16, Brayman telegraphed to USG. "I have received Gov. Johnson's Proclamations ordering the Election in the ninth and tenth Districts, on the twenty-ninth (29th) instant." ADfS, *ibid.*; telegram received, DNA, RG 393, Dept. of the Tenn., Telegrams Received. Previously, a convention held in the 9th Congressional District of Tenn., in northwestern Tenn., had determined to hold an election on Dec. 13 unless Johnson formally proclaimed another date, and an election was held then before many voters knew of his proclamation. On Johnson's election day of Dec. 29, C.S.A. Brig. Gen. Nathan B. Forrest's raid had so disrupted the area that Hurlbut postponed the election to Jan. 20, 1863, but again many voters went to the polls. On all three dates Alvin Hawkins won overwhelmingly, but was denied a seat by the U.S. House of Representatives because of irregularities in the election process. *CG*, 37-3, 888, 1391, 1540, 1548; *HRC*, 37-3-46. In addition, according to a statement of Dec. 26, 1862, of Sheriff John Aldredge, nearly 800 voters in McNairy County in the 10th Congressional District in southwestern Tenn. voted on USG's date of Dec. 24, with the majority favoring Lt. Col. Fielding Hurst. ADS, DNA, RG 109, Union Provost Marshals' Files of Papers Relating to Two or More Civilians. No claimant from this district appeared before Congress.

On Jan. 16, 1863, USG telegraphed to Johnson. "The Union men here deem it advisable not to hold an election in this District now and ask that it be postponed until an election be ordered for Governor members of the Legislature and Representatives. If you will postpone it notify me by telegraph" Copies, DLC-USG, V, 18, 30; DNA, RG 393, Dept. of the Tenn., Letters Sent.

On Dec. 16, 1862, Brig. Gen. Leonard F. Ross, Oxford, Miss., wrote to Richard H. Parham. "Yours of the 12th Inst is recd and I have today had an interview with Gen Grant on the subject of our correspondence—The General thinks that he has no power to act in the matter—that in the absence of any order from the President on the subject, the people must act primarily—He recommends the holding of public meetings throughout the District for the purpose of ascertainig the sentiment of the people, and the organization of a Government *de novo* —that it must originate with the people—The time as you remark is too short and the condition of the country too unsettled to hold a formal election before the 1st of January—but could you not hold a public meeting—agree upon a day to select a delegate—appoint judges & clerks—and let a delegate to Congress be selected? The delegate thus selected might not be recognized as a member of Congress, but he would be, to say the least a citizen of Mississippi authorized to speak and act for those who have sent him—The time is short and if any action is taken it must be at once—Let me hear from you—I am expecting to move again in a couple of days" ALS, *ibid.*, RG 217, Southern Claims Commission, Claim No. 360.

To Maj. Gen. Henry W. Halleck

Oxford Miss. 5 P M
Decr. 9, [*18*]62.

MAJ GEN HALLECK.

The number of prisoners taken on the advance here proves over 1.200[1] Besides these many deserters come in daily to take the oath of allegiance & return hom to the border states. I have permitted a great many from Ky, Tennessee & Missouri, of those taken in arms to take the oath & go home,   A letter from Gen McClernand,[2] just rec'd states that he expects to go forward in a few days. Sherman has already gone   The enterprise would be much safer in charge of the latter

U. S. GRANT
Maj Genl

Telegram received, DNA, RG 94, Generals' Papers and Books, Telegrams Received by Gen. Halleck; *ibid.*, RG 107, Telegrams Collected (Bound); *ibid.*, Telegrams Collected (Unbound); copies, *ibid.*, Telegrams Received in Cipher; *ibid.*, RG 393, Dept. of the Tenn., Hd. Qrs. Correspondence; DLC-USG, V, 5, 8, 24, 88, 91. *O.R.*, I, xvii, part 1, 475. See letter to Maj. Gen. John A. McClernand, Dec. 18, 1862.

1. On Dec. 9, 1862, Lt. Col. John A. Rawlins wrote to Col. John V. D. Du Bois, Holly Springs. "One Brigade has been ordered to report to you at

Waterford from Gen. Sherman's command. You will make such disposition of them as to guard the Rail Road from that place south to Abbeville. All prisoners of War you now have at Holly Springs cause triplicate rolls of them to be made, and send duplicates of same to Dept. Hd Qrs. at Holly Springs to be forwarded to Washington, and the prisoners in charge of a Commissioned Officer to Cairo to report to Gen. Tuttle to be forwarded on Cartel boat to Vicksburg, Miss." Copy, DLC-USG, V, 91. This message is entered as written by USG, *ibid.*, V, 18, 30; DNA, RG 393, Dept. of the Tenn., Letters Sent.

    2. This letter has not been found. In view of Maj. Gen. John A. McClernand's regular habit of retaining copies of outgoing correspondence, USG probably derived this information from a letter addressed to someone else.

To Maj. Gen. William S. Rosecrans

———

                    By TELEGRAPH FROM Oxford [*Dec. 9, 1862*]
To MAJ GEN ROSECRANS

    The following despatch just recd—Washington Eleven five A M to Maj Genl Grant Oxford,

        Rolls Genl Rosecrans prisoner have not arrived   cannot duplicate be sent   exchange cannot be made till they are recd   rolls of about ~~one hundred~~ one thousand delivered at vicksburg by capt E M Wood[1] C. S. have been received (Signed) W HOFFMAN[2] C. G. P.[3]

    Please answer col Hoffman

                    U S GRANT
                    Maj Genl

Telegram received, DNA, RG 393, Dept. of the Cumberland, Telegrams Received; copies, *ibid.*, Dept. of the Tenn., Letters Sent; DLC-USG, V, 18, 30, 91. On Dec. 9, 1862, Maj. Gen. William S. Rosecrans telegraphed to USG. "The duplicates were left with the official reports at Corinth Gen McKeans officers gave one of them to the Rebel officers" Telegram received, DNA, RG 393, Dept. of the Tenn., Telegrams Received; copies, *ibid.*, Dept. of the Cumberland, Telegrams Sent; *ibid.*, RG 107, Telegrams Collected (Unbound). On Dec. 10, Brig. Gen. Grenville M. Dodge, Corinth, telegraphed to Col. William Hoffman. "I find in the old P. M. Genl office Rolls of prisoners taken at Iuka Corinth & Hatchie. Shall they be copied for safety before sending or sent by messengers" Telegram received, *ibid.*

    On Dec. 1, Hoffman had telegraphed to USG. "To effect exchanges duplicate rolls of prisoners captured by Genl Rosecrans are required. Have any been forwarded, where." ALS (telegram sent), *ibid.*, RG 249, Letters Sent (Press); telegram received, *ibid.*, RG 393, Dept. of the Tenn., Telegrams Received. On the same day, USG telegraphed to Hoffman. "Instructions were given to Gen Rosecrans to forward to A Genl office at Washn D C the proper Roll of prisoners captured & paroled those captured by Genl Ord & Hurlbut were forwarded" Telegram received, *ibid.*, RG 249, Telegrams Received; *ibid.*, RG 107, Telegrams Collected (Bound); copies, *ibid.*, RG 393, Dept. of the Tenn., Letters Sent; DLC-USG, V, 18, 30, 91.

On Dec. 7, Hoffman wrote to Col. Edward D. Townsend, AGO, that only partial rolls of prisoners captured at Iuka and Corinth had reached him. On Jan. 7, 1863, Townsend endorsed a copy of this letter to USG. Copy, DNA, RG 393, Dept. of the Tenn., Letters Received. On Dec. 19, 1862, Hoffman telegraphed to USG. "Duplicate rolls should accompany prisoners sent to Vicksburg for exchange one with a receipt to be returned by a message by the Adgt Genl for this office" ALS (telegram sent), *ibid.*, Telegrams Received; *ibid.*, RG 107, Telegrams Collected (Bound); telegram received, *ibid.*, RG 393, Dept. of the Tenn., Telegrams Received.

1. Ephraim M. Wood of Ohio, appointed capt., 15th U.S. Inf., as of May 14, 1861.
2. William Hoffman of N. Y., USMA 1829, fought in the Mexican War as capt., 6th Inf., and spent most of the time between wars on frontier duty. He was taken prisoner at San Antonio, Tex., in 1861. After his exchange, on Aug. 27, 1862, he was promoted to col., 3rd Inf., and appointed commissary gen. of prisoners.
3. Sent on Dec. 9. ALS (telegram sent), *ibid.*, RG 107, Telegrams Collected (Unbound); telegram received, *ibid.*, RG 393, Dept. of the Tenn., Telegrams Received.

To Col. John V. D. Du Bois

Oxford, Miss. Dec 9th 1862

Col. J. V. DuBois
Holly Springs, Miss.

Permission has been granted for Cotton speculators and Citizens of the North generally to come South as far as the Tallahatchie. Instructions from Washington are to encourage getting Cotton out of the country. Department orders have been published regulating this matter and any violation of them can be punished by sending the offender out of the Dept. Any order you have published different from this controvenes Dept orders and will have to be rescinded[1]

U. S. Grant
Maj Genl.

Copies, DLC-USG, V, 18, 30, 91; DNA, RG 393, Dept. of the Tenn., Letters Sent.

On Dec. 9, 1862, USG telegraphed to Brig. Gen. Jeremiah C. Sullivan, Jackson. "The Army now having penetrated far into Mississippi trade may be resumed in Tennessee subject only to Treasury restrictions and such other restrictions as local Commanders may deem necessary to preserve good order and discipline" Telegram received, *ibid.*, 16th Army Corps, 4th Division, Telegrams Received; copies, *ibid.*, Dept. of the Tenn., Letters Sent; DLC-USG, V, 18, 30, 91. *O.R.*, I, xvii, part 2, 396.

On Dec. 10, USG wrote to Lt. Col. Charles A. Reynolds, Holly Springs. "Take measures to secure all confiscated Cotton and Cotton brought in by public teams. Speculators violating orders will be reported to Post Commander who will expel them." Copies, DLC-USG, V, 18, 30, 91; DNA, RG 393, Dept. of the Tenn., Letters Sent. On the same day, USG wrote to Brig. Gen. John McArthur, Abbeville. "Have all Cotton brought in by Govt teams marked C. A. R. Chief Q. M. Holly Springs and when the Cars commence running ship it to him." Copies, *ibid.*

1. On Dec. 8, Col. John V. D. Du Bois, Holly Springs, issued General Orders No. 2. "On account of the scarcity of provisions, All Cotton-Speculators, Jews and other Vagrants having no honest means of support, except trading upon the miseries of their Country, and in general all persons from the North, not connected with the Army, who have no permission from the General Commanding to remain in this town, Will Leave in twenty four hours or they will be sent to duty in the trenches" Copy, Caleb Morgan Papers, Minn. Historical Society, St. Paul, Minn.; letter from Holly Springs, Dec. 9, *Missouri Republican*, Dec. 13, 1862; letter from Oxford, Dec. 11, *Chicago Tribune*, Dec. 18, 1862. In a letter to the editor, *Morning Chronicle*, Washington, Sept. 29, 1868, Du Bois stated that: "This order was revoked by Gen Grant and I was relieved from command on account of it." ALS, Morgan Papers, Minn. Historical Society. The possibility that Du Bois was responsible for USG's General Orders No. 11, Dec. 17, 1862, is discussed but dismissed in Bertram Wallace Korn, *American Jewry and the Civil War* (Philadelphia, 1951), pp. 138–40.

To Maj. Gen. Henry W. Halleck

Oxford Miss Dec 10, 12 M [*1862*]

MAJ GEN H W HALLECK

Following dispatch just recd from Corinth Miss Dec 10th 1862.

MAJ GENL U. S. GRANT

The news from Bragg is that Kirby Smith is at Mumfreesboro Breckenridge at Shelbyville[1] Bragg Short distance

from Tullahoma   The Rail Road is finished from ~~at H~~ Athens[2]
to Tenn. River thence to Huntsville. This may a/c for the
accelerating accumulation of forage on R R which runs from
Florence to that Rail Road. I have seen several men from
Braggs with 20 days furlough. They say Bragg intends to
stay where he is.

Provisions getting very scarce in Tennessee Valley &
North of it.   Signed M M DODGE[3] Brig Genl

U. S. GRANT
Maj Genl

Telegram received, DNA, RG 94, Generals' Papers and Books, Telegrams
Received by Gen. Halleck; *ibid.*, RG 107, Telegrams Collected (Bound); copies,
ibid., RG 393, Dept. of the Tenn., Hd. Qrs. Correspondence; DLC-USG, V, 5, 8,
24, 88, 91. *O.R.*, I, xvii, part 1, 475.

On Dec. 10, 1862, 3:00 P.M., USG again telegraphed to Maj. Gen. Henry W.
Halleck. "One of our soldiers who escaped from Rebels and returned reports
Price fifteen miles south of Grenada on the Yazoo   From other sources I learn
that their army is retreating to Jackson" Telegram received, DNA, RG 94,
Generals' Papers and Books, Telegrams Received by Gen. Halleck; *ibid.*, RG 107,
Telegrams Collected (Bound); copies, *ibid.*, Telegrams Received in Cipher; *ibid.*,
RG 393, Dept. of the Tenn., Hd. Qrs. Correspondence; DLC-USG, V, 5, 8, 24,
88, 91. *O.R.*, I, xvii, part 2, 475.

1. Shelbyville, Tenn., on the Duck River, about twenty-three miles north-
west of Tullahoma.

2. Athens, Tenn., on the East Tennessee and Georgia Railroad, about fifty
miles northeast of Chattanooga.

3. On Dec. 7, Lt. Col. John A. Rawlins had telegraphed to Brig. Gen.
Grenville M. Dodge, Corinth. "What news, if any from up the Tenn. or Bragg's
Army." Copies, DLC-USG, V, 18, 30, 91; Dodge Papers, IaHA; DNA, RG 393,
Dept. of the Tenn., Letters Sent. On the same day, Dodge telegraphed to Rawlins.
"I get news from Bragg daily but for a week it has been very conflicting   No
infantry has passed south of Tennessee river this side of Decatur up to yesterday
morning but the scout from Dalton Georgia says troops are going south from
Chattanooga by R R Daily but I do not believe they are anything but sick &
convalescent soldiers   on the Boyle R Road the road from Decatur south & from
Warrentown they are collecting large quantities of forage & stock & have been
at it for two weeks—One brigade of Withers division did not stop at Dalton but
went on to Chattanooga. All these scattering Cavalry North of the Tenn River
have come North & there is at least two thousand stretched along the line from
Cherokee to Saltillo at that place one or two regts of Cavalry & one of infantry
ready to give any time   A man from Mobile tonight says no troops are on that
road only at Meridian where they are moving a large number of cars towards
Jackson Enterprise Columbus & Saltillo. He says they have a large number of

men & wagons at work at Mobile & Columbus day & night on the fortifications. Rhoddy with six hundred 600 paid us a visit yesterday   done but little damage but passed through Iuka   His return with his whole force violating the agreement made as regards that place—Deserters from Price come in daily   one dozen today"   Telegram received, *ibid.*, Telegrams Received. On Dec. 10, Dodge telegraphed to USG. "Yesterday morng there was two Regts of cavalry at Saltillo & a few Infantry at Tupelo   they only form from Enterprise to this place"   Telegram received, *ibid.* Also on Dec. 10, Brig. Gen. Jeremiah C. Sullivan, Jackson, telegraphed to USG. "Scouts from Tennessee River report that Bragg is moving toward Florence. The rebels have large force, say between 6,000 and 8,000, on east side of Tennessee, from Duck River to Florence. My scouts have been sent to the river. I will report as soon as heard from." *O.R.*, I, xvii, part 2, 398. See telegram to Brig. Gen. Grenville M. Dodge, Dec. 11, 1862.

To Maj. Gen. Henry W. Halleck

Oxford Mississippi
December 10th 1862

MAJ. GEN. H. W. HALLECK,
GEN. IN CHIEF
WASHINGTON D. C.
GEN.

Permit me to recommend to you for your influance for promotion to the rank of Brig. Gen. Lieut. Col. Jas. A. Hardie, A. D. C. to Gen. McClellan. Col. Hardie was a classmate of mine and consequently an acquaintance of over twenty-three years has existed. I do not hesitate to say that he is well qualified for the position, having served continuously in the Army from the time of his graduation to the present time, and always enjoying the confidance of those with whom he has been associated.

Whilst a young 2d Lieutenant Col. Hardie was selected for the position of Major to Col. Stevenson's regiment,[1] and during that time was probably personally known to you.

The service is already retarded by the appointment of so many men without Military experiance that I feel as if a great benefit had been done every time an officer of this class is advanced.

I will regard it as a personal favor to myself if you will give this a favorable consideration.

> I am Gen. very respectfully
> your obt. svt.
> U. S. GRANT
> Maj. Gen.

ALS, deCoppet Collection, NjP. James A. Hardie of N. Y., USMA 1843, was capt., 3rd Art., on the eve of the Civil War. As lt. col., he served on the staff of Maj. Gen. George B. McClellan. Appointed brig. gen. of vols. as of Nov. 29, 1862, he declined the appointment to serve as maj., AGO. At the time Hardie solicited USG's endorsement, he also approached other officers; for selections from their letters, see [C. F. Benjamin], *Memoir of James Allen Hardie, Inspector-General, United States Army* (Washington, 1877), pp. 32–33.

1. As maj., 1st N. Y., Col. Jonathan D. Stevenson, Aug. 1, 1846–Oct. 26, 1848, Hardie served briefly as military commandant of San Francisco. *Ibid.*, pp. 13–14.

To Col. T. Lyle Dickey

> Hd Qrs. Dept of the Tenn.
> Oxford, Miss. Dec 10th 1862.

COL. T. LYLE DICKEY,
COMMDG CAVALRY DIVISION

The detail to accompany Col. McCulloughs remains and effects may be made.[1]

The train for provisions for part of your forces is now here. They will have to go to Waterford[2] and possibly Holly Springs.

Three Divisions are going to the front as far as the Yockna. On their approach I want the Cavalry to proceed as far as Water Valley,[3] especially if the bridges are standing to that point.[4]

You need not start on the other expedition[5] until you receive further orders from here.

Respectfully &c

U. S. Grant

Major General.

Copies, DLC-USG, V, 18, 30, 91; DNA, RG 393, Dept. of the Tenn., Letters Sent. *O.R.*, I, xvii, part 2, 398.

1. Lt. Col. William McCullough, 4th Ill. Cav., was killed at the engagement at Coffeeville, Miss., Dec. 5, 1862. See President Abraham Lincoln to Fanny McCullough, Dec. 23, Lincoln, *Works*, VI, 16–17. On Dec. 10, 2:00 P.M., Col. T. Lyle Dickey wrote to USG. "I am urging preparation with every energy—I find the greatest difficulty in the matter of horse shoeing The facilities are so defective that it progresses very slowly—I have directed wagons sent to Oxford for rations of hard bread salt Sugar & Coffee—The flag of truce party sent to recover the body of Lt Col McCullough has not returned—His little son in charge of his effects is at the Hospital at Oxford with Dr Luce 4th Ill Cav—by my direction awaiting the return of the party from Coffeeville—I wish very much to be allowed to detail a small party to take charge of the lad & effects & the body if recovered & take them to Bloomington—I expect the party this evening Where shall we find rations at Oxford & how soon must we start—Allow as much time for preparation as may be if you please" ALS, DNA, RG 393, Dept. of the Tenn., Letters Received. On Dec. 11, Dickey, Springdale, Miss., telegraphed to Lt. Col. John A. Rawlins. "Remains of Col McCollough are here & go forward at once Notify Lt Hyde who stays with Capt Osband to have MuCulloughs son & effects ready Enimies killed at Coffeeville estimated by the Enemy at 30 to 75" Telegram received, *ibid.*, Telegrams Received.

2. Waterford, Miss., about seven miles south of Holly Springs.

3. Water Valley, Miss., on the Mississippi Central Railroad, about seventeen miles south of Oxford.

4. Earlier on Dec. 10, USG wrote to Dickey. "Several Infantry Divisions will move up to the Yocona tomorrow. On their arrival I want the Cavalry moved forward to Water-Valley and as many of the rail road bridges saved as possible." Copies, DLC-USG, V, 18, 30, 91; DNA, RG 393, Dept. of the Tenn., Letters Sent. *O.R.*, I, xvii, part 2, 398.

5. On Dec. 9, Rawlins wrote to Dickey. "In making the detour east concerning which you have received instructions from the Genl. Commdg. select such of your Cavalry as you may deem most suitable for the expedition, leaving about half of your Cavalry force where they now are, for within the next forty eight (48) hours a strong Infantry and Artillery force will be moved from here to the place where you are now encamped and it is the intention to push southward with Cavalry in front." Copies, DLC-USG, V, 18, 30, 91; DNA, RG 393, Dept. of the Tenn., Letters Sent. *O.R.*, I, xvii, part 2, 395.

To Col. James B. Fry

Oxford Miss [*Dec.*] 11th [*1862*]

JAMES B. FRY A A G.

The additional aides De Camp in this Dept are Col. J. V. Dubois[1] Holly Springs W S Hillyer C. B. Lagow J Riggin genl Hallecks Staff & Col G P Ihrie Genl Wools Staff here Capt W L B Jenny Engineer at Memphis & Capt Wm Cassisic[2] Engr at Corinth   the latter in Genl Hallecks Staff

U S. GRANT M G

Telegram received, DNA, RG 94, Letters Received; *ibid.*, RG 107, Telegrams Collected (Bound); copies, *ibid.*, RG 393, Dept. of the Tenn., Hd. Qrs. Correspondence; DLC-USG, V, 5, 8, 18, 24, 30, 88, 91. James B. Fry of Ill., USMA 1847, a 1st lt. on the eve of the Civil War, had served as chief of staff for both Brig. Gen. Irvin McDowell and, after promotion to col., Maj. Gen. Don Carlos Buell. After Buell's removal from command, Fry was transferred to the AGO. On Dec. 10, 1862, Fry telegraphed to USG. "I am directed to call for a report of the Station name and rank of all additional aides de camp on duty with your Staff or who may be acting under your directions. The information is necessary to answer resolutions of inquiry made by the Senate." LS (telegram sent), DNA, RG 107, Telegrams Collected (Unbound); telegram received, *ibid.*, RG 393, Dept. of the Tenn., Telegrams Received.

1. On July 17, John V. D. Du Bois was confirmed as col., additional aide-de-camp, to rank from Feb. 19. Since Sept. 1, 1862, he had ranked as col., 1st Mo. Art., but resigned this position on Oct. 14.
2. Capt. William Kossak.

To Brig. Gen. Grenville M. Dodge

Oxford, Dec 11th 1862

GEN. DODGE, CORINTH, MISS.

Cavalry will leave Springdale[1] on Saturday[2] to strike Mobile road. Send out a force from Corinth to cooperate allowing them to go as far south as Tupelo. if practicable. Keep a sharp lookout for Bragg's force—should he approach I will reinforce you suffi-

ciently   you have a much more important command than that
of a division in the field—it would ~~be probably~~ probably be well
to send towards Iuka ~~to send a~~ at the same time you send south—

U. S. Grant
Maj Genl

Telegram received (incomplete), Dodge Papers, IaHA; copies, *ibid.*; DLC-USG,
V, 18, 30, 91; DNA, RG 393, Dept. of the Tenn., Letters Sent. *O.R.*, I, xvii,
part 2, 399.
On Dec. 11, 1862, Lt. Col. John A. Rawlins telegraphed to Brig. Gen.
Grenville M. Dodge. "Look out for Forrest's Cavalry on line of Rail road. Dis-
patch from Gen. Rosecrans would indicate he is threatening it at some point
though he does not state where." Copies, DLC-USG, V, 18, 30, 91; DNA,
RG 393, Dept. of the Tenn., Letters Sent. *O.R.*, I, xvii, part 2, 400. Rawlins also
sent an identical telegram to Brig. Gen. Jeremiah C. Sullivan, Jackson. Telegram
received, DNA, RG 393, 16th Army Corps, 4th Division, Telegrams Received.
On Dec. 10, Maj. Gen. William S. Rosecrans, Nashville, had telegraphed to USG.
"Tell the authorities ~~along th~~ along the Rail Road to look out for Forrest"
Copies, *ibid.*, RG 107, Telegrams Collected (Unbound); *ibid.*, RG 393, Dept. of
the Cumberland, Telegrams Sent. *O.R.*, I, xvii, part 2, 400; *ibid.*, I, xx, part 2,
150.
On Dec. 11, Dodge telegraphed to USG. "All my cavalry except one company with two regiments of infantry & one section of artillery was in Tuscumbia
this morning unless they met a larger force than I anticipated   I think they will
be back by Saturday morning   will that be in time for me to cooperate south   I
moved with infantry in wagons   I was very uneasy about Rumors that came from
that quarter and desired to ascertain facts"   Telegram received, DNA, RG 393,
Dept. of the Tenn., Telegrams Received. On Dec. 12, Dodge telegraphed to USG.
"One of my men has just arrived here from Murfreesboro via Columbia Waynesboro & Savannah. He brings nothing new from Braggs army but says that Forrest
is moving from Columbia to Waynesboro & thence west   He knows not at what
point. I intercepted a letter today from Pembertons army I judge from Med
Director to Surgeons at Iuka that says they are satisfied that grants army is too
strong for them & that they are going to divide their army into three divisions &
seperate so as to get him (grant) to divide his army. I send it for what it is worth"
Telegram received, *ibid.* On Dec. 12, Sullivan telegraphed to USG. "Scouts from
Tennessee River report at Bethel that Forrest's cavalry are marching via Waynesborough from Columbia, striking the river at Savannah. I will order all the roads
obstructed and try and force them south. Cannonading was heard in the direction
of Yellow Creek to-day from Bethel. The people of this district are flocking in to
take the oath. I allow them until Monday." *O.R.*, I, xvii, part 2, 405. See Col.
Addison S. Norton, La Grange, to Sullivan, Dec. 11, *ibid.*, p. 400.
Also on Dec. 12, USG telegraphed to Act. Rear Admiral David D. Porter.
"A large force of Rebel Cavalry is moving west from Columbia Tennessee
towards Savanah Tenn   Can a light Draft Gun boat get up there at this time"
Telegram received, DNA, RG 45, Correspondence of David D. Porter, Telegrams
Received; copies, *ibid.*, RG 393, Dept. of the Tenn., Letters Sent; DLC-USG,
V, 18, 30, 91. *O.R.*, I, xvii, part 2, 404; *O.R.* (Navy), I, xxiii, 626. On the same

day, Porter, Cairo, telegraphed to USG. "Two gun boats are working their way up Tennessee River but cannot get higher than 'Curds Ford'—one is ashore." ALS (telegram sent), DNA, RG 45, Correspondence of David D. Porter, Mississippi Squadron, General Letters (Press); telegram received, *ibid.*, RG 393, Dept. of the Tenn., Telegrams Received. *O.R.*, I, xvii, part 2, 404; *O.R.* (Navy), I, xxiii, 626.

Apparently a telegram similar or identical to that sent by Rawlins to Dodge and Sullivan was sent to Col. Isham N. Haynie, Bethel. On Dec. 11, Haynie telegraphed to USG. "Your dispatch recd concerning which I learn today from the Tennessee river as follows That rebel forces are making head quarters on Indian Creek 20 miles East of Savannah Bissell & coxs men my scouts do not report reinforcements but say forrest forces are in & about Columbia Rhodes men are said to have crossed to Alabama Not sure of it I expect to get word from Biffels camp tonight I have scouts extending from Hamburg to Clifton on the Tennessee they are citizen scouts but are reliable & active I have furnished them arms they are away from home & need subsistence. may I issue to them" Telegram received, DNA, RG 393, Military Division of the Miss., Letters Received. *O.R.*, I, xvii, part 2, 399. On the same day, USG telegraphed to Haynie. "You can furnish provisions to your scouts." Copies, DLC-USG, V, 18, 30, 91; DNA, RG 393, Dept. of the Tenn., Letters Sent. Also on Dec. 11, Haynie telegraphed to USG. "Scouts Perkins just in from Yellow-Creek 15 miles above Hamburg Reports Roddys men eight hundred 800 strong had left there at daylight this a m says there are several ferry boats on river one at state line ferry one at Yellow Creek & the other above Yellow Creek No report of Forces crossing Perkins gathers from secesh that Roddy is said to be the advance of larger forces souhern scrip in good demand up there returned Confederates say the army is destitute & is comng on this way after supply scouts starts tonight to hunt main forces" Telegram received, *ibid.*, Military Division of the Miss., Letters Received. *O.R.*, I, xvii, part 2, 400.

On Dec. 12, Dodge telegraphed twice to Rawlins. "Will you direct the Topographical Engineer to send me a copy of the sectional map of Eastern Mississippi & Northern Ala if he has it they took only reliable ⚔ sectional map of N. E. Miss. away with them I need one badly" "I shall instruct to strike saltillo at day light sunday morng shall send infanty in wagons with one section of artillery have not over one hundred Cavalry to send will this cooperate with you" Telegrams received, DNA, RG 393, Dept. of the Tenn., Telegrams Received. On the same day, USG telegraphed to Dodge. "Monday morning will be early enough for your troops to strike Saltillo." Copies, DLC-USG, V, 18, 30; DNA, RG 393, Dept. of the Tenn., Letters Sent; Dodge Papers, IaHA. *O.R.*, I, xvii, part 2, 403. Entered in DLC-USG, V, 91 as sent by Rawlins. See letter to Col. John C. Kelton, Jan. 2, 1863.

1. Springdale, Miss., about twelve miles south of Oxford. Misprinted as "Springfield" in *O.R.*, I, xvii, part 2, 399.
2. Dec. 13.

To Col. T. Lyle Dickey

Oxford, Dec 11th 1862 11-30 A. M.
Col. Dickey, Springdale, Miss.

Lieut. Wilson[1] has gone to the front. You need not start east until Saturday.[2] Strike the road as far south as possible and travel North along it doing all the damage possible. I will instruct Dodge to move out a Brigade from Corinth. Send your sick back here.

U. S. Grant
Maj Genl.

Copies, DLC-USG, V, 18, 30, 91; DNA, RG 393, Dept. of the Tenn., Letters Sent. *O.R.*, I, xvii, part 2, 399. On Dec. 11, 1862, Col. T. Lyle Dickey, Springdale, telegraphed to USG. "Flag of truce for Col McCulloughs body not returned third (3d) Mich. Cavaly moving to point south of this & to throw guard forward to R R bridge at Water Valley. Lees Command in Camp 2 miles north of this   I take Hatches Brig & three (3) cos. 2d Iowa from Lees Brig for the detour east when shall I start & by what route. shall I travel   I want orders   shall I send to Oxford the debris of the Camp of the men I take east with me   please send Lt Wilson to me with maps"   Telegram received, DNA, RG 393, Dept. of the Tenn., Telegrams Received. On the same day, Dickey telegraphed to Lt. Col. John A. Rawlins. "I have not been furnished with the Countersigns—Where is R E Goodell? I want to see him   Where is the 11th Ill. Ify? Col Mizner is over the Yacona guarding Water Valley R R bridge   Col Hatch & Lee move tomorrow morning to the outs   Lee West of Watervalley & Hatch E of Watervalley   I move my Head Quarters tomorrow south of Springdale   Why don't Wilson send me a map." Telegram received, *ibid.*

On Dec. 12, Dickey telegraphed to Rawlins three times, from "Near Springdale," "Water Valley," "McKees Farm." "Let Charlie leave his Baggage with your Hd Qrs & taking his blankets & horse come to me near Watervalley Crossing at the force west of the R R at New Spring Dale"   "I have moved my Hd Qrs to McKees farm one mile South East of the free bridge on the road from that bridge to Water valley & about 2 miles South west of Springdale   R E Goodell did not come out with Wilson   where is Charlie Dickey"   "My Div. lies along north bank of ~~Oufie~~ Otuc River about Watervally   citizens from south report main Rebel army at Grenada small force at Jackson   Road pretty well guarded from Jackson to Vicksburg   not a large force at Vicksburg   where is Grierson 6 Ill Cav & the 2d Ill Cav   Gen Grant talked of modifying Brigades   when will this be done   Mizen is better than I expected"   Telegrams received, *ibid.* On the same day, Rawlins telegraphed to Dickey. "Start on your eastward expedition early tomorrow morning. Lieut Charles Dickey left here this morning to join you. Lieut Wilson and Goodell started for the front yesterday"   Copies, DLC-USG, V, 18, 30, 91; DNA, RG 393, Dept. of the Tenn., Letters Sent. *O.R.*, I, xvii, part 2, 403. On Dec. 13, 12:30 A.M., Dickey telegraphed to Rawlins. "Order to start East this morning just recd   will move today to some point near Paris   I did expect written specific instructions & a map to have been sent me   I would be glad to receive them tonight   Lt Dickey has not yet arrived"   Telegram received, DNA, RG 393, Dept. of the Tenn., Telegrams Received.

1. According to his diary, 1st Lt. James H. Wilson rode to see Dickey on Dec. 13. Delaware Historical Society, Wilmington, Del. On Dec. 16, Wilson wrote to USG a protest concerning his need for horses. *Ibid.*
   2. Dec. 13.

Special Field Orders No. 21

────────

Hd. Qrs 13th Army Corps
Dept. of the Tennessee
In Field, Oxford, Miss, Dec 12th 1862.

SPECIAL FIELD ORDERS No 21

1. Distress and all most famine having been brought on many of the inhabitants of Mississippi by the march of the two Armies through the land, and humanity dictating that in a land of plenty no one should suffer the pangs of hunger, the General Commanding directs that the following provision shall be made at all Military Posts within this State.

1st. At each Post one or more loyal persons will be authorized to keep for Sale, provisions and absolute necessities for family use, nothing will be sold except on permits granted by the Commanding Officers of Posts, and no permits will be granted for a greater amount of any one Article than the Commander may believe is necessary for the family of the purchaser

2d. A fund may be created at each post to supply the necessaries of destitute families, gratis, either by levying contributions upon those disloyal persons who are able to pay, taxing Cotton brought to their posts for sale or in any other equitable way.

3d. All contributions so collected will be expended by the Post Commissary on the order of the Commanding Officer and the accounts will be kept seperate from all other accounts.

4th. The Commanding Officers of Posts will require all accounts of these disbursments to be presented for their Examination, weekly, and they will be held responsible that these accounts are properly kept.

5th. All such accounts will be open for inspection to the Inspector General of the Department at any time he may call for them

By order of
Major General U S Grant.
Jno A Rawlins
Asst. Adjt. Genl.

DS, DNA, RG 94, Dept. of the Tenn., General Orders; copies, *ibid.*, RG 393, Dept. of the Tenn., General and Special Orders; *ibid.*, Special Orders; DLC-USG, V, *26, 27, 91. O.R.*, I, xvii, part 2, *405.*

To Abraham Lincoln

Head Quarters, 13th Army Corps
Oxford Miss, Dec. 13th 1862

His Excellency A. Lincol
President of the United States
Washington D. C.
Sir:

Permit me to renew a recommendation for the promotion of an officer that I have made some four or five times before. I refer to Col. C. C. Marsh. Col. Marsh has been under my command since the 1st of Sept./61. Has sustained himself as a regimental and brigade commander with great credit to himself and has won promotion on more than one field of battle.

At Fredericktown Mo. Forts Henry & Donelson and Shiloh he played a conspicuous part. His promotion would not only reward merit but would secure to the service a man well qualified to command all the troops his rank might entitle him to command.

I will add that Col. Marsh has been frequently recommended

by me for this promotion without his knowledge of the fact and solely for what I conceived to be his merit as a soldier.

> I am sir, very respectfully
> your obt. svt.
> U. S. GRANT
> Maj. Gen.

ALS, DNA, RG 94, ACP, M1113 CB 1863. Col. C. Carroll Marsh was nominated on Jan. 19, 1863, by President Abraham Lincoln for promotion to brig. gen. to rank from Nov. 29, 1862, but was not confirmed.

To Col. T. Lyle Dickey

Oxford, Dec 13th 1862

COL. DICKEY COMMDG CAVALRY DIV.

I want you to strike the Mobile road as far South as possible and follow up North, dstroying it all you can. Particular roads to pass over cannot be given. You may encounter difficulties that will defeat the object of the expedition. I do not want any great risk run but leave this entirely to your judgment.

Dodge starts a force of probably 2500. men from Corinth southward to day intended to cooperate with you.[1] If practicable you might continue North until you meet them and return by Pontotoc[2] to the front.

> U. S. GRANT
> Major General.

Copies, DLC-USG, V, 18, 30, 91; DNA, RG 393, Dept. of the Tenn., Letters Sent. *O.R.*, I, xvii, part 2, 410.

On Dec. 13, 1862, Col. T. Lyle Dickey telegraphed to Lt. Col. John A. Rawlins. "Hatch with 1300 will camp tonight near paris twelve miles east of Water Valley   I leave Misner in Command of first & third Brigades near Water Valley to report direct to Maj Gen Grant   I suggest that a strong Cavalry demonstration be made tomorrow from Water Valley toward Coffeevill & east of that road to favor my departure on that road. At Paris I will take eight hundred picked & horses & try the riffle   dispatches recd from you by telegraph"   Telegram received, DNA, RG 393, Dept. of the Tenn., Telegrams Received. On Dec. 14, Dickey telegraphed to Rawlins. "Your directions by Telegraph Just Recd   I start tomorrow morning with eight hundred men without wagons for the post indicated   I send three hundred 300 to make a demonstration towards

Pittsboro tomorrow & returning to Paris   Will fall back with the train of Hatch's Brigade to Markets bridge between this & Oxford & will await our Return there" Telegram received, *ibid.*

On Dec. 13, Col. John K. Mizner, Water Valley, telegraphed frequently to USG. "A Scout sent to Oakland captured a messenger with orders to Maj Blythe to destroy all cotton between the Tallahatchie & Coldwater & all others points accessible   He expected to find Maj Blythe at ~~Hoon~~ Horn lake 14 miles from Memphis   We also learn from him that Price is camped five miles west of Grenada & Van Dorn three miles east of Grenada   force of each fifteen thousand 15000. Six hundred 600 reinforcements arrived from below on thursday   Pemberton is at Grenada   Lovell left for Richmond on Tuesday. Enemy is through up earth works north of Yalobusha   work is done by Negroes. Pickets are seven 7 miles north of grenada   I move at Day light"   Telegram received, *ibid.*, RG 94, War Records Office, Dept. of the Tenn. *O.R.*, I, xvii, part 2, 411. "As directed by Colonel Dickey, chief of cavalry, I report myself in command of the cavalry division, with headquarters at this place. The information I get is that the mass of the rebel army is at Grenada. An outpost of cavalry at Torrance Station; strength about 1,200. The rest of the cavalry are at Stratham's, on Yalabusha. No infantry north of Grenada. Pickets 3 miles south of Coffeeville, with occasional patrols in Coffeeville. I am guarding railroad bridge at this place and the crossings of the Otuckalofa. Let the Sixth Illinois Cavalry come up, if possible." *Ibid.* "A small party of Rebels have made their appearance on the lines of the R R   I have sent out scouts to Cut them off   I will be able to move by day laght in the morng   Col Dickey will not get farther than Paris tonight & as I will have some peparations to make presume mornng will be soon enough for me to move"   Telegram received, DNA, RG 393, Dept. of the Tenn., Telegrams Received. On the same day, USG telegraphed to Mizner. "Move with your Cavalry to the South or southeast slowly to cover the movement of Col. Dickey. You should remain out until Monday evening or Tuesday. Should you discover any movement of the enemy towards Col. Dickey apprize him of the fact or go to his assistance as may seem best." Copies, DLC-USG, V, 18, 30, 91; DNA, RG 393, Dept. of the Tenn., Letters Sent. *O.R.*, I, xvii, part 2, 411. Also on Dec. 13, Mizner telegraphed again to USG. "I am not advised as to Colonel Dickey's intended route. I will move as you direct. No infantry has yet arrived here. I will have to leave a guard over the bridges in this vicinity. Cannot move. Cavalry will be sent to the front to make a considerable demonstration, or is your desire that no advance be made farther than that indicated in your last dispatch?" *Ibid.*, p. 412.

1. On Dec. 13, USG telegraphed to Brig. Gen. Grenville M. Dodge, Corinth. "A Cavalry force leaves our front to strike the Mobile road as far South as possible. They are instructed then to push North destroying the road until they meet the force sent by you if practicable. Your troops should be instructed to be back within six days, and to run no risk of being cut off." Copies, DLC-USG, V, 18, 30, 91; DNA, RG 393, Dept. of the Tenn., Letters Sent; Dodge Papers, IaHA. *O.R.*, I, xvii, part 2, 411. On the same day, Dodge telegraphed to USG. "Am greatly in need of Cavalry & labor under many difficulties for the want of it for this place & all my outposts   I have not got now three hundred effective men   I have used them all up Horses & men.   if you can send me a good Regt it will enable me to keep parted in a circle of Sixty 60 miles and penetrate the

enemy's line east at any time" Telegram received, DNA, RG 393, Dept. of the Tenn., Telegrams Received.

2. Pontotoc, Miss., about thirty-two miles east of Oxford.

To Col. John V. D. Du Bois

Oxford, Dec 13th 1862

COL. DUBOIS, HOLLY SPRINGS,

All prisoners who give themselves up and are not taken in battle may be paroled and set at liberty. All others should be sent for exchange except cases where the Commdg Officer is satisfied that the parties will go North and remain.[1]

Passes through lines will always be given to paroled prisoners. A list must be kept of all such a copy of which will be sent to Washington.

U. S. GRANT
Major General.

Copies, DLC-USG, V, 18, 30, 91; DNA, RG 393, Dept. of the Tenn., Letters Sent. On Dec. 13, 1862, Col. John V. D. Du Bois had telegraphed to Lt. Col. John A. Rawlins. "Please inform me if such confederate prisoners as have reached this place & in good faith are willing to take the oath of allegiance wheuther they will be permitted pass these lines & proceed to their homes" Telegram received, *ibid.*, Telegrams Received.

On Dec. 13, Capt. Theodore S. Bowers, Holly Springs, issued Special Orders No. 46. "The territory from and including Cold Water on the north, to and including Oxford on the south, will constitute the District of the Tallahatchie. Col. R. C. Murphy, 8th Regiment Wisconsin Infantry Volunteers, is assigned to the command of same, and will with the force under his command guard and protect the Railroad through his District." Printed, Oglesby Papers, IHi. Copies are lacking in USG records because of their destruction in the C. S. A. capture of Holly Springs one week later. These orders placed Col. Robert C. Murphy, 8th Wis., in command at Holly Springs instead of Du Bois. On Dec. 13, Murphy telegraphed to Rawlins. "Soldiers are applying here for transportation to Memphis who belongs to Gen Shermans Comd alleging that Gen Sherman is ordered to Memphis where shall I send enlisted men of his Comd" Telegram received, DNA, RG 393, Dept. of the Tenn., Telegrams Received. On the same day, Rawlins telegraphed to Murphy, "Commd'g Holly Springs." "Apply to Capt Bowers at Dept. Hd Qrs. Holly Springs and he will furnish you with a list of troops, and their stations." Copies, DLC-USG, V, 18, 30, 91; DNA, RG 393, Dept. of the Tenn., Letters Sent. On Dec. 16, Murphy telegraphed to USG. "Col DuBois has requested me send 17 Ill to Abbebill I would prefer to send another Reg as I wish place Col Norton a good officer in Comd of post here can I have my own judgement in selecting a Reg. or must I send the 17th Ill Col Norton I have ordered all brige gurads on the south to hurry up there defences have not a piece of artillery in this dist that I know of can you send one out to this post" Telegram received, *ibid.*, Telegrams Received. On the same day, Rawlins issued Special Field Orders No. 25. "Col. C C. Marsh, 20th Illinois Infy. Vols., is hereby assigned to the command of the District of the Tallahatchie and will relieve Col R C. Murphy. Col Murphy is hereby assigned to the command of the Post of Holly Springs, Mississppi." DS, *ibid.*, RG 94, Dept. of the Tenn., General Orders; copies, *ibid.*, RG 393, Dept. of the Tenn., General and Special Orders; *ibid.*, Special Orders; DLC-USG, V, 26, 27, 91.

On Dec. 14, Du Bois, Abbeville, telegraphed to USG. "The road is guard from down to the tank three miles south of Waterford by the 100st 103rd & 109th The Road from the Tank to the river will require nearly a Regt I will then have one Regt left of those which have reported the twenty seventh (27th) Iowa & 12th Indiana Will One Regt be Enough from here to Oxford The Orderly will wait at Abbeville for an answer" Telegram received, DNA, RG 393, Dept. of the Tenn., Telegrams Received. On the same day, USG telegraphed to Du Bois. "There should be two Regts this side of the river. The 17th Ills. will be at Holly Springs if not there now." Copies, DLC-USG, V, 18, 30, 91; DNA, RG 393, Dept. of the Tenn., Letters Sent. On Dec. 15, Du Bois telegraphed to USG. "I will send an order for the Seventeenth 17 Illinois to come this side of the Tallahatchie The bottom of the Tallahatchie will have to be corduroyed if you wish to transport rations with wagons the Railroad bridge over the River is being built very slowly. I will send you a written report of the Railroad guards tomorrow" Telegram received, *ibid.*, Telegrams Received. On the same day, George G. Pride, Abbeville, telegraphed to USG. "The rain this morning has detained our work at the Tallahatchie but I have everything going as possible & think supplies leaving here early wednesday morning early will go without delay" Telegram received, *ibid.*

1. On Nov. 28, Brig. Gen. James M. Tuttle, Cairo, had telegraphed to USG. "Fifty six (56) Prisoners sent Here captured at Corinth who have taken the oath what shall I do with them would it be allowed to let those who wish join our army." Telegram received, *ibid.*

To Julia Dent Grant

Oxford Miss.
Dec. 13th 1862

Dear Julia,

Bowers is here just returning and I take advantage of the occation to write you a few lines. I did intend moving Hd Quarters south to Springdale to-day but as it looks so much like rain and there is no special necessity for it I will not move until Monday[1] or Teusday next. I have had no letter from home since we left Lagrange nor no letter for you, from any quarter, except one from Ford[2] enclosed in one to me. The bottle of Bourbon sent by Mrs. Davies I sent over to Gen. Sherman. Myself nor no one connected with the Staff ever tasted it.

Kiss Jess for me. Remember me to Lagow.

ULYS.

ALS, DLC-USG. Julia Dent Grant, then in Holly Springs, visited USG at Oxford for the weekend beginning Dec. 19, 1862, thus missing the Van Dorn raid of Dec. 20. Mary Hillyer Clarke, "A Personal Experience of the Raid on Holly Springs," typescript, Robert C. W. Hillyer, San José, Costa Rica; *The Personal Memoirs of Julia Dent Grant* (New York, 1975), pp. 107–8.

1. Dec. 15.
2. On Nov. 11, Charles W. Ford, St. Louis, had written to USG. "I wrote you a few days ago and sent the letter per Adams Express, and asking the favor of a permit to send 100 casks of liquor to Memphis. I write now in the hope that this may reach you in time *to stop the permit*. I do not want it—as the market has been thrown open—by a general permit to all parties to import as much liquor as they please, into Memphis. Ubsdell-Pierson & Co—offered me a handsome share in 'a venture,' on dry goods if I could get a permit to send to *Trenton* & points in that Vicinity—say $5.000 worth of goods. What do you think of it? If favorably —can you help me to the permit—I have less *scruples* in asking for this—because it is more legitimate than the whiskey permit. I know you are very busy—but— I cannot resist writing this note" ALS, DNA, RG 393, Dept. of the Tenn., Telegrams Received. It is possible, of course, that USG referred to a later letter from Ford.

To Lt. Gen. John C. Pemberton

Head Quarters, 13th Army Corps.
Dept of the Tennessee.
Oxford, Miss. Dec 14, 1862

LIEUT. GEN. PEMBERTON,
COMMDG CONFEDERATE FORCES
JACKSON, TENN.[1]
GENL:

Your communication in relation to the case of Col. Hedge-path[2] is just received.

I did not even know that Col. Hedgepath was in the Hospital at Memphis and cannot answer as to the misfortunes that may possibly have befallen him in the way of losses sustained. Where there are large Armies, and particularly in large cities, there are always persons ready to *steal* where there is an opportunity occurs and especially have many of our Federal troops who have been so unfortunate as to fall into the hands of the Southern Army found this true.

As to the other, or any other bad treatment towards Col. Hedgepath you will find, when the facts are before you he has received none.

All prisoners of War are humanely treated by the Federal authorities and many a wounded or sick soldier has remonstrated against being sent back for exchange on the ground that the treatment received at the hands of the Union authorities was so much better than they could get among what they denominated their friends.

All prisoners who desire it are sent by the first opportunity that occurs to Vicksburg for exchange. Sick and wounded are paroled in Hospital and as soon as able to travel are furnished passes out of our lines, or are sent with other prisoners to the Depot agreed upon for exchange.

Unless there is some good reason for it Col. Hedgepath has not nor will not be made an exception to the rule

> I am, Sir, Very Respectfully
> Your Obt. Servant.
> U. S. GRANT
> Maj Genl.

Copies, DLC-USG, V, 18, 30, 91; DNA, RG 393, Dept. of the Tenn., Letters Sent. *O.R.*, II, v, 81–82. On Dec. 10, 1862, C.S.A. Lt. Gen. John C. Pemberton, Jackson, Miss., wrote to USG. "I am credibly informed that Lieut Col. Hedgepath. 6th Mo. Infy. C. S. A who was severely wounded in the engagement near Corinth, is now at the Govtm Hospital Memphis subjected to unusually harsh treatment, 'his parole, watch & money taken from him'. If this statement is correct I respectfully request that you will inform me of the reasons why the privileges issued by the Cartel for the exchange of prisoner are denied in Col. Hedgepath's case, and further request that he be either paroled at once, or sent to Vicksburg for exchange by the first opportunity." ALS, DNA, War Records Office, Dept. of the Tenn. *O.R.*, II, v, 57.

1. Jackson, Miss., was intended.
2. Lt. Col. Isaac N. Hedgpeth, 6th Mo., wounded and captured at Corinth, Oct. 3.

To Maj. Gen. Henry W. Halleck

———

Oxford 3 P M Dec 14 [*1862*]

MAJ GENL HALLECK
GEN'L IN CHF
The following desbatch has been recd from Genl Dodge

Corinth Dec 13th 1862.

MAJ GENL GRANT,
    I have just recd a despatch from Col Sweeny in command of the forces sent out   he struck the outputs of the enemy at Cherokee three hundred strong under Col Warren[1]   Pursued them five miles fighting all the way where they met Col Rhoddy with fourteen hundred who after a sharp engagement fell back to Little Bear Creek four miles this side of Tuscumbia from which they were driven after burning their stores camp Equipage & Bridges   Rhoddy had here four cannon & saw Infantry from Braggs army   we captured thirty two (32) prisoners a number of Horses arms &c   The reconnoisance was a success   The artilly & Infantry had just arrived there from Decatur & strengthened the reports of his crossing a force at that point   on the arrival of Col Sweeny I shall know about how strong   a report comes to night that sixteen thousand (16000) Infty have gone to Pemberton by way of merdian   It went down the Chattanooga & Meridian road   this is given by refugees from Alabama who arrived here to day from Walker County   it does not agree with what have heretofore heard except that was one of the roads on which forage & provisions were being collected.
    Signed   G. M. DODGE
    B. Gl.[2]

U. S. GRANT
Maj Genl

Telegram received, DNA, RG 94, Generals' Papers and Books, Telegrams Received by Gen. Halleck; *ibid.*, RG 107, Telegrams Collected (Bound); copies (dated Dec. 13, 1862, 1 P.M.), *ibid.*, RG 393, Dept. of the Tenn., Hd. Qrs. Correspondence; DLC-USG, V, 5, 8, 24, 88, 91.

On Dec. 15, USG wrote to Maj. Gen. Henry W. Halleck. "I have the honor to transmit herewith a Dispatch received from Brig. Genl. G. M. Dodge, Commanding at Corinth, Miss. of the result of a reconnoissance sent out by him towards Tuscumbia." LS, DNA, RG 94, War Records Office, Union Battle Reports. On Dec. 14, Brig. Gen. Grenville M. Dodge, Corinth, telegraphed to USG. "The Tuscumbia force has arrived it seems that the artilley come to Rhoddy about a week ago & he had started the mornng we attacked him to attack our forces at Glendale he had four days rations cooked he fell back towards Decatur & across the river to florence he has at florence two flat boats good ones & two small steamers that have been fitted up in the last 2 months they now run he is repairng boats at that place all the time & his men say that he intends to make a raid down the river as soon as water will permit his force is rising 2000 he has Telegraphic but not R R communication with Bragg Col Sweeny used him up badly & brot in a large amount of his troops Rhoddy burnd his camps stores, & also the fine coverd bridge across Little Bear Creek The force is only an outpost of Braggs but the steamer should be destroyed had he reached Glendale he would have hurt us though I am fortified at that place great praise is due Col Sweeny for the manner in which he carried out the orders & the valuable information he obtaind" Telegram received, *ibid.*; copies, *ibid.*, RG 393, 16th Army Corps, Letters Sent; Dodge Papers, IaHA. *O.R.*, I, xvii, part 1, 541–42. Other reports of this skirmish are *ibid.* On Dec. 16, Dodge telegraphed to Lt. Col. John A. Rawlins. "Col Roddy C S A has 7 of our men picked up in the last two months Can I exchange that No of men of his in comds we took some 40" Telegram received, DNA, RG 393, Dept. of the Tenn., Telegrams Received.

On Dec. 14, USG telegraphed to Halleck. "The following dispatch from Gen Dodge just received." Telegram received, *ibid.*, RG 107, Telegrams Collected (Bound); copies, *ibid.*, RG 393, Dept. of the Tenn., Hd. Qrs. Correspondence; DLC-USG, V, 5, 8, 24, 88, 91. *O.R.*, I, xvii, part 1, 475–76. USG transmitted a telegram of Dec. 14 addressed to him by Dodge. "At the time I sent the force to Tuscumbia I sent a small Cavalry force to cut the roads running from Tuscumbia. Decatur Warrenton & Chattanooga to Columbus & Meriden. They have just returned They penetrated Alabama 100 miles & ascertained that none of Braggs Army had gone to either Columbus or Meridan by way of the east road. The force that was reported to have gone to Meridan were conscripts from Alabama & Georgia & there was quite a force of them Their force at Decatur only one outpost of Braggs Army to watch us & gather provisions—it is small—Several small bands of Cavalry are on all the roads mentioned gathering forage & provisions. The Scout was a very daring & successful one & settles the flying reports from that quarter" Telegram received, DNA, RG 393, Dept. of the Tenn., Telegrams Received; *ibid.*, RG 107, Telegrams Collected (Bound); copies, *ibid.*, RG 393, Dept. of the Tenn., Hd. Qrs. Correspondence; DLC-USG, V, 5, 8, 24, 88, 91. *O.R.*, I, xvii, part 1, 475-76.

1. C.S.A. Lt. Col. James M. Warren, 5th Ala. Cav., who served under Col. Philip D. Roddey. Warren was not killed in this engagement as Dodge later erroneously reported. See telegram to Maj. Gen. Henry W. Halleck, Dec. 16, 1862.

2. Copy, DNA, RG 94, War Records Office, Union Battle Reports. *O.R.*, I, xvii, part 1, 541.

To Maj. Gen. Henry W. Halleck

Oxford Mississippi
December 14th 1862

MAJ. GEN. H. W. HALLECK,
WASHINGTON D. C.
DEAR GEN.

I have just received a private letter from Mr. Washburn[1] in which he speaks of a conversation that he had with you in which you said that anything I would recommend with referance to my Staff you would aid me in.

My individual labors have been harder probably than that of any other Gen. officer in the Army except probably yours and McClellen, with the exception of the time you was present with the Army in the Field. Much of this was due to having an entire Staff of inexperienced men in Military matters.

I now have for Chief of each the Q. M. and C. S. Departments men that are all I want. Also Engineers, Topographical Engineers and Ordnance officers in whom I have great confidance.

Of my individual Staff there are but two men who I regard as absolutely indispensable. One of them is Lt. Col. Rawlins, A. A. Gen. and Capt Bowers A. D. C. and now recommended for the position of Judge Advocate with the rank of Major.

Col. Rawlins I regard as the ablest and most reliable man in his Dept. of the Volunteer service, and with but few equals in the regular Army. Capt. Bowers has been with me for fourteen months, first a private soldier and clerk in the Office. On his promotion I made him A. D. C. and he has continued in reality an Acting A. A. Gen. He is capable, attentive and indispensable to me.

Col. Hillyer is very efficient as Provost Marshal Gen. and relieves me from much duty that I have heretofore had to attend to in person.

Col. Lagow I am very much attached to personally and can endorse him as a true honest man, willing to do all in his power for the service.

My regular Aids are all persons with whom I had previous acquaintance and were appointed by me for what I believed was their merit as men. They give entire satisfaction.

Hillyer and Lagow were my regular Aides but by promotion are Additional Aides. Lagow fills the position of Inspector Gen. an appointment I have not made, or recommended anyone for, and Hillyer is Provost Marshal Gen.

I learn that there will probably be an effort made to defeat the confirmation of all the recent promotions. There are many of them I have no interest in, but in the case of McPherson I am deeply interested.[2] He is now second in command with the Army in the Field and should his name be brought up, and be rejected I would feel the loss more than taking a Division from me. He is worth more than a Division of men in his present position, particularly as his successor to the command of a Wing would be such a person[3] as would leave me to look after that command direct in addition to my duties with the whole.

I am now better situated with regard to Wing and Division commanders than I have ever been before and hope no officers will be sent into the Department who rank those who are now with me. I am sorry to say it but I would regard it as particularly unfortunate to have either McClernand or Wallace sent to me. The latter I could manage if he had less rank, but the former is unmanageable and incompetant.

I would bespeak for Gen. Hamilton promotion. He has earned it on the battle field and is competant. Besides this there is not a single Major Gen. from Wisconsin and some day they may claim one and give the rank to some less worthy person.

The people of Mississippi show more signs of being subdued than any we have heretofore come across. They are very cordial

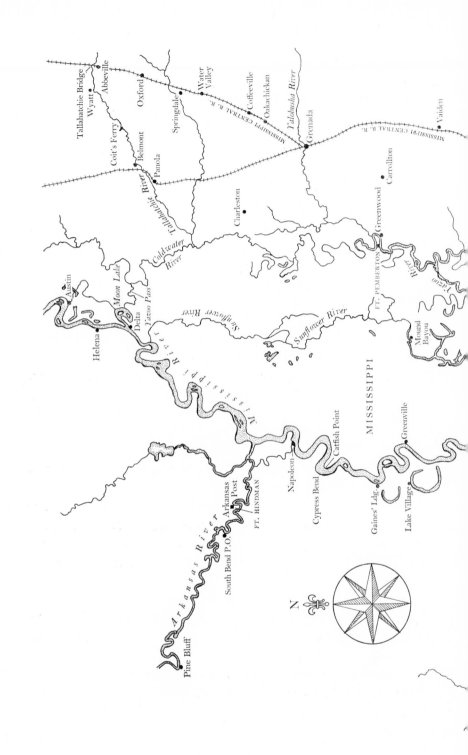

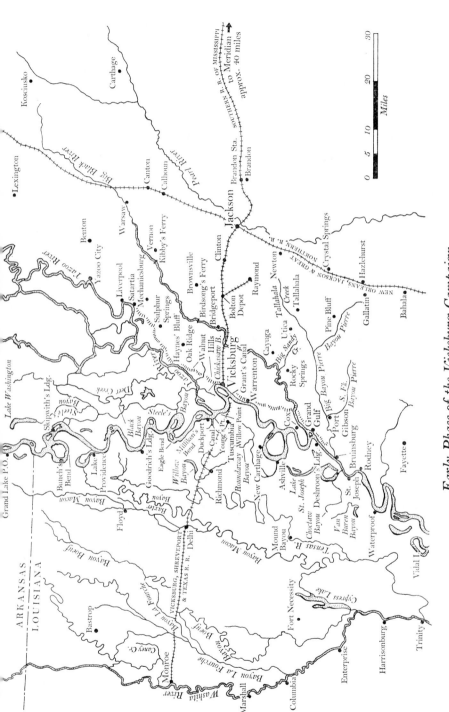

Early Phase of the Vicksburg Campaign

in their reseption of the Federal officers and seem desirous of having trade resumed.

I have been waiting on the reports of the Cavalry commanders before making mine. If they are not handed in within a few days I will make mine and submit theirs when received.

I am under many obligations to you for the confidance which Mr. Washburn says you expressed in me and will endeavor not to disappoint you.

> Yours Truly
>
> U. S. GRANT

ALS, DNA, RG 94, Special File. *O.R.*, I, lii, part 1, 313–14.

1. Although the letter from U.S. Representative Elihu B. Washburne to USG has not been found, a copy was sent to Maj. William R. Rowley, who commented on it in a letter of Dec. 16, 1862, to Washburne. "I hope it will draw out an answer from him of the right kind but I fear he will hardly have the heart to cut loose from the four Colonels. It is *very* important that it should be done. You perhaps can realize the necessity of it. Rawlins rote me last night that he would write you immediately upon the subject and state some facts. I hope that when I am called back from Columbus to find fewer loafers about head Quarters" ALS, DLC-Elihu B. Washburne. Rowley apparently provoked Washburne's letter to USG through a letter of Nov. 20 to Washburne in which he stated that Col. John Riggin, Jr., had been appointed to USG's staff accidentally when USG only intended to compliment his services as a vol. aide. "Gen Grant has four Cols on his staff   3 appointments by Gen Halleck Lagow Regan & Hillyer and I doubt whether either of them have gone to bed sober for a week   The other Col Ihrie is appointed as Ad'n Aide on the staff of Gen Wool and assigned to Gen Grant as I understand without any solicitation on the part of Gen Grant. And he is not much better than the rest although possessing more military talent   he is a protegee of Trumbulls I believe a cousin of Trumbulls Wife, and a sneaking Loco Foco of the N Y Herald stripe." ALS, *ibid.*

2. On Dec. 13, USG telegraphed to Maj. Gen. Henry W. Halleck. "Urge the confirmation of McPherson—he commands a wing of this army & it is of vast importance to the service that he should retain it" Telegram received, DNA, RG 94, Generals' Papers and Books, Telegrams Received by Gen. Halleck; *ibid.*, RG 107, Telegrams Collected (Bound); copies, *ibid.*, RG 393, Dept. of the Tenn., Hd. Qrs. Correspondence; DLC-USG, V, 5, 8, 24, 88, 91. *O.R.*, I, xvii, part 1, 475. The appointment of James B. McPherson as brig. gen. and maj. gen. were both pending, and were confirmed on March 10, 1863.

3. This may be a reference to Brig. Gen. Thomas J. McKean, highest ranking brig. gen. with USG's army in the field after Brig. Gen. Charles S. Hamilton, who commanded the other wing. Evidence of some difficulty is embodied in a telegram of Dec. 9, 1862, from McKean, Waterford, to Lt. Col. John A. Rawlins. "I expect to be transferred to the pay Dept soon pending which I respectfully request to be relieved of my Comd. & permitted to go to Cairo & await orders

in case which will allow me a little time to arrage some unsettled business in that Dept" Telegram received, DNA, RG 393, Dept. of the Tenn., Telegrams Received. On the same day, Rawlins issued Special Field Orders No. 18. "Brig. General Lauman will move one Brigade of his present command to a point convenient for Water on the line of the Railroad and from four to six miles south of Abberville to guard the Road from that point south, the other Brigade to Waterford to report to Col. J V. Du-Bois for further orders. These dispositions being made General Lauman will relieve General McKean in command of the 4th Division and bring it Oxford with as little delay as practicable." DS, *ibid.*, RG 94, Dept. of the Tenn., Special Orders; copies, *ibid.*, RG 393, Dept. of the Tenn., Special Orders; DLC-USG, V, 26, 27, 91. *O.R.*, I, xvii, part 2, 396.

On Jan. 7, 1863, Maj. Gen. Samuel R. Curtis, St. Louis, wrote to USG. "I have twice requested that Brig Genl T. J. McKean might be transfered to my command: but he has been so employed elsewhere it has not been found convenient. He is now here and I wish you would allow the transfer and so recommend orders from Washington" ALS, DNA, RG 94, Generals' Papers and Books, Thomas J. McKean. On the same day, McKean, Cairo, wrote to USG. "You will receive a letter from Genl. Curtis relative to my transfer into his Department— if you can assist the object I shall be glad (not that I dislike to remain in your Department) it will give me facilities for getting into the Pay Dept. which I still hope to accomplish as soon as the General aspect of Affairs improves a little in some other quarters—" ALS, *ibid.* Soon transferred to the Dept. of the Mo., McKean never again served directly under USG.

To Maj. Gen. William T. Sherman

Oxford, Dec 14th 1862

Maj Gen. Sherman.

I have not had one word from Grierson since he left. Am getting uneasy about him. I hope Gen. Gorman[1] will give you no difficulty about returning the troops that were on this side of the river and Steele to command them. The 21.000 men you have with 12.000 from Helena will make a good force. The enemy are as yet on the Yalabusha. I am pushing down towards them slowly, but so as to keep up the impression of a continuous move. I feel particularly anxious to have the Helena Cavalry on this side of the river if not now at least after you start. If Gorman will send them instruct them where to go and how to communicate with me. My Head Quarters will probably be in Coffeeville one week hence. In the mean time I will be at Springdale.

It would be well if you could have two or three small boats suitable for navigating the Yazoo. It may become necessary for me to look to that base for supplies before we get through.

U. S. Grant
Maj Genl.

Copies, DLC-USG, V, 18, 30, 91; DNA, RG 393, Dept. of the Tenn., Letters Sent; DLC-William T. Sherman. *O.R.*, I, xvii, part 2, 412. On Dec. 12, 1862, Maj. Gen. William T. Sherman, Memphis, wrote to USG. "I arrived at 12 M. to day, find Genls A. J. Smith and Morgan here, each in command of a Division. But these old Divisions on arriving at Memphis were mere skeletons and the new Regiments were added thereto. A. J. Smith has twelve Regiments about 8000 men. Morgan has ten Reg'ts about 6000 men. M. L. Smith will be in tomorrow morning with his Division 10 Regiments about 7000 men, making 21,000 men from Memphis. I understand Genl Gorman is now in command at Helena. Steele is with him but Hovey has gone home. All the troops that were over to the Talla-hatchie have returned to Helena   I have just sent an Aid to Helena to ascertain if Col. Grierson got through with your letter, and to know if Gen'l Hallecks dispatch had been received and if I could depend on the 12000 Infantry and 2000 Cavalry. Lest Col. Grierson failed to reach Helena I recapitulated your orders as to their disposition   I will send Capt. Fitch up to Columbus to telegraph you and to keep me advised of the condition of things above and below for a few days. I want him to see to the steamboats, ammunition &c and to dispatch the business generally. I will be ready to embark on the 18th if the boats come and I will instruct Capt. Fitch to telegraph you as fast as boats pass Columbus." Copies (2), DLC-William T. Sherman; DNA, RG 94, Generals' Papers and Books, William T. Sherman, Letters Sent. *O.R.*, I, xvii, part 1, 601–2.

On the same day, Sherman wrote to Capt. Henry S. Fitch, Memphis. "You will proceed to Columbus by boat, on arrival telegraph to Genl. Grant my letter of this date and send original by cars—" Copy, DNA, RG 94, Generals' Papers and Books, William T. Sherman, Letters Sent. On Dec. 14, Fitch, Cairo, twice telegraphed to USG. "The despatch forwarded from here tonight from Gen Sherman Should have left this morning from Columbus   Owing to Some un-explained mistake was not Sent   I will be in Columbus all day tomorrow & next day to forward any dispatches you may Send" "Fifty Steamers are engaged to ~~blow~~ go below   Can Carrey 40,000 troops with artillery & baggage   all coaled   most of them will be here tomorrow On way down   Will send you list of Steamers As well as list of Regts at Memphis tomorrow from Columbus if you desire" Telegrams received, *ibid.*, RG 393, Dept. of the Tenn., Telegrams Received. On Dec. 15, Fitch telegraphed to USG. "I have just seen your Despatch to Gen Sherman inquing about Regts at Memphis   I herewith send list of all Regts at Memphis except those composing Gen Morgan L Smiths Div with which you are familiar . . ." Telegram received, *ibid.*

On Dec. 13, Sherman wrote to Lt. Col. John A. Rawlins. "I wrote at length last night and sent to Columbus by Capt Fitch to be telegraphed through. Today I have to report the arrival of Morgan L Smiths Division in the city. So that my

Memphis force of 3 Divisions are now on hand.—My Aid has gone to Helena to see about that force and will be back tomorrow. General Washburn is up from Helena. He Commanded the Cavalry force which accompanied Hovey. They made a floating Bridge at mouth of Coldwater. Infantry force of 5000 advanced to the Yocana whence the Cavalry force of 2000 proceeded to Oakland, Preston, and within 5 miles of Grenada, where he became satisfied he could not surprise the place and his horses beng fatigued by a ride of 55 miles in one night he caused the Road to be broken about 5 miles from Grenada, & wires cut. He is satisfied now that he could have gone into Grenada, but General Hovey and and he apprehended the enemy would move from Abbeville toward Panola & Coldwater & cut off their retreat. Evidently the Road was very slightly damaged. Gen Washburn. broke one small bridge on the Memphis & Grenada Road about 10 miles north of Grenada, with which exception he thinks the whole from Coldwater to Grenada is in good order. He wants to make a strike at Yazoo City from some point of the River coincident with our movemt south. He also says that they have full 25000 men at Helena, and could spare 15000 easy—but there is some doubt about Gorman permitting any to go unless Curtis orders it—Being no longer in your Department, and only 5000 Infantry having been there, there is a doubt whether Hallecks order embraces them. To make sure Get Halleck to order a specific number of men say 12000 Inf. 2000 Cavalry and some 3 Batteries to be transferred to you   I will have all things ready here by the 18th and expect as a matter of course the transportation. I have ordered the Quarter Master here to hold on to ten steamboats for our use." ALS, *ibid.*, Letters Received. *O.R.*, I, xvii, part 2, 408. On the same day, Sherman endorsed a letter of the same date of Maj. Gen. Stephen A. Hurlbut outlining plans for the military administration of Memphis. "Respectfully forwarded to Genl Grant. Only two Cos of Cavalry 3rd Regulars are now here—There will always be a large force of sick convalescents and dodgers who can go to make up a Garrison. The People must break up the bands of Guerillas or submit to be plundered by them. That is not the business of an army now. The movements below Memphis will remove all force of an attack" AES, DNA, RG 393, Dept. of the Tenn., Letters Received.

On Dec. 16, Sherman wrote to Rawlins. "Yesterday was a very stormy day but again the weather is good and I hope the boats will arrive on time for I am all ready to embark. by the 18th inst—I have perfectly satisfactory letters from Genl. Gorman at Helena and also from Admiral Porter. All enter into our plans with zeal & eagerness and the most perfect harmony exists between all. I now enclose the last Field Report I can make up which contains substantially all the data which the General could wish—I have heretofore stated that I propose to carry along a Million of Rations and a full supply of small arms & Gun ammunition   I will also take some boats along fitted for a ferry & a bridge should I be compelled to cross streams—Our Gunboats are below & have possession of the mouth of Yazoo. The fort up Yazoo is No 24 miles up designed to cover the river against our boats ascending the Yazoo, accounts vary as to the condition of the Enemy's Gunboat fleet up Yazoo, some representing their boats iron-clad-, armed, & ready for service others stating the reverse   The best plan for embarkation also will only be found by personal inspection—I will be able to get 7 steamboats at Helena, 10 here and I hear unofficially that a fleet of empty boats are is coming from Louisville & St Louis   A Mr H____ reports to me that a Planter named B____ has just returned from Jackson Miss. whither he went for permission to load a steam boat with Cotton in the Tallahatchie above the mouth of Yallobusha & move her down to Yazoo City or the mouth of Yazoo—he says he has permission to pass the raft built below the fleet of boats—which raft is provided with a draw but the Navy Officers at the mouth of Yazoo report the ~~river~~ Enemy obstructing the river below the ~~draft~~ with a line of piles—Indeed at this distance our information is unreliable & I will proceed on the basis of your plan as developed to Genl Halleck—Of course attacking Vicksburg at the first movement if deemed possible. This same party represents the talk at Jackson that Bragg would amuse Rosecrans with a pretended attack whilst his army would substantially move towards the Mobile & Ohio Road near Baldwin or Tupelo that we would be allowed to move south almost unopposed, when Bragg from the east & Holmes from the west would close in to the river at Pillow or Memphis, and that the pretended attacks on Kentucky, Clarksburg &c were mere feints. Insomuch as time would be lost I will send to Adjt. Genl. Thomas at Washington for the information of Genl Halleck a short condensed Report of my force— Infantry Cavalry & Artillery that he may judge of its sufficiency to the end in view   You will observe that I only have here three Companies of Cavalry available. I understand Col. Howe may be daily expected with 4 Cos 3d Regular Cavalry   I will leave him with Hurlbut. Hurlbut has erysipelas & prefers to remain. Having no adequate Command for Genls Asboth I leave him also in command of the Fort with its four Regiments & detachments. All detachments belonging to Denver's & Lauman's I have ordered to march to Holly Springs'' Copy, *ibid.*, RG 94, Generals' Papers and Books, William T. Sherman, Letters Sent; DLC-William T. Sherman. On the same day, Sherman wrote to Brig. Gen. Lorenzo Thomas reporting his troop strength for the expedition in detail. ALS, DNA, RG 94, Letters Received. *O.R.*, I, xvii, part 1, 602–3.

1. Willis A. Gorman of Minn. had served in the Mexican War as 1st sergt., then maj., 3rd Ind., and col., 4th Ind. Appointed col., 1st Minn., April 29, 1861, he was confirmed as brig. gen. on March 17, 1862, to rank from Sept. 7, 1861, and assigned to command the District of Eastern Ark. on Dec. 3, 1862. See letter to Brig. Gen. Frederick Steele, Dec. 8, 1862.

To Col. Addison S. Norton

Hd Qrs, Dept of the Tenn.
Oxford, Miss. Dec 14th 1862

Col. A. S. Norton
Commdg 17th Ills. Infy
Col:

Your letter of the 12th[1] is just recd. I can certainly have no desire to keep from you the reason of your removal from LaGrange.

Twice it was reported to me that you permitted Flags of Truce to come to your Hd Qrs, once after your attention had been called to the impropriety of such a thing.[2] Discipline was reported very bad in LaGrange, and the burning of three houses, besides other outrages, come to my knowledge.[3]

On the 2nd I caused you to be telegraphed that trade and travel was opened to Holly Springs. You failed to give passes until Major Bowers was telegraphed on the 5th thereby giving the monopoly of trade to three or four individuals f 4 days.[4]

The discipline of the 17th hast become so bad that the Regt alone will require your whole time.[5]

> Very Respectfully &c
> U. S. Grant
> Maj Genl.

Copies, DLC-USG, V, 18, 30, 91; DNA, RG 393, Dept. of the Tenn., Letters Sent. Addison S. Norton was mustered in as capt., 17th Ill., on May 25, 1861. On July 17, 1862, he was confirmed as maj. and aide, but had already commenced service in this capacity on the staff of Maj. Gen. John A. McClernand. Norton later assumed command of the 17th Ill. as col., retaining his U.S. commission as maj.

Controversy between USG's hd. qrs. and Norton, commanding at La Grange, first surfaced in two letters of Nov. 30 from Lt. Col. John A. Rawlins to Norton. "The 126th Ills. will come forward to Coldwater. Will increase your garrison as soon as it is possible to do so without leaving other places more exposed. The Whiskey belonging to Thornburg & Graham will be held subject to their order. They had a permit from Gen. Hurlbut to bring it to Lagrange. It exceeded his authority but they are not to blame for it." "It is reported that a party of the enemy with flag of truce came into La Grange, exchanged prisoners and returned without interruption and that there are no pickets on roads leading into LaGrange. This should not have been permitted. You have no authority to exchange prisoners and should have had pickets out. The enemy's real object was to learn your strength and position. You may look out for an attempt on their part to destroy our supplies at Grand Junction and LaGrange. The 126th Ills. has been directed to report to you which with the Infantry and Cavalry designated as a Garrison for those places will be, with proper vigilance on your part sufficient to hold them and protect our stores. Picket the several roads leading to Grand Junction and LaGrange at once and keep a sharp look out to the east and west of you." Copies, *ibid*. The second letter is in *O.R.*, I, xvii, part 2, 370.

On Dec. 4, USG telegraphed to Norton. "If there are no troops at Davis' Mills send a Regt there immediately. Lose no time. Answer" Copies, DLC-USG, V, 18, 30, 91; DNA, RG 393, Dept. of the Tenn., Letters Sent. On Dec. 12, USG telegraphed to Norton. "Move to Holly Springs with the 17th and turn over the command to the Officer next in rank. March your troops." Copies, *ibid*.

On Dec. 16, Norton, Holly Springs, wrote to USG. "I have the honor to acknowledge the receipt of your communication of the 14th inst. for which I beg leave to tender my sincere thanks. I shall not presume to address you again upon this subject, but in my own justification send the enclosed Statement, which if satisfactory, as I trust it will be, I am sure will afford you *pleasure* in my justification." ALS, DNA, RG 393, Dept. of the Tenn., Letters Received. *O.R.*, I, xvii, part 2, 416. Norton enclosed a lengthy letter addressed to USG dated the same day, and six documentary exhibits, drawn on in the notes below. ALS (and copies of enclosures), DNA, RG 393, Dept. of the Tenn., Letters Received. *O.R.*, I, xvii, part 2, 416–19.

    1. This letter has not been found.

    2. Norton received flag of truce parties on Nov. 29 and Dec. 8. On the first occasion, Norton received a letter addressed to USG from Col. Robert V. Richardson, Partisan Rangers. "G. W. Tatum, G. W. Clay W E. Ballard were part of escort, of flag of Truce with dispatch of 26th Inst. proposing exchange of Thomas Boyle J. H Simon, & Thos. Simon for James F. Bell. E W. Matthews and Dr Theo Wilkenson. The prisoners were left under Flag of Truce, in custody of Tatum Clay & Ballard near Somerville, while Capt Bell proceeded to your Head Quarters with Dispatches. Maj Mudd ~~arrested~~ captured Tatum, Clay & Ballard, horses & Equipments, besides three horses & a buggy used to convey the prisoners Boyle and two Simons. This is a violation of the Flag of Truce, which it is only necessary to bring to your notice, to have corrected. Capt W Bell and J E Raney are bearers of Flag of truce & This dispatch" On Nov. 30, Norton wrote to Richardson. "I am in receipt of your Flag of Truce, and communication of the 29th inst   Disapproving the act of the officer making the arrest of messers Tatum, Clay and Ballard, I have unconditionally ordered their release, and delivered to Capt Bell, the bearer of your Flag. I am not aware of the name of the officer making the arrest" In his letter of Dec. 16, Norton admitted that the flag of truce party had passed points which should have been picketed, and stated that in releasing the prisoners he believed he was acting as USG would wish.

    On Dec. 8, Norton's pickets properly stopped the flag of truce party; then, through ignorance, escorted it through the lines to Norton. Richardson's letter, addressed to the commander, La Grange, asked the release of ten prisoners on parole. On Dec. 10, Norton wrote to Richardson that he knew nothing of these prisoners.

    3. Norton admitted two fires, also the burning of many fence rails for fuel.

    4. Norton stated that he had received a telegram from USG on Dec. 5, 10:20 P.M., opening trade and travel to Holly Springs, and issued orders implementing this. Post Order No. 19, which he enclosed, was dated Dec. 5.

    5. Norton conceded the poor discipline of some of his officers and said that he was trying to remove them.

To Lt. Gen. John C. Pemberton

————

Head Quarters, 13th Army Corps.
Dept of the Tennessee.
Oxford, Dec 15th 1862.

Lieut. Gen. Pemberton.
Commdg Confederate Forces.
Jackson, Miss.
General:

Your communication of the 13th inst in relation to the detention of Capt. Faulkner and other Guerrillas is just received.

These roving bands have been a pest to communities through which they passed but no detriment to the cause of the Union. They have not observed the rules of civilized warfare and I did not suppose were authorized or under any control except such as they agreed upon among themselves.

As you acknowledge them, however and as most of their belligerance is directed against sympathizers and abettors of this rebellion I will send them to Vicksburg for exchange or turn them loose.

I will state here that this is the third communication from you to Gen. Sherman and myself since the present advance commenced that has been threatening in tone.[1] One of your communications also implied a doubt of my veracity in the statement made by me as to prisoners taken, as well as casting reflection upon the character of those prisoners.

I will now state to you that the number of prisoners taken by my forces on this advance has been, exclusive of *Sick* and *stragglers,* over one thousand.

Most of this latter class have been persons who have become tired of the War and have been *permitted* to take the oath of allegiance and return to their homes.

All communications heretofore received from Officers of the Southern Army have been courteous and kind in spirit and have been replied to in the same tone. I regret the necessity for any other class of correspondence.

On my part I shall carry on this war humanely and do what I conceive to be my duty regardless of threats and most certainly without making any.

> I am, Genl, Very Respectfully
> Your Obt. Servant
> U. S. GRANT
> Maj Genl.

Copies, DLC-USG, V, 18, 30, 91; DNA, RG 393, Dept. of the Tenn., Letters Sent. *O.R.*, II, v, 83–84. On Dec. 13, 1862, C.S.A. Lt. Gen. John C. Pemberton, Jackson, Miss., wrote to USG. "I am credibly informed that Capt W. W. Faulkner, Capt Meriwether, Lieut L. U. Johnson, Lieut Blakemore, and sixteen (16) privates belonging to Partizan Ranger Corps, Confederate States Army, have been refused the benefits of the late Cartel for the exchange of prisoners of war. These officers and men are as much a part of the Confederate States army as are any others composing it, and as much entitled to the benefits of the Cartel as any of your prisoners whom I now hold—I request therefore to be informed of your intentions in reference to the prisoners above referred to; and have to state that I shall cause an equal number of your prisoners to be held in close confinement, if the information conveyed to me be correct—" LS, DNA, RG 109, Unfiled Papers, Robert M. Meriwether; copy, *ibid.*, Dept. of Miss. and East La., Letters Sent. *O.R.*, II, v, 77. See telegram to Maj. Gen. Henry W. Halleck, Oct. 19, 1862, and letter to Col. Jesse Hildebrand, Dec. 15, 1862.

On Dec. 16, Col. John K. Mizner, Water Valley, telegraphed to USG. "Capt Nugent 3d Mch. Cav. sent with flag of truce from Coffeeville has returnd   he went to the enemys grand guard Infy which he found eight miles south of Coffeeville   I have Lt Gen Pemberton autograph letter authorizing Lt Col H R Withers to receve your despatches & his receipt for the   Rusts Div is in front & whole army still at Grenada   Reg of Cav the fourth Ky was at the Oakachima & their pickets but a short distance north"   Telegram received, DNA, RG 393, Dept. of the Tenn., Telegrams Received.

1. See letters to Lt. Gen. John C. Pemberton, Nov. 23, Dec. 14, 1862. On Nov. 19, Maj. Gen. William T. Sherman wrote to Lt. Col. John A. Rawlins discussing and enclosing his correspondence with Pemberton concerning the killing of William H. White of De Soto County, Miss., by troops of the 6th Ill. Cav. following an ambush of U.S. troops near his home. Copy, DNA, RG 94, Generals' Papers and Books, William T. Sherman, Letters Sent. *O.R.*, II, iv, 729–30; *ibid.*, I, xvii, part 2, 870–71. The enclosed correspondence is *ibid.*, pp. 871–73; *ibid.*, II, iv, 702–3, 723–25.

To Maj. Gen. William T. Sherman

Oxford, Dec 15th 1862

Major Gen. Sherman, Memphis, Tenn.
Care Capt. Fitch, Columbus, Ky.

If there is any difficulty about getting possession of the forces at Helena that were thrown to the West bank of the river assume command of them by Gen. Hallecks order and organize them and take them off. I hope Steele will be able to go with them.

It is to be hoped that you will have no trouble in getting possession of these troops but be prepared to act positively if necessary.

U. S. Grant
Major Genl.

Copies, DLC-USG, V, 18, 30, 91; DNA, RG 393, Dept. of the Tenn., Letters Sent. *O.R.*, I, xvii, part 2, 414.

On Dec. 18, 1862, Maj. Gen. William T. Sherman wrote to Lt. Col. John A. Rawlins. "Capt H. S. Fitch arrived last night with your Despatches of Dec 15th & 16th. All right—I am now in full receipt of letters from Col Parsons General Allens Agent for chartering Boats who assures me plenty of Boats will be here today. I am furnished the names of some Sixty Boats. I have some 15 here now loading, and have at Helena about ten, and am momentarily looking for the whole Fleet. As soon as they arrive I will be on board and off for Helena—Admiral Porter is just in from above, having been detained four days, by low water, but his letters are all we could ask. I am also informed that there is a rise in the water above so that the Fleet of Boats ought not to be longer delayed. Evry possible preperation has been made, so that no moment should be lost. If the fleet came today all shall be on board tomorrow and I hope to be at Helena the 20th and at Millikens Bend, Where we shall first begin to act by the 23 or 24th. Nothing is wanting but the Boats and I feel evry assurance they will be here today. I was all ready so that evn the loss of one day must not be charged to me. General Gorman and Steele both write me most satisfactorily from Helena, and indeed we must admit they have fulfilled their parts handsomely. I give Steele full command of the Division at Helena which by the addition of Blairs Brigade, part of which 3 Regts. have passed and the men reported near at hand, will reach near 13 000 men, so that I hope to have 33 000 men. Such a force operating at Vicksburg in concert with the Gunboats will make something to yield and prepare your way. You will have heard that our Iron Clad Gunboat Cairo was sunk in the Yazoo by the Explosion of one of the Infernal machines. The weather is fine, and I repeat I only await the fleet of Transports to be off." ALS, DNA, RG 94, War Records Office, Union Battle Reports. *O.R.*, I, xvii, part 2, 426; *O.R.* (Navy), I, xxiii, 557–58.

On Dec. 19, Sherman wrote to Rawlins. "I estimate we have enough Boats to carry our command—We are now embarking and will be all aboard tomorrow. I will go ahead to Helena tomorrow and conclude the arrangements for the Garison at Friars Point & Cavalry force operating to the Tallahatchee. Enough Boats ~~will~~ have gone forward to carry Steeles Command, so that I calculate to leave Helena. Dec 21, Gavins Landing 22. and be at Vicksburg 24th. No final Returns from Helena but estimated Total 32000. men. Admiral Porter is here and goes to Helena tomorrow. We expect all to meet at Millikens Bend 25 miles above Vicksburg, on the 24th. Shall at once break Railroad West of Vicksburg and then enter the Yazoo. You may calculate on our being at Vicksburg by Christmas.— River has risen some feet and all is now good navigation. Gunboats are at Mouth of Yazoo now, and there will be no difficulty effecting a landing up Yazoo within 12 miles of Vicksburg. General Gorman proposes to move all his force from Helena to Napoleon at mouth of Arkansas. I will see him tomorrow. He says he could then if called brig all his men to Vicksburg, or act up the Arkansas. Colonel Howe & 4 companies of Regular Cavalry have arrived armed with pistols & Sabres. I leave him with the Garrison hitherto detailed for Memphis. I take Thielmans Cavalry, 70 men.   at Helena will make up the necessary Cavalry force   At Vicksburg will act so as to accomplish the original purpose and will calculate to send you rations up the Yazoo. Yazoo City is the best point and can be reached after the reduction of the Battery at Haines Bluff." ALS, DNA, RG 94, War Records Office, Union Battle Reports. *O.R.*, I, xvii, part 1, 603–4. On Dec. 19, Brig. Gen. Frederick Steele, Columbus, Ky., telegraphed to USG. "I am on my way to Helena with one Div   expect another will follow soon"   Telegram received, DNA, RG 393, Dept. of the Tenn., Telegrams Received.

On Dec. 21, Sherman, Helena, Ark., wrote to Rawlins reporting his strength and plans. ALS, *ibid.*, RG 94, War Records Office, Union Battle Reports. *O.R.*, I, xvii, part 1, 604–5.

To Col. Jesse Hildebrand

Hd Qrs, 13th Army Corps.
Dept of the Tennessee.
Oxford, Dec 15th 1862.

Commdg Officer, Alton, Ills.

Col. Faulkner and Capt. Merriweather[1] and their Officers and men now in the Military prison at Alton, Ills. having been recognized by the Conferate authorities as regularly in the Confederate service and entitled to the treatment of Prisoners of War.

You will therefore please send them in charge of a proper escort to Cairo, Ills. and deliver them to the Commdg Officer at that place to be forwarded by him on Cartel ship to Vicksburg for exchange under the provisions of the Cartel agreed upon between the United States and Confederate authorities.

> I am, Sir, Very Respectfully
> Your Ob't. Servant.
> U. S. Grant
> Maj Gen. Commdg.

Copies, DLC-USG, V, 18, 30, 91; DNA, RG 393, Dept. of the Tenn., Letters Sent. On Dec. 19, 1862, Col. Jesse Hildebrand wrote to USG. "In answer to yours of the 15th inst I have to inform you that in transferring a lot of Prisoners from this Prison to Johnstons Island on the 14th of last month, Col Faulkner made his escape and has not been herd of since. Capt Merriweather has been sent to Cairo for exchange" LS, *ibid.*, RG 109, Unfiled Papers and Slips. *O.R.*, II, v, 99. See letter to Lt. Gen. John C. Pemberton, Dec. 15, 1862.

1. Capt. Robert M. Meriwether.

To Mary Grant

Oxford Mississippi
Dec. 15th 1862

Dear Sister,

Yesterday I received a letter from you and the children and one from Uncle Samuel.[1] Today I learn by telegraph that father is at Holly Springs thirty miles North of here. Julia is there and as I expect the rail-road to be completed to here by to-morrow I look for them down.[2] I shall only remain here to-morrow, or next day at farthest; so that Julia will go immediately back to Holly Spri[ngs.] It is a pleasant place and she may as well stay there as elswhere. I will state here before I forget it that I will give father fifty dollars to be used for the children. So you need not wait for anything they may need to get the money.

We are now having wet weather. I have a big Army in front of me as well as bad roads. I shall probably give a good account of myself however notwithstanding all obsticles. My plans are all complete for weeks to come and I hope to have them all work out just as planed. For a conciencious person, and I profess to be one, this is a most slavish life. I may be envied by ambitious persons but I in turn envy the person who can transact his daily business and retire to a quiet home without a feeling of responsibility for the morrow. Taking my whole Department there are an immence number of lives staked upon my judgement and acts. I am extended now like a Peninsula into an enemies country with a large Army depending for their daily bread upon keeping open a line of rail-road runing one hundred & ninety miles through an enemy's country, or at least through territory occupied by a people terribly embittered and hostile to us. With all this I suffer the mortification of seeing myself attacked right and left by people at home professing patriotism and love of country who never heard the whistle of a hostile bullet. I pitty them and a nation dependent upon such for its existence   I am thankful however that although such people make a great noise the masses are not like them.

With all my other trials I have to condend against is added that of speculators whos patriotism is measured by dollars & cents. Country has no value with them compared with money.[3] To illucidate this would take quires of paper so I will reserve this for an evenings conversation if I should be so fortunate as to again get home where I can have a day to myself.

Tell the children to learn their lessons, mind their grandma and be good children. I should like very much to see them. To me they are all obedient and good. I may be partial but they seem to me to be children to be proud of.

Remember me to all at home.

Your brother
ULYS.

ALS, PPRF.

1. For Samuel Simpson, see *PUSG*, 1, 7*n*–8*n*.
2. See letter to Julia Dent Grant, Dec. 13, 1862.
3. On Dec. 15, 1862, Brig. Gen. John McArthur, Abbeville, telegraphed to USG. "There are one hundred & Ten bales cotton here taken from J R Bowles

state senator mostly marked C. S. A. aid legitimately confiscated for which a reciept was given to his overseer   he has turned over said receipt to a Mr Shultz who presents himself to me claimng said cotton by virtue of special feild orders No. 22 from your head quarters   I have declined to deliver it on the ground that the cotton did not originally belong to Shultz nor does now nor ₊ have I any belonging to him which is all the order calls for   It appears by this plan they wish to whip the Devil around the stump   Shultz avers that this was explained to you when the order was issued   Is this so & shall I deliver the cotton"   Telegram received, DNA, RG 393, Dept. of the Tenn., Telegrams Received.

To Richardson, Spence and Thompson

[*Oxford, Miss.*]
[*Dec. 15, 1862*]

You will please make and forward to me a complete suit— coat vest and pants—including Major General's shoulder straps. Make the vest of dark blue cloth.

Also a coat and pants for Col. W. S. Hillyer of my staff.

You have Col. Hillyer's measure taken some time ago. Since then he has increased some three inches in circumference and about 33 pounds in weight. His height is the same. If the coat and pants are made about three inches larger around the waist, you can probably fix the proportions by the old measure.

U. S. GRANT

American Clipper (American Autograph Shop, Merion Station, Pa.), Dec., 1939, p. 899. On Jan. 23, 1863, USG wrote to Richardson, Spence, and Thompson. "Enclosed I send you one hundred & thirty-four dollars (134) the amount of Col. Hillyer's and my last bills for clothing, with 5 pr. ct. off for cash as per accompanying account. The clothing suits both as to quality of goods and fit of the garments." ALS, deCoppet Collection, NjP. Attached to this letter is a document giving detailed measurements for USG. *Ibid.*

To Maj. Gen. Henry W. Halleck

Oxford Miss 6 P M [*Dec.*] 16th [*1862*]
Maj Gen H W Hallack
The following dispatch from Gen Dodge just rec'd:

Corinth Dec 16th 1862
To Maj Gen Grant, I have men in direct from Shelbyville
Tenn, Left the Eighth 8th & crossed the Tenn at Eastport
all the army at Shelbyville & South had been ordered to
Torgue Tenn[1]   also most of Cavalry   the bulk of the stores
were kept at Chattanooga They having eight (8) days on
hand   Johnson has entire command & they intend to make
stand at Torgue   The bridge at Bridgeport[2] is finished,   A
large number of deserters are coming to our lines from
Braggs army west Tenn & Arkansas troops   They corrobo-
rate the above   Generally when these men left most of For-
resters cavalry was up on Cumberland river west of Nashville
Buckner command occupied Shelbyville & Marched to
Torgue Dec 6th   Col Warren was killed in fight in Tuscumbia   Signed   G M Dodge Brig Genl[3]
U. S Grant
Maj Gen

Telegram received, DNA, RG 94, Generals' Papers and Books, Telegrams
Received by Gen. Halleck; *ibid.*, RG 107, Telegrams Collected (Bound); copies,
ibid., RG 393, Dept. of the Tenn., Hd. Qrs. Correspondence; DLC-USG, V, 5, 8,
24, 88, 91. *O.R.*, I, xvii, part 1, 476.
    Also on Dec. 16, 1862, USG telegraphed to Maj. Gen. Henry W. Halleck.
"Bragg is said to be going towards the Tenn. river through Waynesboro.
Rosecrans ought to push them & if possible gunboats be sent up the Tenn."
Telegram received, DNA, RG 94, Generals' Papers and Books, Telegrams
Received by Gen. Halleck; *ibid.*, RG 107, Telegrams Collected (Bound); copies,
ibid., RG 393, Dept. of the Tenn., Hd. Qrs. Correspondence; DLC-USG, V, 5, 8,
24, 88, 91. *O.R.*, I, xvii, part 1, 476. On the same day, USG sent an identically
worded telegram to Act. Rear Admiral David D. Porter. Telegram received,
DNA, RG 45, Correspondence of David D. Porter, Telegrams Received. *O.R.*
(Navy), I, xxiii, 627. Another identical telegram went to Maj. Gen. William S.
Rosecrans. Telegram received, DNA, RG 393, Dept. of the Cumberland, Telegrams Received.

On Dec. 14, Brig. Gen. Jeremiah C. Sullivan, Jackson, wrote to Lt. Col. John A. Rawlins. "The reported crossing of the Tennessee River by a large guerrilla force seems to be false. The country south of Hatchie is not in my command, but I propose to visit it with all my cavalry and three regiments of infantry during this week. I will have at La Grange and Grand Junction, as soon as I can procure arms and equipments, about 500 cavalry. An advance made by Hurlbut toward the Hatchie and my troops marching on the south side toward Somerville will clear all the guerrillas from the haunts in that direction. Commanders of posts and regiments are unable to make their monthly returns for November for want of blanks. I am without any for my own headquarters. Can you supply?" *O.R.*, I, xvii, part 2, 413. On Dec. 15, 6:30 P.M. and 9:50 P.M., Sullivan twice telegraphed to USG. "Forrest is crossing Tennessee at Clifton. A large force of cavalry is crossing above. Bragg's army is reported by scouts to be moving this way, through Waynesborough. It has been raining hard all day." *Ibid.*, p. 415. "I will detain the detachment of fifth O Cav & two 2 Regts infantry a few days until I can by actual observation know what is going on at Tenn River" Telegram received, DNA, RG 393, Dept. of the Tenn., Telegrams Received.

1. Apparently Lavergne, Tenn., on the Nashville and Chattanooga Railroad, about fifteen miles southeast of Nashville.
2. Bridgeport, Ala., on the Tennessee River, about a mile south of the Tenn. state line.
3. Telegram received, *ibid.*

To Maj. Gen. James B. McPherson

Oxford Dec 16—1862

Gen McPherson

I will move head Quarters on ~~the~~ Thursday[1]—Is there a house near the Railroad north side of the River—News from Tennessee is that some of Braggs forces are at waynesboro moving west—Forrest moving on clifton   no special orders for you —Grierson has returned & will join you tomorrow

U S Grant
Maj Gen

Telegram received, McPherson Papers, NjR.
On Dec. 12, 1862, Maj. Gen. James B. McPherson had written to USG. "Enclosed I send you a Sketch showing the relative positions of the different Divisions of my Command. Genl. Denver's Division came up about two P. M. to day and Genl. Lauman's about Four—I have had a large force building and repairing bridges to day & the 'Free Bridge' across the Yick-na-pa-ta-fa will be

Officers of the 47th Illinois, Oxford, Mississippi, December 1862. *Courtesy William M. Anderson, Galesburg, Illinois.*

Maj. Gen. John A. Logan (seventh from left, hand on sword) and Staff. *Courtesy William M. Anderson, Galesburg, Illinois.*

ready to cross on tomorrow morning. The Cavalry has gone to the Front near Water Valley, everything quiet as far as I can learn—Forage is Very Scarce in this Vicinity, as well as everything Else in the Eating line" ALS, DNA, RG 393, Dept. of the Tenn., Letters Received. The sketch is attached.

1. Dec. 18. See telegram to Maj. Gen. James B. McPherson, Dec. 17, 1862.

General Orders No. 11

————

Head Quarters 13th Army Corps,
Department of the Tennessee,
Oxford, Miss. Dec. 17th 1862.

GENERAL ORDERS No. 12.

I. . The Jews, as a class, violating every regulation of trade established by the Treasury Department, and also Department orders, are hereby expelled from the Department.

II. . Within twenty-four hours from the receipt of this order by Post Commanders, they will see that all of this class of people are furnished with passes and required to leave, and any one returning after such notification, will be arrested and held in confinement until an opportunity occurs of sending them out as prisoners unless furnished with permits from these Head Quarters.

III. . No permits will be given these people to visit Head Quarters for the purpose of making personal application for trade permits.

By Order of Maj. Genl. U. S. Grant
JNO. A. RAWLINS
Ass't Adj't Genl.

Copies (designated General Orders No. 12), DLC-USG, V, 13, 14, 95; DNA, RG 94, Dept. of the Tenn., General Orders; *ibid.*, RG 393, Dept. of the Tenn., General and Special Orders. This document, originally designated General Orders No. 11, was incorporated with that number on Dec. 17, 1862, in a telegram from Lt. Col. John A. Rawlins, Oxford, Miss., to Brig. Gen. Mason Brayman, Bolivar, Tenn. Telegram received, Brayman Papers, ICHi. After the discovery that General Orders No. 11, Dept. of the Tenn., had already been issued at La Grange, Tenn., on Nov. 26, to announce the results of recent courts-martial, the number was changed in book records. In the meantime, this document had been widely publicized as General Orders No. 11, and is thus numbered in *O.R.*, I, xvii, part 2, 424. Kenneth P. Williams, *Lincoln Finds a General* (New York, 1949–59), IV, 512, explained the numerical discrepancy on the basis of USG's decision not to issue General Orders No. 9, Nov. 23. If the original number had later been revised downward, this explanation would be appropriate, but the opposite occurred. Since USG issued General Orders No. 11 at Oxford while the bulk of his records were at Holly Springs, accidental misnumbering is more likely. See Rawlins to Enos Ripley, Dec. 20, 1862, ADfS, USG 3.

General Orders No. 11 has inspired considerable discussion and speculation, with much attention given to possible diminution of USG's responsibility for the document. Bertram Wallace Korn, *American Jewry and the Civil War* (Philadelphia, 1951), pp. 140–44, presented several contemporary accounts, including statements by Rawlins and Jesse R. Grant, attributing General Orders No. 11 to orders from Washington. Korn concluded, however, that previous letters written by USG indicated prejudice against Jews, that no subsequent letter of USG supported this contention, and that no record existed of the supposed orders from Washington. It may be added that communications from the War Dept. to USG were routinely copied in Washington, sometimes frequently, then entered in the register of letters received by the Dept. of the Tenn., or copied in letterbooks. Telegrams were also copied both by the War Dept. and at USG's hd. qrs. Records at both ends are so complete that actual messages almost always show up in both places, and no orders authorizing or encouraging General Orders No. 11 have been found. Only one communication from Washington to USG mentioned Jews. On Dec. 1, Philip Wadsworth, Chicago, wrote to the War Dept. "states that Jews are taking large amounts of gold into Kentucky and Tennessee." DNA, RG 107, Register of Letters Received. Wadsworth's letter, received on Dec. 5, was referred to USG, but no copy exists of the letter or endorsement. See following letter.

In the western theatre of war, frequent complaints concerning Jewish involvement in illicit trade appeared in newspapers and in correspondence of persons associated with USG. In 1861, Treasury agent William P. Mellen and Lt. S. Ledyard Phelps denounced the Jews of Paducah. *HRC* 37-3-108, III, 574; *PUSG*, 3, 425. As U.S. forces advanced southward in 1862, commanders blamed Jews for the cotton trade: examples include Brig. Gen. Leonard F. Ross, July 25 (*O.R.*, I, xvii, part 2, 120); Maj. Gen. William T. Sherman to Rawlins, July 30 (*ibid.*, pp. 140–41), Aug. 11 (*ibid.*, III, ii, 349–50); Maj. Gen. Samuel R. Curtis, Aug. 10 (*ibid.*, I, xiii, 553); Brig. Gen. Alvin P. Hovey, Dec. 5 (*ibid.*, I, xvii, part 1, 532). See also testimony of Maj. Gen. Stephen A. Hurlbut, Memphis, May 8, 1863, RG 156, KK 285. Casual anti-Semitism was reflected in a newspaper comment: "From Jackson I learn nothing new or startling. Col. C. C. Marsh, commandant of the post, has expelled a dozen Jewish cotton buyers for dealing in Southern money, and depreciating United States Treasury notes." Letter of "Hal," Cairo, Oct. 31, in *New York Tribune*, Nov. 5, 1862. For similar expressions see *Chicago Tribune*, Nov. 25, 1862, *Missouri Republican*, Nov. 23, Dec. 20, 1862. Jewish merchants in Memphis attracted both heavy contemporary fire and later scholarship. See Albert Deane Richardson, *The Secret Service, the Field, the Dungeon, and the Escape* (Hartford, 1865), p. 264; *Complete History of the 6th Illinois Veteran Volunteer Infantry* (Freeport, Ill., 1866), p. 48; *Extracts from Letters to A. B. T. from Edward P. Williams . . .* (New York, 1903), pp. 18–19; Joseph H. Parks, "A Confederate Trade Center under Federal Occupation:

Memphis, 1862 to 1865," *Journal of Southern History*, VII, 3 (Aug., 1941), 293; Korn, pp. 147–55; James A. Wax, "The Jews of Memphis: 1860–1865," *West Tennessee Historical Society Papers*, III (1949), 39–87. James Grant Wilson, *General Grant* (New York, 1897), pp. 149–50, purported to provide a first-hand account of the author's pursuit of Jewish smugglers while USG commanded at Memphis, but Wilson was not appointed maj., 15th Ill. Cav., until Dec. 25, 1862, and was mustered in on Jan. 9, 1863.

General Orders No. 11 represented the culmination of USG's efforts to regulate the cotton trade in his dept. to the advantage of his army. Concern with the supply of his opponents by unscrupulous businessmen furnished a recurrent theme in his correspondence and orders; see letters to Brig. Gen. Isaac F. Quinby, Nov. 18, 1862, to Mary Grant, Dec. 15, 1862. At the same time, authorities in Washington encouraged trade in order to bring much-needed cotton to northern mills. On Dec. 6, 1862, Capt. Theodore S. Bowers issued Special Orders No. 40 permitting civilians, previously stopped at the Miss. state line, to travel to the Tallahatchie River. DS, DNA, RG 94, Dept. of the Tenn., General and Special Orders; copies, *ibid.*, RG 393, Dept. of the Tenn., Special Orders; DLC-USG, V, 26, 27. On Dec. 11, Bowers issued Special Orders No. 44 extending the travel limits to Oxford. DS, DNA, RG 94, Dept. of the Tenn., General and Special Orders; copies, *ibid.*, RG 393, Dept. of the Tenn., Special Orders; DLC-USG, V, 26, 27; (printed) Oglesby Papers, IHi. *O.R.*, I, xvii, part 2, 400. On Dec. 1, Special Agent of the Treasury David G. Barnitz reported to Mellen that considerable cotton was then passing through Cairo, Ill. ALS, DNA, RG 366, Correspondence of the General Agent.

In 1918, Simon Wolf reported a conversation with USG a half-century earlier in which USG allegedly claimed that he had "nothing whatever to do" with General Orders No. 11, that the person responsible was "one of his staff officers" acting on a complaint by Sherman, and that USG had never set the record straight because to do so might be considered "seeking public applause." *The Presidents I have Known from 1860-1918* (Washington, [1918]), pp. 70–71. But the orders were issued by Rawlins, as demonstrated by his telegram to Brayman cited above, and the issuance of orders in USG's name was not casually done behind his back. Some earlier orders printed in *PUSG* are drafts by USG for Rawlins's signature. Whether USG or Rawlins drafted General Orders No. 11 is moot; that USG knew and approved of them before issuance is certain. *Richardson* (p. 277) described an angry USG issuing the orders over Rawlins's objections. See James Harrison Wilson, *The Life of John A. Rawlins* (New York, 1916), p. 96. For criticism of Wolf's accuracy in another context, see Sylvan Morris Dubow, "Identifying the Jewish Serviceman in the Civil War: A Re-Appraisal of Simon Wolf's *The American Jew as Patriot, Soldier and Citizen*," *American Jewish Historical Quarterly*, LIX, 3 (March, 1970), 357–69.

Whether or not USG actually drafted General Orders No. 11, he had already expressed unfavorable views of Jews in communications to Quinby, July 26, 1862; to Hurlbut, Nov. 9; to Col. Joseph D. Webster, Nov. 10; to Sherman, Dec. 5. See following letter. Although General Orders No. 11 raised a storm of controversy, USG's earlier attitude had not gone unnoticed: a soldier newspaper published in the town which held USG's hd. qrs. called Jews "sharks, feeding upon the soldiers.—General Grant has determined to rate them a nuisance, and abate it suddenly." *Corinth War Eagle*, Aug. 7, 1862. See letter from Corinth, Aug. 16, 1862, in *Chicago Times*, Aug. 22, 1862.

USG's thoughts in issuing General Orders No. 11 probably involved the arrival of his father in Holly Springs intent on obtaining permits to trade in cotton. Jesse R. Grant agreed to use his influence to further the enterprise of Mack & Brothers, a Jewish firm of Cincinnati, in return for one quarter of the profits. Jesse Grant later unsuccessfully sued the Macks for withholding payment; his petition of Dec. 21, 1863, is in the *New York Tribune*, Sept. 19, 1872. The decision was reported in the *Cincinnati Enquirer*, May 17, 1864. See Walter B. Stevens, "Joseph B. McCullagh . . . Third Article," *Missouri Historical Review*, XXV, 4 (April, 1931), 427–28; *Richardson*, p. 277; Jesse R. Grant to Elihu B. Washburne, Jan. 20, 1863, DLC-Elihu B. Washburne; anonymous letter to Robert Bonner, Feb. 24, 1868, DLC-USG; Sylvanus Cadwallader, "Four Years with Grant," pp. 48–49, IHi. Jesse Grant's involvement in the cotton trade provides a psychological explanation for the orders, though hardly a justification—USG expelled the Jews rather than his father—and also may explain why USG issued these orders shortly after revoking similar orders issued at Holly Springs. See telegram to Col. John V. D. Du Bois, Dec. 9, 1862.

Orders expelling Jews, "as a class," for violation of U.S. Treasury regulations created uncertainty in enforcement. On Dec. 18, 1862, Brig. Gen. Grenville M. Dodge, Corinth, telegraphed to Rawlins to ask if the orders applied to Jewish sutlers. Telegram received, DNA, RG 393, Dept. of the Tenn., Telegrams Received. On Dec. 19, Col. Robert C. Murphy, Holly Springs, telegraphed to Rawlins to ask if he had been correct in expelling Jewish sutlers. Telegram received, *ibid*. On Dec. 24, Col. James B. Weaver, 2nd Iowa, and other officers, Corinth, wrote to USG's hd. qrs. to ask that L. S. Flersham [Florsheim ?] and his brother, who were Jews, be allowed to continue as sutlers. *Ibid*., Register of Letters Received; DLC-USG, V, 21. On Dec. 31, Rawlins endorsed this letter. "Brig Genl Dodge is hereby especially authorized to grant the permit asked for if it meets his approval" Copies, *ibid*., V, 25; DNA, RG 393, Dept. of the Tenn., Endorsements. On Dec. 31, Lt. Col. George H. Campbell, Jackson, Tenn., telegraphed to Rawlins to ask about Jewish sutlers. Telegram received, *ibid*., Telegrams Received. These officers saw the orders in relation to sutlers, and neglected a broader interpretation applying to soldiers. But on March 3, 1863, Capt. Philip Trounstine, 5th Ohio Cav., Moscow, Tenn., wrote to Maj. Charles S. Hayes that because he was "either fortunately or unfortunately born of Jewish parents," he was "deeply hurt" by USG's orders and subject to "taunts and malice." He therefore submitted his "immeadiate and unconditional resignation." ALS, *ibid*., RG 94, Carded Records, Vol. Organizations, Civil War, 5th Ohio Cav. See Benjamin P. Thomas, ed., *Three Years with Grant as Recalled by War Correspondent Sylvanus Cadwallader* (New York, 1955), p. 40.

U.S. Senator Lazarus W. Powell stated that he had documents showing that about thirty Jewish male citizens of Paducah were expelled on twenty-four hour notice along with their wives and children. Jan. 9, 1863, *CG*, 37-3, 245. Information concerning enforcement on other civilians, though less precise, indicates that the orders were followed. See Korn, pp. 123–24.

On Jan. 4, Maj. Gen. Henry W. Halleck telegraphed to USG. "A paper purporting to be a Genl Order No. 11 issued by you Dec 17th has been presented here. By its terms it expells all Jews from your Dept. If such an order has been issued, it will be immediately revoked." ALS (telegram sent), DNA, RG 107, Telegrams Collected (Bound); copies, *ibid*., RG 108, Telegrams Sent; *ibid*., RG 393, Dept. of the Tenn., Hd. Qrs. Correspondence; DLC-USG, V, 5, 8, 24,

88. *O.R.*, I, xvii, part 2, 530. On Jan. 5, Col. John C. Kelton wrote to USG. "Permit me to inform you unofficially the objection taken to your Genl Order No 11. It excluded a whole class, insted of certain obnoxious individuals. Had the word 'pedler' been inserted after Jew I do not suppose any exception would have been taken to the order. Several officers and a number of enlisted men in your Dept are Jews. A Govr of one of the Western states is a Jew." ALS, DNA, RG 393, Dept. of the Tenn., Letters Received. This letter was not received until Jan. 12, so it was solely in response to Halleck's telegram that on Jan. 6, Rawlins issued General Orders No. 2. "In pursuance of directions from the General-in-Chief of the Army, General Orders No. 12, from these Head Quarters, dated Oxford, Miss., December 17th, 1862, is hereby revoked." Copies, DLC-USG, V, 13, 14, 95; DNA, RG 393, Dept. of the Tenn., General and Special Orders. On the same day, Rawlins telegraphed to Brig. Gen. Charles S. Hamilton. "By direction of the General in Chief of the Army at Washington the General Order from these Head Quarters expelling Jews from this Department is hereby revoked" Copies, DLC-USG, V, 18, 30; DNA, RG 393, Dept. of the Tenn., Letters Sent. Rawlins telegraphed an identical message to Brig. Gen. Thomas A. Davies (telegram received, *ibid.*, Dept. of Ky., Telegrams Received) and to Dodge (undated telegram received, Rawlins Papers, ICHi). Printed as a circular, dated Jan. 7, *O.R.*, I, xvii, part 2, 544. On Jan. 21, Halleck wrote to USG. "The President has directed that so much of Arkansas as you may desire to control, be temporarily attached to your Department. This will give you control of both banks of the river. In your operations down the Mississippi you must not rely too confidently upon any direct cooperation of Genl Banks and the lower flotilla, as it is possible that they may not be able to pass or reduce Port Hudson. They, however, will do every thing in their power to form a junction with you at Vicksburg. If they should not be able to effect this, they will, at least, occupy a portion of the enemy's forces, and prevent them from reinforcing Vicksburg. I hope, however, that they will do still better, and be able to join you. It may be proper to give you some explanation of the revocation of your order expelling all Jews from your Dept. The President has no objection to your expelling traders & Jew pedlars, which I suppose was the object of your order, but as it in terms prescribed an entire religious class, some of whom are fighting in our ranks, the President deemed it necessary to revoke it." ALS, DNA, RG 94, War Records Office, Dept. of the Tenn. *O.R.*, I, xxiv, part 1, 9.

In the meantime, numerous protests against the orders reached Washington. On Dec. 29, 1862, a telegram was sent to President Abraham Lincoln by D. Wolff & Bros., Cesar F. Kaskel, and J. W. Kaskel, Paducah. "Genl. order No. 11, issued by Genl Grant Oxford Miss, december the 17th Commands all post Commanders, to expel all Jews without distinction within twenty four hours from his entire Dept   the undersigned good & Loyal Citizens of the U. S. & residents of this town for many years engaged in legitimate business as Merchants feel greatly insulted & outraged by this inhuman order the carrying out of which would be the grossest violation of the U. S. Constitution & our rights as good Citizens under it & would place us besides a large number of other Jewish families of this town as outlaws before the whole world; we respectfully ask your immediate attention to this enormous outrage on all law & humanity & pray for your effectual & immediate interposition. We would respectfully refer you to the Post Commander & Post Adjt as to our loyalty & to all respectable Citizens of this Community as to our standing as Citizens & merchants. We respectfully ask for immediate instructions to be sent to the Commander of this Post—" Telegram received, DNA, RG 107, Irregular Series, Letters Received. *O.R.*, I, xvii, part 2, *506*. On Dec. 31, Halleck endorsed this telegram. "Respectfully referred to Genl Grant for report." AES, DNA, RG 107, Irregular Series, Letters Received. On Jan. 15, 1863, USG endorsed the telegram. "Respectfully returned to Headquarters of the Army, Washington, D. C. and attention invited to enclosed copies of General Orders from this Department." ES, *ibid.*

On Jan. 5, Rabbi Isaac M. Wise, Cincinnati, wrote to Secretary of War Edwin M. Stanton. "Without having received an answer to my letter of December 30, I must trouble you again. Notwithstanding my oppositions deputations from Louisville Ky. Paducah Ky., Cincinnati and elsewhere have been appointed to see the President on General Grant's order expelling the Jews, and I *must* go with them to Washington. In similar cases Mr. Van Buren and Mr. Buchanan disposed of the subject matter previous to the call of the committees, and gained the laurels of paternal care. I respectfully suggest the same policy. Enclosed a copy of the order." ALS, *ibid.* An account by Wise of his visit to Washington, printed in *The Israelite*, Jan. 16, 1863, is reprinted in Morris U. Schappes, *A Documentary History of the Jews in the United States 1654–1875* (3rd ed., New York, 1971), pp. 473–76. On Jan. 5, S. M. Isaacs & Son, office of the *Jewish Messenger*, wrote to Halleck. "We have been informed that, at the instance of the President, you have rescinded the General Order issued by Gen Grant excluding 'all Jews' from his department. May we trouble you to kindly notify us as to the truth of this statement, in order that we may communicate the same to the Jewish public in our pages this week?" ALS, DNA, RG 108, Letters Received. On the same day, Rabbi Bernhard Felsenthal, Sinai Congregation, Chicago, wrote Stanton a long protest against the orders. ALS, *ibid.*, RG 107, Letters Received. On Jan. 10, Asst. Secretary of War Peter H. Watson wrote to Felsenthal that the orders had "been rescinded by order of the President." LS, American Jewish Historical Society, Waltham, Mass. On Jan. 6, John M. Krum, St. Louis, telegraphed to Halleck. "Have you revoked Genl Grants order expelling Jews—great indignation here against his order Answer paid here—" Telegram received, DNA, RG 107, Telegrams Collected (Bound). On Jan. 9, Halleck telegraphed to Krum. "Genl Grants order expelling Jews revoked some time ago." ALS (telegram sent), *ibid.* On Jan. 13, Myer S. Isaacs, Board of Delegates of American Israelites, New York, sent to Stanton resolutions condemning the orders and commending Halleck for their revocation. ALS, *ibid.*, Letters Received. The resolutions are *ibid.*, and in RG 108, Letters Received. A third copy was to be sent to USG. Other reactions are discussed in Korn, pp. 124–32.

Resolutions condemning the orders were introduced in the U.S. House of Representatives by George H. Pendleton of Ohio and in the Senate by Lazarus W. Powell of Ky., but were tabled in the House by a vote of 56-53, and in the Senate 30-7. *CG*, 37-3, 184, 222, 245–46. On Jan. 6, U.S. Representative Elihu B. Washburne wrote to Lincoln that General Orders No. 11 were "the wisest order yet made . . ." ALS, DLC-Robert T. Lincoln. On Jan. 8, Washburne wrote to USG. "Your order touching the Jews has kicked up quite a dust among the Israelites. They came here in crowds and gave an entirely false construction to the order and Halleck revoked it. I went to see him about it yesterday and he said it was so broad in the way it was construed he had to revoke it.—That construed as it was undoubtedly intended—that is, to exclude Jew peddlars, &c. it would be all right, but to apply it to all the Jew residents, would be a hardship. He said, further, if you would only express precisely in your order what you meant (as he supposed) to exclude these Jew traders it would be all right. You will see by the paper I send you they moved in regard to it in our House yesterday, but they did not make anything by it. All the democrats were fierce to censure your action. We have just got the news of Sherman's repulse and all feel badly." ALS, USG 3. No reply by USG to this letter is known, and the issue apparently submerged until the presidential campaign of 1868. See letter to Isaac N. Morris, Sept. 14, 1868.

To Christopher P. Wolcott

Head Quarters, 13th Army Corps.
Dept of the Tennessee
Oxford, Dec 17th 1862

HON. C. P. WOLCOTT
ASST. SECTY OF WAR
WASHINGTON, D. C.
SIR:

I have long since believed that in spite of all the vigilance that can be infused into Post Commanders that the Specie regulations of the Treasury Dept. have been violated, and that mostly by Jews and other unprincipled traders. So well satisfied of this have I been that I instructed the Commdg Officer at Columbus to refuse all permits to Jews to come south, and frequently have had them expelled from the Dept. But they come in with their Carpet sacks in spite of all that can be done to prevent it. The Jews seem to be a privileged class that can travel any where. They will land at any wood yard or landing on the river and make their way through the country. If not permitted to buy Cotton themselves they will act a Agents for some one else who will be at a Military post, with a Treasury permit to receive Cotton and pay for it in Treasury notes which the Jew will buy up at an agreed rate, paying gold.

There is but one way that I know of to reach this case. That is for Government to buy all the Cotton at a fixed rate and send it to Cairo, St Louis or some other point to be sold. Then all traders, they are a curse to the Army, might be expelled.

> I am, Sir, Very Respectfully
> Your Obt Servant
> U. S. GRANT
> Maj Genl.

Copies, DLC-USG, V, 5, 8, 24, 88, 91; DNA, RG 393, Dept. of the Tenn., Hd. Qrs. Correspondence. *O.R.*, I, xvii, part 2, 421–22. Christopher P. Wolcott of Ohio, brother-in-law of Secretary of War Edwin M. Stanton, was confirmed as asst. secretary of war on June 11, 1862, replacing Thomas A. Scott. Wolcott died in Jan., 1863. During the time Wolcott was in office, USG wrote him only one letter. Possibly this letter went to Wolcott because he endorsed the letter of Philip Wadsworth, mentioned in the preceding note. A book of copies of endorsements by the office of the secretary of war in DNA, RG 107, which does not record the endorsement on the Wadsworth letter, does show that of thirty-two endorsements in the period Dec. 1–15, 1862, Wolcott signed eighteen.

To Maj. Gen. James B. McPherson

> Head Quarters, Dept. of the Ten.
> Oxford, Miss., Dec. 17th 1862.

MAJ: GEN. McPHERSON
COMD'G. LEFT WING &c.,
GEN:

I wish you as soon as practicable to make a reconnoisance to the front as far as Otoolattah creek[1] with the view of making an advance to that point. I will not move my Hd' Qrs. until Saturday[2] and then probably to Springdale.

> Respectfully &c.,
> U. S. GRANT.
> Maj: Gen.

Copies, DLC-USG, V, 18, 30, 91; DNA, RG 393, Dept. of the Tenn., Letters Sent. *O.R.*, I, xvii, part 2, 423. On Dec. 18, 1862, Maj. Gen. James B. McPherson, "Camp Yocknapatafa," wrote to USG. "Your dispatch received. I was down to Water-Valley and examined the roads & ground in the Vicinity of the 'Otuckalofa Creek' day before yesterday with a view to a forward movement—The ground along the banks of this creek is well adapted for camping being high and rolling, with plenty of good water, I have enclosed a 'Sketch' showing the relative positions of of my troops & the routes by which they can march to the position designated. Col: Leggett's Brigade is now encamped on the *South* side of the 'Yuckna,' the advance being within three miles of Water Valley. Lee's & Mizner's Cavalry is encamped near this creek, Lee's Head Qrs. being about one mile west of Water Valley & Mizner's a short distance east of that place—I can move forward with Logan's Division tomorrow ~~tomorrow~~ to the Otuckalofa, leaving Denver's and Lauman's Divisions to come up the next day, or I can move them all forward tomorrow, in either case leaving a Regiment temporarily to guard the bridges across the Yuckna—Since writing this, your dispatch in relation to 'Train loaded with provisions' has just been handed me, The *first Train load* better be left at the 'Yuckna' Station, and the remainder sent forward to Springdale or *Water Valley* if the whole of my command moves forward tomorrow & the day following"   ALS, DNA, RG 393, Dept. of the Tenn., Letters Received. *O.R.*, I, xvii, part 2, 428–29.

    1. Otuckalofa Creek, which crossed the Mississippi Central Railroad just south of Water Valley, Miss., about six miles south of Springdale.
    2. Dec. 20.

To Brig. Gen. Charles S. Hamilton

Head Quarters, Dept of the Tenn.
Oxford, Miss. Dec 17th 1862.

Genl. C. S. Hamilton.
Commdg. Left. Wing. &c
Genl:

    You may instruct McArthur to move up with his Division taking position to the east of Yockna Station. By starting tomorrow at 12 P. M he will be able to make the march by next day evening.

    McArthur's Division will furnish a guard for the Station and stores that will be there tomorrow and for that purpose, if practicable, two companies should be sent forward with the Cars.

Respectfully &c
U. S. Grant
Maj Genl.

Copies, DLC-USG, V, 18, 30, 91; DNA, RG 393, Dept. of the Tenn., Letters Sent. *O.R.*, I, xvii, part 2, 422–23.

To Brig. Gen. Jeremiah C. Sullivan

———

By Telegraph from Oxford [*Dec.*] 18 [*17*], *1862*
To Gen Sullivan

Get the position of the Troops that have crossed the Tenn &
collect your forces all that can be spared from the rail road &
attack them   You can take one regiment & the Tenn cavalry
from Bolivar & get one regiment from Davies & probably two
from Dodge   Let me know your plans. Telegraph through Gen
Davies to Genl Lowe at Fort Henry movements of enemy

U. S. Grant
Maj Genl

Telegram received, DNA, RG 393, 16th Army Corps, 4th Division, Telegrams
Received; copies (dated Dec. 17, 1862), *ibid.*, Dept. of the Tenn., Letters Sent;
DLC-USG, V, 18, 30, 91. Dated Dec. 18 in *O.R.*, I, xvii, part 2, 429. On Dec. 17,
Brig. Gen. Jeremiah C. Sullivan telegraphed to USG. "Couriers sent by Captain
Carter, Tennessee cavalry, report force of several thousand rebel cavalry with
battery 7 miles this side of Clifton, near McCorkle's, estimated 10,000. I have
had out since yesterday p. m. 600 cavalry with a section, with orders to proceed
to Clifton. I have heard nothing from them." *Ibid.*, p. 423.

On Dec. 17, Maj. Gen. William S. Rosecrans, Nashville, telegraphed to
USG. "Bragg was in Murfreesboro this morning. Withers, Cheatham & Breckenridge, there yesterday reviewed there by Jeff Davis Saturday. Hardee at Trinue
12 miles west on same day. Scouts from Waynesboro two days ago, no troops
moving that way then. Davis said Middle Tenn. must, could & should be held.
Forrest cavalry may & probably will cross & make a raid on you. They have too
many cavalry for my little force. I dont think any more will be done. Jeff Davis
left on Sunday for Mobile." Copy, DNA, RG 393, Dept. of the Cumberland,
Telegrams Sent. *O.R.*, I, xx, part 2, 192. This telegram is printed *ibid.*, I, xvii,
part 2, 423, as addressed to Sullivan.

To Elihu B. Washburne

———

Oxford Mississippi
December 17th 1862

Hon. E. B. Washburn,
Dear Sir:

Permit me to introduce to you Capt. G. A. Williams of the
1st United States Infantry.

Capt. Williams is one of the most efficient as well as one of the most experienced officers in my Department. For his merit alone I have twice recommended him for promotion to the rank of Brig. Gen.[1] and hope you will give him your support.

The Army has already been much afflicted by the appointments of inefficient Brigade & Division Commanders. With such commanders as Capt. Williams would make, throughout the entire Army, I do not hesitate to say that twenty-five per cent would be added to its effectiveness.

Capt. Williams has served as Instructor of Tactics at West Point and Commandant of the Corps of Cadets. He has served with me since the Siege of Corinth with distinction, in command of his regiment. I have no doubt but that Gen. Halleck will bear me out in this recommendation. In a letter to the Gen several weeks since I made the same recommendation and hoped before this to have seen the appointment made.

Should Capt. Williams be advanced to the position of Brig. Gen. it is my desire that he be assigned to duty in this Department.

Yours Truly
U. S. GRANT

ALS, Mrs. Walter Love, Flint, Mich.

1. See letter to Maj. Gen. Henry W. Halleck, Nov. 2, 1862.

To Act. Rear Admiral David D. Porter

————

By TELEGRAPH FROM Oxford [*Dec. 18*] *186*[*2*]
To ADMIRAL PORTER CAIRO

I am informed that there is now four (4) feet of water in the Tennessee[1]—Gunboats there would be of immense value   Forest and Napier[2] are now on this Side the river with from five (5) to ten thousand (10000) men—and have got near to Jackson   I hope my forces will be able to drive them to the river—I have been concentrating troops all day to meet them

U. S. Grant

Maj Gen—

Telegram received, DNA, RG 45, Correspondence of David D. Porter, Telegrams Received; copies, *ibid.*, RG 393, Dept. of the Tenn., Letters Sent; DLC-USG, V, 18, 30, 91. *O.R.*, I, xvii, part 2, 426; *O.R.* (Navy), I, xxiii, 629. On Dec. 18, 1862, Act. Rear Admiral David D. Porter was at Memphis; Capt. Alexander M. Pennock, Cairo, telegraphed to USG. "Five light draught gun boats left Ohio river for Tenn. River on 15th Inst they draw about three feet & have orders to go up with the rise They are only ~~masked~~ musket proof" Telegram received, DNA, RG 94, War Records Office, Dept. of the Tenn. *O.R.*, I, xvii, part 2, 426; *O.R.* (Navy), I, xxiii, 629.

1. On Dec. 18, Brig. Gen. Grenville M. Dodge, Corinth, telegraphed to USG. "There are four feet of water reported in the Tennssee if so a light Gun Boat could Run to Savanah or Clifton & destroy all the flat Boats which would bother forrest he crossed his train in flats" Telegram received, DNA, RG 393, Dept. of the Tenn., Telegrams Received.

2. Col. T. Alonzo Napier, 10th Tenn. Cav., who was killed on Dec. 31 during this raid.

To Maj. Gen. John A. McClernand

Head Quarters, Dept. of the Ten.

Oxford Miss. Dec. 18th 1862

Maj. Gen. J. A. McClernand.

Gen.

I have been directed this moment by telegraph from the Gen. in Chief of the Army to divide the forces of this Department into four Army Corps, one of which to be commanded by yourself, and that to form a part of the expedition on Vicksburg.[1]

I have drafted the order and will forward it to you as soon as printed.[2] The Divisions now commanded by Brig. Gen. Geo. W. Morgan[3] and Brig. Gen. A. J. Smith will compose all of it that will accompany you on this expedition, and the Divisions of Brig. Gen. F. Steele and Brig. Gen. M. L. Smith will accompany you and will be commanded directly by Maj. Gen. W. T. Sherman, who will command the Army Corps of which they are a part.

Written and verbal instructions have been given Gen. Sherman[4] which will be turned over to you on your arrival at Memphis.

I hope you will find all the preliminary preparations completed on your arrival and the expedition ready to move.

I will cooperate with the river expedition from here commanding this portion of the Army in person.

Maj. Gen. Hurlbut will have command of the 3d Army Corps, most of which is here with me. He will therefore be directed to report immediately to these Head Quarters for orders.

The instructions now with Gen. Sherman provides for the Garrison of Memphis and and forms a part of the 2d Army Corps.

The District of Columbus is attached to your command, but for the present will report direct to these Head Quarters and will receive orders direct also.

It is desirable that there should be no delay in starting. If unforeseen obsticles should be in your way however inform me of it by messenger to Columbus and by telegraph from there. Also send me a Field return of your entire command, that is of the river expedition, before starting.

> I Am Gen. Very respectfully
> your obt. svt.
> U. S. GRANT
> Maj. Gen. Com

ALS, McClernand Papers, IHi. *O.R.*, I, xvii, part 2, 425. See letter to Maj. Gen. John A. McClernand, Dec. 28, 1862.

1. On Dec. 18, 1862, Maj. Gen. Henry W. Halleck telegraphed to USG. "The troops in your Dept including those from Genl Curtis command which join the down-river expedition will be divided into four Army corps. It is the wish of the President that Genl McClernand's Corps shall constitute a part of the river expedition and that he shall have the immediate command under your direction." ALS (telegram sent), DNA, RG 107, Telegrams Collected (Bound); telegram received, *ibid.*, RG 393, Dept. of the Tenn., Telegrams Received. *O.R.*, I, xvii, part 1, 476. On the same day, USG telegraphed to Brig. Gen. Thomas A. Davies, Columbus, Ky. "Please send the following dispatch to Gen. Sherman at Memphis. . . . Inform Gen. Sherman that his army corps will be composed of Steels forces

and Gen. Morgan L. Smith Division, and Gen McClernands of the Divisions of Genls. A. I. Smith and Morgan and that Genl. McClernand and him descend the river." Copies, DLC-USG, V, 18, 30, 91; DNA, RG 393, Dept. of the Tenn., Letters Sent; *ibid.*, Hd. Qrs. District of Columbus, Telegrams Received. *O.R.*, I, xvii, part 2, 425. On Dec. 21, Col. John C. Kelton telegraphed to Maj. Gen. John A. McClernand a copy of Halleck's telegram to USG. Telegram received, McClernand Papers, IHi. On Dec. 18, Col. Edward D. Townsend issued AGO General Orders No. 210. "By the direction of the President, the troops in the Department of the Tennessee, and those of the Dept. of the Missouri, operating on the Mississippi River, will be divided into four Army Corps, to be numbered the 13th, 15th, 16th, and 17th. Major General J. A. McClernand is assigned to the command of the 13th Army Corps; Major General W. T. Sherman to the command of the 15th Army Corps; Major General S. A. Hurlbut to the 16th Army Corps; and Major General J. B. McPherson to the command of the 17th Army Corps" Copy, DNA, RG 94, Letters Received. *O.R.*, I, xvii, part 2, 432-33.

2. On Dec. 22, Lt. Col. John A. Rawlins issued General Orders No. 14 dividing the troops of the Dept. of the Tenn. into the 13th Army Corps, commanded by McClernand; the 15th Army Corps, commanded by Maj. Gen. William T. Sherman; the 16th Army Corps, commanded by Maj. Gen. Stephen A. Hurlbut; and the 17th Army Corps, commanded by Maj. Gen. James B. McPherson. Copies, DLC-USG, V, 13, 14, 95; (printed) DNA, RG 94, Dept. of the Tenn., General Orders; (2) *ibid.*, RG 393, General and Special Orders; (printed) Oglesby Papers, IHi. *O.R.*, I, xvii, part 2, 461.

3. George W. Morgan, born in Pa. in 1820, left Washington College to fight in Tex., then entered USMA in 1841, but left in his second year. He abandoned a law practice at Mount Vernon, Ohio, to serve as col., 2nd Ohio, and col., 15th Inf., in the Mexican War. Appointed brig. gen. as of Nov. 12, 1861, he drove the C.S.A. from Cumberland Gap before his transfer to Memphis.

4. See letters to Maj. Gen. William T. Sherman, Dec. 8, 14, 15, 1862.

To Maj. Gen. James B. McPherson

Oxford, Miss. Dec. 18th 1862

MAJ: GEN. McPHERSON.
COMD'G. RIGHT WING &C,
GEN.

All the provisions yet arrived have been left here, the chief Commissary reporting that the facilities at Yocna Station were not sufficient for unloading there except to be immediately issued

If you are about out of rations send your trains back here to draw five days, and move forward after they reach you.

Forrest and Napier have crossed the Tennessee river and are

now near Jackson. I have directed such a concentration of Troops that I think they will not many of them get back to the East bank of the Ten.

They will probably succeed however in cutting the road and wires so as to interrupt communication North for a day or two.

Yours &c.

U. S. Grant

Major General.

Copies, DLC-USG, V, 18, 30, 91; DNA, RG 393, Dept. of the Tenn., Letters Sent. *O.R.*, I, xvii, part 2, 428. In a telegram dated only "18," probably sent on Dec. 18, 1862, Maj. Gen. James B. McPherson telegraphed to USG. "Is there anything special going on on the extreme left   there is a good deal of canndnading & musketry fire" Telegram received, DNA, RG 393, Dept. of the Tenn., Telegrams Received.

Also on Dec. 18, Lt. Col. John A. Rawlins issued Special Field Orders No. 27 regulating foraging parties. DS, *ibid.*, RG 94, Dept. of the Tenn., Special Orders; copies, *ibid.*, RG 393, Dept. of the Tenn., Special Orders; *ibid.*, General and Special Orders; DLC-USG, V, 26, 27, 91. *O.R.*, I, xvii, part 2, 433. On Dec. 29, Rawlins issued Special Field Orders No. 35. "Foraging parties will leave, for the use of families and their servants, a sufficient supply of provisions for sixty days, and when families have a less supply on hand, no part of it will be taken as long as a supply beyond this is found in the country, within reach of the Army. This order is not, however, to be construed to deprive the soldier of his rations whilst the country affords it. If suffering must fall on one or the other, the citizen must bear it." Copies, DLC-USG, V, 26, 27; DNA, RG 393, Dept. of the Tenn., Special Orders; *ibid.*, General and Special Orders; (printed) Oglesby Papers, IHi. *O.R.*, I, xvii, part 2, 505–6.

On Dec. 18, USG telegraphed to Lt. Col. Charles A. Reynolds, Holly Springs. "Issue no forage from that brought from the north until it becomes an absolute necessity." Copies, DLC-USG, V, 18, 30, 91; DNA, RG 393, Dept. of the Tenn., Letters Sent. On Dec. 18, however, Reynolds was in Cairo when he telegraphed to Capt. Theodore S. Bowers concerning "unserviceable stock." Telegram received, *ibid.*, Telegrams Received.

To Brig. Gen. Grenville M. Dodge

Oxford Dec. 18th 1862.

Genl. Dodge,

Corinth. Miss.

Gen. Sullivan is directed to collect forces and attack the enemy who are now west of the Tennessee River. Send forces from your

command either to hold Bethel and relieve that Garrison to join
him or send direct to Jackson.

U. S. GRANT
Maj. Genl.

Telegram, copies, DLC-USG, V, 18, 30, 91; DNA, RG 393, Dept. of the Tenn.,
Letters Sent; Dodge Papers, IaHA. *O.R.*, I, xvii, part 2, 427. On Dec. 18, 1862,
USG again telegraphed to Brig. Gen. Grenville M. Dodge. "If safe leave your
Post to a reliable Officer and take such forces as can be spared, and with the troops
at Jackson, attack Forrest and drive him East of the Tennessee." Copies, DLC-
USG, V, 18, 30, 91; DNA, RG 393, Dept. of the Tenn., Letters Sent; Dodge
Papers, IaHA. *O.R.*, I, xvii, part 2, 427. On the same day, Lt. Col. John A.
Rawlins telegraphed to Dodge. "Have received no dispatches from the officer
commanding the expedition, but, from guard in charge of Prisoners captured and
sent in learn that they have reached the Mobile & Ohio RailRoad and cut it in
several places, they are still going ahead with but little opposition." Copies,
DLC-USG, V, 18, 30, 91; DNA, RG 393, Dept. of the Tenn., Letters Sent;
Dodge Papers, IaHA. On the same day, USG again telegraphed to Dodge. "Move
to night with all the force you can spare from Corinth, to Jackson if you can get
there. If not strike them in the flank or rear.   be governed by your own judgement
when you get near them." Copies, *ibid. O.R.*, I, xvii, part 2, 427.

Also on Dec. 18, Dodge sent four telegrams to USG, the last at 10:00 P.M.
"one of my men arrived just now left Shelbyville friday Columbia Saturday went
to Tuscumbia   could not get through & returned to waynesboro   left there
yesterday at two oclock   forrest left with 2 thousand to twenty five hundred cavalry
& five pieces of artillery left Columbia Saturday crossed the Tenn at Clifton or
near there Tuesday   napier with from two to three thousand & four pieces of
artillery crossing at Carrollville monday to join forrest   they reported that they
were to strike Jackson first & Bethel next their intention being to stop supplies
to our army   no infantry had left Shelbyville west but there was a movement of
all Forces taking place north   some said they were to go west but these facts
could not be ascertained   no infantry accompanied Forrest to columbia.   the
scout that brings this has never yet failed & I believe his statement   he saw
Forrests cavaly & artilly but did not see Napiers command but saw men from
Carrollville who did see it"   "Have you heard from the force that went south to
Tupello"   "I move at day light with 2000 Men & two batteries"   "My troops
are on road   I will join them at Purdy in morng going to Bethel by cars   Col
Morris at Jacinto on his return has seventy prisoners   Rhoddy has fallen back
to Courtland   If the wire shold be cut there is a line of Couriers from Chewalla
to Bolivar"   Telegrams received, DNA, RG 393, Dept. of the Tenn., Telegrams
Received. The first of these telegrams is printed in *O.R.*, I, xvii, part 2, 431–32,
as addressed to Brig. Gen. Jeremiah C. Sullivan.

On Dec. 29, Dodge wrote to Rawlins reporting in detail his unsuccessful
pursuit of C.S.A. Brig. Gen. Nathan B. Forrest, Dec. 18–24. LS, DNA, RG 94,
War Records Office, Union Battle Reports. *O.R.*, I, xvii, part 1, 549–50.

To Brig. Gen. Jeremiah C. Sullivan

By Telegraph from Grants Head Qrs [*Dec. 18*] *186*[*2*]
To Gen Sullivan

Col Lowe is instructed to move from Fort Heiman with ten to twelve hundred to get in rear of the Enemy   Dodge will also be up with a force   there are now five 5 light draft gun boats in Tennessee so that if you get Enemy on retreat & push them I Expect to hear a good account from Jackson tomorrow

U S Grant
Maj. Genl

Telegram received, DNA, RG 393, 16th Army Corps, 4th Division, Telegrams Received; copies, *ibid.*, Dept. of the Tenn., Letters Sent; DLC-USG, V, 18, 30, 91. *O.R.*, I, xvii, part 2, 431. Earlier on Dec. 18, 1862, USG telegraphed to Brig. Gen. Jeremiah C. Sullivan, Jackson. "Have you made preperations to get forces from Corinth   Dont fail to get up a force & attack the enemy. Never wait to have them attack you"   Telegram received, DNA, RG 393, 16th Army Corps, 4th Division, Telegrams Received; copies, *ibid.*, Dept. of the Tenn., Letters Sent; DLC-USG, V, 18, 30, 91. *O.R.*, I, xvii, part 2, 430. See letter to Maj. Gen. James B. McPherson, Dec. 19, 1862.
    Also on Dec. 18, Col. Robert C. Murphy, Holly Springs, telegraphed to USG. "Have recd the following from Lagrange   I am ordered by Gen Sullivan to send our force at this point & Grand Junction to Jackson   he orders me to notify to you to send troops to these points   Send immediately by Rail that I may have trains to send forward the forces at this place   Signed J Richmond Cmdg   Shall I send what troops I can spare to Lagrange & Grand Junction"   Telegram received, DNA, RG 393, Dept. of the Tenn., Telegrams Received. On the same day, Lt. Col. John A. Rawlins telegraphed to Murphy. "You have no troops to send that can be spared from their present duties. So notify Brig.-Genl. Sullivan" Copy, DLC-USG, V, 91. On the same day, Murphy telegraphed to Rawlins. "Genl Sullivan has ordered his troops at Lagrange & Grand Junction to Jackson & requests Col Richmond at Lagrange to ask me to supply their place by troops from here   shall I send the 62d Ills & 2 co's of the 29th to Lagrange & Grand Junction   I can get cars in about an hour"   Telegram received, DNA, RG 393, Dept. of the Tenn., Telegrams Received. On the same day, Rawlins telegraphed to Murphy. "Send the 62nd Illinois and two Companies of the 29th Illinois to LaGrange and Grand Junction to garrison those places as soon as possible and if cars are not needed to move troops from those places to Jackson—let the cars return immediately to Holly Springs where they may be needed" Copies, DLC-USG, V, 18, 30; DNA, RG 393, Dept. of the Tenn., Letters Sent. Also on Dec. 18, Rawlins telegraphed to Murphy. "Send the 62nd Ills and two companies of 29th Ills through to Jackson   if they have gone forward from Holly Springs Telegraph to Grand Junction to the officer in command to go on to Jackson. A regiment will

be sent from here to Grand Junction. If no guards are at Grand Junction leave the two companies of the 29th Ills to be disposed of in such manner as best to guard our stores at that place and La Grange" Copies, *ibid.* On the same day, Murphy telegraphed to Rawlins. "Despatch recd the 62d & 2 Cos of 28th will be off in one hour have ordered Col True to leave 2 Cos at Grand Junction if there is not sufficient force to protect ~~to protect~~ public Stores & to proceed with his Reg to Jackson & report to Gen Sullivan" Telegram received, *ibid.*, Telegrams Received. On the same day, Col. C. Carroll Marsh, Holly Springs, telegraphed to Rawlins. "Sixty second (62d) started for Jackson 2 cos 29th for Gnd Junct—" Telegram received, *ibid.*

Also on Dec. 18, USG telegraphed to Col. Joseph D. Webster, Jackson. "Can you send at once from Grand Junction and Holly Springs Cars sufficient to move from this place to Jackson Two thousand or twenty five hundred men?" Copies, DLC-USG, V, 18, 30, 91; DNA, RG 393, Dept. of the Tenn., Letters Sent. On the same day, USG again telegraphed to Webster. "I will send one brigade from here Cars here now to take 700 Can you have Cars here by morning" Telegram received, *ibid.*, 16th Army Corps, 4th Division, Telegrams Received; copies, *ibid.*, Dept. of the Tenn., Letters Sent; DLC-USG, V, 18, 30, 91. On the same day, Rawlins wrote to Col. John M. Loomis, Oxford. "Send two companies for fatigue duty to the depot to unload cars immediately as cars are required to move Brigade of troops from this place to Jackson. One train arrive one hour from this time, another at 2. a. m to night See that there is no delay in their reporting at the depot for work. Please report compliance with this order" Copies, *ibid.*; DNA, RG 393, Dept. of the Tenn., Letters Sent.

On Dec. 19, USG telegraphed to Sullivan. "Have you had any engagement today What are the appearances now" Telegram received, *ibid.*, 16th Army Corps, 4th Division, Telegrams Received. On the same day, Sullivan wrote to USG. "This morning as I was preparing to advance, information was brought me that the enemy were advancing in force. At the same time I received news that the station on Columbus [road] ~~eight~~ 8 miles from here was attacked at daylight, the guard of 87. men captured, the stationhouse burned, and road at switch destroyed. A few moments later news from Corinth Road was received, giving news that the bridges ~~twelve~~ 12 miles south were burned, and that a large force had crossed going towards railroad leading to Bolivar. Almost at same time the enemy opened their artillery on my advance force, and drove them into within ~~three~~ 3 miles of Jackson. My men skirmished up to ~~three~~ 3 o'clock, at which time the brigade of Col. Fuller's command arriving, two regiments reporting, I immediately advanced six regiments under Gen'l. Brayman who drove them back and at present are bivowacking in front ~~six~~ 6 miles out. I move at daylight with my force leaving 2,000 men to hold this place. Prisoners taken to-day confirm reports of their having crossed the Tennessee River in flats and pontoon bridges,—a full cavalry regiment crossing with horses, and wagons, in half a day. Forest has six or seven colonels, but can get no estimate of force. Chatham's brigade is on this side, and Napier's also. I need no more reinforcements, and can surely save all your rear communications this way. I have ordered a cavalry dash at midnight on their position." Copy, *ibid.*, RG 94, War Records Office, Union Battle Reports. *O.R.*, I, xvii, part 1, 551–52.

To Col. William W. Lowe

———

Oxford, Miss. Dec. 18th 1862

Col. Low
Fort Henry, Tenn.

Forrest is now West of the Ten. Take 1500 of your command
and attack him   You can take them from Henry and Heiman
and order troops from Donelson to take their place. This should
be done at once. Troops are now on the way from Jackson to
attack

U. S. Grant
Maj Gen.

Telegram, copies, DLC-USG, V, 18, 30, 91; DNA, RG 393, Dept. of the Tenn.,
Letters Sent. *O.R.*, I, xvii, part 2, 428. Earlier on Dec. 18, 1862, USG had telegraphed to Col. William W. Lowe. "The enemy are reported crossing the
Tennessee River at Wrights Island. Three Thousand already across. Make a
demonstration with all the force you can possibly spare, to harrass and prevent
him crossing any more troops." Copies, DLC-USG, V, 18, 30, 91; DNA, RG 393,
Dept. of the Tenn., Letters Sent. *O.R.*, I, xvii, part 2, 428.

To Maj. Gen. James B. McPherson

———

Head Quarters Dept. of the Ten.
Oxford, Miss., Dec. 19th 1862.

Maj: Genl. McPherson
Comd'g. Right Wing &c.,
Gen.

There will be no farther advance of our forces until further
directions. The enemy under Forrest have crossed the Ten. below Clifton, and are now near to Jackson. Communication is cut
off so that I cannot hear from there. Sullivan reports the strength
of the enemy at from five to ten thousand and still crossing.
Dodge however had a scout among them before they commenced
crossing who estimates their force at about five thousand

Ingersoll's[1] Cavalry watched their movements for the last twenty five miles, and yesterday had an engagement with them at Lexington,[2] resulting in a defeat for us Col. Ingersoll and two pieces of Artillery falling into the hands of the enemy.[3] Last night Sullivan brought them to a halt about six miles from Jackson   I have reinforced Sullivan to the full extent of the capacity of the road to carry troops partly from Columbus, partly from Corinth, one Brigade from here and by concentrating of the forces of the District of Jackson. Lowe is also moving from Heiman. I think the enemy must be annihilated, but it may trouble and possibly lead to the necessity of sending further forces from here.

A dispatch from Gen. Halleck received late last night, directs me to divide my forces into four Army Corps one of which to be commanded by Maj Genl. McClernand, and he to have the chief command of the Vicksburg expedition, but under my direction[4] I was in hopes the expedition would be off by this time and it may be that they are about starting

We must be ready for any move, I think however it will not be a retrograde one

Yours &c.

U. S. Grant

Maj Genl. Comd'g.

Copies, DLC-USG, V, 18, 30, 91; DNA, RG 393, Dept. of the Tenn., Letters Sent. *O.R.*, I, xvii, part 2, 435–36.

On Dec. 19, 1862, Maj. Gen. James B. McPherson, "Camp Yaknapatafa," telegraphed to USG. "A Rept has been brought down by a surgeon from Oxford that Lawler & his whole Command at Jackson has been taken prisoners & has been circulated to a certain extent in the camps   is it true or not as I wish to have it contradicted if it is not so"   Telegram received, DNA, RG 393, Dept. of the Tenn., Telegrams Received. On the same day, Lt. Col. John A. Rawlins wrote to McPherson. "The report of the Surgeon is untrue. Order his arrest for being an alarmist. The following dispatch just received from Gen. Sullivan says, 'I will move and attack in front this afternoon—The enemy are within are within three miles of this place. They have burned the bridges on the Corinth and Bolivar roads. I have force enough to drive what force they have here to the river. The river is falling very rapidly.' Gen Dodge moved last night from Corinth with a force of at least two thousand is probably within striking distance of their flank or rear. Col. Lowe was ordered to move with all his available force against the enemy two O'clock yesterday afternoon from Fort Henry. The order reached him promptly. He is perhaps near them. One Brigade, Col. Fullers, was sent from here last night, and it is to be hoped we will not only be able to whip the enemy but will prevent his recrossing the Tennessee." Copies, DLC-USG, V, 18, 30, 91; DNA, RG 393, Dept. of the Tenn., Letters Sent. *O.R.*, I, xvii, part 2, 436. The telegram of Brig. Gen. Jeremiah C. Sullivan, Dec. 19, was transmitted to USG by Capt. William L. Barnum, Bolivar. Copy, Brayman Papers, ICHi.

Also on Dec. 19, McPherson wrote to USG. "I enclose you Copy of Letter from Col: Mizner Water Valley—In Answer to Col: Mizner's request I have sent Col: Leggetts Brigade of Infantry to Water Valley, and directed Col: Grierson to report to Mizner with his Cavalry—I think the Rebel Cavalry he speaks of are after Col: Dickey, and have suggested that it would be a good plan to assemble all his Cavalry & go to Dickeys relief by pushing out after the Rebels towards Pontotoc   I have ordered another Brigade across the 'Yuknapatafa' to take the place of Leggetts when he moves forward—" ALS, DNA, RG 393, Dept. of the Tenn., Letters Received. *O.R.*, I, xvii, part 2, 437–38. In his letter of Dec. 19 to McPherson, Col. John K. Mizner, Water Valley, reported that C.S.A. forces might be leaving Grenada for the south, and asked for more inf. to free his cav. for scouting. *Ibid.*, p. 438. On the same day, USG telegraphed to McPherson. "Send a brigade with one (1) battery to Water valley to relieve the Cavalry of a part of their picket duty & to enable the Cavalry to do more scouting" Telegram received, McPherson Papers, NjR. See telegram to Col. John K. Mizner, Dec. 19, 1862.

1. Robert G. Ingersoll, born at Dresden, N. Y., in 1833, the son of a clergyman, practiced law at Shawneetown and Peoria, Ill., and was an unsuccessful Democratic candidate for U.S. Representative in 1860. Commissioned col., 11th Ill. Cav., on Oct. 22, 1861, he led his regt. in battle at Shiloh and Corinth, and was named chief of cav. by Brig. Gen. Jeremiah C. Sullivan on Dec. 2, 1862. Ingersoll's postwar career as politician, orator, and agnostic generated a substantial literature best approached through Gordon Stein, *Robert G. Ingersoll: A Checklist* (n.p. [Kent State University Press], 1969).

2. Lexington, Tenn., about twenty-five miles east of Jackson.

3. See telegrams to Brig. Gen. Jeremiah C. Sullivan, Dec. 17, 18, 1862. On Dec. 18, Sullivan sent six telegrams to USG, the first at 2:00 A.M., the third at 5:00 P.M., the last at 7:10 P.M. "The following was received from our cavalry scout sent out yesterday: Captain O'Hara, who went out at daylight yesterday, reports that the enemy are crossing the Tennessee at Wright's Island in considerable force. At noon yesterday 3,000 infantry, 800 cavalry, and six pieces had crossed and were still crossing. O'Hara had 70 men; fell back to where I now am, at Buck River, 5 miles southeast of Lexington. When first seen the enemy were 10 miles from the Tennessee. Their pickets are now within 6 miles of me. I have sent out two companies of Colonel Hawkins' to reconnoiter. I will keep you as well informed as possible. Intend to push on in the morning. I believe they are going on the Bolivar and Clifton road. I have now 450 men. Our pickets are now in sight of the enemy's. R. G. INGERSOLL, Colonel Eleventh Illinois Cavalry." "As far as I can learn the rebels are near Mifflin. My force here is so small, numbering only 1,300, that until the troops I have ordered in arrive I cannot move. General Brayman will be here this afternoon with 700 men and one battery. The Thirty-ninth Iowa will be here this evening. I have ordered from Union City and Trenton all the available force, say 700 men. I will attack the rebels in the morning if they do not first attack me. My preparations for defense are good. I can hold

Jackson against all their force if it numbers 10,000, and meet and whip them if they are 5,000 strong." "General Dodge telegraphs there are no cars at Corinth. I have to send train from here, and at present we have no spare engine. Will send train as soon as possible. Want of information from Colonel Ingersoll as to direction the enemy are marching keeps me still. I have sent out another party to find their position and will move to attack them at once. A rumor is here that Ingersoll's cavalry has been whipped and dispersed; know nothing about it." "The enemy have attacked my cavalry. They have been fighting all day between Mifflin and Lexington. I will hold this post till the last." "The enemy are within 4 miles of this place. My infantry regiments have checked their advance, which seems to be cavalry. General Dodge is moving against their flank and I will attack in front to-morrow morning." *O.R.*, I, xvii, part 2, 429–30. "My cavalry was whipped at Lexington to-day, Col. Ingersoll taken prisoner and section of artillery captured. The enemy are reported to be from 10,000 to 20,000 and still crossing the river. They are now within six 6 miles of my outposts. I will try and find their number by daylight." Copy, DNA, RG 94, War Records Office, Union Battle Reports. *O.R.*, I, xvii, part 1, 551. Ingersoll's Dec. 27 report of the skirmish at Lexington is *ibid.*, pp. 553–55; that of Brig. Gen. Nathan B. Forrest is *ibid.*, p. 593. See also V. Y. Cook, "Forrest's Capture of Col. R. G. Ingersoll," *Confederate Veteran*, XV, 2 (Feb., 1907), 54–55.

4. See letter to Maj. Gen. John A. McClernand, Dec. 18, 1862.

To Brig. Gen. Grenville M. Dodge

By Telegraph from Oxford [*Dec. 19*] *1862*
To Genl Dodge
by courier from Bolivar

Jackson is now moving North with a cavalry force of about three thousand (3000) He will probably be near the Talla-hatchie tonight   I will have him followed with cavalry   look out for him

U. S. Grant
Maj Gen

Telegram received, Brayman Papers, ICHi; copies, DLC-USG, V, 18, 30, 91; DNA, RG 393, Dept. of the Tenn., Letters Sent; Dodge Papers, IaHA. *O.R.*, I, xvii, part 2, 436.

On Dec. 19, 1862, USG sent telegrams, similar to that to Brig. Gen. Grenville M. Dodge, to the commanding officers, Holly Springs, Davis' Mill, Grand Junction, La Grange, and Bolivar. "Jacksons Cavalry Has gone North with the Intention probably of striking the Rail Road north of this place and cut off our communication   Keep a sharpe lookout and defend the Road at all Hazard   a heavy cavalry force will be in persuet of him from here" Telegram received,

Brayman Papers, ICHi; copies, DLC-USG, V, 18, 30, 91; DNA, RG 393, Dept. of the Tenn., Letters Sent. *O.R.*, I, xvii, part 2, 439. On the same day, Lt. Col. John McDermott, 15th Mich., Grand Junction, telegraphed to USG. "The twenty fifth (25) Ind are at Davis Mills & Lamar fifteenth 15 Mich at grand Junction four (4) companies one hundred & twenty sixth (126) Ill at Lagrange" Telegram received, DNA, RG 393, Dept. of the Tenn., Telegrams Received.

Also on Dec. 19, Capt. William L. Barnum, Bolivar, telegraphed to USG. "Two hundred and twenty-seven infantry, 24 cavalry, two 6-pounder James rifled cannon, and 29 artillerymen; this is all within 2 miles of these headquarters. Your dispatch to Brigadier-General Dodge started all right." *O.R.*, I, xvii, part 2, 440. On the same day, Barnum sent two more telegrams to USG. "A line of couriers is established on the south side of the Hatchie from here to Corinth communicating with Brig Gen Dodge" "Col Sprague in Command of the train your dispatch did not reach him at Grand Junction Sixty third 63d Ohio & forty third 43d Ohio on board what shall be done do." Telegrams received, DNA, RG 393, Dept. of the Tenn., Telegrams Received; copies, Brayman Papers, ICHi. On the same day, Barnum transmitted to Brig. Gen. Jeremiah C. Sullivan a telegram from Lt. Col. John A. Rawlins to Col. John W. Sprague, 63rd Ohio. "Disembark your command at Bolivar and make such disposition of them as best to defend our line of communication to this place." *O.R.*, I, xvii, part 2, 440. On Dec. 20, Barnum telegraphed to USG two messages from Dodge dated Dec. 19. "My force will move on road from Purdy to Melftim [*Mifflin*] on road from which will enable me to strike towards Jackson or Lexington as case may require" "I shall camp to night at Sweetley creek twelve (12) miles north of Purdy—The first nights and days march on the men is rather severe—Message sent to me via Bolivar and thence to Chewalla will reach me here—I should like to know the result of the fight at Jackson" Telegram received (incomplete), DNA, RG 393, Dept. of the Tenn., Telegrams Received; copy, Brayman Papers, ICHi.

On Dec. 22, Barnum telegraphed to Sullivan the text of two Dec. 21 telegrams, 2:00 A.M. and 2:00 P.M., from Dodge, Lexington, to USG. "I have moved 24 miles all gone North 400 men and two 2 pieces of artillery joined Forrest today—I will push for him tomorrow—expect to hear from Gen Sullivan tonight" "I am pushing here towards Spring Creek as Forrest I learn is there. It seems to me we should get the R R. clear first We are getting along distance from Corinth. I may be wrong but it appears to me all importan[t] that we should open your commu[nica]tion north." Copies, DNA, RG 393, 16th Army Corps, 4th Division, Telegrams Received. *O.R.*, I, xvii, part 2, 457.

To Brig. Gen. Charles S. Hamilton

Head Quarters, Dept. of the Ten.
Oxford Miss. Dec. 19th 1862.

SPECIAL ORDERS.

Brig. Gen. Hamilton will detach two Brigades from his command, one from Quinby's and one from Ross' Divisions to proceed to-morrow to Pontotoc Miss. taking with them five days rations. They will return to their present Camps by the time their rations run out.

Each Brigade will take with it one Battery of Artillery and one Caisson to each Battery. This will enable them to attach an addition pair of horses to each team. Brig. Gen. Ross is assigned to the command of the whole.

Col. Mizner has been directed to send a regiment of Cavalry with the expedition.

Arriving at Pontotoc the officer in command will cause reconnoisances to be made as far to the South and East as practicable and should any further advance be necessary to rescue Col. Dickey, or to drive back an inferior force of the enemy it will be made.

It is desirable that on this march there should be no straggling from the ranks and all pilag should be prevented.

ADf, DLC-USG, V, 91. Another hand has altered this document to convert it to a letter addressed to Brig. Gen. Charles S. Hamilton, and the document is copied elsewhere as altered. Copies, *ibid.*, V, 18, 30; DNA, RG 393, Dept. of the Tenn., Letters Sent. *O.R.*, I, xvii, part 2, 435.

To Col. John K. Mizner

Oxford, Dec., Dec. 19. 1862.

COL. MIZNER
WATER VALLEY, MISS.,

I have no information from Col. Dickey. The forces that went from Corinth to co-operate have returned to their post having captured quite a number of prisoners.

I will send two Brigades to Pontotoc taking with them five days Rations.[1] I want you to send at least one regiment of Cavalry with the expedition with instructions to reconnoitre as far to the east and south as practicable.

U. S. GRANT
Maj: Gen.

Copies, DLC-USG, V, 18, 30, 91; DNA, RG 393, Dept. of the Tenn., Letters
Sent. *O.R.*, I, xvii, part 2, 437. On Dec. 19, 1862, Col. John K. Mizner wrote to
USG. "Scouts which returned last night bring information that a heavy cavalry
force passed from Grenada to Graysport and toward Pontotoc on Tuesday morning, and it was rumored that it was to cut us off. News of Colonel Dickey's move
had probably reached them. The scout returning from Banner and Paris was fired
on from ambush 9 miles east of here. One man was killed and Lieutenant McEntee
and 2 men wounded, the lieutenant mortally, I fear. Captain Nugent, of another
scout, brought in 9 prisoners and 12 horses. Lieutenant Corbyn and 1 man of his
command were wounded. Jeff. Davis was at Grenada Sunday, and General J. E.
Johnston is also said to be there. There is a rumor of a heavy force at Pontotoc,
spoken of as a portion of Bragg's army. Do you hear from Colonel Dickey? I am
scouting well out and would like to be advised of any information you have, to act
and plan accordingly." *Ibid*. On the same day, Mizner telegraphed to Lt. Col.
John A. Rawlins. "Have you any information to enlighten us a little down here
have heard nothing for days   Has Col Dickey returned and where is he   what
is particularly expected of us on this front   any news of a force East of us"   Telegram received, DNA, RG 393, Dept. of the Tenn., Telegrams Received. On the
same day, Mizner twice telegraphed to USG. "A scout employed by Gen. Logan
just in reports a column of four Regiments of Cavalry moving up the Pontotoc
road this all north east also that heavy artillery convalescents & Commissary
stores are being sent south & that the force at Grenada is prparing to fall back to
Jackson that the Cavalry is sent out to cover this movement   I have scouts out
south & southeast & may have more news soon"   "Having so much of my cavalry force on Guard picket & scouting think it would be well to have some
infantry sent here as a sort of grand guard and in order to make the whole cavalry
force available should any of the heavy columns of Rebel cavalry reported to be
in motion make an attack here"   Telegrams received, *ibid*. *O.R.*, I, xvii, part 2,
437–38.

1. See preceding letter.

To Col. John K. Mizner

Oxford, Miss., Dec. 19. 1862

COL: MIZNER
WATER-VALLEY

I want you to take all the available cavalry including the 6th
Ill. but excluding that just returned with Col. Dickey[1] and take
the most direct route for Rockey Ford   When you get on Jacksons trail follow him until he is caught or dispersed. Jackson must

be prevented from getting to the Rail Road in our rear if possible.
I have ordered Col. Grierson to meet you hear with his command.

U. S. GRANT

Maj Genl.

Copies, DLC-USG, V, 18, 30, 91; DNA, RG 393, Dept. of the Tenn., Letters
Sent. *O.R.*, I, xvii, part 2, 439. Later on Dec. 19, 1862, USG wrote to Col. John K.
Mizner. "Send orders to 6th Ills Cavalry to report to you at once. Collect all the
forces possible and proceed without delay as per order" Copies, DLC-USG, V,
18, 30, 91; DNA, RG 393, Dept. of the Tenn., Letters Sent. *O.R.*, I, xvii, part 2,
439. On the same day, Mizner telegraphed to USG. "The Seventh 7 Kansas
fourth 4 Ill & third 3 Mich Cavalry regts are here   much of it is out scouting &c.
Probably a force of twelve hundred 1200 in all could go   the Sixth Ill I have Just
learned is with Genl Denver   why it has not reported to me I do not know   if
Jackson passed pontotoc yesterday he is not less than Seventy miles from here
now   It is fifty 50 miles here to Pontotoc   Jacksons force that left Grenada was
reported to be Seven thousand   probably however not half that number or perhaps Seven Regts   nearly the whole of the third Mich Cavalry is out but I will
collect all I can tonight if you desire me to do so"   Telegram received, DNA,
RG 393, Dept. of the Tenn., Telegrams Received. *O.R.*, I, xvii, part 2, 439.

1. On Dec. 20, Col. T. Lyle Dickey wrote Lt. Col. John A. Rawlins a lengthy
report of his cav. expedition, Dec. 14–19. LS, DNA, RG 94, War Records Office,
Union Battle Reports. *O.R.*, I, xvii, part 1, 496–99. On Dec. 28, Dickey, Holly
Springs, wrote to his wife. "I then took 800 picket men & started S. E—for the
~~Ohio &~~ Mobile & Ohio Rail road—made a march of 200 miles in six days—drove
from that Rail Road its guards consisting of 400 infantry & some 600 Cavalry—
burnt all the bridges & trisle work from Saltillo—to Ocolona (say 34 miles)
embracing 3 important bridges—2 less important & about three miles of trestle
work—a large amount of commissary stores—40,000 bushels corn—four R. R.
cars—& a large quantity of infantry equipments—captured two wagon loads of
C. S. leather important maps of the Country and one hundred & fifty prisoners—
Returning with 700 men (I had sent back 100 men with prisoners & spoils from
Pontotoc as I went out) we run square against Van Dorn with 6000 or 7000
mounted men—Striking his right flank about a mile & a half from the rear of his
column—We captured six of his men—wounded two & maneuvered my column
round his rear & brought my men safely into Oxford without losing a man—
brought notice that Van Dorn's force was moving north on thursday at 6. P. M—
the 19th & this was telegraphed up the line & saved every station on this road
except this Holly Springs & ought to have saved this—" ALS, Wallace-Dickey
Papers, IHi.

To Col. Robert C. Murphy

———

Oxford, Dec. 19. 1862.

COL. MURPHY
HOLLY SPRINGS

Jackson is moving north with a large force of Cavalry. Will probably be at Rocky Ford to night. Send out all the Cavalry you can to watch their movements. I am sending Cavalry from the front to follow Jackson. Let the 2nd join them in the pursuit.

U. S. GRANT
Maj Genl.

Telegram, copies, DLC-USG, V, 18, 30, 91; DNA, RG 393, Dept. of the Tenn., Letters Sent. *O.R.*, I, xvii, part 2, 439. On Dec. 19, 1862, Col. Robert C. Murphy telegraphed to USG. "Have ordered out all my Cavalry as you order. Where is Rocky Ford you Speak of   I found no map here & have none but what I have made of surrounding Country that are reliable   Shall have Cavalry on the new albany & Pontotock road   will tha[t] be the course" Telegram received, DNA, RG 393, Dept. of the Tenn., Telegrams Received. *O.R.*, I, xvii, part 2, 440. On the same day, 9:00 P.M., Murphy telegraphed to USG. "My cavalry are 'boots and saddles' and ready to move. Where is Rockyford? I have no maps of the country except those I have made myself." *Supplement to [Wisconsin] Assembly Journal of Friday, March 13, 1863*, p. 13. On the same day, USG telegraphed to Murphy. "Rocky ford is on the Tallahatchie about 20 miles above Abberville or Rail Road crossing. In the morning will be early enough for your Cavalry to start and then go due East from Holly Springs to watch the enemy. They must be on their guard not to be caught and if they can retard the movements of Jackson until Mizner can get up." Copies, DLC-USG, V, 18, 30, 91; DNA, RG 393, Dept. of the Tenn., Letters Sent. *O.R.*, I, xvii, part 2, 440.

On Dec. 20, Murphy telegraphed twice to Lt. Col. John A. Rawlins. "Contraband just in reports Van Dorn only 14 miles from here with 5,000 cavalry, intending to destroy stores here, and then dash on Grand Junction. He is on the Ripley [road] and expected to reach here by daylight. Have ordered out my cavalry, but my force is only a handful." "Have ordered out my cavalry to the east. Have sent some trains on to bring up my troops on the north as far as Coldwater and the south as far as the tank. I have now here, exclusive of cavalry, less than 500 men. Van Dorn was informed of this fact by paroled prisoners on yesterday." *Ibid.*, p. 444. At 7:00 P.M. on Dec. 20, Murphy wrote to Rawlins. "Although you telegraphed me last night at 11. oclock that it was unnecessary to send out my Cavalry to look after Jackson who was advancing North with a large force, until this morning—yet from information from a Contraband at 5. oclock this morning that Genl Van Dorn was advansing on me with 22 regiments or 12,000 men & would be here at daylight inducd me to act at once & make every disposition for a faithful defence. Accord'gly I ordered the whole Cavalry force under Col McNeil to report to me at once, at the rail road depot, & proceeded there to issue orders for trains to bring me reinforcements in accordance with a telegram which I sent you. Just as the trains were ready to move & all my orders were issued a force of the enemy some 6.000, come dashing in to the Rail Road depot & on my infantry camp (my left) which did not contain over 200 effective men—My last message expressed the fact that about 5 or 6000 men of the enemy were in sight. Before this I had called on Mr Wilson, Train Supt of RR to furnish me with all the aid he had to borricade with cotton bales around the depot & public stores—At the same time I had ordered the commanding Officers of the detachment of the 62 22d Ills & 29th, to concentrate all their available forces at the R Road depot immediately— The two trains nearly ready to move, the one to the South as far as the *tank*, the other to the north as far as Cold Water were to carry orders to to all commanders of stations to hasten to this point with nothing but their available men & all their amunition. As all these dispositions were made, the enemy made their appearance in the force mentioned (6000) & charged by two roads, the right led by Genl. Van Dorn on my small infantry camp, the left & centre on the road which led direct to the depot. In attempting to escape by the rear of the depot building in order to join my infanty forces I was captured by a company of cavalry. I was taken to the rear and found the force of the enemy to be 22 regiments of cavalry or about 10.000 men. My own force was less than Five Hundred men (500) & they, scattered in four posts or pickets & in general guard duty over the city. It was impossible for me to concentrate at one given point in the time allowed more than 150 [men.] *The cavalry never reported to me at all as I had ordered*—but I hear from Lt. Edinger Ordinance Off they behaved badly in town when they encountered the enemy, & instead of cutting their way through the force sent into the town to capture me personally (thinking I was not yet up) they recieved two volleys from the enemy & then cleared out taking I am told the Pigeon Roost road. I have no fault to find with the fighting of the Infanty—they did all they could, they were taken in detail as the posts were of necessity so, & there was no time for concentration. What orders I did give were forwarded on information from a contraband which I telegraphed you this morning at 5.30. My Pickets both cavalry & Infantry were out, & faithful but the force was so large that they were overwhelmed & in every instance killed wounded or taken prisoners before daylight. Genl. Van Dorn burnt up all the stores, Depot Buildings, armory & ordinance buildings, in fact a large portion of the business part of the town is in ruins. There is no supplies here for the paroled prisoners, & the sick, & what shall be done for them. My fate is most mortifying. I have wished a hundred times today I had been killed—I have done all in my power, in truth my force was inadequate. I have foreseen this and have so advised—No works here, & no force to put in them, if they were here & yet I know Genl. Grant is not to blame—he has done all for the best & so did I. I have obeyed orders, & have been unfortunate in so doing. The misfortune of war is mine. This railroad line cannot be maintained without an imense force. They make a feint on *Jackson*, & the real attack on *Holly Springs*—the *first* depletes the *latter* & makes the move almost certain. Col. I send this by an Officer who was here & knows the facts—he can tell you many things I can not write. . . . P. S. I am not able now to give my loss in killed wounded & taken prisoners but will do so as soon as possible" ALS, DNA, RG 94, War Records Office, Union Battle Reports. *O.R.*, I, xvii, part 1, 508–9.

On Dec. 23, Surgeon Horace R. Wirtz wrote to Rawlins reporting the capture of Holly Springs, and, on Dec. 26, USG endorsed this report to the AGO. AES, DNA, RG 94, War Records Office, Union Battle Reports. *O.R.*, I, xvii, part 1,

510–11. On Feb. 6, 1863, USG endorsed to the AGO a report of Dec. 27, 1862, from Maj. John J. Mudd, 2nd Ill. Cav., to Rawlins concerning the capture of Holly Springs. ES, DNA, RG 94, War Records Office, Union Battle Reports. *O.R.*, I, xvii, part 1, 512–14. On Dec. 29, Capt. Arnold Hoeppner wrote to Maj. Gen. Henry W. Halleck reporting that he was on parole after capture at Holly Springs, that he had reported by letter to USG, and that he considered the surrender shameful. LS, DNA, RG 94, War Records Office, Union Battle Reports. On Dec. 31, Halleck endorsed this letter to USG. "Respectfully referred to Major Genl Grant, for report in regard to the defense of Holly Springs by Col Murphy." AES, *ibid*. See letter to Col. John C. Kelton, Dec. 25, 1862.

To George G. Pride

Head Quarters 13th Army Corps
Dep't of the Tennessee
Oxford, Miss. Dec 19. 1862

COL GEO G PRIDE
SUP'T MIL. R. R. EAST FROM VICKSBURGH
COLONEL,

You will proceed to St. Louis, and Chicago if you find it necessary, and purcure such material, Machinery, tools, teams and wagons as you think are required for a rapid construction and for running the Rail Road east from Vicksburgh. You will also engage such employees as you may deem proper, and fix the rate of wages for same. All materials and men so procured will be forwarded at once to Cairo, and be ready to be shipped south at short notice, and will himself direct the shipping of the same, and all steamboats and barges necessary for shipment will be moved south under his direction. The Chief Quartermaster and chief Commissary at St Louis are requested to furnish such supplies as may be required by you for the expedition   You will report as frequently as possible to these Head Quarters.

Lieut Col C. A. Reynolds, chief Quartermaster of this Department will detail a quartermaster to report to you for this duty

U. S. GRANT
Maj Genl

Copies, DLC-USG, V, 18, 30; DNA, RG 393, Dept. of the Tenn., Letters Sent. *O.R.*, I, xvii, part 2, 434.

To Maj. Gen. James B. McPherson

——————

Hd Qrs, Dept of the Tenn
Oxford, Miss. Dec 20. 1862

Maj Gen. McPherson
Commdg Right. Wing
Army in the field
Genl:

Fall back with your entire command to the north side of the Tallahatchie the troops retiring by the same routes they advanced on.

I will instruct the Cavalry to advance towards Grenada to keep up the idea of an advance as much as possible.[1] Keep your transportation as well to the front as possible and instruct your Commissaries to collect all the Cattle they can fit for beef; and corn meal from the mills. Destroy all the mills within reach of you and the bridges after you are done using them.

Respectfully &c.
U. S. Grant
Maj Genl.

Copies, DLC-USG, V, 18, 30, 91; DNA, RG 393, Dept. of the Tenn., Letters Sent. *O.R.*, I, xvii, part 2, 445. On Dec. 20, 1862, Maj. Gen. James B. McPherson, Camp "Yocknapatafa," wrote to USG. "Genl. Lauman's Division will move to the position occupied by General McArthur's, near the 'Yockna' Station at 6 o'clock tomorrow morning—I send you extract of a letter from Col: Leggett giving some information brought in by a Scout from his Command whom we sent out—If this information is correct & it seems to be confirmed at least partially from other sources I am decidedly of the opinion that the rebels are concentrating their forces at Jackson & Vicksburg, with a view of throwing them all into Vicksburgh if necessary—and that our policy is to have as many or more men at that point than they can bring to bear—~~That~~ In view of the fact that the Rail Road from Granada to Memphis is so seriously damaged, that it will take some weeks to open it, and that with our present *long* line of communication interrupted, and liable to be so again when reopened, we cannot well go beyond Granada and

~~Commun~~ form a junction with the forces moving down the River. I think it best to fall back to the north side of the Tallahatchie, hold that line, and then send as many as two Divisions to Memphis to be added to the Force collecting for the Vicksburg Expedition—Open the Rail Road from Memphis to Grand Junction and establish an easy & rapid communication which I think could be protected with our strong Cavalry force, and a ~~Strong~~ body of Infantry and Artillery on the Tallahatchie, Holly Springs, Hernando &c. I have merely suggested these remarks in consequence of the note at the bottom of your letter, and I will also add that in consequence of *orders* from washington placing *General McClernand* in charge of the Expedition *under you*, that I would *if in your place* proceed to Memphis & take command of it myself—It is the great feature of the Campaign and its execution rightfully belongs to you. In case you go I would like to accompany you with two Divisions Laumans & Logans—but am ready for any place or position to which you may assign me—" ALS, DNA, RG 393, Dept. of the Tenn., Letters Received. *O.R.*, I, xvii, part 2, 446. On the same day, Col. Mortimer D. Leggett, Water Valley, had written to McPherson. "He has just returned. He did not succeed in reaching Grenada but says he got within four miles & spent several hours with the enemys Pickets. They told him that the enemy had moved all his sick, Convalescents, and large guns back to Jackson and they thought there was but one battery left at Grenada. He reports having seen three Regts of Cavalry pass the post at which he was,—in a Northerly direction on the Pontotoc Road. He could not learn their destination officially but a Private remarked, 'We'll cut off their grub & the damed Yankees will eat you up, before we get back' I dont believe *they* mean to *fight* us *at Grenada. Would like* to *try them.* The Telegraph line is still down somewhere the office here gets no responses." Copy, DNA, RG 393, Dept. of the Tenn., Letters Received.

On Dec. 21, McPherson wrote to USG. "I am just in receipt of your Dispatch, will order Leggett's Brigade back to this point this afternoon, and will move for the north bank of the Tallahatchie with my whole command tomorrow morning at 6 o'clock—I am anxious to know something about the Cavalry as a portion of their Train is at Water Valley & if I destroy the Bridges across the 'Yoknapatafa' which I have had built and repaired they cannot well get back. I do not wish to have a bridge left standing and therefore desire to have an understanding with the officer in command of the Cavalry as to ~~the~~ what *bridge* or *bridges* I am to leave for him to cross on and then destroy" ALS, *ibid.* Misdated Dec. 20 in *O.R.*, I, xvii, part 2, 445–46.

1. On Dec. 20, 9:00 P.M., Lt. Col. John A. Rawlins wrote to Col. Edward Hatch. "You will at once break all the Cavalry Camps in the front and send the trains, camp and Garrison Equipage and ambulances to this place. You will then take all the effective cavalry force south of the Yocknapatafa river and make a demonstration as far towards Grenada, as you can go, without serious resistance and thence return to this place, destroying thourghly on your return all bridges on Rail Road and wagon Roads, and all mills on the line of your march." Copies, DLC-USG, V, 18, 30, 91; DNA, RG 393, Dept. of the Tenn., Letters Sent. *O.R.*, I, xvii, part 2, 442–43.

To Brig. Gen. Charles S. Hamilton

Head Quarters, Dept. of the Ten.
Oxford Miss. Dec. 20th 1862

Brig. Gen. Hamilton
Comd.g Left Wing
Army in the Field.
Gen.

Direct Quinby to fall back to Oxford to-morrow. I shall be compelled in order to keep up supplies as well as it being otherwise a matter of policy, to fall back to North side of the Tallahatchie. I want all mills within reach of our retreat destroyed and all meal and meat taken for the use of the Army. Bridges should also be destroyed as we are done using them.

Quinby's Div. may remain at Oxford for several days possibly.

Respectfully &c.
U. S. Grant
Maj. Gen. Com

ALS, Ritzman Collection, Aurora College, Aurora, Ill.

To Col. C. Carroll Marsh

Oxford, Dec 20th 1862

Col. C. C. Marsh.
Waterford, Miss.

Two regiments will be at Abberville in one hour on the Cars. If you require them telegraph to them and they will go up at daylight. Mizner will join you to-night with 2000. Cavalry.[1] I want those fellows caught if possible and any support you can give towards it with your Infy and Artillery, I want you to do it.

U. S. Grant
Maj Genl.

Telegram, copies, DLC-USG, V, 18, 30, 91; DNA, RG 393, Dept. of the Tenn., Letters Sent. *O.R.*, I, xvii, part 2, 442. On Dec. 20, 1862, Col. C. Carroll Marsh sent three telegrams to USG, the first two from Waterford, the last from "North side of River." "Enemy still at Holly Springs. Scout just in from their pickets. They are burning ammunition and stores. I start at daylight for Springs. Think I have all the force I need. Train can come here safely." "Colonel Buckland with two regiments close here. I left one of his regiments at the river. If you have one more to spare I can use it to advantage. Shall be in Holly Springs or be whipped to-morrow morning." "Lieutenant Carter informs me that the enemy are in possession of Holly Springs and Waterford; that Jackson and Forrest are united. They have some artillery. I think it prudent to return the train from here. Their advance has been within 2 miles of here this morning. I have formed line of battle, thrown out skirmishers, and will feel my way cautiously. If you think necessary to send me re-enforcements and some cavalry do so by train." *Ibid.*, pp. 442, 443.

On Dec. 21, Col. Ralph P. Buckland, 72nd Ohio, Waterford, telegraphed to USG. "Arrived here last Evening after dark with two Regts & & waterhouse battery   we are entirely out of rations" Telegram received, DNA, RG 393, Dept. of the Tenn., Telegrams Received. An undated telegram from Buckland to USG was probably sent the same day. "I have communicated with Col Marsh through my aid. He directs me to leave one Regiment at the Tallahatchie & move to Oxford with balance which I am doing—Hope to reach there to night" Telegram received, *ibid.*

1. On Dec. 20, Col. John K. Mizner, Abbeville, telegraphed to USG. "Colonel Marsh is at Waterford. I could not overtake him, and am encamped near Colonel Buckland, at the Tallahatchie. I learn from the surgeon of Bissell's Engineer Regiment, who left Holly Springs at 11 a. m. to-day, that every man was taken, supplies of all kinds burned; also 3 locomotives and 40 cars. The rebel cavalry number 4,000. Jackson and Armstrong are with Van Dorn. The doctor was a prisoner. The town was taken a little after daylight. It was a surprise; not above 40 shots were fired. The rebels took citizens, sutlers, and everybody. They are paroling them. They destroyed everything they could not carry away." *O.R.*, I, xvii, part 2, 443. On the same day, USG telegraphed to Mizner. "Go forward and join Col. Marsh to night. as you were instructed. Dont allow him to be cut up by piece meal" Copies, DLC-USG, V, 18, 30, 91; DNA, RG 393, Dept. of the Tenn., Letters Sent. *O.R.*, I, xvii, part 2, 443. Also on Dec. 20, Marsh, Waterford, telegraphed to USG. "My Column moving   Misner Just arrived says he cannot leave here for three hours" Telegram received, DNA, RG 393, Dept. of the Tenn., Telegrams Received. On the same day, USG telegraphed to Marsh. "Col Mizner was ordered to join you tonight. He is camped at the Tallahatchie. Has been ordered again to proceed tonight and join you. If in the morning he shows any reluctance in the pursuit, arrest him and turn the over the command to the next in rank." Copies, DLC-USG, V, 18, 30, 91; DNA, RG 393, Dept. of the Tenn., Letters Sent. *O.R.*, I, xvii, part 2, 443.

To Maj. Gen. Henry W. Halleck

Oxford Miss
Dec 21st 1862 8 P M

MAJ GEN H W HALLECK
GEN IN CHIEF

The Rebel cavalry commanded by Van Dorn made dash into Holly Springs yesterday at daylight   captured the troops stores &c   Their movement from the Yallabusha was very rapid   I heard of them crossing and ordered force to Pontatac to intercept them but they travelled as rapidly as the Scouts who brought the news—next their departure from Pontotoc going north was reported   All my available cavalry was ordered in pursuit and are still out—as the rebels out number them three to one I dont expect much   When communication was broken with the north I had troops concentrate to resist attack on Jackson   Dont know the result   If Enemy falling back north of the Tallahatchie I may find it necessary to send forces to Corinth. I would like to send two Divisions more to Memphis and join the River Expedition with them   This would make it necessary to fall back to Bolivar   The Enemy are falling back from Grenada—

U S GRANT
Maj Gen Comdg

Telegram received, DNA, RG 94, Generals' Papers and Books, Telegrams Received by Gen. Halleck; *ibid.*, RG 107, Telegrams Collected (Bound); copies, *ibid.*, Telegrams Received in Cipher; *ibid.*, RG 393, Dept. of the Tenn., Hd. Qrs. Correspondence; DLC-USG, V, 5, 8, 24, 88, 91. *O.R.*, I, xvii, part 1, 477. This telegram was not received at Washington until 8:45 P.M., Dec. 26, 1862. On Dec. 27, Maj. Gen. Henry W. Halleck telegraphed to USG. "I think no more troops should at present be sent against Vicksburg. I fear you have already too much weakened your own forces. Concentrate and hold only the more important points." ALS (telegram sent), DNA, RG 107, Telegrams Collected (Bound); copies, *ibid.*, RG 108, Telegrams Sent; *ibid.*, RG 393, Dept. of the Tenn., Hd. Qrs. Correspondence; DLC-USG, V, 5, 8, 24, 88. *O.R.*, I, xvii, part 1, 478.

To Maj. Gen. James B. McPherson

Hd Qrs, Dept of the Tennessee.
Oxford, Miss. Dec 21st 1862.

MAJ GEN. McPHERSON.
GENL:

I have ordered two Divisions back to Corinth and facts may develop through the day which will make it necessary to send much more force to that point.[1] It is now reported that Bragg is in motion for Corinth. If so our whole force will be required for its defense.

You will fall back therefore to the North bank of the Tallahatchie by which time facts enough will be developed to determine upon our further course.[2]

My present plan is to send Quinby's and Logan's Divisions to Memphis and either you or Hamilton in command and to go myself, if allowed and send the other two Divisions to Bolivar from which position they can be made available for any point that may be threatened

If the rebels get such a check as to leave the road in a condition to be repaired in one week I shall hold the line of the Tallahatchie for the present.

If I go to Memphis I shall take either you or Hamilton leaving the other in command of all the forces except those accompanying the river expedition.

Respectfully &c
U. S. GRANT
Maj. Genl.

Copies, DLC-USG, V, 18, 30, 91; DNA, RG 393, Dept. of the Tenn., Letters Sent. *O.R.*, I, xvii, part 2, 451–52. On Dec. 21, 1862, Maj. Gen. James B. McPherson, "Camp Yucknapatafa," wrote to USG. "I will commense my march for the 'Tallahatchie' tomorrow morning—I would like very much to see the Officer who is to remain in chg of the Cavalry to have some definite understanding about destroying the Wagon road Bridges as we retire—I propose to have a Regt. of Infantry move back along the line of the R. R. and destroy every bridge and Trestle work from the 'Otuck' north—I sent over to General Denver yester-

day afternoon to destroy the bridge (McFarlands) about Five miles to the west
of him across the 'Yuckna,' thinking perhaps the Rebel Cavalry might return
from their raid into Holly Springs, by that route & we might thus be enabled to
make some of them repent of their rashness—I issued an order this morning putting my men on ¾ rations and by so doing have enough Provisions on hand to
last ten days—Leggett is Still at Water Valley and I shall not make any move to
the rear until the Cavalry is ready to make the demonstration in Front & screen
our movements—unless I hear from you"   ALS, DNA, RG 393, Dept. of the
Tenn., Letters Received. *O.R.*, I, xvii, part 2, 452. On the same day, McPherson
wrote to Brig. Gen. James W. Denver, Brig. Gen. Jacob G. Lauman, and Brig.
Gen. John A. Logan, concerning the withdrawal. *Ibid.*, pp. 452–53.

1. On Dec. 21, Col. William S. Hillyer, Holly Springs, telegraphed to USG.
"Have sent to Corinth Two Sources   nothing further in the way of the news"
Telegram received, DNA, RG 393, Dept. of the Tenn., Telegrams Received.
On Dec. 23, USG telegraphed to the commanding officer, Corinth. "Did scout
and two Cavalrymen sent through from Holly Springs on Sunday with dispatches
arrive." Copies, DLC-USG, V, 18, 30, 91; DNA, RG 393, Dept. of the Tenn.,
Letters Sent.
2. In connection with the withdrawal, on Dec. 21, 1st Lt. Joshua Ricketts,
Bissell's Mo. Engineers, Water Valley, Miss., telegraphed to USG. "The ~~ral~~
Railroad is in Condition for trains to run on to this place   Run not to Exceed
Eight miles per hour"   Telegram received, *ibid.*, Telegrams Received.

To Brig. Gen. Charles S. Hamilton

Head Quarters, Dept of the Tenn.
Oxford, Miss. Dec 21st 1862.

Brig. Gen. C. S. Hamilton
Genl:

You will instruct the Divisions of McArthur[1] and Ross[2] to
move immediately upon Corinth by the most practical routes.—
The troops should be instructed to be as careful as possible of
their rations. Organized foraging parties should be formed to
collect all the provender and food that may be required as see to
its proper distribution.

In entering Corinth if it is ascertained that communications
are cut North as large a supply of forage as possible should be
carried in with the troops.

If it is learned that a move is being made on Corinth the

troops should make a forced march to reach their destination

All Mills on the route should be destroyed and the means of supporting an Army carried off as far as practicable or destroyed also.

> Respectfully &c
> U. S. GRANT
> Major Genl. Commdg.

Copies, DLC-USG, V, 18, 30, 91; DNA, RG 393, Dept. of the Tenn., Letters Sent. *O.R.*, I, xvii, part 2, 451.

1. On Dec. 21, 1862, Brig. Gen. John McArthur, Abbeville, Miss., telegraphed to USG. "Telegram Recd   ambulances will be pushed ahead to Holly Springs for that duty as fast as possible"   Telegram received, DNA, RG 393, Dept. of the Tenn., Telegrams Received.

2. On Dec. 21, Brig. Gen. Charles S. Hamilton, "Gen Grant's Hd. Qrs.," wrote to Brig. Gen. Leonard F. Ross. "Please come here in person as soon as possible." Julia Sweet Newman, List No. 243.

To Col. C. Carroll Marsh

———

Oxford, Dec 21st 1862.

COL. C. C. MARSH
WATERFORD, MISS[1]

Try to get messenger through North to all the stations where we have troops and direct them to fall back to Bolivar taking with them all they can and destroying the balance. You will have to supply your troops from the country.

> U. S. GRANT
> Maj. Genl.

Telegram, copies, DLC-USG, V, 18, 30, 91; DNA, RG 393, Dept. of the Tenn., Letters Sent. *O.R.*, I, xvii, part 2, 448. On Dec. 21, 1862, Col. C. Carroll Marsh, Holly Springs, telegraphed twice to USG. "Am here. Van Dorn left for north yesterday p. m. Have started messengers north and sent two companies of cavalry to hover in their rear for information. Mizner has turned over his command to Grierson. Lee is on one road, Grierson on the other. Will follow in pursuit if not ordered to the contrary." "Cavalry here or close by. Your message forwarded." *Ibid.*, pp. 448–49.

Also on Dec. 21, USG sent two more telegrams to Marsh. "The enemy should be pursued. If they have gone North pursuit may prevent them doing further. damage and by throwing Infy. and Arty. off in the direction they wish to return they might be considerably damaged. There will be two Divisions in Holly Springs tomorrow." "Send a company of Cavalry through to learn what news from Jackson. The Co. can go to Grand Junction and call on Commdg Officer there for another Company if the wires are not at work to send by telegraph. They can go until an office is found that has communication Forward the enclosed for Gen. Halleck." Copies, DLC-USG, V, 18, 30, 91; DNA, RG 393, Dept. of the Tenn., Letters Sent. *O.R.*, I, xvii, part 2, 449. On the same day, Marsh sent three telegrams to USG. "Scouts returned from Lamar. No enemy in that vicinity. All information leads to the belief that after going a short distance north they took a southeasterly course toward Rocky Ford." "Nothing yet from troops sent north. Information varies as to direction taken by enemy. It is certain that a portion, and that a large one, moved back on the road they came in on. Their numbers have been underrated by us." "Shall I endeavor to countermand orders to fall back from Grand Junction and to destroy property?" *Ibid.* On the same day, USG telegraphed to Marsh. "By all means send orders countermanding any order for falling back from posts north of you." Copies, DLC-USG, V, 18, 30, 91; DNA, RG 393, Dept. of the Tenn., Letters Sent. *O.R.*, I, xvii, part 2, 450.

On Dec. 22, Marsh twice telegraphed to USG. "Send 50 men and tools, and road can be opened north in six hours after they reach here. Engine from Bolivar came below Coldwater last evening." "I never saw your instructions to the cavalry, and was not informed that you had given such orders." *Ibid.*, pp. 454, 455. On the same day, Marsh sent three additional telegrams to USG. "All quiet above this morning nothing heard from Scouts sent towards Salem yesterday" "Shall grierson leave the three co's of cavalry" "What shall be done with paroled prisoners left here" Telegrams received, DNA, RG 393, Dept. of the Tenn., Telegrams Received. Also on Dec. 22, Marsh sent two additional telegrams to USG. "Have sent company cavalry to Grand Junction Expect Every moment to hear from there not heard from them near Lagrange & all right there" "Cavalry mostly here they may as well be at the front leave me all you can spare of them" Telegrams received, *ibid.*, RG 94, War Records Office, Dept. of the Tenn. The latter telegram is in *O.R.*, I, xvii, part 2, 455. On the same day, USG telegraphed to Marsh. "Send Col. Mizner with the 3rd Mich. Cavalry through to Grand Junction and Bolivar if necessary to ascertain the condition of the road to our rear and to reestablish the garrisons if they have been deserted. Send the balance back here." Copies, DLC-USG, V, 18, 30, 91; DNA, RG 393, Dept. of the Tenn., Letters Sent. *O.R.*, I, xvii, part 2, 455.

1. On Dec. 21, Col. Willard A. Dickerman, 103rd Ill., Waterford, Miss., telegraphed to USG. "Cannot muster over four hundred (400) Effective men will be ready & give the best we have" Telegram received, DNA, RG 393, Dept. of the Tenn., Telegrams Received.

To Col. John K. Mizner

Oxford, Dec 21st 1862.

Col. Mizner, Waterford

Your apparent reluctance at starting from here and the want
of alacrity in complying with my orders has so shaken my confidence in you that no matter how well qualified you may be to
command such an expedition as the one you have started on I
should feel insecure with you in command. My instructions to
turn the command over to the next in command will therefore
be obeyed.

U. S. Grant
Maj Genl.

Telegram, copies, DLC-USG, V, 18, 30, 91; DNA, RG 393, Dept. of the Tenn.,
Letters Sent. *O.R.*, I, xvii, part 2, 448. On Dec. 21, 1862, Col. C. Carroll Marsh,
Waterford, Miss., telegraphed to USG. "No signs of Mizner yet. Shall I move
without him? Rations needed here to-day" *Ibid.*, p. 447. On the same day, USG
telegraphed to Col. John K. Mizner, Waterford. "Turn your command over to
the officer next in rank with the instructions you have received." Copies, DLC-
USG, V, 18, 30, 91; DNA, RG 393, Dept. of the Tenn., Letters Sent. *O.R.*, I,
xvii, part 2, 448. On the same day, Mizner telegraphed to USG. "I marched until
6.30 p. m. yesterday, and learning that Colonel Marsh was at Waterford, 9 miles
farther on, my horses, I believed, would not stand a farther journey. I started at
2 this morning, and would have been here an hour before day but for the difficulties
attending crossing the Tallahatchie Bottom in the dark. I reached here at broad
daylight, and every officer must say that I made no unnecessary delay. I make
this statement in justice to myself, for I believe circumstances demand it of one
who has in good faith honestly endeavored to do his duty." *Ibid.*

On Dec. 23, Lt. Col. John A. Rawlins issued Special Field Orders No. 32.
"Col Mizner, of the 3rd Regt Michigan Cavalry Vols, will proceed by first train
north and resume the Command of the Cavalry wherever he finds them and will
pursue the Enemy as long as they can be heard from in this Department, with all
vigor, foraging and subsisting upon the Country." DS, DNA, RG 94, Dept. of
the Tenn., General Orders; copies, *ibid.*, RG 393, Dept. of the Tenn., Special
Orders; DLC-USG, V, 26, 27, 91.

To Brig. Gen. Charles S. Hamilton

Oxford, Dec 22nd 1862.

GEN. HAMILTON, HOLLY SPRINGS.

The Cavalry need not start tonight, if not already started. Their Camp equipage is all ordered to Abberville when they will remain until further orders.[1]

You may retain Lee's Cavalry with you. Open communication with the North if possible and get information from Corinth. I telegraphed you instructions to-day to send one Division to Holly Springs. One at Waterford.[2] I will give Quinby instructions here.[3] You need not move from positions indicated here without further directions.

U. S. GRANT
Major. General.

Telegram, copies, DLC-USG, V, 18, 30, 91; DNA, RG 393, Dept. of the Tenn., Letters Sent. *O.R.*, I, xvii, part 2, 456.

On Dec. 22, 1862, Brig. Gen. Charles S. Hamilton, Waterford, Miss., telegraphed to USG. "Two dispatches received. McArthur's division goes to Holly Springs to-night. Ross stops here. Will push cavalry to the north. If no cavalry at hand will send forward Marsh with brigade to-night. Shall be in Holly in one hour." *Ibid.*, p. 455. On the same day, Hamilton, Holly Springs, telegraphed to USG. "Van Dorn went to Salem; then to Davis' Mill, where he was repulsed; then down south bank Wolf to Moscow. He pulled up some rails near Davis' Mill. He started north from Moscow at 3 o'clock this morning. All right at Corinth. I think I will send a brigade to Salem to head Van Dorn." *Ibid.*, p. 456. On the same day, USG telegraphed to Brig. Gen. Jeremiah C. Sullivan, Jackson. "What news from Jackson? Is the Road and wires right north of you?" Telegram received, DNA, RG 393, 16th Army Corps, 4th Division, Telegrams Received. *O.R.*, I, xvii, part 2, 458. On the same day, 7:45 P.M., Sullivan telegraphed to USG. "Jackson, Humboldt, and Bolivar all right. The rebels are in strong force all around us—entirely cavalry. I am busy repairing the road north, and will use all my force to keep it open. Trenton was taken by Forrest. Our loss, no one killed and but 2 or 3 wounded. All surrendered. The wires are not in order above here." *Ibid.*, p. 456. USG endorsed this telegram with a message to Hamilton. "Send word to Marsh to push on to Grand Junction to-night. There is a large force of cavalry in north of them. There are about 100,000 rations at Grand Junction." *Ibid.* Also on Dec. 22, Hamilton telegraphed to USG. "Marsh starts soon with four regiments. Grierson is here; also Lee. Can use both to great advantage in heading off Van Dorn. Shall I keep both?" *Ibid.*, p. 455. On the same day, Hamilton telegraphed to USG. "McArthur with Div is here   Ross & Div at waterford Grierson gone to Abberville   Lee remains here.   there is every reason to believe

Van Dorn Crossed Road to the north & was this morning at Moscow   Shall I push a brigade to Grand Junction   *G*—3d Mich gone north under your instructions   we have a deserter & two niggers from Van Dorn   think he may be trying to make circuit of your army   all right yet at Grand Junction & Jackson bridge over wolf at Lagrange destroyed   two small R R bridges reported destroyed between here & Coldwater   McArthur will repair in morning   will push marsh & brigade forward tonight   Messengers are sent to Corinth—" Telegram received, DNA, RG 393, Dept. of the Tenn., Telegrams Received. At the end of this message USG drafted another telegram, probably for Hamilton. "There is now telegraphic communication with Corinth. No message received from there yet." ADf, *ibid*. On the same day, Hamilton again telegraphed to USG. "Have you recd any Telegram from Rosecrans"   Telegram received, *ibid*. At the end of this telegram USG wrote the word "None" ADf, *ibid*. On the reverse he drafted another telegram, probably for Hamilton. "Rebel Cavalry passed LaGrange at 8 towards Bolivar   Trenton taken" ADf, *ibid*.

Also on Dec. 22, Col. William S. Hillyer, Holly Springs, telegraphed to USG. "Grierson impatient to pursue enemy; has been after me several times to telegraph to you on subject. He has been ready to pursue ever since yesterday noon." *O.R.*, I, xvii, part 2, 457. USG endorsed this telegram with a message to Hamilton. "Let Grierson, Lee, and Fifth Ohio Cavalry push after enemy until they find him. They may travel over West Tennessee in pursuit of the enemy until it will no longer support an army." *Ibid*. On the same day, Hamilton twice telegraphed to USG. "Grierson & Lee will go straight to Grand Junction & be there before day light—My operator at Grand Junction Just Telegraphs skirmishing Going on at Lagrange   think VanDorn will find ~~smaller one~~ smaller hole ~~to get~~ thro which to get back than in coming out"   "The third Mich has gone North   an Opr has gone up the road & will report the condition at different points   I will strain Every nerve to open communications north   Cavalry pursued enemy only a short distance assuming command of all & had no instructions to follow ~~the~~ A deserters from rebels say rebels went to Lagrange   send instructions to me & all will go right   Lees & Grierson Cav will go to Oxford in an hour under your orders"   Telegrams received, DNA, RG 393, Dept. of the Tenn., Telegrams Received. Also on Dec. 22, Col. Benjamin H. Grierson, Holly Springs, telegraphed to USG. "Road to Abbeville blocked by train difficult to pass in night Shall I remain here till further orders. Have ordered Coll Lee to report to Genl Hamilton   3d Mich gone north   forage here   None towards Abbeville" Telegram received, *ibid*.

    1. On Dec. 22, Col. Addison S. Norton, Abbeville, twice telegraphed to USG. "I have instructed my Officers to build block house along the road towards Oxford   shall I continue them"   "Your order relating to Cavalry Encamping is Recd & will be obeyed"   Telegrams received, *ibid*.

    2. On Dec. 22, Lt. Col. John A. Rawlins telegraphed to Brig. Gen. John McArthur. "If your entire Division has moved let it continue to Waterford and camp for the night." Copies, DLC-USG, V, 18, 30, 91; DNA, RG 393, Dept. of the Tenn., Letters Sent. *O.R.*, I, xvii, part 2, 454. On the same day, McArthur, Waterford, telegraphed to USG. "My Division has arrived here & going into Camp as Ordered   Great difficulty in getting wagon train through the Tallahatchie bottom. Will probably not be able to get an Early start   Ross' Div train is in rear of mine with three regts of Infy   shall I forward ambulances to Holly

Springs"   Telegram received, DNA, RG 393, Dept. of the Tenn., Telegrams
Received.

3. On Dec. 22, USG telegraphed to Hamilton. "Concentrate one of your
Divisions at Holly Springs and one at Waterford   I will give Quinby directions
here. They need not move on towards Corinth without further directions unless
you get information making it necessary"   Copies, DLC-USG, V, 18, 30, 91;
DNA, RG 393, Dept. of the Tenn., Letters Sent. *O.R.*, I, xvii, part 2, 455. On
the same day, Rawlins wrote to Brig. Gen. Isaac F. Quinby. "You will move
from here to morrow morning with your command, and concentrate it in the
neighborhood of Lumpkins Mills, it is not necessary that this should be done in
one day. Genl Denver has been ordered to move to Abberville and there encamp
to morrow night." Copies, DLC-USG, V, 18, 30, 91; DNA, RG 393, Dept. of
the Tenn., Letters Sent. *O.R.*, I, xvii, part 2, 456.

To Maj. Gen. James B. McPherson

Holly Spring, Dec 23rd 1862

GEN. MCPHERSON, OXFORD, MISS.

A force of rebel Cavalry are now encamped at the mouth of
Tippah creek[1] going south with a large number of led horses and
mules. Probably those captured here. The main body of the rebels
went North from here. Send this word to Hatch.[2] By properly
directing his course he may recover much that was lost here.

U. S. GRANT

Maj Gen

Telegram, copies, DLC-USG, V, 18, 30, 91; DNA, RG 393, Dept. of the Tenn.,
Letters Sent. *O.R.*, I, xvii, part 2, 468. On Dec. 23, 1862, Maj. Gen. James B.
McPherson twice telegraphed to USG, the second time at 10:00 P.M. "Having
learned that a strong cavalry force was 5 miles east of Waterford at 3 o'clock,
I have ordered Colonel Hatch, with his entire command, to move immediately
toward Pontotoc and see if he cannot get on track of the rebels. Have also sent
orders to General Lauman, General Denver, and the officers in command of guards
for trains to be on the alert, and guard especially against any cavalry dash." "I
have already given directions to Colonel Hatch, and his whole command will be
here to start in a few minutes in an east-northeasterly direction until he strikes
the road running from the mouth of Tippah Creek to Pontotoc, and try, if possible,
to head the rebels off. I think he will reach this road before daylight and have
instructed him to use all efforts to ascertain the whereabouts of the enemy and
ambush them." *Ibid.*, pp. 468, 469. On the same day, Col. Edward Hatch, 2nd
Iowa Cav., "Near Oxford," telegraphed to USG. "My command found the
enemy's pickets about 2 miles north of Coffeeville on the morning of the 22d;

drove them south of Coffeeville 3 miles, where I found the enemy in force; destroyed the railroad trestle-work south of Coffeeville and between that point and the Yocknapatalfa." *Ibid.*, p. 466.

On Dec. 22, Lt. Col. John A. Rawlins, Oxford, wrote to Col. John M. Loomis, "Commanding Post," Oxford. "Upon Gen McPherson moving his last Division from here you will break up this Post and proceed with your command to Holly Springs Miss., keeping with Gen. McPherson Division as far as it moves on the same road" Copy, DLC-USG, V, 91. Entered as written by USG at Oxford on Dec. 23, *ibid.*, V, 18, 30; DNA, RG 393, Dept. of the Tenn., Letters Sent. *O.R.*, I, xvii, part 2, 469. The earlier date appears preferable because all other communications of Dec. 23 place USG at Holly Springs.

1. Tippah Creek, flowing in a southerly direction, joins the Tallahatchie River about five miles east of Abbeville, Miss.

2. Edward Hatch, born in Maine in 1832, attended Norwich University for two years, and eventually settled in Iowa. Appointed capt., 2nd Iowa Cav., he rose to col. by June 13, 1862, and commanded the second cav. brigade, Dept. of the Tenn. His report of the pursuit of Maj. Gen. Earl Van Dorn is *ibid.*, I, xvii, part 1, 502–3.

To Brig. Gen. Grenville M. Dodge

Holly Springs Dec. 23d 1862.

GEN. G. M. DODGE.

CORINTH,

Rebel Cavalry have gone north. Our Cavalry is in pursuit. Send me the papers you speak of. I will direct forage and beef collected and sent to you

U. S. GRANT
Major Gen'l.

Telegram, copies, DLC-USG, V, 18, 30, 91; DNA, RG 393, Dept. of the Tenn., Letters Sent; Dodge Papers, IaHA. On Dec. 23, 1862, Brig. Gen. Grenville M. Dodge, Corinth, telegraphed to USG. "Col Chetlain informs me that two Cavalry men only got here last evening   they lost the ~~escort~~ scout somewhere   they brought a verbal message only   two young men have arrived ~~from~~ here from Mobile with Mobile papers of sixteenth (16th) & seventeenth (17th)   their information for preparations to attack Mobile & news of papers if you have not seen it ought be of importance. to you   shall I send it or have you later news   also is there any cavalry force of enemy north of you   if so when shall I look for them I am about out of rations   Have been on half rations for several days   Could not you order a lot of beef & forage brought or ~~pres~~ pressed for me at Jackson   you know there is nothing of the kind in this vicinity." Telegram received, DNA, RG 393, Dept. of the Tenn., Telegrams Received. On the same day, Dodge wrote to USG. "On an examination of men from Mobile, I consider their statement and reliability, so important that I send it, L. W. Pierce who gives most of the information was in Q M. Dept. of 2d Iowa Infantry, Member of Co. "C" was captured in front of Corinth last August, was taken to Tupelo a prisoner of war, escaped 2d day, met Chas. Davenport of Boston an Engineer on M & O. R. R with whom he was acquainted and being an Engineer himself through Davenports influence got a situation as Engineer on M & O. R. R   They both escaped by running away with an Engine, on plea of examining the damage done by us to R. R. They left Mobile Tuesday night, says a large fleet off Mobile and great consternation existed as only two Regiments of Infantry remained in Mobile, Gen Forney having joined Price, with the other forces. Three weeks ago they transported to Pemberton 18000 men, were two weeks doing it, and that they came to Mobile from Chattanoga   both agree in the statement as to time and numbers   since that time no troops have gone that way except conscripts though they have been expecting more every day. The talk in Columbus was that Braggs Army was coming but he could get no foundation for it, except rumor for a week past. He has been transporting the machinery of Arsenal at Columbus to Selma and Montgomery, also a part to Georgia. The same has gone over the Road from Jackson and Greneda. He says Pembertons force does not exceed 40,000 men and that your advance has created great excitement   The troops from Mobile to this place are ten Companies of Infantry at Meridian and Bartolp Cavalry at West Point. They were going to move to Okolona, at Columbus there are no Troops. At Marion 4 miles above, Meridian all the stock of the Memphis & Charleston R. R is laid up, and when Van Dorn advanced on Corinth they employed a large number of Engineers, expecting to resume that road. He also gives full statement of the vessels in Mobile Harbor. Their armament and especially of the Florida, New Oveide, which run in there some time ago   says he has been on her and had offered him the place of 4th Asst Engineer that she has shipped two crews expecting shortly to run the Blockade, one crew being for a Ship in England. She is not an Iron Clad but has about a foot of pressed Cotton between her inner and outer hull &c. It appears to me, that the information contained in his statement of armed vessels in Mobile Bay should be sent to Secy of War, by Telegraph. He also brings plans of approach to Mobile Harbor and approach to Mobile by land.   both men are very intelligent and young. Pierce is vouched for by his whole Regiment. I knew him in Iowa and he was then a good citizen   He has all his papers to show by whom employed in South Pass exempting him from conscription &c"   Copy, *ibid.*, 16th Army Corps, Letters Sent; Dodge Papers, IaHA.

Earlier on Dec. 23, Dodge had telegraphed to USG. "I arrived here today all my Command will be in Before night—I marched one hundred & thirty (130) miles in four (4) days going to Lexington Junos & thence to Mifflin & Hendersen where I put the command aboard of the car & returned thence Here—I could not find any Enemy in force   they were still north of me & I think scattered about in Small parties—I sent my Cavalry to Clifton thence up the river to Pittsburg Landing & up to last night there was no force of any size on this side—near Clifton about two hundred & fifty (250) men were guarding the boats & raft— I do not think forest had over five thousand men if that if & Intended—to rtr break up the rail road   they say Clifton   He intended to return in three weeks his men were all mounted   crossed with five or six pieces of artillery—all Quiet here—"   Telegram received, DNA, RG 94, War Records Office, Military Division of the Miss.

To Brig. Gen. Jeremiah C. Sullivan

By Telegraph from Holly Springs [*Dec. 23*] 186[*2*]
To Gen Sullivan

Instruct all your Post Commanders to collect all the forage beef cattle and fat hogs in their vicinity belonging to Secessionists and have them issued by the commissary & Quarter-Master— Send some forage and Cattle to Corinth immediately or as soon as possible; they are out of rations

U S. Grant
Maj Gen

Telegram received, DNA, RG 393, 16th Army Corps, 4th Division, Telegrams Received; copies, *ibid.*, Dept. of the Tenn., Letters Sent; DLC-USG, V, 18, 30, 91. *O.R.*, I, xvii, part 2, 465. On Dec. 23, 1862, 11:00 A.M., Brig. Gen. Jeremiah C. Sullivan, Jackson, telegraphed to USG. "An order was issued for the troops at Grand Junction and La Grange to fall back to Bolivar. They were unable to obey on account of the enemy being in their rear. Shall I reissue the order? No news of the rebels. I will be able to reach Trenton to-day with cars." *Ibid.*, p. 464. On the same day, USG telegraphed to Sullivan. "The order to fall back to Bolivar was countermanded   I now have three Rgiments of cavalry and four of infantry besides the old garrison there   think they will be able to take care of all the rebels this side of Bolivar" Telegram received, DNA, RG 393, 16th Army Corps, 4th Division, Telegrams Received; copies, *ibid.*, Dept. of the Tenn., Letters Sent; DLC-USG, V, 18, 30, 91. *O.R.*, I, xvii, part 2, 464. On the same day, Sullivan sent two additional telegrams to USG, the second at 6:20 P.M. "Colonel Ingersoll has just come in. He thinks the rebels have gone to Columbus and then to cross over and destroy Rosecrans' line of railroad. They number at least 7,500 men. Their intention was to destroy stores at Jackson, having been informed of our exact force by a Tennessee officer in United States forces. I am ordering my available force north and will try and have the road repaired in a week." "I will occupy Trenton to-morrow. I have sent a force toward Denmark and north side of Hatchie. General Haynie is pushing north on railroad with a force strong enough to open the road." *Ibid.*, p. 465.

Also on Dec. 23, Brig. Gen. Isham N. Haynie, Humboldt, telegraphed to USG. "I left Oxford the next morning after ~~you~~ I saw you   came to Jackson Same day   found forces concentrated there & trouble Generally   I declined to proceed further reported to Gen Sullivan for duty & after the rebels fell back from Jackson I was directed to take Command of the forces ordered toward Columbus & reestablish Communications I am now trying to do so—Come here last night Will go to trenton tomorrow Rebels are on ahead so reported —When I shall go through I do not know I sent a courier to Gen Davies this morning requesting him to move down this way & check Forrest so that we can drive him off of R R or whip him I want to get home & before I get there my furlough will expire I would like to have it so changed so as allow me to have a leave that wont expire before it begins I am progressing well & will bend all energies to get road through to Columbus & send stores down—'' ALS (telegram sent), DNA, RG 393, Military Division of the Miss., Letters Received. *O.R.*, I, xvii, part 2, 467. On the same day, Lt. Col. John A. Rawlins telegraphed to Haynie. "Your leave for ten days will be given as soon as Gen'l. Sullivan can relieve you from the duty you are now on.'' Copies, DLC-USG, V, 18, 30; DNA, RG 393, Dept. of the Tenn., Letters Sent.

To Col. John V. D. Du Bois

Head Quarters, Dept of the Ten.
Holly Springs, Miss Dec. 23d. 1862

COL. J. V. DuBOIS
COL.

You will proceed by first train of Cars going North from this place to Benton Barracks, Mo., in charge of the prisoners paroled at this place on the 20th inst.

Cause complete rolls to be made of the Prisoners on the route there and furnish one copy to the Commanding Officer at Benton Barracks and send one roll to these Hd. Quarters.

Rations can be drawn at the different Posts on the route as required, taking enough from Columbus or Cairo to last through to Saint Louis

Having performed this duty report to the Gen. in chief of the Army, by letter for further instruction

Respectfully &c.,
U. S. GRANT
Maj. Gen.

Copies, DLC-USG, V, 18, 30, 91; DNA, RG 393, Dept. of the Tenn., Letters Sent.

On Dec. 23, 1862, Lt. Col. John A. Rawlins telegraphed to the commanding officers, Bolivar, Grand Junction, and Jackson. "Arrest & return to this ~~office~~ place all officers and men who may find their way to your Post claiming to be paroled & permit no one connected with the army under any pertext to pass north without written authority from these Head Quarters sending back under proper guards all who do not belong to your Post" Telegram received, *ibid.*, 16th Army Corps, 4th Division, Telegrams Received; copies, *ibid.*, Dept. of the Tenn., Letters Sent; DLC-USG, V, 18, 30, 91. *O.R.*, I, xvii, part 2, 464; *ibid.*, II, v, 115. On Dec. 25, Rawlins issued Special Field Orders No. 34 specifying that paroled prisoners would march to Memphis, then travel by steamboat to Benton Barracks, St. Louis. DS (dated Dec. 24), DNA, RG 94, Dept. of the Tenn., Special Orders; copies (dated Dec. 25), *ibid.*, RG 393, Dept. of the Tenn., Special Orders; DLC-USG, V, 26, 27.

On Jan. 21, 1863, USG wrote to Brig. Gen. Lorenzo Thomas. "I have the honor herewith to transmit, list of Federal Prisoners, paroled by the Rebels, at Holly Springs and vicinity, on the 20th day of December, 1862." LS, DNA, RG 249, Letters Received. On Jan. 24, USG transmitted to Thomas a duplicate list of prisoners. LS, *ibid.*

To Col. Benjamin H. Grierson

Holly Springs, Dec 23rd 1862.

COL. GRIERSON, GRAND JUNCTION.

Pursue the enemy with all vigilance wherever they may go reporting whenever you can reach a telegraph office   Take the 3rd Mich with you.[1]

U. S. GRANT
Maj Genl

Telegram, copies, DLC-USG, V, 18, 30, 91; DNA, RG 393, Dept. of the Tenn., Letters Sent. *O.R.*, I, xvii, part 2, 465. On Dec. 23, 1862, Col. Benjamin H. Grierson, Grand Junction, telegraphed to USG. "Just received the following from Bolivar: Col. B. H. GRIERSON: The enemy are going north. Come here and I will put you on their track. M. BRAYMAN. Column moving northeast. Have halted them. Shall I act on the above?" *Ibid.* On the same day, USG telegraphed to Grierson. "If you are on the track of the enemy follow him. Don't be turned off by directions from Post Commanders unless you think you will get after the enemy by a shorter route or in a more effective manner by doing so." Copies, DLC-USG, V, 18, 30, 91; DNA, RG 393, Dept. of the Tenn., Letters Sent. *O.R.*, I, xvii, part 2, 466. On the same day, Grierson telegraphed to USG. "I am moving as rapidly as possible north to Bolivar." *Ibid.*

Also on Dec. 23, Grierson, Grand Junction, telegraphed to USG and Brig. Gen. Charles S. Hamilton. "Mistake about rebels being near La Grange. Colonel

Richmond says they were 3 miles below Somerville at 3 p. m. yesterday, giving the impression that they were going to unite with Johnston at Jackson. I will move northward, striking between Bolivar and Somerville. Third Michigan has arrived." *Ibid.*, p. 483. Although the only source of this telegram provides the date Dec. 25, Grierson was not at Grand Junction on Dec. 25, was joined by the 3rd Mich. Cav. on Dec. 23, and did move northward from Grand Junction on Dec. 24. See *ibid.*, I, xvii, part 1, 518–19, for Grierson's report of his movements at this time. On Dec. 25, USG received a telegram from Grand Junction. "The following dispatch to Col Greson just recd here   I do not know where to reach him   Bolivar 25 Col B. H. GRIERSON Comdg Cav. Enemy appear to be crossing river above bearing towards Jackson   I fear the main body have got away from you   your Train will start for Junction in morning. M BRAYMAN Brig Gen" Telegram received, DNA, RG 393, Dept. of the Tenn., Telegrams Received. On the same day, Brig. Gen. Mason Brayman wrote to USG. "Yesterday morning the Enemy in large force, drove in our pickets and advanced in line of battle, from the west. The Cavalry of Grierson and Lee having arrived, met the Enemy. The attacking force divided. The larger portion went to Middleburgh, Seven miles below, ~~attacking~~ and Summoned Col Graves to surrender. He refused. The fight lasted two and a half hours. The Enemy lost twelve (12) killed, 30 wounded, and fourteen prisoners. ~~A portion are still in this~~ They abandoned the attempt. They broke the wire, which is being repaired. They also set track on fire in four places, but it was soon extinguished. ~~So~~ A portion is still in this neighborhood, but I have force enough. A train from Jackson Just in." ADfS, Brayman Papers, ICHi.

On Dec. 28, USG telegraphed to the commanding officers, Bolivar and Grand Junction. "Order down all the cavalry ambulances &c that were left. at. Bolivar by Col Grierson when there"   Telegram received (dated Dec. 29), *ibid.*; copies (dated Dec. 28), DLC-USG, V, 18, 30; DNA, RG 393, Dept. of the Tenn., Letters Sent. On Dec. 29, Brayman telegraphed to USG. "The Cavalry ambulances, &c, which Col. Grierson left here, departed south on the morning of the 27th. Bodies of rebel cavalry are still in this neighborhood. I have no sufficient force to pursue them." ADfS, Brayman Papers, ICHi.

1. On Dec. 23, Col. Addison S. Norton, Abbeville, telegraphed to USG. "train of third Mich Cavalry reported for orders   I have sent them to the north side of Tallahatchie to await orders   shall I send all Cavalry trains forward—" Telegram received, DNA, RG 393, Dept. of the Tenn., Telegrams Received.

To Lt. Col. John McDermott

Holly Springs, Dec 23rd 1862

COL. McDERMOTT, GRAND JUNCTION

Has Col. Marsh joined you? I wish him to remain at Grand Junction, Lagrange and Davis Mills until otherwise directed unless he sees an opportunity to operate against the enemy advantageously. Show this to Col. Marsh.

U. S. GRANT

Maj Genl

Telegram, copies, DLC-USG, V, 18, 30, 91; DNA, RG 393, Dept. of the Tenn., Letters Sent. *O.R.*, I, xvii, part 2, 467. On Dec. 23, 1862, USG again telegraphed to Lt. Col. John McDermott. "Has Col. Marsh joined you?" Copies, DLC-USG, V, 18, 30; DNA, RG 393, Dept. of the Tenn., Letters Sent. On the same day, McDermott telegraphed to USG. "Col Marsh has arrived   his Command has not yet arrived" Telegram received, *ibid.*, Telegrams Received.

Also on Dec. 23, Col. C. Carroll Marsh, Grand Junction, telegraphed to USG. "Have seen your dispatch to Col McDermott   I reported to you by telegraph two hours ago" Telegram received, *ibid.* On the same day, Marsh sent two additional telegrams to USG. "Arrived here at 2 o'clock with four regiments of infantry. Cavalry just leaving here for the north." "Colonel Richmond telegraphs that his pickets have been fired on to-night. He calls for re-enforcements." *O.R.*, I, xvii, part 2, 468. Another telegram from Marsh, Grand Junction, to USG was probably sent on Dec. 23. "Bridges destroyed between Lagrange & Moscow   Scouts sent out towards somerville found all bridges destroyed. Courier from Maj Myers 3d Mich Cav reports that twelfth 12th Mich Infy were attacked this morning at Middleburg & repulsed the Enemy taking Some prisoners   Maj Taylor of 3d Mich Cav reports a prisoner taken who States that van dorn expected to make a Junction with Price tomorrow morning & attack Bolivar   Maj Myer was moving towards Spring Hill" Telegram received, DNA, RG 94, War Records Office, Dept. of the Tenn. Misdated Dec. 22 in *O.R.*, I, xvii, part 2, 454.

On Dec. 22, McDermott had telegraphed to USG. "I received dispatch today for all troops north of Holly Springs and south of Bolivar to fall back to Bolivar, signed by General Grant. I could not fall back, as the enemy was in our rear. Was the order genuine? Everything quiet, but the enemy in large force near." *Ibid.*, p. 458. USG endorsed this telegram with a reply to McDermott. "Barricade with cotton-bales if you have them. A force is moving north from Holly Springs to your assistance; will reach you by morning." *Ibid.*, p. 459. On the same day, McDermott telegraphed to USG. "We are now skirmishing with the enemy and will hold them in bay until morning." *Ibid.* On Dec. 23, McDermott telegraphed to USG. "Five regiments cavalry here and moving on in pursuit of enemy. It is absolutely necessary to leave one company here. I have no cavalry." *Ibid.*, p. 467.

To Maj. Gen. James B. McPherson

———

Holly Springs Miss Dec 24, 1862

Maj Gen'l. J. B McPherson
Oxford Miss

The following dispatch is just received. Send it to Col Hatch tomorrow morning if possible.

"Near Bolivar Dec 24, 1862

Maj Gen'l Grant

I arrived in Bolivar 11 O'clock last night. Pickets at that place were driven in last night. Our presence no doubt saved the place, as it is evident they did not know of our presence until this morning. We struck their trail on Middleburg[1] road this morning, evidently a large force 7 or 8000. My column is now moving. Have been skirmishing all the morning, a number of the enemy killed and wounded : no loss on our side.

Later Middleburg Dec 24

The enemy repulsed from this place by our Infantry, we came up with their rear : they struck off to the left toward the Van Buren road, we are in close pursuit : their number from 5 to 7000. I have but one thousand four hundred men. Cannot the 7th Illinois 3d Iowa and balance of the 3d Mich be sent after me ? From latest information they appear to be going Southeast. Will keep you advised as well as possible   B. H. Grierson Commdg

U. S. Grant Maj. Gen'l

Copies, DLC-USG, V, 18, 30; DNA, RG 393, Dept. of the Tenn., Letters Sent. *O.R.*, I, xvii, part 2, 474. The copy in DLC-USG, V, 18, is misdated Dec. 23, 1862. On Dec. 24, 8:30 P.M., Maj. Gen. James B. McPherson, "North side of Tallahatchie," wrote to USG. "My command is in camp on the North side of the Tallahatchie, with the exception of Col Leggett's Brigade, which I left at Abbeville, with one battery of Artillery, to assist in guarding the cotton &c until it can be removed. Left Oxford at 12 oclock 'M.' Everything in that vicinity quiet. Co'l Hatch left Oxford at 12. o'clock last night in an east, north east direction, to try and intercept the rebels. Have not heard from him yet. Your despatch enclosing one from Co'l Grierson just received. Will immediately send thirty of my escort with it to Co'l Hatch if he can be found." Copies, DNA, RG 393, 17th Army Corps, Letters Sent; *ibid.*, Bolivar, Tenn., Letters Sent. *O.R.*, I, xvii, part 2, 473. Earlier on the same day, McPherson wrote to USG. "I have been examining into the ration question this morning. General Denver has only enough, on three-quarter rations, to include the 28th instant; General Logan to include the 31st; General Lauman to include the 30th." *Ibid.*, p. 472.

Also on Dec. 24, 8:00 A.M., Brig. Gen. Mason Brayman, Bolivar, telegraphed to USG. "Cols Grierson & Lee are here with their commands   pickets Exchanged shots at Six this morning four miles out on whiteville road   I think the Enemy is moving north to Join Forrest—I do not consider Bolivar & Jackson now in danger   the Col Grierson starts at once"   Telegram received, DNA, RG 393, Dept. of the Tenn., Telegrams Received; ADfS, Brayman Papers, ICHi. On the same day, Col. Benjamin H. Grierson, Bolivar, telegraphed to USG. "Arrived at 11, o'clock last night. Pickets driven in here this morning. Think only a feint. Think they have gone North to join Forrest. My column now moving East of North ~~East~~. Will keep you advised as far as possible." Telegram received, *ibid. O.R.*, I, xvii, part 2, 474. Later the same day, Grierson, Saulsbury, Tenn., telegraphed twice to USG. "Have just arrived at this place; enemy still going southward, their rear only a mile ahead. We are constantly picking up their stragglers. Have just learned that they talk of turning to the left a short distance. Shall throw out scouts and observe their movements, and camp to-night without camp-fires. I sent you dispatch from Middleburg and also from Van Buren." "Your dispatch received this evening. I am camped within 2½ miles of the enemy. I sent out scouts, who reported to me an hour ago that they had left, still going south. I start in pursuit in one hour and will follow them to their den." *Ibid.*, p. 475.

Also on Dec. 24, Lt. Col. John A. Rawlins telegraphed to Grierson. "Your despatches from near Middleburg and Van Buren have been sent to the commanding officer at Salem whose forces consist of Infantry and Artillery, and is about fifteen miles east of here. Also to Col. Hatch who started last evening with his cavalry force to the mouth of Tippah creek, on the Tallahatchie, in pursuit of a portion of the enemy near there. He may be able to join you after you cross the Tallahatchie, and may intercept the enemy's retreat. Make every possible exertion to harrass and destroy the enemy. Take Hatch with you in the pursuit if you meet with him." Copies, DLC-USG, V, 18, 30; DNA, RG 393, Dept. of the Tenn., Letters Sent. *O.R.*, I, xvii, part 2, 474–75. Rawlins sent this telegram to Col. C. Carroll Marsh, Grand Junction. "Send the above to Col. Grierson by courier at once. He was at Van Buren about 4, o'clock, in pursuit of the enemy going directly south. Give Grierson any supplies. Please acknowledge receipt of this." Copies, DLC-USG, V, 18, 30; DNA, RG 393, Dept. of the Tenn., Letters Sent. On the same day, Marsh telegraphed to USG. "Despatch for Col Grierson with me directing to forward by Courier recd   will forward immediately"   Telegram received, *ibid.*, Telegrams Received. On the same day, Col. John K. Mizner, Grand Junction, telegraphed to USG. "I have read your dispatch to Colonel Grierson. I will leave at once to join the command at Saulsbury. I hope as much cavalry as possible will be thrown out east to intercept the enemy's retreat, that they may be effectually used up. I will keep you advised, reporting as often as practicable." *O.R.*, I, xvii, part 2, 472.

Also on Dec. 24, Rawlins telegraphed to Marsh. "Notify troops at Davis'

Mills to be in readiness to repel any attack that may be made." Copies, DLC-USG, V, 18, 30; DNA, RG 393, Dept. of the Tenn., Letters Sent. *O.R.*, I, xvii, part 2, 472. On the same day, Marsh twice telegraphed to Rawlins. "Dispatch received. I notified Colonel Morgan at 6 o'clock to be prepared for attack, and that if attacked I would go to his assistance. I send dispatch to Colonel Grierson to Saulsbury." "I have re-enforced Colonel Morgan and Colonel Richmond to the extent of my ability, and am prepared to co-operate with either of them in case of attack at Davis' Mill or La Grange." *Ibid.* On the same day, Marsh twice telegraphed to USG. "A contraband Just in reports that he left the rebels at Salisbury at four oclock & that they threatened to take Lagrange   I am ready for them" "The Quarter Master of my Regts are all at Holly Springs   I have telegraph Lt Boas my quartermaster to notify them to start with their trains using the men left behind for Escort"   Telegrams received, DNA, RG 393, Dept. of the Tenn., Telegrams Received. On the same day, USG telegraphed to Marsh. "Will you, if it is possible, ascertain if any damage is done to the Rail Road near La Grange or Moscow?" Copies, DLC-USG, V, 18, 30; DNA, RG 393, Dept. of the Tenn., Letters Sent.

1. Middleburg, Tenn., on the Tennessee and Ohio Railroad, about five miles southwest of Bolivar.

To Brig. Gen. Charles S. Hamilton

Head Quarters, Dept. of the Ten
Holly Springs Miss. Dec. 24th 1862

GEN. HAMILTON,

Enclosed herewith I send you copies of dispatches just received from Col. Grierson.[1] One a little later from Grand Junction says fighting is now going on North of that place. It is probable therefore that the enemy are now turning their course South.

The force at Salem should be informed of this fact and be on the lookout for them to give them a salute as they pass. Send notice at once.

Yours &c.
U. S. GRANT
Maj. Gen.

ALS, George V. Rountree, Chicago, Ill. On Dec. 24, 1862, Lt. Col. John A. Rawlins wrote to Brig. Gen. Charles S. Hamilton, Holly Springs. "You will, please move Ross' Divn of your command tomorrow morning the 25th inst to Davis Mills, Grand Junction and Lagrange." Copies, DLC-USG, V, 18, 30, 91; DNA, RG 393, Dept. of the Tenn., Letters Sent. *O.R.*, I, xvii, part 2, 473.

1. On Dec. 24, 4:00 P.M., Col. Benjamin H. Grierson, Van Buren, telegraphed to USG. "The rebels have just passed through this place and are going directly south. Van Dorn in command; they are moving towards Salisbury, 5½ miles from here. We are still in close pursuit and constantly skirmishing with their rear. They broke the telegraph, set fire to the culverts and tressel work and destroyed dwellings and barns. The garrison at Middleburg killed, wounded and captured a number, giving them a hot reception and fighting nobly. I dispatched you from Middleburg." Copies, DLC-USG, V, 18, 30; DNA, RG 393, Dept. of the Tenn., Letters Sent. *O.R.*, I, xvii, part 2, 473–74. These sources place the Grierson telegram in the body of USG's letter.

To Brig. Gen. Isaac F. Quinby

Holly Springs, Miss., Dec. 24. 1862

BRIG. GEN'L. J. F. QUINBY,
WATERFORD, MISS.,

If I go to Memphis, your Division goes also.[1] It is now reported however from the South that Vicksburg is now in our possession.[2]

Your Division will all be concentrated at Lumpkin's Mills until further orders.

U. S. GRANT,
Maj. Gen'l.

Copies, DLC-USG, V, 18, 30; DNA, RG 393, Dept. of the Tenn., Letters Sent.
O.R., I, xvii, part 2, 473.

1. On Dec. 25, 1862, Lt. Col. John A. Rawlins issued Special Field Orders No. 34 sending the division of Brig. Gen. Isaac F. Quinby to Memphis to escort wagon trains sent for supplies. DS (dated Dec. 24), DNA, RG 94, Dept. of the Tenn., Special Orders; copies (dated Dec. 25), *ibid.*, RG 393, Dept. of the Tenn., Special Orders; *ibid.*, General and Special Orders; DLC-USG, V, 26, 27. Dated Dec. 25 in *O.R.*, I, xvii, part 2, 485. On Dec. 25, Rawlins wrote to Quinby. "In escorting the trains to Memphis it will not be necessary to march your whole Divisions into Memphis, but can encamp 15 or 20 miles from there, sending a sufficient escort for guards with train, and await their return with the remainder of your Division. The paroled prisoners will proceed with you." Copies, DLC-USG, V, 18, 30; DNA, RG 393, Dept. of the Tenn., Letters Sent.
2. On Dec. 23, Maj. Gen. James B. McPherson, Oxford, telegraphed to USG. "A Contraband has Just came in who left vicksburg last wednesday   he repts himself as a Servt of Capt Roberts of the 15th Miss   he says vicksburg was

taken by our forces from New Orleans after Shelling the place for half a day & that the rebel forces fell back to Jackson Most of their heavy guns having been removed to that place   he also reports Grenada strongly reinforced & being heavily fortified Also large bodies of troops at Jackson   Col Hatch has came up & his command is about five miles South of this   I have directed him thoroughly Scout the country south & east of this place tomorrow early"   Telegram received, *ibid.*, Telegrams Received.

To Col. John C. Kelton

Headquarters Department of the Tennessee
Holly Springs, Miss. Dec 25, 1862

COL. J. C. KELTEN
A. A. GEN'L
WASHINGTON, D. C.
COLONEL:

I am just sending a large wagon train to Memphis after supplies, and avail myself of the opportunity, the first now for over a week, to communicate with the authorities at Washington.

I had timely notice of the advance of Forrest on the railroad in the neighborhood of Jackson, and took every means to meet it. Gen. Sullivan was reinforced from the Army with me, and forces from Corinth, Forts Henry, Heiman and Donelson were sent to co-operate. As the enemy's force was all Cavalry, and Gen. Sullivan's nearly all Infantry, it is probable that they have succeeded in evading our troops, so as do some damage to the Railroad, but to what extent I have not yet learned.

Before any decisive move had been made by Gen Sullivan against the enemy, or by the enemy on our roads, communications were cut between us, and a formidable move of Cavalry from Grenada, was reported going North.

This force assembled first at Pontotoc, and as Col. Dickey was out to the East on the Mobile road with about half of my available Cavalry, I concluded that the object was to cut him off.—I immediately ordered all the Cavalry that could be spared

to Pontotoc, and two Brigades of Infantry with them, with directions to operate from there for the relief of Col Dickey. Before
these troops got in motion, however, I learned of the Rebel
Cavalry passing North from Pontotoc, and of Col. Dickey passing
safely by their rear. I immediately notified all Commanders
North of me, to Bolivar, of this move of the enemy, and to be
prepared to meet them, and to hold their respective posts at all
hazards. Excepting this place, all have done well, the enemy
being repulsed at Cold-Water, Davis' Mills,[1] Bolivar, and at
Middleburg. This place was taken whilst the troops were quietly
in their beds. The Commanding Officer of the Post, Col. R. C.
Murphy, of the 8th Wisconsin Vols. took no steps to protect the
place, or resist the enemy, not even having notified a single officer of his command of approaching danger, although he, himself, had received warning, as hereinbefore stated.[2] The troops
cannot be blamed in the matter, for they found themselves surrounded by from five to seven thousand cavalry.—the first intimation of the approach of an enemy.

Notwithstanding this surprise, many of the troops behaved
nobly, refusing to be paroled, and after making their escape from
the enemy, attacked him without regard to their relative strength.
Conspicuous among these latter, was the detachment of the 2nd
Illinois Cavalry, consisting of six Companies, that was stationed
here at the time.

Our loss here will probably amount to $400.000. in property,
and 1500 men taken prisoners.

As soon as I learned that the rebel cavalry had moved North
from Pontotoc, and that Col. Dickey was safe, I ordered all the
Cavalry that could be spared for the purpose, about 1500 men,
to pursue the enemy, and not leave them until they were captured
or completely broken up. They found them near Bolivar, and
were close on their heels all day yesterday, compelling the enemy
to change his course southward, killing and capturing quite a
number. Last night Federals and Rebels encamped near Salsbury,
and I presume the pursuit is still going on.

Gen. Hamilton sent a Brigade of Infantry, with one Battery,

to Salem, to operate against the enemy. [if] he should return by that route. Have also sent the remainder of the Cavalry force that returned from the expedition to the Mobile road, to intercept the enemy wherever he may attempt to cross the creeks of the Tallahatchie.

I yet hope the enemy will find this a dearly bought success.

I am now occupying the line of the Tallahatchie, with the road strongly guarded to the rear, waiting for communications to be opened to know what move next to make.

It is perfectly impracticable to go further south by this route, depending upon the roads for supplies; and the Country does not afford them. Our immense train has so far been fed entirely off of the country, and as far as practicable the troops have also been subsisted.

For fifteen miles East or West of the railroad from Coffeeville to La Grange nearly everything for the subsistence of man or beast has been appropriated for the use of our Army, and on leaving our advanced position, I had the principle mills destroyed.

The expedition under Col. Dickey was quite successful. Whilst out he captured about two hundred confederate soldiers with a fair proportion of horses, arms and equipments. He destroyed large quantities of Corn, which had been collected on the Mobile and Ohio Railroad, and also a few cars. The road was completely and thoroughly broken up from Saltillo to a point south of Tupelo.

Reports will be forwarded to you as fast as they can be got in

> I am, Col,
> Very Respectfully
> Your Ob't Serv't
> U. S. GRANT
> Maj. Gen Com'd'g

LS, DNA, RG 94, Vol. Service Division, T684 (vs) 1862. *O.R.*, I, xvii, part 1, 477–78.

1. On Dec. 26, 1862, Col. Jonathan Richmond, 126th Ill., La Grange, wrote to USG reporting his defense of Davis' Mill. Copy, DNA, RG 94, War Records Office, Union Battle Reports. *O.R.*, I, xvii, part 1, 520–21. On Jan. 8, 1863,

Lt. Col. John A. Rawlins issued General Orders No. 4 congratulating the garrisons of Coldwater, Davis' Mill, and Middleburg for "their successful repulse of an enemy many times their number. . . . The only success gained by Van Dorn was at Holly Springs, where the whole garrison was left by their commander in ignorance of the approach of danger." Copies, DLC-USG, V, 13, 14, 95; DNA, RG 393, Dept. of the Tenn., General and Special Orders. *O.R.*, I, xvii, part 1, 525.

2. See telegram to Col. Robert C. Murphy, Dec. 19, 1862. On Dec. 23, 1862, Murphy wrote to USG. "Will you do me the favor to grant me a personal interview, and to name the hour by the return orderly?? I am too unwell to leave my room except to avail of such a favor." Copy, DNA, RG 94, Vol. Service Division, T684 (vs) 1862. USG endorsed this note. "Col Murphy can see me at any hour." Copy, *ibid.* On Dec. 25, USG wrote to Brig. Gen. Charles S. Hamilton. "I told Col Murphy to day that he being in bad health could have leave to go to his home to await his exchange." Copy, *ibid.* On Dec. 24, Rawlins issued Special Field Orders No. 33 severely criticizing Col. Robert C. Murphy for the capture of Holly Springs. DS, *ibid.*, Dept. of the Tenn., 13th Army Corps, General Orders; copy, DLC-USG, V, 27; copies (dated Dec. 23), *ibid.*, V, 26; DNA, RG 94, War Records Office, Union Battle Reports; *ibid.*, RG 393, Dept. of the Tenn., General and Special Orders; *ibid.*, Special Orders. *O.R.*, I, xvii, part 1, 515–16. On Dec. 28, USG wrote to Maj. Gen. Stephen A. Hurlbut. "Arrest and detain Col. Murphy of the 8th Wisconsin Vol. Inf.y. He is a paroled prisoner now on his way out by my authority. He will not be permitted to leave Memphis until again authorized from these Head Quarters." ALS, DNA, RG 94, Compiled Service Records, Vol. Organizations, 8th Wis.

On Jan. 5, 1863, Maj. Gen. Henry W. Halleck endorsed USG's letter to Col. John C. Kelton, Dec. 25, 1862, printed above. "I respectfully recommend that Col. Murphy be ~~cashier~~ dismissed the service." AES, *ibid.*, Vol. Service Division, T684 (vs) 1862. On Jan. 10, Secretary of War Edwin M. Stanton approved this endorsement, and Murphy was dismissed by AGO General Orders No. 11, Jan. 10. ES, *ibid. O.R.*, I, xvii, part 1, 516. On Jan. 8, Rawlins had already issued General Orders No. 4. "Col. R. C. Murphy, of the 8th regiment Wisconsin Infantry Volunteers, having, while in command of the post of Holly Springs, Miss., neglected and failed to exercise the usual and ordinary precautions to guard and protect the same; having, after repeated and timely warning of the approach of the enemy, failed to make any preparations for resistance or defense, or show any disposition to do so; and having, with a force amply sufficient to have repulsed the enemy, and protect the public stores intrusted to his care, disgracefully permitted him to capture the post and destroy the stores—and the movement of troops in the face of an enemy rendering it impracticable to convene a Court Martial for his trial, is therefore dismissed the Service of the United States, to take effect from the 20th day of December, 1862, the date of his cowardly and disgraceful conduct." Copies, DLC-USG, V, 13, 14, 95; DNA, RG 393, Dept. of the Tenn., General and Special Orders. *O.R.*, I, xvii, part 1, 516.

On Feb. 2, Murphy wrote a lengthy letter to President Abraham Lincoln. *Supplement to [Wisconsin] Assembly Journal of Friday, March 13, 1863*, pp. 2–10. On May 26, Lincoln forwarded this letter and accompanying documents to Col. Joseph Holt, judge-advocate-gen. "This is the case of Col. Murphy—Holly Springs, Miss.—Will the Judge Advocate General please examine it, & give me his opinion of it?" ALS, DNA, RG 94, Vol. Service Division, T684 (vs) 1862. On May 30, Holt wrote a lengthy opinion favorable to Murphy on the grounds that his force was small and his instructions confusing, and that no clear neglect of duty occurred. Holt recommended that Murphy's dismissal be revoked, and that Murphy report to USG for a court-martial. Copy, *ibid.* On Oct. 24, Lincoln endorsed this report. "Let the order dismissing Col. Murphy be revoked, and he ordered to report to Gen. Grant as above advised, with the modification that the ordering a Court Martial be in the discretion of Gen Grant." AES, *ibid.* On Oct. 28, Col. Edward D. Townsend, AGO, endorsed the report with the comment that since another col., 8th Wis., had already been properly appointed, he needed instructions from the War Dept. ES, *ibid.* On Nov. 9, Asst. Secretary of War Peter H. Watson endorsed the report back to Lincoln with the comment that his instructions were "impracticable." ES, *ibid.* Lincoln took no further action.

On June 13, 1867, Bvt. Brig. Gen. Thomas M. Vincent forwarded to USG a report on the Murphy case prepared in response to an inquiry made by U.S. Senator Charles D. Drake of Mo. ES, *ibid.* On June 24, USG endorsed this report. "Respectfully returned to the Secrety of War. The record of Col. Murphy at Holly Springs, Miss., and prior to that at Iuka, Miss., is so much against him that I cannot make any recommendation in his favor." ES, *ibid.* Between 1877 and 1880, efforts were made through the War Dept., and through congressional action (46th Congress, 2nd Session) to revoke Murphy's dismissal on the basis of Lincoln's endorsement of the Holt report, but no action resulted. Documents concerning the matter are *ibid.*

To Maj. Gen. Stephen A. Hurlbut

Head Quarters, Dept. of the Ten
Holly Springs Miss. Dec. 25th 1862

MAJ. GEN. S. A. HURLBUT
MEMPHIS, TEN.
GEN.

Just as Forrest's raid upon our rail-roads was commenced I received a dispatch from the Gen. in Chief of the Army to divide my command into four Army Corps, giving one to Gen. McClernand and placing him in chief command, under my direction, of the expedition on Vicksburg.

I immediately wrote the order giving you command of the 3d Army Corps and directed Gen. McClernand to order you here to take command of it.

Before this got off all communication was cut off with the North and has not yet been resumed. Gen. McClernand consequently has not received my directions and orders.

Communications now being cut off, and the probabilities being that Vicksburg is already in our hands, a change of plans will probably be be adopted and also a change of organization of Army Corps. I would direct therefore that you retain command of the District of Memphis until receipt of orders arranging Army Corps in accordance with the instructions refered to.

I will be glad to hear from you and to learn when the river expedition sailed and any other news you may have to communicate.

I Am Gen.

Your obt. svt.

U. S. Grant

Maj. Gen.

ALS, DNA, RG 393, District of West Tenn., 4th Division, Letters Received. *O.R.*, I, xvii, part 2, 480–81. See letter to Maj. Gen. John A. McClernand, Dec. 18, 1862.

To Maj. Gen. John A. McClernand

Head Quarters, Dept. of the Ten

Holly Springs Miss. Dec. 25th 1862

COMD.G OFFICER,

EXPEDITION DOWN MISSISSIPPI,

SIR:

Raids made upon the rail-road to my rear by Forrest Northward from Jackson and by Van Dorn North from the Tallahatchie have cut me off from supplies so that a further advance by this route is perfectly impracticable. The country does not afford supplies for troops and but a limited supply of forage.

I have fallen back with my advance to the Tallahatchie and will only be able to hold the enemy at the Yallabusha by making demonstrations in that direction or towards Columbus and Meredian.

News received here from the South, apparently very reliable, says that Vicksburg is now in our hands. Gen. Butler[1] with Farrigut's fleet are said to have assended the river and to have been successful in their attack. This does not come however in sufficiently reliable a form to base any order or change of plan upon it.

These raids have cut off communication so that I have had nothing from the North for over a week.

Telegraph will probably be working through by to-morrow and rail-road within five days.

> Respectfully &c.
> U. S. GRANT
> Maj. Gen. Com.

ALS, McClernand Papers, IHi. Copies (misdated Dec. 23, 1862), DLC-USG, V, 18, 30; DNA, RG 393, Dept. of the Tenn., Letters Sent. *O.R.*, I, xvii, part 2, 463. On Dec. 25, Lt. Col. John A. Rawlins wrote to the commanding officer, Memphis. "Inclosed find communication for Gen. J. A. McClernand, which you will deliver to him if he be at Memphis; if he has gone down the river you will please forward it to him. The original letter was sent to the Commanding Officer at Cairo, with instructions to deliver it to Gen. McClernand if he had not already passed that point going South, and if he had to send it to him at Memphis. Communication North was cut off and probably did not reach him." LS, DNA, RG 393, District of West Tenn., 4th Division, Letters Received. *O.R.*, I, xvii, part 2, 480.

1. Benjamin F. Butler, born in N. H. in 1818, graduated from Waterbury College (Colby), practiced law in Lowell, Mass., and entered politics as a Democrat. Although a supporter of the Southern Democrats in 1860, he led a regt. to D. C. in 1861, and was appointed maj. gen. as of May 16. His controversial administration of New Orleans, which began on May 1, 1862, ended on Dec. 16, when Maj. Gen. Nathaniel P. Banks assumed command of the Dept. of the Gulf.

To Maj. Gen. James B. McPherson

————

> Holly Springs, Miss., Dec. 25 1862

MAJ. GEN'L. J. B. MCPHERSON,
ABBEVILLE, MISS.,

Send one Brigade of your command to Lumpkin's Mill and keep it running. Both Divisions that were there have been removed, one to Davis' Mill, the other as escort to Wagon train.

Relieve Gen'l. Smith from command of his Brigade and order
him to report to me. Ross is in arrest,[1] and I want Smith to take
his Division.

U. S. GRANT,

Maj. Gen'l.

Copies, DLC-USG, V, 18, 30; DNA, RG 393, Dept. of the Tenn., Letters Sent.
O.R., I, xvii, part 2, 478.

    1. On Dec. 25, 1862, Brig. Gen. Leonard F. Ross, Holly Springs, wrote to
Lt. Col. John A. Rawlins. "I have been placed under arrest and relieved of my
Command by Brig Genl Hamilton Comd'g Left Wing of the Army of the Tenn,
I await the Orders of the Comdg Genl—If agreeable to the Commanding Genl
would be pleased to visit him in person and explain my position in the matter."
ALS, DNA, RG 156, Court-Martial Records, KK 703, Leonard F. Ross. On the
same day, Brig. Gen. Charles S. Hamilton endorsed the letter. "Gen Ross has
been placed in arrest for a positive refusal to obey an order given by me, that he
should report to Gen Quinby by telegraph, for instructions as to where & when
his Division train should report, for the trip to Memphis. The request to visit
the Maj Gen Comd'g is respectfully referred to him. I see no objections" AES,
ibid. Also on Dec. 25, USG wrote to Hamilton. "Direct Gen'l. Ross to proceed
to La Grange, Grand Junction or Davis' Mill's, where his command will be, and
await action on his arrest." Copies, DLC-USG, V, 18, 30; DNA, RG 393, Dept.
of the Tenn., Letters Sent. On Dec. 26, Ross, La Grange, telegraphed to USG.
"I am here & await your orders   how soon may I expect an investigation of the
charges against me" Telegram received, *ibid.*, Telegrams Received. On Dec. 27,
USG telegraphed to Ross. "I will order a court as soon as possible" Copies,
DLC-USG, V, 18, 30; DNA, RG 393, Dept. of the Tenn., Letters Sent. On the
same day, by Special Orders No. 54, Rawlins appointed a court-martial for Ross
for Dec. 31. DS, *ibid.*, RG 94, Special Orders, Dept. of the Tenn.; copies, *ibid.*,
RG 393, Dept. of the Tenn., Special Orders; DLC-USG, V, 26, 27. The court-
martial found Ross guilty of refusal to obey orders, quoting his refusal to report
by telegraph to Brig. Gen. Isaac F. Quinby for orders concerning his wagon train:
" 'I shall **not** do it. I have played orderly to General Quinby and other Generals
long enough,' or words to that effect." Ross was sentenced to a reprimand from
USG, which was embodied in General Orders No. 1, Dept. of the Tenn., Jan. 4,
1863. "Findings and Sentence approved. Brigadier General Leonard F. Ross,
having been guilty of disobedience of the orders of his commanding officer, thereby
setting a bad example to his juniors, is deserving of the serious reprimand of the
General Commanding; but from long service with him, the General Commanding
is satisfied that he was not wilfully guilty of conduct so prejudicial to the service,
but acted under the impulse of the moment, and the belief that a wrong was being
done him. Brig. Gen. Ross is relieved from arrest, and will assume command of
his Division." Copies, *ibid.*, V, 13, 14, 95; DNA, RG 393, Dept. of the Tenn.,
General and Special Orders; (printed) *ibid.*, RG 156, Court-Martial Records,
KK 703, Leonard F. Ross. On Feb. 21, USG forwarded a transcript of the court-
martial to the AGO. ES, *ibid*.

To Maj. Gen. James B. McPherson

Holly Springs Miss Dec 25 1862

MAJ GEN'L J B McPHERSON

ABBEVILLE MISS

The office at Abbeville can be moved back to your Head Quarters or another established. No news from Grierson to day. Parties in from the East report hearing Artillery off toward Rocky Ford for several hours this forenoon Communication will be opened with Columbus tomorrow, Sullivan reports road much less damaged than he expected.[1] Will be in order by Monday or Tuesday. All in order now to Jackson Dodge reports Roddy at Guntown with 1500 Cavalry and some Artillery moving West. If our Cavalry get Van Dorn under good headway towards Pontotoc I would like them to give Mr Roddy a dash

U S GRANT

Maj Genl

Copies, DLC-USG, V, 18, 30; DNA, RG 393, Dept. of the Tenn., Letters Sent. *O.R.*, I, xvii, part 2, 478.

On Dec. 25, 1862, Lt. Col. John A. Rawlins twice telegraphed to Maj. Gen. James B. McPherson. "You will please direct the Officer in command of the Cavalry now camped on the Tallahatchie to send a train of fifty wagons giving same instructions as to your own Regimental trains, to report to Gen. Quimby for further use" "The Genl Commanding desires to know if you received order to send trains to Memphis for supplies, telegraphed you this morning. Please answer" Copies, DLC-USG, V, 18, 30; DNA, RG 393, Dept. of the Tenn., Letters Sent. On the same day, McPherson telegraphed to USG. "Fifty teams of the Cavalry division will leave here shortly escorted by One hundred 100 Cavalry for TallaLoosa with positive orders to report to Gen Quinby at twelve 12 Oclock tomorrow After turning over their train they are instructed to make a scout to the South & southwest to the Tallahatchie I would like to have a telegraph office established on this north side of the river" Telegram received, *ibid.*, Telegrams Received; copies, *ibid.*, 17th Army Corps, Letters Sent; *ibid.*, Bolivar, Tenn., Letters Sent. On the same day, McPherson wrote to Rawlins. "Dispatch received. Division trains will be at Tallaloosa at 12. 'M,' to morrow (26th Inst). Order for Col Hatch enclosing Copy of despatches from Co'l Grierson, sent to Col Hatch and received by him at one A. M. this morning. His command would start immediately in the direction of 'Rocky Ford and Ripley. All our Cavalry have left Oxford and I presume a small force of Rebel Cavalry are in the place, as the Cavalry pickets were fired on early this morning. I have notified Co'l Leggett, at Abbeville, that all our Cavalry has been removed from his front, in the direction of Oxford, and that his sentinels and Out-posts must be on the alert to guard against surprise. I shall order Co'l Leggett's Brigade from Abbeville, to this side of the river, as soon as the cotton &c is removed   I have given orders to have the rebel works on the South side of the river (Tallahatchie) levelled." Copies, *ibid.*

1. On Dec. 25, 4:00 P.M., Brig. Gen. Jeremiah C. Sullivan, Jackson, telegraphed to USG. "The road to Columbus is not so badly hurt as supposed. I hold Trenton. My forces whipped Forrest yesterday at Obion. General Brayman beat him off at Bolivar. I think the road will be in running order by the first of next week. I will send a large force in that direction to protect Colonel Webster and his repairs. I have secured Jackson in such a manner that all the rebels cannot take it. The surrender of Trenton mortifies me, but the damage to road is not worth grieving about." *O.R.*, I, xvii, part 2, 483. On the same day, USG telegraphed to Sullivan. "Three miles north of Toons Station are three Bridges ungarded   you will at once protect them"   Telegram received, DNA, RG 393, 16th Army Corps, 4th Division, Telegrams Received; *ibid.*, Dept. of the Tenn., Letters Sent; DLC-USG, V, 18, 30. *O.R.*, I, xvii, part 2, 483.

To Brig. Gen. Grenville M. Dodge

————

Holly Springs Miss., Dec. 25. 1862

BRIG. GEN'L. G. M. DODGE

CORINTH, MISS.,

Parole the prisoners you have and turn them loose. Send a complete roll of them to the Adjutant General of the Army, a retain a copy.

Van Dorn was at Salisbury last night   Our cavalry close on him. He was repulsed at every place except here. It is possible that Van Dorn turned east of Salisbury.

Have you any news from Rosecrans or Bragg?

U. S. GRANT.

Maj. Gen'l.

Telegram, copies, DLC-USG, V, 18, 30; DNA, RG 393, Dept. of the Tenn., Letters Sent; Dodge Papers, IaHA. *O.R.*, I, xvii, part 2, 482. On Dec. 25, 1862, Brig. Gen. Grenville M. Dodge had telegraphed to Lt. Col. John A. Rawlins. "Morgan has tried a raid in the rear of Rosecrans at same time it was tried on us   do not know what success he had   I heard from Braggs Army   Scout seven days on the road   Every thing was in same position as I left Reported except on brigade at Shelbyville has been mounted   I expect more news tomorrow   Rhoddy left Tuscumbia last Saturday with his whole command   Camped monday night at Bay Springs was out at Guntown tuesday & going west he had about fifteen hundred 1500 mounted men five pieces Artillery I have scouts on his track I have some Taxans of withers brigade who were dismounted when they left Arkansas Since they fell back from Holly Springs the whole brigade has been remounted the horses came from Texas I have two hundred prisoners taken in the last week Cannot I send them through the lines where is van Dorns Cavalry" Telegram received, DNA, RG 94, War Records Office, Military Division of the Miss. *O.R.*, I, xvii, part 2, 482–83.

To Col. George P. Ihrie

By TELEGRAPH FROM Holly Springs [*Dec. 25*] *186[2]*
To COL IHRIE HUMBOLT

Nothing has been recd. from Genl. Sullivan for a number of days except by Telegraph—there has been no other communication and consequently no opportunity for him to send the papers referred to—I presume they will be sent when the cars resume their running—These querries are embarrasing and detrimental to the service and ought to be avoided if practicable—Genl Sullivan had a perfect right to release Col Rodgers if he thought the good of the service required it—He is the Commander of the district and communication was cut off with department Head Quarters—All officers my staff included who happened to be in his department at the time were subject to his orders

U. S. GRANT

~~John~~ J Maj Genl.

Telegram received, DNA, RG 393, 16th Army Corps, 4th Division, Telegrams Received; copies, *ibid.*, Dept. of the Tenn., Letters Sent; DLC-USG, V, 18, 30.

On Dec. 20, 1862, Col. George P. Ihrie, riding as a passenger on a train from Jackson, Tenn., to Columbus, Ky., learned that a railroad bridge over the Forked Deer River, near Humboldt, Tenn., was under attack by C.S.A. cav. As Ihrie reported to Lt. Col. John A. Rawlins on Dec. 31, he assumed command of troops on the train, another force on another train commanded by Col. John A. Rogers, 7th Tenn., and the troops at the bridge, drove away the C.S.A. cav., recaptured Humboldt, and was preparing an expedition to retake Trenton, Tenn., on the evening of Dec. 22 when relieved by Brig. Gen. Isham N. Haynie. Shortly before Haynie arrived, Ihrie arrested Rogers for disobedience of orders. ALS, DNA, RG 94, War Records Office, Union Battle Reports. *O.R.*, I, xvii, part 1, 562–66. On the same day, Ihrie wrote to Rawlins criticizing the defense of

Trenton, and accusing Brig. Gen. Thomas A. Davies, commanding at Columbus, of being stampeded. ALS, DNA, RG 94, War Records Office, Union Battle Reports. *O.R.*, I, xvii, part 1, 566–67. Ihrie's General Orders No. 1, Dec. 20, assuming command, and General Orders No. 2, Dec. 22, 10:00 P.M., surrendering command, are *ibid.*, I, xvii, part 2, 876–78.

On Dec. 22, Ihrie telegraphed to USG. "The troops under my Command after some brisk skirmishing recaptured this place day before yesterday little after dark driving out the rebel Cavalry & causing them to drop some of their plunder We also saved two of our trains the road is cut up to Union City in numerous places & telegraphic Communication with Columbus is destroyed If I had had a single piece of Artillery I should have fought my way to Union City" Telegram received, DNA, RG 393, Dept. of the Tenn., Telegrams Received. *O.R.*, I, xvii, part 1, 566. On Dec. 23, Brig. Gen. Jeremiah C. Sullivan, Jackson, telegraphed to USG. "George. P. Ihrie Col. on your Staff has been useing your name to interfere with military movements made by myself I ask you to order him to report to you untill I can make out Charges—his conduct has been reported to me by several as having been ~~do~~ decidedly unmilitary—" Telegram received, DNA, RG 94, Staff Papers, Ihrie. On the same day, Rawlins telegraphed to Sullivan. "Order Col. Geo. P. Ihria to this place under arrest" Telegram received, *ibid.*; copies, *ibid.*, RG 393, Dept. of the Tenn., Letters Sent; DLC-USG, V, 18, 30, 91.

Also on Dec. 23, Ihrie telegraphed to USG. "I ~~P~~ Placed Capt Williams 1st U. S. infy on Duty as actg asst adjt Gen His Leave of absence will have to be dated today tomorrow as it is impossible I suppose for me to overhaul Gen Sherman I would Like to Pass the Holidays in St Louis Have I your permission" Telegram received, DNA, RG 393, Dept. of the Tenn., Miscellaneous Letters Received. On the same day, USG telegraphed to Ihrie. "You may go to S Louis & spend the Christmas Holidays any charges Genl Sullivan has against you can be investigated on your return" Telegram received, *ibid.*, 16th Army Corps, 4th Division, Telegrams Received; copies, *ibid.*, Dept. of the Tenn., Letters Sent; DLC-USG, V, 18, 30, 91. On the same day, Rawlins twice telegraphed to Ihrie. "Charges have not been received. Gen'l. Grant telegraphed you to proceed to St. Louis, and can answer charges on your return." "Gen Sullivan has preferred charges against you for assumption of Authority. Your order to go to Saint Louis is revoked." Copies, *ibid.*, V, 18, 30; DNA, RG 393, Dept. of the Tenn., Letters Sent. The second telegram is also in DLC-USG, V, 91.

Also on Dec. 23, Ihrie twice telegraphed to Rawlins. "If I had not assumed authority by taking Command the 2 trains with heavy mails & large amt. of money would have been Captured by the Confed. cavalry this is the unanimous of every unprejudiced person on board does Gen'l Grant intertain the Charges please answer I wrote Genl Grant an unofficial today explainig everything" Telegram received, DNA, RG 393, Dept. of the Tenn., Telegrams Received. "Additional I refused for some time to take Comd. & did so at request of several passengers & offices beside according to the decision of the War Dept The case of Col Stevenson of Mo. I was the ranking officer present & in the trying situation & under the Circumstances in which we were placed did I not taken Comd. I would have been highly Censureable I dont Care a chip about the Charges as they will recoil upon ~~their~~ erudite officer who preferred them but I wish to go St Louis as there are those there who will be griviously disappointed Sullivan has ordered Haynie to arrest me The order is illegal as I am not under

Sullivans or Haynies Comd   Haynie cannot arrest one of Gen Grants aids   Please ask Gen Grant to put a stop to Sullivans conduct   the arrest is by order of Gen Grant   has Gen Grant authorized it"   Telegram received, *ibid.*, Miscellaneous Letters Received. On the same day, Capt. George A. Williams telegraphed to Rawlins. "I am requested by Col Ihrie to telegraph you my opinion of what would have occurred if he had not taken Comd of troops on our way from Jackson to this place   I am perfectly satisfied that had he not done so train together with all of the passengers & troops who could not save themselves by running would have been captured   he took command at request of many who saw the necessity of it" Telegram received, *ibid.*, Telegrams Received. On the same day, J. A. Van Buskirk, conductor of the military train, telegraphed to Rawlins. "I desire to inform you that my opinon both trains from Jackson en route for Columbus on the 20th Inst together with valuable mail would have been captured by Rebel Cavaly had not Col Ihrie assumed command of the troops"   Telegram received, *ibid.*

On Dec. 24, Ihrie telegraphed to Rawlins. "Did Genl Grant authorize Sullivan to have me arrested   I ask to be released   please answer immediately" ADfS, *ibid.*, RG 94, Staff Papers, Ihrie. On the same day, Rawlins telegraphed to Sullivan. "You will release Col Geo P Ihrie from arrest & permit him to proceed to S Louis   on his return his case can be fully Envestigated"   Telegram received, *ibid.*, RG 393, 16th Army Corps, 4th Division, Telegrams Received; copies, *ibid.*, Dept. of the Tenn., Letters Sent; DLC-USG, V, 18, 30, 91. On Dec. 25, Ihrie telegraphed to Rawlins. "Have you recieved the official papers including my serious charges against Col Rogers which I enclosed to Gen Sullivan for his Information to be sent to genl Grant   they left him yesterday morning" Telegram received, DNA, RG 393, Dept. of the Tenn., Miscellaneous Letters Received.

On Dec. 29, 7:30 P.M., Ihrie, Cairo, telegraphed to Col. John C. Kelton. "I have just arrived from Trenton Tenn accross lots   I am of the opinion that certain officers commanding have been badly Stampeded & laid the road open. It is very badly cut up   It will take a ~~ye~~ week yet to repair it. I am alarmed about supplies for Grants Army—No telegraphic communication with Gen'l Grant. Troops with construction train should be sent out from Columbus—at least two days ago" Telegram received, *ibid.*, RG 107, Telegrams Collected (Bound).

To Col. C. Carroll Marsh

Holly Springs, Miss. Dec. 25. 1862

Col. C. C. Marsh,
Grand Junction, Tenn.,

You will send two companies as Rail Road guard to Hickory Valley.[1] Instruct the guards to patrol the Rail Road through the Bridge this side of Middleburg.

U. S. Grant,
Maj. Gen'l.

Telegram, copies, DLC-USG, V, 18, 30; DNA, RG 393, Dept. of the Tenn.,
Letters Sent.
　　Later on Dec. 25, 1862, USG telegraphed to Col. C. Carroll Marsh. "Brig.
Gen. Ross' Division has been ordered up to garrison the post around Grand
Junction. On this arrival you will return and resume command of your old Brigade"
Copies, *ibid*. On the same day, Marsh telegraphed to USG. "An escaped prisoner
reports that Van Dorn encamped last night at Jonesburg, on Corinth road, heading
toward Corinth." *O.R.*, I, xvii, part 2, 484.

　　1. Hickory Valley, Tenn., on the Tennessee and Ohio Railroad, about midway between Bolivar and Grand Junction.

To Col. Joseph D. Webster

Holly Springs, Miss., Dec. 25. 1862

Col. J. D. Webster,
Jackson, Tenn.,

　　Do you know if the Rail-Road is in order between Jackson
and Grand Junction? If so, have a train of. box cars ready to come
here on dispatch from here. How many Engines and cars have
you at Jackson?

U. S. Grant,
Maj. Gen'l.

Telegram, copies, DLC-USG, V, 18, 30; DNA, RG 393, Dept. of the Tenn.,
Letters Sent.
　　Later on Dec. 25, 1862, USG again telegraphed to Col. Joseph D. Webster.
"How much is the Rail Road damaged between Jackson and Columbus, and how
soon can it be repaired? Answer in detail. Department papers all right" Copies,
ibid. On the same day, Webster twice telegraphed to USG, the second time at
10:20 P.M. "The damage to the road is not known beyond the trestlework next
north of trenton which will be passible tomorrow—We hear that the rebels were
repulsed from attack on big Obion bridge so that we hope now that the damage is
not so great as we feared yesterday　a party is out today to ascertain particulars
as far north as possible　Have not heard from them yet　we run trains now to
trenton north & to corinth & bolivar South　between Bolivar & Grand Junction
there is some damage done but It is thought to be inconsiderable　a few hours
work will repair it　The gun cars at Bolivar now　we have forty 40 Cars here
& forty at Humbolt　Will have a train ready tomorrow morning with empty box
cars which I think can go through　will send guard with it—Major Tweedale of
Engineer Regiment is pushing repairs north with despatch　we hope to be through
to Columbus in a few days　how many cars shall I send you—" "Reports from

above less favorable   Gen Haynie has report that our forces at Union City were defeated & the bridge over Obion burn   Cols Ihirie & Williams started to go through but came back bringing the above report   forrest was said south east of Union City with 7000 men & eight pieces of artillery   The location looks probable   The nos exaggerated   rumors are numerous"   Telegrams received, *ibid.*, Telegrams Received.

On Dec. 23, Webster had telegraphed to Lt. Col. John A. Rawlins. "The road is open to Humboldt   Enemy have left Trenton but we do not know which way they have gone   there will be more work to do in that direction than south   I want first (1st) Battalion of Engr Regt. sent here as soon as possible   let them bring their tools   will send train to meet them at Cold Water if necessary" Telegram received, *ibid.* On the same day, Rawlins telegraphed to Webster. "The road between here and Grand Junction will be in condition probably tomorrow. The Engineer Regt will be here tomorrow night ready to proceed to you. Will telegraph you when to send up train." Copies, DLC-USG, V, 18, 30, 91; DNA, RG 393, Dept. of the Tenn., Letters Sent.

On Dec. 25, Sol Palmer telegraphed to USG. "I have sent hand Car & men back to Holly Springs   they will do all work that you want till I get back   I shall get line to work to Columbus before I return"   Telegram received, *ibid.*, Telegrams Received.

Also on Dec. 25, Rawlins telegraphed to Col. Addison S. Norton, Abbeville. "Have your advance guards on Rail Road to Oxford drawn in? If they have not drawn them in at once. The Rail Road is to be abandoned from Abbeville to Oxford. Keep out guards for defence of Abbeville only. (Answer.)" Copies, DLC-USG, V, 18, 30; DNA, RG 393, Dept. of the Tenn., Letters Sent. *O.R.*, I, xvii, part 2, 483.

To Maj. Gen. James B. McPherson

Holly Springs Dec 26 1862

MAJ GENL J B McPHERSON
ABBEVILLE MISS

I hardly think it would pay to detach a Division so far from the main body, but if you think it would you can send Denver[1] to Wyatt   No news from Van Dorn or our Cavalry   The rebels are encamped up near Kenton   I expect they will do serious damage to the road near Union City

U S GRANT
Maj Genl

Telegram, copies, DLC-USG, V, 18, 30; DNA, RG 393, Dept. of the Tenn., Letters Sent. *O.R.*, I, xvii, part 2, 487. On Dec. 26, 1862, Maj. Gen. James B.

McPherson twice telegraphed to USG. "Dispatch received. Every means will be taken to secure everything in the [way] of provisions which this section will supply. I have directed my command to be placed on half rations until it is definitely known how soon we will get a supply over the railroad. Colonel Leggett's command will remain at Abbeville to-day and possibly to-morrow, depending somewhat upon the weather and news of the enemy's movements. No word as yet from Colonel Hatch." "I have selected a place on this side of the river near one of the new rebel batteries for the cars to stop at when they run down with supplies, &c. The mills which General Sherman had in operation where Colonel Buckland's brigade was are on the south side of the Tallahatchie, on Hurricane Creek, and about 12 miles from here. By moving Denver's division to Wyatt and rebuilding the bridge across the river I could place a brigade at the mills and set them to running again. Colonel Leggett has a small mill in operation near Abbeville, and will, I think, have another started soon." *Ibid.* On the same day, USG twice telegraphed to McPherson. "Send Denver Division to morrow and La Fayette. I will commence opening that road" "There is said to be a considerable quantity of Meal at the Mill near where Col Bucklands Division was encamped. If practicable send for it" Copies, DLC-USG, V, 18, 30; DNA, RG 393, Dept. of the Tenn., Letters Sent. The first telegram is in *O.R.*, I, xvii, part 2, 488. An undated telegram from McPherson to USG, 3:00 P.M., may have been sent on Dec. 26. "Four Regts & 2 batteries of Genl Denvers Division are Just starting the balance of the division will follow early in the morning Genl D will call on you for further instructions" Telegram received, DNA, RG 393, Dept. of the Tenn., Telegrams Received.

On Dec. 27, USG telegraphed to McPherson. "What road did Gen'l Denver take going to Moscow and Lafayette, and where will he camp tonight?" Copies, DLC-USG, V, 18, 30; DNA, RG 393, Dept. of the Tenn., Letters Sent. On the same day, McPherson wrote to USG. "Fifty teams from General Denver's division went out on a forage expedition under Colonel Stevenson and have not yet returned, so that he could not start to-day. He will take the road via Holly Springs and Hudsonville, and his orders, given after the receipt of your first dispatch, were to start as soon as possible. He will see you in Holly Springs. Two companies of cavalry will report to you to-morrow by 9 o'clock. From information gathered from citizens it appears that a large force of rebels under General Holmes are moving northeast from Grenada. I shall not place much reliance upon it unless confirmed from other sources. To-morrow morning the telegraph office will be at my headquarters, and I can then communicate immediately; now it takes fully three hours." *O.R.*, I, xvii, part 2, 497.

1. James W. Denver, born at Winchester, Va., in 1817, graduated from Cincinnati Law School, practiced law and edited a newspaper at Platte City, Mo., then served as capt., 12th Inf., in the Mexican War. Attracted by the gold rush to Calif., he entered politics as a Democrat, serving as U.S. Representative (1855–57), commissioner of Indian affairs, and governor of Kans. Territory. Appointed brig. gen. as of Aug. 14, 1861, he served first in Kans., then with the Army of the Tenn.

To Maj. Gen. James B. McPherson

Head Quarters
Holly Springs [*Dec.*] 26th [*1862*]

Gen McPherson—

Van Dorn passed Ripley yesterday going South. Our Cavalry was after him but from six (6) to ten (10) miles in the rear   Van Dorn got the start they making a march when he had apparently encamped for the night.[1] The hope is now that Hatch may have succeeded in heading him until other Troops come up   I think by foraging liberally we will give the men more than half rations but would not give more from the supply on hand. The road North of Trenton is worse than first reported—I have directed work to progress towards Memphis. I ordered Sullivan to mount Infantry to pursue these fellows up North. He reports that he can mount fifteen hundred (1500) at once.

U S Grant
Maj Genl

Telegram received, McPherson Papers, NjR; copies, DLC-USG, V, 18, 30; DNA, RG 393, Dept. of the Tenn., Letters Sent. *O.R.*, I, xvii, part 2, 488.

1. On Dec. 25, 1862, 3:30 p.m., Col. John K. Mizner, Ripley, telegraphed to USG. "We have followed the enemy all day, but have not been able to come up close enough to engage him. Van Dorn left his camp, 2 miles south of Saulsbury, at 8 p. m. yesterday and moved 10 miles south on Ripley road, where he remained till daylight. They are now on the Pontotoc road and probably 6 miles south of here. I shall move on, and if I do not succeed in coming up with them to-night will camp 5 miles south, on Pontotoc road. I joined the command at 8 a. m. this morning. I have been joined here by a portion of the Second Illinois. Colonel Deitzler came into the Ripley road 10 miles north of here, I am informed, after we passed. If Hatch can get south of Van Dorn and block the roads we may get a fight out of them. I will continue on early in the morning. Van Dorn is making his way back to Grenada or below as fast as he can travel. I have several prisoners, but have had no fight." *Ibid.*, p. 484. On Dec. 26, Brig. Gen. Grenville M. Dodge, Corinth, telegraphed to Lt. Col. John A. Rawlins. "It is reported that van dorn is Coming this way on Salem & Ripley Road   Do you know where he is   reported also that canonnading was heard at Ripley & Salem last night" Telegram received, DNA, RG 393, Dept. of the Tenn., Telegrams Received. On the same day, USG telegraphed to Dodge. "Van Dorn passed Ripley yesterday going South, Our Cavalry in pursuit   A deserter from Van Dorn is now in, he reports that no part of this force went North" Copies, DLC-USG, V, 18, 30; DNA, RG 393, Dept. of the Tenn., Letters Sent; Dodge Papers, IaHA.

To Brig. Gen. John E. Smith

———

Holly Springs Miss Dec 26 1862

BRIG GENL J E SMITH
DAVIS MILLS

Assume command of all the forces at La Grange, Grand Junction and Davis Mills, and you will retain command of them at any other point to which they may be sent for duty   The balance of the Division will be returned as soon as Forrest is driven out of West Tennessee

The Regiment ordered to occupy the road between LaGrange and Moscow may go on to Moscow, to hold the bridge at that place until Denver's Division arrives when it will return and guard the road indicated in the first order. You can place your Artillery at the diffirent posts within your command according to your judgement

At all bridges the men should build Block houses

U S GRANT
Maj Genl

Copies, DLC-USG, V, 18, 30; DNA, RG 393, Dept. of the Tenn., Letters Sent. *O.R.*, I, xvii, part 2, 492–93. On Dec. 26, 1862, Lt. Col. John A. Rawlins issued Special Orders No. 53. "Brig. Genl. John E. Smith is hereby assigned to the command of the 8th Division, Leeft Wing, Army of the Tennessee and will report at once to Brig. Genl. C S. Hamilton"   DS, DNA, RG 94, Dept. of the Tenn., Special Orders; copies, *ibid.*, RG 393, Dept. of the Tenn., Special Orders; DLC-USG, V, 26, 27. *O.R.*, I, xvii, part 2, 492. See telegram to Maj. Gen. James B. McPherson, Dec. 25, 1862, note 1.

On Dec. 26, USG telegraphed to Brig. Gen. John E. Smith. "Sullivan is calling for more troops to drive the rebels out of the north part of Tenn. I have notified him that I will send four Regiments if he will send Cars. You may hold them in readiness from your command, to imbark on arrival of Cars"   Copies, DLC-USG, V, 18, 30; DNA, RG 393, Dept. of the Tenn., Letters Sent. *O.R.*, I, xvii, part 2, 492. On Dec. 27, Smith telegraphed to USG. "Your despatch recd this morng eight oclock   will hold four Regiments ready for the Cars—have but five Regts & four batteries in all"   Telegram received, DNA, RG 94, War Records Office, Dept. of the Tenn. On the same day, USG telegraphed to Smith. "Col Marsh has sent the 93rd Indiana to Moscow from Grand Junction. This leaves you one Regiment to protect Batteries, and four to send to Sullivan. The Regiment Marsh sends to Moscow is sufficient to guard bridge there"   Copies, DLC-USG, V, 18, 30; DNA, RG 393, Dept. of the Tenn., Letters Sent. On the same day, Smith telegraphed to USG. "If I send four Regts to Sullivan cant send back for ammunition & camp equipage left at Coldwater as I have but one Reg left to take charge of four batteries" Telegram received, *ibid.*, RG 94, War Records Office, Dept. of the Tenn.

To Brig. Gen. John E. Smith

Holly Springs Mis Dec 26 1862

BRIG GENL J E SMITH
DAVIS MILLS

Send one Brigade of your command to Moscow leaving one Regiment between LaGrange and Moscow. Instructions will be sent for the repairs to the road. They should start the Mill at Moscow and gather all the forage and supplies possible. Send with this Brigade such portions of the Pioneer Corps[1] formed by Gen Ross as you have with you

U S GRANT
Maj Genl

Copies, DLC-USG, V, 18, 30; DNA, RG 393, Dept. of the Tenn., Letters Sent. *O.R.*, I, xvii, part 2, 492. On Dec. 26, 1862, USG telegraphed to Brig. Gen. John E. Smith. "By Courier from La Grange orders to move Brigade to Moscow Countermanded" Copies, DLC-USG, V, 18, 30; DNA, RG 393, Dept. of the Tenn., Letters Sent.

1. On Dec. 12, George G. Pride, Abbeville, wrote to USG. "Will it not be a good plan to furnish immediately to each Division of this Army a supply of framing tools for Pioneer Corps & from each division can be found Mechanics say to the number of seven hundred & fifty (750) which can be temporarily be organized under command of a Commissioned Mechanic or Engineer Each Division shall have the tools with them in hands of Quarter Master of division By this means as we move on each division when quitting can do whatever work is before them: The Engineer Regt is very good in name but not over one third ⅓ are fit to handle tools. If this meets your views please issue the necessary orders to the divisions & I will make up a memorandum of tools for Col Reynolds to order immediately with these arrangements we could have been at Oxford three days since I think we can finish here by the time we can get the cars to the River probably on Tuesday Please answer" Telegram received, *ibid.*, Telegrams Received. On Dec. 13, Lt. Col. John A. Rawlins issued Special Orders No. 22, 13th Army Corps, Dept. of the Tenn., detaching 150 men from each division to form a "Pioneer Corps." DS, *ibid.*, RG 94, Dept. of the Tenn., Special Orders; copies, DLC-USG, V, 26, 27, 91; (printed) Oglesby Papers, IHi.

To Brig. Gen. Jeremiah C. Sullivan

By Telegraph from Holly Springs [*Dec. 26*] 186[*2*]
To Gen Sullivan

VanDorn went to Bolivar pursued by our Cavalry, then struck south-east through Saulsbury & Ripley. Our Cavalry was still in pursuit at that point & have not since been heard from. This was yesterday. They are now near Grenada   Two deserters came in from Van Dorn today; they left him ten 10 miles north of New-Albany[1] at 10 oclock last night,—still going south—If there is any cavalry north of the Hatchie it must be some small irregular band.—Send cars to Davis' Mills and I will order four 4 Regiments more up to you   Collect all the bacon; beef, hogs sheep and grain you can from Planters.

Mount all the Infantry you can and drive Forrest east of the Tennessee

U S Grant
Maj Gen

Telegram received, DNA, RG 393, 16th Army Corps, 4th Division, Telegrams Received; copies, *ibid.*, Dept. of the Tenn., Letters Sent; DLC-USG, V, 18, 30. *O.R.*, I, xvii, part 2, 489. On Dec. 26, 1862, Brig. Gen. Jeremiah C. Sullivan, Jackson, telegraphed to USG. "Colonel Webster will furnish the cars to-morrow. The cars will probably follow the mail train in the morning. I can secure the road as you wish. I have organized my forces to meet Forrest. I have made every attempt to mount infantry but cannot succeed in procuring more than 1,000 horses. I believe by moving toward Dresden and Paris Forrest will be compelled to pass behind Bolivar and Jackson to escape. Unless he has arrangements for crossing the Tennessee lower than Clifton, your cavalry can meet him." *Ibid.*, p. 491.

Also on Dec. 26, USG telegraphed to Sullivan. "How are your forces now located"   Telegram received, DNA, RG 393, 16th Army Corps, 4th Division, Telegrams Received; copies, *ibid.*, Dept. of the Tenn., Letters Sent; DLC-USG, V, 18, 30. *O.R.*, I, xvii, part 2, 489. On the same day, Sullivan telegraphed twice to USG, the second time at 11:20 A.M. "General Haynie has at Trenton about 1,000 men, at Humboldt 475; Colonel Lawler has 1,000 men just returning from pursuits. General Brayman has two regiments Fuller's brigade, Forty-third Illinois, Twelfth Michigan, Fiftieth Indiana. I have two regiments of Fuller's brigade and scattering forces at Bethel, Forty-eighth and Forty-ninth Illinois and one battery at Bolivar, one section with Haynie, one with Lawler; balance here." "I have one-third of my force opening road to Union City, under command of General Haynie. I have under Colonel Lawler 1,000 men who have been after the rebs, and will to-day be at Toone's Station or on their return. I will send immediately that force north on railroad. I am unable to get nearer the enemy than within sight, when they immediately retreat. My cavalry was entirely broken up, and it is difficult to reorganize it. All my officers telegraph that they are collecting forage and cattle, but have received no statement of amount. Van Dorn is reported to have escaped our cavalry, and, crossing the Hatchie, has made his way to join Forrest. Reports from Obion are less favorable, but as they are merely rumors I do not place much reliance on them." *Ibid.*, pp. 489, 492.

Also on Dec. 26, Brig. Gen. Charles S. Hamilton, Holly Springs, wrote to USG. "Col Fuller telegraphs from Jackson. that his officers & men are in a sad condition without tents, without change of under-clothes no cooking utensils, and greatly desires to get to his baggage—& get his brigade together. If it can be spared from Jackson, would it not be well to order the brigade to join the Division at Davis Mill. Or if it is important that it should remain at Jackson—then to have its baggage sent on to that point." ALS, DNA, RG 393, Dept. of the Tenn., Telegrams Received. On the same day, USG telegraphed to Sullivan. "If Col Fullers brigade is no longer required send it to join the division at Davis Mills if you still require them send to Davis Mills for their baggage" Telegram received, *ibid.*, 16th Army Corps, 4th Division, Telegrams Received; copies, *ibid.*, Dept. of the Tenn., Letters Sent; DLC-USG, V, 18, 30. On Dec. 27, Brig. Gen. Mason Brayman, Bolivar, telegraphed to USG. "The forty third 43 & Sixty third 63 Ohio came here while I was at Jackson leaving their camp & garrison Equipage at oxford   the Sixty third went to Jackson this morning under Gen Sullivan's order   if they do not return to Oxford cannot their stuff be sent there   it rains & they suffer" Telegram received, DNA, RG 393, Dept. of the Tenn., Telegrams Received.

On Dec. 26, USG telegraphed to Sullivan. "What steps are you taking to drive out the enemy. Are you collecting forage & supplies." Telegram received, *ibid.*, 25th Army Corps, Telegrams Received; copies, *ibid.*, Dept. of the Tenn., Letters Sent; DLC-USG, V, 18, 30. On the same day, Sullivan telegraphed to USG. "I have taken all steps necessary to procure forage & subsistence   I will most gladly visit the citizens   they have no love for me now & of course I have nothing to lose" Telegram received, DNA, RG 94, War Records Office, Dept. of the Tenn. On the same day, USG telegraphed to Sullivan. "What success do you have in collecting forage & subsistence? You had better collect the bacon & meal from the Secessionists in town to us[e] in case of Emergency   if they dont like the association of yo[u] let them move South among their friends" Telegram received, *ibid.*, RG 393, 16th Army Corps, 4th Division, Telegrams Received; copies, *ibid.*, Dept. of the Tenn., Letters Sent; DLC-USG, V, 18, 30. *O.R.*, I, xvii, part 2, 490.

Also on Dec. 26, USG sent four more telegrams to Sullivan. "Can you collect horses and mules enough to mount three or four Regiments of Infantry to pursue Forrest? If you can do so." "Have you a force moving north sufficient to drive out the rebels from the road? Those fellows should be kept off the road at least." Copies, DLC-USG, V, 18, 30; DNA, RG 393, Dept. of the Tenn., Letters Sent. *O.R.*, I, xvii, part 2, 490. "It is important that the Road between you & Corinth & the Junction Sh[ould] be secured beyond a peradv[enture.]   have you made arrangemen[ts] to send for 4 Regts at davis Mills"   "My Cav'y is now in pursuit of VanDorn & must be near Grenada—I will be well ~~tried~~ tired out by [the] time they return   do you hear anything of the force ordered from Fort Henry to co ope[rate] with you" Telegrams received, DNA, RG 393, 16th Army Corps,

4th Division, Telegrams Received; copies, *ibid.*, Dept. of the Tenn., Letters Sent; DLC-USG, V, 18, 30. *O.R.*, I, xvii, part 2, 490. On the same day, Sullivan telegraphed to USG. "I have recd no news from Col Lowe   my Scouts reported that a large Column of rebel Cavalry was marching towards paris some three days ago   I knew it was Lowes Cavalry but have heard nothing since"   Telegram received, DNA, RG 94, War Records Office, Dept. of the Tenn. At 3:30 P.M., Sullivan again telegraphed to USG. "The following dispatches I have this moment received from General Haynie, dated at Trenton at noon to-day: GENERAL: We arrived here at noon. I met one of my scouts who went up toward Columbus day before yesterday. He reported to me that all I have heard of the favorable condition of the road and bridges is untrue; says that Union City was taken and all or nearly all the bridges and trestles are burned that high up, and that it will take a long while to repair them. The rebel force is large. I can move after Forrest, but then I leave points unguarded; and a force of several hundred are threatening the road between Humboldt and this point north of Brownsville. Colonel Dawson has a regiment, and John Irwin, brother-in-law of Cheeny, of Savannah, reports another force of cavalry or mounted infantry as crossing the Tennessee. I can possibly mount 1,500 men. I will do so and attack if I can." *O.R.*, I, xvii, part 2, 491. Later on the same day, Sullivan again telegraphed to USG. "The following recd—Trenton 7 30 P M   to Gen Sullivan   P. H. Krol Chaplain of 109th Ill has just come in   he has been up as far as Crocket passing Dyer Station Rutherford & Kenton along the road   he confirms the bad condition of the bridges   forrest is forty 40 miles he says off from Crocket Station   Forrest so the chaplain says had ten thousand 10000 men on the Road burning & destroying it   He had also other forces out [w]ith him on this side Kenton but K saw 100 rebels on Picket   Signed I N HAYNIE Brig Gen"   Telegram received, DNA, RG 94, War Records Office, Dept. of the Tenn.

Also on Dec. 26, 7:30 P.M. and 8:30 P.M., Sullivan telegraphed twice more to USG. "Van Dorn seems to be in north of Hatchie with a large force. Forrest is near Union City. Mr. Spears brings me information that Van Dorn is planning an attack on Jackson. I think now, general, that a sufficient force should be speedily sent here to capture the whole of this force. I am not able with my small force to assume the offensive and guard what we yet hold." "Every available man is now north. I will send this evening troops that have just returned from a fatiguing march. I have no doubt that the design of the rebels is to weaken this post by making me send off my men, and then, marching rapidly to the rear, capture and destroy the stores. What can be done shall be done." *O.R.*, I, xvii, part 2, 491. On the same day, USG again telegraphed to Sullivan. "Make the best disposition you can to drive Forrest out & comm[u]nicate with me often wha[t] you are doing   Good night"   Telegram received, DNA, RG 393, 16th Army Corps, 4th Division, Telegrams Received; copies, *ibid.*, Dept. of the Tenn., Letters Sent; DLC-USG, V, 18, 30. *O.R.*, I, xvii, part 2, 490.

Also on Dec. 26, Brig. Gen. Grenville M. Dodge telegraphed to USG three times. "Gen Sullivan desires me to send him one Reg. to aid in opening Road   unless you direct otherwise I shall a Reg. in the morng to remain untl Road is open" "My scouts are in front from East of Tenn river left waynesboro & clifton yesterday   at latter place are about 500 Mississippi Cavalry   at Clifton about 100   at Oldtown, a large lot of hogs are collected in charge of Robertsons cavalry   yesterday the citizens at Savannah had a fight with some of Robinsons Co   wounded two & took six prisoners which the scouts brought here   Some of my cavalry crossed tonight to help them through—In wayne Co. are some two hundred 200 armed union men who the Mississippi Cavalry ~~who~~ have been sent to put down at Old Carrollville Forrest has his trains & what he has captured a good regt of cavalry could capture the lot or a force up the river from fort Henry could catch them—men from Clifton who saw forrest cross say he did not cross over three thousand five hundred 3500 I think he will return for them down the river. River is very low no movement of Bragg that I can discern. Jeff Davis in Chattanooga last Sunday Johnson with him" Telegrams received, DNA, RG 393, Dept. of the Tenn., Telegrams Received. "One of our men arrived yesterday from Tullahoma, Tenn.; ten days on the road. The main body of Bragg's army was there. They were retreating to Chattanooga. All the stores were being sent there and they were collecting all the corn and stock and forage, taking it to Chattanooga. On his road he met fifteen droves of hogs, cattle, and sheep, in Lincoln and Giles Counties, all being driven to the same place. They saw men from Bragg's army in three counties to the Tennessee River, collecting produce and stock and taking it all that way. He brings same report as sent two days ago of force south of Tennessee River." *O.R.*, I, xvii, part 2, 489. On Dec. 27, USG telegraphed to Sullivan. "Dodge learns from persons who saw Forrest cross the Tennessee river, that he has but 3500 men at the furthest. Act on the theory that he has no more" Copies, DLC-USG, V, 18, 30; DNA, RG 393, Dept. of the Tenn., Letters Sent. Dated Dec. 26 in *O.R.*, I, xvii, part 2, 490. On the same day, Sullivan telegraphed to USG. "Forrest has left for Tennessee River, supposed crossing at Reynoldsburg. I am pursuing on Huntingdon road. The Tennessee River has risen 2 feet since Sunday. I will not leave him until he is out of the district." *Ibid.*, p. 498. On the same day, USG telegraphed to Sullivan. "Have all supplies collected put in the hands of the Commissary so that they may be regularly issued without waste" Telegram received, DNA, RG 393, 16th Army Corps, 4th Division, Telegrams Received; copies, *ibid.*, Dept. of the Tenn., Letters Sent; DLC-USG, V, 18, 30. On the same day, Sullivan telegraphed to USG. "I have arrested a cotton buyer find on him four thousand (4000) pound sterling & letters for the Rebel army I will await orders from you as to his future—I am on the track of others" Telegram received, DNA, RG 94, War Records Office, Dept. of the Tenn.

1. New Albany, Miss., on the Tallahatchie River, about thirty-two miles southeast of Holly Springs.

To Col. Joseph D. Webster

Holly Springs Miss Dec 26. 1862

COL J D WEBSTER
JACKSON TENN

Will you send down to this point tomorrow a train to bring mails and other necessities.

Instruct Conductor to bring express package for Col Pride

from Jackson and Bolivar. Engineer Regiment with load to go to you in the morning with all their tools. Telegraph here when your train leaves to come here, so we may instruct them where to meet train from here. Let them report at Bolivar and Grand Junction for orders. Answer.

U S GRANT
Maj Genl

Telegram, copies, DLC-USG, V, 18, 30; DNA, RG 393, Dept. of the Tenn., Letters Sent. On Dec. 26, 1862, 9:00 P.M., Col. Joseph D. Webster, Jackson, Tenn., telegraphed to USG. "Train will leave here with mail at eight & half 8½ tomorrow morning will report as ordered will send six box cars and fourteen 14 flats—what does Col Pride want flats for—My estimate of ten 10 days is confirmed since by Maj Twedale" Telegram received, *ibid.*, Telegrams Received.

Also on Dec. 26, USG telegraphed to Webster. "Do you not think it advisable for me to open the road to Memphis for temporary purposes?" Copies, DLC-USG, V, 18, 30; DNA, RG 393, Dept. of the Tenn., Letters Sent. On the same day, Webster telegraphed to USG. "Yes decidedly I was telling Lyford so an hour ago" Telegram received, *ibid.*, Telegrams Received. On the same day, USG twice telegraphed to Webster. "I am sending four more Regiments from Ross' Division to Jackson. There has been a Pioneer Regiment organized from this Division, which you can use in reparing Rail Road, and call for such additional details as you may want. I think I will I use the Engineer Regiment to open the Memphis Road temporarily until the other is repaired." "What prospect for mounting Infanty sufficient to drive Forrest of out of West Tennessee" Copies, DLC-USG, V, 18, 30; DNA, RG 393, Dept. of the Tenn., Letters Sent. On the same day, Webster telegraphed to USG. "Not good But a few hundred horses to be had here Although Forrests numbers are probably exaggerated 7000 prudence will hardly justify us in disregarding altogether so many concurrent reports" Telegram received, *ibid.*, Telegrams Received.

Also on Dec. 26, USG telegraphed to Webster. "What is the shortest time you can open the road through to Columbus, if we send all the Engineer Regiment and their tools? No Pile driver in this region" Copies, DLC-USG, V, 18, 30; DNA, RG 393, Dept. of the Tenn., Letters Sent. On the same day, Webster sent four more telegrams to USG, the third at 7:15 P.M. "I have no more definite Information than that furnished by Gen Haynies desphes Telegraphed to you by Gen Sullivan I have little hope of being able to open Road to Columbus in less than 10 days with Engr Reg. fear it will take more time." "That is if I am rightly informed as to its Condition west of Lagrange" "Maj Tweedale reports making reconnoissance on Rail Road to Dyer station 34 miles from here Can have the repaired to that place by saturday no one noon he saw Lt Milliken who went over road yesterday to near Crockett he reports all bridges destroyed & much of track torn up Saw rebel camp near Kenton forty three miles from here & was informed that a large force was near Crockett still engaged in destroying road" Telegrams received, *ibid.*, Telegrams Received. "I fear very much that this road will take two weeks or more" Telegram received, *ibid.*, RG 94, War Records Office, Dept. of the Tenn.

To Maj. Gen. James B. McPherson

Holly Springs Miss Dec 27. 1862

Maj Genl J B McPherson
Abbeville Miss

So soon as the Cavalry returns[1] I want two Companies, the freshest that can be got, to send through to Memphis   From what I understand that road can be put in order in a few days   I want in that case to order Quinby to return by the state line road guarding the road from Germantown until he meets the Cars, with his Division, and send his supplies through by [r]ail[2]

U S Grant
Maj Genl

Copies, DLC-USG, V, 18, 30; DNA, RG 393, Dept. of the Tenn., Letters Sent. *O.R.*, I, xvii, part 2, 499. On Dec. 27, 1862, Maj. Gen. James B. McPherson, Abbeville, telegraphed to USG. "Will send Two companies of Cavalry to Report to you as soon as some come in   have not heard a word from Col Hatch since he left Oxford in [the] direction of Rocky Ford & t[aking] all the Cavalry I had in cam[p] [—] the escort companies were [—] out early this morng to the [—] under Comd of Col Stevenson who has gone out with 3 Regts of Infy & one hundred & fifty (150) wagons on a grand foraging expedition"   Telegram received, DNA, RG 393, Dept. of the Tenn., Telegrams Received. On Dec. 29, McPherson telegraphed to USG. "Colonel Hatch returned with his cavalry last evening without having met the enemy. He went within 10 miles of Pontotoc, to Rocky Ford, and New Albany." *O.R.*, I, xvii, part 2, 505.

1. On Dec. 26, Col. John K. Mizner, "19 miles south of Ripley," wrote to USG. "Van Dorn is making his way back to Pemberton as fast as he can go. I have followed him as closely as possible. I am 19 miles from Pontotoc, but may go there. Unless I can learn that a force of ours is south of Van Dorn, further pursuit will be useless   to-morrow I shall turn back towards Oxford—If I can make him fight I will do so. I have taken many prisoners." ALS, DNA, RG 393, Dept. of the Tenn., Letters Received. *O.R.*, I, xvii, part 2, 493. On Dec. 27, 4:00 P.M., Mizner, "Pott's Farm 15 miles S. W. from Holly Springs," wrote to USG. "Col Hatch with his Command arrived at New Albany four hours after I had passed. I continued the pursuit nine miles south of that place, when being convinced that farther pursuit would be fruitless and, having gone to a point further south than our lines extended, I turned west and camped at King's Bridge 7 miles west of New Albany last night. Col Hatch reported to me by letter at 6 P. M. he was at New Albany. I directed ~~with~~ him to proceed by the most practicable route to our advance post. He will go via Water ford to Abbeyville. My Command is exhausted from fatigue & were drenched by the rain last night, I

shall camp here to-night; finding an abundance of forage & will proceed to Holly Springs in the morning. Some ambulances & wagons belonging to the command were left at Bolivar & were ordered to Grand Junction, will you have them ordered to meet us. Our trains should also be ordered to join us at Holly Springs, as the command is without a change of clothing & in such a condition as to require rest. . . . I sent a line to you by Maj Mudd   We pressed the enemy hard & took many prisoners," ALS, DNA, RG 393, Dept. of the Tenn., Letters Received. *O.R.*, I, xvii, part 2, 498–99.

2. On Dec. 28, McPherson telegraphed to USG. "Gen Denvers train will not be in till towards night having gone some 20 miles west foragining   shall I give orders for two Regs of each Brigade with batteries to start immediately & let balance of Division start soon as the train comes"   Telegram received, DNA, RG 393, Dept. of the Tenn., Telegrams Received. On the same day, USG telegraphed to McPherson. "By all means start what troops you can of Denver's Division at once   We want the work in Memphis road to progress as rapidly as possible. I expect the cars to meet Quinby within thirty miles of Memphis and let the wagons go back for a second load of supplies"   Copies, DLC-USG, V, 18, 30; DNA, RG 393, Dept. of the Tenn., Letters Sent.

On Dec. 29, McPherson telegraphed to USG. "The 27 Iowa is in Camp near me & are not reporting to any one   what shall I direct them to do"   Telegram received, *ibid.*, Telegrams Received. On the same day, Lt. Col. John A. Rawlins twice telegraphed to McPherson. "Order the 27th Iowa forward to this place with their camp and garrison equipage"   "Please countermand order for 27th Iowa to proceed to Holly Springs and hold them in readiness to move at eight O'clock tomorrow morning with their entire camp and garrison equipage by Railroad to Jackson Tenn   Cars will be at Waterford promptly at the time or whenever you may wish them to embark. Please answer and designate the place"   Copies, DLC-USG, V, 18, 30; DNA, RG 393, Dept. of the Tenn., Letters Sent. On the same day, USG twice telegraphed to McPherson. "I will have cars sent down for the sick of the 27th Iowa as soon as possible"   "Direct the Cavalry to move their equipage to the Railroad   I will send the cars after it"   Copies, *ibid.*

To Brig. Gen. Grenville M. Dodge

Holly Springs Miss Dec 27. 1862

BRIG GENL G M DODGE
CORINTH MISS

There are now five light draught Gun Boats in the Tennessee River waiting to run up on the first rise.

They will naturally destroy all means of crossing the river   I wish however to make sure, you would send a request for them to do so

If you can get a messenger through to Lowe, instruct him
to destroy Forrest's train

U. S. GRANT
Maj Genl

Telegram, copies, DLC-USG, V, 18, 30; DNA, RG 393, Dept. of the Tenn.,
Letters Sent; Dodge Papers, IaHA. *O.R.*, I, xvii, part 2, 497. On Dec. 27, 1862,
Brig. Gen. Grenville M. Dodge telegraphed twice to USG. "The tennessee is
rising & if a gunboat could come up and destroy the flats on the river it would
draw forrest off—I have destroyed all I could reach but below Clifton there are
a large number which I have no doubt Forrests intends to use his trains being at
Carrollville & below   I can get a message through to Fort Henry should you
desire"   "One of the scouts is in from near Murfreesboro   he went by way of
Decatur Huntsville & returned by way of Columbia Waynesboro Hamburg
&c   reports small forse at at Decatur & Huntsville & on the road collecting
stock & sending it to bragg to Chattanoogo   Bragg's Army was from Shelbyville
North when he left on tuesday. Says they were going to attack or talked so—met
no troops this way from Columbia except small parties collecting stock provisions
& conscripts   Says he heard but did not see that a part of forrests train had gone
back that way   Cavalry attack on Clifton had scared them   He thinks most of
the train is on the river & says Forrest has instructions to remain this side &
break up the railroad as long as possible   up to Tuesday Braggs forces had made
no move west or south"   Telegrams received, DNA, RG 393, Dept. of the Tenn.,
Telegrams Received.

On Dec. 29, Dodge telegraphed to USG. "All my Cavalry with Hursts west
Tenn Cav have gone down the Tenn   have been gone two days   genl Brayman
Orders Hursts Cavalry back immediately to Bolivar   it will be a great impro-
priety for them to leave now   Cannot they remain until the expedition returns
They Are on both sides of Tennessee & we can damage Forrest materially   They
have already destroyed Boats Stores &c   Please answer"   Telegram received,
ibid. On the same day, USG telegraphed to Dodge. "By all means keep Hursts
cavalry until the object of the expedition is ended—"   Telegram received, *ibid.*,
RG 107, Telegrams Collected (Unbound); copies, *ibid.*, RG 393, Dept. of the
Tenn., Letters Sent; DLC-USG, V, 18, 30; Dodge Papers, IaHA. On the same
day, USG telegraphed to Brig. Gen. Mason Brayman, Bolivar. "Countermand
your order for return of Hursts cavalry until object of present expedition is
accomplished   Bolivar is no present danger with proper vigilence"   Telegram
received, Brayman Papers, ICHi; copies, DLC-USG, V, 18, 30; DNA, RG 393,
Dept. of the Tenn., Letters Sent. On the same day, Brayman telegraphed to USG.
"I have ordered the West Tenn Cav to remain & receive Orders from Gen Dodge
or yourself   Bolivar is safe   I ordered their return to organize & equip them
and not on account of Danger here"   Telegram received, *ibid.*, Telegrams
Received; ADfS, Brayman Papers, ICHi.

Also on Dec. 29, Dodge telegraphed to USG. "I have scouts in from Tennessee & alabama   One left waynesboro saturday night   Says there is a small
force of Cavalry at Buffalo Creek & three hundred 300 Mississippi Cavalry under
Col Burton at waynesboro   came there wednesday from Okolona   forrest has
not returned but has moved his flats down the river   Bragg is in old position

Says he heard Morgans Raid was a failure There evidently is no force of any amount this side of Bragg but they are ~~scouring~~ skinning the country of produce Leather stock & conscripts all of which goes to huntsville Chattanooga &c Everything tends that way & says all talk as though Bragg would fall back after he has got all he can out of the state though they protest that they will tennessee —Everything in alabama is tending towards montgomery the evidence is so strong & from so many sources that there can be no mistake about the direction of all these stores" Telegram received, DNA, RG 393, Dept. of the Tenn., Telegrams Received.

To Col. C. Carroll Marsh

———

Holly Springs Miss Dec 27. 1862

Col C C Marsh
Grand Junction

The Rail Road from Junction west will be opened Let the Regiment understand that the bridge to be guarded is the Railroad Bridge Engineer men will go on tomorrow by train Camp equippage of Regiment that goes tonight, can go by train tomorrow, but the Regiment to guard must reach there tonight

U S Grant
Maj Genl

Telegram, copies, DLC-USG, V, 18, 30; DNA, RG 393, Dept. of the Tenn., Letters Sent.
On Dec. 27, 1862, USG sent three additional telegrams to Col. C. Carroll Marsh. "Notify Genl Smith to send one Rg't any one that can be best spared to occupy the road between LaGrange and Moscow" "The Bridge at Moscow is not destroyed, send a Regiment there tonight if possible. Answer when it will start" "Instruct Reg't going to Moscow that the bridge is one half mile beyond Moscow, and must be protected at all hazards tonight" Copies, *ibid.* On the same day, Marsh telegraphed to USG. "Regt will go through to Bridge tonight ~~to be~~ instructions to Comdr as directed" Telegram received, *ibid.*, Telegrams Received.
Also on Dec. 27, USG telegraphed to Col. Jonathan Richmond, La Grange, Tenn. "Is the Bridge at Moscow burned or destroyed? If you do not know positively in regard to it send out immediately and ascertain" Copies, DLC-USG, V, 18, 30; DNA, RG 393, Dept. of the Tenn., Letters Sent. On the same day, Richmond twice telegraphed to USG. "The RR bridge the other side of Moscow across the Wolf is just as our troops left it nearly completed—the wagon bridge

this side is all right" "I have learned since sending you last despatch that bridge a Moscow was standing last night" Telegrams received, *ibid.*, Telegrams Received.

To Col. Joseph D. Webster

Holly Springs Miss Dec 27. 1862

COL J D WEBSTER
JACKSON TENN

The majority of your locomotives and Cars had best be sent at once to Grand Junction. You will please transfer the other two Regiments. from Davis' Mills to Jackson. and such camp equipments as are needed, and furnish other necessary transportation on the Rail road as you deem best, but I want what other rolling stock you have not in use at Grand Junction—

U S GRANT
Maj Genl.

Telegram, copies, DLC-USG, V, 18, 30; DNA, RG 393, Dept. of the Tenn., Letters Sent.

On Dec. 27, 1862, USG again telegraphed to Col. Joseph D. Webster. "There is no restriction to travel   Mr Keith can come to La Grange" Copies, *ibid.* On the same day, Webster had telegraphed to USG. "Mr Keith of Chicago a friend of mine & all right wishes permission to go to Lagrange" Telegram received (misdated Dec. 28), *ibid.*, Telegrams Received. On the same day, Webster again telegraphed to USG. "Will send down two trains of 20 cars each tomorrow Morning   if one can bring the troops from Davis Mills the other will be for service there   who commands the pioneer Corps—Will it report to me—Engine No 15 had better come up & go into Shop for repair   Can replace it easily now   Shall require a construction train a wood train & ~~one~~ an other of say fifteen cars and a spare engine or two   Will send the rest to grand Junction   No news from above" Telegram received, *ibid.*

To Abraham Lincoln

Holly Springs Mississippi
December 28th 1862

HIS EXCELLENCY, A. LINCOLN
PRESIDENT OF THE UNITED STATES,
WASHINGTON D. C.
SIR:

Permit me to renew recommendations that I have frequently made before for promotion to the rank of Brigadier General of Col. J. D. Webster of the 1st Ill. Artillery,[1] Col. C. C. Marsh, 20th Ill. Infantry and to add the name of Col. John Mason Loomis[2] of the 26th Ill. Infantry.

Col. Webster has rendered most efficient service from the beginning of the War, having been with me in every engagement where I have had the honor of commanding   Col. Marsh has rendered most excellent service as regimental, Brigade and Post commander.

Col. Loomis is an active intelligent and efficient officer of much experience and well qualified for advanced rank. His services have not come so much under my notice until latterly as the two former, but as a Brigade commander on the recent advance of this Army, and as commander of the post of Oxford Miss. I had an opportunity of observing him and do not hesitate to cordially recommend his promotion.

I am very respectfully
your obt. svt.
U. S. GRANT
Maj. Gen

ALS, DNA, RG 94, ACP, W1016 CB 1865. On Feb. 28, 1863, this letter was favorably endorsed by Governor Richard Yates of Ill., Lt. Governor Francis A. Hoffman, Secretary of State Ozias M. Hatch, Treasurer William Butler, and AG Allen C. Fuller. *Ibid.*

1. On Dec. 3, 1862, President Abraham Lincoln wrote to Secretary of War Edwin M. Stanton. "Let Col. James D. Webster, of Illinois, be appointed as

Brigadier General of Volunteers." ALS, *ibid*. On Dec. 4, U.S. Representative Isaac N. Arnold of Ill. wrote to John G. Nicolay. "I gave the name of Col Webster to the President as *Jas*. D. It is *Joseph D. Webster*   Please advise him & oblige" ALS, *ibid*. On Dec. 5, Lincoln endorsed Arnold's letter. "It seems that 'Joseph D. Webster' and not 'James D. Webster' is the name of the officer, I wrote to have appointed a Brigadier General." AES, *ibid*. On Dec. 9, Arnold wrote to Lincoln urging Webster's promotion. ALS, *ibid*. On Dec. 11, Lincoln endorsed Arnold's letter. "Submitted to the War Department." AES, *ibid*. On Dec. 9, Arnold had written to USG. "Asks for papers recommending J. D. Webster as a Brig. Genl. States that he will see that they reach the President, and thinks he will secure his commission as Brig. Genl." DLC-USG, V, 21; DNA, RG 393, Dept. of the Tenn., Register of Letters Received. Lincoln nominated Webster as brig. gen. on Feb. 11, 1863; the nomination was confirmed on March 9.

2. John M. Loomis, born at Windsor, Conn., in 1825, settled in Milwaukee, Wis., in 1846, entered the lumber business, and transferred his firm to Chicago in 1852. On Aug. 9, 1861, he was commissioned col., 26th Ill., and served at that rank until his resignation on April 30, 1864.

To Maj. Gen. Stephen A. Hurlbut

Head Quarters, Dept. of the Ten.
Holly Springs Miss. Dec. 28th 1862

MAJ. GEN. S. A. HURLBUT
COMD.G DIST. OF MEMPHIS,
GEN.

Please forward the accompanying letter to its address by the first opportunity.

Gen. Hallecks instructions to me were that I could retain that portion of the Helena forces sent to this side of the river under Gen. Hovey.[1] Immediately on receiving his dispatch to this effect I sent orders for one regiment of Infantry & one battery to remain at Friars Point and Garrison that place and the Cavalry to take a station about the mouth of Coldwater. When this order reached Friars Point these troops had gone back to Helena and I have not since learned whether they have been returned. If you are aware of the fact that they have not been returned please destroy the letter addressed to Comd.g Officer Friars Point and advise me.

> I am Gen. Very respectfully
> your obt. svt.
> U. S. GRANT
> Maj. Gen. Com

ALS, DNA, RG 393, District of West Tenn., 4th Division, Letters Received.
O.R., I, xvii, part 2, 503. See following letter.

1. See letter to Maj. Gen. William T. Sherman, Dec. 8, 1862.

To Commanding Officer, Friar's Point, Miss.

──────

> Head Quarters Dept of the Tennessee
> Holly Springs Miss Dec 28 1862

COMMANDING OFFICER
FRIAR'S POINT MISS

The falling back of my forces from the Yocona to the Tallahatchie river renders it unnecessary longer to keep a force at Friar's Point. You will therefore order the entire Cavalry force at Friar's Point to proceed by the most practicable route to Holly Springs Miss keeping north of the Tallahatchie river, where it can be used to great advantage in clearing out the Country of rebel Cavalry.

The Infantry and Artillery you will send to Memphis Tenn The Quartermasters Department at Memphis will furnish you the necessary transportation. The Cavalry should report here as son as practicable

> U S. GRANT
> Maj Genl

Copies, DLC-USG, V, 18, 30; DNA, RG 393, Dept. of the Tenn., Letters Sent.
O.R., I, xvii, part 2, 503–4.
    On Dec. 21, 1862, Maj. Gen. William T. Sherman wrote to Brig. Gen.
Willis A. Gorman, Helena, Ark., requesting a cav. diversion in Miss. in USG's
behalf. *Ibid.*, p. 877. On Dec. 23, Gorman wrote to USG. "I will Start 2000.

Cavalry to the TalleHatchie tomorrow, will be at mouth of Cold Water the 25th. If they can cross, they will come to Oxford   If not will wait a day or two to hear from you. But if it comes on ~~to~~ rain, we must return to the Miss River, as they cannot cross the river bottom, and would be cut off by mire & overflow. Genl Sherman will be at the mouth of Yazoo on the 24th. I have Infantry at Friars point"   ALS, DNA, RG 393, Dept. of the Tenn., Letters Received. *O.R.*, I, xvii, part 2, 464. On Dec. 27, Gorman wrote to Maj. Gen. Stephen A. Hurlbut. "If you have a chance to Send a dispatch Safely through to Genl Grant I respectfully ask that he may be informed that agreeable to his request, I sent Genl Washburn with 2000 Cavalry and 4 pieces of Artillry to Cold Water, and with orders to make his way to Genl Grant if possible. That I have garrisoned Friars Point, with Infantry Artillery and Cavalry. Genl Washburn found the bottom lands so utterly impassible that he was compelled to return, and when the least rain falls at this Season of the year the bottoms are impassable at all points between the Miss & TalleHatchie. That evry effort has been made to get a communication with Oxford but it is impossible from the causes stated   There is no enemy in force this side the TalleHatchie." ALS, DNA, RG 393, Dept. of the Tenn., Letters Received. *O.R.*, I, xvii, part 2, 496.

To Maj. Gen. John A. McClernand

Head Quarters, Dept. of the Ten.
Holly Springs Miss. Dec. 28th 1862

MAJ. GEN. J. A. McCLERNAND
MEMPHIS TEN.
GEN.

The mail taken over by the train, escorted by Gen. Quinby, contains a letter of instructions addressed to you, care of Gen. Tuttle, Cairo. This letter was written the same evening the dispatch from the Gen. in-chief was received and immediately mailed. But when the cars got as far as Jackson they found they could proceed no further. Since this there has been no communications with the North prior to this train under Gen. Quinby.

I do not know what facilities you will be able to get for reaching your command. I have no controll over the gunboats and no communication with the North except by way of Memphis. You can then Gen. better make arrangements for a passage down the river than I can.

I hope soon to be connected with Columbus and Cairo by telegraph and to learn more from there.

> I am Gen. very respectfully
> your obt. svt.
> U. S. GRANT
> Maj. Gen. Com

ALS, McClernand Papers, IHi. See letter to Maj. Gen. John A. McClernand, Dec. 18, 1862.

On Dec. 28, 1862, Maj. Gen. John A. McClernand, Memphis, wrote to USG. "I avail myself of the first moment, to communicate the accompanying papers: No. 1. is the order of the Secretary of War recognizing the Miss. Expedition, and assigning me to the command of it. The President's indorsement thereon manifests the interest he feels in the Expedition. No. 2., is the copy of an order issued by the Genl. in Chief to you, which I send, lest the original has failed to reach you. This order, while giving to me the immediate command of the Expedition, makes it a part of your general command. No. 3. is an extract from an order, issued by the Secty. of War, relieving me from duty at Springfield, Ills., and instructing me to report to you for the purpose specified in order No. 2. No. 4 is an extract from a communication from the Secretary of war. I have the honor to ask your instructions in the premises, and that you will be kind enough to afford me every proper facility in reaching my command. I found the reports, that the Miss. river between Cairo and this place was invested by guerillas, unfounded. At the expiration of twenty four hours, after leaving Cairo, I reached here, without hindrance or interruption. General Hurlbut informs me, that, Genl. Sherman left Helena last Tuesday; and, that a steamer coming up last night, brings the report that the enemy have planted a battery at Bolivar, nearly opposite the mouth of the Arkansas river. With a gunboat and detachment from Helena, I could test the truth of the report. I regret that the expectation, that I would find you here, is disappointed. I have much that I would like to communicate to you. Much valuable information could be obtained by you, at once, here, respecting the operations of your command, not only in General Davis' District, but on the Lower Miss. At this time, access can be obtained without difficulty, to all parts of your command, from this place, at least above Bolivar. I shall anxiously watch events upon the river, until I hear from you." LS, DNA, RG 393, Dept. of the Tenn., Letters Received. *O.R.*, I, xvii, part 2, 501–2. The enclosures are printed *ibid.*, pp. 502–3. On the same day, McClernand wrote to Maj. Gen. Stephen A. Hurlbut. "Having important dispatches to communicate to Maj Genl Grant, at Holly Springs, Miss. I am constrained by a proper precaution to ask of you a cavalry escort for the officers charged with bearing them. If the officer should find a friendly force on the road to Holly Springs he will order the return of the cavalry." Copy, McClernand Papers, IHi. On the same day, Hurlbut wrote to Lt. Col. John A. Rawlins. "I have the honor to report every thing quiet here, except a small force of Guerillas on the East & North of this place. Genl. McClernand has arrived & is very anxious to send a message across. I reluctantly spare him ten men as an Escort to the officer who bears it. I have advised him to wait until Quimby comes in but he insists on its being sent and as I do not know the

contents of this Dispatch except as he says they are *very important*, I have sent
them across. Serious charges are made as to the conduct of Genl. Daviess at
Columbus. I forward his own report which I opened. I have sent him a letter to
day directing the troops detained by him to be sent down to Helena & this place.
unless otherwise ordered from Washington. I will explain more fully by letters
which will be brought by return train. He does not need more than 1500 to 2,000
men at Columbus. We have abundance of supplies here . . . I would write more
fully but do not consider the transit safe"   ALS, DNA, RG 393, Dept. of the
Tenn., Letters Received.

  The report of Brig. Gen. Thomas A. Davies, to which Hurlbut referred,
dated Dec. 25 and addressed to Rawlins, discussed at length his actions during
the preceding five days while unable to communicate with USG's hd. qrs. Davies
had concentrated troops at Columbus, Ky., in the belief that he was threatened by
an army of 6,000 or more. ALS, *ibid. O.R.,* I, xvii, part 2, 481–82. During this
period and later, Davies telegraphed directly to Maj. Gen. Henry W. Halleck.
Ibid., pp. 441–42, 453–54, 462–63, 470, 479, 493–94, 500, 505, 520. On Dec. 27,
Col. Josiah W. Bissell, Memphis, wrote to USG's hd. qrs. that Davies had "acted
in an unsoldierly and cowardly manner and has Shown great lack of skill and
judgement. Will prefer charges against him." DLC-USG, V, 21; DNA, RG 393,
Dept. of the Tenn., Register of Letters Received. See telegram to Col. George
P. Ihrie, Dec. 25, 1862.

To Maj. Gen. James B. McPherson

Holly Springs Miss Dec 28th 1862

MAJ GEN J B McPHERSON
ABBEVILLE MISS
  Dispatch from Sullivan says Forrest is making for the Tennessee river he—Sullivan in close pursuit. The Tennessee has
risen two feet. Last dispatch received from Navy Department
said there was five light draught Gunboats in the Tennessee
river three feet draught waiting to go up on the first rise

U S GRANT
Maj Gen

Copies, DLC-USG, V, 18, 30; DNA, RG 393, Dept. of the Tenn., Letters Sent.
See telegram to Brig. Gen. Grenville M. Dodge, Dec. 27, 1862.

  On Dec. 29, 1862, 8:06 P.M., Brig. Gen. Jeremiah C. Sullivan, Huntingdon,
Tenn., telegraphed to USG. "I reached Huntingdon before the rebels knew I had
left Trenton. I have Forrest in a tight place, but he may escape by my not having
cavalry. The gunboats are up the river as far as Clifton, and have destroyed all

the boats and ferries. To escape, Forrest must pass as far south as Savannah. My troops are moving on him in three directions, and I hope for success." *O.R.*, I, xvii, part 2, 505. On the same day, telegraph operator John C. Holdridge, Trenton, Tenn., telegraphed to USG. "A Scout just in from Paducah reports that Forrests flat boats are all torn up & floating down the river   forrest seems to be surrounded by our forces as near as we can learn this evening"   Telegram received, DNA, RG 393, Dept. of the Tenn., Telegrams Received.

To Brig. Gen. Isaac F. Quinby

Holly Springs Miss Dec 28. 1862

BRIG GENL J F QUINBY
COMM'G 7TH DIVISION

Fearing that damages to the Rail Road north to Columbus, will take several weeks to repair, I, have directed the opening of the Memphis road. Investigation shows that but little damage has been done it at Moscow, and consequently cars can be run in a day or two at least as far as Lafayette 21 miles west of Grand Junction.[1] The roads from Memphis to that point are good. I have directed therefore that cars be got as far West as practicable to meet you on your return, and have also sent troops to guard the road to Lafayette and I think for some miles further west You will then return by the state line road until you meet the cars, and then in the absence of further orders dispose of your troops to guard the road westward as the work progresses. We may find it necessary to send the wagons back to get a second load of supplies. This will depend however on the extent of damages to be repaired, both on the road north and the Memphis road

I have no idea of keeping the Memphis road except for temporary purposes

It may become necessary however to send more troops to Vicksburg   In that event the road will be very convenient

U S GRANT
Maj Genl

Copies, DLC-USG, V, 18, 30; DNA, RG 393, Dept. of the Tenn., Letters Sent.
O.R., I, xvii, part 2, 504.

    1. On Dec. 28, 1862, USG telegraphed to Col. Joseph D. Webster, Jackson.
"Should it not be well to direct that all the cars running West and south from
Grand Junction receive their directions from Col Pride at least while the work
on the Memphis road is progressing. Col Pride will be at La Grange or the Junction where he can attend to it and trains will have to run by telegraph and not on
time" Copies, DLC-USG, V, 18, 30; DNA, RG 393, Dept. of the Tenn., Letters Sent.

To Col. Lewis B. Parsons

———

Holly Springs Miss Dec 28 1862

Col. L B Parsons A Q M
St Louis Mo.

The six locomotives ordered sometime since I would like to
have ready for shipment at the earliest possible moment but do
not want them sent until advised from here where to send them

They may be required at Memphis Columbus or Vicksburg
The particulars point not yet determined

One hundred more cars might also be ordered to the former
order one half of them flat cars

U S Grant.
Maj Genl.

Copies, DLC-USG, V, 18, 30; DNA, RG 393, Dept. of the Tenn., Letters Sent.
    On Dec. 14, 1862, USG had telegraphed to Col. Lewis B. Parsons. "Instead
of the four Locomotives ordered by telegraph last night, purchase Six Locomotives and get them to Columbus at the earliest possible moment." Copies,
ibid.; DLC-USG, V, 91.

To Col. Joseph D. Webster

Holly Springs Miss
Dec 29th 1862

Col J D Webster
Jackson Tenn

The paper of the 21st contains no news of "Special" interest.—Burnside is north of the Rappahanock[1] still. Davies has
had a big scare with 5000 men near Columbus. Thinks the enemy
with a Division under Cheatham within three miles of him

Burnside and his Generals have been before the Committee
on the conduct of the war. Public opinion sustains him. Possible
that Banks[2] may have cooperated with forces against Vicksburg.
Dont know this to be so. Report from the South says Vicksburgh
in our possession. McClernand is in Memphis on his way to take
command

U S Grant
Maj Gen

Copies, DLC-USG, V, 18, 30; DNA, RG 393, Dept. of the Tenn., Letters Sent.
On Dec. 29, 1862, 9:10 P.M., Col. Joseph D. Webster telegraphed to USG. "Is
there any important news from the East   we have nothing later than the 17th"
Telegram received, *ibid.*, Telegrams Received. On the same day, telegraph operator John C. Holdridge, Trenton, Tenn., telegraphed to USG. "I have paper of
23d   shall I send you telegraf Items"   Telegram received, *ibid.*

1. Ambrose E. Burnside of Ind., USMA 1847, served in the Mexican War,
and resigned on Oct. 2, 1853, with the rank of 1st lt. After a venture at manufactur-
ing breech-loading rifles, he worked for the Illinois Central Railroad. Appointed
col., 1st R. I., on May 2, 1861; brig. gen. on Aug. 6; maj. gen. on March 18, 1862;
on Nov. 10 he replaced Maj. Gen. George B. McClellan in command of the Army
of the Potomac. Following a disastrous defeat at Fredericksburg, Va., on Dec. 13,
Burnside withdrew across the Rappahannock River, where he remained until his
replacement on Jan. 25, 1863.
2. Nathaniel P. Banks, born in Waltham, Mass., in 1816, largely self-
educated while he worked in a cotton-mill, entered politics as a Democrat, winning
election as a U.S. Representative in 1852. Reelected in 1854 as an American
(Know-Nothing), he was elected Speaker of the House in 1856, then resigned in
1857 after his election as governor of Mass. as a Republican. Appointed brig.
gen. as of May 16, 1861, he served without distinction in the Shenandoah Valley,
and, on Dec. 16, 1862, replaced Maj. Gen. Benjamin F. Butler in command of the
Dept. of the Gulf.

To Col. Joseph D. Webster

Holly Springs Miss
Dec 29th 1862

Col J D Webster
Jackson Tenn

As Jackson Corinth and the Army here will have to supplied from Memphis until the road north is repaired all cars that can be spared out to sent to Grand Junction at once

U S Grant
Maj Gen

Copies, DLC-USG, V, 18, 30; DNA, RG 393, Dept. of the Tenn., Letters Sent. On Dec. 29, 1862, Col. Joseph D. Webster, Jackson, twice telegraphed to USG. "Will send all cars to Grand Junction commencing tomorrow on through freight time   Have been north to three miles beyond Dyer   Things are going on well train to Rutherford tonight   Cannot tell how much damage beyond   Some reason to hope road is uninjured beyond Union City   no distress for Subsistence here"   "I understand it is ~~per~~ proposed to send a large number of sick men from Holly Springs   Would it not be better to send them to Memphis in cars going for Subsistence & so economise transportation   they can be put on hospital boats there"   Telegrams received, *ibid.*, Telegrams Received.

On Dec. 30, USG telegraphed to S. W. Wilson, railroad agent. "All the sick at the Depot will have cars furnished for them immediately to the exclusion of everything els. All orders interfering with this are countermanded." ALS (telegram sent), Mr. and Mrs. Philip D. Sang, River Forest, Ill.

Also on Dec. 30, Webster telegraphed twice to USG, the second time at 10:00 P.M. "Train to Rutherford today   stong party working south from union City   distance between reduced to Eleven (11) miles   hope to make connection in few days   Gen Sullivan went east from Trenton sunday morng   nothing from him since   Rebel camp discovered today at Milan East of Humboldt"   "Some of Regts which are to be replaced by those now coming north are probly absent from line of the Road with Gen Sullivan   There is little excitemnt in consequence of our cavalry having been driven in yesterday mornng & some spies having been seen in town we are making little preparation as matter of prudence   I attend to the East side of town Lawler west"   Telegrams received, DNA, RG 393, Dept. of the Tenn., Telegrams Received.

To Commanding Officer, Jackson

Holly Springs Miss Dec 29th 1862

COMMANDING OFFICER
JACKSON TENN

Send back to Grand Junction Col Fuller's Brigade[1] by every train coming south. Other troops that have not yet been Brigaded will be sent from here to take their place

U S GRANT
Maj Gen

Telegram, copies, DLC-USG, V, 18, 30; DNA, RG 393, Dept. of the Tenn., Letters Sent. On Dec. 29, 1862, Col. Michael K. Lawler, Jackson, telegraphed to Lt. Col. John A. Rawlins. "Telegram Recd & forwarded to Brig Gen Sullivan who is East of trenton on road to Dresden with Col Fullers brigade" Telegram received, *ibid.*, Telegrams Received. On the same day, Col. Oliver Wood, 22nd Ohio, Trenton, telegraphed to USG. "Gen Sullivan is near Huntington   Col Fullers brigade is with him   forrest was in Dresden last night" Telegram received, *ibid.* Also on Dec. 29, USG telegraphed to Lawler. "I do not want Col Fuller's Brigade recalled from any expedition they may be on to return to their Division. When they return however I want to exchange other unbrigaded troops to replace them" Copies, DLC-USG, V, 18, 30; DNA, RG 393, Dept. of the Tenn., Letters Sent. On Dec. 30, Lawler telegraphed to USG. "Your despatch ordering that Col Fullers Brigade shall not be recalled from any Expedition they may be on has been recd & forwarded" Telegram received, *ibid.*, Telegrams Received. On the same day, 7:00 P.M., Lawler again telegraphed to USG. "Major Funke, Eleventh Illinois Cavalry, reports a ferry-boat at Lowrey's Ferry, on the Hatchie. He was followed from there through Brownsville on his return by 300 cavalry; their number on both sides of the river is reported at 1,000. If you send me a regiment of infantry I will drive the rebels across the river." *O.R.*, I, xvii, part 2, 509.

An undated telegram from Col. Joseph D. Webster, Jackson, 4:00 P.M., was probably sent on Dec. 31. "Heavy firing heard this a m for several hours about 25 miles north east near Independence   suppose Gen Sullivan has come up with Forrest   Col Lawler goes east immediately to Lexington   hopes to intercept Rebels in retreat   Lowe north of this within hearing distance   will report further" Telegram received, DNA, RG 393, Dept. of the Tenn., Telegrams Received.

1. John W. Fuller, born in England in 1827, the son of a Baptist minister, established a business as bookseller and publisher in Utica, N. Y.; after a disastrous fire in 1857, he reestablished his business in Toledo. Commissioned col., 27th Ohio, on Aug. 18, 1861, in 1862, he commanded the Ohio Brigade: the 27th, 39th, 43rd, and 63rd Ohio.

To Maj. Gen. Stephen A. Hurlbut

———

Holly Springs Miss
Dec 30th 1862

MAJ GEN S A HURLBUT
COMM'DG DISTRICT OF MEMPHIS TENN

Your communication enclosing dispatch from Washington[1] was duly received. As you are not in sufficient health to take the field I will be very glad to retain you in command at Memphis for the present

In fact I have been somewhat troubled who I could send there to relieve you. Genl Davies has a force of 5000 at Columbus, where one Regiment is the greatest abundance to hold the place and has been during all of the late scare—I have directed him to reduce his garrison to what I was before sending all the spare troops to Memphis.[2] My Cavalry force is very weak, but if the 2000 Cavalry belonging to Hovey's command are still on this side of the river, I will be able to send you one Regiment of it. I have ordered this Cavalry to report here.[3] I am now opening the Memphis and Charleston road and have placed a large force on the road to protect it. With the additional forces you will receive from Columbus you will be able to hold the road to Germantown. The balance will be provided for from here. No special news here. An unofficial dispatch received last evening from Humboldt says that our troops now have Forrest in a tight place

The Tennessee has risen and our troops I believe have destroyed all the flats on the river. With a sufficient Cavalry force Forrest's fate would be sealed. Infantry however he may succeed in evading

U S GRANT
Maj Gen

Copies, DLC–USG, V, 18, 30; DNA, RG 393, Dept. of the Tenn., Letters Sent. *O.R.*, I, xvii, part 2, 508. On Dec. 30, 1862, Maj. Gen. Stephen A. Hurlbut, Memphis, wrote to Lt. Col. John A. Rawlins. "I desire to report to the Major

Genl Comg Department that Genl Quimby with his Division escorting a heavy supply train arrived at this Post yesterday. Every preparation had been made in advance to facilitate the loading, but the teams were fatigued & Genl Quimby deferred commencing until this morning. We have an abundance of Rations and the C. S. has been notified by Col. Haines to keep always four millions on hand. I have obtained 700,000 feet of Lumber & propose to Erect within the Fort a store House for two millions—which with our other accommodations will give abundant storage. It will also be necessary to erect a Barrack Hospital within the ramparts. The ground in front of the Fort is now being cleared of Houses &c to a distances of about 250 yards & Capt Prime proposes to erect a flank work at the North End to cover the Quarter Masters & Commissary's Depots & flank the heavy guns. The garrison is all within the Fort except one Regiment on Provost duty at the Square in the City. The strength of the command is shown by the Returns herewith. I stopped the 36th Iowa for a few days but have sent them on. The City is restless but cowed—I have not hesitated to announce that an attack would involve the destruction of Memphis. I am enrolling the Union Club as Home Guards & propose to arm them. Since Genl. Sherman took away the force from here smuggling has been unlimited   I occasionally catch them with cavalry patrols & confiscate. I have ordered Gen. Daviess to send down all forces destined originally for Memphis & Helena & stopped by him and have forwarded to day the order of Maj Genl Grant to the same effect. I regret to say that it is my opinion from all I can learn that the good of the service demands inquiry into the conduct of Genl Daviess. The destruction and abandonment of Island No. 10.—this unnecessary accumulation of troops, this keeping these troops so accumulated under arms night after night and the neglect to push out forces into the country are strongly reported to me by rumour   These rumors may be unjust but I fear they are not altogether so. I regret to report that the paroled prisoners arrived here in the wildest disorder. Col. Ferrell of the 29th Ills. who commanded after the Maj Genl. relieved Col. Murphy from duty exercised no authority over his Officers & men, and when the command arrived at the Nonconnah 7 miles out abandoned them and rode in an ambulance with his wife. The example spread & officers & men came in in squads & parties & spread all over the City. I was compelled to order the Provost Guard to arrest all officers & men & force them to the Fort. Col. Ferrell is under arrest: & I have no doubt when you receive the Report of Genl Quimby will be mustered out of service for disobedience of orders & desertion of his men. I shall be able to get them off to St Louis tomorrow. Col. Murphy has been arrested & waits orders   Col Howes 3d Regular Cavalry about 200 Strong is here, a fine body of men but armed only with Pistol & Sabre. They all by education mounted Riflemen. If the Maj. Genl will send me Grierson's Regt —I would be glad to send Howe's in exchange.   two companies of 3d U. S. are at Corinth. My reason for asking for Grierson is that he is thoroughly acquainted with this Country & will be more useful than any other. I am of opinion that Genl Gorman has with drawn most of his force from this side of the River—and I learn from him that the Cavalry made an ineffectual attempt to cross from Friar's Point to Oxford but were prevented by mud. He is ordered both by Genl Curtis & Halleck to move by the 3d January toward Little Rock in a combined movement with Blunt Herron & Schofield. A fleet of light draft boats are now passing down to him so that I suppose he will proceed up Arkansas or White River both now full. I have no report from Sherman, except Stories brought up by different persons that Sherman was at Vicksburgh landed & within 6 miles of the Town moving on & Banks below the City. I do not think that any troops will come to this place from Helena but hope for a Regiment or more from Columbus when Daviess lets them go. I have been compelled to postpone the Election for Member of Congress from the 29 Dec. to 20 January on account of this Raid—by that time I hope the Country will be quiet. I beg you will state to the General that Major Genl John A McClernand went down the River this morning on the Tigress. He will need convoy to get through below. I am sorry that my health hitherto good is failing me—I am unable for the field on account of an obstonate Erysipelas which annoys me exceedingly about the face & eyes & has prevented my riding for two weeks —I am however fit for Office work & to hold Memphis especially as Halleck will not let me go home—" ALS, DNA, RG 393, Dept. of the Tenn., Letters Received. *O.R.*, I, xvii, part 2, 506–8.

    1. No record of the enclosure has been found.
    2. See letter to Maj. Gen. John A. McClernand, Dec. 28, 1862, and telegram to Maj. Gen. Henry W. Halleck, Jan. 2, 1863.
    3. See letter to Maj. Gen. Stephen A. Hurlbut, Dec. 28, 1862.

To Maj. Gen. James B. McPherson

————

Holly Springs [*Dec.*] 30 [*1862*]
Maj Gen McPherson.

    I have det[ained] Denvers Division here & sent McArthur to Lafayette & Moscow thus keeping the commands more together—I have rebrigaded the cavalry making 2 Brigades the one commanded by Grierson to be assigned to you[1]—For the present they are encamped East of Holly Springs a few miles out[2] They had better remain where they are but be ready for an Expedition in any direction. Do you hear anything from the front[3]—I have had 2.000. Cavalry at Friars Point that made an unsuccessful attempt to reach me at Oxford   I have now ordered them to get here ~~they~~ by the most practicable route   they may have gone back to Helena however

                    U S Grant
                    Maj Genl

Telegram received, McPherson Papers, NjR; copies, DLC-USG, V, 18, 30; DNA, RG 393, Dept. of the Tenn., Letters Sent. *O.R.*, I, xvii, part 2, 509.

    1. On Dec. 30, 1862, Lt. Col. John A. Rawlins issued Special Orders No. 57 creating cav. brigades under Col. Benjamin H. Grierson and Col. Albert L. Lee.

At the same time, Col. T. Lyle Dickey, chief of cav., was sent to Springfield, Ill., to hurry forward additional cav. DS, DNA, RG 94, Dept. of the Tenn., Special Orders; copies, *ibid.*, RG 393, Dept. of the Tenn., Special Orders; DLC-USG, V, 26, 27.

2. On Dec. 31, USG telegraphed to Maj. Gen. James B. McPherson. "The wagon trains of the Right Wing of the army ~~of~~ in the field will arrive at Lafayette & be ready to start from there ~~here~~ to join their respective Divisions by about 12 M on the 1st Proximo. You will send cavalry to escort them to be ready by that time. Three hundred (300) men will be sufficient. . . . P. S. Foregoing order has been given to Col Grierson" Telegram received, McPherson Papers, NjR; copies (dated Dec. 30, addressed to Grierson), DLC-USG, V, 18, 30; DNA, RG 393, Dept. of the Tenn., Letters Sent. On Dec. 31, McPherson telegraphed to USG. "I understand that three hundred 300 Cavalry will go from Col Griersons Command to escort train & that I am not to send any from here" Telegram received, *ibid.*, Telegrams Received. On the same day, USG telegraphed to McPherson. "I have ordered Cavalry from here to escort wagon trains back from Lafayette to their divisions—Cavalry will leave here after muster" Telegram received, McPherson Papers, NjR; copies, DLC-USG, V, 18, 30; DNA, RG 393, Dept. of the Tenn., Letters Sent.

3. On Dec. 30, McPherson twice telegraphed to USG. "I have no special news from the front   am Expecting this Evening some scouts whom I sent out three days ago with directions to go to grenada if possible   two of them went as far as Tray a few miles N W of grenada where they were stopped by the rebel pickets   One was turned back & the other got a pass to go in & it is the latter whom I am Expecting back tonight   There has been some rebel cavalry in Oxford & a company came up very near Abbeville—I sent over Early this morning four hundred 400 cavalry with instructions to scout on the Pontotoc & Oxford roads & to go as far as Oxford or beyond   Hatchs cavalry came back with their horses very much jaded   as soon as they rest a little I will send them out in" Telegram received (incomplete), *ibid.*, Telegrams Received. "Colonel Hatch's cavalry went into Oxford to-day; captured 2 prisoners belonging to Colonel Slemons' regiment. They scouted country 2 miles south of Oxford; encountered and chased about 60 rebel cavalry. Failed to find out anything about movements of enemy." *O.R.*, I, xvii, part 2, 509.

To Brig. Gen. Charles S. Hamilton

Holly Springs Miss Dec 30th 1862

Brig Gen C. S. Hamilton
LaGrange Tenn

Lee's Brigade of Cavalry has been ordered to you immediately after muster. McPherson's Cavalry will escort his wagons back to their Divisions

Lawler reports Guerilla bands of about 1000 in all on the two sides of the Hatchie. Try and clear them out. You can have cooperation from Jackson of Forrest has got out

U S Grant
Maj Gen

Copies, DLC-USG, V, 18, 30; DNA, RG 393, Dept. of the Tenn., Letters Sent.

To Commanding Officer, Grenada, Miss.

Head Quarters Department of the Tennessee
Holly Springs Miss Dec 31st 1862

Commanding Officer
Southern Forces
Grenada Miss
Sir:

Leiut D H Gile[1] of the 4th Illinois Cavalry as bearer of flag of truce goes to the lines of the Confederate Army in charge of seven paroled prisoners of war who I propose to exchange for an equal number of Federal prisoners who I have detained for the purpose of effecting this exchange. Those retained by me are as follows towit Privates Wm H Hessan 78th Ohio Napoleon Trembly 1st Illinois Artillery F E Lovejoy Jno Farrar & Chas Water 4th Illinois Cavalry, D N Johnson 1st Kansas and A Remington 10th Iowa. Should this exchange be consented to, you are at liberty to regard the release of the prisoners sent to your lines as full and unconditional. If no response is received in eight days I will also regard the exchange as having been properly effected and will return the within named privates to duty

Very Respectfully &c
U S Grant
Maj Gen

Copies, DLC-USG, V, 18, 30; DNA, RG 393, Dept. of the Tenn., Letters Sent.
On Dec. 31, 1862, USG wrote to Maj. Gen. James B. McPherson. "Herewith I send you seven prisoners of war to be delivered to the nearest Southern

Military post together with a letter to the Commanding Officer. I have named Lieut Gile of your Staff as the Officer to bear the flag of truce but you are at liberty to change this and substitute any other Officer of your command that you wish" Copies, *ibid*. On Jan. 1, 1863, McPherson telegraphed to USG. "The prisoners to be sent South to be exchanged have just arrived. I will send them early tomorrow morning under flag of truce in charge of Lt Giles" Telegram received, *ibid*., Telegrams Received.

Also on Jan. 1, Col. Joseph D. Webster, Jackson, telegraphed to USG. "A Messenger is here from the rebels with a flag of truce has the paroles of some prisoners of an Iowa regt which he says he wishes a p approved by a general officer The thing looks so like a pretence that I have detained him till I can hear from you particularly as I do not see any necessity of his going out to give any information to the enemy tonight. all quiet here Have no Force to spare to send out East—Lawler is in just the right place" Telegram received, *ibid*. On the same day, Lt. Col. John A. Rawlins telegraphed to Webster. "Detain party with Flag of Truce until such time as in your Judgment will prevent it from carrying information to the enemy that can do us damage." Copies, DLC-USG, V, 18, 30; DNA, RG 393, Dept. of the Tenn., Letters Sent.

1. David H. Gile of Chicago, commissioned 1st lt., Co. A, 4th Ill. Cav., as of Aug. 23, 1861.

To Maj. Gen. James B. McPherson

Holly Springs [*Dec.*] 31st [*1862*]

GEN MCPHERSON.

At Memphis all reports confirm the taking of Vicksburg by Sherman, but no particulars can be obtained—Gen McClernand & 49 Staff Officers chartered the Tigress & started for Vicksburg yesterday Hurlbut thinks the Enemy have erected Batteries on the River that will prevent him getting down—Holmes is moving against Helena but there is sufficient ~~force~~ force there to protect the place—Genl Gorman moving on Little Rock by steamer. No damage has been done Rail Road between Lafayette & Memphis There has been a great deal of cannonading today East of Henderson station, I Hope Sullivan has Forrest in a tight place.[1] I will try & get down to see you on the Second

U. S. GRANT
Maj Genl

Telegram received, McPherson Papers, NjR; copies, DLC-USG, V, 18, 30; DNA, RG 393, Dept. of the Tenn., Letters Sent. *O.R.*, I xvii, part 2, 511. The source of the news from Memphis was a telegram of Dec. 31, 1862, from Capt. Theodore S. Bowers to Lt. Col. John A. Rawlins, *ibid.*, p. 510.

1. On Dec. 31, USG telegraphed to Brig. Gen. Grenville M. Dodge. "Do you hear anything from down the Tennessee? Heavy cannonading reported off from Henderson." Copies, DLC-USG, V, 18, 30; DNA, RG 393, Dept. of the Tenn., Letters Sent; Dodge Papers, IaHA. On the same day, Dodge sent three telegrams to USG. "I have heard nothing since yesterday when my Cavalry were some place in Decatur to & have had several sharp fights   they reported no heavy force of the Enemy   the river would let a light draft gunboat up   I think my messengers must have reached fort Henry two nights ago—messengers will be in tonight"   "I have a scout in from south   left Columbus 26th & brings sketch of the Fortification &c   says that there are 3 Companies of artillery there & a few militia that the 42d Ala. Infy left there Christmas Eve for Vicksburg that the stores & machinery are being taken to Salma Ala & Atlanta Ga   he went down just before Cavalry dash on the Road south   says they were panic stricken & expected us at Columbus that no regular trains run on road now & gives the forces this side as few cavaly   says that a Report was there that Van Dorn & Forrest were to join their forces but Van Dorn failed   that Christmas They fired salute at Columbus in honor of the success of the two Raids & the Capture of Corinth   no forces gone to Pemberton since forces some six weeks ago that came up from Mobile though heard it talked then that force was to Come from Ark.   says Vicksburg is being reinforced"   "A prussian refugee a very intelligent man has arrived here   left Morristown Dec 15   was at Chattanoogo Tenn twenty first 21st & went to atlanta ga the 22d or 23d & returned same night   met several trains loaded with Kirby Smiths & Stephensons troops going to Jackson Miss Says Kirby Smith & Stephenson with their forces are ordered there   Estimated at thirty thousand 30000   also that McGowan has four thousand 4000 men at Cumberland gap   I have heard such rumors as this before but placed no reliance in them but this man tells a straight forward story & I send it as given   I have a man in Chattanoogo & also one in Murfreesboro unless they are taken   if this is a fact they will hurry back"   Telegrams received, DNA, RG 393, Dept. of the Tenn., Telegrams Received. On Jan. 1, 1863, USG telegraphed to Dodge and Brig. Gen. Charles S. Hamilton. "Following dispatch just received: Parker's Cross Road, between Lexington and Huntington. December 31st, 1862— 6. O'clock P. M. Maj. Gen. Grant: We have achieved a glorious victory, We met Forrest 7,000 strong,   after a contest of four hours completely routed him with great slaughter,   We have captured six guns, over 300 prisoners, over 350 horses, a large number of wagons and teams, and large quantity of small arms. Col. Napier killed Col. Cox and Maj. Strain, Forrest's Adjt. and one A. D. C. and a number of other officers captured. Col. Raniker slightly wounded,   I will telegraph particulars of our loss. J. C. SULLIVAN. Brig. Gen." Copy, *ibid.*, RG 94, War Records Office, Union Battle Reports. *O.R.*, I, xvii, part 1, 552. On Jan. 1, Dodge telegraphed to USG. "My Cavalry report meeting Forrests forces six 6 miles this side of clifton   they are now between bethel & clifton   I shall move & endeavor to intercept him"   Telegram received, DNA, RG 393, Dept. of the Tenn., Telegrams Received.

To Maj. Gen. James B. McPherson

[*Dec. 31, 1862*]

MAJ GEN J B MCPHERSON
ABBEVILLE MISS

I saw a man who said he had heard somebody else say that some one he had forgotten who, had seen somebody else who had seen a Copy of the Chicago Times of the 27th which said that Lee was near Washington Halleck was removed the place offered to McClellan Cabinet dissolved[1] and things generally in confusion. I received a dispatch from Halleck dated Washington Dec 27th, 12.30 P. M signed General-in-Chief.[2] Sullivan is out after Forrest and is supposed to have him in a tight place. The Tennessee river has risen and our troops from Corinth and probably from Fort Henry have destroyed all the flats on the river. Cars will be running to Memphis by the 3rd and to Columbus by the 12th Jany   Any news I get I will send to you for distribution

U S GRANT
Maj Gen

Copies, DLC-USG, V, 18, 30; DNA, RG 393, Dept. of the Tenn., Letters Sent.

1. Only this portion of the news had any validity: both Secretary of State William H. Seward and Secretary of the Treasury Salmon P. Chase had resigned. By Dec. 22, 1862, both had agreed to resume their duties. Lincoln, *Works*, VI, 11–13.
2. Probably the telegram of Dec. 27 from Maj. Gen. Henry W. Halleck to Maj. Gen. Stephen A. Hurlbut. "Memphis must be held at all hazards. I have asked General Curtis to re-enforce you. Endeavor to communicate with General Grant; also with gunboats down the river. There are none above." *O.R.*, I, xvii, part 2, 496.

To Brig. Gen. Charles S. Hamilton

Holly Springs Miss
Dec 31st 1862

Brig Gen C S Hamilton
La Grange Tenn

Instructions were sent to Quinby at Memphis to return by the state line road until he meets the cars then to guard the road from there to Memphis as the work progresses. Davies was ordered to send all his spare force to Memphis and Hurlbut to guard the road to Germantown as soon as they arrive. Cavalry has been ordered from here to escort wagons back to their Divisions   Hawkins has gone or will go to La Fayette and is instructed to send all the wagons of your command on with their provisions or a part of it. Same with Denver's train. Some provisions will have to be taken out to send to Corinth

U S Grant
Maj Gen

Telegram, copies, DLC-USG, V, 18, 30; DNA, RG 393, Dept. of the Tenn., Letters Sent. On Dec. 30, 1862, Brig. Gen. Charles S. Hamilton, La Grange, telegraphed to USG. "Two of McArthur's brigades are at Moscow; the other (Crocker's) will reach La Fayette to-morrow. I will recall Smith's regiments from those places. McArthur reports large numbers of guerrillas along the road west. I hope the cavalry will reach Moscow to-morrow" *O.R.*, I, xvii, part 2, 509. On Dec. 31, Hamilton telegraphed to USG. "Have instructions been sent to Gen Quinby what to do with his trains when he reaches the cars   the 93d Ind will be withdrawn from Moscow & placed midway to this place"   Telegram received, DNA, RG 393, Dept. of the Tenn., Telegrams Received.

Also on Dec. 31, USG sent two additional telegrams to Hamilton. "McArthur can guard the road from five to ten miles west of La Fayette and Quinby the rest of the way to Memphis until Hurlbut receives his reenforcements from Columbus. Both Division Commanders can then draw eastward"   "I have ordered Lee to go immediately forward to Moscow and report to you from there by telegraph. The road is all in good order from La Fayette to Memphis but will be destroyed by Guerillas if not protected. Send word to Quinby to dispose of his force for its protection and patrol with the Cavalry as soon as it gets up"   Copies, DLC-USG, V, 18, 30; DNA, RG 393, Dept. of the Tenn., Letters Sent. On Jan. 1, 1863, Hamilton telegraphed to USG. "There were indications of a rebel force a few miles north of this place last night, and confirmed this morning. We are all right here. In ordering me here last night I intended to clean out this force. It may be a part of Forrest's force, but think it is only a congregation of guerrillas to the number of perhaps 1,500. No fear of Grand Junction or this place. Your dispatch of last night received. I have sent Lee his instructions at Moscow." *O.R.*, I, xvii, part 2, 518.

Also on Dec. 31, USG telegraphed to George G. Pride, La Fayette, Tenn. "I have just telegraphed to Hamilton to have McArthur hold the road from Moscow five or ten Miles west of La Fayette and Quinby from there to Memphis until Hurlbut receives reenforcements" Copies, DLC-USG, V, 18, 30; DNA, RG 393, Dept. of the Tenn., Letters Sent. On Dec. 30, Pride, La Grange, telegraphed to USG. "I hope day after tomorrow night to run into Lafayette & probably next day to Memphis" Telegraph received, *ibid.*, Telegrams Received. On Dec. 31, Pride, La Fayette, telegraphed to USG. "We will want a Telegraph operator soon as he can get to Germantown hope to get to Memphis day after tomorrow Col Crocker with his Brigade just arrived" Telegram received, *ibid.* On the same day, Pride telegraphed twice to Lt. Col. John A. Rawlins. "Day before yesterday two men who are intelligent belonging to the regt on duty at this place were captured & today returned & report that Somerville is well provided with Supplies procured at Memphis & that enemy procure everything they require in that manner direct from Memphis I learn from Gen McArthur that his division will reach to Layfayette Quinby to Germantown & Hurlbut from there to Memphis Is this correct I hope to run to Memphis day after tomorrow" "We are at the bridge three 3 miles west of Lafayette & are three 3 miles East of Lafayette how far west will Mcarthurs troops go guarding Railroad please answer tonight Gen Hamilton Telegraphs that Hurlbuts to guard to germantown Quinby thence to Lafayette Mcarthurs Lafayette & Moscow leaving fifteen miles to Hurlbut is this right" Telegrams received, *ibid.*

To Maj. John J. Mudd

Holly Springs Miss
Dec 31st 1862

Major Mudd
Comm'dg 2nd Illinois Cavalry.

You will proceed to Memphis Tenn with all the effective men of your command with as little delay as praticable keeping south of the State line road to Germantown From that point to Memphis take any route you may desire. Any Guerilla Bands you may hear of to your right of left break up if praticable Returning you can take any route that information you may receive will most thoroughly clear out the country between this and Memphis of small bands of the enemy's Cavalry. You can remain in Memphis two days to rest horses and men and draw clothing &c to replace that lost them in the recent capture of this place by the enemy   By taking the Muster Rolls of your command it is possible that you will be able to draw pay at least for a part of the time due. Learn from Genl Hurlbut on your arrival if the Cavalry crossed over from Helena is still on this side of the river and if I am to expect it here. Telegraph me from Memphis on this subject as soon as the Office there is open. If not open during your stay request Gen Hurlbut to do so as soon as it is

U S GRANT
Maj Gen

Copies, DLC-USG, V, 18, 30; DNA, RG 393, Dept. of the Tenn., Letters Sent.
    On Dec. 29, 1862, Maj. John J. Mudd and fourteen other officers of the 2nd Ill. Cav. addressed a petition to USG. "In justice to our Regiment and the service, we ask that the Colonel Silas Noble may be dismissed the service for incapacity inefficiency and indolence which is so notorious with yourself and all the old troops of this department that we deem it superfluous to give particulars." DS, *ibid.*, RG 94, Vol. Service Division, Letters Received, N756 VS 1862. On Dec. 31, USG endorsed the petition. "Respectfully forwarded to Head Quarters of the Army—Washington, D. C., with the urgent recommendation that Col. Noble be mustered out of service. Although a very clever old gentleman, he is entirely unfit for any Military position whatever, and being the senior Cavalry officer in the Department, he cannot be disposed of otherwise than prejudicially to the service. It is also unjust to the other officers of the regiment to retain him. I have twice ordered Boards in conformity to Act. of Congress; entitled an Act to Authorize the Employment of Volunteers &c., approved July, 21st 1861., Sec. 10. but for some reason, the sudden removal of troops, I believe, he was never brought before them." ES, *ibid.* On Jan. 24, 1863, Noble, Chicago, wrote to U.S. Representative Elihu B. Washburne that USG had been influenced by Mudd to arrange for the petition. ALS, DLC-Elihu B. Washburne. On Feb. 16, by Special Orders No. 76, Hd. Qrs. of the Army, Col. Silas Noble was mustered out "for inefficiency." Copy, *ibid.* See letter to Brig. Gen. Lorenzo Thomas, April 14, 1863.
    On Jan. 7, Maj. Gen. John A. McClernand wrote to USG. "I hope it will be convenient and agreeable to you to assign Major J. J. Mudd 2d Ills Cav. under instructions, immediately to report to me for duty   I hope to be at the mouth of the White River in the morning." DfS, McClernand Papers, IHi; copy, *ibid.*

To Maj. Gen. James B. McPherson

Holly Springs Miss Jany 1 1863,

MAJ GENL J. B MCPHERSON
ABBERVILLE MISS

I have just heard most. reliably from all south of us. There is but about. 8.000 Troops at Grenada   Vandorn is about Coffeeville with the Cavalry   Very few troops at Jackson   all have gone to Vicksburg   Kirby Smiths forces have gone and are on the road[1]   Banks has superseded Butler   I wish you could come here to morrow, I will not be able to go down

U. S. GRANT
Maj Genl

Telegram, copies, DLC-USG, V, 18, 30; DNA, RG 393, Dept. of the Tenn., Letters Sent. *O.R.*, I, xvii, part 2, 519. On Jan. 1, 1863, Maj. Gen. James B. McPherson telegraphed to USG. "Cavalry scouts just in and confirm report that Van Dorn is this side of Coffeeville with part of his cavalry force. I will come up to-morrow, leaving here at 7 o'clock." *Ibid.*

1. See letter to Maj. Gen. James B. McPherson, Dec. 31, 1862, note 1. C.S.A. Lt. Gen. Edmund Kirby Smith, then at Knoxville, Tenn., commanding the Dept. of East Tenn., was assigned to command the Southwestern Army of West La. and Tex. on Jan. 14. *O.R.*, I, xxii, part 2, 772. On Jan. 1, Brig. Gen. Grenville M. Dodge, Corinth, telegraphed to USG. "The man stationed at Stevensons has got in tonight   he says that two divisions of Kirby Smiths Army passed through Stevensons going to Chattanooga & & Jackson Miss from the 21st to the twenty sixth 26th   that one division was Stephensons & that he considers them about ten thousand 10,000 to a Division with Considerable artillery   Says they came from Murfreesboro & all said they were going to reinforce Price & van Dorn   one thing certain they have gone South   Says no troops of consequence this side of Stevenson   he came to Decatur thence to Athens & thence to Horace [*Florence*] & Eastport   Bragg with him on East river & who says no troops in East Tenn except McGowan at Cumberland gap   I have sent three 3 of my best men to Meridian to watch"   Telegram received, DNA, RG 393, Dept. of the Tenn., Telegrams Received. On Jan. 3, Dodge telegraphed to USG. "Have a scout in from East   reports Kirby Smith moved his troops by rail to reinforce price   also says that Kirby Smiths wagon train crossed Tenn last week at Head of Muscle Shoals   says that there was only one hundred & fifty 150 wagons in the train that he saw cross & that they all said they were ordered to Jackson Miss   that there had been a battle between Bragg & Rosecrans near Nashville but could not learn the result   Says rebels claim a victory but does not think they had any reliable news only that there had been a battle. He left athens Dec thirty first 31st & crossed river at Savannah   reports forrest advance ~~of~~ on waynesboro road going

East   a scout in from Down the river reports a battery of heavy guns at mouth of Duck river   Says the guns was taken off of steamer Hannibal   the River has raised three feet in last week & is in good boating order   Saw nothing of gunboats"   Telegram received, *ibid.*, RG 94, War Records Office, Military Div. of the Miss.

To Maj. Gen. James B. McPherson

Holly Springs [*Jan.*] 1st [*1863*]

Gen McPherson.

News just ~~recd~~ brought in to Corinth says there has been a sharp fight near Nashville. Johnsons. army badly cut up & falling back.[1] Do you get anything from Grenada or South East.

U. S. Grant
Maj Genl

Telegram received, McPherson Papers, NjR; copies, DLC-USG, V, 18, 30; DNA, RG 393, Dept. of the Tenn., Letters Sent. On Jan. 1, 1863, Maj. Gen. James B. McPherson telegraphed to USG. "The defeat of Johnston [*Bragg*] is good news for New Year's day. I have nothing definite from Grenada or the southeast. The scout whom I expected back from Grenada has not returned. I have sent three more, one southeast, one in south of Panola, and one toward Grenada, but it is very difficult to get good scouts here. The citizens generally don't know anything, and when they do are not to be trusted, unless corroborated from other sources. The cavalry are out every day, but thus far have got no news of the enemy's movements." *O.R.*, I, xvii, part 2, 518.

Also on Jan. 1, McPherson telegraphed to USG. "Would it not be well to move Colonel Leggett's brigade to this side of the Tallahatchie? There is nothing left at Abbeville, and the rebel fortifications on the south side have been leveled down by the contrabands. The bridges can be guarded from this side and I can keep a good force of cavalry at Abbeville to scour the country. The road across the bottom is very bad, making communication somewhat difficult." *Ibid.*, p. 519. On the same day, USG telegraphed to McPherson. "Leave Leggett in Abbyville until after you have been up here." Telegram received, McPherson Papers, NjR; copies, DLC-USG, V, 18, 30; DNA, RG 393, Dept. of the Tenn., Letters Sent.

1. In the battle of Murfreesboro or Stone's River, Tenn., Dec. 31, 1862–Jan. 2, 1863, the armies of C.S.A. Gen. Braxton Bragg and Maj. Gen. William S. Rosecrans fought inconclusively, though U.S. losses were greater.

To Brig. Gen. Charles S. Hamilton

Holly Springs Jan 1 1863.

BRIG GENL C. S. HAMILTON
LaGRANGE TENN

I would forage off the neighborhood of Somerville but destroy nothing not even the Mill   we can use all they have

Sullivan caught up with Forrestt and gave him a tremendious thrashing   carptured six peices of his artillery and killed and wounded a great many   took his baggage and several hundred prisoners   The Gunboats got up and destroyed all his ferries. Dodge says that a scout brings in the news that Roscran has had a fight and whipped the enemy badly

Vicksburg is not taken   Kirby Smith is reinforceing that place with his Army Corps 30.000 Strong

U S GRANT
Maj Genl

Telegram, copies, DLC-USG, V, 18, 30; DNA, RG 393, Dept. of the Tenn., Letters Sent. On Jan. 1, 1863, Brig. Gen. Charles S. Hamilton, La Grange, Tenn., had telegraphed to USG. "Richardson's guerrillas are hovering about Somerville, 800 to 1,200 strong. Is it best for Lee to forage in the neighborhood, so that the scoundrels can't subsist there? To do that it may be necessary to burn the mills. I want to see them cleaned out. I propose to send a couple of infantry regiments to Somerville in a few days on a foraging expedition, and see if Somerville bacon is good. Quinby is at La Fayette. Train of cars goes there in the morning." *O.R.*, I, xvii, part 2, 518. On Jan. 3, Hamilton telegraphed to USG. "Lee has returned to near Moscow. Richardson ran off. Lee got 8 prisoners and 170 horses and mules. Shall begin moving infantry. Sullivan is here." *Ibid.*, p. 525.

To Brig. Gen. Isaac F. Quinby

Holly Springs Miss
Jan 1 1863

Brig Genl. J F Quimby
LaFayeete Tenn

If Col Hawkins is at LaFayette he has instructions from me how to dispose of the rations   if Hawkins is not there I want one train of cars loaded for the Post at Corinth and the rations for Logan and Lauman sent by rail to the Tallahatchie

I have sent a Cavalry escort to conduct the wagons back to their Divisions. Denvers rations can come in the wagons here. A Brigade of Cavalry has been sent to Hamilton with which he will be able to clear out the Guerillas, I also sent a Cavalry force to Memphis to day to scour the country there and back   I have directed Hamilton to protect the road to Memphis until Hurlbuts receives his regiments, the the latter will hold it to Germantown

U S Grant
Maj Genl.

Copies, DLC-USG, V, 18, 30; DNA, RG 393, Dept. of the Tenn., Letters Sent. On Jan. 1, 1863, Brig. Gen. Isaac F. Quinby telegraphed to USG three times: first from Colliersville, Tenn.; from La Fayette, Tenn., at 2:30 P.M.; then again from La Fayette. "The head of my column has just reached this place   I shall move on to LaFayette today where I hope to meet cars   I have three hundred wagons loaded with subsistences stores   any instructions you may have will be waited for at LaFayette"   "Shall the provisions brought here by the wagon train from Memphis be sent to the several commands by wagons or by R R   The teams are not in a condition to go farther than this today   Not knowing that troops had yet reached here I brought with me two Brigades leaving one Eckleys just west of collierville. After the trains are dispatched to their destination which will be this evening I will take the other two brigades to occupy the road from forest Hill to Memphis unless you otherwise order"   "Col Hawkins is not here & in the absence of instructions from him to Capt Ferry I have directed Gen Denvers wagons to take out fifty thousand assorted rations in the morning & all other wagons loaded with commissary stores to be unloaded ~~with Col~~ & sent under cavalry escort to their respective Divisions   the teams are now unloading at the depot & will continue all night if necessary—I understand you that Denver is at Holly Springs." Telegrams received, *ibid.*, Telegrams Received; copies, *ibid.*, RG 107, Telegrams Collected (Unbound). Earlier on Jan. 1, Brig. Gen. Charles S. Hamilton had telegraphed to USG. "Gen Quinby is this side Colliersville   will be at Lafayette at four P M today his instructions have been sent it is desirable that his camp equipage now at Holly Springs shall be sent him by train as quickly as possible Will you please give the necessary orders" Telegram received, *ibid.*, RG 393, Dept. of the Tenn., Telegrams Received. Also on Jan. 1, George G. Pride, Moscow, Tenn., telegraphed to USG. "Shall load 2 & probably 3 trains Comsy stores at Lafayette tomorrow for such points as Col Hawkins directs who is with me" Telegram received, *ibid.*

On Jan. 2, USG telegraphed to Quinby. "If arrangements are not yet made for getting your Camp and Garrison equippage and Artillery to you Select an Officer to attend to shipping it, and call on Col Pride to give order for cars to report to him for transporting it." Copies, DLC-USG, V, 30; (misdated Dec. 2, 1862) *ibid.*, V, 18; DNA, RG 393, Dept. of the Tenn., Letters Sent. On Jan. 2, Pride twice telegraphed to USG. "Gen Quinby left here this morning to place his troops on the railway told me he would have it done tomorrow hope to work throught to Memphis tomorrow night if you have any dispatches for Memphis & I will get them through trains with rations left for Corinth & Holly" "I have instructed Condrs to charge for passengers to & from Memphis tenn 10 cents a mile it is easier calculated than 6 cents am I right" Telegrams received, *ibid.*, Telegrams Received; *ibid.*, RG 107, Telegrams Collected (Unbound). On the same day, USG telegraphed to Pride. "Your are right" Copies, DLC-USG, V, 18, 30; DNA, RG 393, Dept. of the Tenn., Letters Sent.

On Jan. 3, USG telegraphed to Hamilton. "Quimby has sent down here all the wagons belonging to the Cavaly Division Lee's and all You will have give directions for their return, and send the escort to send them back It seems the Cavalry might have looked a little better after their wagons and saved there coming down here empty, to go immediately back" Copies, *ibid.* On the same day, Hamilton telegraphed to USG. "Your dispatch Recd & will be carried out forthwith" Telegram received, *ibid.*, Telegrams Received.

To Maj. Gen. Henry W. Halleck

———

Holly Springs Miss
Jany 2nd 8. a m 1863

Maj Gen H. W. Halleck
Gen in Chief

Sherman had not succeeded in landing at Vicksburg on Tuesday.[1] Kirby Smith has gone there with thirty thousand reinforcements. There is but about Eight thousand Infantry and Artillery at Grenada. I will make a dash at Enemy's Lines of communication that if successful will leave West Tennessee easily held so

as to be able to send large reinforcements to Vicksburg if necessary   Sullivan has succeeded in getting a fight out of Forrest &
whipped him badly—captured Six pieces of artillery a great many
horses & prisoners. Van Dorn was repulsed at every point ~~but~~
except this and with heavy loss.

   Davies should be relieved from duty.[2]

   Gen McClernand left Memphis for Vicksburg on the 30th
Dec'r   Gen Banks is said to be in New Orleans

U. S. GRANT
Maj Gen Com'dg

Telegram received, DLC-Robert T. Lincoln; DNA, RG 107, Telegrams Collected (Bound); *ibid.*, Telegrams Collected (Unbound); copies, *ibid.*, Telegrams
Received in Cipher; (dated Jan. 1, 1863) *ibid.*, RG 393, Dept. of the Tenn., Hd.
Qrs. Correspondence; DLC-USG, V, 5, 8, 24, 88. Dated Jan. 2 in *O.R.*, I, xvii,
part 1, 479.

   1. Dec. 30, 1862.
   2. See letter to Maj. Gen. Stephen A. Hurlbut, Dec. 30, 1862. On Dec. 29,
USG wrote to Brig. Gen. Thomas A. Davies. "Forward to Memphis immediately
all the forces you have detained at Columbus. The forces you had before Forrests
raid is abundant to garrison that place." ALS, DNA, RG 393, District of Western
Ky., Unentered Letters Received. On Jan. 1, 1863, Davies telegraphed to Maj.
Gen. Henry W. Halleck a justification of his conduct, quoting USG's telegram.
Telegram received, *ibid.*, RG 107, Telegrams Collected (Bound). *O.R.*, I, xvii,
part 2, 520. On the same day, Davies wrote a fuller explanation to Maj. Gen.
Stephen A. Hurlbut, which was then copied and sent to USG. Copy, DNA, RG
393, Dept. of the Tenn., Letters Received. *O.R.*, I, xvii, part 2, 519–20. On
Jan. 9, Davies sent Lt. Col. John A. Rawlins a lengthy report of his activities
Dec. 18, 1862–Jan. 3, 1863. LS, DNA, RG 94, War Records Office, Union Battle
Reports; copy, *ibid.*, RG 393, Hd. Qrs. District of Columbus, Letters Sent. *O.R.*,
I, xvii, part 1, 548–49; (incomplete) *O.R.* (Navy), I, xxiii, 656. On Jan. 24,
USG endorsed this report. "Respectfully forwarded to Head Quarters of the Army
Washington D. C." AES, DNA, RG 94, War Records Office, Union Battle
Reports. On Jan. 11, Rawlins issued Special Orders No. 11. "Brig Gen. A. Asboth
is hereby relieved from duty at Memphis, Tenn, and will proceed without delay
to Columbus, Ky. and relieve Brig Gen. T. A. Davies in the command of the Dist
of Columbus. Brig Gen. T. A. Davies is hereby relieved from duty in the Dist of
Columbus, and will turn over the command of the same to Brig Genl. A. Asboth
and report in writing to the Head Quarters of the Army, Washington, D. C. for
orders," Copies, DLC-USG, V, 26, 27, 98; DNA, RG 393, Dept. of the Tenn.,
Special Orders. *O.R.*, I, xvii, part 2, 554. See letter to Maj. Gen. Stephen A.
Hurlbut, Jan. 3, 1863.
   On Jan. 17, Davies telegraphed to Rawlins. "Will Gen Grant so modify
special order no 11 as to allow me to visit Memphis"   Telegram received, DNA,
RG 393, Dept. of the Tenn., Telegrams Received. At the foot of this telegram,

Capt. Theodore S. Bowers drafted a reply. "Gen Grant has gone ~~below~~ down the river." ADfS, *ibid.*; copies, *ibid.*, Letters Sent; DLC-USG, V, 18, 30. On Jan. 19, Halleck telegraphed to Davies. "If you have been relieved by Genl Grant, you will report for duty to Genl Curtis at St Louis." ALS (telegram sent), DNA, RG 107, Telegrams Collected (Bound); copy, *ibid.*, RG 108, Telegrams Sent. *O.R.*, I, xxii, part 2, 55. On March 9, Davies, St. Louis, wrote to USG. "A friend of mine was informed by President Lincoln that I was relieved from my Command of the District of Columbus on your report to the War Department of my *incompetency* Will you do me the favour to inform me if this is correct, and if not what report you did make to that Department prejudicial to me. I must confess it took me some what by surprise as I never had received from you the slightest intimation of your displeasure of the manner in which I had performed my duties in your Department." ALS, DNA, RG 94, Generals' Papers and Books, Davies. No reply to this letter has been found.

On Nov. 17, 1862, Col. John C. Kelton had telegraphed to USG. "Brigr Genl Asboth has been directed to report to you for orders." ALS, *ibid.*, RG 108, Letters Sent by Gen. Halleck (Press). On Nov. 22, Brig. Gen. Alexander Asboth, Cincinnati, wrote to USG. "Having been relieved by Special Order Nos. 123 Head Quarters Department of the Ohio from duty in that department, I have the honor to report ~~I have the honor~~ that pursuant to instructions received from Head Qrs of the Army dated 17th inst. I will leave tomorrow for the Department of the Tennessee under your command. My Staff Transportation and private horses being in St Louis I have to take my route via St Louis to Columbus Ky. where I would respectfully request to have my orders directed." ADfS, *ibid.*, RG 94, Generals' Papers and Books, Asboth. On Dec. 3, Rawlins telegraphed to Asboth, Columbus, Ky. "Orders were sent you at Columbus to proceed to Memphis and there report to the Commdg Officer. You will report there accordingly." Copies, DLC-USG, V, 18, 30, 91; DNA, RG 393, Dept. of the Tenn., Letters Sent.

On Jan. 6, 1863, Rawlins issued Special Orders No. 6. "Brig. Gen'l A. Asboth is hereby relieved from duty at Memphis, Tennessee, and will report in person without delay to these Headquarters for orders." Copies, DLC-USG, V, 26, 27; DNA, RG 393, Dept. of the Tenn., Special Orders. *O.R.*, I, xvii, part 2, 542. On Jan. 10, Asboth wrote to USG. "I beg to submit herewith pursuant to the interview granted me this morning, correct Copies of appointments, Orders, Certificates and endorsements in regard to my services actually rendered as Brigadier and Acting Major General in the U. S. Army from Aug. 1st 1861.—" LS, DNA, RG 393, Dept. of the Tenn., Letters Received. USG probably asked Asboth for the attached documents because of his irregular appointments earlier in the war. See telegram to Brig. Gen. Alexander Asboth, Oct. 1, 1861.

To Maj. Gen. Henry W. Halleck

Holly Springs Miss
Jan 2 1863

Maj Gen Halleck
Gen in Chief

Orders limiting this Department specially attach Forts Henry and Donelson to it   I am also in telegraphic communication with these points over Government wires[1]—

Gen Rosecrans now calls my attention to interferences with these Posts by my Generals & wants me to correct   If they are parts of Gen Rosecrans command I have no desire to interfere[2]— Answer

U S Grant
Maj Genl

Telegram received, DNA, RG 107, Telegrams Collected (Bound); copies, *ibid.*, RG 393, Dept. of the Tenn., Hd. Qrs. Correspondence; DLC-USG, V, 5, 8, 24, 88. *O.R.*, I, xvii, part 1, 479. On Jan. 2, 1863, USG telegraphed the first two sentences of the above telegram to Maj. Gen. William S. Rosecrans. Telegram received, DNA, RG 107, Telegrams Collected (Bound); (dated Jan. 5) *ibid.*, RG 393, Dept. of the Cumberland, Telegrams Received; copies (dated Jan. 2), *ibid.*, Dept. of the Tenn., Letters Sent; DLC-USG, V, 18, 30. On Jan. 2, USG again telegraphed to Maj. Gen. Henry W. Halleck. "Will you order the Regt of heavy Artillery from St Louis to report to me? I want six Companies at Memphis and six at Corinth" Telegram received, DNA, RG 107, Telegrams Collected (Bound); *ibid.*, Telegrams Collected (Unbound); copies, *ibid.*, Telegrams Received in Cipher; *ibid.*, RG 393, Dept. of the Tenn., Hd. Qrs. Correspondence; DLC-USG, V, 5, 8, 24, 88. *O.R.*, I, lii, part 1, 318. On Jan. 3, Halleck telegraphed to USG. "Forts Henry & Donelson are in your Dept. I will consult Gen'l Curtis about the heavy artillery. Genl Banks will ascend the Mississippi as rapidly as possible, and assist at Vicksburg. Do not scatter your forces too much. Columbus, Memphis, Grand Junction, and Corinth are the most important points to hold till Vicksburg is taken. If Bragg has been defeated he may fall back upon your line." ALS (telegram sent), DNA, RG 107, Telegrams Collected (Bound); copies, *ibid.*, RG 108, Telegrams Sent; *ibid.*, RG 393, Dept. of the Tenn., Hd. Qrs. Correspondence; DLC-USG, V, 5, 8, 24, 88. *O.R.*, I, xvii, part 1, 479–80.

1. On Jan. 11, telegraph superintendent William G. Fuller, Cairo, telegraphed to USG. "The Telegraph Line between Smithland and Fort ~~Donelson~~ Henry is being cut by Guerrillas. It should be ~~paroled~~ patroled by Cavalry. Will you please give the necessary orders." Telegram received, DNA, RG 107, Telegrams Collected (Unbound).

2. On Dec. 21, 1862, Rosecrans telegraphed to USG. "By general orders hundred sixty eight 168 all Tennessee east of Tennessee river Therefore Fort Henry is within dept Cumberland   your generals do not apparantly understand this & are giving orders to post commanders interfering with mine   please regulate This" Telegram received, *ibid.*, RG 393, Dept. of the Tenn., Telegrams Received; copy (dated Dec. 20), *ibid.*, Dept. of the Cumberland, Telegrams Sent. Later telegrams between Rosecrans and officials in Washington concerning control of the forts are *ibid.*, RG 107, Telegrams Collected (Bound). See *O.R.*, I, xxiii, part 2, 9–10. On Jan. 25, 1863, Halleck telegraphed to USG. "Forts Henry & Donelson have been transferred to the Dept of the Cumberland." ALS (telegram sent), DNA, RG 107, Telegrams Collected (Bound); telegram received, *ibid.*, RG 393, Dept. of the Tenn., Telegrams Received. On Feb. 4, Halleck telegraphed to USG and Rosecrans. "Fort-Hindman, as an appendage to Fort-Henry, will be attached to the Dept of the Cumberland." ALS (telegram sent), *ibid.*, RG 107, Telegrams Collected (Bound); telegram received, *ibid.*, Telegrams Collected (Unbound). *O.R.*, I, xxiii, part 2, 43. On March 31, Halleck returned control of Fort Heiman to USG. *Ibid.*, p. 195.

To Col. John C. Kelton

Head Quarters, 13th Army Corps.
Department of the Tennessee.
Holly Springs, Miss.s Jany. 2nd 1863.

Col. J. C. Kelton
A. A. Genl.
Washington D. C.
Col:

Herewith I enclose you reports of Genl Dodge and Col. Mersey of the 9th Ills. Infy of an expedition from Corinth on the Mobile & Ohio Road.[1]

I at the same time sent Col. Dickey of the 4th. Ills Cavalry with about one thousand men from Springdale, Miss., to co-operate. No official report is yet recieved from Col. Dickey[2] but his expedition was eminently successful. He struck the Railroad about Tupelo, and traveled south about thirty five mile[s] destroying all the bridges and culverts for the whole of that distance, and a large amount of grain that had been collected along the line of the road for the use of the Rebel Army. He also destroyed some cars, captured about one hundred and twenty (120) prisoners some teams and Camp and Garrison equipage.

> I am, Col. Very respectfully
> Your obt. Servt.
> U. S. GRANT
> Maj Gen.

Copies, DLC-USG, V, 5, 8, 24, 88; DNA, RG 94, War Records Office, Union Battle Reports; *ibid.*, RG 393, Dept. of the Tenn., Hd. Qrs. Correspondence. *O.R.*, I, xvii, part 1, 478–79.

1. See telegram to Brig. Gen. Grenville M. Dodge, Dec. 11, 1862. On Dec. 26, 1862, Dodge wrote to Lt. Col. John A. Rawlins reporting the expedition, enclosing the report of Col. August Mersy, 9th Ill., Dec. 17. LS, DNA, RG 94, War Records Office, Union Battle Reports. *O.R.*, I, xvii, part 1, 544–46. Mersy, who had commanded a div. of the Baden revolutionary army in 1848 and later settled in Belleville, Ill., was appointed lt. col., 9th Ill., on July 26, 1861, and promoted to col. as of Sept. 3.

2. On Dec. 20, 1862, Col. T. Lyle Dickey wrote to Rawlins reporting the expedition. LS, DNA, RG 94, War Records Office, Union Battle Reports. *O.R.*, I, xvii, part 1, 496–99.

To Maj. Gen. James B. McPherson

Holly Springs Jan 2nd 1863

MAJ GENL. J B. MCPHERSON,
ABBERVILL MISS.

A citizen says the Grenand Appeal of 31st gives vicksburg to Sherman   Dispatches reached Helena on the 31st and one just now from Sherman and Naval commander direct   Sherman was then hotly engaged inland three miles from Vicksburg and the Gunboats engaged the Batteries. Vicksburg is ours or Sherman is whipped before this   Gwin is reported mortaly wounded.[1] Forestt reports his loss 1500   Hurlbut reports Rebel Cavalry working north by way of Panola

> U. S. GRANT.
> Maj Genl

Copies, DLC-USG, V, 18, 30; DNA, RG 393, Dept. of the Tenn., Letters Sent. On Jan. 2, 1863, Maj. Gen. James B. McPherson telegraphed to USG. "Scout just in from Grenada and confirms report that a considerable portion of the force there has gone south, though those remaining are still fortifying. No attempts have been made to repair the railroad this side of Grenada, and only sufficient repairs on the dirt roads to facilitate the passage of cavalry. Van Dorn is very popular since his return, and the report is that his forces are concentrating near Pontotoc for another movement. Hatch says there has been a regiment of rebel cavalry near Rocky Ford, but nothing more, he thinks. He has sent out four companies of cavalry to reconnoiter. The whole country is full of small parties hovering near our lines to pick up stragglers and watch our movements. I sent scouts in the direction of Panola yesterday morning, but they have not returned." *O.R.*, I, xvii, part 2, 521. On Jan. 4, McPherson telegraphed to USG. "The battalion of cavalry sent out day before yesterday to Rocky Ford has not returned. They were instructed to push on until they met the enemy or learned something of his movements, and as they have not returned or sent any word back I think they have gone beyond Rocky Ford." *Ibid.*, p. 533.

1. Lt. Commander William Gwin, U.S.S. *Benton*, was mortally wounded on Dec. 27, 1862, on the Yazoo River.

To Brig. Gen. Mason Brayman

By Telegraph from U S Grants Hd Qurs [*Jan. 2*] *1863*
To Gen Brayman
Stockades must be built at every Military post or Station.[1] A cavalry Raid under Van Dorn may be looked for any day & must be resisted   He is now consentrating his Cavalry at Pontotoc   notify every Officer of your command to be ready and on alert   Acknowledge receipt of this Order
                                             U S Grant
                                             Maj Gen

Telegram received, Brayman Papers, ICHi. This telegram was sent to "All Commanders From Holly Springs to Jackson and Memphis." Telegram received, DNA, RG 94, War Records Office, 17th Army Corps; copies, *ibid.*, RG 393, Dept. of the Tenn., Letters Sent; DLC-USG, V, 18, 30. *O.R.*, I, xvii, part 2, 523.
    On Jan. 2, 1863, Lt. Col. John A. Rawlins telegraphed to Brig. Gen. Mason Brayman. "It is rumored that a large force of the enemys cavalry is again moving north   you will give such orders as to secure proper vigilance on the part of your command against an attack"   Telegram received, Brayman Papers, ICHi; copies, DLC-USG, V, 18, 30; DNA, RG 393, Dept. of the Tenn., Letters Sent. On the

same day, Brayman telegraphed to Rawlins. "All possible vigilance will be used. I have only 45 mounted men, not enough for pickets, and will rely on infantry. Colonel Mizner, with the Third Michigan Cavalry, passed toward Jackson this morning. Richardson's band of guerrillas is west of here, 300 strong. I want cavalry very much; our defenses are strong, and Bolivar is safe, but I wish to clear the neighborhood." *O.R.*, I, xvii, part 2, 521.

1. On Dec. 26, 1862, Col. William H. Morgan, 25th Ind., reported his defense of Davis' Mill, Miss., on Dec. 21 against the cav. of C.S.A. Maj. Gen. Earl Van Dorn, emphasizing the importance of a blockhouse he had constructed of cotton bales and railroad ties. *Ibid.*, I, xvii, part 1, 521–23. On Jan. 2, 1863, Brig. Gen. Charles S. Hamilton endorsed this report. "A copy of Colonel Morgan's modest report having come into my possession it is respectfully forwarded to the general commanding. I desire to call special attention to it as being an affair of such gallantry as to deserve, in my opinion, special commendation." *Ibid.*, p. 523. On Jan. 4, Col. Josiah W. Bissell, La Fayette, Tenn., telegraphed to USG. "I have four Com Companies here & vicinity   Shall I build block houses or send them up to help above Jackson"   ALS (telegram sent), DNA, RG 107, Telegrams Collected (Unbound); telegram received, *ibid.*, RG 393, Dept. of the Tenn., Telegrams Received. On the same day, Rawlins telegraphed to Bissell. "Send the four companies with you, with their tools &c to Jackson to repair roads north of that place"   Copies, DLC-USG, V, 18, 30; DNA, RG 393, Dept. of the Tenn., Letters Sent.

To Brig. Gen. Jeremiah C. Sullivan

————

Holly Springs Miss Jan 2 1863.

Brig Genl J. C. Sullivan
Jackson Tenn

You have done a fine job[1]   Retrieved all lost at Trenton and north of you   I sent a fine regiment of Cavaly to you   they left here on the 31st.[2] Clear out west Tennassee of all roving Cavalry   if it is necessary mount as much infantry as you think necessary. what do you estimate the loss on each side? Dodge is now out after Forestt band[3]

U S Grant Maj Genl.

Copies, DLC-USG, V, 18, 30; DNA, RG 94, War Records Office, Union Battle Reports; *ibid.*, RG 393, Dept. of the Tenn., Letters Sent. *O.R.*, I, xvii, part 1, 553. On Jan. 2, 1863, Brig. Gen. Jeremiah C. Sullivan, Jackson, telegraphed to USG three times, first at 3:00 P.M., last at 11:00 P.M. "Just arrived here from Lexington. Left Col. Lawler with 3,000 men old troops and eight pieces of artillery to follow the retreating enemy to the river. Forrest's army is completely broken up they are scattered over the country without ammunition, we need a good cavalry regt. to go through the country and pick them up. I left a regiment at the battle ground and two at Huntington. Captured six pieces of artillery (the enemy burst over nine caissons) over 400 prisoners, 500 horses, a portion of his train, all his ammunition but one wagon, three wagon loads of small arms and a large quantity of our captured clothing. Will report further when I receive reports from brigade commanders." "Flag of truce came into Jackson last night. This morning it was started out on Trenton, with orders to proceed via Trenton to Tennessee river. This evening the same flag of truce is found on Lexington road, following, our troops; I had it brought back, and now await your orders as to whether it shall be sent via Cairo to Vicksburg, or south through Corinth. The rebel loss as estimated by Forrest is 1,500 men killed, wounded, and missing. Their dead I have good reason to believe is 200 their prisoners over 400 my loss will not exceed 100 killed and wounded; prisoners, 63" Copies, DNA, RG 94, War Records Office, Union Battle Reports. *O.R.*, I, xvii, part 1, *552.* "Despatch received Shall make all preperations" Telegram received, DNA, RG 94, War Records Office, Dept. of the Tenn.

1. See letter to Maj. Gen. James B. McPherson, Dec. 31, 1862, note 1. On Feb. 22, Brig. Gen. Grenville M. Dodge transmitted to USG's hd. qrs. a report of Col. John W. Fuller, 27th Ohio, of the battle of Dec. 31, 1862, at Parker's Cross-Roads, Tenn. On March 14, 1863, USG endorsed Dodge's letter. "Respectfully forwarded to Head Quarters of the Army, Washington, D. C." Copies, DLC-USG, V, 25; DNA, RG 393, Dept. of the Tenn., Endorsements. For Fuller's report, see *O.R.*, I, xvii, part 1, 568–72.

2. On Jan. 3, USG telegraphed to Sullivan. "Has the 3rd Michigan Cavalry joined you?" Copies, DLC-USG, V, 18, 30; DNA, RG 393, Dept. of the Tenn., Letters Sent. On the same day, 1st Lt. Alexander S. Buchanan, aide to Sullivan, telegraphed to USG. "The Third 3 Mich Cavalry reported here today the genl left for Holly Springs this P M" Telegram received, *ibid.*, Telegrams Received. Earlier on Jan. 3, Sullivan, La Grange, had telegraphed to USG. "I am at this place visiting my different posts if it meets with your consent I would like to visit Holly Springs tomorrow" Telegram received, *ibid.*, RG 94, War Records Office, Dept. of the Tenn. On the same day, Lt. Col. John A. Rawlins telegraphed permission. Copies, DLC-USG, V, 18, 30; DNA, RG 393, Dept. of the Tenn., Letters Sent.

3. On Jan. 2, Dodge, Corinth, telegraphed to USG. "My forces are between here & Pittsburg Landing I go out this moring My Cav. fought him yesterday six miles this side of Clifton says he only had two pieces of artillery I find my Cavalry are badly cut up but as they are the other side of Forrest do not know they killed 26 of Forrests men that we know of have not heard from them" Telegram received, *ibid.*, Telegrams Received. On Jan. 3, Dodge twice telegraphed to USG. "Forrest escaped the river at Clifton at 7 a m Jany 1st having travelled all the time. Since his fight & immediately attacked my cavalry they kept him from the river until night when they found they were surrounded by a very heavy force & two pieces of artillery they cut their way out down river & got into his rear next morning forrest commenced crossing that night his men on rafts his horses swam the cavalry attacked again the second 2d & this morning he had every thing across by ten 10 oclock a m today—I could not reach him

with my forces but sent forward all the mounted men I could raise with one section of artillery   they will get to Clifton today   No gunboats in the River   heard nothing from Sullivans forces   our cavalry have lost considerable in killed & wounded but not many prisoners   they took several of forrests men   I have just returned"   Telegram received, *ibid.*, RG 94, War Records Office, Military Div. of the Miss.; copy, *ibid.*, Union Battle Reports. *O.R.*, I, xvii, part 1, 551. "My cavalry are all at & about Clifton seventy 70 miles from here   will keep out my scouts   had I better recall them before the coast is clear in that direction"   Telegram received, DNA, RG 393, Dept. of the Tenn., Telegrams Received. On the same day, USG telegraphed to Dodge. "You can exercise your Judgement about when to recall your Cavalry. I have sent a Regiment of Cavalry to Sullivan" Copies, DLC-USG, V, 18, 30; DNA, RG 393, Dept. of the Tenn., Letters Sent. On Jan. 4, Dodge telegraphed to USG. "Forrest has halted back of Savannah   the cavalry at Waynesboro & one battery or part of battery have gone to him   the scout says that infantry & large bodies of cavalry have crossed Tenn at Head of Muscle Shoals since Dec 28th   this since Kirby Smiths troops went south which he thinks did not exceed fifteen thousand   I believe these men tell the truth   have you anything that tends to confirm these reports"   Telegram received, *ibid.*, RG 94, War Records Office, Military Div. of the Miss.

To Maj. Gen. Stephen A. Hurlbut

Head Quartes Dept of the Tennessee
Holly Springs Miss Jan 3 1863.

MAJ GENL S. A HURLBUT.
COMD.G DISTRICT OF MEMPHIS

Some citizens of Memphis were overheard to say that there was a dertermination that we should not run the M & C. R. R. That it will be easier to interrupt that and force us to move the Army to Memphis for supplies than to come here to fight the main army.

It is my determination to run the road as long as we require it and if necessary I will remove every family and every species of personal property. between the Hatchie and Cold Water rivers[1]   I will also move south every family in Memphis of doubtful loyalty whether they have taken the oath of illagiance or not if it is necessary for our security and you can so notify them

For every raid or attempted raid by Geurillas upon the road I want ten families of the most noted secessionists sent south if the enemy with his regularly organized force attacks us I do not propose to furnish non Combatant citizens for it but these Guerillas received suport and countenance from this class of citizens and by their acts will bring punishment upon them

In this matter I wish you to give this letter all the force of an order

U. S. GRANT,
Maj. Genl.

Copies, DLC-USG, V, 18, 30; DNA, RG 393, Dept. of the Tenn., Letters Sent. *O.R.*, I, xvii, part 2, 525. On Jan. 2, 1863, Maj. Gen. Stephen A. Hurlbut wrote to USG. "I send this by an express scout, and will send a copy on the other road. Affairs do not look well; it is reported, but not, I think, reliable, that a force of cavalry from the Grenada army is working up between your line and the river, indicating toward Panola and Senatobia. No news here; have heard nothing from Quinby since he left. Great activity and a new impetus to guerrillas below, burning cotton and wood-piles to hinder navigation. Kirby Smith and Morgan are in Kentucky—Morgan at Glasgow. Rosecrans still stationary; in God's name, why does he not move? We have 4,000,000 rations due here and to be kept on hand at that amount. Gorman moves from Helena, leaving only a garrison in fort; this move is in conjunction with Curtis' force toward Little Rock. Gorman's dispatch within will explain more fully matters below." *Ibid.*, p. 522; (incomplete) *O.R.* (Navy), I, xxiii, 604. The enclosed letter is *ibid.* On the same day, Lt. Col. John A. Rawlins wrote to Hurlbut. "Some of the rebel cavalry captured between here and Memphis were armed with perfectly new carbines which evidently were procured in Memphis. These merauders are probably also getting all other contrabands supplies from there   I know it is impossible with your present small force to prevent smuggling in contraband articles entirely but I would suggest that the Provost. Marshal be directed to make a descent upon all business houses and if any are found to be carrying on illegal traffic confiscate there stock in trade and ship the offenders south of our lines   Have you heard from Davies whether he is sending you reinforcements or from Gorman, whither the Cavalry of Hoveys command is coming here? I require them very much   I am taking measures to clear out the country from here to Memphis of all Guerillas. If it cannot be done in any other way I will be compelled to take and destroy the last bushel of grain between the Hatchie and the Tallahatchie, and all the stock   I will make it the interest of the citizens to leave our lines of communication unmolested   Sullivan has whipped Forrestt and has entirely broken up his band   He has killed and wounded great numbers, captured over 400 prisoners all their trains and several wagons load of small arms six peices of Artillery over 500 horses, and recaptured much of the clothing and other property taken from our posts that surrendered" Copies, DLC-USG, V, 18, 30; DNA, RG 393, Dept. of the Tenn., Letters Sent. *O.R.*, I, xvii, part 2, 522–23. The style of this letter indicates that it was drafted either by or for USG.

On Jan. 3, USG telegraphed to Hurlbut. "Retain the second Illinois cavalry at Memphis until the paymasters start here & then so dispose of them as to give special protection to them. In addition send an infantry escort with the cars as far as Lafayette to be returned from there and their place supplied by another detail"

Telegram received, DNA, RG 393, District of West Tenn., 4th Division, Telegrams Received; copies, *ibid.*, Dept. of the Tenn., Letters Sent; DLC-USG, V, 18, 30. On the same day, Paymaster Edwin D. Judd, Cairo, twice telegraphed to USG, first at 10:30 A.M. "We leave for Memphis today   Can you secure us a safe journey with proper escort to your quarters"   "We leave at Daylight tomorrow on gunboat glide for Memphis"   Telegrams received, DNA, RG 107, Telegrams Collected (Unbound); *ibid.*, RG 393, Dept. of the Tenn., Telegrams Received. On the same day, USG telegraphed to Judd. "the cars will run through from memphis   I wil give you a Special car in addition." Telegram received, *ibid.*, RG 107, Telegrams Collected (Unbound); copies, *ibid.*, RG 393, Dept. of the Tenn., Letters Sent; DLC-USG, V, 18, 30. Also on Jan. 3, Brig. Gen. Thomas A. Davies, Columbus, Ky., telegraphed to Rawlins. "Capt Ross has just arrived on his way to Memphis with eighty five Sacks containing one million three hundred & forty two thousand Seven hundred & fifty two ~~bes~~ ~~letters~~ dollars besides papers   mail goes to Memphis tonight   Howitzers goes as soon as road is open"   Telegram received, DNA, RG 393, Dept. of the Tenn., Telegrams Received.

On Jan. 2, USG had twice telegraphed to Davies. "Send six (6) eight (8) inch Howitzers you have directed to Captain Phillips first U. S. Infantry to Corinth as soon as possible." "Have you forwarded any troops to Memphis. are you guarding the road to Union City" Telegrams received, *ibid.*, Dept. of Ky., Telegrams Received; copies, *ibid.*, Dept. of the Tenn., Letters Sent; DLC-USG, V, 18, 30. On the same day, Davies telegraphed to Rawlins. "I have sent two 2 despatches to Gen Grant one by Memphis & one by Jackson to say that his orders should be obeyed as regards troops going to Memphis as soon as transportation can be furnished" Telegram received, DNA, RG 393, Dept. of the Tenn., Telegrams Received; copy, *ibid.*, Hd. Qrs. District of Columbus, Letters Sent. On the same day, Davies wrote to Rawlins. "The order received from Maj General Grant as regards sending troops to Memphis shall be complied with as soon as transportation can be furnished" LS, *ibid.*, RG 94, War Records Office, Dept. of the Mo. *O.R.*, I, xvii, part 2, 521.

On Jan. 3, Davies telegraphed to Rawlins. "The Road is guarded to Union city & I have a heavy construction train at work   as I understand the trains are within eight or ten 10 miles of each other I am going to get off one regt today & send balance troops as soon as boats can be procured   Your telegram about six (6) eight 8 inch Howitzer I cannot understand" Telegram received, DNA, RG 393, Dept. of the Tenn., Telegrams Received; copy, *ibid.*, Hd. Qrs. District of Columbus, Letters Sent. On the same day, Rawlins telegraphed to Davies. "The howitzers referred to are those that were sent direct from Washington directed to Capt Phillips at Corinth, and that were it is understood detained by you. they will be sent forward to Corinth without delay." Telegram received, *ibid.*, Dept. of Ky., Telegrams Received; copies, *ibid.*, Dept. of the Tenn., Letters Sent; DLC-USG, V, 18, 30. On Jan. 16, USG wrote to Brig. Gen. Alexander Asboth, Columbus. "There are now at Columbus Ky. some 8 inch Howitzers which were destined, and ordered, for Corinth. I wish now to have them sent to Memphis by the first opertunity to be sent on down to use with the Mississippi river Expedition. You will please attend to this as soon as possible." ALS, DNA, RG 393, District of Western Ky., Unentered Letters Received. On Jan. 17, Asboth telegraphed to USG. "Six eight inch howitzers are mounted at Fort Halleck Columbus. They will be brought to the river at daybreak tomorrow and shipped with the ammunition as soon as possible. During the snowstorm yesterday Col. Lowe comdg.

Fort Henry sent out an expedition to Waverly which captured one Major two
Captains one Quarter Master, one Lt, one Sergeant and seven privates belonging
to different Regts of the Confederate army, together with horses arms etc."
Telegram received, *ibid.*, RG 94, War Records Office, Remount Station; copy,
ibid., Union Battle Reports; *ibid.*, RG 393, Hd. Qrs. District of Columbus, Letters
Sent. Misdated Jan. 18 in *O.R.*, I, xvii, part 2, 573–74. See telegram to Maj.
Gen. Henry W. Halleck, Jan. 4, 1863, note 1.

    1. On Jan. 2, USG telegraphed to Brig. Gen. Charles S. Hamilton. "Let Lee
collect Horses mules saddles and bridles and mount as many infantry as possible
to clear out the Guerillas between the Hatchie and Tallahatchie"   Copies, DLC-
USG, V, 18, 30; DNA, RG 393, Dept. of the Tenn., Letters Sent. *O.R.*, I, xxiv,
part 3, 141. On Jan. 3, USG telegraphed to Brig. Gen. Isaac F. Quinby, "in charge
of commanding officer Lafayette to be forwarded to him at once." "Give notice
to the citizens on the road to Memphis that if necessary to secure the Rail Road
every family and every vestage of property except land itself between the Hatchie
and the Cold Water will be removed out of these limits or confiscated—arrest
and parole all citizens between eighteen (18) and fifty (50) years of age   Collect
forage as far as practicable from south side of the road." Telegram received, DNA,
RG 94, War Records Office, 17th Army Corps; copies, *ibid.*, RG 393, Dept. of
the Tenn., Letters Sent; DLC-USG, V, 18, 30. *O.R.*, I, xvii, part 2, 524.

To Maj. Gen. Henry W. Halleck

Holly Springs, Miss,
Jan 4, 1863, 1 P M

Maj Gen Halleck
Gen in Chf U S A.

    Dispatches from Sherman & Naval commander were rec'd at
Helena on 31st. Gunboats were engaging the Enemy's batteries.
Sherman was inland 3 miles from Vicksburg, hotly engaged.
From rebel sources I learn that Grenada Appeal of 31st says the
Yankees have got possession of Vicksburg. If this statement is
confirmed I will fall back to line of Memphis & Corinth. Since
the late raids this Dept except troops on the river have subsisted
on the country.

    There will be but little in North Mississippi to support guer-
rillas in a few weeks more

U S Grant
M G Comdg

Telegram received, DLC-Robert T. Lincoln; (2) DNA, RG 107, Telegrams Collected (Bound); *ibid.*, (Unbound); copies, *ibid.*, Telegrams Received in Cipher; *ibid.*, RG 393, Dept. of the Tenn., Hd. Qrs. Correspondence; DLC-USG, V, 5, 8, 24, 88. *O.R.*, I, xvii, part 1, 480. See telegram to Maj. Gen. Henry W. Halleck, Jan. 7, 1863.

To Maj. Gen. Henry W. Halleck

Holly Springs Miss
Jany 5th [4] 4 P M/63

Maj Gen. H. W. Halleck
Gen in Chief

Dispatch just received from Vicksburg to 29th   Sherman has had a terrific fight—Loss probably three thousand killed & wounded. Sherman captured a Fort & nine guns at the point of bayonet also Enemys Rifle Pits and main Fort but was obliged to fall back owing to failure of troops to come to his support— Fleet was seen coming up the river when the boat left Vicksburg no doubt it was Gen'l Banks[1]—This is from Gen'l Gorman who did not hear from Sherman direct   I am firm in the belief that news from the South that Vicksburg has fallen is correct

U S. Grant
Maj Gen'l Comdg

Telegram received, DNA, RG 107, Telegrams Collected (Bound); (dated Jan. 5, 1863) *ibid.*, Telegrams Collected (Unbound); copies, *ibid.*, Telegrams Received in Cipher; (dated Jan. 4) *ibid.*, RG 393, Dept. of the Tenn., Hd. Qrs. Correspondence; DLC-USG, V, 5, 8, 24, 88. Dated Jan. 5 in *O.R.*, I, xvii, part 1, 480. On Jan. 3, Maj. Gen. Stephen A. Hurlbut, Memphis, wrote to USG. "I have recd. dispatches from Gorman. Sherman has had a bitter fight, forced the first line of entrenchments Captured and holds one Nine Gun Battery. Captured their Main Fort on Walnut Hill at the point of the bayonet but the supports did not come up and our men were driven out with great Slaughter. Morgan Smith is Wounded Giles Smith Col 8. Mo and Wyman 13th Ills Killed. loss about 3000 Killed & Wounded. No official report from Sherman. Price and Joe Johnston are at Vicksburgh. Steamers from below are seen bringing up troops. I fear Sherman is over matched. he has sent for ammunition. I send him to day all I have 230,000 rounds and have sent his order forward to be telegraphed from Cairo. He wants 4,000 000 rounds. The Blue Wing with Ammunition was taken below Helena and has gone up the Arkansas. I this day send three barges of coal for the Fleet which they greatly need. Davies still holds the troops above and says he does it by orders of General Halleck. Sherman ought to be reinforced. I think they out number him besides the advantage of Position. Nothing heard from Banks. I have suggest to Gorman the propriety of throwing his whole available force except Fort Garrison to Vicksburgh. The Messenger Schultz who was bringing your reply was captured but destroyed his dispatches. The road from here to Germantown is full of Gurrillas and some Regular Cavalry. I trust the Rail Road may be forced through rapidly. It must be strongly guarded down to the Depot as I cannot spare any guards. Shermans wounded will be here before long I suppose and am preparing Hospital Buildings in case they arrive. I require more force even for ordinary Guards, and especially Cavalry to beat up these Gurrillas. Major Blythe is within 14 miles on the Hernando Road. Richardson near Wolfe river about Germantown." Copy, DNA, RG 393, District of Memphis, Letters Sent. *O.R.*, I, xvii, part 2, 526. Hurlbut's reply to Brig. Gen. Willis A. Gorman is *ibid.*, pp. 526–27.

On Jan. 4, USG telegraphed to Bvt. Maj. Franklin D. Callender, St. Louis. "Have you sent Ordnance Stores to Vicksburg? Sherman requires four-hundred thousand rounds assorted small arms ammunition immediately." Copy, DLC-USG, V, 18, 30; DNA, RG 393, Dept. of the Tenn., Letters Sent. On Jan. 5, Callender telegraphed to USG. "Dispatch Recd   shipping today a large quantity of small arm ammunition to Memphis for Gen Sherman & ammunition for field guns including a large supply for ten & 20 pounder parrott to Replace that captured on the steamer Blue wing" Telegram received, *ibid.*, Telegrams Received. *O.R.*, I, xvii, part 2, 537.

1. See telegram to Maj. Gen. Henry W. Halleck, Jan. 2, 1863. On Jan. 4, USG telegraphed to Hurlbut. "Banks is coming up the Mississippi with reinforcements to Sherman. I have again ordered Davies to send you troops." Telegram received, DNA, RG 393, District of West Tenn., 4th Div., Telegrams Received; copies, *ibid.*, Dept. of the Tenn., Letters Sent; DLC-USG, V, 18, 30. On the same day, USG telegraphed to Brig. Gen. Thomas A. Davies, Columbus, Ky. "Send a part of your forces immediately to Memphis." Copies, *ibid.* On the same day, Davies telegraphed to Lt. Col. John A. Rawlins. "The trouble is transportation   have telegraphed to St Louis   none to be had   one 1 Regt will leave in the morning on the Swallow   I am stopping all boats up & down as fast as they arrive to send troops as ordered   they will go as soon as boats can be had   the battery left this morning" Telegram received, DNA, RG 393, Dept. of the Tenn., Telegrams Received; copy, *ibid.*, Hd. Qrs. District of Columbus, Letters Sent. *O.R.*, I, xvii, part 2, 535. On Jan. 5, USG telegraphed to Davies. "You can retain at Columbus about (1000) one thousand Men over your former garrison" Telegram received, DNA, RG 393, Dept. of Ky., Telegrams Received; copies, *ibid.*, Dept. of the Tenn., Letters Sent; DLC-USG, V, 18, 30.

On Jan. 4, George G. Pride, Memphis, telegraphed to USG. "Railroad all right here—Shall start trains with supplies East Monday morning—.Have sent Hurlburts dispatches—Hurlburt says he can raise steamboat Transportation south for twelve thousand men—Please instruct me if I shall go on to St Louis to carry out the Vicksburgh Railroad order—Hurlburt wishes you were here—" Telegram received, DNA, RG 107, Telegrams Collected (Unbound); *ibid.*, RG 393, Dept. of the Tenn., Telegrams Received. On Jan. 3, USG had telegraphed to Pride. "Go to St Louis and be prepared to execute the mission you were going on but make no contracts until you receive further dispatches from me   There is a possibility of change of plan being ordered from Washington"   Copies, DLC-USG, V, 18, 30; DNA, RG 393, Dept. of the Tenn., Letters Sent.

To Maj. Gen. James B. McPherson

Holly Springs, Miss. Jan. 4, 1863

BRIG. GEN'L. J. B. MCPHERSON,
ABBEVILLE, MISS.,

It looks evident that Van Dorn, Forrest and Roddy are going to unite their forces and attack Corinth, or make a general raid upon the roads. Van Dorn is now marching towards Jacinto. Roddy is at Tuscumbia, and Forrest back of Savanna. There is no special object longer in holding the Tallahatchie.[1] You may therefore fall back as far as you can to-morrow.

U. S. GRANT,
Maj. Gen'l.

Copies, DLC-USG, V, 18, 30; DNA, RG 393, Dept. of the Tenn., Letters Sent. *O.R.*, I, xvii, part 2, 532.

On Jan. 4, 1863, USG telegraphed to Maj. Gen. James B. McPherson. "A wagon train was attacked near the Tallaloosa this evening. I have no Cavalry to send after them. If Grierson is where he can be sent send him immediately." Copies, DLC-USG, V, 18, 30; DNA, RG 393, Dept. of the Tenn., Letters Sent. On the same day, McPherson wrote to USG. "I have sent to Colonel Grierson at Waterford to move with two battalions of cavalry immediately toward Tallaloosa. Colonel Hatch has three companies of cavalry at Chulahoma, and I have directed him to send two companies more to the same point, and then to move from there up to the south and west of Chulahoma." *O.R.*, I, xvii, part 2, 533–34.

1. On Jan. 3, McPherson had telegraphed to USG. "The river is rising so fast there is danger of its carrying bridges away & I think of ordering Col Leggetts Brig. over to this side   what is to be done with Capt Forts Co. & the Contrabands   I did not exactly understand yesterday whether it was understood between Capt. Prince & yourself that I was to order them to Holly Springs"   Telegram received, DNA, RG 393, Dept. of the Tenn., Telegrams Received. *O.R.*, I, xvii, part 2, 525. On the same day, USG telegraphed to McPherson. "Order Leggett to this side of the river   send the Camp of contraband here. I will send them to memphis"   Copies, DLC-USG, V, 18, 30; DNA, RG 393, Dept. of the Tenn., Letters Sent. On Jan. 12, Col. John W. Sprague, Corinth, telegraphed to USG.

"Company D Capt J W Fouts that you ordered to Join my Regt when at Oxford has not yet reported   they have been detached five months   I should be glad to have them back"   Telegram received, *ibid.*, RG 94, War Records Office, Dept. of the Tenn.

On Jan. 4, McPherson wrote twice to USG. "The recent rains have raised the Tallahatchie and all the Streams running into it very much, and the former is still rising. The water is running over the center of the lower Bridge, and washing away the abutment of the upper one. They are both so far gone that Teams cannot cross. Col Leggett's Brigade is on this side with all his Transportation, though he left a small quantity of Forage, which we can get over on rafts or the R. Road Bridge. The question of Forage is becoming a very serious one. We have managed thus far to get plenty of Corn, but fodder or long forage is very scarce, and all the Animals are suffering and many of them dying for the want of it. Unless the roads dry up very rapidly, it will be impossible to keep up the supply of corn for the command, if it remains at this point. I shall send Col Hatch's Regiment over to the westward beyond Wyatt. Col Prince's to the Eastward near Tippah Creek, and let Col Grierson remain in the vicinity of Waterford for the present as Forage is much more abundant there than here." Copy, *ibid.*, RG 393, 17th Army Corps, Letters Sent. "My command will march to the vicinity of Holly Springs to-morrow. Shall I destroy the railroad bridge over the Tallahatchie? I understand that I cannot leave a force of infantry here, but have Colonel Leggett's brigade march back as far as Lumpkin's Mill at least, and then follow on after everything there and at Waterford has been removed." *O.R.*, I, xvii, part 2, 533. On the same day, USG telegraphed to McPherson. "I think it is not necessary to destroy the Tallahatchie bridge. The road is destroyed so far south that the enemy cannot use it for some time, and we may want it, at least we will keep up the appearance of wanting it. Move your whole force back however, leaving one Brigade at Lumpkins Mill's" Copies, DLC-USG, V, 18, 30; DNA, RG 393, Dept. of the Tenn., Letters Sent. *O.R.*, I, xvii, part 2, 533.

To Maj. Gen. James B. McPherson

Holly Springs Miss Jan. 4th, 1863,

BRIG GENL J B. MCPHERSON
ABBERVILLE, MISS

If the report of Vicksburg being in our possession proves true I will fall back to the line of Memphis and Corinth at once   There is no objection to your falling back to the Waterford and Tchulahoma road leaving a small force on the road near the river.

A long dispatch from Vicksburg on the 29th was Just received. Sherman had had a desperate fight in which he had lost 3.000 men killed and wounded, he had carried the enemys rifle pits and a

fort of nine guns & also their principal Fort, but from this latter
he had been forced to fall back owing to support not comeing up
in time. Morgan Smith and and his brother wer both wounded
the former probably dead[1]   When the boat left a fleet was coming up the river, probably Banks. I have news overland of his
arrival in New Orleans, and a dispatch today from Genl Halleck
says that he is to push up the river.[2]

U. S. GRANT,
Maj Gnl.

Copies, DLC-USG, V, 18, 30; DNA, RG 393, Dept. of the Tenn., Letters Sent.
O.R., I, xvii, part 2, 531.

    1. Brig. Gen. Morgan L. Smith was severely but not mortally wounded at
Chickasaw Bayou on Dec. 28, 1862.
    2. See telegram to Maj. Gen. Henry W. Halleck, Jan. 2, 1863.

To Brig. Gen. Grenville M. Dodge

Grants. Hd. Qurs [*Jan. 4, 1863*]

G M DODGE
    am not informed that force at Pontotoc is yet moving   think
it is not   If I ascertain that there is combined movement of Rodys
forces & the forces said to be at Pontotoc I will send divission to
you if I can   as it is now Reported Vicksburg is ours I can send
you divission any way. My latest advices from Vicksburg direct
are of the twenty ninth   there had then been desperate fighting.
Shrman had lost about three Thousand (3000) men, killed &
wounded but had carried Enemys Rifle Pits & one 1 fort of nine
(9) Guns. I hear from citizens that Grenada appeal thirty first
(31st says Yankees had Possession of Vicksburg

U. S. GRANT
Maj Gen

Telegram received, DNA, RG 393, District of West Tenn., Telegrams Received;
copies, *ibid.*, Dept. of the Tenn., Letters Sent; DLC-USG, V, 18, 30. *O.R.*, I,
xvii, part 2, 530.

To Brig. Gen. Grenville M. Dodge

Holly Springs, Miss., Jan. 4, 1863

BRIG. GEN'L. G. M. DODGE

CORINTH, MISS.,

Scout just in from Pototoc.[1] Found out nothing reliable but report said Van Dorn had gone east   Was getting up all the Cavalry and partizan rangers he could. He evidently means mischief. I will direct rations to be sent to you as fast as possible, and order Sullivan to send you forage.[2]

U. S. GRANT,

Maj. Gen'l.

Telegram, copies, DLC-USG, V, 18, 30; DNA, RG 393, Dept. of the Tenn., Letters Sent. *O.R.*, I, xvii, part 2, 532.

On Jan. 3, 1863, USG had telegraphed to Brig. Gen. Grenville M. Dodge. "The enemys Cavalry and mounted Infantry has been collecting at Pontotoc with a design no doubt of getting into our rear or possibly to reinforce Forrestt. Keep a sharp lookout for him and dont let him get across the Tuscumbia if it can be helped" Copies, DLC-USG, V, 18, 30; DNA, RG 94, War Records Office, 16th Army Corps; *ibid.*, RG 393, Dept. of the Tenn., Letters Sent. *O.R.*, I, xvii, part 2, 524. On Jan. 4, Dodge telegraphed to USG. "Have you any information which way the force is moving that was at Pontotoc or its strength   Citizens bring report that a division is to camp near Jacinto tomorrow night   it is not safe to go far away from here & take the forces that are necessary to successfully accomplish any thing   from some reports that the scouts bring in I am satisfied they know exact strength   I have no fears for this place but if they come near me would like to go after them   there are reports today of forces crossing the Tenn at head of muscle shoals   it comes direct but is not from my own men   it may be guard to Smiths train   Rhoddy has had one regt of conscripts come within the last week & appears to be accumulating considerable stores at florence Tuscumbia"   Telegram received, DNA, RG 393, Dept. of the Tenn., Telegrams Received.

1. On Jan. 4, Maj. Gen. James B. McPherson wrote to USG. "Scout just returned from Pontotoc. Only a few cavalry there; he could not learn anything of Van Dorn's movements that was definite, though reports said he had gone east toward the Mobile and Ohio Railroad, and was collecting all the cavalry, Partisan Rangers, &c., that he could. The battalion of cavalry has just returned from Rocky Ford; found no enemy except few straggling guerrillas on this side of the Tallahatchie, and only heard of a small force being on the other side. Lieutenant Gile has not returned yet with flag of truce." *O.R.*, I, xvii, part 2, 533.

2. On Jan. 3, Dodge had telegraphed to USG. "I understand that road is open to Memphis   I have been out of rations of bread for a long time & on half

rations of Every thing else & it is almost impossible to get any thing in this portion of the country for man or animal   I am very anxious to get a supply   should I be cut off by any large force it will be difficult to get any thing   you are aware of the condition of the surrounding country & if possible I wish you would order rations to me   thire are so many between me & supplies I fear I shall be cut out with out your aid"   Telegram received, DNA, RG 393, Dept. of the Tenn., Telegrams Received. On Jan. 4, USG telegraphed to Dodge. "I have instructed the cheif commissary only to keep the other posts supplied for the time being until you get 400.000 rations   possibly one train may reach you to morrow   You had better order only three quarters rations issued   a sufficient supply is on hand   I instructed sullivan to send you all the forage he could"   Copies, DLC-USG, V, 18, 30; DNA, RG 393, Dept. of the Tenn., Letters Sent. On the same day, Lt. Col. John A. Rawlins telegraphed to Dodge. "Four hundred thousand (400.000) rations have been ordered to you   First train will probably reach you to day haveing arrived at Jackson last night. Rations will be forwarded to you as rapidly as possible"   Copies, *ibid*. On Jan. 5, Dodge telegraphed to USG. "Am on half rations   shall remain so until I get full supply   have five feet of water in Tenn & rising"   Telegram received, *ibid.*, Telegrams Received.

On Jan. 3, Lt. Col. John P. Hawkins, La Fayette, Tenn., telegraphed to USG. "I go towards Memphis today   hope to get through   I would like to have orders as to what amount to fill up Holly Springs   have sent stores to Lagrange Jackson & Corinth"   Telegram received, *ibid.*; *ibid.*, RG 107, Telegrams Collected (Unbound). On the same day, USG telegraphed to Hawkins. "We want all the rations the Rail Road can possibly carry at present   Corinth should have 400.000 rations as rapidly as they can be got there keeping other points supplied"   Copies, DLC-USG, V, 18, 30; DNA, RG 393, Dept. of the Tenn., Letters Sent. On Jan. 4, USG twice telegraphed to Hawkins. "Get at supply of ten days rations distributed to all parts of the Department before accumulating beyond that amount at one place. While the supply of meat of the country holds out I see no necessity of Beef contractors coming here nore them bringing more than half rations of pork." "Push rations to Corinth as speedily as possible. Supplies must be sent there to the exclusion of other points, which may be kept down to two days supply." Copies, *ibid*.

To Brig. Gen. Charles S. Hamilton

Holly Springs, Miss., Jan. 4, 1863

Brig. Gen'l. C. S. Hamilton
La Grange, Tenn.,

A scout just in reports that there are but few troops at Pontotoc. Van Dorn is said to have gone east, and is collecting all the Cavalry and Partizan Rangers he can. Dodge says also that he understands a Division of Rebels will be at Jacinto to-morrow night. Roddy is at Tuscumbia. Probably they will join in a raid. Have your cavalry ready for a pursuit if necessary.

U. S. GRANT,
Maj. Gen'l.

Telegram, copies, DLC-USG, V, 18, 30; DNA, RG 393, Dept. of the Tenn., Letters Sent. *O.R.*, I, xvii, part 2, 532. On Jan. 3, 1863, Brig. Gen. Charles S. Hamilton had telegraphed twice to USG. "D̶. C̶. Dr David C Hibbitt returning from near Nashville to his home in Dyer Co N W Tenn came through Pontotoc on the 1st inst   he says there was but a small cavalry force one 1 company there he was told in Pontotoc that Pembertons army was in Oxford & was advancing hibbitt is Secesh & is unwilling to take the oath   I Shall keep him   he had heard nothing of vandorn"   Telegram received, DNA, RG 393, Dept. of the Tenn., Telegrams Received. "Is it not probable that Van Dorn is preparing to go to Forrest's aid rather than to make another attack on the railroad? There is no point now where he can cross Wolf River. If he goes to Forrest he must go by Chewalla, and Dodge may head him on the Tuscumbia." *O.R.*, I, xvii, part 2, 524. On Jan. 4, Hamilton telegraphed to USG. "I am told to-day that Morgan, of Kentucky, had united his cavalry with Van Dorn, and was with him at Holly Springs. I have no doubt it was so, and that he is with him again." *Ibid.*, p. 530.

On Jan. 4, USG telegraphed to Hamilton. "There is no doubt of concentrating troops for the purpose of attacking Corinth. It will be necessary to strengthen that place with at least a Division   If Fullers Brigade has not yet returned instruct them to go there and I will send the balance of the Division as son as they can be replaced by troops from here"   Copies, DLC-USG, V, 18, 30; DNA, RG 393, Dept. of the Tenn., Letters Sent. *O.R.*, I, xvii, part 2, 531. On the same day, Hamilton telegraphed to USG. "Fuller's brigade yesterday had gone to Clifton. All the troops from my command sent to Sullivan have pushed far to the east and north. I have telegraphed Sullivan to send Fuller immediately." *Ibid.* Also on Jan. 4, USG telegraphed to Hamilton. "If you have anyone that you can send out towards Carrolville to discover if there is a movement towards Jacinto from Potatoc, I wish you would send them   I have no one here and no Cavalry to send"   Copies, DLC-USG, V, 18, 30; DNA, RG 393, Dept. of the Tenn., Letters Sent. On the same day, Hamilton telegraphed to USG. "I can start some Cavalry tomorrow   Chickasaw & Reed my best men are at Corinth   Dodge has men entirely at home in the region from which you wish intelligence   Orders for Commission Recd"   Telegram received, *ibid.*, Telegrams Received.

To Brig. Gen. Charles S. Hamilton

———

Holly Springs Miss Jan 4th 1863,
BRIG GENL C. S. HAMILTON
LAGRANGE TENN

The Soldiers referred to should be tried by a Military commission[1]   send the names of three Officers to compose it and the commission will at once be ordered

A Despatch of 29th or 30th date not given from Sherman and the Commander of naval fleet, says gunboats were then engageing enemies batteries   Sherman was inland three miles from Vicksburg. hotly engaged the enemy   not a word said of prospect. From secession sources I learn that the Grenada Appeal of 31st says the Yankees have taken Vicksburg

Eighty five bags of mail matter passed down to Memphis last night for the army

U. S. GRANT.
Maj Genl.

Telegram, copies, DLC-USG, V, 18, 30; DNA, RG 393, Dept. of the Tenn., Letters Sent.

1. On Jan. 4, 1863, Brig. Gen. Charles S. Hamilton had telegraphed to USG. "A party of soldiers of 11th Mo have been apprehended for Robbing a farm house in the night   the farmer killed one & mortally wounded another & was badly wounded himself   the men should be made an example of   how shall they be tried   what news from vicksburg" Telegram received, *ibid.*, Telegrams Received.

To Brig. Gen. Jeremiah C. Sullivan

———

Holly Springs, Miss. Jan. 4, 1863.
BRIG. GEN'L J. C. SULLIVAN,
JACKSON, TENN.,

Van Dorn has gone East from Potatoc, and is gathering all the Cavalry and Partizan Rangers he can. Roddy is about Tuscumbia. The probabilities are that he will be heard from about Corinth, Bethel or Bolivar. Have the two latter on their guard. If possible send Dodge forage promptly.

U. S. GRANT,
Maj. Gen'l.

Telegram, copies, DLC-USG, V, 18, 30; DNA, RG 393, Dept. of the Tenn., Letters Sent. *O.R.*, I, xvii, part 2, 532.

To Col. William S. Hillyer

Holly Springs Miss Jan 4 1863.

COL W. S. HILLYER
LAFAYETTE TENN

A dispatch Just received from General Halleck says that Banks. in pushing up the Mississippi to Vicksburg. This with the news from Vicksburg that a fleet is seen coming up the river is satisfactory that Sherman is reinforced before this   it would take me four days to get reinforcements for him to Memphis unless I should abandon the Rail Road   Inform Hurlbut of these facts

U. S. GRANT,
Maj. Genl.

Telegram, copies, DLC-USG, V, 18, 30; DNA, RG 393, Dept. of the Tenn., Letters Sent. *O.R.*, I, xvii, part 2, 531. On Jan. 4, 1863, Col. William S. Hillyer, La Fayette, Tenn., telegraphed to USG. "Train just arived from Memphis   I will detain train to Memphis till you have time to send dispatches   Morgan L Smith is reported dead"   Telegram received, DNA, RG 393, Dept. of the Tenn., Telegrams Received; *ibid.*, RG 107, Telegrams Collected (Unbound).

To Maj. Gen. Stephen A. Hurlbut

———

Holly Springs, Miss, Jan: 5th 1863.
MAJ: GENL' S. A. HURLBUT.
MEMPHIS, TENN:

Furnish each prisoner with a parole. Have duplicate lists made out of all the prisoners, and them receipted by one of the officers among them, furnish them with three days rations and have them landed below the city, at some point convenient for them to get back South, send the small pox patients where you deem best into Arkansas, or down the river. The certificate of officer in charge of Cartel Ship, that the prisoners had been taken to Vicksburgh and refused, should be attached to the rolls.

U. S. GRANT
Maj Genl'.

Telegram, copies, DLC-USG, V, 18, 30; DNA, RG 393, Dept. of the Tenn., Letters Sent. On Jan. 4, 1863, Maj. Gen. Stephen A. Hurlbut had telegraphed to USG. "I have one Thousand prisoners refused at Vicksburgh on Steamer Minnehaha—They are sickly and have seven cases of small pox. what shall I do with them. I have taken off the small pox cases and ordered the rest and the Boat thoroughly cleaned & kept in quarantine till I hear from you. I do not want them here both on account of the Contagion and the want of Hospitals and Guards answer as soon as possible." Telegram received, *ibid.*, Telegrams Received; *ibid.*, RG 107, Telegrams Collected (Unbound).

On Jan. 5, USG telegraphed to Hurlbut. "Have you any news from Vicksburgh since the 29th" Copies, DLC-USG, V, 18, 30; DNA, RG 393, Dept. of the Tenn., Letters Sent.

To Maj. Gen. Stephen A. Hurlbut

———

Holly Springs, Miss. Jan: 5th 1863
MAJ GENL' S. A. HURLBUT
MEMPHIS, TENN:

You will please forward the following dispatch to Comm'dg Officer at Vicksburgh by first opportunity:

"Holly Springs, Miss Jan: 5th 1863.

Commanding Officer
River Expedition
        The following dispatch just received from the General in
Chief.

                                                    Washington Jan: 2nd 1863
Genl' Grant.
        No officers prisoners of War will be released on parole
until further orders

                                                    H. W. Halleck
                                                    Genl' in Chief.[1]
You will retain as prisoners all confederate officers, parole none

                                                    U. S. Grant.
                                                    Maj General

Telegram, copies, DLC-USG, V, 18, 30; DNA, RG 393, Dept. of the Tenn.,
Letters Sent. On Jan. 5, 1863, Lt. Col. John A. Rawlins had telegraphed to Maj.
Gen. Stephen A. Hurlbut an almost identical message with a modified final para-
graph. "You will therefore retain all confederate officers within your lines. Parole
none, including those on Cartel Ship. If boat has started bring them back." Copies,
ibid. Rawlins also sent similar messages to Brig. Gen. Mason Brayman, to Brig.
Gen. Grenville M. Dodge, and to Brig. Gen. Jeremiah C. Sullivan. Copies, *ibid.*
On Jan. 3, USG had telegraphed to Sullivan. "Send your prisoners to Cairo to be
Kept there until sent by Truce ship to Vicksburg"   Copies, *ibid.*

        1. On Dec. 30, 1862, Maj. Gen. Henry W. Halleck had telegraphed to USG
and to seven other commanding gens. "No officers prisoners of war will be re-
leased on parole till further orders." ALS (telegram sent), *ibid.*, RG 107, Tele-
grams Collected (Bound); telegram received, *ibid.*, RG 393, Dept. of the Tenn.,
Telegrams Received. *O.R.*, II, v, 130. On Jan. 2, 1863, Brig. Gen. Thomas A.
Davies telegraphed the text of this telegram to Rawlins. Telegram received,
DNA, RG 393, Dept. of the Tenn., Telegrams Received; copy, *ibid.*, Hd. Qrs.
District of Columbus, Telegrams Sent.

To Brig. Gen. Charles S. Hamilton

Holly Springs, Miss., Jan. 5. 1863

Brig. Gen'l. C. S. Hamilton,
La Grange, Tenn.,

I foresee the necessity of consolidating the Districts of Jackson and Columbus, and send you there to command. Guerilla parties come in on the road in small parties and pick up operators when they choose.

U. S. Grant,
Maj. Gen'l.

Telegram, copies, DLC-USG, V, 18, 30; DNA, RG 393, Dept. of the Tenn., Letters Sent. On Jan. 5, 1863, USG sent three additional telegrams to Brig. Gen. Charles S. Hamilton. "On the arrival of Logan's Division, order Ross to Corinth. The Regiments at Grand Junction and that vicinity not Brigaded order to Jackson. The Regiment in charge of Contrabands may remain where it is until further orders from me." "Has Quinby got his Artillery up yet?" "You need not move any of the Unbrigaded troops until I get up." Copies, *ibid*. On the same day, Hamilton sent four telegrams to USG. "Sullivan has seven Regts of Smiths Division four of fullers brigade two of Bucklands one of Mowers will you send him orders to send them to Corinth of the rest of Smiths division one regt is at Davis Mill one at Grand Junction two here & one between here & Moscow these last can be put on the cars in very short time but they ought to be replaced" "Is it your wish I should send Morgans Regt which is on R R from Davis Mills to Coldwater to Jackson except that Reg there are only four Cos unbrigaded in this vicinity those are guard of Town" "I hope the order may be delayed for a few days I expect to hear from Washington today as the commucation of LaGrange & Grand Junction is entirely with Memphis Cannot these places be included in the Memphis Dest I would like to see you before my command is changed" "The Troops must go by R R or if they march ~~march~~ they must go via Bolivar the Rains have sent all rivers out of their banks & no doubt the Temporary bridges on state line Road over Tuscumbia & hatchie are swept away Can they be sent by Rail" Telegrams received, *ibid*., Telegrams Received. On the same day, Lt. Col. John A. Rawlins telegraphed to Hamilton. "We have not cars to spare. They must march via Bolivar" Copies, DLC-USG, V, 18, 30; DNA, RG 393, Dept. of the Tenn., Letters Sent.

Also on Jan. 5, USG twice telegraphed to Brig. Gen. Jeremiah C. Sullivan, Jackson. "Have you replaced the guards on the line of the Rail Road? It should be done at once. Send the troops from Ross' Division as rapidly as possible to Corinth. You can retain two Regiments until they are replaced from here." "I have three good Regiments between here and Grand Junction not Brigaded that I will send to you as soon as possible. You can retain that number of Regiments until the others arrive" Copies, *ibid*. On the same day, Sullivan telegraphed to USG. "Six of my regiments are now returning from pursuit of Forrest across the river. Colonel Fuller's brigade is ordered to report to Corinth. Three regiments will be at Trenton to-day that will also be forwarded to Corinth. My line of road has been guarded all the time, but when I send the regiments belonging to Ross' division away I will be very short. There are plenty of men at Columbus that can be ordered here. The six regiments mentioned above have been ordered to Bethel; from there to Corinth." *O.R.*, I, xvii, part 2, 538.

To S. W. Wilson

Holly Springs, Miss: Jan: 5th 1863.

S. W. WILSON
GRAND JUNCTION, TENN:

Dont unloard any cars that are intended for Jackson and Corinth, supplies must be sent there as fast as possible. Let one train run between Grand Junction and here. As trains going from Corinth and Jackson to Memphis pass, they can drop empty cars and hitch on to the loaded ones from here. All the sick and freight must be moved from this place.

U. S. GRANT
Maj Genl'.

Telegram, copies, DLC-USG, V, 18, 30; DNA, RG 393, Dept. of the Tenn., Letters Sent.
    On Jan. 4, 1863, railroad superintendent S. W. Wilson, Grand Junction, telegraphed to USG. "From what point is the transportation required" Telegram received, *ibid.*, Telegrams Received. On the same day, USG telegraphed to Wilson. "From Holly Springs to Tallahatchie, I want cars to move cotton and stores, from this place north." Copies, DLC-USG, V, 18, 30; DNA, RG 393, Dept. of the Tenn., Letters Sent. Also on Jan. 4, Wilson telegraphed to USG. "The road is badly washed near waterford   will you order a detail with shovels picks & bars to accompany the train from Holly Springs South to repair—My men are all at work on a break north of Holly   Have the detail report to Mr Cain at the depot   please answer" Telegram received, *ibid.*, Telegrams Received. On the same day, Lt. Col. John A. Rawlins telegraphed to Wilson. "Instruct the train master to put negroes aboard with the tools, or call on the Commanding Officer at Waterford for men." Copies, DLC-USG, V, 18, 30; DNA, RG 393, Dept. of the Tenn., Letters Sent.
    On Jan. 5, Wilson twice telegraphed to USG. "One train has arrived from Memphis & gone to Corinth"   "I will send every thing I have to Holly Springs today   all our cars & Engines are now at Memphis loading with stores   Shall I unload the cars designed to go north at this point & send them to Holly   will order every thing from Jackson down at once"   Telegram received, *ibid.*, Tele-

grams Received. On the same day, USG twice telegraphed to Wilson. "We want no more stores here, but want a daily train to carry off every thing" "Send the stores now on the cars forward to Corinth. The 45th Illinois Reg't is here, it will move north to Coldwater to-morrow." Copies, DLC-USG, V, 18, 30; DNA, RG 393, Dept. of the Tenn., Letters Sent.

Also on Jan. 5, USG telegraphed to Lt. Col. John P. Hawkins, La Fayette, Tenn. "We want no more stores at Holly Springs" Copies, *ibid.* On the same day, George G. Pride, Memphis, twice telegraphed to USG. "Wilson Telegraphs me you wish R R transportation Our train leaves here tonight for Holly with Comsy stores please telegraph Wilson Grand Junction if you wish cars unloaded this side of Holly" "Your dispatch recd it is necessary for me to remain here a few days to get things in working order please instruct me if you ne wish me to hasten to St Louis the quarter master & comsy want me to extend tracks to river it can be done but will take a week to do it Shall I set to work at it if you keep the road open it had better be done please answer" Telegrams received, *ibid.*, Telegrams Received; *ibid.*, RG 107, Telegrams Collected (Unbound). On the same day, USG telegraphed to Pride. "Extend tracks as required by quartermaster and Commissary" Copies, DLC-USG, V, 18, 30; DNA, RG 393, Dept. of the Tenn., Letters Sent. On Jan. 6, Pride, Jackson, telegraphed to USG. "Must stop here this eveing have you any orders for me here" Telegram received, *ibid.*, Telegrams Received. On Jan. 7, Pride, Memphis, telegraphed to USG. "I have been requred here until now so soon as telegraph is open I shall go to St Louis shall I then turn over Road to Col Webster Supt please answer to end of telegraph line as messenger will be waiting" Telegram received, *ibid.* On Jan. 7, USG telegraphed to Pride. "When you are ready turn over the Superintendency to Col Webster and proceed as per your order to St Louis." Copies, DLC-USG, V, 18, 30; DNA, RG 393, Dept. of the Tenn., Letters Sent. A second telegram of the same date to Pride may represent a telegraphic transformation of the first. "Turn over the road to Col.. Webster as soon as you leave" Telegram received, *ibid.*, RG 107, Telegrams Collected (Unbound).

On Jan. 6, USG telegraphed to Wilson. "You were directed yesterday to have a train run between this place, and Grand Junction. When will you be able to make that arrangement. There is a large amount of property here that requires moving at once." Copies, DLC-USG, V, 18, 30; DNA, RG 393, Dept. of the Tenn., Letters Sent. On the same day, Wilson telegraphed to USG. "The train which I had designed to be at Holly last night with 22 cars was by your Order sent to Corinth I notified Col Webster yesterday morning that you required transportation he promised me 15 cars & Engine at day light this morning I can hear nothing from there three heavy trains should have been here at nine this morning from Memphis but have not yet arrived & there being no telegraph I can hear nothing from them will notify you at once as soon as I can hear from them" Telegram received, *ibid.*, Telegrams Received. On the same day, USG sent three more telegrams to Wilson. "The Cars for moving Commissary stores from Waterford will not be required" "In the absence of instructions from Colonel Hawkins, where the supplies to arrive are to be sent, you can send one of the three trains to Corinth, and one to Jackson, the third you can send to La Grange, or Grand Junction, which latter, after unloading, to run down here to take up a load" "Keep the train now here to run between this place and the Junction. Let them bring here empty Cars, and those they take up loaded attach to other trains, and send them on to Memphis" Copies, DLC-USG, V, 18, 30;

DNA, RG 393, Dept. of the Tenn., Letters Sent. Also on Jan. 6, Wilson twice more telegraphed to USG. "Every Engine has her train   not an idle car on the line   a train will unload at Lagrange this P M   I shall send it to Holly this Evening to load tonight & leave at 7 a m"   "One train just left here for Holly one from Memphis with stores will leave for Jackson at 12 M   a call to move troops at Jackson uses train I should have had from there this morng"   Telegrams received, *ibid.*, Telegrams Received.

To Maj. Gen. Henry W. Halleck

Holly Springs Miss
Jany 6th 12. M 1863

MAJ GEN H. W. HALLECK
GEN IN CHIEF

To obtain supplies of Forage am gradually falling back to line of Memphis and Corinth. Will leave Holly Springs about tenth. One Division goes to Corinth. Supplies coming over Memphis & Charleston Rail Road but so many cars being shut up at Columbus forage and fresh meat must be obtained from country. Supply will last thirty days yet. I seize all mills in Country and issue corn meal to great extent. Contraband question becoming serious one. What will I do with surplus Negroes? I authorized an Ohio philanthropist few days ago to take all that were at Columbus to his state at Government expense.[1] Would like to dispose of more same way.

U. S. GRANT
Maj Gen'l Com'dg

Telegram received, DNA, RG 107, Telegrams Collected (Bound); *ibid.*, Telegrams Collected (Unbound); copies, *ibid.*, Telegrams Received in Cipher; *ibid.*, RG 393, Dept. of the Tenn., Hd. Qrs. Correspondence; DLC-USG, V, 5, 8, 24, 88. *O.R.*, I, xvii, part 1, 481.

1. On Jan. 3, 1863, Brig. Gen. Thomas A. Davies, Columbus, Ky., telegraphed to USG. "A man here from Ohio proposes to take all the Contrabands from here to that state provided the Govt. furnish the transportation   shall I send them   thier condition here is terrible"   Telegram received, DNA, RG 393, Dept. of the Tenn., Telegrams Received; copy, *ibid.*, Hd. Qrs. District of Columbus, Letters Sent. On the same day, Lt. Col. John A. Rawlins telegraphed to Davies. "You are hereby authorized to furnish the necessary transportation for

contrabands at Columbus, to the State of Ohio as per proposal of the Gentleman from Ohio mentioned in your despatch." Telegram received, *ibid.*, Dept. of Ky., Telegrams Received; copies, *ibid.*, Dept. of the Tenn., Letters Sent; DLC–USG, V, 18, 30. On Jan. 9, Davies telegraphed to Rawlins. "The Chaplain of the 7th ills is here & proposes to take the contrabands to Ohio   Mr Wright who undtook it is Sick   Can he be detailed from his regt for that purpose   his name is Perkins" Telegram received, DNA, RG 393, Dept. of the Tenn., Telegrams Received.

On Jan. 17, W. H. Ladd, New York City, wrote to Secretary of War Edwin M. Stanton. "Just recd information from Cincn that Gen. Grant has ordered all negroes at Columbus &c not in employ of Gov. shipped to Cin. If he ships several thousand negroes in there unprovided for, in the face of existing prejudice. It will be very impolitic" ALS, *ibid.*, RG 108, Letters Received. Stanton added an undated endorsement. "I think Grant should countermand the order if he has made one. Please direct him to do so immediately." AES, *ibid.* On Jan. 19, Maj. Gen. Henry W. Halleck telegraphed to USG. "I am directed by the Secty of War to say that if you have ordered the shipment of Negroes from the Slave states to Cincinnati, you will countermand the order." ALS (telegram sent), *ibid.*, RG 107, Telegrams Collected (Bound); copy, *ibid.*, RG 108, Telegrams Sent. *O.R.*, I, lii, part 1, 323.

On Jan. 22, Rawlins telegraphed to Brig. Gen. Alexander Asboth, who had succeeded Davies in command at Columbus, that the order for the contrabands should be countermanded if not already implemented. Telegram received, DNA, RG 393, Dept. of Ky., Telegrams Received; copies, *ibid.*, Hd. Qrs. District of Columbus, Telegrams Received; *ibid.*, Dept. of the Tenn., Letters Sent; DLC–USG, V, 18, 30. On the same day, Asboth telegraphed twice to Rawlins. "Pursuant to telegram of 3d head quarters Dept of the tennessee Contrabands were forwarded to Cairo Ill on the Twelfth & thirteenth inst as follows two hundred & twelve 212 men two hundred 200 women & two hundred & three 203 children Am not informed whether they have gone to Ohio or not but will ascertain at once"   "The contrabands enumerated in my Telegram of this evening are still at Cairo without proper shelter   shall they remain there, or be forwarded to Cincinnati" Telegrams received, DNA, RG 393, Dept. of the Tenn., Telegrams Received; copies, *ibid.*, Hd. Qrs. District of Columbus, Letters Sent. On Jan. 23, Rawlins telegraphed to Asboth that the contrabands could be left at Cairo or returned to Columbus, "whichever place they can be of most use and best cared for." Copies, *ibid.*, Telegrams Received; *ibid.*, Dept. of the Tenn., Letters Sent; DLC–USG, V, 18, 30.

To Brig. Gen. Charles S. Hamilton

Holly Springs, Miss. Jan: 6th 1863.

Brig Genl' C. S. Hamilton
La Grange, Tenn:

The baggage belonging to Buckland's Brigade should be sent to them.[1]

One Regiment from Jackson has gone to Corinth, but as Sullivan reports rebels crossing the Tennessee river again, I have directed him to keep the troops he has till we learn the facts. The balance of the Division will go to Corinth via Bolivar.

The order, by direction of the President, making 13th, 15th 16th and 17th Army Corps, and assigning commanders to each has arrived[2]

U. S. GRANT
Maj General.

Telegram, copies, DLC-USG, V, 18, 30; DNA, RG 393, Dept. of the Tenn., Letters Sent.

    1. On Jan. 6, 1863, Brig. Gen. Charles S. Hamilton telegraphed to USG. "Bucklands Regts with Sullivan will get back to Jackson tomorrow   is there any prospect that the Div will not be wanted at Corinth   the 7 Regts to Sullivan have been without baggage or cooking"   Telegram received (incomplete), *ibid.*, Telegrams Received. On Jan. 8, Brig. Gen. Jeremiah C. Sullivan telegraphed to Lt. Col. John A. Rawlins. "Col Fullers Brig Ross Div. is at Buthel on way to Corinth   I retain col Bucklands Brig Three Regts for present   the Tenn is reported raising very Rapidly   I have ordered Citizens along line of road to be pressed into services to set to work helping repair R R   It works well   We are in great need of Blank muster Rolls &c"   Telegram received, *ibid.*, RG 94, War Records Office, Dept. of the Tenn.
    2. See letter to Maj. Gen. John A. McClernand, Dec. 18, 1862.

To Brig. Gen. Charles S. Hamilton

———

Holly Springs, Miss. Jan: 6th 1863.

BRIG GENL' HAMILTON
LA GRANGE, TENN:

I expect you were right in arresting the officer of Engineer Reg't at Davis Mills. That Reg't, from the nature of its duties and the necessity of moving it constantly from one part of the Dept to another, and to prevent conflicting orders being given it, has been specially placed under the Sup't of the Rail Road, and is no more subject to orders from others commanders than troops of one Division are subject to the orders of their superiors in another Division. This however does not justify disrespect. When an officer of the Engineer Regiment is arrested it should always be reported immediately to Col Webster, so that he may appoint some one else to superintend the work they may be overlooking at the time

U. S. Grant
Maj General

Copies, DLC-USG, V, 18, 30; DNA, RG 393, Dept. of the Tenn., Letters Sent. Earlier on Jan. 6, 1863, Lt. Col. John A. Rawlins telegraphed to Brig. Gen. Charles S. Hamilton. "You will please release Lieut Goodrich of the Engineer Regiment at Davis' Mills, and order him to resume his duties at that place" Copies, *ibid.* On the same day, Hamilton telegraphed to USG. "Three days since I sent word to Lt Goodrich through Col Morgan to give up an ox team & wagon that have been at the mill six or eight weeks   Lt Goodrich sent me back an insolent reply that he would not obey any order of mine no matter what it is   if he had obeyed the order & then made a protest I should have thought it all right but his conduct was insubordinate & insulting & without cause. I shall release him as you direct"   Telegram received, *ibid.*, Telegrams Received.

To Brig. Gen. Charles S. Hamilton

Holly Springs, Miss Jan: 6th 1863.
Brig Genl' C. S. Hamilton
La Grange, Tenn:

Nothing from Corinth to-day. Rosecrans has whipped Bragg badly at Murfreesboro', and forced him to fall back. Probably Van Dorn is going there. Sullivan telegraphs that rebels are crossing the Tennessee again.[1] I can hardly think it.

The Tennessee is now up, and the Naval Commander at Cairo says there are several Gunboats up the river.[2]

I do not know what day I will be going to Memphis[3] You can go then, or as soon as the troops arrive to replace Ross' Division, which will be to-morrow

Let Lee clean Richardson out if he can[4]

U. S. Grant.
Maj General.

Copies, DLC-USG, V, 18, 30; DNA, RG 393, Dept. of the Tenn., Letters Sent.
O.R., I, xvii, part 2, 541.

   1. On Jan. 6, 1863, Brig. Gen. Jeremiah C. Sullivan, Jackson, telegraphed
to Lt. Col. John A. Rawlins. "Scouts from Tenn River Rept that another force is
crossing that the rebels say Gen Rosecrans whipped Bragg & that braggs Army
retreated west with Sixty pieces of artillery"   Telegram received, DNA, RG 94,
War Records Office, Dept. of the Tenn. On the same day, USG telegraphed to
Sullivan. "Send out the 3rd Michigan Cavalry to the Tennessee River, to watch
the movements of any rebel forces that may be crossing and to protect it if possible
The naval commander at Cairo says that Gun boats have gone up the Tennessee"
Copies, DLC-USG, V, 18, 30; DNA, RG 393, Dept. of the Tenn., Letters Sent.
On the same day, Sullivan telegraphed to Rawlins. "I have had Colonel Mizner
out in that direction for three days, and intend to keep him there. I am so completely enveloped with roaming squads of rebel cavalry that it is almost impossible
to get courier through. Colonel Lawler has orders to watch movements closely,
and in case the force is too large to fall back slowly until I can re-enforce him."
O.R., I, xvii, part 2, 540. Also on Jan. 6, USG again telegraphed to Sullivan.
"You can keep the balance of the troops with you until the facts are learned about
troops crossing the Tennessee River. I can hardly credit the story, but we must
be on our guard." Copies, DLC-USG, V, 18, 30; DNA, RG 393, Dept. of the
Tenn., Letters Sent. On the same day, Sullivan telegraphed to USG. "Lieutenant
Hart, of the Tennessee Cavalry, reports to me that Buckner and Cheatham are
crossing the river at Saltillo and Shannonville. The report of General Rosecrans
whipping Bragg is received from same source and that this portion of the rebels
made their way to the river. Had I not better hold my troops here and re-enforce
Corinth, if it should be attacked? I sent off to General Dodge to-day one regiment." *O.R.*, I, xvii, part 2, 540. On the same day, USG again telegraphed to
Sullivan. "Enquire of Quartermaster if he has any shoes on hand, and if so send
what he can spare to La Grange"   Copies, DLC-USG, V, 18, 30; DNA, RG 393,
Dept. of the Tenn., Letters Sent.
   2. On Jan. 4, USG telegraphed to the naval commander, Cairo. "Some light
draught Gunboats now in Tennessee would be of great value. Forest has got to
the East bank, but there are strong signs of his recrossing in the vicinity of
Savannah. Can any be sent"   Telegram received, *ibid.*, RG 45, Correspondence
of David D. Porter, Telegrams Received; *ibid.*, RG 107, Telegrams Collected
(Unbound); copies, *ibid.*, RG 393, Dept. of the Tenn., Letters Sent; DLC-USG,
V, 18, 30. *O.R.*, I, xvii, part 2, 530; *O.R.* (Navy), I, xxiv, 5. On Jan. 5, Capt.
Alexander M. Pennock, Cairo, telegraphed to USG. "have already ordered all
available boats to ascend Tennessee with the rise"   Telegram received, DNA,
RG 107, Telegrams Collected (Unbound). *O.R.* (Navy), I, xxiv, 5. On Jan. 6,
Brig. Gen. Grenville M. Dodge, Corinth, twice telegraphed to USG. "Are there
any gunboats in Tenn   the Crossing at Florence should be destroyed   a gunboat can go there   Every creek &c is full of hidden flat boats & the only sure
way of disposing of them is by way of river   I get nothing definite from south
Reports continue to come in of crossing at head of Muscle shoals   up Dec. 31 no
troops had passed meridian"   "Scouts in from the south state Van Dorn with
heavy cavalry force is at Okalona   that he expects reinforcements from east
more Scouts will be in in mornig"   Telegrams received, DNA, RG 393, Dept.
of the Tenn., Telegrams Received. On Jan. 6, Rawlins telegraphed to Col. William

W. Lowe, Fort Henry. "There are said to be large numbers of flat boats and other craft for crossing the Tennessee River hid away at the mouths of streams emptying into the Tennessee. You will therefore please request the Gunboats which are reported to be up the river, to use every means for their destruction, that the enemy may be prevented from crossing into West Tennessee and Kentucky. They should proceed up the river as far as the water will permit. Answer if you are in communication with the Gunboats, and their whereabouts." Copies, DLC-USG, V, 18, 30; DNA, RG 393, Dept. of the Tenn., Letters Sent. *O.R.*, I, xvii, part 2, 541; *O.R.* (Navy), I, xxiv, 5–6.

3. On Jan. 6, USG telegraphed to Brig. Gen. Charles S. Hamilton. "I cannot say when I will be up. Will probably go to Memphis in a day or two. Glad to hear the news from Washington." Copies, DLC-USG, V, 18, 30; DNA, RG 393, Dept. of the Tenn., Letters Sent. On the same day, Hamilton telegraphed to USG. "Have you any thing further from Corinth or about vandorn I would like to accompany you to Memphis & look at my command along the line is it likely I will be wanted to the Eastward for two or three days I want to clean out Richardson" Telegram received, *ibid.*, Telegrams Received.

4. Robert V. Richardson, born in N. C. in 1820, was a lawyer and business-man in Memphis when the Civil War began. After organizing the 1st Tenn. Partisan Rangers, which he commanded as col., he operated under orders from Lt. Gen. John C. Pemberton. *O.R.*, I, xvii, part 1, 797–98. On Jan. 6, 1863, Hamilton telegraphed to USG. "Col Lee telghs from Moscow his scout just in from Mt Pleasant reports a rebel mounted force of some two 3000 some artillery Camped last night at Tallalosa he says the source not entirely reliable but the report was they would strike road near German town or Collierville I cannot beleve the report but troops along line have been notufied Wall Texas legion is reported as part of the force if this is true they must have crossed Tallahatchie at Watts" Telegram received, DNA, RG 393, Dept. of the Tenn., Telegrams Received. On the same day, USG telegraphed to Hamilton. "Gen Logan has been directed to place one Brigade at Davis' Mills, One at Grand Junction, and one at La Grange, and to guard the road to Moscow" Copies, DLC-USG, V, 18, 30; DNA, RG 393, Dept. of the Tenn., Letters Sent.

To Brig. Gen. Isaac F. Quinby

Holly Springs, Miss. Jan. 6th 1863.
Brig Genl' I. F. Quinby
La Fayette, Tenn:

I shall go to Memphis, as soon as possible and regulate matters. I am told that things are going at loose ends there. In the meantime you may let Cotton pass into Memphis, but allow no contraband articles to pass out, and specie is one of them.

U. S. Grant.
Maj General.

Copies, DLC-USG, V, 18, 30; DNA, RG 393, Dept. of the Tenn., Letters Sent. On Jan. 6, 1863, Brig. Gen. Isaac F. Quinby, "Crossing of Pidgeon Roost Memphis & Charleston R R" telegraphed to USG. "There is a continuous stream of wagons loaded with Cotton coming from Miss. over pidgeon Roost road taking there return all stores of supplies the owners acknowling themselves to be disloyal   this thing is so manifestly wrong that I have taken responsibility of stopping & sending back all Cotton in hands of orignal owners who cant produce satisfactory proof of loyalty. It is reported to me that buyers in Memphis are paying specie for Cotton   I hope you will sustain me in this course which is manifestly vital to our cause"   Telegram received, *ibid.*, Telegrams Received; copy, *ibid.*, 15th Army Corps, District of Corinth, Letters Sent. *O.R.*, I, xvii, part 2, 542. On Jan. 7, Quinby telegraphed to USG. "I would like to see you personally about the Cotton trade   as at present conducted it outrages common sense   I will endeavor to comply with you teleg order of yesterday strictly" Telegram received, DNA, RG 393, Dept. of the Tenn., Telegrams Received.

On Jan. 16, USG wrote to Brig. Gen. John A. Logan. "The railroad is run exclusively for the benefit of troops and not for cotton speculators. Your complaint will be attend to immediately. Cotton or private goods can be put out at any point where there is a guard when the cars are necessary for military purposes." Copy, DLC-John A. Logan.

To Maj. Gen. Henry W. Halleck

Holly Springs Miss
Jany 7th 6 P M 1863

MAJ GEN H. W. HALLECK
GEN IN CHIEF.

All supplies not taken from the country are now brought from Memphis. Think it advisable to complete Railroad to Columbus to get rolling Stock on this side & possibly to hold it for short time. Am throwing large supply Subsistence into Corinth. With use of two or three light draft Gunboats the Tennessee can be used.[1] Nothing from Sherman since my last dispatch. Will be ready to reinforce him from Memphis if necessary—Will move heavy Artillery from East bank of River. Is Helena Ark in my Dept ?[2] Can have troops at Corinth to operate from there soon as supplies can possibly be got there

U. S. GRANT
Maj Genl

Telegram received, DNA, RG 107, Telegrams Collected (Bound); _ibid._, Telegrams Collected (Unbound); copies, _ibid._, RG 393, Dept. of the Tenn., Hd. Qrs. Correspondence; DLC-USG, V, 5, 8, 24, 88. _O.R._, I, xvii, part 2, 543; _O.R._ (Navy), I, xxiv, 7. On Jan. 6, 1863, Maj. Gen. Henry W. Halleck had telegraphed to USG. "I suggest the propriety of imediately concentrating your forces as proposed in a former telegram so as to be able to reinforce Sherman, should it be necessary, or if not, to cooperate with Rosecrans against Bragg's army   In connexion with this, should not all artillery be removed from points on the east side of the river between Memphis & Columbus, so as to prevent its falling into the hands of the enemy. New Madrid & Helena must be held on the west side. Without heavy artillery the enemy can make no logments on the river from which they cannot be driven by the Gunboats. Cannot Corinth now be supplied from Memphis or during the winter from Pittsburg more securely than from Columbus, & thus avoid the necessity of guarding the Mobile & Ohio R. Road?" ALS (telegram sent), DNA, RG 107, Telegrams Collected (Bound); telegram received, _ibid._, RG 393, Dept. of the Tenn., Telegrams Received. _O.R._, I, xvii, part 1, 480.

On Jan. 7, USG again telegraphed to Halleck. "I never consented or proposed to send the Kentucky Cavalry away. I have about four hundred and fifty of them at Paducah." Copies, DLC-USG, V, 5, 8, 24, 88; DNA, RG 393, Dept. of the Tenn., Hd. Qrs. Correspondence.

1. On Jan. 7, Brig. Gen. Jeremiah C. Sullivan, Jackson, transmitted to Lt. Col. John A. Rawlins a telegram from Col. William W. Sanford, Bethel. "A man just from Florence, Ala., reports that Roddey has raised the steamboat Dunbar, sunk by our gunboats last winter, and is trying to fix up her engines; also that Kirby Smith's command crossed the river about there last week, going to reenforce Price. He is vouched for as a Union man and one that is reliable." _O.R._, I, xvii, part 2, 543; _O.R._ (Navy), I, xxiv, 6–7. On the same day, USG telegraphed to Brig. Gen. Grenville M. Dodge, Corinth. "am now sending Reinforcements to you. will it not be Practiciable for you when you get them to drive Roddy to the north bank of the River & destroy his Boats"   Telegram received, Dodge Papers, IaHA; copies, DLC-USG, V, 18, 30; DNA, RG 393, Dept. of the Tenn., Letters Sent. _O.R._, I, xvii, part 2, 543.

On Jan. 9, USG telegraphed to Capt. Alexander M. Pennock, Cairo. "There is no gunboat in Tennessee River above Fort. Henry—there is ten (10) feet water and rising"   Telegram received, DNA, RG 45, Correspondence of David D. Porter, Telegrams Received; copies, _ibid._, RG 393, Dept. of the Tenn., Letters Sent; DLC-USG, V, 18, 30. _O.R._ (Navy), I, xxiv, 7. On the same day, Pennock telegraphed to USG. "Two light draught gunboats have gone up Cumberland as convoy for supplies for Gen Rosecrans—Two have orders to ascend Tennessee with rise—The fifth is disabled and now undergoing repair—I have no others to send—They are only bullet proof." ALS (telegram sent), DNA, RG 107, Telegrams Collected (Unbound); telegram received, _ibid._. _O.R._ (Navy), I, xxiv, 8. Misdated Jan. 6 in _O.R._, I, xvii, part 2, 541; _O.R._ (Navy), I, xxiv, 6. On Jan. 10, USG telegraphed to Pennock. "Col. Lowe, Fort Henry will furnish the required number of Enlisted men from his command to man the guns on board the Gun Boat. you sent up the Tenn. river"   Copies, DLC-USG, V, 18, 30, 98; DNA, RG 393, Dept. of the Tenn., Letters Sent. On the same day, Pennock ordered the gunboats _Alfred Robb_ and _General Pillow_ up the Tennessee River. _O.R._ (Navy), I, xxiv, 8.

On Jan. 10, Dodge twice telegraphed to USG. "I have news from Gunboats up to thursday mornig   they were then at duck River removing the obstructions thought they would all be out in twenty four (24) hours—the rebels guard the east side of the river at all points   have two (2) pieces of artillery at Clifton and 2 at Savannah that arrived there yesterday   I have Hursts cavalry watching this side from Decaturville to EastPort   that cavalry is thoroughly posted in that country & it would be of benefit to service to keep them along the river for present   I understand that they belong to Genl Braymans command"   "I was mistaken about GunBoats in the river   it was transports   there are no Gun Boats but Col Lowe was sent a transport which arrived at Pittsburg today with artillery & infantry to protect her   she brings stores & forage—come through all right   passed Clifton in night"   Telegrams received, DNA, RG 393, Dept. of the Tenn., Telegrams Received. On Jan. 12, Col. William W. Lowe, Fort Henry, telegraphed to USG. "Have sent one transport with stores for Gen Dodges command & just recd word that it arrived safely   Another now here & will go up as soon as I can get it loaded   Our gunboat the Pillow reached here last night but its power is so small it will be a long while getting up   Another is promised" Telegram received, *ibid.*; copy, *ibid.*, Fort Donelson, Telegrams Sent. On Jan. 13, Dodge telegraphed to USG. "I succeeded in destroying two of Roddys ferries across the Tenn today. my cavalry had sharp work & lost from 150 to 200 men" Telegram received, *ibid.*, Dept. of the Tenn., Telegrams Received.

2. See General Orders No. 11, Dec. 17, 1862.

To Brig. Gen. Charles S. Hamilton

Holly Springs Miss Jan 7. 1863.

BRIG GENL C. S. HAMILTON
LA GRANGE TENN.

On further questioning Capt. Metcalf[1] who has charge of shipping captured Cotton, I find that he did not give up the Cotton I telegraphed you about and for the reason that the amount covered by the order was greater than the amount seized   I have settled the difficulty by leaving with Capt. Metcalf an order in favor of Mix & Co.[2] for the amount actually taken, on proof of his paying the parties owning the Cotton and Government charges   Mix is undoubtedly a dangerous man to act on the statements of

Capt. Metcalf is asking for a short leave of absence. You are at liberty to grant it for twenty days or less, to go to any place except Washington

U. S. GRANT
Maj Genl

Copies, DLC-USG, V, 18, 30; DNA, RG 393, Dept. of the Tenn., Letters Sent. Earlier on Jan. 7, 1863, USG had telegraphed to Brig. Gen. Charles S. Hamilton. "Cotton released here by your order proves to be nearly double the amount claimed to have been lost by the parties losing it, and for that little they have received no consideration from the parties taking it   No property seized should be turned over to any but the parties owning it, and then only on proper investigation. The same claims are now coming up again, and will cause annoyance at least." Copies, *ibid*. On the same day, Hamilton telegraphed to USG. "In giving order for cotton I acted on contracts signed by the producers   no lists of the owners terms or amount seized were furnished by Quinby or Mcarthur   Only that seized by my own order is properly accounted for. I [h]ave orders that purchasers should furnish receipts from producers for amounts paid and did not for a moment suppose any cotton would be given up until that was done"   Telegram received, *ibid*., Telegrams Received.

Also on Jan. 7, USG telegraphed to Col. Joseph D. Webster, Jackson. "I have directed the station agent here to ship Cotton from this place in the following order. 1st All the Government Cotton   2nd That which was brought from Oxford, and Abbeville according to its priority of receipt here. 3rd That which has been purchased here in the order of its receipt." Copies, DLC-USG, V, 18, 30; DNA, RG 393, Dept. of the Tenn., Letters Sent. On the same day, Lt. Col. John A. Rawlins wrote to station agent T. W. Jones, Holly Springs. "Verbal instructions in reference to the Shipment of Cotton from here have been given you as follows. 1st All Cotton belonging to the Government   2nd All Cotton that came from Oxford, since the raid on this place, in accordance to its priority of its receipt here. 3rd and last. such as has been purchased and delivered here in the order of its receipt   No attention will be paid to orders for Cars for Shipment of Cotton given by anyone else than the Dept Commander. Men holding's receipts for freight on Cotton to Columbus prior to 20th Dec. will form no exception to this rule. Wherever this order of shipment is violated, the Cotton will be seized for the benifit of Gov't, and the Officer or Agent conniving at such violation, summarily punished. You will acknowledge the receipt of this." Copies, *ibid*.

1. Capt. Lyne S. Metcalf of Ill., appointed asst. q. m. of vols. on April 14, 1862.

2. On Nov. 18, USG had telegraphed to Hamilton. "I have made the order for Mix and Cohen to leave this Department by the 20th inst, on pain of being sent to Alton if found here after that time"   Copies, *ibid*. On Nov. 19, Maj. Gen. James B. McPherson telegraphed to Hamilton. "The charges against Mr Mix are of an indefinate charact[er] but sufficient in Maj Genl. Grants opinion to warrant, sentence him out of the department. in view of the slight regard paid by cotton buyers to regulations & orders." Copy, *ibid*., District of Corinth, Telegrams Received. In 1871, James Mix was awarded $5,318.27 by the U. S. Court of Claims for twenty-four bales of cotton seized at Grand Junction, Tenn. *HED*, 44-1-189, p. 18. See letter from Cairo, Dec. 21, in *New York Herald*, Dec. 26, 1862.

To Elihu B. Washburne

Holly Springs, Mississippi,
Jan. 7th, 1863.

Hon. E. B. Washburn, M.C.,
Washington, D. C.
Dear Sir:

Learning that additional Medical Inspectors, with the rank of Lieut. Col., are to be appointed, I want to urge the appointment of Surgeon J. H. Brinton, who is now on duty in Washington, having been selected as one to compile the Medical History of this rebellion.

I have selected you to write to on this subject because you have always shown such willingness to befriend me. I acknowledge the many obligations I am under to you and thank you from the bottom of my heart for them. I will feel further obligation if you can give this matter your attention and support.

Dr. Brinton has served with me and messed with me. I know him well. He is an honor to his profession and to the service both for his moral worth and attainments in and out of his profession.

Although yet but a young man you will find that Dr. Brinton has won for himself, in Philadelphia where he resides, a reputation attained by but few in the country, of any age, and by none others as young as himself.

I am now feeling great anxiety about Vicksburg. The last news from there was favorable, but I know that Kirby Smith is on his way to reinforce Johnson. My last advices from there were to the 31st. If Banks arrived about that time all is well. If he did not Sherman has had a hard time of it.

I could not reinforce from here in time, and too much territory would be exposed by doing it if I could.

Yours truly,
U. S. Grant.

Personal Memoirs of John H. Brinton (New York, 1914), pp. 355–56.

To Maj. Gen. Henry W. Halleck

Holly Springs Miss
Jany 8th 9 35 P M [*1863*]

MAJ GEN H. W. HALLECK
GEN IN CHIEF.

Scouts just in to Corinth from South & East report Enemy moving East from Jackson & north on Mobile Road—fortifying near Meridian   have been moving Several days   This is not confirmatory of Richmond report—¹Some of Braggs forces are passing South on line of Athens & Nashville road²

U. S. GRANT
Maj Gen'l

Telegram received, DNA, RG 107, Telegrams Collected (Bound); copies, *ibid.*, RG 393, Dept. of the Tenn., Hd. Qrs. Correspondence; DLC-USG, V, 5, 8, 24, 88. *O.R.*, I, xvii, part 2, 544.

1. On Jan. 7, 1863, Maj. Gen. Henry W. Halleck twice telegraphed to USG. "Richmond papers of the 5th and 6th say that Sherman has been defeated and repulsed from Vicksburg. Every possible effort must be made to reenforce him. We cannot communicate with Banks, but he has been urged to lose no time in cooperating. Curtis has been directed to give you all he can spare   Take everything you can dispense with in Tenn. & Miss. We must not fail in this if within human power to accomplish it." ALS (telegram sent), DNA, RG 107, Telegrams Collected (Bound); copies, *ibid.*, RG 108, Telegrams Sent; *ibid.*, RG 393, Dept. of the Tenn., Hd. Qrs. Correspondence; DLC-USG, V, 5, 8, 24, 88. *O.R.*, I, xvii, part 2, 542. "Give us the earliest possible information of affairs at Vicksburg, as movement of troops here depends upon the capture of that place." ALS (telegram sent), DNA, RG 107, Telegrams Collected (Bound); telegram received, *ibid.*, RG 393, Dept. of the Tenn., Telegrams Received. *O.R.*, I, xvii, part 2, 542. Also on Jan. 7, Secretary of War Edwin M. Stanton telegraphed to several gen. officers including USG. "Richmond papers of the 6th say General Rosecrans is in possession of Murfreesboro and the Rebel army has retreated thirty miles and that this opens eastern Tenn. and if General Rosecrans takes possession of it two hundred thousand Rebel troops cannot drive him out." Copy, DNA, RG 107, Telegrams Collected (Bound). *O.R.*, I, xx, part 2, 307. On Jan. 8, 3:00 A.M., USG telegraphed to Halleck. "Will get off re-inforcements to Sherman without delay. I have no reports to confirm statements of the Richmond papers." Telegram received, DNA, RG 107, Telegrams Collected (Bound); *ibid.*, Telegrams Collected (Unbound); copies, *ibid.*, Telegrams Received in Cipher; *ibid.*, RG 393,

Dept. of the Tenn., Hd. Qrs. Correspondence; DLC-USG, V, 5, 8, 24, 88. *O.R.*,
I, xvii, part 2, 544.

On Jan. 7, USG had telegraphed to Maj. Gen. Stephen A. Hurlbut, Memphis.
"Give me the earliest possible information from Vicksburg   it is important for
me to know" Telegram received, DNA, RG 393, District of West Tenn., 4th
Div., Telegrams Received; copies, *ibid.*, Dept. of the Tenn., Letters Sent; DLC-
USG, V, 18, 30. On Jan. 8, Hurlbut telegraphed to USG. "I have no news from
vicksburg   no boat has come to Helena since the minnehaha which left 19th Dec
the first news will be telegraphed" Telegram received, DNA, RG 393, Dept.
of the Tenn., Telegrams Received; copy, *ibid.*, District of Memphis, Letters Sent.
On the same day, George G. Pride, Memphis, telegraphed to USG. "There has
been no news of any kind or boat from South of Helena for six days" Telegram
received, *ibid.*, Dept. of the Tenn., Telegrams Received. On the same day, USG
telegraphed to Hurlbut. "What number of troops have you transportation in
Memphis   I will send at least fifteen thousand (15 000) more down river &
want transportation ready for them   Send word if you can send down river that
reinforcements are going to them" Telegram received, *ibid.*, District of West
Tenn., 4th Div., Telegrams Received; copies, *ibid.*, Dept. of the Tenn., Letters
Sent; DLC-USG, V, 18, 30. USG's telegram as forwarded to Brig. Gen. Willis A.
Gorman is in *O.R.*, I, xvii, part 2, 548. Also on Jan. 8, Hurlbut twice telegraphed
to USG. "I have no transportation here, but if you order, will have it here as soon
as it can be obtained. Will send word down River by first Boat that troops will be
sent. Will hold all Boats arriving" "I have ordered Genl Gorman to send me
all the Boats he can spare from his fleet—He has some (25) twenty five but do
not know how many he requires under his orders—Will hold all Boats that come
down or up" LS and ALS (telegrams sent), DNA, RG 393, District of Memphis,
Letters Sent; telegrams received, *ibid.*, Dept. of the Tenn., Telegrams Received.
On the same day, USG telegraphed to Hurlbut. "Will be in Memfis in few days
remain there till I arrive" Telegram received, *ibid.*, District of West Tenn.,
4th Div., Telegrams Received; copies, *ibid.*, Dept. of the Tenn., Letters Sent;
DLC-USG, V, 18, 30. On the same day, Hurlbut telegraphed to USG. "Shall
remain in Memphis as you have ordered" Telegram received, DNA, RG 393,
Dept. of the Tenn., Telegrams Received. On the same day, USG telegraphed to
Hurlbut. "I have dispatched the Q M in St Louis for transportation—a scout from
south reports that the Enemy have been moving East for several days ~~for~~ over the
Jackson & Meridian road   this looks favorable" Telegram received, *ibid.*, Dis-
trict of West Tenn., 4th Div., Telegrams Received; copies, *ibid.*, Dept. of the
Tenn., Letters Sent; DLC-USG, V, 18, 30.

Also on Jan. 8, USG telegraphed to Col. Robert Allen, St. Louis. "I want at
Memphis soon as possible railroad transport for eleven 000 infantry and 1 000
artillery" Telegram received, DNA, RG 107, Telegrams Collected (Unbound);
copies, *ibid.*, RG 393, Dept. of the Tenn., Letters Sent; DLC-USG, V, 18, 30.
On the same day, USG telegraphed to Col. Thomas J. Haines, St. Louis. "Col
Hawkins is not here   Memphis will be our main Depot." Copies, *ibid.* Also on
Jan. 8, USG telegraphed to Capt. Alexander M. Pennock, Cairo. "Can I have
Gunboats at Memphis to Convoy Reinforcements to vicksburgh. I will want them
by the Eleventh." Telegram received, DNA, RG 45, Correspondence of David
D. Porter, Telegrams Received; *ibid.*, RG 107, Telegrams Collected (Unbound);
copies, *ibid.*, RG 393, Dept. of the Tenn., Letters Sent; DLC-USG, V, 18, 30.
O.R., I, xvii, part 2, 544. On Jan. 9, 1:00 P.M., Pennock telegraphed to USG.

"Will send one Light Draught Gunboat bullet proof. one fourth manned. I can do no more. cant you place under the command of her captain. Soldiers enough to work her guns." ALS (telegram sent), DNA, RG 107, Telegrams Collected (Unbound); telegram received, *ibid.*; *ibid.*, RG 94, War Records Office, Dept. of the Tenn. *O.R.*, I, xvii, part 2, 550.

2. On Jan. 8, Brig. Gen. Grenville M. Dodge, Corinth, telegraphed to USG. "Forrest passed through waynesboro going East yesterday   scout from Meridian says troops have been going East on Jackson road & north on M & O R R for several days that I considerable force is at Okolona & ~~Marietta~~ Marietta that they are throwing up works short distance north of Meridian   their large amount of R R stock at Marion & Meridian is being removed South that streams are all high & most of bridges gone   scout from East says a part of braggs force is coming south near the line Athens & Nashville R R   there is ten feet of water on bars in Tenn river & rising"   Telegram received, DNA, RG 393, Dept. of the Tenn., Telegrams Received.

On Jan. 7, Brig. Gen. James M. Tuttle, Cairo, twice telegraphed to USG. "Murfreesboro advices report the federal victory complete   the entire rebel army is fleeing toward Tullahoma in great disorder   All quiet on the Rappahannock   Will inform you more as soon as papers come in this P M   the monitor foundered" "3 days hard fighting at Murfreesboro   our troops victorious   have taken the town—Enemy in full retreat—our loss 5500 wounded 1000 killed   Enemys loss much larger"   Telegrams received, *ibid.*; (2) ALS (telegrams sent), *ibid.*, RG 107, Telegrams Collected (Unbound).

To Brig. Gen. George W. Cullum

Head Quarters Department of the Tennessee
Holly Springs, Miss., Jan. 8th 1863.

BRIG. GENL. G. W. CULLUM
CHIEF OF STAFF OF ENGINEERS
WASHINGTON D. C.
GENERAL,

I would respectfully request that if deemed practicable authority be granted for the transfers of such enlisted men as are mechanics' and desired to be transferred to the Engineer Regiment of the West, commanded by Col. Bissell by and with the consent of their company and Regimental commanders.

In this manner the Regiment would soon be filled to the maximum number, and would add greatly to the efficiency of the Regiment.

> I am General
> Very Respectfully
> Your Obt: Servt.
> U. S. GRANT
> Maj. Genl.

Copies, DLC-USG, V, 5, 8, 24, 88; DNA, RG 393, Dept. of the Tenn., Hd. Qrs. Correspondence. On Feb. 2, 1863, Col. John C. Kelton endorsed this letter to USG. "Resp: returned to Maj. Genl Grant. Transfers from one Vol. Regts. to another is not approved by the War Department." Copy, *ibid.*, RG 108, Register of Letters Received.

On Feb. 16, Col. Josiah W. Bissell wrote to USG concerning problems in obtaining pay for his engineer regt. ALS, *ibid.*, RG 393, Dept. of the Tenn., Letters Received.

To Maj. Gen. James B. McPherson

Holly Springs Miss Jan 8 1863

BRIG GEN J B McPHERSON
HOLLY SPRINGS MISS

As soon as all public Stores Sick &c are removed from Holly Springs fall back with the troops now occupying the place to the vicinity of La Grange Grand Junction or Davis' Mills[1]

When you arrive there examine the Rail Road to the East, and ascertain the practicability of supplying troops at Pocohontas by rail and trains   If practicable, and you think it advisable, Denver's Division may be moved to that place

The 25th Iowa and 90th Illinoiss now doing Rail Road duty, will be added to Genl Denver's Division, giving him 12 Regiments   By taking two Regiments from the old Brigades, ~~and~~ a new one can be formed

> U. S. GRANT
> Maj Genl

Copies, DLC-USG, V, 18, 30; DNA, RG 393, Dept. of the Tenn., Letters Sent. *O.R.*, I, xvii, part 2, 545. Earlier on Jan. 8, 1863, USG telegraphed to Maj. Gen. James B. McPherson. "Order Denver to move immediately to take Logan's place, Logan to move west and relieve McArthur until Lauman can be pushed to Moscow and La Fayette. A Dispatch from Genl Halleck just received says, that Richmond papers of the 5th say that Sherman has been repulsed, and to re inforce him with all troops possible to spare" Copies, DLC-USG, V, 18, 30; DNA, RG 393, Dept. of the Tenn., Letters Sent. *O.R.*, I, xvii, part 2, 545. See telegram to Maj. Gen. James B. McPherson, Jan. 13, 1863.

1. On Jan. 7, S. W. Wilson, Grand Junction, twice telegraphed to USG. "I start a tran for   at one oclock   if you think proper the sick had better be sent by this train as they are tight box cars   If not I will load freight" "I want to send a train to bring up the water tank & train of wood from Malon & 3 miles south of waterford   are there troops there yet" Telegrams received, DNA, RG 393, Dept. of the Tenn., Telegrams Received. On the same day, USG telegraphed to Wilson. "When will the train be down which is to go for the Water tank" Copies, DLC-USG, V, 18, 30; DNA, RG 393, Dept. of the Tenn., Letters Sent. Also on Jan. 7, USG wrote to McPherson. "The train of cars expected in in a few minutes will go south of Waterford to bring up the Water tank from there   I wish you to instruct the Commanding Officer at Waterford to afford any protection the cars may require, and when all the stores are moved from Waterford to join his Division with his command" Copies, *ibid.*

On Jan. 8, USG sent four telegrams to Wilson. "I want a train to leave here about 11 O'clock, tomorrow if possible to move Head Quarters. Two cars will take the horses and one car the balance. I do not want a special train" "Send all the cars here you can, Send to Jackson if necessary for more trains. I want to take everything from here tomorrow" "Unload all trains both ways at Grand Junction or La Grange and send them here until everything is removed" "What is to prevent the construction train that is now here, taking Cotton &c to Grand Junction?" Copies, *ibid.* Three undated telegrams from Wilson to USG were probably sent on Jan. 8. "I had supposed until this moment that the construction train was loaded with cotton   it can be at once & ready for the next train" "Two trains just left Holly & two trains just left this point for Holly   I will send them more by 12 P M and one for you in mornig" "I cannot get another car or Engine from Jackson   none there   had I better unload the cotton here that comes from Holly today   it will give us more trains   one here now   can unload in an an hour" Telegrams received, *ibid.*, Telegrams Received.

To Brig. Gen. Charles S. Hamilton

Holly Springs Miss Jan 8, 1863

BRIG GENL C S HAMILTON
LA GRANGE TENN

It meets my views for you to go to Memphis   should it be necessary to send reinforcements to Vicksburg you will go in command of them, or Hurlbut will and leave you in command of the remainder of his corps[1]   This I will leave entirely to Hurlbut. I will be in La Grange tomorrow and I think go on to Memphis immediately

U S GRANT
Maj Genl

Telegram, copies, DLC-USG, V, 18, 30; DNA, RG 393, Dept. of the Tenn., Letters Sent. Earlier on Jan. 8, 1863, Brig. Gen. Charles S. Hamilton telegraphed to USG. "smiths Div has moved except the Regt on R R which will be relieved & moved today   I Shall have then no troops here   if Hurlbut Corps now embraces my Comd I have no Command at all   shall be glad of a speedy assignment to duty & do not wish to remain idle"   Telegram received, *ibid.*, Telegrams Received. On the same day, USG twice telegraphed to Hamilton. "Genl Hurlbut has not yet reported for duty with his Army Corps, and cannot for a number of days. In the meantime your command will not be changed   When Hurlbut does arrive you will probably be assigned as indicated in a former dispatch, that is to the command of two Districts or Divisions in the Field"   "Have Quinby and McArthur ready to move to Memphis at once. They must move along the line of the road to protect it and only leave their present places as other troops arrive to take them"   Copies, DLC-USG, V, 18, 30; DNA, RG 393, Dept. of the Tenn., Letters Sent. On the same day, Hamilton again telegraphed to USG. "Will you be here   order for Mcarthur & Quinby is sent   I will go to Memphis in the morning"   Telegram received, *ibid.*, Telegrams Received.

Also on Jan. 8, Brig. Gen. Jeremiah C. Sullivan, Jackson, telegraphed to Lt. Col. John A. Rawlins. "The last orders I have recd place Lagrange in my district   Gen Logan has Assumed Command   should I not be notified"   Telegram received, *ibid.*, RG 94, War Records Office, Dept. of the Tenn. On the same day, USG telegraphed to Sullivan. "Your District will not include LaGrange and Grand Junction during the stay of troops organized into Brigades and Divisions"   Copies, DLC-USG, V, 18, 30; DNA, RG 393, Dept. of the Tenn., Letters Sent.

1. See letter to Maj. Gen. Stephen A. Hurlbut, Dec. 30, 1862. On Jan. 6, 1863, Rawlins issued Special Orders No. 6. "Maj Gen'l S H. Hurlbut is relieved from duty at Memphis Tenn, and will assume command of the 16th Army Corps

Brig Gen'l James C. Veach is hereby assigned to the Command of the District of Memphis, and will immediately proceed to Memphis Tenn and assume command accordingly." Copies, DLC-USG, V, 26, 27; DNA, RG 393, Dept. of the Tenn., Special Orders. *O.R.*, I, xvii, part 2, 542. On Dec. 20, 1862, Brig. Gen. James C. Veatch, Evansville, Ind., had telegraphed to USG. "I am returning Shall I come to you by Columbus & Jackson or by way of Memphis answer to Cairo" Telegrams received (2), DNA, RG 393, Dept. of the Tenn., Telegrams Received. On Jan. 10, 1863, Rawlins issued Special Orders No. 10. "On account of ill health, leave of ~~health~~ absence for twenty days is hereby granted Maj Gen. S. A. Hurlbut, to go beyond the limits of the Dept. with permission to apply to Hd Qrs. of the Army for leave to visit Washington, D. C. Brig Gen. C. S. Hamilton is hereby assigned to the command of the 16th Army Corps Dept of the Tenn. and will relieve Maj Genl. S. A. Hurlbut to enable him to take the benefit of a leave of absence this day granted him." Copies, DLC-USG, V, 26, 27, 98; DNA, RG 393, Dept. of the Tenn., Special Orders. Incomplete in *O.R.*, I, xvii, part 2, 553.

To *William G. Fuller*

Holly Springs Jan 8. 1863.

H. G FULLER
SUPT MIL TEL. CAIRO ILL

Whose order is it that originals of all telegrams passing over Military lines be saved and sent to Washington? An order for the disposal of Military telegrams would come through me from some one authorized to give me orders. Private despatches I care nothing about. You can make your own regulations concerning them, Answer and send me copy of order

U S GRANT
Maj Genl

Telegram, copies, DLC-USG, V, 18, 30; DNA, RG 393, Dept. of the Tenn., Letters Sent. William G. Fuller, born in 1827, whose father died in 1838, served as a seaman in the Mexican War, then became a telegrapher. On the eve of the Civil War, Fuller was superintendent of a telegraph co. based in Cincinnati. On Jan. 8, 1863, Fuller telegraphed to USG three times. "I have the honor to report to you that I have been ordered to take charge of the military Telegraph lines in your Dept. permit me to add that my whole aim & desire is to make the Telegraph as useful to you as possible & trust that I shall be able to give entire satisfaction please address all orders for changes of officers &c to me & I will endeavor to meet your wishes as soon as I can get property & accts straightened up I will endeavor to consult you in person" "I am ordered to have the original copies of all dispatches sent over the mil lines properly filed & forwarded to the Dept at Wash" "The order referred to is Embraced in a letter of instructions originating from Col Anson Stager Gen Supt of mil Tel Washn City" ALS (telegrams sent), *ibid.*, RG 107, Telegrams Collected (Unbound); telegrams received, *ibid.*, RG 393, Dept. of the Tenn., Telegrams Received. On the same day, USG telegraphed to Fuller. "Col Stager has no authority to demand the originals of Military despatches, and cannot have them. I keep a record of all my despatches, and destroy the originals   I appreciate your informing of the order you had received before acting upon it   Inform Col Stager that he transcends his authority when he demands the Military Correspondence taking place in this department" Copies, DLC-USG, V, 18, 30; DNA, RG 393, Dept. of the Tenn., Letters Sent. On Jan. 17, Fuller telegraphed to USG a copy of the orders concerning telegrams. ALS (telegram sent), *ibid.*, RG 107, Telegrams Collected (Unbound); telegram received, *ibid.*, RG 393, Dept. of the Tenn., Telegrams Received.

Also on Jan. 8, Fuller telegraphed to USG. "Latest in the morning papers from Nashville state our loss 3000 killed & missing 7000 wounded   rebel loss more than double   rebels retreating & Rosecrans pursuing near Tullahoma   Col Carter reported to have destroyed large no of railroad bridges east of Knoxville thus cutting off Richmond from the west" Telegram received, *ibid.*; *ibid.*, RG 107, Telegrams Collected (Unbound). On Jan. 9, Fuller telegraphed to USG. "The Cypher clerk at Washington desires me to inform you that the despatch dated 2 30 P M on the 7th was not intended for you   It was sent to you through a mistake" Telegram received, *ibid.*, RG 393, Dept. of the Tenn., Telegrams Received.

To Maj. Gen. Henry W. Halleck

———

Holly Springs Miss.
1. P. M. Jan. 9. 1863.

Maj Gen H W. Halleck,
Gen in Chf

Sherman has returned to Napoleon.[1]

His loss was small. Will send you the particulars as soon learned.

I will start for Memphis immediately[2] and will do everything possible for the capture of Vicksburg.

U. S. Grant.
Maj. Gen. Comd'g

Telegram received, DNA, RG 107, Telegrams Collected (Bound); *ibid.*, Telegrams Collected (Unbound); copy, *ibid.*, Telegrams Received in Cipher. *O.R.*, I, xvii, part 2, 549; *O.R.* (Navy), I, xxiii, 603. On Jan. 9, 1863, 11:00 A.M., Maj. Gen. Henry W. Halleck telegraphed to USG. "Ewing's brigade has been sent by Genl Wright to report to you at Memphis. How many troops has Sherman, and how many more can you send him, and when?" ALS (telegram sent), DNA, RG 107, Telegrams Collected (Bound); telegram received, *ibid.*, RG 393, Dept. of the Tenn., Telegrams Received. *O.R.*, I, xvii, part 2, 550. On the same day, 9:00 P.M., USG, La Grange, telegraphed to Halleck. "Gen'l Sherman has thirty two thousand men less casualties. I can send from twelve to fifteen thousand more I am on my way to Memphis to attend to all wants of the Expedition" Telegram received, DNA, RG 107, Telegrams Collected (Bound); *ibid.*, Telegrams Collected (Unbound); copy, *ibid.*, Telegrams Received in Cipher. *O.R.*, I, xvii, part 2, 550.

On Jan. 12, Lt. Col. John A. Rawlins, Memphis, wrote to Brig. Gen. Hugh Ewing. "You will proceed immediately and without delay with your entire command and the fleet of transports on which it is now embarked to the mouth of White river and report to the commanding officer of the Mississippi expedition against Vicksburg   Should you not find said expedition at that point you will not proceed with your command up white River but report in writing to the Commanding Officer of said Expedition wherever it may be for orders"   Copies, DLC-USG, V, 18, 30, 98; DNA, RG 393, Dept. of the Tenn., Letters Sent. On the same day, Rawlins issued Special Orders No. 12 assigning Ewing's brigade to the 15th Army Corps, Brig. Gen. Morgan L. Smith's div. Copies, DLC-USG, V, 26, 27, 98; DNA, RG 393, Dept. of the Tenn., Special Orders. *O.R.*, I, xvii, part 2, 556. On Jan. 13, USG wrote to Capt. Asher R. Eddy. "You will please furnish transportation to Gen Ewing to carry the troops now aboard of the Silver Moon." Copies, DLC-USG, V, 18, 30, 98; DNA, RG 393, Dept. of the Tenn., Letters Sent.

    1. Napoleon, Ark., about 145 miles by river above Vicksburg.

    2. On Jan. 9, USG telegraphed to Maj. Edwin D. Judd, paymaster. "Remain in Memphis until I get there"   Copies, DLC-USG, V, 18, 30; DNA, RG 393, Dept. of the Tenn., Letters Sent. On the same day, USG telegraphed to Maj. Gen. Stephen A. Hurlbut. "Despatches for me today send to La Grange"   Copies, *ibid.* On the same day, Hurlbut twice telegraphed to USG. "I am detaining all boats here in view of the news. from Gen'l Sherman. Shall I continue to do so" "this despatch reached me at Eleven (11) a m this day—" Telegrams received, *ibid.*, Telegrams Received.

To Act. Rear Admiral David D. Porter

———

Head Quarters, Dept. of the Ten.
Memphis Ten. Jan. 10th 1863

REAR ADMIRAL D. PORTER
COMD.G MISS. FLEET,

SIR:

I send Col. Bissell, of the Eng. Regt. of the West, to report to you for the purpose of surveying the ground and determining the practicability of reopening the Canal across the tongue of land oposite Vicksburg.[1]

Any suggestions from you I would be most happy to receive.

I have not had one word from the expedition which left Helena on the 22d of Dec. officially, since that time and am consequently very much at a loss to know how to proceed. I am however preparing to reinforce Gen. McClernand and can do it to the extent of 20000 men certainly and possibly more.

By the same boat that takes this I am writing to Gen. McClernand and expect to get such reply as will enable me to act more understandingly.

I am Admiral, very respectfully,
your obt. svt.
U. S. GRANT
Maj. Gen.

ALS, MdAN. *O.R.*, I, xvii, part 2, 551–52; *O.R.* (Navy), I, xxiv, 149. On Jan. 14, 1863, Maj. Gen. William T. Sherman endorsed this letter to Act. Rear Admiral David D. Porter. "am much obliged for the perusal of this letter. Full Reports were made to Gen Grant via Columbus, but his Rail Road was cut and he lost his mail. What we need at Vicksburg is a force approaching from the Rear. We have as many men as we can manage afloat. Bissell is an excellent man for the Canal." AES, MdAN.

1. See telegram to Maj. Gen. Henry W. Halleck, Jan. 27, 1863.

To Maj. Gen. John A. McClernand

Head Quarters, Dept. of the Ten.
Memphis Ten. Jan. 10th 1863
Maj. Gen. J. A. McClernand
Comd.g Expedition on Vicksburg,
Gen.

Since Gen. Sherman left here I have been unable to learn anything official from the expedition which you now command.[1]
Your wants and requirements all have to be guessed at. I am
prepared to reinforce you immediately with one Division from
my old command one brigade from Gen. Curtis' and one brigade
coming from Gen. Wright's Dept. I can also further reinforce
you with one more Division from my old command besides sending all other troops that come to me from elswhere.

This expedition must not fail. If there is force enough within
the limits of my controll to secure a certain victory at Vicksburg
they will be sent there. But I want to be advised of what has been
done; what there is to contend against, and an estimate of of
what is required.—I take it for granted that Ordnance stores,
rations &c. will be required for the command now with you in
addition to what they now have and to a full supply for all
reinforcements.

I would like to have a full report immediately for my guidance
as to what is to be done.

Troops are assembling here, and all transports coming into
port or being detained. If you have any not required for the troops
with you release them to come here.[2]

I am Gen. very respectfully
your obt. svt.
U. S. Grant
Maj. Gen. Com

ALS, McClernand Papers, IHi. *O.R.*, I, xvii, part 2, 551. On Jan. 10, 1863, USG
again wrote to Maj. Gen. John A. McClernand. "In sending reinforcements to

you gunboats will be required to convoy them. They cannot be obtained at Cairo. Please request Admiral Porter, if practicable, to detach boats from his fleet for that purpose." ALS, McClernand Papers, IHi. *O.R.*, I, xvii, part 2, 551; *O.R.* (Navy), I, xxiv, 148. On the same day, Lt. Col. John A. Rawlins wrote to Brig. Gen. Clinton B. Fisk. "You will please proceed on the Steamer Ruth with all possible dispatch to Vicksburg, Miss or until you can communicate in person with Maj Gen. John A. McClernand or the officer Commanding the Mississippi Expedition, when you will release said Steamer to return to this place." Copies, DLC-USG, V, 18, 30, 98; DNA, RG 393, Dept. of the Tenn., Letters Sent. On the same day, Fisk wrote to USG. "I am in receipt of your favor of this date—as therein requested I will with all possible haste proceed down the Mississippi, until I meet Genl McClernand or the Commanding Officer of the Mississippi Expedition in person—" ALS, *ibid.*, Letters Received.

On Jan. 14, McClernand, "Post of Arkansas," wrote to USG. "I have the honor to acknowledge the receipt, this moment, of your despatch of the 10th inst., and hasten to say, that in former despatches I informed you of the repulse of the Miss. river Expedition under General Sherman, near Vicksburg; of my assuming command on the fourth inst., at Milliken's bend; of my departure from that place on the same day; of my arrival at the mouth of the White river, and subsequently at Notrib's landing near this place, and of my attack upon and reduction of the Post of Arkansas on the 11th inst. I am left to infer that these dispatches had not reached you on the 10th inst., but doubtless some, if not all of them, have reached you since that date. I have only to add now, in view of your dispatch, that, although I had hoped to be able to push my successes further in this direction, I will immediately return with my command to Napoleon, on the Miss. river, and unless otherwise ordered, after such brief delay as may be necessary, will return from there to Milliken's Bend, or some other point near Vicksburg, where I will await the arrival of the reinforcements mentioned by you, unless sooner joined by them. In compliance with your instructions, I have requested Rear Admiral Porter to send a Gunboat to Memphis to convoy the transports, upon which will be borne the reinforcements, on their way to join me. Genl. Fisk's Brigade, sent by you under orders to join me, was diverted by Genl. Gorman, as I am informed to day, up the White river. If I can get a gunboat, I will immediately send an order for the Brigade to join me at Napoleon, or wheresoever it may find me. I am glad to be informed by you, that you have anticipated the wants of my command by ordering commissary, ordnance and other stores to be sent to it. I may say, however, that before leaving the Miss. river for this place, I had dispatched officers connected with each of those departments for such stores. Having previously communicated my opinion as to the most feasible plan for the reduction of Vicksburg, I will not enlarge upon that subject now. I find that our success here is more extensive than I at first supposed. So soon as the Corps Commanders send in their reports, which will probably be soon, I will forward to you a formal report of our operations in advancing upon and reducing the Post. Herewith you will find an approximate estimate of the strength of my command, based upon the reports of Corps Commanders, which, as the troops are most of the time moving upon the transports, cannot be correct. I will send an accurate statement as soon as it can be obtained. On December 31st 1862 the number of enlisted men was: 27.480, the aggregate 21,753. Deduct from this our loss at Vicksburg and Post of Arkansas, say, about 2000; and there remains an aggregate of about 29.753. . . . P. S. Admiral Porter informs me this very moment that there are two gun boats at Memphis, one of which is ready to convoy the troops down here, when you are ready to send them." ALS, *ibid*. *O.R.*, I, xvii, part 2, 561–62.

    1. On Jan. 3, Maj. Gen. William T. Sherman, Milliken's Bend, La., addressed to Rawlins a lengthy report of his expedition. ADfS (dated Jan. 1), Sherman Papers, InNd; (dated Jan. 3) LS, DNA, RG 94, War Records Office, Union Battle Reports; copy, *ibid*., Generals' Papers and Books, William T. Sherman, Letters Sent. *O.R.*, I, xvii, part 1, 605–10; (incomplete) *O.R.* (Navy), I, xxiii, 606–8. On Jan. 4, Sherman wrote to Rawlins about the plans for an expedition to Arkansas Post. ALS, DNA, RG 94, War Records Office, Union Battle Reports; copy, *ibid*., Generals' Papers and Books, William T. Sherman, Letters Sent. *O.R.*, I, xvii, part 1, 612. Obviously, neither communication had reached USG.

    2. On Jan. 10, Col. Robert Allen, St. Louis, telegraphed to USG. "Some twenty (20) steamboats are idle at Helena. Send for them. This River is almost destitute of Boats—I have ordered all the boats coming up to be turned back, and have sent an Officer express on this service. I hope to have the requisite number of boats, but you must crowd them of necessary—All the boats on the Ohio have been sent to Gen Rosecrans" Telegram received, DNA, RG 107, Telegrams Collected (Unbound). *O.R.*, I, xvii, part 2, 552. On the same day, USG wrote to Capt. Asher R. Eddy, q. m. at Memphis. "All transports now detained carrying less than four hundred troops may be at once released and until further directions no vessel of such small capacity detained." Copies, DLC-USG, V, 18, 30, 98; DNA, RG 393, Dept. of the Tenn., Letters Sent.

To Maj. Gen. Henry W. Halleck

Memphis Tenn.
3.30 P M Jan 11 1863.

MAJ GEN H W HALLECK.
GEN IN CHF

    Genl. McClernand has fallen back to White river and gone on a wild goose chase to the _____ part of Arkansas.[1]

    I am ready to re-inforce, but must await further information before knowing what to do.

U. S. GRANT.
Maj Gen. Comd'g.

Telegram received, DNA, RG 107, Telegrams Collected (Bound); *ibid*., Telegrams Collected (Unbound); copies, *ibid*., Telegrams Received in Cipher; *ibid*., RG 393, Dept. of the Tenn., Hd. Qrs. Correspondence; DLC-USG, V, 5, 8, 24,

88, 98. *O.R.*, I, xvii, part 2, 553; *O.R.* (Navy), I, xxiv, 106. On Jan. 12, 1863,
Maj. Gen. Henry W. Halleck telegraphed to USG. "You are hereby authorised,
to relieve Genl McClernand from command of the Expedition against Vicksburg,
giving it to the next in rank, or taking it yourself." ALS (telegram sent), DNA,
RG 107, Telegrams Collected (Bound); telegram received, *ibid.*, RG 393, Dept.
of the Tenn., Telegrams Received. *O.R.*, I, xvii, part 2, 555. On Jan. 12, Lt. Col.
John A. Rawlins wrote to Maj. Gen. John A. McClernand. "In accordance with
authority from Hd. Qrs. of the Army Washington D. C. you are hereby relieved
from the Command of the Expedition against Vicksburg and will turn over the
same to your next in rank." Copies, DLC-USG, V, 18, 30, 98; DNA, RG 393,
Dept. of the Tenn., Letters Sent. Rawlins noted on this letter, "Not sent." See
following letter.

1. Arkansas Post or Fort Hindman, Ark., about fifty miles upstream from
the mouth of the Arkansas River.

To Maj. Gen. John A. McClernand

Head Quarters, Department of the Tennessee
Memphis, Tenn. Jany 11, 1863.

MAJOR GENL. MCCLERNAND.
COMMDG EXPEDITION ON VICKSBURG.
GENL:

Unless absolutely necessary for the object of your expedition
you will abstain from all moves not connected with it. I do not
approve of your move on the "Post of Arkansas" whilst the other
is in abeyance. It will lead to the loss of men without a result. So
long as Arkansas cannot reinforce the enemy East of the river we
have no present interest in troubling them. It might answer for
some of the purposes you suggest but certainly not as a Military
movement looking to the accomplishment of the one great result,
the capture of Vicksburg.

Unless you are acting under authority not derived from me
keep your command where it can soonest be assembled for the
renewal of the attack on Vicksburg.

Major Genl. Banks has orders from Washington to cooperate
in the reduction of Vicksburg and if not already off that place may

be daily expected. You will therefore keep your forces well in hand at some point on the Mississippi river where you can communicate with Gen. Banks on his arrival. Should you learn before you have an opportunity of communicating with him, that he is making an attack on Vicksburg move at once to his support. Every effort must be directed to the reduction of that place.

From the best information I have; Milliken's Bend[1] is the proper place for you to be, and unless there is some great reason of which I am not advised, you will immediately proceed to that point and await the arrival of reinforcements and Genl. Bank's expedition, keeping me fully advised of your movements.

I am, Genl, Very Respectfully,
Your Ob't. Servant.
U. S. GRANT.
Maj Genl.

Copies, DNA, RG 94, War Records Office, Union Battle Reports; (dated Jan. 12, 1863) *ibid.*, RG 393, Dept. of the Tenn., Letters Sent; DLC-USG, V, 18, 30, 98. Dated Jan. 11 in *O.R.*, I, xvii, part 2, 553–54. USG's comment in his letter to Maj. Gen. John A. McClernand, Jan. 13, that the letter of Jan. 11 had not yet been sent, the absence of a copy of this letter in the McClernand Papers, and McClernand's failure to acknowledge its receipt all strongly suggest that USG decided not to send it. On Jan. 8, McClernand, "Steamer 'Tigress,'" wrote to USG. "When I arrived at the mouth of the Yazoo river, I found that our army, having been repulsed near Vicksburg, was re-embarked, under Gen'l Sherman's order, for conveyance to Milliken's Bend, on the Mississippi River. On the next day, the 4th, while the troops were still on the transports, I assumed command of the land forces of the Miss. River Expedition, and immediately determined, with the co-operation of Admiral Porter, to sail with my whole command for the Post of Arkansas, *via* the mouth of White River, the cut off, and the Arkansas river, for the reduction of that Post. I am now here and will immediately resume my voyage to the appointed destination. The reasons justifying and requiring this movement may be briefly stated as follows: 1st The failure of the Miss. Riv. Expedn. in the object of reducing Vicksburg, and the present impracticability of reducing that place with the forces under my command by a front attack, unsupported by a co-operative movement in the rear of the place. 2d The importance; nay, duty of actively and usefully employing our arms, not only for the purpose of subduing the rebellion, but to secure some compensation for previous expense and loss attending the expedition. 3rd The importance of reducing the Post as a means of freeing the navigation of the Mississippi river in the vicinity of the mouths of White and Arkansas rivers from molestation by the enemy. 4th The importance of making a diversion of the enemy, who are alledged to be marching to certain points in Missouri, and of co-operating with Gen'l Curtis' column in Arkansas. 5th The counteraction of the moral effect of the failure of the attack near Vicksburgh and the re-inspiration of the forces repulsed, by making them the champions of new, important and successful enterprizes. 6th The intense desire of all worthy officers and men to be usefully employed. I will despatch officers on transports from this place, for additional supplies of Quarter Masters, Commissary's, and Ordnance Stores. The same transports will bear all who were wounded near Vicksburg, in our hands, to the Hospitals above. I expect, after completing any operations undertaken in Arkansas, unless otherwise directed, to return with my command to a point on the Miss. river near Vicksburg, and direct my attention to the following objects:—The seizure of Monroe, on the Vicksburgh and Shreveport R. Road, and if possible New Carthage on the Miss. below Vicksburgh, and some point on the Red River. Also to the practicability of isolating Vicksburgh—by opening another channel for the Mississippi. Having been *en route* on their transports since starting from Milliken's Bend, and my taking command, I have been unable to obtain and, consequently am unable to furnish reports of the strength and condition of my forces. I will do this at the earliest practicable moment." LS, DNA, RG 94, War Records Office, Union Battle Reports. *O.R.*, I, xvii, part 2, 546–47.

On Jan. 10, McClernand wrote to USG. "I am landed within three miles of the Post of Arkansas, and am marching Sherman's Corps by a detour upon the enemy's works. Genl. Morgan's Corps will follow with the Artillery as rapidly as possible. A brigade with a section of Artillery is landed on the right bank and is marching across a neck to take a position on the river above the fort commanding the river. The enemy's force is variously estimated at from 7000 to 12.000 men. Genl. Gorman sends word that he is moving with 12 000 men from Helena towards Duvall's Bluff on the white river and Brownsville. More anon!" ADfS, McClernand Papers, IHi; copies, *ibid.*; DNA, RG 393, Dept. of the Tenn., Letters Received; *ibid.*, 13th Army Corps, Letters Sent. *O.R.*, I, xvii, part 2, 552. See letter to Maj. Gen. John A. McClernand, Jan. 13, 1863.

1. Milliken's Bend on the Mississippi River, about fifteen miles above Vicksburg.

To Col. John C. Kelton

Head Quarters, Department of the Tennessee.
Memphis, Tenn. Jany 12th 1863.

COL. J. C. KELTON,
ASST. ADJT. GENL.
WASHINGTON, D. C.
COL:

I have the honor to transmit herewith the report of Major Genl. W. T. Sherman of the operations of the forces under his command before Vicksburg up to and including the 3rd inst. with the following enclosures.

1st   Copies of orders General and Special relating to operations before Vicksburg.

2nd: Report of Brig Genl. G. W. Morgan.

3rd   ”   ”   ”   ”   Fred Steele.

4th   ”   ”   ”   Col. David Stuart.

5th   ”   ”   ”   Genl. A. J. Smith.

6th   Abstract list of casualties and missing.

7th   Letter from Major Gen Sherman of date the 4th inst.

8th   Major Genl. John A. McClernand's order assuming command of the expedition against Vicksburg.

9th. Gen. McClernand's letter of date Jany 8th 1863.

10th. Copy of my letter in answer to Gen. McClernand's of the 8th inst.

> I am, Col. Very Respectfully,
> Your Ob't. Servant.
> U. S. GRANT
> Major Genl.

LS, DNA, RG 94, War Records Office, Union Battle Reports. The report of Maj. Gen. William T. Sherman and the first seven enclosures are in *O.R.*, I, xvii, part 1, 601–53. For the eighth, see *ibid.*, I, xvii, part 2, 534–35. For the last two, see preceding letter.

To Maj. Gen. James B. McPherson

Memphis, Jany 12. 1863.

MAJ GENL. MCPHERSON
LAGRANGE.

Jackson with a large force of Cavalry say 6000,[1] is moving to attack the Rail Road at some point between here and Lagrange. Be prepared for him and hold the Cavalry ready to follow a repulse.

> U. S. GRANT
> Maj Genl.

Operator will furnish the Commdg Officer at each post on the
line of the R. R. with a copy of the above dispatch.

Copies, DLC-USG, V, 98; (dated Jan. 11, 1863) *ibid.*, V, 18, 30; DNA, RG 393,
Dept. of the Tenn., Letters Sent; (addressed to commanding officer, dated Jan. 12)
ibid., 17th Army Corps, Telegrams Received; *ibid.*, RG 107, Telegrams Collected
(Unbound); Brayman Papers, ICHi. On Jan. 12, USG transmitted to Maj. Gen.
James B. McPherson and to other commanding officers a telegram of the same
date from Brig. Gen. Grenville M. Dodge, Corinth, to USG. "Scouts from South
west report a heavy body of Cavy making north towards you   reports say another
rail road raid   I get this report from both pontotoc & Ripley   have sent Scout
to pocahontas"   Telegram received, DNA, RG 393, Dept. of the Tenn., Telegrams Received; copies, *ibid.*, Letters Sent; DLC-USG, V, 18, 30, 98; Brayman
Papers, ICHi. Also on Jan. 12, USG transmitted to McPherson a telegram of the
same date from Brig. Gen. Mason Brayman, Bolivar, to USG. "The Enemy are
reported in this neighborhood   Infantry force here is small but can hold the
fortifications & defend the bridges   Have no cavalry & cannot pursue   I need a
battalion of cavalry very." Telegram received, DNA, RG 393, Dept. of the Tenn.,
Telegrams Received; copies, *ibid.*, Letters Sent; DLC-USG, V, 18, 30, 98.
    Also on Jan. 12, McPherson sent three telegrams to USG. "Your despatch
recd   Have Cautioned the different Div Commanders"   "Copies of dispatches
from Genl Brayman & Genl Dodge recd"   "Will it not be possible to have some
hay & oats sent here   corn we can get plenty of buts Hay & Oats are very much
needed to bring up the Cav & Arty Horses"   Telegrams received, DNA, RG
393, Dept. of the Tenn., Telegrams Received. On Jan. 13, McPherson telegraphed
to USG. "I will send four companies of 4th Ill cavalry now here to Bolivar to
report to Genl Brayman   I have telegraphed him to know what force is reported
near trains & troops are in all right from Holly Springs   Col Griffin after sending
in his trains from near Lamar this morning started for Holly Springs with the it
fifth & seventh cavalry having heard some Rebel cavalry were in the place   no
report has come in from him yet   Hatch is camped East of Logans Division at
Collierville   two at Lafayette   Laumans division at Moscow   Davies here &
at Grand Junction & Davis Mills   do you wish Logans division any further
East"   Telegram received, *ibid.*
    On Jan. 9, Brig. Gen. Charles S. Hamilton, La Grange, wrote to USG. "Lee
had cavalry all over the country yesterday for 20 miles south of railroad, and
reports only about 400 guerrillas under Blythe not far from Hernando. There is
no danger of attack." *O.R.*, I, xvii, part 2, 550. On the same day, Col. Albert L.
Lee, La Fayette, telegraphed to USG. "It seems to be well established from
information my scouting parties bring that Walls Texas Legion is camped a
short distance west of Tallaloosa   their designs do not seem to be offensive—"
Telegram received, DNA, RG 393, Dept. of the Tenn., Telegrams Received.
    Also on Jan. 9, Dodge telegraphed to USG. "I have two men in from Akalono
Left monday night   they say that Van Dorn has gone East leaving only about
three Hundred (300). Cavalry at that place   that he is to connect with Roddy &
Forrest   they also say that a small portion of his Cavalry left Pontatock & went
to Put a battery at some place on Mississippi River to fire into our transports
Roddy has moved down to Centreville with a portion of his Command but I cannot get track of Van Dorn East of the R R   these men met Col Rodgers with the

fourth Miss Cavalry near Pontatac   say they have been up to Oxford   they also say that there reports current at Okolona that Vicksburg had not been taken up to monday night but that there had been fight for five days   I captured a letter from a captain in Forrests command which says that Forrest has been ordered to Mount Pleasant." Telegram received, *ibid.* On Jan. 14, Dodge telegraphed to USG. "A scout who accompanied Kirby Smiths train to forks of road leading to Tuscalossa & Columbus has just came in   reports a large train guarded by cavalry & infantry   artillery horses as were along   he said they were ordered to Columbus but when they got to Forks of road where he left it they had been ordered to go to Tuscaloosa & took that road   all conscripts & military in alabama were being concentraty at Columbus   Smiths troops all went by cars   met no troops between here & there except stragling cavalry"   Telegram received, *ibid.*

On Jan. 12, Lee, Colliersville, telegraphed to USG. "Col Marsh Comdg this post informs me that he has information from you by way of Gen Logan that Jackson is moving on this road in strong force   I was just starting north in obedience to your order   Shall I remain on the line of road or go after Richardson please give me any information you have"   Telegram received, *ibid.* On the same day, Lt. Col. John A. Rawlins telegraphed to Lee. "You will hold your forces on line of road where you now are, ready to move at a moments notice. Evidence accumulates that another raid is intended on our line of Rail Road" Copies, DLC-USG, V, 18, 30, 98 (2); DNA, RG 393, Dept. of the Tenn., Letters Sent. Also on Jan. 12, Rawlins transmitted to Lee a telegram from Brig. Gen. Jeremiah C. Sullivan, Jackson, to USG. "I have driven Richardson across the Hatchie taking a number of prisoners   a regt of cavalry sent towards Somerville can head him off"   Telegram received, *ibid.*, RG 94, War Records Office, Dept. of the Tenn.; copies, *ibid.*, RG 393, Dept. of the Tenn., Letters Sent; DLC-USG, V, 18, 30, 98. *O.R.*, I, xvii, part 2, 555.

1. C.S.A. Brig. Gen. William H. Jackson, ordered to harass USG's withdrawing forces, had about 2,500 men present for duty in his cav. brigade. *Ibid.*, pp. 827, 829.

To Brig. Gen. Willis A. Gorman

Hd Qrs Dept of the Tenn
Memphis Tenn Jany 12, 1863

BRIG GENL GORMAN
COMDG HELENA ARK.
    The following dispatch is just received

St Louis. Jany 11th 1863

    MAJ GENL GRANT.
        Please use the following dispatch at your discretion.
    BRIG GEN W A GORMAN
    HELENA. ARK
        Continue to regard the Vicksburg move of primary importance let all other moves delay if deemed necessary. Send Boats & men for that object but do not weaken Helena so as to endanger the position

SAMUEL R CURTIS
Maj Genl[1]

You will therefore in accordance with the Spirit of the above dispatch please send forward to report to the Comd'g Officer of the Expedition against Vicksburg every available man that can be spared from your command keeping in view the safety Helena. Gen Banks Expedition has been ordered from Washington to co-operate in the reduction of Vicksburg and I have sent orders to the expedition from here to repair to a point on the Miss River where communications can most likely be had with Gen Banks on his arrival

I am Gen Very Respectfully
Yr obt Serv't
U. S. GRANT Maj Genl

Copies, DLC-USG, V, 18, 30, 98; DNA, RG 393, Dept. of the Tenn., Letters Sent. *O.R.*, I, xvii, part 2, 555.
    On Jan. 13, 1863, USG wrote to Brig. Gen. Willis A. Gorman. "You will please send me as soon as practicable all the River transportation you can possibly spare for the transporting of troops now in readiness at this place to Embark to

join the the Vicksburg Expedition" Copies, DLC-USG, V, 18, 30, 98; DNA, RG 393, Dept. of the Tenn., Letters Sent.

1. ALS (telegram sent), *ibid.*, RG 107, Telegrams Collected (Unbound); copies, *ibid.*, RG 393, Dept. of the Mo., Telegrams Sent; Curtis Papers, IaHA. *O.R.*, I, xxii, part 2, 34.

To Maj. Gen. Henry W. Halleck

[*Jan. 13, 1863*]

MAJ. GEN. HALLECK WASHINGTON D. C.
The following dispatch is just received.

U. S. GRANT
Maj. Gen.

Head Quarters, Army of the Mississippi,
Post of Arkansas January 11th, 1863,

MAJ. GENL. U. S. GRANT.
COMMD.G DEPARTMENT OF TENN.

I have the honor to report, that the forces under my command attacked the Post of Arkansas, today, at one o'clock P. M.; and at four and a half o'clock, having stormed the enemy's works, took a large number of prisoners, variously estimated at from 7,000 to 10,000, together with all his stores, animals, and munitions of war.

Rear Admiral David D. Porter, commd.g the Mississippi Squadron, efficiently and brilliantly co-operated in accomplishing this complete success.

Respectfully Yours,
JOHN A. MCCLERNAND
Maj. Genl. Comg.

ALS (telegram sent), DNA, RG 393, Dept. of the Tenn., Letters Sent. USG wrote his message above the letter received from Maj. Gen. John A. McClernand.

LS, *ibid. O.R.*, I, xvii, part 1, *699; O.R.* (Navy), I, xxiv, 114. For reports of
Arkansas Post, see letter to Col. John C. Kelton, Feb. 7, 1863.

To Maj. Gen. John A. McClernand

Head Quarters, Dept. of the Ten.
Memphis Ten. Jan. 13th 1863

Maj. Gen. McClernand,
Comd.g Ex. on Vicksburg
Gen.

On the 11th inst. I wrote to you disapproving of the diversion
of your expedition from the main object but owing to the difficulty of geting a convoy the dispatch has not yet got off   I am
in receipt of yours of same date and have forwarded it to Washington.[1]

I cannot tell positively what is best for you to do but unless
there is some object not visible at this distance your forces should
return to Millikin's Bend or some point convenient for operating
on Vicksburg and where they can cooperate with Banks should
he come up the river. Banks was in New Orleans on the 16th of
December and under orders to push up the river with all possible
dispatch. What difficulties he may have had to encounter below
I do not know but understand that Port Hudson has been made
very strong. Should he get past that place however it is our duty
to be prepared to cooperate.

One Brigade assigned to the Div. of Morgan L. Smith, goes
down to join you at the same time with this. I understand also
that there are still other forces coming down the river with the
same destination, but of this I am not officially informed. I will
still further reinforce with two Divisions from here unless the
next few days prove it to be unnecessary.

The transports in the river available for moving troops is
becoming very limited in consequence of the great number now

with you. You will therefore discharge any not absolutely necessary for your purposes and order them to report here without delay.

> I am Gen. very respectfully
> your obt. svt.
> U. S. Grant
> Maj. Gen. Com

ALS, McClernand Papers, IHi. *O.R.*, I, xvii, part 2, 559. On Jan. 16, 1863, Maj. Gen. John A. McClernand, Arkansas Post, wrote to USG. "Your dispatch of the 16th [*13th*] inst. came to hand at 6 o'clock P. M. this day, and I hasten, at the same moment, to answer it. I take the responsibility of the expedition against Post Arkansas, and had anticipated your approval of the complete and signal success which crowned it, rather than your condemnation. In saying that I could not have effected the reduction of Vicksburg with the limited force under my command after its repulse near that place under General Sherman, I only repeat what was contained in a previous dispatch to you. From the moment you fell back from Oxford and the purpose of a front attack upon the enemy's works near Vicksburg was thus deprived of co-operation, the Mississippi river Expedition was doomed to eventuate in a failure. I had heard nothing of General Banks when I left Milliken's Bend on the 4th inst., and if, as you say, Port Hudson has been made 'very strong,' it will be some time before he will be in a situation to receive the co-operation of the Miss. river Expedition, unless he should prove more successful than the latter. Had I remained idle and inactive at Millikens Bend with the Army under my command until now, I should have felt myself guilty of a great crime. Rather had I accepted the consequences of the imputed guilt of using it profitably and successfully upon my own responsibility. The officer who, in the present strait of the country, will not assume a proper responsibility to save it, is unworthy of public trust. Having successfully accomplished the object of this expedition, I will return to Milliken's Bend, according to my intention, communicated to you in a previous dispatch, unless otherwise ordered by you." ALS, DNA, RG 393, Dept. of the Tenn., Letters Received. *O.R.*, I, xvii, part 2, 567. On the same day, McClernand wrote to President Abraham Lincoln enclosing a copy of this letter to USG and complaining of persecution by a "clique of West-Pointers." ALS, DLC-Robert T. Lincoln. *O.R.*, I, xvii, part 2, 566–67.

Also on Jan. 16, McClernand wrote to Lt. Col. John A. Rawlins reporting an expedition to South Bend, Ark., on Jan. 14 to gather corn. The party was attacked by guerrillas, and McClernand sent a retaliatory party under Col. Warren Stewart to South Bend the next day. Copies, NHi; McClernand Papers, IHi; DNA, RG 393, 13th Army Corps, Letters Sent. *O.R.*, I, xvii, part 1, 700. For Stewart's report, see *ibid.*, pp. 720–21. On Jan. 20, USG forwarded the letter and report to Washington. DNA, RG 94, Register of Letters Received.

1. See preceding telegram.

To Maj. Gen. James B. McPherson

————

Memphis Jany 13. 1863

MAJ GEN MCPHERSON
LAGRANGE TENN

It is my present intention to command the expedition down the river in person. I will take two divisions with me, Logans & McArthurs I think.[1] It will not be necessary for Logan to move however until further orders. I do not know where McClernand is but have sent orders to him to proceed to Milikens Bend and remain there or cooperate with Banks should he be coming up the river   was Holly Springs destroyed, report here says so. ?[2]

U. S. GRANT
Maj Genl

Telegram, copies, DLC-USG, V, 18, 30, 98; DNA, RG 393, Dept. of the Tenn., Letters Sent. *O.R.*, I, xvii, part 2, 557.

On Jan. 13, 1863, USG again telegraphed to Maj. Gen. James B. McPherson. "Have you any Spare horses or mules with your army corps   Gen Dodge being deficient in Cavalry wishes to mount a regiment of Infantry and where he is, is a poor place for picking up stock"   Copies, DLC-USG, V, 18, 30, 98; DNA, RG 393, Dept. of the Tenn., Letters Sent. On the same day, McPherson telegraphed to USG. "We have some spare mules & I will have a thorough overhauling of all the stock here & think I may be able to send Genl Dodge a couple of hundred through a majority of them are rather inefficient animals"   Telegram received, *ibid.*, Telegrams Received. Earlier on Jan. 13, Brig. Gen. Grenville M. Dodge, Corinth, telegraphed to USG. "I have only four hundred 400 effective Cavaly one third of which are mississippians & albamians & at no time can I muster for a march of two hundred while the Enemy have massed their cavaly & move only in bodies of five hundred to a thousand   my Cavalry have fought them nearly every day for two weeks & b̶r̶ bravely too but have been outnumbered & driven every time   I have to b̶e̶ keep infantry out all the time but they never get near enough to fight   if it is possible I wish you would send me a Regiment of Cavaly or order a Regiment of infantry to be mounted   I have lost since forrest crossed the river forty killed wounded & missing   have done about the same damage. and taken some seventy two prisoners including four officers"   Telegram received, *ibid.* On the same day, USG telegraphed to Dodge. "I have no Cavalry that can be spared to send to you   If you can mount a regiment of Infantry you may do so and I think for that purpose the Qr Mr at LaGrange may be able to furnish you at least a portion of the horses"   Copies, DLC-USG, V, 18, 30, 98; DNA, RG 393, Dept. of the Tenn., Letters Sent.

1. On Jan. 12, Lt. Col. John A. Rawlins wrote to Brig. Gen. Charles S.

Hamilton. "You will please direct Brig Gen. McArthur's Division of the 16th Army Corps to hold itself in readiness with its Camp and Garrison Equipage to embark at an early hour on the morning of the 14th inst. on board the Steamers now lying at the Wharf at this place." Copies, *ibid*. On the same day, Rawlins telegraphed to McPherson. "Please relieve Brig Gen Logan's Division in the guarding of the Rail Road by either Denver or Lauman's Divisions as may be most practicable, and order Logan's Division with its Camp and Garrison Equipage to proceed without delay to Memphis, Tenn." Copies, *ibid*. On Jan. 14, USG telegraphed to McPherson. "I find that it will be from ten to fifteen days before the fleet down the river can be got together again ready for a move on Vicksburg. It will therefore be some time before I shall want Logans Division to come in. McClernand reports the capture of the entire garrison at the post of Arkansas with from 7 to 10 thousand prisoners" Copies, *ibid*.

2. On Jan. 13, McPherson telegraphed to USG. "In accordance with instructions received from Colonel Rawlins last night, I sent orders to General Logan to move to Memphis with his entire command as soon as relieved by General Lauman. I have now sent orders for them to remain as they were until further orders from you. Holly Springs was not burned, only a few houses, comparatively, burned; all frame buildings except the Magnolia Hotel, and none of them occupied. I have had cavalry scouts out south and southeast, and they report no movement of enemy. I will endeavor to be prepared for them if they come." *O.R.*, I, xvii, part 2, 558. On the same day, McPherson wrote to USG. "Having just seen in one of the late Memphis papers, rumors to the effect that Holly Springs, was burned by our Troops, and that a large Rebel force followed us, entering the Town shortly after we left; I will simply state the facts in the case, to show that these reports are all untrue. On Friday evening after you left I telegraphed to the Train-Master at Grand Junction to ascertain how many Trains he could send down the next day, and he replied that he would have three in Holly Springs before noon. These I thought sufficient to carry off all the property, and accordingly issued orders for the Ammunition Train and Quartermaster's Trains to start for Lagrange at 7 a. m. Saturday morning escorted by two Regiments of Infty and Maj Bush's battalion, 2d Ills Cav. Learning that numerous threats had been made to burn the Town, I sent word to Co'l Loomis to double the Guards, and exercise increased vigilance, and turned out a part of my escort, and the Company of Regular Cavalry there, as mounted Patrols to drive all soldiers not belonging to the Guard back to their camps, ordered strong camp guards to keep them in, and sent all stray Negroes to the Contraband Camp. I was riding about the Town a great part of the night with Co'l Loomis and succeeded in putting out several fires and preventing any important houses from being burned, except the 'Magnolia Hotel,' though there were a number of small unoccupied, frame structures on the North and East side of Town destroyed. Saturday at 7 a. m. the Wagon Trains started as directed. The patrols were kept up during the day, and no one allowed in Town except on business, and Citizens ordered to stay at Home. At 12 'M,' Gen'l Lauman was directed to strike his Camp, and have his command ready to march at a moments notice. Cotton and property of various kinds had during the forenoon accumulated to such an extent at the Depot, that two more trains, making five in all, would be necessary to remove everything. These I telegraphed for and the answer came back that they would be down before dark. At 3 P. M Gen'l Lauman was directed to send all his Train to the North Side of 'Cold Water,' escorted by two Regiments of Inft'y and park there. When the last

Train arrived, the Pickets were called in and the Column put in motion for 'Cold Water,' just as the Train was loaded and ready to return with every thing on board, except two boxes of Cavalry Equipments, which were accidentally left. I remained until after nine o'clock when all the Troops had left except four hundred of Co'l Grierson's Cavalry, which had orders to Scour the Town and remain until next morning, when they could fall back to their camp, at Cold Water. There were no houses on fire when I left, and Co'l Grierson reports that none were burned during the night. The Command camped at 'Cold Water,' and the next morning was put in motion for Lagrange and Moscow, which points were reached that same evening without accident or molestation. The Troops along the line of the R. Road were instructed to fall back and join their respective commands as soon as all property was removed from Hudsonville and Lamar. Sunday morning after our Cavalry left, about forty of Mitchell's Guerillas came in Town but remained only a short time. Monday Co'l Grierson went in with two Regt's of Cavalry, remained from 9 A. M. until nearly one P. M. scouted the country in every direction, and could see or hear nothing of any enemy." LS, DNA, RG 94, War Records Office, Union Battle Reports. *O.R.*, I, xvii, part 1, 487–88.

On Jan. 10, McPherson had telegraphed to USG. "the property is not all removed from the depot yet & I shall not be able to leave here much before dark but will march the rear guard to cold water tonight   I want to get the command out of town or it will be burned up   several houses were burned last night & today in spite of everything guards & patrols could do"   Telegram received, DNA, RG 393, Dept. of the Tenn., Telegrams Received. On the same day, S. W. Wilson, Grand Junction, telegraphed to USG. "the last train left Holly Spgs at 7 oclock   we have taken 106 cars from there brought up all the cotton from Hudsonville & Lamar"   Telegram received, *ibid.* On Jan. 11, McPherson twice telegraphed to USG, first from Holly Springs, then from La Grange, Tenn. "All the Public property having been removed from Holly Springs I left there last night shortly after Dark, Camped on Cold Water, and left there at 7 oclock this morning—Grierson's Cavalry remained in Holly Springs After the Infantry had left, & I have had no report from him yet." "The head of Genl Lauman's Division Entered Moscow at 6 P. M. and the Advance of the Ammunition & Qr. Masters Trains reached this place at 6.30—I directed the Train Master at Grand Junction yesterday to send a Train to Hudsonville & Lamar Stations to bring away the Cotton &c, and sent Orders to the Troops and guards along the road to fall back, and join their Commands as soon as all the property was removed—No news— Everything worked well to day, and no delay except from the heaviness of the roads—There were no houses burned in Holly Springs that were occupied—and only two or three of any importance, though a good many small frame structures stables &c were destroyed" Telegrams received, *ibid.*, RG 107, Telegrams Collected (Unbound). The second telegram is in *O.R.*, I, xvii, part 2, 554. On Jan. 12, McPherson telegraphed to USG. "Col Grierson is Just in from Holly springs having left there at half past twelve   No Enemy in that vicinity" Telegram received, DNA, RG 393, Dept. of the Tenn., Telegrams Received.

To Maj. Gen. Henry W. Halleck

———

Memphis Tenn
Jany 14 1863

Maj Genl H W Halleck
Genl in Chief

I learn by special messenger sent to the fleet in Arkansas that it will be fifteen days before they can act ifficiently again   I had hoped to get off early next week but will have to defer until all things are ready   I will go down to the fleet in a day or two and by consultation with McClernand Sherman and Porter will have a better understanding of matters than I now have   McClernand is now I believe moving on balls bluff.[1] orders have been sent him to assemble his forces on the mississippi convenient to co-operate with any force that may be coming up the river

U. S. Grant

Telegram received, DNA, RG 107, Telegrams Collected (Unbound); copies, *ibid.*, Telegrams Received in Cipher; *ibid.*, RG 393, Dept. of the Tenn., Hd. Qrs. Correspondence; DLC-USG, V, 5, 8, 24, 88, 98. *O.R.*, I, xvii, part 2, 560; *O.R.* (Navy), I, xxiv, 165–66. The printed sources place the time of sending at 12:30 A.M. On Jan. 14, 1863, Brig. Gen. Jeremiah C. Sullivan telegraphed to Lt. Col. John A. Rawlins. "The line is not working to cairo today   Expect to get working this afternoon   the genls dispatch to Halleck has not gone" Telegram received, DNA, RG 94, War Records Office, Dept. of the Tenn.

1. Devall's Bluff, Ark. See telegram to Maj. Gen. Henry W. Halleck, July 6, 1862.

To Maj. Gen. John A. McClernand

———

Head Quarters, Dept. of the Ten
Memphis Jan. 14th 1863.

Maj. Gen. McClernand
Comd.g Miss. Expedition,
Gen.

By directions from Head Quarters of the Army no more Commissioned officers hereafter taken prisoners of War will be released on their parole.

The confederate authorities having refused to receive at Vicksburg the last prisoners sent to them no more will be sent there for the present.

The prisoners you have got will either be released on parole in Arkansas, taking duplicate roles of them to be forwarded to Washington, or send them here for disposal.

I would reniew directions already given to keep your force in the Mississippi river at the most suitable point for operating on Vicksburg and cooperating with Gen. Banks should he succeed in reaching that place.

> very respectfully
> your obt. svt.
> U. S. GRANT
> Maj. Gen. Com.

ALS, McClernand Papers, IHi. On Jan. 14, 1863, Maj. Gen. John A. McClernand wrote to USG. "I have all the prisoners embarked for Saint Louis, Mo. My reasons for sending them are these—1st. I have received no orders to exchange them 2nd. The Head Quarters of the Commissioner for the Exchange of prisoners are there. 3rd. It would seem to me criminal to send the prisoners to Vicksburg if they may be properly sent elsewhere. To send them would be to reinforce a place with several thousand more prisoners at the moment we are trying to reduce it. I would sail from here to Little Rock and reduce that place but for want of sufficient supply of water in the channel of the Arkansas River. This being the case I will proceed so soon as I have completed the demolition of the enemy's work here to Napoleon by which time I hope to hear from you." Copies, *ibid.*; DNA, RG 393, Dept. of the Tenn., Letters Received; *ibid.*, 13th Army Corps, Letters Sent. *O.R.*, I, xvii, part 2, 561; *ibid.*, II, v, 176.

To Silas Hudson

> Memphis Ten.
> Jan. 14th 1863

DEAR COUSIN,

Your second letter on the subject of appointments on my Staff is just received. The first reached me at Oxford during the late raid and when it was not practicable to get Mails out of the country.

My understanding of the law authorizing the President to organize Army Corps is that when organized the commanding officer is entitled to a certain Staff and has the privelege of nominating them himself. In accordance with this view of the matter I made my recommendations and supposed the commissions would be issued at once. I will write again renewing the recommendations.

Peter[1] need not get any outfit until after he joins me. For his uniform he can send to the Tailor in New York that makes mine or buy here. Everything required can be got in Memphis.

The surrender of Holly Springs was the most disgraceful affair that has occured in this Dept. Col. Murphy had a force of effective and convalescent men of over 2000, and any quantity of cotton bales and brick walls to protect himself. He also had warning the evening before that a large force of rebel Cavalry were moving North to attack the road some where, and again nearly three hours before the attack that they would be upon him at daylight. I am here looking to Vicksburg and intend to go in person. Of this however you need not speak for the present. It is now known that Vicksburg is very strongly garrisoned and the fortifications almost impregnigable. I will see however what can be done with them.

My respects to your family.

Yours Truly
U. S. GRANT

To SILAS A. HUDSON, ESQ.
BURLINGTON IOWA

ALS, CoHi.

1. See letter to Edwin M. Stanton, Nov. 27, 1862.

To Maj. Gen. Henry W. Halleck

Memphis Tenn
Jany 15th 12 30 a m 1863

Maj Gen H W. Halleck
Gen in Chief

I will send McArthur's Division (all I have transports for)
immediately to join the Expedition on Vicksburg. Send Logans
in a few days and hold Quimby ready to embark when called for—
abandon the Rail Road north from Jackson at once and move the
Machine Shop and public Stores from that place here and hold all
the troops from Grand Junction toward the Rail Road to Corinth
in readiness to be placed on the line from here east. I will go
down and take McPherson leaving Hamilton to command &
carry out instructions for those changes in the Old District of
West Tennessee.

U. S. Grant M. G.

Telegram received, DNA, RG 107, Telegrams Collected (Bound); *ibid.*, Telegrams Collected (Unbound); copies, *ibid.*, Telegrams Received in Cipher; *ibid.*,
RG 393, Dept. of the Tenn., Hd. Qrs. Correspondence; DLC-USG, V, 5, 8, 24,
88. *O.R.*, I, xvii, part 2, 564.
    On Jan. 15, 1863, Lt. Col. John A. Rawlins issued Special Orders No. 15
implementing these plans. Copies, DLC-USG, V, 26, 27; DNA, RG 393, Dept.
of the Tenn., Special Orders; *ibid.*, General and Special Orders; (incomplete)
MiU-C. *O.R.*, I, xvii, part 2, 565–66.

To Maj. Gen. James B. McPherson

Memphis Jany 15, 1863

Gen McPherson
LaGrange

Direct Logan to move to Memphis at once. There will be no
necessity for a forced march however as there are not transports
yet to move him,

I have now determined that you shall accompany. me and will

take three Divisions, Logans, Quinbys, and McArthurs,
The order will be sent you where you are,

U. S. Grant
Maj Genl

Telegram, copies, DLC-USG, V, 18, 30, 98; DNA, RG 393, Dept. of the Tenn., Letters Sent. On Jan. 15, 1863, Maj. Gen. James B. McPherson twice telegraphed to USG. "Dispatch recd Will order Logan to move as soon as relieved by Lauman & will Lauman to move immediately" Telegram received, *ibid.*, Telegrams Received. "What disposition shall I make of the 26th Ill Col Loomis whose regt is now here & of the 15th Mich now at Grand Junction Genl Denver has eleven regts or twelve including the 109th which has been disarmed" Telegram received, *ibid.*; copy, *ibid.*, 17th Army Corps, Letters Sent. On the same day, Lt. Col. John A. Rawlins telegraphed to McPherson. "The 15th Michigan has been assigned to Denver's Division in place of the 25th Indiana ordered here. The 26th Illinois will be assigned to duty at LaGrange" Copies, DLC-USG, V, 18, 30; DNA, RG 393, Dept. of the Tenn., Letters Sent.

On Jan. 16, McPherson telegraphed to USG. "I am just in receipt of orders assigning me to the command of a portion of the forces to operate against Vicksburg. I cannot express to you the gratification it gives me, and I shall most assuredly do my utmost to merit your confidence. I shall leave here as soon as Gen'l Logan's Division is on the march probably to morrow, as Gen'l Lauman was ordered last night to move forthwith. The roads however are in a horrible condition, and the movements will necessarily be slow. But as Logan and his whole Division are keen to go, they will move to Memphis as rapidly as circumstances will admit. I intend to send out a Cavalry expedition this morning, to try and break up the Guerillas in north and west of Summerville, as they could be tracked to their place of rendezvous, but the roads are so very bad, and the horses ball up so badly with snow, that they cannot travel, I was forced to abandon it for the present." Copies (2), *ibid.*, 17th Army Corps, Letters Sent. *O.R.*, I, xvii, part 2, 569. On the same day, USG telegraphed to McPherson. "You may come into Memphis and take immediately charge of troops designated to form part of the river Expedition. General Hamilton will command all others in the District of West Tennessee" Copies, DLC-USG, V, 18, 30; DNA, RG 393, Dept. of the Tenn., Letters Sent.

To Maj. Gen. Henry W. Halleck

Memphis Tenn
Jany 17th [*16*] [*18*]63 4.30 P M

Maj Gen H W Halleck.
Genl in Chief

I start immediately to the fleet. My design is to get such information from them as I find impossible to get here   I will

return here in a few days and in the meantime reinforcements
will be forwarded with all dispatch

U S Grant
Maj Genl

Telegram received, DNA, RG 107, Telegrams Collected (Bound); *ibid.*, Tele-
grams Collected (Unbound); copies, *ibid.*, Telegrams Received in Cipher; (dated
Jan. 16, 1863) *ibid.*, RG 393, Dept. of the Tenn., Hd. Qrs. Correspondence;
DLC-USG, V, 5, 8, 24, 88. Dated Jan. 17 in *O.R.*, I, xvii, part 2, 570; *O.R.*
(Navy), I, xxiv, 179.

To Maj. Gen. Samuel R. Curtis

Head Quarters, Dept. of the Ten.
Memphis Ten. Jan. 16th 1863.

Maj. Gen. S. R. Curtis,
Comd.g the Dept. of the Mo.
St. Louis Mo.
Gen.

I was just starting down the river to join the Miss. expedition
when I met some Steamers loaded with prisoners ordered by
Maj. Gen. Sherman to St. Louis. I find no dispatches to myself
and do not know what there may be directed to yourself. As I am
leaving Memphis and can make no orders for the disposal of these
prisoners I hope you will have the kindness to take charge of
them and communicate with the Gen. in Chief as to their final
disposition. You can state that the last prisoners sent to Vicksburg were refused by the Southern Commander there.[1]

I have received instructions from Washington that no more
Commissioned officers are to be paroled. This I presume is in
retaliation for a course pursued by Southern authorities towards
our prisoners.

I am Gen. Very respectfully
your obt. svt.
U. S. Grant
Maj. Gen. Com

P. S. The probable reason the last prisoners were not received at Vicksburg was in consequence of the attack having commenced before their arrival.

I am opposed to sending more troops to Vicksburg just at this time however if I knew they would be received because they would go at once to reinforce the very point we wish to reduce.

U. S. G.

ALS, DNA, RG 94, War Records Office, Dept. of the Mo. *O.R.*, I, xvii, part 2, *566*; *ibid.*, II, v, 180. On Jan. 23, 1863, Maj. Gen. Samuel R. Curtis wrote to USG. "The Prisoners are arriving here, and what to do with them is a difficult question. I have them on Arsenal Island without shelter. I am obliged to put them where a small gaurd will do, for I have sent everything down to help you in the down river matters. I telegraphed General Gorman through you at Memphis on the 11th inst to, 'Continue to regard the Vicksburgh movement of primary importance,' 'let all other moves delay, if deemed necessary, send boats and men for that object, but do not weaken Helena, so as to endanger the position.' Now, I receive orders, extending your Command, over, 'all troops in Arkansas, which may be within reach of his orders, that portion of Arkansas, occupied by such troops will be temporarily attached to the Department of the Tennesse.' You will please inform me, at your earliest convenience, what troops, and what territory, you will assume, as I must arrange my supervision of affairs to your orders. I suppose you will include Helena, in the enlargement of your Command. If Holmes, and Hindman, mass all their forces, this side of the Arkansas river, they may give me trouble, but I hope you will close out Vicksburgh, before they can do much, and return to my Command, all the force necessary to clean out Arkansas." LS, DNA, RG 94, War Records Office, Dept. of the Tenn. *O.R.*, I, xvii, part 2, 578–79; (incomplete) *ibid.*, II, v, 203.

1. On Jan. 7, Brig. Gen. James M. Tuttle, Cairo, telegraphed to USG. "I Sent on 16th Dec on Steamer 900—rebels to Vicksburgh for exchange   by some delay they got behind Sherman—Admiral porter Sent them to Helena   they were sent from there to Memphis & from Memphis back here and arrived this A. M. I have no place to put them. Shall I send them down the river again or shall I send them to St Louis"   LS (telegram sent), DNA, RG 107, Telegrams Collected (Unbound); telegram received, *ibid.*, RG 393, Dept. of the Tenn., Telegrams Received. On the same day, USG telegraphed to Tuttle. "Send the prisoners to St Louis"   Copies, DLC-USG, V, 18, 30; DNA, RG 393, Dept. of the Tenn., Letters Sent. On Jan. 12, Tuttle telegraphed to USG. "I Sent one lot 800 paroled prisoners of war to St Louis   I have now 700 more & no good place to keep them   shall I send them down for exchange or shall I send them to St Louis" ALS (telegram sent), *ibid.*, RG 107, Telegrams Collected (Unbound); telegram received, *ibid.*, RG 393, Dept. of the Tenn., Telegrams Received. On Jan. 15, Tuttle telegraphed to USG. "1000 prisoners from Murphreesboro here enroute for Vicksburgh   shall I allow them to go forward"   ALS (telegram sent), *ibid.*, RG 107, Telegrams Collected (Unbound); telegram received, *ibid.*, RG 393, Dept. of the Tenn., Telegrams Received. On Jan. 17, Lt. Col. John A. Rawlins drafted a reply at the bottom of Tuttle's telegram. "Dispatch just Recd. Send

Prisoners to Benton Barricks St Louis. Cause complete duplicate rolls to be made of them, if it has not been done." ADfS, *ibid.*; telegram received, *ibid.*, RG 107, Telegrams Collected (Unbound).

To Brig. Gen. Willis A. Gorman

Helena Ark. Jany. 17th 1863

BRIG. GEN. W. A. GORMAN
COMDG. DIST. OF EASTERN ARK.
GEN.

I am now just on my way to the mouth of the White river, or to the fleet holding the Mississippi river expedition, wherever it may be and would have been glad to have met you here.

My understanding of orders from Washington to Genl. Curtis and from Gen. Curtis to yourself, is, that all the force that can be spared after leaving Helena secure are to cooperate in the expedition against Vicksburg whenever they may be required. I cannot say now how soon that may be, but I am making all the dispatch possible. The great drawback to contend against is to obtain sufficient transportation. Genl. Rosecranz is retaining about all on the Ohio river to supply his army, and a great share of that on the Mississippi is with the troops on the lower river. I hope you will send me all the help you can in the way of transportation, retaining enoug[h] for such troops as in your judgement, can be detached temporarily when their services are required at Vicksburg.

The tendency of your present expedition is [*n*]o doubt is to releive Helena of the presence of a force threatening her, or that might threaten ~~th~~ when left with a small garrison.

Wishing you every success,
I remain, General
Very Respectfully
Yr. Obt. Servt.
U. S. GRANT,
Maj. Genl.

Copy, DLC-USG, V, 101.

To Maj. Gen. Henry W. Halleck

——————

Napolion Arkansas
Jany 18th [*1863*]

MAJ GEN H W HALLECK
GENL IN CHIEF

McClernands command is at this place   Will move down the River today   Should Banks pass Port Hudson this force will be ready to cooperate on Vicksburg at any time   What may be necessary to reduce the place I do not yet know but since the late rains think our troops must get below the city to be used effectively—

U S GRANT
Maj Genl

Telegram received, DNA, RG 107, Telegrams Collected (Bound); *ibid.*, Telegrams Collected (Unbound); copies, *ibid.*, Telegrams Received in Cipher; *ibid.*, RG 393, Dept. of the Tenn., Hd. Qrs. Correspondence; DLC-USG, V, 5, 8, 24, 88, 101. *O.R.*, I, xvii, part 2, 573. The telegram was transmitted from Memphis, Jan. 20, 1863, 10:30 A.M.

To Maj. Gen. John A. McClernand

——————

Head Quarters, Dept. of the Ten.
Napoleon Ark. Jan. 18th 1863

MAJ. GEN. J. A. MCCLERNAND
COMD.G MISS. RIVER EXPEDITION,
GEN.

Before leaving Memphis I made arrangements for geting such mining tools as will be required for carrying out the plan spoken of this morning, and also for securing a full supply of all kinds of Ammunition for a long siege.[1]

I will see that all other stores are sent as required including fuel for the fleet.

So many boats being now used in this fleet the Quartermaster at St. Louis finds it impossible to furnish transportation required for the number of troops I design sending. ~~that~~ I wish you would, as soon as practicable, detach from here such as can be spared.

Respectfully
your obt. svt.
U. S. GRANT
Maj. Gen Com

ALS, McClernand Papers, IHi. On Jan. 17, 1863, Maj. Gen. John A. McClernand, Napoleon, Ark., wrote to USG. "Since leaving Vicksburg our supply of fuel has been almost entirely dependent on what fence rails and scattering wood we could pick up; in consequence of which the expedition has been much delayed. Since leaving Memphis we have received but four barges containing about forty thousand (40,000) bushels of Coal, and one of these we were obliged to turn over to the Admiral, as he was out. I understand there is a large amount of Coal at Memphis—will you not see that the Quartermaster forwards us as soon as possible, say one hundred thousand (100,000) bushels?" DfS, *ibid.*; copies, *ibid.*; DNA, RG 393, 13th Army Corps, Letters Sent.

On Jan. 18, McClernand wrote to USG. "General Ewing's Brigade has been attached to Genl Shermans Corps in pursuance of your order. This addition gives Genl Sherman's Corps 31 Regiments and, according to his last official returns, 25.042 men to 23 Regiments and 18.000 men in Genl Morgan's Corps. I wish to call your attention to this disparity, not doubting in the absence of any good reason to the contrary, you will at once equalize the strength of the Corps. It would be agreeable to Genl Morgan that Genl Osterhaus' old brigade, consisting of the 3d 12th & 17th Mo and the 4th Ohio Battery; and the 76th Ohio, Colonel Woods, should be transferred to the 2nd Division; commanded by Genl Osterhaus, of Genl Morgans Corps. The same Division was formerly commanded by Genl Morgan himself. Nor would this arrangement be disagreeable to anyone, so far as I know. With this arrangement Genl Sherman would have 27 Regiments to Genl Morgans 27. Neither the supplies of Ordnance, Commissary, and Quartermaster Stores sent for by me, or referred to in your dispatch of the 13th Inst., as ordered by you, having arrived, although sufficient time has elapsed, I have to urge that you will cause such supplies to be forwarded without delay. To be caught without such stores, particularly, *ordnance Stores*, at so remote a point as the vicinity of Vicksburgh, with the river infested by guerillas in the rear, would indeed be a dilemma." LS, *ibid.*, Dept. of the Tenn., Letters Received. *O.R.*, I, xvii, part 2, 574.

Also on Jan. 18, Lt. Col. John A. Rawlins, Napoleon, wrote to McClernand. "You will disembark one wing of your command at Young's Point, and all of it if you think proper, at least one wing will be disembarked at this point." LS, McClernand Papers, IHi.

1. On Jan. 18, 2nd Lt. Stephen C. Lyford, St. Louis, telegraphed to USG. "I have received Order No 15, but do not understand whether you wish me to furnish this supply & ship to Memphis or for Col Duff to act—Please inform me

what you wish—There is not enough ammunition in all my depots to furnish such a supply and if necessary I shall have to get it from the east—Neely informs me that he has enough or will have soon to keep up his quota, that is 7,000,000 to 8,000,000, but this will not be enough to fill your requisitions—" ALS (telegram sent), DNA, RG 107, Telegrams Collected (Unbound); telegram received, *ibid.*; *ibid.*, RG 393, Dept. of the Tenn., Telegrams Received. For Special Orders No. 15, Dept. of the Tenn., Jan. 15, see *O.R.*, I, xvii, part 2, 565–66.

To Maj. Gen. Henry W. Halleck

Head Quarters, Dept. of the Ten.
Memphis Ten. Jan. 20th 1863.

Maj. Gen. H. W. Halleck,
Gen. in Chief, Washington,
Gen.

I returned here last night from a visit to the expedition under Gen. McClernand.

I had a conversation with Admiral Porter, Gen. McClernand and Gen. Sherman. The former and latter, who have had the best oportunity of studying the enemies positions and plans, agree that the work of reducing Vicksburg is one of time and will require a large force at the final struggle. With what troops I have already designated from here no more forces will be required for the present but I will suggest whether it would not be well to know beforehand where they are to come from when required if required atal.

The enemy have the bluffs from Hains' Bluff,[1] on the Yazoo, (this is where the raft across the river is constructed) to the Mississippi and down until they recede from the river completely and thoroughly fortified.

I propose runing a Canal through starting far enough above the old one, commenced last summer, to receive the stream where it impinges against the shore with the greatest velocity. The old canal left the river in an eddy and in a line purpendicular to the stream and also to the crest of the hills oposite with a battery directed against the outlet. This new canal will debouch below the bluffs on the oposite side of the river and give our gunboats a fare chance against any fortifications that may be placed to oppose them.

But for the intolerable rains that we have had and which have filled all the swamps and Bayou so that they cannot dry up again this Winter, a landing might be effected at Milligans Bend and roads constructed through to the Yazoo above the raft, or Hains Bluff, and the enemy's works turned from that point. Once back of the entrenchments on the crest of the bluffs the enemy would be compelled to come out and give us an open field fight or submit to having all his communications cut off and be left to starve out.

I would make no suggestions unasked if you was here to see for yourself, or if I did not know that as much of your time is taken up with each of several other Departments as with this. As however I controll only the troops in a limited Department, and can only draw reinforcements from elswhere by making application through Washington, and as a demonstration made upon any part of the old District of West Tennessee might force me to withdraw a large part of the force from the vicinity of Vicksburg, I would respectfully ask if it would not be policy to combine the four Departments in the West under one commander. As I am the senior Department commander in the West I will state that I have no desire whatever for such combined command but would prefer the command I now have to any other that can be given.[2]

I regard it as my duty to state, that I found there was not sufficient confidance felt in Gen. McClernand as a commander, either by the Army or Navy, to insure him success. Of course all would cooperate to the best of their ability but still with a distrust.

This is a matter I made no enquiries about but it was forced upon me. As it is my intention to command in person, unless otherwise directed, there is no special necessity of mentioning this matter, but I want you to know that others besides myself agree in the necessity of the course I had already determined upon pursuing. Admiral Porter told me that he had written freely to the Sec. of the Navy on this subject, with the request that what he said might be shown to the Sec. of War.[3]

Gen. Gorman had gone up the White river with most of his forces taking a greatdeel of the river transportation with him. I find great difficulty in geting boats to transport the troops. With the orders I gave however to release boats as fast as they can be dispensed with I hope to remedy all difficulties of this kind

Very respectfully

U. S. GRANT

Maj. Gen. Com

ALS, DNA, RG 94, War Records Office, Union Battle Reports. *O.R.*, I, xxiv, part 1, 8–9. On Jan. 20, 1863, 11 :30 A.M., USG telegraphed to Maj. Gen. Henry W. Halleck. "I found the Mississippi Expedition at mouth of Arkansas and started them immediately to Youngs Point   A canal will be at once surveyed and cut The weather is highly unfavorable for operations and Streams all very high and rising   The work of reducing Vicksburg will take time and men but can be accomplished   Gorman has gone up the White River with a great part of his force   So many Transports being kept there makes it most impossible to get transportation for troops—Both banks of the Mississippi should be under one Commander at least during present operations—" Telegram received, DNA, RG 107, Telegrams Collected (Bound) ; *ibid.*, Telegrams Collected (Unbound) ; copies, *ibid.*, Telegrams Received in Cipher; *ibid.*, RG 393, Dept. of the Tenn., Hd. Qrs. Correspondence; DLC-USG, V, 5, 8, 24, 88. *O.R.*, I, xxiv, part 1, 9. See letter to Brig. Gen. Willis A. Gorman, Jan. 22, 1863.

1. Haynes' Bluff on the Yazoo River, about twenty-three miles upriver from the junction with the Mississippi River. References to Haynes' Bluff in U.S. correspondence frequently indicated the main C.S.A. fortifications three miles below at Snyder's Bluff. Bruce Catton, *Grant Moves South* (Boston and Toronto, 1960), p. 527.

2. James Harrison Wilson, *Under the Old Flag* (New York and London, 1912), I, 148–49, claims to have suggested and drafted this paragraph for USG. On Jan. 20, Wilson wrote to Capt. Adam Badeau. "Just after my arrival here I was requested by General Grant to accompany him to the army acting down the river. Colonels Rawlins and Logan accompanied; during the trip we discussed everything, and I am happy to say General Grant approved of my system of army organization and adopted without qualification my view of the necessity of a united command in the Mississippi Valley, and what's more as soon as we returned here, he wrote an earnest letter to General Halleck earnestly urging a united command west, under some competent general—and the necessity of making everything tend towards the grand object. He declined accepting the supreme control and urged that he be left to the command of his present Department. Read me his entire letter, asked for any other points that might occur to me and readily adopted the suggestions made." Typescript, Bender Collection, Wy-ar.

3. While this letter has not been found, Act. Rear Admiral David D. Porter did present an unfavorable view of Maj. Gen. John A. McClernand in a letter of Jan. 16 to Asst. Secretary of the Navy Gustavus V. Fox. Robert Means Thompson and Richard Wainwright, eds., *Confidential Correspondence of Gustavus V. Fox* (New York, 1918–19), II, 153–56. See *O.R.* (Navy), I, xxiii, 602.

To Brig. Gen. Charles S. Hamilton

Memphis Tenn Jan 20th 1863

BRIG GEN C S HAMILTON
COM'DG DIST WEST TENN

Complaints have come in from Somerville from the few Union men of the outragious conduct of the 7th Kansas and in one case of Col Lee's conduct where he was informed of the status of the party

This was the case of Mr Rivers[1] who called on Lee to try and get him restrain his men and was replied by being made to dismount and give up the animal he was riding. If there are further complaints well substantiated, I wish you to arrest Col Lee and have him tried for incompetency and his Regiment dismounted and disarmed. The conduct of this Regiment at New Albany in their pursuit of Van Doren stopping to plunder the citizens instead of pursuing the enemy when they were so near them and again after Richardson about the 8th of this month they passed near where they knew or at least were informed he was and went on to the town for the purpose of plunder

All the laurels won by the Regiment and their Commander on the pursuit of the enemy from Holly Springs to Coffeeville has been more than counterbalanced by their bad conduct since. Their present course may serve to frighten women and children and helpless old men but will never drive out an armed enemy

U S GRANT
Maj Gen

Copies, DLC-USG, V, 18, 30; DNA, RG 393, Dept. of the Tenn., Letters Sent. *O.R.*, I, xvii, part 2, 575. See letter to Maj. Gen. Henry W. Halleck, March 24, 1863.

On Jan. 8, 1863, Brig. Gen. Mason Brayman, Bolivar, wrote to Lt. Col. John A. Rawlins. "Please afford Hon. *Thos. Rivers, W. A. Williamson* and *Thomas J. Roach*, Esqs. a personal interview with Major Genl. *Grant*, if agreeable to him. Mr. Rivers was member of Congress from this District, and is recognized as one of the most upright and honorable men of Western Tennessee. He has been throughout these troubes a bold, consistent and loyal union man—having the confidence of our friends, and the object of persecution from the Enemy. The other gentlemen are also worthy of confidence. They reside in Somerville, Fayette County. They visit Genl. Grant t̶o̶ in behalf of their fellow-citizens to represent their grievances during the unfortunate and disastrous visit of the 7th Kansas Cavalry to Somerville on Saturday last. I think it due to the honor of the army, to the cause of Justice, and the claims of humanity, that Genl. Grant be fully and correctly advised." ALS, DNA, RG 109, Union Provost Marshals' File of Papers Relating to Individual Citizens. On Jan. 9, John H. Bills, Bolivar, wrote to USG. "This is intended to introduce to your friendly regard the bearer Genl. Tho Rivers of Fayette County T. Genl Rivers visits you for redress of grievances, suffered by the people of Sommerville from a late visit by a portion of the Federal Cavalry—the high social position he occupies in our society, & his constant Union proclivities intitle his representations to the fullest confidence & respect. Your kind attention to him & his associates will but add another to many kindnesses I have had at your hands." ALS, *ibid.* For the incident at Somerville, see Stephen Z. Starr, *Jennison's Jayhawkers: A Civil War Cavalry Regiment and its Commander* (Baton Rouge, La., 1973), pp. 230–34.

On Jan. 7, Brig. Gen. Charles S. Hamilton, La Grange, telegraphed to USG. "8th Wis. going to Corinth   Maj J W Jefferson ought to be relieved from the Military Commission   I recommend 2 Lt. G W Cutler Adjt 1st Mo. Arty for his successor   Col Ruger 3d Wis nominated for Brig.   I wish you would apply for him   he is one of best men in the army   a mutiny on 7 Kansas & an officer shot   will need a Genl Court Martial   Charges will be in today" Telegram received, DNA, RG 393, Dept. of the Tenn., Telegrams Received. On the same day, Rawlins telegraphed to Hamilton. "2nd Lieut G. W Cutler Adg't First Missouri Arty is hereby detailed on the Military Commission now in session at La Grange Tenn in the place of Major J W Jefferson 8th Wisconsin Vols.   Major J W Jefferson 8th Wisconsin Vols is relieved from duty on the Military Commission now in session at La Grange Tenn. and will report in person and without delay to these Head Quarters   His Regiment will march to Corinth, under command of the senior Captain   Send in names for Court Martial in the case of 7th Kansas Cavalry." Copies, DLC-USG, V, 18, 30; DNA, RG 393, Dept. of the Tenn., Letters Sent. Also on Jan. 7, Rawlins telegraphed to Col. William S. Hillyer, Memphis. "Please see Lieut Sperlock and find out the substance of statements of the Major of the 8th Wisconsin Vols. in the Guyosa House at Memphis, against Gen Grant, and also the names of persons who heard it, and send by telegraph at once" Copies, *ibid.* On the same day, Hamilton telegraphed to USG. "Order reliving Maj Jefferson 8 Wis recd   the Reg is under comd. of Leut Col Robbins & therefore will not agree to be turned over to the Capt" Telegram received, *ibid.*, Miscellaneous Letters Received.

1. Thomas Rivers, born in Franklin County, Tenn., in 1819, a lawyer and a brig. gen. in the state militia, was elected by the American Party to serve as U.S. Representative 1855–57.

To Lt. Col. Charles A. Reynolds

———

Head Quarters, Dept. of the Ten.
Memphis Ten. Jany 21st 1863.

LIEUT. COL. C. A. REYNOLDS
CHIEF Q. M.
COL.

Whilst with the fleet Gen. Sherman's Q. M. reported to me that there was on hand with the expedition—about one thousand extra mules.

With this stock below and the number of teams to be left behind by troops yet to be forwarded, and again the great surplus of transportation reported at Helena, I think Gen. Allen should be advised to ship no more mules here.[1] In fact if they are required for any other Dept. Chartered boats going up the river empty might take mules and save the purchase above.

Respectfully &c.
U. S. GRANT
Maj. Gen. Com

ALS, OClWHi.

On Jan. 21, 1863, USG again wrote to Lt. Col. Charles A. Reynolds. "You will please make arrangements to keep the steamer 'Post Boy' permanently for the use of the Medical Department   She is now so employed, but either a standing Charter should be made or the boat purchased. The latter I think preferable on the score of economy"   Copies, DLC-USG, V, 18, 30; DNA, RG 393, Dept. of the Tenn., Letters Sent.

On Jan. 22, USG wrote to Reynolds. "I would suggest the propriety of releasing three steamers to form a regular daily Mail liner between this and Cairo. . . . and carry the United States Mails, and any Government freight or troops offering, to the exclusion of every thing else. . . ." American Art Association, March 12, 1920. On Jan. 25, USG wrote to Reynolds ordering the release of the steamboat *Tycoon* "as no boats will be required here under five or six days to transport troops. . . ." Anderson Auction Co., May 15, 1908, p. 14. On Jan. 31, USG wrote to Reynolds. "If the services of the Jeanie Deans is not absolutely required, you may release her. . . ." *Ibid.* On Feb. 13, USG wrote to Reynolds. "I am sending boats up from here to bring down the remainder of McPherson's command. . . . I will want soon not only all the boats that have been here but many more. . . ." *Ibid.* On March 23, USG wrote to Reynolds ordering him to give five bales of cotton to an agent of the Wis. Sanitary Commission "to aid them in the manufacture of 'quilts' for sick soldiers. . . ." *Ibid.*

1. On Jan. 13, Col. Thomas J. Haines, St. Louis, had telegraphed to USG. "I desire to send beef cattle down the river   Col Allen wishes to send mules to memphis   shall we send both or must the mules give way to the cattle or the reverse   Cattle are much needed below memphis & but little transportation can be procured from here"   Telegram received, DNA, RG 393, Dept. of the Tenn., Telegrams Received.

To Maj. Gen. John A. McClernand

Head Quarters, Dept. of the Tenn.
Memphis Ten. Jan. 22d 1863.

Maj. Gen. J. A. McClernand
Comd.g 13th Army Corps.

In view of future operations I would suggest that stringent orders be made looking to the saving of all ~~gunny~~ sacks emptied by the Army and placing them in the charge of an Engineer officer.

When it comes to erecting batteries these sacks will come in play most conveniently.

I am doing all I can to get forward a proper supply of Ammunition and Mining tools. I presume several thousand spades and picks will reach you in a few days.

By orders which will accompany this you will see that the troops under Gen. Gorman have been added to your Army Corps.[1] I do not think it desirable that they should be moved from their present position, or from Helena, until near the time when their services may be required.

I have here two more Divisions ready to move when they get transportation. But as I am expecting siege guns to forward, and there are many other supplies not yet arrived, there is no great hurry about starting them. I hope the work of changing the channel of the Mississippi is begun, or preparations at least being made to begin.

On the present rise it is barely possible that the Yazoo pass[2] might be turned to good account in aiding our enterprize, particularly if Banks should be fortunate enough to get above Port Hudson. Do you hear from Banks?

Respectfully &c.

U. S. GRANT

Maj. Gen. Com

ALS, McClernand Papers, IHi. *O.R.*, I, xxiv, part 3, 6. On Jan. 22, 1863, Maj. Gen. John A. McClernand, Young's Point, La., wrote to USG. "I arrived here safely yesterday, at 2 o'clock P. M. with all my transports and my command. Before nightfall I reconoitered the country within three quarters of a mile of the canal, and by nine o'clock this morning quite to and beyond it. The water of the Mississippi River, which is rising rapidly, is in the upper end of the canal and must run through in a few hours, if the rise continues. Further reconnoisances have been made to day along the river bank some two miles below the canal. The line of the canal is now occupied by forces deemed sufficient to hold it. It is believed that by tomorrow night all my forces will have gained positions at the same time defensible and commanding. Copies of the 'Vicksburgh Whig' dated yesterday and to day have been captured. I learn from them that Genl Banks is fortifying at Baton Rouge. A rebel force of three thousand is said to be encamped at Delhi on the Vicksburgh and Shreveport R.R. some forty miles from this place. The report is doubtless well founded. Another rebel force estimated at six thousand is said to be encamped on the Mississippi river some eighty miles below Vicksburgh. Prisoners captured report that the enemy is concentrating a large force at Vicksburgh from all points including Richmond, Va., and that he is determined to make a desperate stand there. I will immediately commence enlarging the present, or cutting a new canal, for the purpose of diverting the channel of the river, as circumstances transpiring within a few hours, may suggest. Additional implements, however, will be required to enable me to work effectively in diverting the channel of the stream. The transports which are now being unloaded will be returned at the earliest possible moment, except such as the public service may require to remain here. None of the Quartermaster Commissary or ordnance stores expected, have arrived, nor any of the reinforcements promised by you, when you were at Napoleon." LS, DNA, RG 393, Dept. of the Tenn., Letters Received. *O.R.*, I, xxiv, part 3, 7. On Jan. 23, McClernand wrote to USG. "I add this as a supplement to my letter of yesterdays date   By to-morrow evening I expect to be able to command the Mississi river a few miles below Vicksburgh, with a Battery of twenty pounder Parrotts which I intend to plant upon the bank"   ALS, DNA, RG 393, Dept. of the Tenn., Letters Received. *O.R.*, I, xxiv, part 3, 8.

Also on Jan. 23, USG wrote to McClernand. "The Quartermasters Dept. here complain that barges sent to the Mississippi Expedition are not returned and consequently they are retarded in sending Coal and forage. Please direct the Q. M. in charge of this branch of business to have all empty barges sent back as rapidly as possible." ALS, McClernand Papers, IHi. On Jan. 24, McClernand wrote to USG. "I write to report the progress made since the date of my last despatch. The desired Quartermaster and Ordnance stores arrived yesterday. Also General McArthur's division. I will order back to Memphis all the transports that can be safely spared to bring down the remaining reinforcements. My order will also include instructions to General Gorman to send back as many steamboats as he can spare for the same purpose. Great prudence needs to be exercised in detaching transports from this fleet to return to Memphis, as the Mississippi river is rising, rapidly, and may deluge our troops at any time. You will at once percieve the great importance of this caution, as it involves the very existence of the army here. The waters of the Mississippi are now running through the canal a foot deep. I will see in a short time what effect this diversion will have upon the main channel. Yesterday evening, in company with General David Stuart and some of my staff officers, I reconnoitered the West shore of the Mississippi several miles below Vicksburg. The river is quite wide in that vicinity. We made a critical examination of the bluffs on the opposite shore. We saw a number of ~~batteries~~ earth works, but came to the conclusion that, with one or two exceptions, guns had not been mounted on them. Two rebel transports of a small and inferior character were all that were seen on the river. These I hope to intercept or sink by some Parrot guns which I am establishing on the bank of the river below the city. The promised supply of coal has not yet arrived. One of the best officers in the United States service fell yesterday by a random shot from a detachment of the enemy near New Carthage below here on the Mississippi. I allude to Colonal Warren Stewart, whose death all who were acquainted with him must ~~piequantly mourn and~~ deeply deplore   A considerable portion of the forces at Vicksburg are represented to be Virginia troops who participated in the late engagements at Harper's Ferry and other points on the Potomac   Before closing this despatch I wish to say that the transports ordered back to Memphis should be returned here at the earliest possible moment, if the Mississippi river continues to rise." Copy, DNA, RG 393, Dept. of the Tenn., Unregistered Letters Received.

On Jan. 26, McClernand wrote to USG. "I have only to add to my despatch of the 24th inst. that the Mississippi River is still rising.—that three crevasses occur within twenty miles of the lower end of the canal, and that the country for some twelve miles above New Carthage is being rapidly overflown. The first of this series of crevasses occurs about three miles below the canal, and about one mile below my left wing,—the second four miles below the first,—and the third ten miles below the second. Two others occur in front of my right wing, and demand the indefatigable labor of details, with the few implements I have, to mend them. Thus the implements are needed, not only for the purpose of cutting the canal, but to avert the necessity of leaving here until sheer necessity may compel it—With the threatened danger of a flood before me, I am confirmed in my determination to retain enough transports here to move my command if forced to that dire necessity.—The water flows three feet deep in the canal, but gives no evidence of diverting the channel of the river. I have ordered all the men I can employ, with the limited number of implements available, to make a lateral cut from the main trunk, terminating higher up the river. These men worked all last night and today.—I am doubtful that even this change will prove successful, but as it will cost but comparatively little time and labor, I thought I would try it. I am causing such examinations and surveys as present necessities, and flooded sloughs, bayous, and marshes, will permit, contingently, with the view of cutting a canal higher up the river. I compassed the front of my right wing to-day, passing from the river to the rail-road, and found three flat cars and twenty-eight trucks on the track.—The crast on the west bank of the river for twenty miles below Vicksburg, as well as on both banks above to Memphis, has been abandoned by almost all proprietors, who have retired from this vicinity with their negroes and moveables to Monroe. In many cases they have left foreigners, chiefly Irishmen, behind to take care of their houses.—Having received no confirmation of a report two days old that Genl. Banks had taken Port Hudson, I am not authorized to accept it as true. Since the disembarkation of the troops on the Yazoo bottom, near Haynes Bluff, sickness has prevailed among them to an alarming extent. If the new troops here could be replaced by older ones, it would be better in all respects. The weather continues rainy. It has rained more or less every day for several days in succession. The rain has been occasionally accompanied by winds, chiefly from the South." LS, *ibid.*, RG 94, War Records Office, Dept. of the Tenn.; copies, McClernand Papers, IHi. *O.R.*, I, xxiv, part 3, 12–13.

1. See following letter.
2. Yazoo Pass in Miss. on the Mississippi River about eight miles below Helena, Ark., led through Moon Lake to the Coldwater River, the Tallahatchie River, and the Yazoo River.

To Brig. Gen. Willis A. Gorman

———

Memphis Tenn Jan 22 1863

BRIG GENL W. A. GORMAN
COMMD.G DISTRICT OF HELENA
The following despatch is just received.

Washington D. C. Jan 21 1863

MAJ GENL GRANT.

By direction of the President Maj Genl Grant will assume command of all troops in Arkansas which may be in reach of his orders. the portion of Arkansas occupied by such troops will be temporarily attached to the Department of the Tennessee

Signed   H W HALLECK
Genl in chief[1]

In conformity with the above I have attached your command to the 13th Army Corps Maj Genl McClernand commanding. I will have you furnished soon with all such past Orders as are necessary for your guidance

I wish you to return to Helena with your command as soon as possible and discharge all the steamers that can be possibly

spared   do not understand this as an order to abandon any enterprise for breaking up the enemy, in his strong holds if you are
near the accomplishment of such a result

The Mississippi River enterprise must take preecedence over
all others and any side move made must simply be to protect our
flank and rear   so long however as the enemy have Steamers in
the White and Arkansas rivers it is necessary for the safe navigation of the Mississippi to the Vicksburg to break up all their
forces on those two Rivers and if possible get possession of their
boats.

I will be going down the river in a few days when I hope to
meet you at Helena

U. S. GRANT,
Maj. Genl.

Copies, DLC-USG, V, 18, 30; DNA, RG 393, Dept. of the Tenn., Letters Sent.
O.R., I, xxiv, part 3, 5–6. On Jan. 22, 1863, Lt. Col. John A. Rawlins issued
Special Orders No. 22 assigning the command of Brig. Gen. Willis A. Gorman
to the 13th Army Corps. Copies, DLC-USG, V, 26, 27; DNA, RG 393, Dept. of
the Tenn., Special Orders. *O.R.*, I, xxiv, part 3, 7; *ibid.*, I, xxii, part 2, 68. On
Jan. 24, Gorman wrote to USG reporting his White River expedition. *Ibid.*, I,
xvii, part 2, 579. This may be the report enclosed in a letter of Jan. 25 from Maj.
Gen. John A. McClernand addressed to USG and Secretary of War Edwin M.
Stanton. "I have the honor to enclose herewith a copy of Brig Genl W. A. Gorman's Report of his Expedition up White River. The retirement of the enemy
south of the Arkansas river was anticipated as a sequence of the reduction of Post
Arkansas. Since the date of Genl Gorman's letter, he has returned to Helena as
I am informed. The order for Gen Fisk to join me, was predicated upon your
order as reported to me by Genl Fisk"   DfS, McClernand Papers, IHi; copies,
ibid.; DNA, RG 393, 13th Army Corps, Letters Sent. On Jan. 29, Gorman wrote
to Maj. Gen. Samuel R. Curtis to ask whether he should send reports to Curtis
as well as to USG. ALS, *ibid.*, Dept. of the Tenn., Letters Received. On Feb. 4,
Curtis endorsed this letter to USG. "Respectfully referred to Maj Genl. Grant
Commanding Department of the Tennesse"   ES, *ibid.*

1. ALS (telegram sent), *ibid.*, RG 107, Telegrams Collected (Bound); telegram received, *ibid.*, RG 94, War Records Office, Military Div. of the Miss.
O.R., I, xxii, part 2, 65. For the incorporation of these instructions in a letter,
see General Orders No. 11, Dec. 17, 1862.

To Brig. Gen. Charles S. Hamilton

Memphis Tenn Jan 22 1863.

BRIG GENL C. S. HAMILTON
COMMD.G DISTRICT OF WEST TENN

Have moved from the east bank of the river from this place to Columbus all large guns still remaining and also the guns from Island No 10 and from the floating battery below there   these guns or such of them that can be used may be brought to Memphis the remainder sent to Cairo

It will be necessary to keep up a small garrison at New Madrid Island No 10 Hickman and possibly at Fort Pillow   This latter however should be inspected before establishing a garrison[1]

as soon as practicable relieve the 15th Regular Infantry from Columbus and bring them to this place preparatory to being sent down the river   The same with the 1st Infantry at Corinth There are three companies of Cavalry belonging to Cornyns Missouri Regt[2] at Columbus and three companies here   I wish them to be collected at Memphis as soon as possible   The other six companies of this Regiment are at Helena and will be ordered here immediately

As soon as it can be possibly done send a Regt of Cavalry to Corinth   One of the new Regtmints to arrive can be put in charge of the heavy guns in the fort and drilled by some Artillery Officer of experience   same at Corinth   all the rolling stock of the Rail Road should be got away from Columbus as soon as possible

U. S. GRANT.
Maj Genl

Copies, DLC-USG, V, 18, 30; DNA, RG 393, Dept. of the Tenn., Letters Sent. *O.R.*, I, xxiv, part 3, 6.

1. On Jan. 25, 1863, Brig. Gen. Charles S. Hamilton, Columbus, Ky., telegraphed to USG. "No heavy guns at Fort Pillow   floating battry is under water guns cannot be got out. plenty of spiked guns on Island 10. carriages not burned liaven instruction for me if you go before I arrive"   Telegram received, DNA, RG 94, War Records Office, Dept. of the Tenn. *O.R.*, I, xxiv, part 3, 11.

2. Col. Florence M. Cornyn, 10th Mo. Cav. On Jan. 23, USG wrote to Brig. Gen. Willis A. Gorman, Helena. "You will forward to Memphis with as little delay as practicable the six companies of the 10th Missouri Cavalry now at Helena, also the two Howitzers taken by Genl Fisk" Copies, DLC-USG, V, 18, 30; DNA, RG 393, Dept. of the Tenn., Letters Sent.

To Brig. Gen. James C. Veatch

Memphis Jan 22 1863

BRIG GENL J C VEATCH
COMMD'G DISTRICT OF MEMPHIS

I would suggest of having all the roads leading into the city except about three strongly Barricaded so that vehicles or animals cannot get out or in and require all travel to pass by the open road   These three could be pickited and all persons attempting to enter the city or pass out by any other route should be arrested

From the number of horses being stolen, and even Soldiers caught and paroled in the street[1] very stringent regulations will have to be made

If the proper goverment of the city requires it I will not oppose driving out every man woman and child who will not live strictly up to all requirements

U S GRANT
Maj Genl

Copies, DLC-USG, V, 18, 30; DNA, RG 393, Dept. of the Tenn., Letters Sent. James C. Veatch, born in Harrison County, Ind., in 1819, a lawyer-politician of Spencer County, Ind., was appointed col., 25th Ind., on Aug. 19, 1861, and confirmed as brig. gen. on April 28, 1862.

1. On Jan. 23, 1863, Brig. Gen. Alexander Asboth, Columbus, Ky., telegraphed to Lt. Col. John A. Rawlins. "Five Enlisted men of the 14th Wis and 16th Iowa came from Fort Pillow with written paroles dated January 19th   they state that they were taken in the Heart of the city of Memphis on the 17th Inst six oclock P M by Rebels dressed in our uniforms. my impression that the men are deserters & will detain them for such until further orders from Department Hd Qrs." Telegram received, *ibid.*, Telegrams Received; copy, *ibid.*, Hd. Qrs. District of Columbus, Letters Sent. On the same day, USG telegraphed to Asboth. "Send the five (5) deserters taken at Columbus back to their regiments in charge of an officer. It is a violation of the Cartel to parole soldiers before sending them to points agreed upon" Copy, *ibid.*, Telegrams Received.

To Col. John C. Kelton

———

Head Quarters, Department of the Tennessee
Memphis, Tenn., Jan. 23rd, 1863.

Col. J. C. Kelton A. A. G.
Washington D. C.

Lieut J. H. Wilson, Topographical Engineer, having been appointed Inspector General with the rank of Lt. Col. and attached to the 10th. Army Corps, I would respectfully ask a suspension of the order taking him away from here. This Department is almost entirely without Staff Officers of the Regular Army, and Col. Wilson of all others ~~can~~ is the one I can least spare at this time.

Lt. Col. Wilson is now going to Youngs Point[1] on duty. If his order to report for duty to the 10th Army Corps, is to be complied with immediately please answer by telegraph, and I will order him back at once

Cannot Col. Wilson be assigned to this Department with his present rank? at least temporarily

Very Respectfully &c.,
U S. Grant
Maj. Genl.

Copies, DLC-USG, V, 5, 8, 24, 88; DNA, RG 393, Dept. of the Tenn., Hd. Qrs. Correspondence. On Jan. 20, 1863, USG had telegraphed to Maj. Gen. Henry W. Halleck. "Lieut. Col. Wilson of the 10th. Army Corps is on duty with me. His services are absolutely necessary. May I retain him?" Copies, *ibid.* Also on Jan. 20, Maj. Gen. David Hunter had issued orders naming 1st Lt. James H. Wilson as asst. inspector-gen. with the rank of lt. col. *O.R.*, I, xiv, 392. According to Wilson, USG said: "I see old David Hunter and go him one better. He has made you lieutenant colonel and inspector general of the Tenth Corps, but I shall nominate you inspector general of the Army of the Tennessee. That beats him and you will remain with us!" *Under the Old Flag* (New York and London, 1912), I, 147.

On Jan. 29, Halleck telegraphed to USG. "If Col Wilson is actually engaged in a seige he can remain temporarily but he cannot be detached from his proper command" Telegram received, DNA, RG 393, Dept. of the Tenn., Telegrams Received; copies, *ibid.*, Hd. Qrs. Correspondence; *ibid.*, RG 107, Telegrams Collected (Bound); *ibid.*, RG 108, Telegrams Sent; DLC-USG, V, 5, 8, 24, 88.

1. Young's Point, La., on the Mississippi River about eight miles above Vicksburg.

To Col. Joseph D. Webster

Memphis Ten Jan 23 1863

Col J·D Webster
Jackson Tenn

Can you not run three trains a day from here, one not to go beyond Grand Junction; one every other day to Jackson and one each day to Corinth. There is much complaint for want of forage

U S. Grant.
Maj Genl.

Telegram, copies, DLC-USG, V, 18, 30; DNA, RG 393, Dept. of the Tenn., Letters Sent. On Jan. 22, 1863, USG wrote to Lt. Col. Charles A. Reynolds. "The cry for forage from La Fayette to Corinth is great. I wish you would strain every thing to get through a supply. I will telegraph Col. Webster to know if three trains a day cannot be run." ALS, ICU. On Jan. 24, Col. Benjamin H. Grierson, La Grange, telegraphed to Lt. Col. John A. Rawlins. "Forage very scarce here teams returned tonight without aparticle   horses dying daily   please order hay & oats to be sent to us immediately"   Telegram received, DNA, RG 393, Dept. of the Tenn., Telegrams Received.

On Jan. 20, USG telegraphed to Col. Joseph D. Webster. "Until Corinth is abundantly supplied with rations and forage suspend running a passenger train" Copies, DLC-USG, V, 18, 30; DNA, RG 393, Dept. of the Tenn., Letters Sent. On the same day, Webster telegraphed to Maj. Theodore S. Bowers. "I have a despatch directing discontinuance of passenger train to Corinth & purporting to come from Gen Grant   is it so   I am transporting all the forage which Qr Mr. Dept. offers for shipment   a passenger car on train will make no difference   The trains are all of the mixed sort"   Telegram received, *ibid.*, Telegrams Received. On Jan. 21, USG telegraphed to Webster. "There are about 600 men at Collierville under orders for this place who are without shoes. Please order the cars today to bring them"   Copies, DLC-USG, V, 18, 30; DNA, RG 393, Dept. of the Tenn., Letters Sent. On the same day, Webster twice telegraphed USG. "Just returned from break in rail-road near Crockett. Late rains raised water in Obion so as to stop work. The road can be repaired with certainty and despatch only by using a steam pile driver at a cost of say $3000. The traffic would pay that in a few days if the road were repaired so as that we could get the new cars from Columbus. The pile driver will be worth its cost in opening any other road. Shall I order it?" "The soldiers along the line burn up our wood at such a rate that two trains cannot keep up the supply. It is cut of proper length for engines and if they continue to burn it, it will cause great delay. This is particularly the case between Grand junction and Memphis. I am going North to the break this mornig. If proper would like a copy of the order in reference to withdraw of troops for Rail Road &c. issued to Gen. Hamilton last week." ALS (telegram sent), *ibid.*, RG 107, Telegrams Collected (Unbound); (2) telegram received, *ibid.*, RG 393, Dept. of the Tenn., Telegrams Received. On Jan. 22, Webster telegraphed to

Rawlins. "Has the general decided about the pile driver? for the rail-road. It is a larger expenditure than I like to go into without his authority." ALS (telegram sent), *ibid.*, RG 107, Telegrams Collected (Unbound); telegram received, *ibid.*, RG 393, Dept. of the Tenn., Telegrams Received. At the foot of the telegram received, Rawlins wrote to USG. "Will please indicate answer to the above" ANS, *ibid.*

On Jan. 23, USG twice telegraphed to Webster. "You will please send forward at once to this place all the companies of Bissells Engineer Regiment now at or in the vicinity of Jackson Tenn with all their tools and camp equipage" "No more work need be done on the road north of Jackson I have given orders to have the rolling stock brought from Columbus by water" Copies, DLC-USG, V, 18, 30; DNA, RG 393, Dept. of the Tenn., Letters Sent. On the same day, Webster telegraphed to USG. "May I ask who has charge of the removal of the rolling stock from Columbus to Memphis? Great saving of time and money can be made by judicious management. I would like to try to arrange to have it sent by barges and flat boats towed by steamers. If sent by steamers only the expense with be very great." ALS (telegram sent), *ibid.*, RG 107, Telegrams Collected (Unbound); telegram received, *ibid.*, RG 393, Dept. of the Tenn., Telegrams Received. At the foot of the telegram received, Rawlins wrote to USG. "Will Genl Grant please send me the answer." ANS, *ibid.*

To Surgeon John G. F. Holston

Headquarters Depart of the Tennessee
Memphis Jany 23d 186[3]

SURG J. G F HOLSTON U S A
SIR.

On your leaving this Depart. at least temporarily allow me to express my regrett that the necessity for doing so, should be caused by failing health, no doubt the result of over-exertion in the performance of your duties Allow me to express my appreciation of your services both as Medical Director on my staff and in a subordinate capacity.

Our relations have been ever cordial and it is but just to say that you have shrunk from no duty, no matter how laborious, nor from any danger

Upon the field of battle and in camp, you have ever been the same, at your post.

Hoping that you may soon be restored to health and duty with me again in the field I remain

> Your's obed serv
> U S Grant
> Maj Gen

Copies, DNA, RG 94, Personal Papers, Medical Officers and Physicians, Holston; *ibid.*, ACP, H 83 CB 1863. On Jan. 23, 1863, Surgeon John G. F. Holston wrote to USG. "Being relieved of all duty, without a fresh assignment, and being completely worn down, body & mind, through hard labour, in my Department I have the honour to present the within, certificate of disability, approved by the highest medical authorities—and in reference thereto ask sick leave for 30 days and that I have leave to report to the Surg. Genrl. at Washington or the Asst. Surg. Genrl. St. Louis. Added, my warmest thanks, for many acts of kindness & craving God's blessing on you & yours" ALS, *ibid.*, Personal Papers, Medical Officers and Physicians, Holston.

To Maj. Gen. Henry W. Halleck

> Memphis Tenn
> Jany 25th 1. P. M 1863

Maj Gen H. W. Halleck
Gen-in-Chief

I leave for the fleet at Vicksburg tomorrow. Since leaving there one week ago I have not had one word from them. The constant rains and tremendous rise in the river may operate against us for the time being

> U S. Grant
> Maj Gen'l

Telegram received, DNA, RG 107, Telegrams Collected (Bound); *ibid.*, Telegrams Collected (Unbound); copies, *ibid.*, Telegrams Received in Cipher; *ibid.*, RG 393, Dept. of the Tenn., Hd. Qrs. Correspondence; DLC-USG, V, 5, 8, 24, 88. *O.R.*, I, xxiv, part 1, 10.

Also on Jan. 25, 1863, USG wrote to Maj. Gen. James B. McPherson. "In view of the present rise of water it is uncertain whether troops can land opposite Vicksburg where their services are now wanted   I would therefore direct that Genl Logans'. Division await further orders here before embarking   I will go down myself in the morning and if it is found practicable to use the troops advantageously below will send back orders for them immediately" Copies, DLC-

USG, V, 18, 30; DNA, RG 393, Dept. of the Tenn., Letters Sent. *O.R.*, I, xxiv, part 3, 11.

On Jan. 26, USG wrote to Act. Vol. Lt. George W. Brown, U. S. S. *Forest Rose.* "I shall be going down the river to-morrow to join the fleet near Vicksburg, and will be glad to have you convoy the steamer in which I go. I will be on the steamer Magnolia. Officers just up from the fleet report having been fired into by artillery and musketry from the east bank of the river at Island No. 32." *St. Louis Globe-Democrat*, Aug. 1, 1885. According to the news story, discussing the presentation of the original letter by Brown to the New York Maritime Exchange, the letter was dated July 26, 1863, but internal and external evidence indicates a Jan. date. The same story in the *Boston Herald*, Aug. 1, 1885, gives the Jan. date.

To Brig. Gen. Charles S. Hamilton

Memphis Tenn Jan 25 1863.

BRIG GENL C. S. HAMILTON
COMMD'G DISTRICT WEST TENN

My attention has been called to a notice given to me Mr Jones occupying the house of Genl Williams to vacate to make room for your Head Quarters   Mr Jones is said to have been always a Union Man and is now paying rent to the Goverment for the house he occupies

I am opposed to working any hardships upon such people when it can be avoided and especially where there are so many undeserving people occupying houses suitable for Officers Quarters   Orders published at Holly Springs make it the duty of Quartermasters to assign quarters and orders published here prohibit turning Union families out to make room for Officers[1] Where there is a great Military necessity for taking private houses from any class of people it will be done but even then the disloyal will be visited first

U S GRANT
Maj Genl.

Copies, DLC-USG, V, 18, 30; DNA, RG 393, Dept. of the Tenn., Letters Sent.

1. General Orders No. 9, Dept. of the Tenn., Jan. 25, 1863. Copies, DLC-USG, V, 13, 14, 95; DNA, RG 393, Dept. of the Tenn., General Orders. *O.R.*, I, xxiv, part 3, 11.

To Brig. Gen. Charles S. Hamilton

Head Quarters, Dept. of the Ten.
Memphis Ten. Jan. 25th 1863.

Brig. Gen. Hamilton
Comd.g Dist. of W. Ten.
Gen.

As soon as it possibly can be done relieve the two regiments at Bethel and with them and two regiments from the new troops arrived or to arrive, form a Brigade to be added to the 8th Division, Gen. J. E. Smith Commanding.

If it is possible to finish the road through from Columbus in a few days, as it is now reported to me is the case, it will be better to do it and bring all the rolling stock of the road over in that way.

Respectfully &c.
U. S. Grant
Maj. Gen. Com

ALS, CSmH. *O.R.*, I, xxiv, part 3, 11.

On Jan. 25, 1863, Brig. Gen. Charles S. Hamilton, Columbus, Ky., telegraphed to USG. "Yours Recd. I shall be in Memphis Monday Evening" Telegram received, DNA, RG 393, Dept. of the Tenn., Telegrams Received. Hamilton appears to have been responding to a telegram which has not been found.

To Commanding Officers

Memphis, Tenn Jan 26 1863

To Commanding Officers at all
Stations from Memphis to Grand Junction

Fortify and build block-houses at all points guarded by troops. A raid may be expected by Van Dorn at any time when the roads will possibly admit of it. He is now said to be North of Grenada.

Guard against surprise, and be prepared to hold your positions at all hazards.

U. S. GRANT
Maj Genl'

Copies, DLC-USG, V, 18, 30; DNA, RG 393, Dept. of the Tenn., Letters Sent. For a similar message, see telegram to Brig. Gen. Mason Brayman, Jan. 2, 1863.

To Maj. Gen. Henry W. Halleck

———

Memphis Tenn
Jany 27th 7. P. M. [*1863*]

MAJ GEN H. W. HALLECK
GEN IN CHIEF

News just received from Vicksburg says water now in old canal—and rising rapidly. In a short time our Batteries of Parrott guns will command the river below town. Vicksburg papers say that Gen'l Banks is fortifying Baton Rouge. I hold two Divisions here ready to reinforce the Expedition as soon as wanted   also Gormans forces.

U S. GRANT
Maj Genl Comdg

Telegram received, DNA, RG 107, Telegrams Collected (Bound); copy, *ibid.*, Telegrams Received in Cipher. *O.R.*, I, xxiv, part 1, 10. On Jan. 25, 1863, 10:40 P.M., Maj. Gen. Henry W. Halleck had telegraphed to USG. "Direct your attention particularly to the canal proposed across the point   the President attaches much importance to this." ALS (telegram sent), DNA, RG 107, Telegrams Collected (Bound); telegram received, *ibid.*, Telegrams Collected (Unbound); *ibid.*, RG 94, War Records Office, Military Div. of the Miss. *O.R.*, I, xxiv, part 1, 10.

Since a correspondent noted that USG arrived at Helena, Ark., about 5:00 P.M., Jan. 27, the telegram to Halleck must have been prepared much earlier than the time shown on the telegram received. Letter of "Bas," Helena, Jan. 27, in *Missouri Democrat*, Feb. 3, 1863.

To Julia Dent Grant

———

Youngs Point, La.
Jan. 28th 9 P M./63

Dear Julia,

We have just arrived here all safe and well, but being after dusk and the troops ashore will not learn anything of the situation of affairs until morning.

If I find that I shall not go back to Memphis until the reduction of Vicksburg is attempted I will write to you so that you can go and make the children a visit.—The trip, with nothing to bother me, makes me feel well. The living on the boat is very fine and my appetite good. The Capt. and owner of the boat is Capt. Shinkle of Covington Ky.[1]

Kiss Jess for me.

Ulys.

ALS, DLC-USG.

1. Probably O. P. Shinkle, whose reminiscent letter appeared in E. W. Gould, *Fifty Years on the Mississippi: or, Gould's History of River Navigation* (St. Louis, 1889; reprinted, Columbus, Ohio, 1951), pp. 705–6.

To Maj. Gen. Henry W. Halleck

———

Vicksburg Miss
Jany 29th 1863 5. P M

Maj Gen H. W. Halleck
Gen in Chief

Water in the canal is five feet deep and river rising   There is no wash however and no signs of its enlarging. I will let the water in from the Yazoo up and try the effect. I have ordered troops from Helena escorted by a Gunboat—the whole in charge of Colonel Wilson Topographical Engineer to cut the Levee

across Yazoo Pass & to explore through to the Cold water if
possible

U. S. GRANT
Maj Gen'l

Telegram received, DNA, RG 107, Telegrams Collected (Bound); *ibid.*, Telegrams Collected (Unbound); copies, *ibid.*, Telegrams Received in Cipher; *ibid.*,
RG 393, Dept. of the Tenn., Hd. Qrs. Correspondence; DLC-USG, V, 5, 8, 24,
88. *O.R.*, I, xxiv, part 1, 10. On Jan. 31, 1863, USG telegraphed to Maj. Gen.
Henry W. Halleck. "I am pushing everything to gain a passage—avoiding Vicksburg   Prospects not flattering by the canal of last Summer. Other routs are being
prospected and work in the meantime progressing on the old canal"   Telegram
received, DNA, RG 107, Telegrams Collected (Bound); *ibid.*, Telegrams Collected (Unbound); copies, *ibid.*, Telegrams Received in Cipher; *ibid.*, RG 393,
Dept. of the Tenn., Hd. Qrs. Correspondence; DLC-USG, V, 5, 8, 24, 88. *O.R.*,
I, xxiv, part 1, 10.

To Col. John C. Kelton

————

Head Quarters, Department of the Tenn.
Youngs Point, La., Jany. 29th./63.

COL: J. C. KELTON
ASST. ADJT. GENL.
WASHINGTON, D. C.
COL:

Dispatch of the 21st. asking by what authority, the 8th, 12th,
and 14th, Iowa Regiments were sent to Davenport, is just received,

These three Regiments with the 58th. Ills formed what was
called the Union Brigade numbering less than four hundred men
for duty. The 58th. Ills. was ordered back for reorganization by
the Secretary of War. This left but a very small organization for
duty, and from its mixed character of but little service.

I authorized Genl. Dodge, therefore, as soon as he could dispense with them to, send them back to their State for reorganization, same as had been done by the 58th. Ills.

These Regiments were composed of convalescents &c., who were left after the capture of said Regts. at Shiloh.

I acted as I thought for the best interests of the service, and in accordance, with, what I supposed to be the wishes of the War Dept. from the action in the case of the 58th. Ills. which was in the same condition.

Their reorganizations, I am satisfied can be much sooner effected under the immediate supervision of the Governor of the State, than in the field.

> I am, Col. Very respectfully
> Your obt: servt:
> U. S. GRANT
> Maj. Genl.

Copies, DLC-USG, V, 5, 8, 24, 88; DNA, RG 393, Dept. of the Tenn., Hd. Qrs. Correspondence. On Jan. 21, 1863, Maj. Gen. Henry W. Halleck had written to USG and Maj. Gen. Samuel R. Curtis. "It is reported here that the 8th 12th & 14th Iowa volunteers have been sent to Davenport, Iowa. You will immediately report by what order and under what authority these regiments were sent to Iowa" Copy, *ibid.*, Letters Received; *ibid.*, RG 108, Letters Sent (Press).

On Feb. 9, Halleck wrote to USG. "Your report of January 29th in regard to the ordering of the 8th 12th and 14 Iowa regiments from your Department to Davenport, Iowa, is just recieved. Numerous applications were recieved by the Secty of War for such an order, all of which were refused, on the ground that to permit the regiments of one state to return home to reorganize would render it necessary to grant the same favor to others. The Governor of Iowa was repeatedly informed that the application for the abovementioned regiments could not be granted, and that the exchanged officers and men must rejoin and reorganize the regiments in the field. After these repeated refusals information is recieved here that the portions of these regiments in your Dept., and those portions in other Depts., which had been ordered to join your command, had all been sent to Iowa. The exercise of such authority by Generals in the face of repeated orders of the War Dept against it, caused no little surprise, and I recieved direction to ascertain and report upon the facts. Your report will be submitted to the Secretary. In regard to the 58th Illinois, the order sending it to Illinois must have been given without the Secretary's knowledge, for all such applications have been refused." ADf, *ibid.*, RG 94, Generals' Papers and Books, Henry W. Halleck, Letters Sent (Press).

To Brig. Gen. Willis A. Gorman

Near Vicksburgh, Jan: 29th 1863.

BRIG GENL' W. A. GORMAN
COMMANDING DISC'T OF HELENA

Send a stern wheel Steamer, with as many troops as it can conveniently carry, to the entrance of Yazoo Pass, for the purpose of cutting the levee and letting the water from the Mississippi in.

The GunBoat by which this is sent will accompany the expedition. The party should remain at the Pass until they see the work effectually done, and then return to Helena

I shall certainly not want Genl' Fitch's Brigade here for several days.

U. S. GRANT.
Maj General.

Copies, DLC-USG, V, 18, 30; DNA, RG 393, Dept. of the Tenn., Letters Sent. On Feb. 1, 1863, Brig. Gen. Willis A. Gorman, Helena, wrote to USG. "Your order to place men at the disposal of Col Wilson to cut the Levee at the mouth of the Yazoo pass, and watch it until the work is effectually done and then explore it as far as possible, has been rec.d And Tomorrow morning at 9 A. M. the force will leave here. No news, except that Genl Burnside has resigned, Genls Franklin & Sumner relieved and Genl Hooker placed in Command of the army of the Potomac   Much feeling seems to be manifested from the information I get from my Correspondence from Washington. I trust that a good providence may save that Army from any more misfortune, as it really seems as if the efforts of man have mostly failed   The hope of the great West is Concentrating on your efforts to open this great throat of Commerce and I feel the most unbounded Confidence in your Success." ALS, *ibid.*, Letters Received. See letter to Brig. Gen. Willis A. Gorman, Feb. 1, 1863.

To Act. Rear Admiral David D. Porter

Young's Point, La Jan: 30th 1863.

REAR ADMIRAL D. PORTER
COMD'G WESTERN FLOTILLA.

By inquiry I learn that Lake Providence which connects with Red River through Tansas Bayou Washita and Black Rivers is a wide and navigable way through.

As some advantage may be gained by opening this, I have ordered a Brigade of troops to be detailed for the purpose, and to be embarked as soon as possible.

I would respectfully request that one of your light Gun Boats accompany this expedition if it can be spared.

U. S. GRANT
Maj General

Copies, DLC-USG, V, 18, 30; DNA, RG 393, Dept. of the Tenn., Letters Sent. *O.R.*, I, xxiv, part 3, 17; *O.R.* (Navy), I, xxiv, 211–12.

To Maj. Gen. John A. McClernand

Head Quarters, Dept. of the Ten.
In the Field Near Vicksburg
Jan. 30th 1863.

MAJ. GEN. J. A. MCCLERNAND
COMD.G 13TH ARMY CORPS.
GEN.

Upon enquiry from the best information at hand I find that Lake Providence some sixty miles above here, wich connects with Red River through Tensas Bayo Washita and Black rivers, is a wide and navigable way. The distance to be cut to enter it from the Mississippi not great. With this open a vast foraging district would be opened and our gunboats, of light draft, would be enabled to cut off the enemies commerce with the West bank of the river.

I have determined to make the experiment at all events and for this purpose will want a Brigade detailed' and embarked as soon as possible.

They will be accompanied by one of the gunboats.

All the tools required can be got by calling on Capt. Reno,[1] A. Q. M. on the Steamer Adelia.

Respectfully &c.

U. S. GRANT

Maj. Gen. Com

ALS, McClernand Papers, IHi. *O.R.*, I, xxiv, part 3, 17–18. On Jan. 30, 1863, Maj. Gen. John A. McClernand twice wrote to USG. "Your dispatch of this date is received. I have accordingly ordered a brigade to be detailed to cut the proposed canal between Lake Providence & Bayou Tensas   If this project should fail of success it might be well to inquire into the practicability of connecting the Miss river at Lake Village (nearly opposite Greenville) with the Washata and the Red river"   "I have unofficially learned that two officers of the Engineers attached to the Dept of the Tennessee are here, but am not advised whether they are under orders to examine and report respecting the practicability of diverting the course of the Miss river through the present canal, or any other that may be cut in this vicinity. I have ordered certain modifications of the present canal as explained to you yesterday   If they prove unsuccessful the uselessness of the present canal will have been demonstrated. I think the Engineers referred to might profitably turn their attention in some other direction for a suitable line for a new cut.— From all I can learn an effective dredging machine would be equal, nay superior to the labor of many thousand men in opening a canal after water had flown through it. Would it not be advisable to send to Louisville for one or more at once. Time presses and every practicable method to make this army available for great results should be tested"   LS, DNA, RG 393, Dept. of the Tenn., Letters Received; McClernand Papers, IHi. *O.R.*, I, xxiv, part 3, 18–19. On Jan. 30, USG wrote to McClernand. "The Gunboat to accompany the expedition to Lake Providence has reported. Please inform me who goes in command so that I may direct the Capt. to report for orders." ALS, McClernand Papers, IHi.

1. Benjamin F. Reno, born in Pa., was commissioned 2nd lt., 2nd Iowa Cav., as of Sept. 5, 1861. On March 13, 1863, Reno was confirmed as capt. and asst. q. m. as of Nov. 17, 1862. On June 3, 1863, Lt. Col. Judson D. Bingham wrote to Lt. Col. John A. Rawlins. "I have the honor to report that I have relieved Capt. B. F. Reno A. Q. M. from duty, and respectfully request that he may be ordered to report to the Chief Quartermaster at St. Louis, for assignment beyond the limits of this Department." ALS, DNA, RG 94, Staff Papers, Reno.

To Maj. Gen. John A. McClernand

Head Quarters, Dept. of the Ten.
Before Vicksburg, Jan. 30th 1863.
Maj. Gen. J. A. McClernand
Comd.g 13th Army Corps.
Gen.

Col. Parsons and Col. Dunlap happened in my office this morning after my note had been sent to you calling for a detail of one Brigade to go on the expedition to cut into Lake Providence. I mentioned the matter and Col. P. remarked he had not been notified to get the boats in readiness but he would do so in anticipation of the order. He now informs me that the boats have been in readiness for some time but no order has come for them. I have directed him to send the boats to report to Gen. McArthur at an early hour in the morning. Lieut. Col. Duff will accompany the expedition as Engineer officer, the officers of Gen Morgan's Staff requested by me this morning having failed to report.[1]

I am Gen. very respectfully
your obt. svt.
U. S. Grant
Maj. Gen. Com

ALS, McClernand Papers, IHi.

1. On Jan. 30, 1863, Lt. Col. John A. Rawlins twice wrote to Maj. Gen. John A. McClernand. "Please direct Captains Lyon, and Patterson of Genl. Morgans Staff (with his permission) to report to the Major General, Commanding, for Special Service." "I am instructed by the Major General Commanding, to say, in answer to your communication this moment received; the Brigade will be in charge of its own Commanding officer, and that he has no engineer officer to send with it. The officers of Genl. Morgans Staff, he requested you to order to report to him this morning, were intended for that purpose, but as they have not yet reported, you will please send one of your engineer officers with the expedition, with directions to report here at once for instructions" LS, *ibid.* On the same day, Lt. Col. Walter B. Scates, adjt. for McClernand, wrote to Rawlins. "I am directed by Genl McClernand to state that the order for a detachment of a Brigade from Genl McArthurs command, with. Arms. & twenty days rations, to report to Head Quarters of. Genl McClernand, was sent, Genl McArthur had very heavy details out working on the crevasse just below him. Having also to load baggage

tents &c on Steamer—time is necessarily consumed and he may not be able to report before morning. He has Transports enough with his command & it was unnecessary to order any more up. Sidney. E. Lyon Engineer with Genl Morgan has been ordered to report forthwith. Genl McClernand countermanded his order for the return of the Transports North, directing them to remain until further orders   He has sent a heavy detail to wood the fleet, some eighteen miles up the River where he has had a large quantity of wood cut so as to have them in readiness for any movement required." DfS, *ibid.*; copy, DNA, RG 393, 13th Army Corps, Letters Sent. Also on Jan. 30, USG wrote to Brig. Gen. John McArthur. "Boats have been ordered to report to you at an early hour to-morrow morning to take on board a Brigade of your Division directed this morning by General McClernand. Lieut Col Duff goes in charge of the Engineering part of the Expedition, and if you have an officer acquanted with that branch of service, I wish you would let him accompany Col. Duff." Copies, DLC-USG, V, 18, 30; DNA, RG 393, Dept. of the Tenn., Letters Sent.

To Brig. Gen. Charles S. Hamilton

Young's Point, La. Jany 30th 1863.

BRIG GENL' C. S. HAMILTON
COMD'G DISC'T WEST TENN.

If the present good weather holds for a few days, or if it does not, than as soon as possible an expedition should be got up, mostly of Cavalry, to penetrate, if possible as far South as the Tallahatchie Bridge   I would like to have that bridge destroyed, and as much destruction to the road as possible from that point to Holly Springs. North of Holly Springs, I do not care to have the road injured.

In addition to the Cavalry ordered up from Helena, I am sending up one Regiment from here, and want the 2nd Illinois Cavalry to replace them. Send this latter Regiment down without delay.

U. S. GRANT
Maj General

Copies, DLC-USG, V, 18, 30; DNA, RG 393, Dept. of the Tenn., Letters Sent.

To Col. Jesse Hildebrand

————

Head Quarters, Dept. of the Ten.
Before Vicksburg, Jan. 30th 1863.

COMD.G OFFICER
ALTON PRISON
SIR:

You have confined at Alton a man by the name of Carroll H. Rawlings who has been in the Southern Army but who gave himself up voluntarily to the Federal Army at Oxford Miss. for the purpose of escaping service and was passed out by me,   He should not have been arrested except for offences committed afterwards and I presume was arrested by Gen. Tuttle without a knowledge of these facts.

Please release him on his taking the oath of allegiance.

Respectfully &c.
U. S. GRANT
Maj. Gen. Com

ALS, DNA, RG 109, Unfiled Papers and Slips, Rawlins, Carroll H.
On Jan. 22, 1863, USG wrote to Col. Jesse Hildebrand. "Please release the following political prisoners sent to Alton by some of the officers of my command: towit: William R James, Hiram Twitty, John Robertson and B. H. F. Barnett. The above are all citizens of Tishamingo Co. Miss. and, if released, will require passes to go to their homes." ALS, *ibid.*, RG 249, Records of Prisoners Confined at Alton, Ill.

To Col. Lewis B. Parsons

————

Head Quarters, Dept. of the Ten.
Before Vicksburg, Jan. 30th 1863.

COL. PARSONS,
SIR:

I ordered Gen. McClernand this morning to have a Brigade detailed and placed aboard of steamers for an expedition and supposed he had given all the orders in accordance to my directions. I am informed by the Gen. that he designated the troops from Gen. McArthur's Division. In that case the steamers will not be wanted down here. Please send the steamers to report to Gen. McArthur at an early hour in the morning.

> Respectfully &c.
> U. S. GRANT
> Maj. Gen. Com

ALS, Parsons Papers, IHi.

On Jan. 30, 1863, Col. Lewis B. Parsons wrote to USG. "I expect to send about twenty or twenty five boats immediately up the river, and as many more in a day or two. Do you desire that any of these boats should be detained at Memphis to bring down additional troops? Please advise me what you wish as I expect to go up myself with the first division of the fleet. If any are detained would it not be well that they should be from the next division of the fleet going up." LS, *ibid.* On the same day, Lt. Col. John A. Rawlins endorsed this letter. "The Boats to be detained will be detained from the next division of the fleet going up." ES, *ibid.* Also on Jan. 30, USG wrote to Parsons. "Retain all the Boats except sufficient to move the Cavalry now under orders for Washington, and such other Boats as it may be necessary to send after Coal, forage and other supplies. A move make take place at any time requiring the use of all our transportation" Copies, *ibid.*; DLC-USG, V, 18, 30; DNA, RG 393, Dept. of the Tenn., Letters Sent.

On Jan. 27, Parsons had written to USG. "Some days since I addressed Col. Reynolds, by the 'Warsaw' stating that we should send a number of boats within a day or two to bring down two divisions of your army. The next day I was ordered to keep an ample supply of boats to reembark this whole army; consequently I have been unable to send any boats. The river—already very high—is still rising rapidly with a strong prospect of flooding this whole country in a few days, which ~~has~~ would rendered it necessary to reembark the whole army. I therefore send but two boats & those only for the purpose of carrying the sick; without them or some other boats it would be impossible to remove all the Animals of this expedition. I trust therefore that the sick may be disposed of at Memphis & the boats returned as early as consistent. As yet I have received no coal since we left Memphis except four barges one of which we gave to the Navy & are almost destitute of fuel. I have written fully to Col. Reynolds upon the subject & trust that the tow boats will immediately be sent bringing us fuel, or that any other boats coming down will tow some barges, which they can readily do—" Copy, Parsons Papers, IHi.

To Act. Rear Admiral David D. Porter

Jan. 31st 1863.

Admiral D. D. Porter
Comd.g Flotilla,
Sir,

Did one of the rams run the blockade last night? I warned our batteries to be on the lookout for her and not to fire into her if she should come by.

I send you with this the result of yesterdays reconnaisance towards the city.

Respectfully &c
U. S. Grant
Maj. Gen.

ALS, Washington University, St. Louis, Mo. At this time Act. Rear Admiral David D. Porter was preparing the U.S. ram *Queen of the West* to run the blockade to attack the C.S.A. steamboat *City of Vicksburg*. On Feb. 1, 1863, Maj. Gen. William T. Sherman wrote to USG. "I am almost absolutely certain the Vicksburg is exactly where she was yesterday, for I have her watched by Commissioned officers and no Report of any Change in affairs has been made. I will send an aid Capt McCoy to see with his own eyes and to report to you on board the Magnolia. You would be safe in reporting as much to the Admiral adding that in two hours you will have the official Report of a responsible officer. I will myself ride round and give orders to my Batteries. Notify the Admiral the best place for his Ram [to] round to will be immediately in front of the Biggs House, where the Ferry boat lay when he visited her." ALS, PPRF. USG added an undated endorsement probably intended for Porter. "If the Vicksburg has changed position I will inform you of the fact as soon as it is ascertained. No further communication from me this afternoon will indicate this fact. Should your boat not run the blockade to-night I will have the position of the Vicksburg watched to-morrow and in case of any change will report the fact." AES, *ibid.* On Feb. 1, Porter wrote to USG. "I may be ready to night, to send down the Ram to destroy the Steamer 'Vicksburg,' in which case our Ram will be distinguished (after performing the duty,) by three vertical lights.—She will come to, if she gets past, at or near our batteries, when she will have her lights down.—If you could ascertain if the Vicksburg is there at sunset, you would much oblige me—I am packing the Ram with cotton bales so that she cannot be injured—If she does not go to night, she certainly will to-morrow night.—" LS, DNA, RG 45, Correspondence of David D. Porter, Mississippi Squadron, General Letters (Press). *O.R.* (Navy), I, xxiv, 217. For reports of the ensuing engagement, see *ibid.*, pp. 217–22. On Feb. 4, Porter wrote to USG. "In case the 'Queen of the West' shall come up the river from below Vicksburg at night she will carry three vertical lights. I mention this so that she will not be fired upon by our batteries—" LS, DNA, RG 45, Correspondence of

David D. Porter, Mississippi Squadron, General Letters (Press). *O.R.* (Navy), I, xxiv, 234.

To Maj. Gen. John A. McClernand

———

Head Quarters, Dept. of the Ten
Before Vicksburg, Jan. 31st 1863.

MAJ. GEN. J. A. MCCLERNAND
COMD.G 13TH ARMY CORPS.
GEN.

The intention of Gen. Orders No 13 is that I will take direct command of the Miss. river expedition which necessarily limits your command to the 13th Army Corps.

In charging the 13th Army Corps with Garrisoning the West bank of the river I add to it all the forces belonging to my command on that bank not already assigned to other Corps, and instead of weakening your force in the field it will strengthen it by about 7000 men, still leaving a proper garrison at Helena the only place I now deem necessary to garrison.

All forces, and posts garrisoned by the 13th Army Corps, are under your command subject of course to directions from these Head Quarters.

I regard the President as the Commander-in-Chief of the Army and will obey every order of his, but as yet I have seen no order to prevent my taking immediate command in the field, and since the dispatch refered to in your note I have received another from the Gen. in-Chief of the Army authorizing me directly to take command of this Army.

I at first thought I would publish no order taking command but soon saw that it would be much more convenient to issue orders direct to Corps Comdrs, whilst present with the Command, than through another commander.

your obt. svt.
U. S. GRANT
Maj. Gen. Com

ALS, McClernand Papers, IHi. *O.R.*, I, xxiv, part 1, 13. On Jan. 30, 1863, Lt. Col. John A. Rawlins issued General Orders No. 13. "Major General U S Grant, Commanding Department of the Tennessee, hereby assumes the immediate command of the expedition against Vicksburg and Department Headquarters will hereafter be with the expedition   Army Corps Commanders will resume the immediate command of their respective Corps and will report to and receive orders direct from these Headquarters. As Army Corps to be effective should be complete in their organization, and ready at all times for any move they may be called on to make without looking to Department or other Headquarters for anything more than the replenishing of their supplies, no changes or transfers will be made by Department orders unless absolutely necessary for the interests of the service. The 13th Army Corps, Maj. Genl. J A McClernand commanding, is charged with garrisoning the Post of Helena, Arkansas, and any other point on the west bank of the river it may be necessary to hold south of that place." DS, McClernand Papers, IHi; DNA, RG 94, War Records Office, Union Battle Reports; copies, *ibid.*, Generals' Papers and Books, U. S. Grant; DLC-Edwin M. Stanton; (numbered General Orders No. 11) DLC-USG, V, 13, 14, 95; (2) DNA, RG 393, Dept. of the Tenn., General and Special Orders. Numbered General Orders No. 13 in *O.R.*, I, xxiv, part 1, 11.

On the same day, Maj. Gen. John A. McClernand wrote to USG. "General orders No 13 is this moment received. I hasten to inquire whether its purpose is to relieve me from the command of all, or any portion, of the forces composing the Miss. River Expedition, or, in other words, whether its purpose is to limit my command to the 13th Army Corps. I am led to make this inquiry, because while such seems to be the intention, it conflicts with the order of the Secretary of War, made under the personal direction of the President, bearing date Octo. 31st. 1862 of which the following is an extract—'Major General McClernand is directed to proceed to the States of Indiana, Illinois & Iowa to organize the troops remaining in those states . . . and forward them . . . to Memphis, Cairo, or such other points, as may hereafter be designated . . . to the end that when a sufficient force not required by the operations of Genl. Grant's command, (then in West Tenn) shall be raised, an expedition may be organized under General McClernand's command against Vicksburg and to clear the Miss. to New Orleans.' Also; with the order of the Genl. in Chief, to you, dated Dec. 18th. 1862 of which the following is an extract. 'It is the wish of the President that Genl. McClernands corps shall constitute a part of the river expedition and that he shall have the *immediate* command under your *direction*.' Also; with your communications of the same date, based on the preceding order and giving me command of the expedition; and with your verbal assurance, of yesterday, that my relations to the forces here would continue undisturbed. I repeat that I respectfully ask for an explanation of this seeming conflict of authority and orders that I may be enabled to guide my action intelligently. By Genl. Orders No. 22 you extend your command as far West from the Miss River as your orders may reach. By Genl. Orders No. 13 you charge the 13th. Army Corps with garrisoning Helena and other points south. Is it to be understood that my command, West of the Miss, is co-extensive with the purview of Genl. Orders No. 22. Again; you charge the 13th. Army Corps with garrisoning the West bank of the Miss. Am I to understand that I am to act on my own judgement in fixing the number, strength, and location of those garrisons, or simply by your directions. It is quite obvious that the whole or a large portion of the 13th. Army Corps must be absorbed by these garrisons if the purpose is to afford complete protection to all lawful vessels navigating the river; and thus while having projected the Miss River expedition & having been by a series of orders assigned to the command of it, I may be entirely withdrawn from it. For the reason last stated; and because the portion of the 13th. Army Corps, taking part in this expedition, is very much smaller than any other corps of your command; and because my forces are here and those of others have yet to come; why not detach from the latter to garrison the river shore and relieve all those here from liability to that charge ?" LS, DNA, RG 393, Dept. of the Tenn., Letters Received; DLC-Robert T. Lincoln. *O.R.*, I, xxiv, part 1, 12–13.

Although USG's assumption of command had been authorized and intended for some time, correspondence of Jan. 30 helps to explain why it happened then. On that day, Rawlins wrote to McClernand. "You will please direct the respective Quartermaster's of the troops most contiguous to the several Hospitals of your command, to make arrangements for, and bury the dead of such Hospitals, in accordance with the requirements of General Orders, No. 33. A. G. O., Paragraph II. of date April, 3rd., 1862. Also direct the 54th. Indiana Volunteers, to move their Camp outside the limits of the Camp Hospital, where they now are, and to furnish guards for said Hospital." LS, McClernand Papers, IHi. On the same day, McClernand wrote twice to USG. "Your dispatch of this date respecting the burial of the dead is recd   I enclose herewith an order dated an 26th inst which explains how your wishes in that respect have been anticipated. If any further arrangements are necessary doubtless I would have been advised of it by Major McMillan the Medical Director. If any thing further is required I will see that it is provided for"   LS, DNA, RG 393, Dept. of the Tenn., Letters Received. "Your order directing me to move the camp of the 54th Indiana Volunteers outside the limits of the Camp hospital, and to furnish guards for said hospital, is recieved. The officer who brought you a complaint upon this subject should not have troubled you, but should have come to me; or, having come to you, I think ought, regularly, to have been referred to me. I denounce his complaint as an act of insubordination. Please advise me who made the complaint. If I am to be held responsible for the safety of this camp, I must be permitted to dispose of the forces within it as I may think proper. The internal organization of the camp and the disposition of its forces are matters that properly belong to me, as their immediate commander. The 54th. Indiana was assigned to the position coveted by the Medical Director or the Hospital Surgeon, for strategic reasons before the Camp hospital was located. Those reasons are in part explained by the correspondence a copy of which is herewith enclosed. Nevertheless, upon the application of the Medical Director, or rather upon my own suggestion, the huts occupied by the 54th were vacated by them, and assigned for hospital uses, and the regiment ordered to encamp as far away as was consistent with strategic considerations. This they did. Still, complaint came,—the surgeon objected to the neighborship of the regiment, the Colonal complained of the insolence of the surgeon and stated that his men had voluntarily cared for the sick who had been brought out and left on the ground uncared for. I settled the question as already mentioned, by giving the huts and necessary space to the surgeon, and moving the regiment as far away as was considered proper. With this statement it remains for you to decide what ought to be done in the premises. The enforcement of your order will be the subversion of my authority at the instance of an inferior, who deserves to be arrested for his indirection and spirit of insubordination. And having said thus much, General, it is proper that I should add one or two other words. I understand that orders are being issued from your Head Quarters directly to Army Corps Commanders, and not through me. As I am invested, by order of the Secretary of War, endorsed by the President,—and by order of the President communicated to you by the General-in-Chief, with the command of all the forces operating on the Mississippi river, I claim that all orders affecting the condition or operations of those forces should pass through these Head Quarters. Otherwise I must lose a knowledge of current business, and dangerous confusion ensue. If different views are entertained by you, then the question should be immediately referred to Washington, and one or other, or both of us relieved. One thing is certain: two Generals cannot command this army, issuing independent and direct orders to subordinate officers, and the public service be promoted" LS, *ibid.*, RG 94, War Records Office, Union Battle Reports; DfS, McClernand Papers, IHi. *O.R.*, I, xxiv, part 3, 18–19.

On Feb. 1, McClernand wrote to USG. "Your dispatch of this date, in answer to mine of yesterday, is received. You announce it to be the intention of Genl. Orders No. 13., to relieve me from the Command of the Miss. river Expedition and to circumscribe my command to the 13th Army Corps, and undertake to justify the order by authority granted by the Genl. in Chief. I acquiesed in the order, for the purpose of avoiding a conflict of authority, in the presence of the enemy—but, for reasons set forth in my dispatch of yesterday, (which for anything disclosed I still hold good,) I protest against its competency and justice; and respectfully request that this, my protest, together, with the accompanying paper may be forwarded to the General in Chief, and through him to the Secretary of War and the President. I request this, not only in respect for the President and Secretary, under whose express authority I claim the right to command the Expedition, but in justice to myself as its author and active promoter." ALS, DNA, RG 94, War Records Office, Union Battle Reports. *O.R.*, I, xxiv, part 1, 13–14.

On the same day, McClernand again wrote to USG. "It seems to be probable, if not certain, that the fresh rise of the Mississippi river will drive our forces, here to withdraw upon the transports. In view of such a misfortune, I request that you will allow my command to embark, and reinforced by such troops as may be safely detached from Helena, ascend the Arkansas river, if practicable, to Pine Bluff, and march upon Arkidelphia, an extensive depot of rebel stores, and capture it, together with its Garrison; thence to Little Rock and capture that place, or to sail directly to the latter place, if practicable, and after capturing that place, march upon Arkidelphia; or to sail to Gain's Landing, and march from there to Arkidelphia, as may, upon further investigation, be found most advantageous. From Pine Bluff to Arkidelphia it is 75 miles; and from there to Little Rock it is the same distance; and from Gain's Landing to Arkidelphia it is 87 miles. This movement would consummate the expedition begun in the reduction of the Post of Arkansas, and would forward Genl. Curtis views and meet with his hearty approbation. In addition; if rapidly executed, might betray into our hands a number of the enemy's transports, said to be at Arkidelphia and thus furnish us with transports with which to descend the Washita and Red rivers into the Mississippi. These transports could be used to convey our troops to Port Hudson to co-operate with Genl. Banks in the reduction of Port Hudson, preparatory to a combined movement by land and naval forces against Vicksburg. Without such a movement what can be done but to lose valuable time and let our forces be idle? Even if it were preferable for them to remain here; under existing circumstances, comparatively few men could hold our present position with entire safety. The Army can do nothing here now, and must according to present pregnant indications be driven away by high water in a few hours." LS, DNA, RG 393, Dept. of the Tenn., Letters Received. McClernand's first letter of Feb. 1 led to USG's letter of that date to Col. John C. Kelton; the second received no written response. On Feb. 2, McClernand sent a copy of the second letter to President Abraham Lincoln. ALS, DLC-Robert T. Lincoln. See letter to Maj. Gen. John A. McClernand, Feb. 18, 1863.

To Capt. John W. Cornyn

Young's Point, La Jan 31st 1863.

CAP'T CORNYN
17TH OHIO INF'TY VOLS.

You will proceed on Steamer to Millikens Bend; and explore the system of Bayous from that point to Carthage,[1] with a view of determining the practicability of turning sufficient water from, the Mississippi through that way to navigate with our fleet.

It is not expected that you will do any work but ascertain about the amount that will have to be done to effect the object.

You will want to take with you one or more light yaul-boats, which can be carried by your men from the river to the water in the Bayou, and over any dry places you may encounter.

At Millikens Bend you will take Big Bayou pass, through that into Willow Bayou thence into Roundaway Bayou and through Bayou Vidal to the Mississippi River at Carthage.

You will take every precaution against surprise by small bodies of the enemy that you may encounter by the way.

U S GRANT
Maj General

Copies, DLC-USG, V, 18, 30; DNA, RG 393, Dept. of the Tenn., Letters Sent. John W. Cornyn was appointed capt., 78th Ohio, as of Jan. 11, 1862. On Feb. 5, 1863, Cornyn wrote to USG. "In accordance with your instructions of the 31st ultimo, I proceeded with 300 men on steamer Diligent to Milliken's Bend, and landed at Buckson's plantation. I here found on inquiring that Big Bayou was 3 miles distant, and that it ran much nearer the river at the Omega plantation. I re-embarked on the steamer, and passing up to that point found the head of the bayou; and on inquiry learned that boats of no description could be used in it.

Here I took 25 men, and proceeded 1½ miles to the Omega plantation quarters, and pressed a wagon, six mules, and driver, to haul our rations. I returned to the river, loaded the rations, and started the wagon and 275 men, under Captain Hart of the Eighth Missouri, on the main road, whilst I took an escort of 25 men and proceeded carefully to survey the bayou, with the following result: From the head of the bayou to the river would require an excavation of 300 yards in length, and a width of 50 feet at top and 25 feet at bottom, and a depth of 15 feet. From the point thus made to Willow Bayou there is a depth of 15 feet, by a width of 50 to 25 feet. The channel being much obstructed by heavy timber, drift-wood, logs, &c., some few points (in order to give room for boats to turn) require cutting off. The channel at many places would require an excavation of 3 to 5 feet in depth. It is my opinion that the whole amount of excavation required in Big Bayou would be equal to 500 yards in length, and a width of 50 to 25 feet, and a depth of 15 feet; the distance from the river to the junction of Willow Bayou being 8 miles. Willow Bayou opens with a width of 100 feet, and an average depth of 5 feet water, with 10-foot banks, which character it retains, except that the banks gradually recede for 2 miles, when the whole merges into a swamp of 3 miles in length, with an average width of 300 yards. Embankments of 3 miles in length would be required through this swamp, 20 feet width at base and 10 feet at top, with an average height of 10 feet. From this point the bayou could easily be made navigable by clearing away a small quantity of timber. The main length of Willow Bayou is 9 miles. Roundaway Bayou opens with a fine sheet of water. It has an average width of 75 yards, with 10 to 15 feet of water and 10-foot banks, and but little labor would be required, such as cutting away timber along its banks, in order to give free passage to the boats. I explored about 4 miles of Roundaway Bayou, 1½ miles below the railroad. I was here compelled to abandon my exploration from the fact that there was no possible pass on this side of the bayou, and as all bridges and ferries have been destroyed by the enemy in order to prevent our crossing, I did not deem it safe to cross with my small command, with no means of falling back should we be attacked by a heavy force, and for the further reason that I was convinced the whole project is impracticable at this season of the year. During low water it would be a matter of labor and time. We were fired upon just after kindling our fires on the morning of the 4th, wounding one of the Thirtieth Ohio Volunteer Infantry seriously; and again while with a guard of 6 men I was trying to find a road by which to pursue my survey, wounding a private of the Eighth Missouri. I was much indebted to Captain Hart, of the Eighth Missouri, and all the officers with me, for their ready co-operation, and to Dr. A. L. Flint for his attention and efficiency, and am pleased to say that the entire march was marked by the best of order." *O.R.*, I, xxiv, part 3, 33–34.

1. New Carthage, La., on the Mississippi River about twenty miles downriver from Vicksburg.

To Julia Dent Grant

Near Vicksburg Jan. 31st 1863

DEAR JULIA,

I shall not return to Memphis until the close of this campaign. You had better make your visit to the children at once. As soon as I am stationary I will write to you to join me again.

Vicksburg will be a hard job. I expect to get through it successfully however.

I just learned that a boat was going out this evening as I was about starting to take a ride through the camps and write in great haste. This is a terrible place at this stage of water. The river is higher than the land and it takes all the efforts of the troops to keep the water out.

I am still living on board of the steamer Magnolia but will go into camp as soon as a definite plan is fixed upon.

Kiss all the children for me and accept the same for yourself.

ULYS.

ALS, DLC-USG.

General Orders No. 12

Head Quarters, Dep't of the Tennessee.
Young's Point, La. Feb. 1. 1863.

GENERAL ORDERS, No. 12.

The proceedings of the Court of Inquiry convened at Holly Springs, Miss., by Special Orders No. 2., of date January 2nd 1863, from these Head Quarters, and of which Lieut. Col. Dewitt C. Loudon, of the 70th Ohio Volunteer Infantry, was President, to inquire into and investigate the allegations and charges of disloyalty against the 109th Illinois Infantry Volunteers, exonerates said regiment, as a regiment, from all suspicions of disloyalty, satisfactorily vindicates its innocence, and places it where the General Commanding hoped to find it, among the pure and patriotic in their country's defence; that whatever cause for suspicion or charges of disloyalty there was, arose from the conduct and declarations of the following named officers, who are hereby dismissed the service of the United States, with forfeiture of pay and allowances, to take effect from this date for the offences of which they are severally shown to be guilty:

Lieut. Col. Elijah Willard, for disobedience of orders, and deserting his command in the face of an enemy, that he might be taken prisoner.

Captain John M. Richie, for disobedience of orders, encouraging his men to desert, and discouraging his men from fighting in the face of the enemy.

Captain Thomas Boswell, for encouraging his men to desert, that they might be captured and paroled, and advising them to apply for discharges for slight causes; also, for trying to impress upon the minds of the officers and men of his regiment that they were embraced in the surrender of Holly Springs, by Col. Murphy, on the 20th day of Dec. 1862, well knowing the same to be false.

Captain John I. Mc.Intosh, for declaring in the hearing of his men, and in the presence of the enemy, that he would not fight if attacked, near Holly Springs, Miss., on the 20th day of December, 1862.

Captain Penninger, of Co. G., for proposing a plan by which the Regiment could be surrendered to the enemy, and attempting to induce others of the Regiment to aid in carrying it into execution during the raid of the enemy's cavalry on Holly Springs, on the 20th day of December, 1862.

2nd Lieut. John Stokes, for straggling from his command and procuring for himself, and a number of his men fraudulent paroles from a rebel citizen.

2nd Lieut. Daniel Kimmell, for advising the Colonel of his Regiment if attacked by the enemy to surrender, and on feigned sickness, procuring a Surgeon's certificate to go to the Hospital at Holly Springs, Miss., by reason of which he was captured and paroled by the enemy during the raid on that place.

1st Lieut. and Adjutant James Evans, for inciting disatisfaction among the men of his Regiment, and speaking in an improper manner of the War and the President, in violation of the 5th Article of War.

Commissary Sergeant Joshua Weisenheimer, is reduced to the ranks for declaring that he would never fire a gun upon the enemy, and on hearing a camp rumor that Maj. Gen. Burnside was defeated with a loss of twenty thousand men, wishing it was so.

By Order of Maj. Gen. U. S. Grant
JNO. A. RAWLINS
Ass't Adj't Genl

Copies, DLC-USG, V, 13, 14, 95; (2) DNA, RG 393, Dept. of the Tenn., General and Special Orders. *O.R.*, I, xvii, part 2, 586–87.
    Raised during the summer of 1862 primarily in Union County in southern Ill., the 109th Ill. was mustered in on Sept. 11. Shortly afterwards, the Preliminary Emancipation Proclamation greatly diminished the enthusiasm of the 109th. As the 109th passed through Cairo, a local newspaper claimed that there were only seven Republicans in the regt. and four of them condemned the Proclamation. *Cairo Gazette*, Oct. 23, 1862. On Oct. 31, Brig. Gen. Thomas A. Davies, Columbus, Ky., wrote to Maj. John A. Rawlins. "The Provost. Marshal reports, that he has not much confidence in the 109th Ills being composed of many 'Knights of the Golden Circle' I have releived them from Gaurd duty over prisoners, they having allowed some 8 or 9 to escape without any apparent reason. They compose a large share of the Infantry force here, and the amount of Public property at this place I have been informed amounts to some $13.000,000.—Most of Infantry are recruits On conversing with those officers who have been here for some time, I am Satisfied a small force of the Enemy, could do us much harm, tho I know of no immediate danger. I feel it my duty to acquaint you of these facts and ask if you have any suggestions to make" Copy, DNA, RG 393, Hd. Qrs. District of Columbus, Letters Sent.
    The troops also resented the quality of their weapons, and the adjt. asserted that "rocks would be as serviceable against the enemy." *Jonesboro Gazette*, Sept. 27, Dec. 20, 1862. On Nov. 23, Brig. Gen. Isaac F. Quinby, Moscow, Tenn., telegraphed to Rawlins. "The 72d Ills Vols arrived here yesterday & the 109th is just in. The latter Regt is badly off for arms it having four (4) different patterns mostly without bayonets & with locks so weak that they will not explode a cap please call attention of the matter to Genl Comdg & ask him to do what he can to replace the defective arms—" Telegram received, DNA, RG 393, Dept. of the Tenn., Telegrams Received. On Nov. 26, Quinby telegraphed to USG. "You must excuse me for again calling your attention to the miserable arms of the 109

Ill Vols   the whole Reg should be rearmed"   Telegram received, *ibid.* On the same day, USG telegraphed twice to Quinby. "What is the calibre of the 109th Reg't Illinois Infantry. Cannot suitable ammunition be obtained for their arms" "All the arms we have at Jackson were sent for yesterday. I doubt whether the 109th can be benefited. I tried since while at Corinth I believe and since to get arms for this Department but failed"   Copies, DLC-USG, V, 18, 30; DNA, RG 393, Dept. of the Tenn., Letters Sent.

When C.S.A. Maj. Gen. Earl Van Dorn captured Holly Springs on Dec. 20, the 109th Ill., guarding bridges to the south, was not under attack, but the reluctance of the troops to fight and their eagerness to surrender, their demoralization and high desertion rate, brought the regt. to USG's attention. On Dec. 31, Rawlins issued Special Orders No. 58. "It having been alleged that the 109th Regt. Illinois Infy Vols. have shown indications of disloyalty, and many members of the Regiment having Voluntarily hunted up Citizens in the neighborhood of their Camp to surrender and obtain paroles from, is hereby placed in arrest. The regiment will be disarmed by the Commander of the Brigade to which the Regiment is temporarily attached, and the arms and ammunition of the Regiment turned over to the Ordnance Officer, Lieut Carter, to be disposed of as may hereafter be ordered. Officers and men will be confined within Camp limits until otherwise ordered. The conduct of Co "K" of said Regiment being in honorable contrast with the balance of the Regiment, is exempt from the effect of the above order and will be placed on duty with the Brigade to which said Regiment is attached." Copies, DLC-USG, V, 26, 27; DNA, RG 94, Dept. of the Tenn., Special Orders; *ibid.*, RG 393, Dept. of the Tenn., Special Orders. *O.R.*, I, xvii, part 2, 511. On Jan. 2, 1863, Rawlins issued Special Orders No. 2 appointing a court of inquiry to investigate the charges against the regt. Copies, DLC-USG, V, 26, 27; DNA, RG 393, Dept. of the Tenn., Special Orders. *O.R.*, I, xvii, part 2, 523.

The court completed work on Jan. 14. On Jan. 20, USG telegraphed to Col. Joseph D. Webster, Jackson, Tenn. "The 109th Illinois at Grand Junction is ordered into Memphis and have no transportation to bring them   Send cars by the 22nd." Copies, DLC-USG, V, 18, 30; DNA, RG 393, Dept. of the Tenn., Letters Sent. On Feb. 11, USG endorsed the proceedings of the court. "Respectfully forwarded to Headquarters of the Army, Washington, D.C. and attention called to the enclosed printed Order dismissing the officers therein named from the service with the request that the same be approved by the President." Copies, DLC-USG, V, 25; DNA, RG 393, Dept. of the Tenn., Endorsements. A copy of the proceedings is *ibid.*, RG 94, Vol. Service Div., T99 vs 1863. On April 10, Brig. Gen. Lorenzo Thomas issued Special Orders No. 6 discharging officers of the 109th Ill. and transferring the men to the 11th Ill. *O.R.*, I, xvii, part 2, 590–91.

To Col. John C. Kelton

Head Quarters Dept. of the Ten.
Before Vicksburg, Feb. 1st 1863.

COL. J. C. KELTON
A. A. GEN.
WASHINGTON D. C.
COL.

Herewith I enclose you copy of Gen. Orders No 13 from these Hd Qrs. and of correspondence between Gen. McClernand and myself growing out of it.

It is due to myself to state that I am not ambitious to have this or any other command. I am willing to do all in my power in any position assigned me.

Gen. McClernand was assigned to duty in this Dept. with instructions to me to assign him to the command of an Army Corps operating on the Miss. river and to give him the chief command under my direction. This I did, but subsequently receiving authority to assign the command to any one I thought most competant, or to take it myself I determined to at least be present with the expedition.

If Gen. Sherman had been left in command here such is my confidance in him that I would not have thought my presence necessary. But, whether I do Gen. McClernand injustice or not, I have not confidance in his ability as a soldier to conduct an expedition of the magnitude of this one successfully. In this opinion I have no doubt but I am born out by a majority of the officers of the expedition though I have not questioned one of them on the subject.

I respectfully submit this whole matter to the Gen. in Chief and the President. Whatever the decision made by them I will cheerfully submit to and give a hearty support.

I am Col. very respectfully
your obt. svt.
U. S. GRANT
Maj. Gen. Com

ALS, DNA, RG 94, War Records Office, Union Battle Reports. *O.R.*, I, xxiv, part 1, 11. For the enclosures, see letter to Maj. Gen. John A. McClernand, Jan. 31, 1863.

On Jan. 28, 1863, Secretary of War Edwin M. Stanton wrote to Capt. William J. Kountz. "I have received your letter of the 25th instant, and have this day instructed the Quartermaster General to direct you to report for duty to Major General John A. McClernand. The letter of instructions of the Quarter Master General is herewith returned." Copy, DNA, RG 107, Letters Sent. On Feb. 25, Kountz, Pittsburgh, wrote to McClernand. "I have just returned from Washington where I had a very pleasant interview with Sec Stanton. That he wanted me to accompany you down the river I have no doubt. But by some over sight I never got notice of my appointment until the first of this—month which appointment was made Nov 26th at the time I was in springfield Ills with you   If my services is desired on your staff you will please let me know imedeately & I will be with you at once—I have an order from Mr Stanton to Genl Megs QMGenl to report to you for specal duty which order I will hold untel I hear from you—I have ompened a banking house here but am willing to leave the business with my partner and give my service to the Gov if I can make my self useful . . . P. S. Stanton is evedently your Friend—I have some thing to say to you which I will not put on paper"   ALS, McClernand Papers, IHi. On March 12, McClernand wrote to Kountz. "Your communication of the 25th ulto is received. Your order to report to me for Special duty, to which you refer I suppose relates to the Superintendence of river transports when I have occasion to use them. In that Capacity you could be useful and are desirable. I expect to move soon by water." DfS, *ibid.* On March 15, McClernand wrote to President Abraham Lincoln. "Permit to present to you Capt Kountz an honest and riliable gentleman. I would add more but he must embark." ALS, DLC-Robert T. Lincoln. On the reverse of this letter, Kountz wrote an undated note. "On the 13th of March 1863 Genl. Grant I am informed was Gloriously drunk and in bed sick all next day   If you are averse to drunken Genls I can furnish the Name of officers of high standing to substantiate the above"   ANS, *ibid.* On March 16, Lt. Col. John A. Rawlins wrote to McClernand. "If W. J. Kountz, late a Quartermaster is at Millikens Bend you will please cause to be ascertained by what authority he is there and on what business and report the same to these Headquarters"   Copies, DLC-USG, V, 19, 30; DNA, RG 393, Dept. of the Tenn., Letters Sent; *ibid.*, 13th Army Corps, Letters Received. On March 17, McClernand wrote to Rawlins. "Captain Kountz left there yesterday going up the river. I think I understood that he had been at Dept Head Quarters—He left on city of Memphis the same day he came from Youngs Point"   DfS, McClernand Papers, IHi; copy, DNA, RG 393, 13th Army Corps, Letters Sent. See endorsement to Capt. William J. Kountz, Jan. 29, 1862.

To Brig. Gen. Willis A. Gorman

Before Vicksburgh, Feby 1st 1863.

BRIG GENL W. A. GORMAN
COMD'G DIST OF EAST ARK.

In view of the present rise in the river, making it possible that all the country will be overflowed, the troops from Helena designed to operate with this Army will not be required until further orders

It may become necessary also to move our forces from here to higher ground. To do this there is not sufficient transportation at present. You will therefore send down immediately, to report to Col. Parsons, Master of Transportation the Boats designed to move General Fisk's Brigade.[1]

There should be no delay, as these Boats may be required as soon as they possibly can get here. Direct them to take on all the coal they can.

U. S. GRANT.
Maj General.

Copies, DLC-USG, V, 18, 30; DNA, RG 393, Dept. of the Tenn., Letters Sent.
On Feb. 1, 1863, Col. Lewis B. Parsons, Young's Point, wrote to USG. "Under your own or Genl. McClernand's orders I have within the last seven or eight days sent to Memphis six or seven boats loaded with sick, prisoners or animals requiring transportation. I gave orders in all cases, except one, to be sure to unload at Memphis & return *immediately*. It has been so customary to take boats without reference to what orders they had, that with the continued rise of the river I feel some anxiety in regard to their return lest they may be detained by the orders of some other officer; & would therefore suggest that an order be sent, on a tow boat which I will send to day, similar to the ~~one I inclose~~ following. ('Quartermasters at Helena & Memphis. The Strs 'Forest Queen,' Von Phul, J. C. Swan, City of Alton, Di Vernon, Warsaw, City of Memphis—Iatan, Nebraska, Roe & Jenny Deans, have been sent up from this fleet with orders to return *immediately*. as yet none of them have come back. The river—already very high —is still rising & threatens soon to inundate the whole country. It is therefore *imperatively* necessary that six or seven of these boats or a number of others eqivalent in capacity be sent down here *immediately*. If there are such at Helena or Memphis you will order them to take on board as soon as possible a sufficient quantity of of Coal & report here without delay; if not you will send down the first that come. By order of Maj Gen U. S. Grant'), As but twenty thousand

bushels of Coal have come since the fleet left Arkansas Post I would be glad if you could instruct the Q Ms at Memphis to send it forward more rapidly." Copy, Parsons Papers, IHi. On the same day, USG wrote to Lt. Col. Charles A. Reynolds. "Send forward Coal as rapidly as possible. But three Barges of Coal have arrived since the fleet returned from Arkansas Post." Copies, DLC-USG, V, 18, 30; DNA, RG 393, Dept. of the Tenn., Letters Sent.

On Feb. 4, Brig. Gen. Willis A. Gorman wrote to Lt. Col. John A. Rawlins. "I rec.d the dispach of the Genl Comd.g Dept of Tenn. directing me not to send the troops at this place down to Vicksburg for the present, and ordering me to send all the Transports now here to Col Parsons to remove the forces to higher ground   I found on the 'Forest Queen' going down a lot of Convalesent soldiers, attaches, citizens, &c. I deemed it prudent to stop all such here, until further orders, as they were not armed, and they could only be in the way. I did not think proper to stop the 250 Contrabands as I thought the Genl might yet need them." ALS, *ibid.*, Unregistered Letters Received. On the same day, USG wrote to Gorman. "The object in sending for the transports at Helena to be brought to this place was that we might have transportation sufficient to take on board all the troops, Artillery and public property in case of the rise in the river driving us out. Whilst this contingency exists, I do not want the troops from Helena brought down   When I know it to be perfectly safe I will send Boats from here to bring these troops down, hence there is no necessity for retaining transports at Helena, or sending for others to be used there"   Copies, DLC-USG, V, 18, 30; DNA, RG 393, Dept. of the Tenn., Letters Sent.

1. Clinton B. Fisk, born in N. Y., was an insurance agent in St. Louis on the eve of the Civil War. He organized the 33rd Mo. and was appointed col. as of Sept. 5, 1862. A prominent Methodist layman active in prohibition work—he was the Prohibition presidential candidate in 1888—his religious connections assisted his appointment as brig. gen. as of Nov. 24, 1862. James E. Kirby, Jr., "How to Become a Union General Without Military Experience," *Missouri Historical Review*, LXVI, 3 (April, 1972), 360–76. For Fisk's assignment by USG, see letter to Maj. Gen. John A. McClernand, Jan. 10, 1863. On Jan. 14, 1863, Fisk, St. Charles, Ark., wrote to USG. "When I left Memphis the Steamer John D. Perry with the 33d Iowa Vols of my command with me from St Louis and Columbus —was just ready to back out for Helena—as I supposed—I have not seen the Regiment since—not heard of any cause for its detention—the 21st Mo was to have reached Helena on Sunday from Columbus—but had not when our Expedition sailed—it is very important that the two Regiments come foward at once as the Garrison at Helena is not strong enough without them—We are pushing up White River—have found no Enemy yet—I learn they are in force at Pine Bluff and Little Rock—We found twenty five hundred Bushels of corn at this Post— left here by the Steamer Blue Wing—on Monday last—the Regiment that was here arrived at old Post—just in time to be swallowed up by Genl McClernand— I hope we shall all be soon summoned to the Mississippi—to join you in taking Vicksburgh—it seems to me that is the first mission of the western Army—" Copy, DNA, RG 393, Dept. of the Mo., Letters Sent. On Jan. 21, Fisk, "Mouth of White River," wrote to USG. "Arrived at this point a few moments since. I proceed at once to Helena to organize my Brigade and join you at earliest possible moment. The fact that my Brigade is scattered among the forces of the White River Expedition, renders it necessary for me to go there for reorganization.

Awaiting your further pleasure." Copy, *ibid*. On Jan. 24, USG wrote to Fisk. "You will leave the steamer Ruth and call upon the Quartrmaster for transportation to your command for yourself   The Ruth is a vessel of fine capacity, and the Goverment is now pressed for transportation"   Copies, DLC-USG, V, 18, 30; DNA, RG 393, Dept. of the Tenn., Letters Sent.

To Brig. Gen. James C. Veatch

Before Vicksburgh, Feby 2nd 1863

Brig. Genl. J. C. Veatch
Comd'g Dis't of Memphis

Hereafter I will send all telegraphic dispatches and important letters for Washington to your care.

I wish you to see that dispatches get off promptly from Memphis if the lines are working, if not send them to Cairo to be telegraphed from there

One of our Rams run the blockade this morning, and will prove a great annoyance to the enemy[1]

U S Grant
Maj General.

Copies, DLC-USG, V, 18, 30; DNA, RG 393, Dept. of the Tenn., Letters Sent.

1. See letter to Act. Rear Admiral David D. Porter, Jan. 31, 1863.

To Col. George W. Deitzler

Before Vicksburgh, Feby 2nd 1863.

Col. Geo. W. Deitzler.
Comd'g Expedition to Lake Providence.

Collect as many able bodied negro men as you can conveniently carry on your transports, and send them here to be employed on the canal.

If you are likely to remain where you are for several days, collect as many as you can of these people and send them down at once, with instructions for the Boats to return to you again. The boat taking this dispatch may also be loaded.

U. S. GRANT

Maj General

Copies, DLC-USG, V, 18, 30; DNA, RG 393, Dept. of the Tenn., Letters Sent. For Col. George W. Deitzler, see *Calendar*, Dec. 13, 1862; letter to Col. John C. Kelton, Feb. 4, 1863.

On Jan. 30, USG wrote to Brig. Gen. Willis A. Gorman, Helena. "If you have them send here one hundred able bodied contrabands to be employed on the canal at this place. Send them by any Steamers at your disposal" Copies, DLC-USG, V, 18, 30; DNA, RG 393, Dept. of the Tenn., Letters Sent. On Feb. 3, Gorman wrote to USG. "I Send by the 'Lealie' a lot of Negroes, all I have here, fit for duty. Col Lagow will probably get enough from above. The work on the Yazoo pass Commenced yesterday and will be open in Two days more. It looks favorable for Success." ALS, *ibid.*, Letters Received.

On Feb. 2, Lt. Col. John A. Rawlins wrote to Maj. Gen. John A. McClernand. "Please send by bearer a statement of what details are being furnished from the respective Divisions of your Army Corps, including Genl. McArthur's Division, for work on levies, roads &c. This is necessary to a proper apportionment of those required for work on the canal from yours and Genl. Sherman's commands" LS, McClernand Papers, IHi. On the same day, McClernand wrote to USG. "Herewith you will find the required report of the men on fatigue in the two Divisions of my Corps. You will see that the number, exclusive of men on picket and other guards, exceeds one half of my whole force. These extraordinary drafts are bearing heavily upon the strength and spirits of the men. Prevalent sickness, and exposure to rain and mud are telling with fearful effect.—Above and below Greenville, on the east bank of the Miss. River, many negroes were seen upon my descent to this place. Could not transports be sent to bring them and thus lighten the fatigues of our men?" LS, DNA, RG 393, Dept. of the Tenn., Letters Received; ADfS, McClernand Papers, IHi. Also on Feb. 2, Rawlins wrote to McClernand. "You will detail (800) eight hundred men of your command for work on the canal. They will report to the Engineer Officer at the head of the canal, promptly, at half past seven o'clock, A. M. of to morrow the 3rd, inst:, For efficiency, the detail will be made by Regiments as far as practicable, and continued daily until further orders. You will please report compliance with this order." LS, *ibid.* On Feb. 3, USG wrote to McClernand. "Capt. Freeman reports that he will require five hundred more men than he can get from Gen. McArthur to work on the Crevass above you. Please make the detail from your Corps to report to Capt. Freeman at an early hour tomorrow morning on board the Clara Bell." ALS, *ibid.*

On Feb. 5, Rawlins wrote to McClernand. "The Engineer officer reports that the detail for work on the canal of 800 men did not report to day. Please direct them to report at the hour required tomorrow morning, with the reasons of their non-compliance to day." LS, *ibid.* On the same day, Lt. Col. Walter B. Scates, adjt. for McClernand, wrote to Rawlins. "I have the honor to state, by direction of Genl McClernand, that in a personal interview, the day before yesterday, Genl

Grant authorized him to rescind the order of detail of 800 men of Genl Smiths
Division for work on the canal, upon the ground that the details from the 13th
Army Corps were very heavy and that Genl Sherman could furnish the men for
that work from his Corps nearby   The detail was therefore withheld by his order.
I am further directed by Genl McClernand to inquire if it is desired that the detail
should be renewed." DfS, *ibid.*; copy, DNA, RG 393, 13th Army Corps, Letters
Sent.

On Feb. 11, Rawlins issued Special Field Orders No. 1. "The work on the
Canal across the point opposite Vicksburg will be pushed forward with all possible
dispatch under the general supervision of Capt. Prime Chief Engineer. Details
will be furnished on the requisition of Captain Prime by Army Corps Commanders
as follows: The 15th Army Corps will furnish all details for the work south of the
Rail Road. The 13th Army Corps will furnish the details for all work north of the
Railroad levee to the main levee, and the contrabands will work from that point
north to the river. During the progress of this work all other details will be reduced to the least possible minimum. Capt. Prime will construct a channel at least
sixty feet in width and with as much depth as the high stage of the water will
admit." DS, McClernand Papers, IHi.

To Maj. Gen. Henry W. Halleck

Vicksburg Miss
Feb 3rd 1863 1 P M

MAJ GENL H W HALLECK
GENL IN CHIEF

One of the Rams ran the blockade this morning[1]   This is of
vast importance cutting off the Enemys communication with the
west bank of the River   One Steamboat laying at Vicksburg was
run into but not sunk   Work on the canal is progressing as
rapidly as possible

U S GRANT
Maj Genl Comdg

Telegram received, DLC-Robert T. Lincoln; DNA, RG 107, Telegrams Col-
lected (Bound); copies, *ibid.*, Telegrams Received in Cipher; *ibid.*, RG 393,
Dept. of the Tenn., Hd. Qrs. Correspondence; DLC-USG, V, 5, 8, 24, 88. *O.R.*,
I, xxiv, part 1, 14.

1. Since the ram *Queen of the West*, Col. Charles R. Ellet, ran the blockade
on the morning of Feb. 2, 1863, USG may have misdated his telegram or erred
in his first sentence.

To Col. John C. Kelton

———

Head Quarters, Dept. of the Ten.
Before Vicksburg, Feb.y 4th 1863.

Col. J. C. Kelton
A. A. Gen. Washington City,
Col.

Herewith I enclose your reports from Col. Deitzler and Lieut. Col. Duff from Lake Providence fifty odd miles above here.[1]

On examining the route of the present canal I lost all faith in it ever leading to any practical results. The canal is at right angle with the thread of the current, at both ends, and both ends are in an eddy, the lower coming out under bluffs completely commanding it. Warrenton,[2] a few miles below is capable of as strong defences as Vicksburg and the enemy seeing us at work here have turned their attention to that point.

Our labors however has had the effect of making the enemy divide his forces and spread their big guns over a greatdeel of territory. They are now fortified from Hains bluff to Warrenton. Taking the views I did I immediately on my arrival here commenced, or ordered, other routes prospected. One of these is by the way of Yazoo pass into Coldwater the Tallahatchie and Yazoo rivers. This is conducted by Lt. Col. Wilson from whom no report is yet received.[3] This route, if practicable, would enable us to get high ground above Hains bluff and would turn all the enemy's river batteries.

Another is by Lake Providence and the network of bayous connecting it with Red river. The accompanying reports show the feasability of this route. A third is by the way of Willow & Roundaway bayous, leaving the Mississippi at Millikins bend and coming in at New Carthage.

There is no question but that this route is much more practicable than the present undertaking and would have been accomplished with much less labor if commence[d] before the water had got all over the country.

The work on the present canal is being pushed. New inlet and outlet are being made so that the water will be received when the current strikes the shore and will be carried through on a curren[t.]

Respectfully &c

U. S. GRANT

Maj. Gen.

ALS, DNA, RG 200, Dr. John J. Schneider Collection. *O.R.*, I, xxiv, part 1, 14. On Feb. 4, 1863, USG wrote to Maj. Gen. John A. McClernand. "I am going up the river to Lake Providence. Will be gone until to-morrow evening." ALS, McClernand Papers, IHi.

 1. On Feb. 3, Col. George W. Deitzler, 1st Kan., Lake Providence, wrote to Lt. Col. John A. Rawlins. "Despatch *per War Eagle* just received. I send by same boat 100-able-bodied negroes—all that can be secured at present—will send out tomorrow and collect as many as possible and forward them. The Planter's have sent most of their negroes and Cotton back into the country on *Bayou Macon* some 12 or 15 miles from here, and we shall, therefore, probably not be able to send you many hands to work on the Canal. Col. Duff has permitted me to read his report respecting the object and probable result of our expedition, which covers the ground. The water in the Lake is about 8 feet lower than the surface of the River. In about six days we hope to be able to complete a cut in the Levee, 100 feet wide, which will connect the lake and the river by a channel five feet *deep*. I do not think that we will have any considerable difficulty in finding a passage for Gun Boats and small stern wheel boats through *Baxter's Bayou.* into *Bayou Macon* a distance of from 10 to 15 miles. When the water in Lake Providence rises to the level of the water in the Miss. *Baxter's Bayou* will furnish a passage for large Boats—it will only be necessary to cut a few trees so as not to interfere with chimneys. Once in *Bayou Macon* we shall have a clean coast to Red River. I look upon the prospect as entirely practicable, and shall feel very much disappointed if the Gun Boats do not pass through to *Bayou Macon* within three weeks. At Trenton, one mile above *Monroe* on Washita River the Rebels have several Batteries and a small Infantry force. This force and Batteries were at Monroe until the time our troops destroyed the Depot at *Delhi*. About 35 miles west of Monroe, at Raven's lake the Rebels have extensive salt works. where they employ several thousand Negroes. I learn that these works supply the whole south west with salt and they *ought to be destroyed*. There are in this vicinity many articles on 'the list of loyal Capture'—such as Horses, Mules and Cattle. I can 'gobble up' and send down a large supply of the latter, if desired. When the next boat comes up will you please instruct the Captain to touch at General McArthur's Head Quarters and bring up our mail." Copy, DNA, RG 94, War Records Office, Dept. of the Mo. *O.R.*, I, xxiv, part 1, 15.

 On the same day, Lt. Col. William L. Duff, Lake Providence, wrote to Rawlins. "In consequence of an impenetrable fog and other causes of detention beyond my control, the expedition for the connection of Lake Providence with the Mississippi River, did not reach this place till about 2 P. M. Sunday 1st inst. At the time of landing I was prostrated from a severe billious attack which had set in almost immediately on our leaving the fleet and from which I have not yet recovered. Immediately on landing, Col. Deitzler disembarked and occupied the remainder of the day in making a partial reconnoissance of the relative positions of the Lake and river, returning without coming to any definite conclusion as to the place best suited to make the connection but fully convinced that a connection was entirely practicable. Yesterday morning a party of 80 mounted men under the command of Col. Deitzler, and accompanied by Lieut. Elfurs, Captain Smith of the Gunboat and myself (although still very sick,) made the entire circuit of the lak[e *ta*]king the course along the Bayou on the upper side of the lake, as per accompanying chart, and returning to Providence across Bayou Tensas. The Bayou on the upper side of the lake although very easily connected with the river, and as far as depth of water is concerned, better than the canal finally decided upon, is too crooked and too much obstructed by timber to be made available for navigation within several weeks, while the course of the proposed canal upon which we are now working is short and the work can be done within a week, nature having already done the best part of it, and when completed it will give a depth of five feet, sufficient for any vessel, the dimensions of which would admit of passing through Bayou Tensas or Baxter. Either plan involves the destruction of the town (now nearly deserted,) but neither Col. Deitzler, nor myself thought this a matter of sufficient importance to interfere with the accomplishment of the object in view. On our reconnoisance yesterday we passed down the left bank of Tensas bayou about a mile, and found it navigable   to make sure however whether Tensas or Baxter is best suited to our purpose a strong reconnoitering party has gone out today, which has not yet returned. One of these outlets being decided upon as the best, the other we propose if possible to close before admitting the water from the river. In any event I do not doubt the entire practicability during high water of passing with such vessels as the Musquito fleet from the Mississippi to the Red river   We have heard however of a battery on the Washita near Monroe, planted there, with a view to the defense of extensive salt works in that neighborhood by means of which, I am informed the whole of this part of Rebeldom and the army in Mississippi and Arkansas is supplied with that indispensable article. On this subject I hope to be better informed in a few days when I will immediately advise you. I have sanguine hopes, shared in by Col. Deitzler, that the General Commanding may authorize an expedition to destroy these salt works should the information we have from negroes be confirmed. I should mention that yesterday we met with no obstacles from guerrillas. A few fleeing horsemen were chased when they dismounted and took to the swamps, leaving their horses and arms which were captured. We have also driven in some beef cattle. Trusting that so much as has been done will meet the approval of the Major General Commanding."

Copy, DNA, RG 94, War Records Office, Union Battle Reports. *O.R.*, I, xxiv, part 1, 15–16. On Feb. 4, Maj. Gen. William T. Sherman wrote to USG. "I have hastily read the Reports of the Lake Providence scheme   It is admirable and most worthy a determined prosecution. Come up the design all you can, and it will profit all the conditions of the great Problem. This little affair of ours here on Vicksburg Point is labor lost." ALS, DNA, RG 94, War Records Office, Dept. of the Tenn. *O.R.*, I, xxiv, part 3, 32.

On Feb. 9, Deitzler again wrote to Rawlins. "I stated to the Gen'l Com'd'g, when he was up here, several days since, that there are several families living in this town, who will have to be moved before we let the water into the Lake, and he suggested that they be sent up the river, which I shall do by the first boat. The

Gen'l, also suggested, that if any of them are loyal and have property which they are unable to take with them, they had better exchange it for cotton. One of them 'Hiram Steine' a german with a wife and three children, whose loyalty is and always has been above suspicion, has secured Forty three (43) bales of Cotton, and has applied to me for permission to ship the same to Memphis. As I doubt my power to grant such permission, I respectfully refer the case to you and bespeak for it a favorable consideration. I send this directly to you, instead of through the regular channel, for the reason that Gen'l McArthur will probably be on his way up to this point, while this is going down. I have read Col Duffs report and have nothing to add to it." ALS, DNA, RG 393, Dept. of the Tenn., Letters Received. On the same day, Duff wrote to Rawlins. "The work from the river to Lake Providence is nearly completed but of course the water cannot be let in until the outlet through Bayou Baxter is clear.   this cannot be done with the force now here. I hope therefore that the remainder of the 6th Division will be sent here as soon as practicable. An immense amount of stock has been driven from this region over to the highlands west of Bayou Macon which will be accessible as soon as Baxter is open—As it is now the foraging party on the 'Continental' have pretty well cleaned out what was left   The Rebels cut the ~~bayou~~ levee on Bunch's bend on Saturday but were discovered by our 'mule cavalry' in time to prevent the consummation of their project—They were compelled to repair the Levee and warned that a repetition of the offense would be visited by the burning of every house in the settlement." ALS, *ibid.*, RG 94, War Records Office, Dept. of the Mo. *O.R.*, I, xxiv, part 3, 41–42.

2. Warrenton, Miss., about ten miles downriver from Vicksburg.

3. See letter to Col. John C. Kelton, Feb. 6, 1863.

To Maj. Gen. James B. McPherson

—————

Lake Providence Feb 5, 1863.

Maj Genl J B McPherson
Comm'dg 17th Army Corps

Move one Division of your command to this place with as little delay as practicable, and come with yourself   One Brigade of McArthurs Division is now here, and the balance will be ordered up as soon as I return.

This bids fair to be the most practicable route for turning Vicksburg. You will notice from the Map that Lake Providence empties through the Tansas, Washita, Black and Red rivers into the Mississippi

All these are now navigable to within a few miles of this

place, and by a little digging less than one quarter than has been done across the point before Vicksburg will connect the Mississippi and the Lake, and in all probability will wash a channel in a short time

You will want to bring with you all the intrenching tools you can   forage and Beef Cattle can be got here near you in great abundance. You want to come however with some forage.

Direct the Division you leave behind to be in readiness to move at a moments warning.

On your arrival here you will find the work progressing which it is expected your command will complete   I will be up to see you soon after your arrival

Cotton speculators will follow you in spite of every effort to prevent it   Make orders excluding all citizens from coming within your lines so that if any of these fellows get outside they can be kept out[1]

U S Grant
Maj Genl.

Copies, DLC-USG, V, 18, 30; DNA, RG 393, Dept. of the Tenn., Letters Sent. *O.R.*, I, xxiv, part 3, 33. On Feb. 8, 1863, Maj. Gen. James B. McPherson, Memphis, wrote to USG. "Your dispatch of the 5th inst was received at 10 a. m. yesterday—Logan's Division is all ready and will embark as soon as Transports can be provided—There are not enough here now, but Graham thinks some will be up this evening—I hope to get away from here with Logan's Div—by tuesday night at latest—Quinby's Division is just relieved from Rail Road duty and marching in to day—His command will be in good shape, and ready to move at a moments notice—Bissell has just shown me an order requiring him to move with Logan's Division, with his Regt. Ponton Train, Tools &c and I have given Graham orders to assign him a Boat, which he is now loading, I hope soon to be with you, and aid in carrying out the plan which strikes me as the best and most feasible that has been presented"   ALS, DNA, RG 94, War Records Office, Dept. of the Tenn. *O.R.*, I, xxiv, part 3, 40. See letter to Maj. Gen. James B. McPherson, Feb. 12, 1863.

1. On Feb. 8, USG wrote to Brig. Gen. John McArthur. "On taking command at Lake Providence La positively prohibit cotton speculators from going into the country to purchase and bring in cotton. Enforce that Article of War which says that any person, citizen or soldier, passing beyond the outer pickets shall be shot. These people with the army are more damaging than the small pox or any other epedemic." ALS, IC. See letter to Brig. Gen. John McArthur, Feb. 15, 1863.

To Col. John C. Kelton

Head Quarters, Dept. of the Ten.
Before Vicksburg, Feb. 6th 1863.

Col. J. C. Kelton,
A. A. Gen. Washington, D. C.
Col.

Enclosed I send you report of Lt. Col. Wilson of the prospects of effecting a safe passage into the Yazoo river by the way of Yazoo Pass.

Admiral Porter will have this pass thoroughly explored by light draft gunboats upon which I am puting six hundred riflemen from the army.

It is to be hoped that this expedition will be able to capture all the transports in the Yazoo and tributaries, and destroy two gunboats said to be in course of construction. They will also attempt to ascend the Yalobusha to Grenada and if possible destroy the rail-road bridges.

The ram that run the blockade on the 2d inst. has returned to the lower end of the peninsular oposite Vicksburg.

She went as far as Red river and some miles up it capturing and destroying three steamboats loaded with commissary stores and about sixty prisoners.

I send dispatches every day or two to be telegraphed from Memphis, but as I do not know that they get through think it necessary to notify you of the fact.

respectfully
your obt. svt.
U. S. Grant
Maj. Gen. Com

ALS, DNA, RG 94, War Records Office, Union Battle Reports. *O.R.*, I, xxiv, part 1, 17. USG enclosed reports of Feb. 2, 1863, 8:00 p.m., and Feb. 4, 8:00 a.m., from 1st Lt. James H. Wilson, Yazoo Pass, to Lt. Col. John A. Rawlins. "We reached Helena last night and had all arrangements complete to start from there this morning at 10 A.M. Gen'l Gorman accompanied me, sending under my command 500 men, provided with two days rations and implements complete for the necessary labor. He returned to Helena this evening and will send down all the provisions, tents &c: needed. I arrived at the levee across the Pass about noon and found a much more favorable state of affairs than I at first anticipated; the stream looks quite navigable and I am sure will allow the boats now here to navigate it without difficulty. I had the men at work cutting the embankment by two oclock and by tomorrow night will have a water way twenty yards wide, cut. The difference of level between the water outside and inside of the levee is eight and a half feet. The steamers Henderson and Hamilton came in the pass this afternoon, landed against the embankment and turned about without difficulty—and went back into the Mississippi. The following rough sketch will convey an idea of the state of affairs here at present. . . . From the above you will perceive that there are two entrances into the pass; the lower one is the one *formerly* used, but the upper, is the one thro' which our boats passed to day, and is the best. You will also perceive that the levee is a very heavy one, and therefore will require a good deal of work to cut through, but from the fact that there is 8½ feet difference of level between the water inside and out, once opened the crevasse will enlarge very rapidly. The back country both north and south of the Pass is partially overflowed, by water from crevasses in the levee. I think boats can go through our cut in three days. The under taking promises *fine* results." "The Pass is open, and a river 75 or 80 yards wide is running through it—with the greatest velocity! I wrote you on the evening of the 2nd that by the next (yesterday) evening the water would be let through. About 7 o'clock, after discharging a mine in the mouth of the 'cut,' the water rushed through. The channel was only about five feet at first, though the embankment was cut through in two places, with an interval of about 20 feet between them; the 'cut' through which the water was first started being considerably the larger. By eleven o'clock P. M. the opening was 40 yards wide and the water pouring through, like nothing else I ever saw, except Niagara Falls. Logs, trees and great masses of earth were torn away with the greatest ease. The work is a perfect success. The pilots and the captain of the gun boat Forest Rose think it will not be safe to undertake to run through the pass for four or five days—on account of the great rapidity and fall of the water. It will take several days to pile up the country so much as to slacken the current. A prominent rebel living near Helena, 'Gen'l. Alcorn,' says there will be no difficulty whatever in reaching the Yazoo River with boats of medium size. Capt. Brown will go in with the gun boat at the very earliest moment the passage becomes practicable.—" ALS, DNA, RG 94, War Records Office, Union Battle Reports. *O.R.*, I, xxiv, part 1, 371–73. The sketch is reproduced *ibid.*

To Act. Rear Admiral David D. Porter

Head Quarters, Dept. of the Ten.
Before Vicksburg Feb. 6th 1863.

REAR ADMIRAL D. D. PORTER,
COMD.G MISS. RIVER SQUADRON,
ADMIRAL,

I would respectfully advise the following programs to be followed, as near as practicable, by the expedition through Yazoo Pass.

They necessarily go through the pass into Coldwater river thence down that stream into the Tallahatchie which with its junction with the Yalobusha forms the the Yazoo which it is the great object of the enterprise to enter.

At the town of Marion on the Yazoo river the enemy were said at one time to have had a battery.[1] But it has since been removed and unless a mistrust of our present design has induced the enemy to reoccupy that point no guns will be found there. It would be well to approach it carefully.

Below Marion the river divides forming a very large island, the right hand branch, descending, being known as the Big Sun Flower, or at least connecting with it, and the left hand branch retains the name of Yazoo. On this is Yazoo City where in all probability steamers will be found, and if any Gunboats are being constructed it is likely at this place.

According to the information I receive most of the transports are up the Sun Flower river. I would therefore advise that both of these streams, and in fact all navigable bayous, be well reconnoitered before the expedition returns.

The Yalobusha is a navigable stream to Grenada. At this place the rail-road branches one going to Memphis, the other to Columbus Ky. These roads cross the river on different bridges.

The enemy are now repairing boath these roads and on the upper one, the one leading through the middle of West Tennessee, have made considerable progress. I am liable at all times to be compelled a large to divert from the Miss. river expedition a large portion of my forces on account of the existance of these roads. If these bridges can be destroyed it would be a heavy blow to the enemy and of much service to us.

I have directed six hundred men, armed with rifles, to go up on transports to Delta, leaving here to-morrow to act as Marines to the expedition.[2] Have also ordered the regiment spoken of this morning to report at Steamer Magnolia at 10 a. m. to-morrow to join your service.

Respectfully &c.
U. S. GRANT
Maj. Gen. Com

P. S. I have directed the troops sent with the Yazoo expedition to take fifteen days rations with them.

U. S. G.

ALS, DNA, RG 45, Correspondence of David D. Porter, Mississippi Squadron, General Letters (Press). *O.R.*, I, xxiv, part 3, 36; *O.R.* (Navy), I, xxiv, 249–50.

1. Probably a reference to Fort Pemberton, near Greenwood, Miss.
2. See letter to Commanding Officer, Yazoo Expedition, Feb. 7, 1863.

To Maj. Gen. William T. Sherman

Head Quarters, Dept. of the Ten.
Before Vicksburg, Feb. 6th 1863.

MAJ. GEN. W. T. SHERMAN
COMD.G 15TH ARMY CORPS,
GEN.

Detail the regiment of which we were speaking last evening for service on the Gunboats. Let them report here at 10 a. m. to-morrow with one officer to each comp.y. The balance of the officers can be put on any detached service you may desire.

You may also detail about six hundred men to go up the river to-morrow on the Yazoo expedition. As the Gunboats to be used on this expedition are now up the river this detail will have to be sent from here on transports. I will send you word in time what steamer. They can commence embarking immediately after breakfast and take with them fifteen days rations.

Respectfully &c.

U. S. GRANT

Maj. Gen. Com

ALS, ICHi.

To Brig. Gen. Willis A. Gorman

Before Vicksburg Feb 6th 1863.

BRIG GEN'L. W. A. GORMAN

COMD.G DIST EAST ARK.

I send by the Steamer that takes this six hundred men intended to accompany a fleet of GunBoats down the Yazoo river if found practicable   The Steamer goes to Helena after a barge of coal for this fleet   If the Navy have any coal at Helena they will take that; if not, send a barge belonging to the Q. M. Department. Admiral Porter has called my attention to the fact that army transports, have been in the habit of taking coal, belonging to the Navy Dep't. This should not be allowed, except in cases of great emergency and then any coal taken, should be returned as soon as possible   The two branches. of service are supplied out of diffirent appropriations, hence the necessity of being particular in this matter. As it is of the utmost importance that this Expedition should get off, and cannot do it without the coal, if there is none on hand, send a Steamer forthwith to Memphis after some, with directions to return as soon as possible. Should a Steamer be sent up, if they meet a tow coming down with coal, let them take one of their barges and return immediately. If it should be necessary to send the Steamer that has the troops aboard, let them debark at Helena, and await her return. Some other Steamer should be sent however if practicable.

U. S. Grant Maj Genl

Copies, DLC-USG, V, 18, 30; DNA, RG 393, Dept. of the Tenn., Letters Sent. Misdated Feb. 8, 1863, in *O.R.*, I, xxiv, part 3, 39. On Feb. 10, Brig. Gen. Willis A. Gorman, Helena, wrote to Lt. Col. John A. Rawlins. "In reply to certain instructions contained in an autograph letter recieved from Major General Grant, dated the 6th inst. I desire to say that the Coal has been provided for the fleet which is to go through the 'Yazoo Pass'; Also that the suggestions of General Grant in reference to our use of the Navy Coal shall be strictly observed. I do not remember however, that any Coal belonging to the Navy has been used, except in a single case of great emergency, and then, with the consent of the Officer in Command of the Mortar Boats, Mr. Wheelock. The Quarter Master informs me that in this instance, the Coal has been promptly returned." ALS, DNA, RG 393, Dept. of the Tenn., Letters Received.

On Feb. 6, USG again wrote to Gorman. "I have been informed that about one hundred Federal prisoners were brought down the Arkansas river, and turned over to one of our Gun Boats. I requested Admiral Porter to send them to Helena When they arrive send them by first Steamer to the Commanding Officer at Memphis who will receive orders from me for their further disposal." Copies, DLC-USG, V, 18, 30; DNA, RG 393, Dept. of the Tenn., Letters Sent. On the same day, USG wrote to Brig. Gen. James C. Veatch, Memphis. "I have directed Genl Gorman to send you some prisoners, Federal, sent down from Little Rock. When they arrive forward them to Benton Barracks by first opportunity under the charge of a proper Officer" Copies, *ibid*. On Feb. 7, USG wrote to Gorman. "You will place under guard the prisoners brought down from Little Rock, and whom I directed in a note of yesterday to be sent to Memphis Tenn. On reflection but few or none of these men could have been legitimately captured, and I am determined to deal with all others as deserters . . . P. S. Should Major Horton of the 97th Illinois Vols. be among the Prisoners referred to, I want special pains taken to see that he is returned here" Copies, *ibid.*

To Brig. Gen. Charles S. Hamilton

Head Quarters, Dept. of the Ten.
Before Vicksburg, Feb. 6th 1863.

Brig. Gen. C. S. Hamilton
Comd.g Dist. of West Ten.
Gen.

From Southern papers I have seen notices of some of Van Dorn's forces arriving at Holly Springs. There is also evidence that they are working dilligently repairing the rail-road North from Grenada.

That demonstrations will be made on your lines of communication to divert troops from this expedition is almost certain. If we get Vicksburg, and the balance of the Mississippi river it may also be expected that all their troops now holding it will be suddenly diverted to Rosecrans front and into West Ten. I will keep a sharp lookout however for this move.

I will leave Quinby's Div. until the last moment but hope that will not be a great while. If any demonstration should be made requiring the strengthening of some other point in your command Quinby's Div. can be used about the city so as to enable you to spare a greater number from your command proper.

I think my order in relation to the sale of cotton a just one and still adhere to it. If wrong, and so decided by competant authority, the Quartermaster can refund the whole amount received for the cotton, deducting all proper charges. You will direct therefore, that the sale proceed under my order.

Respectfully &c.

U. S. GRANT

Maj. Gen. Com

ALS, Warren A. Reeder, Hammond, Ind. *O.R.*, I, xxiv, part 3, 35. On Feb. 2, 1863, Brig. Gen. Charles S. Hamilton had written to USG. "The Eighty-seventh Illinois Infantry will arrive here to-day. The Tenth Missouri Cavalry is all here but one company. The Second Wisconsin Cavalry from Helena, and a battalion First Missouri Cavalry are here. The Fifteenth Regulars from Columbus are here. The First Regulars from Corinth are under orders, and will be here in a day or two. I have ordered the Thirty-fourth Wisconsin (*en route*) to be stopped at Columbus, and that portion of Thirty-fifth Iowa there to go to Tuttle, at Cairo. I think I shall send the Tenth Cavalry, Colonel Cornyn, to Dodge, at Corinth, but Dodge is nearly starved for forage, and I may want the regiment here, for I learn of something every day that confirms the indications that Van Dorn is ready to move on this road as soon as these divisions of Logan's and Quinby's get away. Undoubted information of yesterday says Van Dorn has returned from Tupelo, and moved across Yalabusha, at Grenada, with considerable artillery, moving on railroad, which is running to Coffeeville. Repairs on railroad were about complete to Oxford. General Stanley reports to me to-day that a noted secessionist near his camp said yesterday that no great resistance would be offered at Vicksburg, but that the rebel army would overrun West Tennessee and Kentucky as soon as your forces were diverted down the river. I do not give much credence to such a report, but I have little doubt Van Dorn, with all his cavalry and a division of infantry, will move on this railroad. If he comes, I hope to make him sick of the experiment. Quinby seems averse to going down the river, and wished me to speak to you about it. He must tell you his own reasons. I found, much to my surprise, yesterday, an order from your headquarters directing Captain [Asher R.] Eddy to sell all the cotton in Government possession, and it was advertised to be sold to-day. Believing you have not understood the matter fully, I ordered a postponement of sale until you could investigate and decide. It will not do to sell the cotton and pay to the owners 25 cents per pound, the price to be paid by speculators. If the Government has any claim on the cotton, it owns its full value. If the owners can establish their claims, it will not be for a fraction of the value, but for it all. Either the cotton is liable to confiscation and belongs entirely to the Government, or it must all be given to the owners. I mean all the value of the cotton. Some of the claims have been established beyond cavil, and it was to avoid any trouble to you that I have had the sale postponed. If the Government will make a rule to buy all the cotton, taking it out of traders' hands entirely, then it will be fairly entitled to what profit can be made between purchase and sale; but the seizure of the cotton gives the Government no right to a profit or to take the profits by force out of the legitimate traders' hands. Hoping you will soon be here to examine these matters in person, . . . P. S.—Have just received a note from Hurlbut, saying he leaves Cairo for Memphis to-night." *Ibid.*, pp. 30–31. See letters to Maj. Gen. Stephen A. Hurlbut, Feb. 9, 13, 1863.

On Feb. 6, USG again wrote to Hamilton. "If the 1st Infantry has not yet left Corinth leave them there until further orders." Copies, DLC-USG, V, 18, 30; DNA, RG 393, Dept. of the Tenn., Letters Sent.

To Brig. Gen. James C. Veatch

Before Vicksburg Feb 6. 1863.

BRIG GENL J C VEATCH
COMMDG DIST OF MEMPHIS.

When Generals Sherman and McArthurs' Divisions left Memphis, a great number of men were left behind in Hospitals, many of whom must now be convalescent.

I wish you would cause an inspection of the Hospital, and see that proper facilities are given to secure the sending of all men in Hospital back to their Regiments as fast as they are able to do duty

There should be certain days in each week when the Surgeon in charge of Hospitals should make an inspection and order men fit for duty back to ther respective commands, or in case of their belonging to distant commands, report them to the commanding Officer of the Post who should have proper regulations for providing them transportation, and seeing that they leave by the first opportunity

U S GRANT
Maj Genl

Copies, DLC-USG, V, 18, 30; DNA, RG 393, Dept. of the Tenn., Letters Sent.

To Col. John C. Kelton

———

Head Quarters, Department of the Tenn.
Young's Point, La. Febry 7th 1863.

COL. J. C. KELTON.
ASST. ADJT. GENL.

I have the honor to transmit herewith the report of Major Gen. W. T. Sherman of the operations of the forces under his command at the Post of Arkansas, with the following enclosures being duplicates furnished direct to these Head Quarters. The report of Major Genl. J. A. McClernand with the exception of an abstract of lists of casualties and missing has not yet been received.[1] It will be forwarded immediately on its receipt.

1st. Report of Brig Gen. D. Stuart.
2nd   ”   ”   ”   ”   C. E. Hovey.
3rd   ”   ”   ”   Col. Giles Smith.
4th Abstract of lists of Casualties and missing.
5th Letter from Major Gen. Sherman of date the 4th inst.[2]

I am, Col, Very Respectfully
Your Ob't. Servant.
U. S. GRANT
Maj Genl Commdg.

LS, DNA, RG 94, War Records Office, Union Battle Reports. Reports of the Arkansas Post expedition are printed in *O.R.*, I, xvii, part 1, 699–796.

On Jan. 17, 1863, Maj. Gen. William T. Sherman had written to USG. "I take a liberty of writing you direct semi officially. Official Reports will convey to you a pretty clear idea of our success at the Post of Arkansas. I infer from a remark made by General McClernand that you have disapproved the step. If I could believe that Banks had reduced Port Hudson, and appeared at Vicksburg ding our absence I would feel the force of your disapproval, but I feel so assured that we will again be at Vicksburg before Banks is there that I cannot think any bad result of this kind can occur. As long as the Post of Arkansas existed on our flank with Boats to ship cannon and men to the Mouth of Arkansas we would be annoyed beyond measure whilst operating below. The capture of the Blue-Wing was a mere sample. We were compelled to reduce it. Its importance to the enemy cannot be doubted by one who has seen their preparations and heard the assertion of its Garrison that it was deemed impregnable. The fort proper was constructed with great care and its armament as good as it could be made. The Post of Arkansas could only have been taken by a strong force both by land & water as we took it, and had we given any previous notice it would have been strongly reinforced. They had huts built for full 10,000 men, and with 15 000 they could have held the Levee as far down as the Notrib house, and our Landing would have been resisted. Could we have followed up, the capture of Little Rock would have been easy, but even as it is the enemy up the Arkansas can be held in check by a single wooden Gun boat. I assure you when next at Vicksburg I will feel much less uneasiness about our communications. We leave here tomorrow and will be at Millikens Bend or Youngs Point by the next day, and if Banks has taken Port Hudson and appeared below Vicksburg we can easily communicate across. But I do not expect he will be there for some time. It may be he can put some guns in position along the shore of the Mississippi at a point where I had my pickets which might occupy the attention of one set of Batteries and if the Gun boats will assail the city in front we might possibly land right under the Guns, or we may try Hains Bluff, but as to forcing a passage at any point along the Yazoo from its mouth to Haines I doubt it. I wish you would come down and see. I only fear McClernand may attempt impossibilities again if Banks do come up   it may be the approach from the South may be better, but all their old defences of last year look to the south. I saw enough to convince me they have about ten field Batteries, and I should estimate their siege guns at fifty. I saw about thirty. The importance of Vicksburg cannot be over estimated and if possible a larger force should somehow reach the Ridge between Black and Yazoo, so as approach from the Rear. Please give much attention to the quantity of ammunition and tools. I carried down with me 1200 axes, picks & spades, but spite of all efforts many are lost—We built batteries at Yazoo and up at the Post, and you know how details of our careless men neglect tools. We have a good deal of real sickness and still more of that sort which develops on the approach of danger. An attack on Vicksburg will surely draw thither the Grenada force so that I think you might safely join us and direct our movemts." ALS, DNA, RG 94, War Records Office, Union Battle Reports. *O.R.*, I, xvii, part 2, 570–71.

1. On Feb. 4, Maj. Gen. John A. McClernand wrote to USG. "Herewith you will find a statement of the killed and wounded in the battle of the Arkansas. It will be soon followed by a full report, which has been delayed by pressing claims of multiform character, upon my attention; and for the completion of a map intended to accompany it. Until then, I have deemed it proper that sub-reports

should be withheld so that all may be sent and published at once." LS, DNA, RG 94, War Records Office, Union Battle Reports; ADfS, McClernand Papers, IHi. On Feb. 10, USG wrote to Brig. Gen. Lorenzo Thomas. "Please find herewith report of Maj. Gen. J. A. McClernand report of operations against the Post of Arkansas, also sub-reports with the exception of some from the 13th Army Corps not yet handed in but which will be forwarded as soon as received." ALS, DNA, RG 94, War Records Office, Union Battle Reports. On Feb. 13, Lt. Col. Walter B. Scates, adjt. for McClernand, sent to USG's hd. qrs. another report of casualties, which USG forwarded to Washington the same day. DLC-USG, V, 21; DNA, RG 393, Dept. of the Tenn., Register of Letters Received; *ibid.*, RG 94, Register of Letters Received.

2. ALS, *ibid.*, War Records Office, Union Battle Reports. *O.R.*, I, xvii, part 1, 763.

To Commanding Officer

———

Before Vicksburg Feby 7. 1863

COMMANDING OFFICER
YAZOO EXPEDITION

You will proceed without delay to Helena Ark and there take in tow a Barge of Coal, applying to Genl Gorman for the same and return to Delta Miss with it

At Delta you will remain until the arrival of four Gun Boats that have been designated by the Admiral when you will divide your force, and send them aboard the Gun Boats, the number on each to be determined by the Navy department.

As soon as the expedition proceeds you will discharge the Transport on which you ascended the river and direct her to return the empty Coal barge to Helena, and then return to this fleet herself.

Full directions have been given the Navy Department for their guidance on this Expedition

The Infantry go to act as Marines for the occasion   The troops will be under the immediate command of their own Officers, but in no instance are they to exercise control over the vessels or dictate when they are to go or what do.

The troops are designed to give protection to the Vessels on which they are, and to operate on land if the necessity arises

U S GRANT
Maj Genl

Copies, DLC-USG, V, 18, 30; DNA, RG 393, Dept. of the Tenn., Letters Sent. *O.R.*, I, xxiv, part 3, 38.

To Abraham Lincoln

Head Quarters, Dept. of the Ten.
Before Vicksburg, Feb. 8th 1863.

HIS EXCELLENCY
A. LINCOLN
PRESIDENT OF THE UNITED STATES.
SIR:

I have just made an endorsment on the recommendation of Gen. Prentiss for the promotion of Capt R. B. Hatch favoring it. This I regard as a simple act of justice to Capt. Hatch.

He offered his services to his country early in this war and was placed from the start in one of the most trying positions in the Army. At Cairo, with all about him green in the new duties they had to perform, Capt. Hatch had to organize his department and run the machinery of it for many months without a dollar of funds. This necessarily caused great clamoring among Govt. creditors and gave a monopoly of supplying the Army to capitalests. Cairo Vouchers went down in the market and loosers would naturally attribute their misfortunes to those from whom they received them. Capitalests were interested ~~and~~ pecuniarily in keeping up this suspicion   Hence Capt. Hatch was in a position to say the least embarassing and dangerous to his reputation even without a fault being committed by himself. A full investigation has entirely exhonerated him and even shown a most economical administration of his duties.

I am so well satisfied now with Capt. Hatchs official conduct that I regard it as a positive act of duty to him to give this testamonial of my convictions of the injustice that has been done him in the past and of his worthiness of a reward which I believe to be due him.

Again I would most respectfully urge the promotion of Capt. Hatch and his assignment for duty with Gen. Prentiss who is anxious to have his services.

> I am Very respectfully
> your obt. svt.
> U. S. GRANT
> Maj. Gen.

ALS, DNA, RG 94, ACP, 241 CB 1872. Enclosed with this letter was an undated petition to President Abraham Lincoln signed only by Brig. Gen. Benjamin M. Prentiss. "We the undersigned, believing that Capt R. B. Hatch A. Q. M. has, by his conduct as an officer and his unwearied labors in the administration of the affairs of the Quartermaster Department while in charge of the same at the various places where he has been stationed, ask for him that he may be promoted to the rank of Colonel and Aid-de-Camp to Major Genl U. S. Grant Commanding Dept of Tenn. &c with orders to report to Genl B. M. Prentiss for duty as Aid-de-Camp and Quartermaster." DS, *ibid.* On Feb. 8, 1863, USG endorsed this petition. "I take great pleasure in recommending Capt. R. B. Hatch for the promotion asked believing him in every way worthy and entitled to the promotion. I would further recommend that the date of his promotion go back to before the repeal of the law authorizing additional Aides-de-Camp, and that Capt. Hatch be placed on the Staff of a Commander entitled to such additional Aides and be assigned as suggested." AES, *ibid.* On Jan. 14, 1864, Lincoln transmitted these documents to Secretary of War Edwin M. Stanton with a covering letter. "My Illinois Sec. of State, O. M. Hatch, whom I would like to oblige, wants Capt. R. B. Hatch made a Quarter-Master in the Regular Army—I know not whether it can be done conveniently, but if it can, I would like it." ALS, *ibid.*

For the earlier difficulties of Capt. Reuben B. Hatch, see letter to Brig. Gen. Montgomery C. Meigs, Jan. 22, 1862. On Sept. 27, 1862, Lincoln wrote concerning Hatch's return to duty. Lincoln, *Works (Supplement)*, p. 154. On Oct. 12, Hatch requested assignment to USG's command. DLC-USG, V, 21; DNA, RG 393, Dept. of the Tenn., Register of Letters Received. On Feb. 8, 1863, by Special Orders No. 39, Dept. of the Tenn., Hatch was assigned to duty under Prentiss in the District of Eastern Ark. DS, *ibid.*, RG 94, Staff Papers, Reuben B. Hatch; copy, *ibid.*, RG 393, Dept. of the Tenn., Special Orders; DLC-USG, V, 26, 27.

To *Act. Rear Admiral David D. Porter*

Steamer Magnolia
Feb. 8th 1863.

ADMIRAL PORTER,
COMD.G MISS. SQUADRON,
ADMIRAL,

The Major and Adjutant of the regiment sent to serve on the gunboats will be relieved from that duty and can make Hd Qrs. of their regiment at Memphis or Cairo where they will stay.

I find that some of the officers of that regiment are laboring under the mistaken idea that they were selected for that particular duty as a punishment. I would be pleased to have their minds set at rest on this point. They were selected solely because of the necessity existing that you should have more men, and of the reduced numbers of their regiment.

One of the regiments selected for the same service has been with me for nearly eighteen months, and has always proven itself one of the very best I had and of course no indignity would be offered them. Any troops I have can well afford to sail in the same boat with this regiment.

I will endeavor to accomodate the number of officers and men to your wants.

Respectfully Yours
U. S. GRANT
Maj. Gen. Com

ALS, MdAN. On Feb. 8, 1863, Act. Rear Admiral David D. Porter twice wrote to USG. "There were 250 men sent over yesterday: we will only want 350 more altogether. Can you so arrange it that we can only have that number, with but 3 officers? We have now 5 officers more with these men than we want, or can accomodate which is the trouble. The Major and Adjutant, brought their horses, which I am afraid they will have to part with if they stay with us. Hoping you will be able to make arrangements that will suit the occasion," "Company C. mutinied this morning and refused duty: I put them all in irons, and sent them to you, as I could not order a legal court on them. The example was salutary, the rest acquiesced immediately. I would recommend that the non-comissioned officers be broken, and that the others be set to digging ditches. I am sorry to have commenced so roughly, but 'a bad beginning makes a good ending.' I would not hesitate to keep the men I have sent you, did I not think that they will feel the punishments of being dismissed the fleet, when they see their comrades again, and hear how comfortable they are They are pretty drunk now and insensible to reason, and I thought the shortest way was to put them out of sight. Some one gave them a half barrel of whiskey amongst their rations, with which they filled their canteens, and regaled the crew of the 'Benton,' who are some what in a like condition, but more tracteable." LS, DNA, RG 45, Correspondence of David D. Porter, Mississippi Squadron, Letters Sent. *O.R.* (Navy), I, xxiv, 324–25.

On Feb. 3, Porter had written to USG. "A great many applications come to me from the soldiers in the Army for employment in the Squadron, and as I am about to be placed 'hors de combat,' by many of my mens times being out, I lately had to obtain twenty-five men from General McClerland for the Gun Boat 'Chillicothe,' that ship having only ten men. I request that you will let me have about four hundred men who I would like transferred in companies without the commissioned officers—When men are picked out of a Regiment or Company, Officers naturally send the worst, but when a whole company goes one would likely stand a chance of getting some good men.—I think you might at this time be able to spare the number I ask for, for if I was called upon to go into action I should be able to fight but very few of my guns.—In case you should accede to my request, may I ask that those sent have a supply of clothing that will enable them to comply with Naval regulations.—I will promise to send you back the soldiers when I have done with them, the best drilled and best behaved men in the Army.— I would not trouble you, or ask such if I was not in a condition that no Naval officer ever was before, and the Government cannot help me." LS, DNA, RG 94, Letters Received.

On Feb. 9, USG endorsed this letter. "Respectfully forwarded to the Head-quarters of the Army Washington, D. C. I have in compliance with the request of acting Rear Admiral David D. Porter, detailed the 58th Ohio Inf'y Vols a Regiment that has been greatly reduced by casualties for duty with the Miss. Squadron, one officer accompanying each company to make out their returns and Meuster Rolls. there are but few officers remaining these I shall place on detached duty where their services can be made beneficial. I have also ordered the (2) two companies of the 29th Ills. and the (4) four companies of the 101st Illinois Infantry (that escaped capture at Holly Springs Miss.) to this place which will make the complement the Admiral requires, and respectfully ask that my action in the matter may be approved." ES (illegible), *ibid.*; copies, *ibid.*, RG 393, Dept. of the Tenn., Endorsements; DLC-USG, V, 25. On Feb. 26, Col. James B. Fry wrote to USG. "I have the honor to acknowledge the receipt of Admiral Porter's letter of date Feb 3, endorsed by yourself, in reference to the course pursued by you in detailing a part of your command for duty with the Mississippi Squadron, and beg to inform you that your action is approved by the General-in-Chief." LS, DNA, RG 393, Dept. of the Tenn., Letters Received.

To Abraham Lincoln

Head Quarters, Dept. of the Ten.
Before Vicksburg, Feb. 9th 1863.

HIS EXCELLENCY
A. LINCOLN, PRESIDENT
SIR:

Seeing the names said to have been handed in to the Senate for confirmation for Gens. I deem it my duty to call your attention to the effect some of these promotions will have in this Dept. I see the name of N. B. Buford for Maj. Gen.[1] He would scarsely make a respectable Hospital nurse if put in petticoats, and certain is unfit for any other Military position. He has always been a dead weight to carry becoming more burthensome with his increased rank.

There are here worthy men to promote who not only would fill their positions with credit to themselves and profitably to their country, but whos promotion would add weight to our cause where it is needed and give reniewed confidance to a large number of brave soldiers. Conspicuous among this latter class is Brig. Gen. J. A. Logan. He has proven himself a most valuable officer and worthy of every confida   He is entitled to and can be trusted with a command equal to what increased rank would entitle him to. There is not a more patriotic soldier, braver man, or one more deserving of promotion in this Dept. than Gen. Logan. I have mentioned these two cases as strongly contrasting and spoken of them fully. I will now mention some who have been named for promotion who really can render their country no service and others whos promotion would add strength to our cause.

Among the former ~~there~~ I would place N. Brayman, Col. S. D. Baldwin, 57th Ill.[2] I. Pugh, 41st Ill. as being conspicuous. All of them are clever gentlemen but could not command the confidance of men in battle. Of those who could I would mention particularly Col. M. D. Leggett 78th Ohio M. M. Crocker 13th Iowa, G. W. Dietzler 1st Kansas, T. E. G. Ransom 11th Ill. J. D. Stevenson 7th Mo. and B. H. Grierson 6th Mo [*Ill.*] Cavalry.

There are a number of both of these classes that might be mentioned but have not the same claims to be placed with the latter class as those named, or are not so objectionable as the others.

Hoping that this will be received as intended, solely to promote the interests of service,

I remain very respectfully your obt. svt.
U. S. GRANT
Maj. Gen.

ALS, DLC-Robert T. Lincoln. Presumably on the same day, Lt. Col. John A. Rawlins wrote an undated letter to U.S. Representative Elihu B. Washburne. "I see by the papers the name of Napoleon Bonaparte Buford before the Senate for confirmation as Major General, which confirmation would be so unjust to the many brave and deserving men and officers of the 'Army of the Tennessee' that I feel it my duty to call your attention, 'as the friend of this Army' and the one to whom it owes so much for proper representation at Washington, to the fact, that if possible so great a calamity if it has not already fallen, may be prevented. General Buford is a kind hearted and affectionate old gentleman, entertaining views at variance with our republican institutions, and believing the Goverment of England, because of its titled nobility, much preferable, and further that the final result of this war will be the overthrow of our present system and give us Dukes and Lords and titled castes and that his family will be among the nobility. This may seem idle talk and unmeaning declamation, but nevertheless he urged it with great vehemence and earnestness to Genl. Richard Oglesby and myself, as long ago as 1861 at Cairo, Illinois. Genl. Oglesby will remember it, I have no doubt, just as I have stated it. To me, however, it evidenced a diseased and addled brain, a weak and foolish old man. His disobedience of positive orders given him on the field of Battle at Belmont came near losing to the country his entire Regiment which was only saved from such fate by the fire from our gun boats driving him off of the main road, and thereby avoided meeting the enemy. Had he obeyed the orders given him by both Generals Grant and McClernand he would have helped defeat the enemy in the fight coming out of Belmont, saved the lives of many gallant men & embarked his Regiment with the other troops, before reinforcements for the enemy could have crossed from Columbus. As it was, it was the merest accident he was saved. For his conduct at Belmont he was never afterwards trusted by Genls. Grant or McClernand   He was left behind on the expedition into Kentucky, and also against Forts Henry and Donelson. How he demeaned himself under General Pope, I am unable to say but know that since he returned to this command he has been absent from one cause or another most of the time, and when here continuously insisting on the command of some Post not in the field, and has at last succeeded in getting himself assigned by orders from Washington to the command of Cairo, displacing Genl. Tuttle an officer who by his bravery and good conduct leading the 2d. Iowa to the assault of the enemy's works at Donelson won the admiration of that best soldier of the Republic, the late lamented, Major General C. F. Smith. From physical infirmities consequent upon exposure in the Field, Genl. Tuttle is unable for active field duty, but might well command the Post of Cairo. Besides, the promotion of such men as Genl. Buford is establishing too high a rate of pensions, for the Government long to stand. But the greatest calamity to the Army is the dissatisfaction it creates among men who remain in the field and do their duty under all circumstances. He is placed over such men as Logan Oglesby, Lauman and Dodge and others too numerous to mention, all his superiors in everything that constitutes the soldier. Logan deserves promotion for his unflinching patriotism and desire to whip the enemy by any rout or means practicable. He should be made a Major General by all means, and if Buford is promoted, should be dated back to rank him. The same can be said of Oglesby and Dodge of Iowa by every officer or soldier in the army. Genl. Grant has written the President on the subject of promotions to-day. I am glad to see John E. Smith's appointment confirmed. His star will never lighten a coward's path or be disgraced by the one whose shoulder it adorns. Everything here is as favorable as could be expected considering the high water. Work on the canal is progressing. Jones is here, making himself generally useful. Trusting that that which is for the best interests of the country may prevail, . . ." Copy, DLC-Elihu B. Washburne.

On Dec. 29, 1862, Maj. Edwin Moore, 21st Mo., Columbus, Ky., wrote to USG. "The citizens of Hannibal. Mo. and of Keokuk Iowa. having gotten up a petition memororbly signed for the promotion of Colonel. David. Moore 21st Mo. Vol Infy. to the position of Brigadier General of Volunteers. I at the request of the line officers of the regiment take the liberty of asking of you a letter of indorsement to the Honorable John B. Henderson U. S. Senate. Having served in your Army for so long a time we presume you to be acquainted with the services rendered by Colonel Moore and his qualifications for the position." LS, DNA, RG 94, ACP, M1111 CB 1863. On Jan. 14, 1863, USG endorsed this letter. "Col. Moore of the 21st Mo. Vols. has been personally known to me since about the 1st of April 1862. A more gallant man does not command a regiment. At Shiloh Col. Moore lost a leg in action but nevertheless returned and resumed command of his regt. in a few months time, seting an example to absent officers worthy of imitation. I cordially recommend Col. Moore for promotion" AES, *ibid*. Col. David Moore was not promoted to brig. gen. until after the Civil War.

On Dec. 18, 1862, Brig. Gen. Charles S. Hamilton, Oxford, Miss., wrote to Secretary of War Edwin M. Stanton recommending the appointment as brig. gen. for Col. George B. Boomer, 26th Mo. LS, *ibid*., B763 CB 1863. On Jan. 16, 1863, USG endorsed this letter. "I cordially endorse the recommendations of Gen. Hamilton in favor of Col. Boomer, of the 26th Mo. Vols, for promotion to the rank of Brig. Gen. He is now in command of a Brigade and sustains himself well in the position." AES, *ibid*. No appointment resulted.

On Jan. 21, Col. C. Carroll Marsh wrote a letter of resignation which USG endorsed on Jan. 28. "Colonel Marsh has been one of the best Brigade Commanders in the Department and has done most excellent service on the Battlefield and in Camp and he has frequently been recommended for promotion. Seeing so many promoted over him, and feeling as he does on the subject I do not believe the service would be benefitted by retaining him, and therefore recommend the acceptance of his resignation" Copies, DLC-USG, V, 25; DNA, RG 393, Dept. of the Tenn., Endorsements. See telegram to Maj. Gen. Henry W. Halleck, Oct. 21, 1862. On Jan. 19, 1863, President Abraham Lincoln nominated C. Carroll Marsh as brig. gen. The Senate refused to confirm Marsh, and his resignation was accepted as of April 22, 1863. In the interim, on Feb. 14, Maj. Thomas M. Vincent, AGO, wrote to Marsh. "I have respectfully to inform you that your tender of resignation, because your promotion has been ignored, has been returned by the General-in-Chief. 'Disapproved' as the reasons given apply equally to many other officers and are not considered sufficient to warrant its acceptance" Copy, DLC-USG, V, 93. On March 1, Rawlins transmitted this letter to Marsh. Copies, *ibid.*, V, 18, 30; DNA, RG 393, Dept. of the Tenn., Letters Sent.

On Feb. 24, the petition of officers of the 6th Div., 17th Army Corps, Lake Providence, for the promotion of Brig. Gen. John McArthur, was favorably endorsed by Maj. Gen. James B. McPherson. ES, IC. On the same day, USG endorsed the petition. "Gen. McArthur has proven himself a zealous and efficient officer from the begining of this rebellion and has won promotion on the field of battle. I heartily endorse him for promotion." AES, *ibid.* McArthur, however, was not nominated as bvt. maj. gen. until Feb. 1, 1865.

On Feb. 6, 1863, McArthur wrote to Lincoln recommending that Col. Augustus L. Chetlain, 12th Ill., be appointed brig. gen. ALS, DNA, RG 94, ACP, C156 CB 1883. On Feb. 9, USG endorsed this letter. "I heartily endorse the recommendation of Col. Chetlain for promotion. He has proven himself a gallant, vigilent and able officer. His whole time and energy has been given to the service of his country from the breaking out of the rebellion, and on the battle field and in camp he has proven his qualifications for an advanced position." AES, *ibid.* Earlier, McArthur, Brig. Gen. Richard J. Oglesby, and Brig. Gen. Thomas A. Davies wrote to Lincoln recommending the appointment of Chetlain. ALS, *ibid.* On Dec. 8, 1862, USG endorsed this letter. "Col. Chetlain is an efficient and valuable officer who has richly earned promotion and is well qualified for the command increased rank would entitle him to." AES, *ibid.* On Dec. 11, Chetlain wrote to Washburne. "I am glad you have addressed Gen Grant asking him to reccommend me for promotion. The Gen told me last summer that he was under very great obligations to you for what you had done for him & that any request you might make of him would be granted. The Gen endorsed my papers sent forward, but a letter of reccommendation will be infinitely better." ALS, DLC-Elihu B. Washburne. Chetlain, however, was not nominated as brig. gen. until Dec. 31, 1863. See letter to Abraham Lincoln, Dec. 2, 1863.

On March 1, officers of the 2nd Brigade, 2nd Div., 15th Army Corps, prepared a petition recommending the promotion to brig. gen. of Col. Thomas Kilby Smith, 54th Ohio. DS, DNA, RG 94, ACP, 213S CB 1863. Brig. Gen. David Stuart and Maj. Gen. William T. Sherman favorably endorsed the petition, as did USG on March 10. "Respectfully forwarded to Head Quarters of the Army. Besides the high recommendations Col. J. Kilby Smith has from his Division Comd.r and those serving under him I am pleased to add my testamonial to his activity, energy and ability as a soldier. His advancement has been won upon the field of battle, and in camp in discipling his men. Promotion on Col. Smith would be most worthily bestowed and would not fall upon one with whom the question would be 'What will you do with him.' " AES, *ibid*. On Jan. 5, 1864, Lincoln nominated Smith as brig. gen. to rank from Aug. 11, 1863.

1. Although nominated as maj. gen. on Jan. 17, Napoleon B. Buford was not confirmed.

2. On March 26, Rawlins issued General Orders No. 21 which announced and approved the verdict of a court-martial in which Col. Silas D. Baldwin, 57th Ill., had been charged with leaving his troops during the battles of Fort Donelson, Shiloh, and Corinth, found guilty of the Donelson and Corinth charges, and sentenced to be cashiered. Copies, DLC-USG, V, 13, 14, 95; DNA, RG 393, Dept. of the Tenn., General and Special Orders; (printed) USGA. On April 11, USG endorsed a letter of Baldwin concerning Lt. Col. Frederick J. Hurlbut, 57th Ill., who replaced Baldwin as col. as of March 12. "Respectfully returned to Head Quarters of the Army Washington D. C., and attention invited to the accompanying proceedings of the Board of Examiners in the case. Lt. Col Hurlbut of the 57th. Ill. Vols., had command of his regiment in every battle it has been in, and proved himself a good officer. The charges preferred by Col. Baldwin who has since been cashiered by a Court Martial was a deliberate attempt to get him out of the service, because of personal enmity." Copies, DLC-USG, V, 25; DNA, RG 393, Dept. of the Tenn., Endorsements. In response to a petition of citizens of Chicago, on May 31 Lincoln authorized Governor Richard Yates of Ill. to reappoint Baldwin, and Yates did so. Lincoln, *Works* (*Supplement*), pp. 189–90. On July 1, Rawlins issued Special Orders No. 177 announcing that despite Baldwin's reappointment he would "not be mustered into the service, . . . unless ordered from Headquarters of the Army." Copies, DLC-USG, V, 27, 28; DNA, RG 393, Dept. of the Tenn., Special Orders. On June 27, Maj. Gen. Stephen A. Hurlbut, Memphis, wrote to Rawlins that he had refused to muster in Baldwin, using the excuse that his regt. was too small. ALS, *ibid*., RG 94, War Records Office, Dept. of the Mo. On July 2, Rawlins wrote to Hurlbut approving his action. Copies, DLC-USG, V, 19, 101, 103; DNA, RG 393, Dept. of the Tenn., Letters Sent. An extensive file on Baldwin contains copies of several of the documents cited above and letters written in his support which attribute his court-martial to rivalries among the officers of his regt. Records of 57th Ill., I-ar. Nonetheless, Baldwin never served again.

On June 11, Col. Frederick J. Hurlbut wrote to Rawlins that the "national colors" of the 57th Ill. had been left at the office of the *Chicago Evening Journal* by Baldwin and that the editors refused to return them. ALS, DNA, RG 393, 16th Army Corps, Letters Received. On June 24, USG endorsed this letter. "Respectfully forwarded to Head Quarters of the Army Washington D. C. with the request that the necessary order to return to this regiment its Colors—be made" ES, *ibid*.

To Maj. Gen. Henry W. Halleck

———

Before Vicksburg 12 M Feby 9th [*1863*]
MAJ GEN H. W. HALLECK
GEN IN CHIEF
The continuous rise in the River has kept the army busy to keep out of water and much retarded work on the Canal. I hope to be able to say something definite in a day or so of the practicability of the other route mentioned in previous despatches
U. S. GRANT
Maj Gen'l Com'dg

Telegram received, DNA, RG 107, Telegrams Collected (Bound); copies, *ibid.*, Telegrams Received in Cipher; *ibid.*, RG 393, Dept. of the Tenn., Hd. Qrs. Correspondence; DLC-USG, V, 5, 8, 24, 94. *O.R.*, I, xxiv, part 1, 17.

To Maj. Gen. Stephen A. Hurlbut

———

Before Vicksburg Feb 9, 1863.
MAJ GENL S A HURLBUT
COMMDG 16TH ARMY CORPS
Enclosed with this I send you copy of instructions left with Genl Hamilton whilst he was in command of the District of West Tennessee. I wish these instructions carried out

Keep me informed as often as practicable of the condition of affairs within your command, and especially should any formidable move be made towards any part of your lines let me know it.

It is of the utmost importance that all the rolling stock of the road should be got on to the road from Memphis   Corinth should be supplied with provisions and forage to last them until the roads can be reasonably expected to be passable in the Spring, so that should it become necessary to abandon all the Mississippi road north of Grand Junction no inconvenience will be felt.

When the roads are passable Corinth can be supplied from Memphis by using the Rail Road as far East as possible and then again from Chewalla on and using wagons over the Gap

If practicable I would like to have a Cavalry expedition penetrate as far South as possible on the Miss Central R R to destroy it

U S GRANT.
Maj Genl

Copies, DLC-USG, V, 18, 30; DNA, RG 393, Dept. of the Tenn., Letters Sent.
On Feb. 9, 1863, Maj. Gen. Charles S. Hamilton, Memphis, wrote to USG. "I have information direct from Grenada, & Jackson Miss. A young man (Horton) native of Minnesota, and known to many of the Minnesota men, come through from Jackson to avoid the conscription. The last division of troops left Grenada for Vicksburg the day Horton come through Grenada. The total force at Vicksburgh is not believed to exceed 45,000 men, and at Port Hudson there are about 15,000. But four regiments of troops are left at Mobile, and no more troops are available in the south to send to Vicksburg. An expidition fitted out in Mobile to operate against our storeships had failed,—but a much larger one was in preparation, and the men engaged in it were to have one half the captures. This information from Mobile comes through Gen Dodge, who regards it as entirely reliable. I communicated it to Capt Pennock of the navy who sent it to Washington. Roddy has built a small field work on the East bank Tenn. near Eastport, and has a steamer. Dodge wants two or three transports & a gunboat to clean him out. His sphere of operations is in Rosecrans Dept. Hurlbut having assumed command of 16th army corps—limits my command to Districts of Memphis and Corinth, & throws nearly all the *trade business* into my hands. I find enough to do. Both Hurlbut and myself have prohibited circulation of Chicago Times in our commands. I referred the subject of the cotton in the hands of Capt Eddy, to you in a former letter. I shall be pleased if you sanction my course of proceeding. I have simply postponed the sale—but owing to your order to sell it, I have not deemed myself authorized to take any action further than the postponement of sale until your decision could be had. A portion of the cotton is fully liable to confiscation, and the agents of the U. S. Sanitary Commission have applied to me for a few bales to be made into comforters for the Hospitals. If you authorize me to investigate and dispose of the claims of owners—I will do so—but cannot act without specific authority—Will you please give me instructions on the subject by return mail. Where claims of owners are established, the cotton ought to be given up only to the original owner—or on the original owners written order. Such a course will prevent any fraud on the part of speculators. Everything here is working harmoniously. I hope you will be entirely successful in your undertaking. The taking of Vicksburg is *your* right, and I hope it may be added to the laurels which belong to you as the most successful general of the war." ALS, *ibid.*, RG 94, War Records Office, Dept. of the Tenn. *O.R.*, I, xxiv, part 3, 40–41.
On Feb. 12, Maj. Gen. Stephen A. Hurlbut wrote to Lt. Col. John A. Rawlins. "I have the honor to enclose the report of Co Lee as received through Maj Genl Hamilton & also copy of letter signed C S. Hamilton Brig Genl. The report is no completely satisfactory—and no further investigation has been made by

Genl Hamilton. The complaints have never come to me. I am satisfied that the good of the service demands that Maj Genl Hamilton should be assigned to duty elsewhere   I would respectfully suggest that an exchange be effected by which Genl Prentiss may be detailed to this command & Genl Hamilton relieve him   my forbearance is nearly exhausted & if he remains here, I shall be compelled to put him in arrest which I do not wish to do. I can get along with almost any body who has not confidential correspondents in high places. In fact I do not know that I have any necessity for another Maj Genl in these limits, and would prefer that they should earn or dignify their rank in active service & be relieved from the corruptions & dangers of such a place as Memphis"   Copy, DNA, RG 393, 16th Army Corps, Letters Sent. See letter to Brig. Gen. Charles S. Hamilton, Jan. 20, 1863.

On Jan. 30, Hamilton wrote to U.S. Senator James R. Doolittle of Wis. "Hurlbut drinks like a fish—He will soon return here & by virtue of his two days rank—will supercede me & have me out of place or command." ALS, Doolittle Papers, WHi. On Feb. 11, Hamilton again wrote to Doolittle. "You have asked me to write you confidentially. I will now say what I have never breathed. *Grant is a drunkard*. His wife has been with him for months only to use her influence in keeping him sober. He tries to let liquor alone—but he cannot resist the temptation always. When he come to Memphis, he left his wife at LaGrange, & for several days after getting here, was beastly drunk, utterly incapable of doing anything. Quinby & I, took him in charge, watching with him day & night, & keeping liquor away from him, & we telegraphed to his wife & brought her on to take care of him. His wife being here, is authority to hundreds of officers to keep their wives, and to as many more to keep mistresses under the name of wives, and the result is a demoralization that is most fatal to the patriotism and efficiency of the army. Now this is in the *strictest confidence*. Grant is a warm fried of mine, & I of him, and although he is not a great man—yet he is a man of nerve and will not let an opportunity slip to strike the enemy a blow, whenever he can do it. I have seen little of Hurlbut—but the stories of his drunkenness are rife through the city, and he is known oftentimes by the soubriquet of 'drunken Hurlbut   I have never seen him drunk myself but his face & manner give evidence of much intemperance." ALS, *ibid.* Nominated as maj. gen. on Jan. 22, although not confirmed until March 9, Hamilton had begun to sign letters with his higher rank at the end of Jan.

To *Julia Dent Grant*

Before Vicksburg
Feb. 9th 1863.

Dear Julia,

Your letter brought by Capt. Hatch[1] says that you had then received but one letter from me. I have written not less than four others and probably more. Generally I have directed to the care of Hillyer. You had better send to the Post Office to enquire if there are not letters there for you.

The weather continues dismal here and roads almost impassable. Water on a portion of the point of land occupied by our troops would be six feet deep if the Levees were cut. It is most disagreeable and trying to our men, this weather, but so far as I see they are not wanting in cheerfulness.

I shall be going up the river in a few days again, as far as Lake Providence, and possibly to Delta, but I will not be able to go to Memphis, that is, I cannot. My whole time, if not occupied, at least my whole presence with my duties are required.

Since I come down here I have felt the necessity of staff officers. All were away at one point and another on duty and still others have been required, that is of a class that can do something. Such as Capt. Prime, Lieut. Wilson and others. Bowers we feel the loss of but Rawlins feels that more than I do.

I am writing before breakfast because the mail goes out at 12 to-day and I have so much to write to Washington that I could not take a moment after seting down to work.

Kisses for yourself and Jess.

Ulys.

ALS, DLC-USG.

1. See letter to President Abraham Lincoln, Feb. 8, 1863.

To Maj. Gen. John A. McClernand

———

Head Quarters, Dept. of the Ten.
Before Vicksburg, Feb. 10th 1863.

Maj. Gen. McClernand
Comd.g 13th Army Corps,
Gen.

The course pursued by Col. Bennett towards Asst. Surgeon Witt and the men of his regiment taken off by him is right except that he should have taken the Dr. and men back to their regt. by force of Arms and prefered charges against the Dr.

I have advised the Medical Director that Dr. Witt will have to be relieved from his present duties to be tried by Court Martial and that proper application will have to be made for details of nurses and hospital attendants.

Col. Bennett can take Asst. Surgeon Witt, and such men of his regiment as have not been properly detailed, back and have the Dr. tried on charges which he will prefer.

Respectfully

your obt. svt.

U. S. GRANT

Maj. Gen. Com

ALS, McClernand Papers, IHi. On Feb. 8, 1863, USG had written to Maj. Gen. John A. McClernand. "The Col. of the 69th Ia Vols. has been reported for interfeering with hospital details by arresting the Asst. Surgeon of his regiment who had been properly placed on duty on board of the hospital boat City of Memphis. Cols. of regiments lose controll of officers and men of their regiments when they they are properly detached for service elswhere. The name of the Col. I believe is Bennett." ALS, *ibid.* On Feb. 9, Col. Thomas W. Bennett, 69th Ind., Young's Point, wrote to USG's hd. qrs. "Reports Surg. Witt of his Reg't. absent without leave and that he has taken with him several men, none of them detailed as far as he can learn." DLC-USG, V, 21; DNA, RG 393, Dept. of the Tenn., Register of Letters Received.

On Feb. 10, USG wrote to Surgeon Charles McMillan, act. medical director. "Asst Surgeon Witt of the 69th Iowa Vols for insolence and contempt of authority of the Colonel of his Regiment, and absenting himself from his regiment without the authority of his Colonel or informing him by what authority he absented himself, and taking from the regiment nurses and Hospital attendants without their being detailed, will be tried by a Court Martial   You will please therefore detail some other Surgeon to perform his duties, and direct the Surgeon in charge of Steamer 'City of Memphis' to apply for the detail they want. The same men they now have can be detailed if required"   Copies, DLC-USG, V, 18, 30; DNA, RG 393, Dept. of the Tenn., Letters Sent. On the same day, USG wrote to McClernand. "Enclosed please find statements forwarded by Surg. McMillen relating to the case of Asst. Surg. Witt and the detail from the 69th regt. of Ia Vols." ALS, McClernand Papers, IHi.

To Julia Dent Grant

———

Near Vicksburg
Feb.y 11th 1863.

DEAR JULIA,

This evening I leave here to go up to Lake Providence to superintend matters there for a few days. We are not much nearer an attack on Vicksburg now apparently than when I first come down, but still as the attack will be made and time is passing we are necessarily coming nearer the great conflict. I have been remarkably well since leaving Memphis. I now feel about as I did on leaving Memphis last summer.

I met with a great loss this morning. Last night, contrary to my usual habit, I took out my teeth and put them in the wash bason and covered them with water. This morning the servant who attends to my stateroom, blacks my boots &c, come in about daylight and finding water in the bason threw it out into the river teeth and all. I wrote to Dr. Hamline[1] by the same Mail that takes this to bring with him if he should come down here material to take an impression and make me a new sett. If the Dr. is in Memphis I wish you would get one of the officers to hunt him up and tell him of my misfortune.[2]

The river is now so high that the most of this country would be under water if the levees were cut.

Kisses for yourself and Jess. Tell Jess he must be a good boy and learn his lessons. If he learns all his letters before I see him again I will give him something pretty.

Goodbuy

ULYS.

ALS, DLC-USG.

1. Probably Shepard L. Hamlen, listed as a dentist in Cincinnati city directories 1849–64. Information from Frances Forman, Cincinnati Historical Society, Jan., 1976. According to a biographer, "a few months later Grant authorized 'S. L. Hamlen, dentist, to practice his profession anywhere within this military command.' " W. E. Woodward, *Meet General Grant* (New York, 1928), p. 293.
2. Four lines crossed out and illegible.

To Maj. Thomas P. Robb

Near Vicksburg
Feb.y 11th 1863

MAJ. ROBB
SANITARY AGT.
MAJ.

Will you be kind enough to forward the enclosed letter to Dr. Hamline of the Sanitary Agency.

Dr. Hamline lives in Cincinnati but has been spending most of his time in this Dept. for the last six or eight months.

I do not know where a letter would and send this to you in hopes you may know.

By attending to this you will much oblige

Yours truly
U. S. GRANT
Maj. Gen

ALS, Robb Papers, IHi. See preceding letter. For Maj. Thomas P. Robb, see *Calendar*, July 31, 1862.

To Maj. Gen. James B. McPherson

Lake Providence La Feb 12. 1863

MAJ GENL J B MCPHERSON
COMMDG 17TH ARMY CORPS

I have just arrived here expecting when I started to find you, and to spend a day or two with you Before arriving however, from a mail taken from a Boat down from Memphis I learned that you had not transportation for a Division

I send you tonight the Tatum, and tomorrow will send all the Boats here, and also order all that can be spared from Helena. You may bring Quinby's Division as soon as possible, do not delay, however to bring the two Divisions altogether. As soon as Quinby has transportation for a single Brigade, let him forward it, and come with the last Brigade himself. I want you to connect the Mississippi with Bayou Macon or the Tansas whichever may promise best. Bayou Macon is the best stream for navigation, and is also nearer Lake Providence

I will return to Vicksburg, and come up again when you arrive

U S GRANT

Maj Genl

Copies, DLC-USG, V, 18, 30; DNA, RG 393, Dept. of the Tenn., Letters Sent. On Feb. 11, 1863, Maj. Gen. James B. McPherson, Memphis, wrote to USG. "I had hoped to have started last night with Logan's Division for Lake Providence but am still here, with no prospect of getting off for three or four days. I am *very much* annoyed, but see no help for it, as there are not half enough transports here to carry the Division—Six or Seven Boats that were expected down from St. Louis are frozen *fast* and there is no telling when they will get through—I have given orders to detain all Boats—except such as are *absolutely necessary* to bring supplies —until enough are procured—I will do all in my power to get away & carry out my part of the programme. Logan's Division has been ready for the last ten days to embark & you may rest assured we will not delay One minute after the Transports are ready—" ALS, *ibid.*, RG 94, War Records Office, Dept. of the Tenn. *O.R.*, I, xxiv, part 3, 44. See letter to Maj. Gen. James B. McPherson, Feb. 5, 1863.

On Feb. 13, USG wrote to Col. Lewis B. Parsons. "I wish to have sent from this fleet, as soon as possible, steamers enough to bring about 6000 troops, including four batteries, from Memphis to Lake Providence. There is about 16000 to come but I think with the steamers already at Memphis and those ordered by me from Providence and Helena the amount of transportation here named will be sufficient." ALS, Parsons Papers, IHi. On Feb. 17, Parsons, steamboat *Anderson,* wrote to USG reporting the names and carrying capacity of the available steamboats. ALS, DNA, RG 393, Dept. of the Tenn., Letters Received.

On Feb. 18, McPherson wrote to USG. "I enclose herewith a communication from Brig. Genl. Quinby in relation to the matter of granting Furloughs to enlisted men in extreme cases—I shall commence embarking Genl. Logan's Division Friday morning and hope to get off Saturday—The Commissary and Qr. Masters Boat have been loaded for the last Eight days & are ready to haul out into the stream, so that there will be no detention on this account—The roads are in a most horrible condition, but the division will move in promptly if it takes all the horses in the Battery to haul a gun   Genl Quinby's Division will follow Logan's as soon as Transports can be provided. I have been annoyed beyond measure at the delay here, but could not help myself—The 'Ruth' which I had directed the Qr. Master to stop here, and carry a portion of my command, was permitted to go to Cairo for Gov't. supplies, with a promise from the Captain that he would be back by a certain day.   As soon as she got to Cairo she was taken possession of for a Hospital Boat and ordered to St. Louis.   I am very much obliged to you General for your kind letter of the 2nd inst, and should have answered it, but it only reached me four days ago—There is no particular movement of the enemy *in force* in this vicinity but the 'Guerrillas' are very bold and troublesome. Genl. Quinby sent an expedition after 'Blythe' which returned yesterday—The expedition penetrated to the Rebel Camp, captured Twelve Prisoners, Muster Rolls of some of the companies several horses, pistols, guns &c. The main force of the Enemy got wind of our coming and left during the night. Mrs. Grant & Jesse are quite well. I have many things to tell you when we meet and I hope to have that pleasure soon—" ALS, *ibid.*, RG 94, War Records Office, Dept. of the Tenn. *O.R.*, I, xxiv, part 3, 59–60.

To Brig. Gen. Benjamin M. Prentiss

Lake Providence La Feby 12, 1863

Brig Genl B M Prentiss
Comm'dg Dist Eastern Ark.

McPherson has been delayed in getting the balance of his Army Corps here for want of transportation a fact which I did not learn until since leaving Vicksburg   Had I known it there I would have sent Steamers from there to supply the deficiency

As it is he must be supplied from here and Helena   I am ordering up all the boats from here and desire that all now lying at Helena not absolutly required for immediate use at the Post should also be sent

I wish General you would give this matter immediate attention and get the Boats off as promptly as possible

U S Grant
Maj Genl

Copies, DLC-USG, V, 18, 30; DNA, RG 393, Dept. of the Tenn., Letters Sent.
On Feb. 8, 1863, Lt. Col. John A. Rawlins issued Special Orders No. 39 assigning Brig. Gen. Benjamin M. Prentiss to command the District of Eastern Ark., with Brig. Gen. Willis A. Gorman and Brig. Gen. Leonard F. Ross in command of the two divs. of inf., and Brig. Gen. Cadwallader C. Washburn in command of the cav. div. Capt. John O. Pullen, 20th Ill., was appointed provost marshal. Copies, DLC-USG, V, 26, 27; DNA, RG 393, Dept. of the Tenn., Special Orders. *O.R.*, I, xxiv, part 3, 39–40. For the reasons for the change in command, see letter to Act. Rear Admiral David D. Porter, Feb. 15, 1863. On Feb. 13, Gorman wrote to Lt. Col. Walter B. Scates, adjt. for Maj. Gen. John A. McClernand, requesting a reorganization of his command. ALS, McClernand

Papers, IHi. On Feb. 22, USG endorsed this letter. "Not approved at present. A change is contemplated in the organization of the Helena forces on the return of Gen. Ross to Helena such as to enable the older troops to take the field." AES, *ibid.*

On Feb. 7, McClernand wrote to USG. "I have the honor to enclose the accompanying conditional order for your approval, if you shall be pleased to give it. I have acted thus early in the matter that Gen'l Ross's desire to engage in active service may in your discretion, be gratified" Copies, DNA, RG 393, 13th Army Corps, Letters Sent; McClernand Papers, IHi. McClernand enclosed General Orders No. 23, 13th Army Corps. "The troops composing Genl Fisks Brigade, together with such orthers as the Genl Comdg the Dept of the Tenn may choose to add, will constitute the 3rd Division, of the 13th Army Corps, Brig Genl L. F. Ross Commanding. Genl Ross will immediately repair to Helena and take command of said Division. This order will take effect conditionally upon the approval of the General Commanding the Dept of the Tenn." DS, *ibid.* On the same day, Rawlins endorsed these orders "Approved" AES, *ibid.*

On Feb. 13, Prentiss wrote twice to USG. "I assumed Command here today & expect to improve condition of affairs somewhat. Genl Washburne has charge of the Forces at work on Yazoo Pass. he has just arrived from that Point and represents many obstacles which may prevent success but says he will strive to remove them he is possessed of Energy and will succeed if possible Genl Gorman goes down to examine today & report. he is not offended but expresses a desire to cooperate cheerfully—and render such assistance ~~that~~ as I may require I shall endeavour to reduce the expenses at this Point materially" ALS, DNA, RG 393, Dept. of the Tenn., Letters Received. "This day the Steamer Clara Belle arrived at this Point having on board a lot of Cotton said to belong to I G Lacy & Co of Memphis. Mr Lacy was on board and received the Cotton under cover of a Gun Boat. To relieve this District from annoyance I had ordered all Cotton on transports landing here to be taken from the Boats and placed in charge of Chief Quarter Master (having the same marked and designated) unless the Parties claiming produced written authority from you to ship Cotton on Transports. I find this necessary to stop the swarms of buyers that are getting below this Point and shall adhere to it strictly. This lot having been bought by Mr Lacy without knowledge of restrictions, I think it due to let it be forwarded and have promised him to write to you and get your permission to pass it on if you are of the same opinion I am." ALS, *ibid.*, RG 109, Union Provost Marshals' File of Papers Relating to Individual Civilians.

To Maj. Gen. Stephen A. Hurlbut

Head Quarters, Dept. of the Ten.
Lake Providence La. Feb. 13th 1863.
MAJ. GEN. S. A. HURLBUT
COMD.G 16TH ARMY CORPS,
GEN.

The steamers Rose Hamilton and Evansville are reported for violating my orders regulating trade.[1] Not being at Hd Quarters I have not got access to orders to give you No and date of the order refered to but it was published about the 20th of January and prohibits boats landing at other than Military posts or under the protection of Gunboats.[2]

Trade is not opened below Helena and therefore vessels landing atal below there, except for Government, without special authority are liable to seizure.

I wish you would refer this matter to the Provost Marshal for investigation.

I have seen your Gen. Order No 4 Feb. 8th prohibiting the circulation of the Chicago Times within your command. There is no doubt but that paper with several others published in the North should have been suppressed long since by authority from Washington. As this has not been done I doubt the propriety of suppressing its circulation in any one command. The paper would still find its way into the hands of the enemy, through other channels, and do all the mischief it is now doing.

This course is also calculated to give the paper a notoriety evidently saught and which probably would increase the sale of it. I would direct therefore that Gen. Order No 4 be revoked.[3]

Information which I have just received, and which is undoubted, shows that VanDorn with his force went over to the Mobile road, to Okolona.[4] Price is at Grenada with six or seven thousand men, only. North of that point there is no large force on the Miss. C. R. R. Our Cavalry can go to the Tallahatchie without difficulty. The enemy have not got the road repaired yet North of Water Valley. I would like to have the road destroyed as much as possible South of Holly Springs.

It seems to me that Grierson with about 500 picked men might succeed in making his way South and cut the rail-road East of Jackson Miss. The undertaking would be a hazerdous one but it would pay well if carried out.

I do not direct that this shall be done but leave it for a volunteer enterprise.[5]

Gen. Hamilton countermanded, or suspended, an order of mine directing the sale of some captured cotton. I wrote to him saying that the sale should proceed. I wish you would direct Capt. Eddy, if he has not already done so, to proceed in accordance with my order in this matter.[6]

I am Gen. Very respectfully
your obt. svt.
U. S. GRANT
Maj. Gen. Com

ALS, DNA, RG 393, 16th Army Corps, Letters Received. *O.R.*, I, xxiv, part 3, 49–50.

1. Correspondence relating to the seizure of *Rose Hambleton* and *Evansville* is in *O.R.* (Navy), I, xxiv, 340–48. See letter to Act. Rear Admiral David D. Porter, Feb. 15, 1863.

2. On Jan. 20, 1863, Lt. Col. John A. Rawlins issued General Orders No. 7. "All trading, trafficking, or the landing of Boats at points South of Memphis, other than at Military Posts, or points guarded by the Navy, is positively prohibited. All officers of boats violating this order will be arrested and placed in close confinement. The Boats and Cargoes, unless the property of the Government, will be turned over to the Quartermasters Department for the benefit of Government. All officers of the Army passing up and down the river are directed to report all violations of this Order, together with the name of the Boats, place and date, to the first Military Post on their route, and to the commanding officer at the end of their route. The Navy is respectfully requested to co-operate in the enforcement of this Order." Copies, DLC-USG, V, 13, 14, 95; DNA, RG 393, Dept. of the Tenn., General and Special Orders; *ibid.*, Dept. of the Mo., Letters Received. *O.R.*, I, xvii, part 2, 575–76; *ibid.*, I, xxiv, part 3, 3; *O.R.* (Navy), I, xxiv, 183–84.

3. See *Chicago Times*, Feb. 12, 13, 14, 16, 19, 1863; Benjamin P. Thomas, ed., *Three Years with Grant as Recalled by War Correspondent Sylvanus Cadwallader* (New York, 1955), pp. 56–57. On Feb. 19, Joseph Medill, editor of the *Chicago Tribune*, wrote to U.S. Representative Elihu B. Washburne. "Your man Grant

has shown his cloven foot and proves himself to be little better than a secesh. Gens. Hurlburt and Sullivan suppressed the circulation of the infernal copperhead Times in their districts, and thereby excluded it from the army below Cairo. Now what does Grant do ? Why he vetoes their acts and opens the army lines for its circulation—a sheet that is more malignantly rebel than any paper published in rebeldom. Last night the editor sent down 3,000 copies of his treasonable issues to do their work of poison in Grant's Department, to breed more mutiny and demoralization. His army now is almost in a state of insubordination. He has in great measures lost the confidence and respect of the loyal officers and privates, as I hear from a hundred sources. But this dirty act of his, suppressing the police orders of Gen. Hurlburt, issued to protect his men, shows the real sentiments of Grant. He stands confessed as a copperhead and openly encourages the dessemi-nation of secession and treason in his army. Is it any wonder the military affairs of the West have been so woefully managed. First we had Halleck a dough face, order No. 3 and now we have a patron of the copperhead Chicago Times. When do you think the Union is going to be saved out West ? I write to you because it is through your influence mainly that he holds the trust which he thus betrays. No man's military career in the army is more open to destructive criticism than Grant's. We have kept off of him on your account. We could have made him stink in the nostrils of the public like an old fish had we properly criticised his military blunders. Look at that miserable and costly campaign into northern Miss. when he sent crazy Sherman to Vicksburg and agreed to meet him there by land. Was there ever a more weak and imbecile campaign. But we forbore exposing him to the excruciation of the people. But I assure you that if he has become the patron saint and protector of the secession again we shall not be so tender on him in the future." Copy, DLC-Elihu B. Washburne.

4. On Feb. 14, Maj. Gen. Stephen A. Hurlbut wrote to Rawlins transmitting a telegram of the same date from Brig. Gen. Grenville M. Dodge. "Couriers in from my cavalry in Alabama report VanDorns' force as still passing North and crossing at Florence. They have had several skirmishes with them. Have taken a number of prisoners." LS, DNA, RG 94, War Records Office, Dept. of the Tenn. *O.R.*, I, xxiv, part 3, 54.

5. On Feb. 16, Hurlbut wrote to Rawlins. "I have certain information that Van Dorn with 4 Brigades of mounted men commanded by Jackson McCullough Whitefield & Armstrong with 12 peices of Artillery and a *heavy train* is moving by Burleson in Franklin Co. Alabama to the East of Bear Creek. I think he pro-poses to cross at Florince and to remain in Middle Tennessee and operate in rear of Rosecrans. I have telegraphed to Genl Rosecrans & to the Naval officer at Cairo to push a Gun boat up. As I am satisfied this will remove nearly all cavalry from my front—at the suggestion of Genl Hamilton I have ordered Grierson's Brigade to cross the head waters of the Tallahatchie & Yallabusha by way of Pontotoc—cut the wires destroy bridges and demonstrate in that neighborhood while the 2d Iowa Cavalry Col. Hatch pushes night and day toward the Main Road between Meridian & Vicksburgh if possible to destroy the Bridge across Pearl River in rear of Jackson and do as much damage as possible on that line returning by the best course they can make. It appeais perilous but I think can be done & done with safety, & may relieve you somewhat at Vicksburgh. To cover this movement I shall at the same time send Lee toward Holly springs to go to the Tallahatchie or threaten it sufficiently to make them burn the bridge and then sweep round toward Panola & Hernando enveloping Blythe's force and driving

them to the Nonconnah or into the swamp. Dodges Cavalry are in Alabama hanging around VanDorn & delaying him by burning Bridges in his front. They have taken several prisoners right out of his column which by the miserable roads is very long. I shall gradually move out the Cavalry now here as soon as the roads permit and concentrate force enough to whip Van Dorn as he comes back if he does come back. At present the roads are horrible—I desire by the expedition of Lee to ascertain the practicability of reaching the opening through the Yazoo Pass so as to be ready to clear your ground should you determine to land there The City of Memphis has more iniquity in it than any place since Sodom, but certain examples are being made which may do good. As soon as McPherson's Corps leaves I shall be able to keep better order" ALS, DNA, RG 94, War Records Office, Dept. of the Tenn. *O.R.*, I, xxiv, part 3, 58.

6. On Feb. 2, Rawlins wrote to Capt. Asher R. Eddy. "You will seize and sell for the benefit of Government all cotton found on board Steamers from this place or vicinity, unless the claimant has a special permit from these Head quarters. No other permits will be recognized by you." Copies, DLC-USG, V, 18, 30; DNA, RG 92, Letters Received by Capt. A. R. Eddy; *ibid.*, RG 393, Dept. of the Tenn., Letters Sent. See letters to Brig. Gen. Charles S. Hamilton, Feb. 6, 1863, and to Maj. Gen. Stephen A. Hurlbut, Feb. 9, 1863.

To Maj. Gen. Stephen A. Hurlbut

Head Quarters, Dept. of the Ten.
Before Vicksburg, Feb. 13th/63

MAJ. GEN. S. A. HURLBUT
COMD.G 16TH ARMY CORPS,
GEN.

In view of the impending struggle in opening the Miss. river it behooves me to collect for that purpose all the forces possible. I expected to get some of Gen. Curtis' forces now in Northern Ark. or Southern Mo. But I do not see that they are coming. I am also informed that no enemy in any force now threatens any part of the road East from Memphis. With this fact I think one Division more might be brought forward which can be done by transfering it to Sherman's Army Corps and transfering the Dist. of Memphis to yours.

If later information than any I possess does not make it absolutely necessary to retain all the troops you have now you may relieve one of the Divisions between Memphis and Grand

Junction and bring it forward to Memphis and held in readiness to be brought forward at a moments notice.

Please notify me when this is done, and the Div. selected so that I can make the necessary order for the transfer.

Orders were sent to you on the 7th before I learned of your return, assigning you to the command of the Dist. of West Tenn and directing Hamilton to report to you.[1]

> Very respectfully
> your obt. svt.
> U. S. GRANT
> Maj. Gen. Com

P. S. Answer by bearer what Division you will send, and the earliest possible moment it will be ready for embarkation

U S G.

ALS (except for the P. S.), DNA, RG 393, 16th Army Corps, Letters Received. *O.R.*, I, xxiv, part 3, 49.

 Also on Feb. 13, 1863, Lt. Col. John A. Rawlins wrote to Maj. Gen. Stephen A. Hurlbut. "You will please revoke the order of Genl Hamilton to Genl Asboth sending the Missouri troops from the District of Columbus, back to the Department of the Missouri. The request of Genl. Asboth to leave the Garrisons of Forts Henry and Donnellson relieved is impracticable at this time   Upon request no doubt the commanders of any of the Gun Boats in your command would cooperate in any expedition you may seem disposed to make up the Obion. The Genl Commanding will request Adm.l Porter to give the neccessary instructions to his officers. Where troops are required from the District of Columbus you will order forward the Illinois Regiments. Enclosed find dispatches from Genl. Asboth to which this is an answer"   LS, DNA, RG 393, 16th Army Corps, Letters Received. *O.R.*, I, xxiii, part 2, 65. Rawlins enclosed four telegrams of Feb. 9–10 from Brig. Gen. Alexander Asboth, Columbus. Telegrams received, DNA, RG 393, 16th Army Corps, Letters Received. *O.R.*, I, xxiii, part 2, 65–66.

 On Feb. 19, Hurlbut wrote to Rawlins. "I have just recd. a letter from Maj. Genl. Grant requesting another Division to be forwarded   If it is expected that the entire road from Columbus to Jackson Corinth & G. Junction is to be maintained & a proper front shewn to the South of Charleston & Memphis Road— I shall probably require all the troops now in my command—If the line through Jackson is abandoned there will be a surplus of troops   Genl. Quimby's Division is under marching orders for Vicksburgh.—Logan's leave to day—I will pass over the line tomorrow & think I shall select Genl Denver's Division which originally was part of Sherman's Corps. I will write more fully when I return." ALS, DNA, RG 393, Dept. of the Tenn., Letters Received. *O.R.*, I, xxiv, part 3, 60–61.

 1. Special Orders No. 38, Dept. of the Tenn., Feb. 7. Copies, DLC-USG, V, 26, 27; DNA, RG 393, Dept. of the Tenn., Special Orders. *O.R.*, I, xxiv, part 3, 38.

To Julia Dent Grant

Lake Providence La
February 13th 1863.

Dear Julia

I come up to this place last night expecting to find McPherson and intending to stay a day or two and give directions. I find however he has not been able to procure transportation. On the way up we overhawled all boats and got off the Hd Qrs. Mail, and found Lagow and Bowers. I got several letters from you and here we met another boat from Memphis with Ihrie aboard and more letters from you.

Your letter to Jennie[1] was very good. It was moderate and in every way right. All the family have ever been made welcome at our house and you will be at theirs, at least to father and mother. Do just as you told them you were going to do. Go directly home and make a short visit and see if it is not agreeable for Mother to keep the children   If it is not take them to some town in Ohio Indiana or Illinois where they have good schools and take boarding for yourself and them. There is no place half so good for them however as just where they are and I do not think for a moment but what it is agreeable to keep them.

Mrs. McM. that you speak about I know nothing about. Certain it is that I never told her, or anyone els that they could go and take any house they pleased or could board at my expense. I cannot conceive who this woman is unless it is one that come into the office one day at Memphis (not Mrs. Canfield)[2] and represented that she had been aiding about the hospitals for a long time but had never asked for any position and had never received any favors from Government or been any expense. She did not know however but she would have to ask for at least some place to stay. At present she said she was boarding in a sesesh family and it was excessively disagreeable to her. I do not remember what I told her and have never thought about her since.

Do not even remember what she looked like.—Mrs. Perkins has not made her appearance with the fleet and cannot get there. Orders prohibit women from coming down and those who do smuggle themselves down are hunted up by the detectives and ordered back.—I will sign the deed you send me and forward with this if it can be done without going before a Notary. If this is required I will go before a Judge Advocate and sign and forward as soon as possible.

Go home and make a visit and do as I say here. It is not atal probable that I will be up the river again until the decisive action takes place, and whilst here you cannot come down.

Kisses for yourself and children dear Julia. I will send for you whenever it is proper that you should come.

ULYS.

ALS, DLC-USG.

1. Virginia Grant, USG's sister.
2. S. A. Martha Canfield of Medina, Ohio, was the widow of Lt. Col. Herman Canfield, 72nd Ohio, who died of wounds received at Shiloh. Mrs. Canfield devoted herself to war relief activities which included the organization of a "colored orphans' asylum" at Memphis. John Y. Simon, ed., *The Personal Memoirs of Julia Dent Grant* (New York, 1975), pp. 99–101; *History of Medina County and Ohio* (Chicago, 1881), p. 336. On June 15, 1863, Mrs. Canfield, St. Louis, wrote a lengthy letter to USG mentioning her recent visit to him at Walnut Hills, quoting President Abraham Lincoln as praising USG, and complaining that Brig. Gen. Napoleon B. Buford at Cairo permitted a C.S.A. officer on parole to visit his hd. qrs. ALS, USG 3.

To Act. Rear Admiral David D. Porter

Head Quarters Dept. of the Tenn.
Before Vicksburg Feby. 14th, 1863

ADMIRAL D. D. PORTER
COMD'G MISS. SQUADRON
ADMIRAL

I will give directions to have Willow Point[1] visited as you suggest.

I have just returned from Lake Providence. The officer in charge there is very sanguine of being able to get into Bayou Macon.

Lt. Col. Wilson has explored Yazoo Pass to within three miles of Cold Water. Thinks it will be perfectly practicable to get into the Yazoo by that route Citizens have discovered this intention and have fallen timber into the stream

I have ordered down two Divisions more about 16,000 effective men from Memphis to Lake Providence.

Quite a little skirmish occurred back of Lake Providence on the 11th. between about one hundred of our men and three or four hundred of the enemys Cavalry. One man was killed on our side and five or six slightly wounded

The enemy lost five or six killed and about thirty prisoners taken among them several officers.

Blanchard[2] is said to be moving on Lake Providence with five or six thousand men. Our troops will be very glad to see him.

If the gunboats are successful in getting into the Yazoo I expect great results. Destroying the Bridges at Grenada alone will be of immense value to us. I had accurate information by way of Memphis of movements of the enemy North of Jackson received last night. There is a force of five or six thousand in and arround Greneda Commanded by Price The Rail Road destroyed whilst I was down there is not yet completed as reported in the papers—Van Dorn is not up on the Tallahatchie as reported but over on the Mobile Road at Ocolona with a force about the same as Price has only much more Cavalry—

Respectfully &c

U. S. GRANT

Maj. Genl.

Copy, CSmH.

On Feb. 13, 1863, Act. Rear Admiral David D. Porter wrote four letters to USG. "The bearer, B. D. Hurley, a prisoner taken by the rebels at Corinth, and who has escaped from Jackson jail, wants to join his company, the Hatchee Scouts. He may be able to give you valuable information." *O.R.* (Navy), I, xxiv, 358. "I am preparing the mortars and will open on the town and thereabouts, as soon as I can get them in position." LS, DNA, RG 94, War Records Office, Dept. of the Tenn. *O.R.*, I, xxiv, part 3, 49; *O.R.* (Navy), I, xxiv, 356. "I ascertain from Refugees that Yazoo City and all that country is perfectly unprotected and unfortified—and that the gunboat expedition will use them up all round" LS, DNA, RG 393, Dept. of the Tenn., Letters Received. "I have reliable information that two Regiments of Rebels, (about 800 men.) have been sent up the Sunflower, with Aitillery, to annoy vessels passing Greenville, and that neighborhood.— Would it not be a good plan to try and clean out that country.—Three or four hundred cavalry with some light field pieces would do it.—They think we will not molest them.— . . . There is also a battery at Cypress Bend which can be taken by 200 men. I have a gunboat near there." LS, McClernand Papers, IHi. *O.R.* (Navy), I, xxiv, 359. On the same day, Capt. Theodore S. Bowers endorsed the fourth letter. "Genl. Grant being absent, this communication is respectfully referred to Major General J. A. McClernand." ES, McClernand Papers, IHi. On Feb. 14, Lt. Col. Walter B. Scates transmitted to Lt. Col. John A. Rawlins letters and orders concerning the ensuing expedition. LS and copies, DNA, RG 94, War Records Office, Dept. of the Tenn. *O.R.*, I, xxiv, part 3, 52–54.

On Feb. 14, USG wrote to Porter. "The steamer Vicksburg, if sunk atal, is sunk in shallow water. Gen. Sherman sent immediately on the receipt of your note to ascertain certainly whether the report of her being sunk was true but the messenger has not yet returned. Col. Bissell of the Eng. regiment has been down to the point and reports as above." Copy, CSmH; typescript, Delbert S. Wenzlick, St. Louis County, Mo.

1. Willow Point on the La. bank of the Mississippi River about twenty-seven miles upriver from Vicksburg.

2. Albert G. Blanchard of Mass., USMA 1829, resigned as 1st lt. in 1840, settled in New Orleans, then served in the Mexican War as capt. of La. Vols. and as maj., 12th Inf. Appointed C.S.A. brig. gen. on Nov. 21, 1861, Blanchard was probably in La. when USG wrote but commanding no troops because Maj. Gen. Richard Taylor believed that he was incompetent. *O.R.*, I, xv, 983–84; *ibid.*, I, xiv, part 3, 1056–57.

To Julia Dent Grant

Before Vicksburg Miss
Feb.y 14th 1863.

DEAR JULIA,

I have written two or three letters in the last two days and therefore have but little to add now. One thing however was suggested by the letter you forwarded to me from home that I forgot to mention in my letter to you. They say that $82 00 has been received for the children and you speak of sending more by express. Do you not remember that I put fifty-two dollars in a letter that was to have been taken by Col. Carpenter? What ever became of that? I am remarkably well. Hope in the course of ten days more to be making a move. My confidance in taking Vicksburg is not unshaken unless if our own people at home will give their moral support. At present however they are behaving scandalously. A soldier now geting home to Illinois, Indiana or Ohio there is no way of geting him back. Northern secessionest defend and protect them in their desertion. I want to see the Administration commence a war upon these people. They should suppress the disloyal press and confine during the war the noisy and most influential of the advocates.[1]

Kiss the children for me. The same for yourself. I will address my next letter to Covington.

ULYS.

ALS, DLC-USG.

1. See letter to Maj. Gen. Stephen A. Hurlbut, Feb. 13, 1863.

To Act. Rear Admiral David D. Porter

———

Feb.y 15th 1863.

ADMIRAL D. D. PORTER,
COMDG. MISS. SQUADRON,
ADMIRAL,

Representations coming in to me as they have reflecting on Gen. Gorman's administration of affairs at Helena I sent an officer there last week to supersede him in the command. Also a new Quartermaster and provost Marshal.[1]

The steamer refered to in your note were reported to me and directions immediately sent to Memphis to have them seized.[2]

Trade has not been opened below Helena by Military authority not even to purchase and ship cotton. I have thought of doing so as low down as Napoleon but have been waiting to see if the Govt. would not adopt suggestions made by myself and numbers of others; that is for Govt. to take all the cotton and sell it in the loyal states. If it is regarded of prime necessity that the greatest amount should be secured then appoint agts to purchase for Govt. giving the citizens to understand that all the cotton they bring in would paid for at a fixed price, say 20 cts per pound.

No Military commander has a right to divert or order a Naval vessel on any duty much less to give aid in private speculations.

> I am very respectfully
> your obt. svt.
> U. S. GRANT
> Maj. Gen. Com

ALS, MH. *O.R.*, I, xxiv, part 3, 55; *O.R.* (Navy), I, xxiv, 342. On Feb. 14, 1863, Act. Rear Admiral David D. Porter wrote to USG. "I enclose you a letter I write to General Gorman. I find that one of my officers whom I sent on the Yazoo Expedition was assisting a relation of General Gorman (I am told his son) to buy cotton (on a permit from him) which of right belongs to the Government. I placed the officer under arrest and shall have him tried by Court Martial. Cannot we stop this cotton mania? I have given all the naval vessels in the River, strict orders to permit no trade in the Rebel territory, but to seize all Rebel cotton for the Gov't . . . I also enclose copies of permits issued to trade." LS, DNA, RG 393, Dept. of the Tenn., Letters Received. Incomplete in *O.R.* (Navy), I, xxiv, 341–42. A copy of the permit given by Brig. Gen. Willis A. Gorman to the *Evansville*, which Porter enclosed, is printed *ibid.*, p. 339. Porter's letter of Feb. 15 rebuking Gorman is *ibid.*, pp. 343–44. On Feb. 8, Brig. Gen. Frederick Steele forwarded to USG's hd. qrs. charges against Gorman which, "through neglect of his staff," did not reach USG until March 11. DLC-USG, V, 21; DNA, RG 393, Dept. of the Tenn., Register of Letters Received. These charges against Gorman were probably those printed in the *Missouri Democrat*, Feb. 11, which involved earlier transactions in cotton.

1. See letters to President Abraham Lincoln, Feb. 8, and to Brig. Gen. Benjamin M. Prentiss, Feb. 12, 1863.
2. See letter to Maj. Gen. Stephen A. Hurlbut, Feb. 13, 1863.

To Brig. Gen. John McArthur

Before Vicksburg
Feby 15th 1863

BRIG GEN J MCARTHUR
COMM'DG 6TH DIV 17TH ARMY CORPS

I understand there is several thousand bales of cotton in one place near Lake Providence. If this is so have it guarded and brought in for the benefit of the Government as soon as possible. There is a Captain Mitchell formerly Captain of the steamer City of Alton at Lake Providence, who I wish you would order away north, a prisoner if he does not take the first steamer after being notified   Ship all captured cotton to Capt Eddy Memphis

U S GRANT
Maj Gen

Copies, DLC–USG, V, 18, 30; DNA, RG 393, Dept. of the Tenn., Letters Sent. For Capt. Mitchell, see *Calendar*, Oct. 10, 1862.

On Feb. 16, 1863, USG wrote to Brig. Gen. Benjamin M. Prentiss, Helena. "All the cotton seized within your command for the benefit of Government send to Capt Eddy Q M Memphis with a full statement of the circumstances under which I was taken. All claims against such cotton can be adjudicated there and if condemned will bring the highest market Price" Copies, DLC–USG, V, 18, 30; DNA, RG 393, Dept. of the Tenn., Letters Sent.

On March 3, USG wrote. "Approved. The Misses Bosworth will be permitted to ship their cotton to Memphis to be sold for their benefit on any transport going up the river" Copy, *ibid.*, RG 92, Letters, Endorsements, and Memoranda Received by Capt. A. R. Eddy. On March 27, Lt. Col. John A. Rawlins issued Special Orders No. 86. "Captain W M Vogleson C S will issue to the Misses Annie and Ida Bosworth of Carrol Parrish La vouchers on which they can draw their pay for the sixty head of cattle received from them as set forth in his certificate or receipt to them for same of date Lake Providence La March 10th 1863" Copies, DLC–USG, V, 26, 27; DNA, RG 393, Dept. of the Tenn., Special Orders.

In a letter eventually forwarded to USG's hd. qrs., on Feb. 14, M. A. Dickens wrote to Col. George W. Deitzler that he was a loyal man who had come to La. with coal, which had been seized by the C.S.A., and that he wanted to return to Ky. with 105 bales of cotton. ALS, *ibid.*, RG 109, Union Provost Marshals' File of Papers Relating to Individual Civilians. On Feb. 19, Rawlins issued Special Orders No. 50. "M. A. Dickens, of Vista Plantation Lake Providence, La. claiming to be a loyal citizen of the state of Kentucky, detained in the Confederate States, has permission to proceed with his family and house hold goods to the state of Kentucky. Mr Dickens having satisfied the Commanding Officer (Brig

Gen'l J. McArthur) at Lake Providence of his loyalty, is permitted to take with him One Hundred and Five Bales of Cotton, his individual property, to Memphis Tenn, and there dispose of it for his own benefit" Copies (2), *ibid.*, RG 109, Union Provost Marshals' File of Papers Relating to Two or More Civilians; *ibid.*, RG 92, Letters, Endorsements, and Memoranda Received by Capt. A. R. Eddy. This section is missing from letterbook copies of Special Orders No. 50. On March 10, Capt. John G. Klinck wrote to Capt. Asher R. Eddy. "I send by Steamer Niagara the following lots of Cotton the same having been properly released by order from Maj Genl Grant. The permits for same will be shown you should you desire it. The Cotton is subject to the usual Freights & as I was not aware of the rates to be paid refer the same to you; There are also several passengers. You will also collect the same and so fix it that the amount shall be deducted from the charter price if paid to the Captain of the Boat. Rev Mr Hagaman has sixty eight Bales & his household goods. M. A. Dickens, has One hundred & five Bales Cotton The Miss Boswells have Forty nine Bales of Cotton. As soon as I can furnish Boats I shall send to you what Cotton has been seized here and other lots as they are seized if they are not ordered down to the fleet" Copies, *ibid.* Dickens later wrote that he had never received his permit but learned from Klinck that 105 bales had been shipped in his name. On April 14, Rawlins endorsed this letter to Maj. Gen. James B. McPherson "for investigation and report." Copies, DLC-USG, V, 25; DNA, RG 393, Dept. of the Tenn., Endorsements. Brig. Gen. Lorenzo Thomas later charged that the permit for Dickens had been taken by a clerk in the q. m. office at Lake Providence, Pvt. Martin Dickenson, 1st Kan., who had shipped and sold cotton for his own benefit. Thomas to Secretary of War Edwin M. Stanton, LS, *ibid.*, RG 94, Letters Received, 815 A 1863.

On March 23, Col. Addison S. Norton wrote to Rawlins. "Sometime since a Rev. Mr Hagaman, residing in the vicinity of Lake Providence—applied to the Maj. Genl Commd'g and obtained a permit to 'ship his cotton,' I am informed he has shipped about two hundred and sixty Bales, and that he is shipping in his own name, Cotton belonging to other parties." ALS, *ibid.*, RG 109, Union Provost Marshals' File of Papers Relating to Individual Civilians. On March 25, USG endorsed this letter. "Refered to Maj. Gen. McPherson" AES, *ibid.* In response, on March 28, Lt. Col. William W. Belknap wrote to Maj. William T. Clark that he had found no evidence of any shipment by Hageman other than sixty-eight bales on the *Niagara*. ALS, *ibid.*, RG 393, Dept. of the Tenn., Letters Received. For more cotton shipped from Lake Providence, see *Calendar*, March 14, 25, 1863.

On April 1, USG wrote to Capt. Asher R. Eddy. "The cotton detained by you onehalf of which was for Government and the other for Mr. Wagley is a part of some cotton abandoned in the field and picked by Mr. Wagly under an arrangement made with him by Genl McPherson. The onehalf can be released to Mr. Wagley." Copy, DNA, RG 92, Letters Received by A. R. Eddy. See *O.R.*, I, xxiv, part 3, 128. When William C. Wagley wrote that Col. William S. Hillyer, provost marshal at Memphis, threatened to seize his cotton, Rawlins endorsed the letter. "This contract was made by with Mr Wagely in the utmost good faith and must be respected. You will therefore not intefere with shipment of the cotton by seizures or otherwise, unless you pass satisfactory evidence of a violation of the contract on Mr Wagelys part, mere suspicions will not suffice." Copies, DLC-USG, V, 25; DNA, RG 393, Dept. of the Tenn., Endorsements. The Wagley contract and Thomas's condemnation of it is *ibid.*, RG 94, Letters Received, 815 A 1863. See letter to Jesse Root Grant, April 21, 1863.

To Brig. Gen. Benjamin M. Prentiss

Head Quarters, Dept. of the Ten.
Before Vicksburg, Feb. 15th 1863.

Brig. Gen. B. M. Prentis,
Comd.g Dist. E. Ark.
Gen.

I send with this, steamers to take on board Gen. Ross' Division to be used with the Yazoo expedition. Enclosed with this you will find copy of a letter from me to Admiral Porter upon which the Admiral based his instructions to the vessels used in this expedition and which I want to have carried out.[1] Please hand the letter to Gen. Ross for his guidance.

The troops will take with them fifteen days rations, a portion of their tents and cooking utensils but no wagons. When the steamers are adapted one piece might be put on the bow. of each

If this expedition should succeed in geting into the ~~cold water~~ Coldwater I want Gen. Ross to take with him all the force he starts from Helena with. To do this you will want to establish a small garrison at the mouth of Yazoo Pass from the remainder of your force. Lt. Col. Wilson, Topographical Eng. has been with the expedition all the time and knows the wants, and where troops should be placed. Please fill all requisitions from him, for troops or tools, as if from myself.

The only change I would make in the instructions already given is that as soon as they arrive at the mouth of the Yalobusha they turn up that stream and take Grenada and destroy the railroad bridges there before proceeding further down the river. Let there be no delay in this matter. Time now is growing important.

Gen. Ross should take with him all his axes & spades and if

he has not got a good supply then he should be supplied, particularly with axes, from the remainder of your command.

> I am Gen. very respectfully
> your obt. svt.
> U. S. GRANT
> Maj. Gen. Com

ALS, DNA, RG 94, War Records Office, Union Battle Reports. *O.R.*, I, xxiv, part 3, 56. On Feb. 15, 1863, USG telegraphed to Maj. Gen. Henry W. Halleck. "Steamboats through Yazoo Pass have gone to within six (6) miles of Coldwater. Express no fear but they will reach it and the Yazoo" Telegram received, DNA, RG 107, Telegrams Collected (Bound); copy, *ibid.*, Telegrams Received in Cipher. *O.R.*, I, xxiv, part 1, 17. On the same day, Brig. Gen. Willis A. Gorman wrote to Maj. Gen. John A. McClernand reporting his progress on the Yazoo Pass expedition. *Ibid.*, I, xxiv, part 3, 55–56. On Feb. 19, McClernand wrote to USG. "I have the honor to enclose a copy of a Communication from Genl. Gorman, respecting his operations in opening the Yazoo Pass." ALS, McClernand Papers, IHi.

On March 1, Lt. Col. Walter B. Scates, adjt. for McClernand, wrote to Lt. Col. John A. Rawlins. "Genl. Ross reports under date of the 23d inst. that the Gunboats had been in 'Moon Lake' for the previous two days, and would start down the pass on the morning of the 24, also that he was embarking his Division on the 23d with the expectation of following the Gunboats in two days. He has strong hope that the pass will be navigable by our boats, but thinks in consequence of swiftness of current, narrowness of the stream and overhanging timber, some damage may be incurred by them." LS, DNA, RG 94, War Records Office, Dept. of the Tenn. *O.R.*, I, xxiv, part 3, 75–76.

1. See letter to Act. Rear Admiral David D. Porter, Feb. 6, 1863.

To Julia Dent Grant

Feb.y 15th 1863.

DEAR JULIA,

If you have not already disposed of your money save it until you hear from me again, and write to Orvil to know if he can pay what is due you in case you want it. I have written to Mr. Douglas[1] of Chicago, one of the most reliable gentlemen in the city to purchase property there for me to the amount of from eight to twelve thousand dollars cash to be paid down for any sum under ten thousand. We have what Orvil owes, the fifteen hundred you have, and one thousand I can spare from the pay now due me. The balance of ten thousand I can borrow without paying interest and should the purchase reach twelve thousand dollars I can pay it in a year, if the war lasts, and if not having so large an amount paid, and saving four hundred dollars a month will at least reduce the amount so that the balance can be managed.

If you have received all the letters I have written in the last few days you cannot complain of not hearing from me.

We are having a greatdeel of rain here and mud so deep that it is almost impossible to get along on horseback. There is a greatdeel of sickness among the soldiers but not nearly so much as there was when I first come down. George is down with the Small pox. Condition hazardous.

Give my love to all. Write to Orvil the reason you want the money if wanted at all but say nothing about the amount of property you intend buying. Say nothing about it at home.

A few weeks more I hope will settle the business here favorably. Kisses for yourself and all the children.

ULYS.

ALS, DLC-USG.

1. John M. Douglas, born in Plattsburg, N. Y., in 1819, practiced law in Galena, Ill., 1841–56, then moved to Chicago where he became solicitor, then vice president, of the Illinois Central Railroad. On July 15, 1863, Douglas wrote to USG. "Upon my return from NewYork I found yours requesting me to invest in United States bonds—I paid Your five thousand dollars in Treasury note unto the Subtreasurer Mr L Haven of Chicago and he give me the enclosed receipt for $5000 in bonds—The bonds will reach me here in two weeks issued in Your name and will be held subject to Your order—The certificate is number 583 for $5000 in six per-cent united states bonds issued in Your name dated July 13, 1863 signed L Haven—Desig Depository I shall probably be required to surrender this certificate when I get the bonds from Mr Haven—Hence I retain it—A Duplicate has bee sent to Washington—Write if you want these bonds sent to you and I will send them—I shall get them from Washington by the time yours reaches me—You have taken Vicksburg—the greatest thing of the war—the best thing except Donaldson & Vicksburg is that you have written no political letters and made no speeches—It seems to me that if our government have reasonable views, and the rebels any sense at all—this war must be pretty near ended—Give my remem to Rollins— . . . Upon refection I have enclosed the certificate and if you want me to take the bonds out of the subtreasury here you must send it back to me—" ALS, USG 3. On Aug. 19, Douglas wrote to USG. "Yours of July 24th was duly received—I have received from Washington five bonds with coupons

attached issued to you in your own name—I have deposited these five bonds for one thousand each with the coupons in the agency of the Bank of Montreal in Chicago where your interest will be collected until you order otherwise—Enclosed also I send you a letter from our friend Osborne enclosing papers for yourself and family—I shall be glad if you have opportunity soon to use them as your friends will be glad to see you in this part of the country—As your part has no parrallel in success, in putting down this wicked rebellion, I venture to express the hope that your future may be as successful when the proper moment arrives, in bringing back to its old basis our once hapy country—I believe, and I wish you to believe, that you are to be as useful to your country in restoreing our government to the affection of our whole people as you have been in the conduct of this war—If we study the liberal spirit of those who made this government we shall be qualified when this war is over to restore it—"   ALS, *ibid*.

To Elihu B. Washburne

Before Vicksburg
Feb.y 15th 1863

Hon. E. B. Washburn
Dear Sir:

I have just been shown a letter from the President to Brig. Steele stating that his name had been witheld from the Senate for promotion in consequence of charges that had been made against him for returning fugitive slaves to their Masters.[1]

Gen. Steele is one of our very best soldiers as well as one of the most able. He is in every sense a soldier, one who believes, as such, his first duty is obedience to law and the orders of his superiors. No matter how far any policy of the Government might vary from his individual views he would conform to it in good faith. Besides I have never heard him express an opinion against any policy of the Administration and know he would do nothing to weaken the power of the President or any officer serving under him.

Gen. Steele is a Northern man, never gave a vote in his life and I presume never influanced one. He has, I think, four brothers, all but one Republicans, and that one, as you know, a conservative Democratic Member of Congress.[2]

The man who made these charges I understand is a Chaplain at Helena, now postmaster.[3] This man has been reported to me almost daily since Helena has been added to my command for his very bad conduct. I am afraid that he has been instigated to these charges from any other than pure motives, and has probably been backed in them by others. No doubt your brother Gen. Washbur has written to you about matters at Helena. If so he has given you facts within his knowledge which have only been hearsay with me.

In regard to Gen. Steele I can say that I have known him for nearly twenty-four years. We were class mates at West Point. A truer man is not in the Army. He will support the Government and maintain the laws, in good faith without questioning their policy.

I hope the President & the Senate will be disabused of any opinion they may have formed prejudicial to Gen. Steele. I would ask, as a special favor to me that you help Gen. S. in this matter.

Yours Truly
U. S. GRANT

ALS, DLC-Robert T. Lincoln.

1. Printed in part in Lincoln, *Works*, VI, 72–73. Brig. Gen. Frederick Steele explained that the allegation stemmed from his release of an unwilling inmate of a house of prostitution. *Ibid*. On March 6, 1863, President Abraham Lincoln nominated Steele as maj. gen.
2. John B. Steele of N. Y.
3. Jacob G. Forman.

To Maj. Gen. Henry W. Halleck

Head Quarters, Dept. of the Ten.
Before Vicksburg, Feb. 16th 1863.

Respectfully forwarded to Hd Qrs. of the Army, Washington for the information of the Gen-in Chief.

There is a force now diligently at work clearing out Yazoo pass, and four light draft Gunboats, one iron clad, with the party.

I am also sending an additional Division of Infantry, with a few pieces of Artillery, without horses to accompany the expedition. If successful they will clear out the Yazoo and all tributaries of all vessels that can do us any injury, saving them for Government if possible, or as many of them as possible. The first attempt will be to ascend the Yalobusha to Grenada and destroy the rail-road bridges there. The force now at Grenada is not large.

U. S. GRANT

Maj. Gen Com

AES, DNA, RG 94, War Records Office, Union Battle Reports. *O.R.*, I, xxiv, part 1, 376. Written on a letter of Feb. 12, 1863, from Lt. Col. James H. Wilson, "In Yazoo Pass, 14 Ms. from the Miss.," to Lt. Col. John A. Rawlins. "In my letter of the 9th to the General, I informed him of the fact that although eminently successful in opening the levee across the Pass, as well as fortunate in finding it naturally a stream entirely capable of navigation, the rebels had discovered our operations time enough to obstruct the channel by felling trees across and into it. On the morning of the 10th I joined Genl. Washburn over a mile from Moon Lake inside of the Pass. Since then, with three day's constant work we have made somewhat more than five miles—having passed and removed two considerable obstructions of fallen and drift timber. Just in front of us there is another about a half mile long, in which many of the trees reach entirely across the stream. Some of them, cotton woods and sycamores, are four feet through at the butt, and will weigh thirty five tons. To add to the difficulty of removing them, the country near the stream is overflowed; nowhere is there more than a mere strip of land next the bank and that only a few inches out of the water. But with all these things against us, there is no doubt of our ability to remove the obstructions and make the Pass navigable for the largest boats that pass through the Louisville Canal. We have brought three steamers with us all the way; Two of which, the Mattie Cook & Luella have been turned about and run to and from Helena. Our greatest difficulty so far has been to obtain tackle strong enough to resist the strains bro't. upon it; but by tomorrow noon, we expect to have new six inch cables. With these we shall be able to lift the heaviest logs. By sawing in two the larger trees, removing such parts as will not sink, and taking out the smaller trees, entirely, we can remove all the obstructions in time. The narrowness and rapidity of the streams requires everything to be taken out that will not float off or sink. I learned to day what I previously suspected: that rebel sympathisers in Helena, thro.' some means or other obtained information and communicated to their friends the nature of our operations at the levee the day we began. At all events it is certain that while we were engaged in opening the Pass at one end, the rebels were closing it at the other. We are now about seven miles from Moon Lake and by the meanderings of the stream the same distance from the Coldwater, though the maps show both distances scarce six miles. It will take from seven to ten days, possibly longer to reach the end of our work." ALS, DNA, RG 94, War Records Office, Union Battle Reports. *O.R.*, I, xxiv, part 1, 375–76.

On Feb. 9, 6:00 P.M., Wilson had written to USG. "Your note of the 7th is just received by the Steamer Emma. I have been waiting all day for a boat, to return to Vicksburg, in order to report in person the condition of affairs in Yazoo Pass—but as an expedition has already been arranged, and you give me permission to accompany it, I shall go back to the 'Pass' in the morning. After the levee had been cut the pilots thought it unsafe to undertake an entrance for several days—The gun-boat Forest Rose needing repairs, plank &c ran up to Memphis, returned, and on the morning of the 7th we ran down and entered the Pass, with great ease. About a mile inside of the levee we struck Moon lake, ran down it about 5 miles to the point where the Pass leaves it, and from that point I proceeded to make further examinations. I was some what disappointed to find the stream neither so large nor straight as it is nearer the river; I went in it about 3 miles in an open boat, but found no obstruction of a serious nature. However we found three men who had just come through in a 'dug-out' from the Tallahatchie— ostensibly for supplies of 'salt' &c. They said, that the people at the mouth of Coldwater had discovered what had been done at the levee, and that a force of rebels, some thirty or forty, with about a hundred negros had been engaged for several days in felling timber across the stream, at intervals between its junction with Coldwater and a point nearly five miles from Moon Lake.—The next day, yesterday, after—waiting till noon for a small steamer, that I had expected the day-before, I went in again with Capt. Brown's cutter, and crew—and decended the 'Pass' nearly six miles—; during this trip we took two men who had belonged to a company of partizen cavalry—; they spoke of the rebels having been there in small force, engaged in cutting timber—but said they had left the evening before. I saw perhaps, at different points forty trees that had been cut so as to fall in the stream but in no place had it obstructed the channel so as to resist, or prevent the passage of boats. At three places some drift timber had collected against standing trees, so as to contract the waterway—but a a few hours work would open it so as to make the passage easy. The timber or at least all that I saw, which had been cut into the water, had either sunk out of sight or been drifted against the shore so as to hurt nothing;—from this fact, and the opinion of boatmen accustomed to small streams, I am inclined to think that although many more trees may have been cut lower down, and at points opposite each other, they will not materially interfere with navigation. The stream is only about one hundred feet wide (but very deep)—and as the timber over hangs it in many places, it will be necessary to cut out considerable in order to prevent the smoke stacks of the steamers from being knocked down. This will be a more tedious operation than usual from the fact that in many places the banks of the stream are under water. But with all these difficulties, no one here entertains a doubt of our being able to work through. Gen'l. Gorman sent Gen'l. Washburn down yesterday with a thousand men, and sent five hundred more this morning; they have begun operations. I shall go down myself, early in the morning and push matters as rapidly as possible. Before I left there, the Ferry boat 'Luella,' about 100 ft. long had gone into the pass near three miles, *turned about* and returned. Information of no very reliable character has reached Gen'l. Gorman, to the effect that the rebels were aware of our movements and 'were making arrangements for our reception.' Where, or how is not known. I have been thus minute in my statement, so that you could see exactly how the matter stands. I am quite sure that no material advantages in the way of a surprise, can be obtained, unless our expedition gets through within five or six days. I see nothing however except the non arrival of the gunboats to prevent this; unless indeed the obstructions in the other end of the Pass, are more serious than we now think. Should the river fall again eight or ten feet, there is not the possibility of a doubt that Yazoo Pass can be opened to admit a large class of boats—, and after the Coldwater is reached there are no obstacles of any kind— and very little chance of interposing any till you arrive at Yazoo City. There is a bluff there, and the next highland is at Haine's Bluffs. I shall accompany the Yazoo Expedition, unless you direct otherwise. . . . It is called twelve miles from Moon Lake to the junction of the Pass with the Coldwater, and therefore there is only six or seven miles yet unexplored—certainly two miles of which are no more difficult than what I have explored already.—I will keep you informed of our progress.—" ALS, DNA, RG 94, War Records Office, Union Battle Reports. *O.R.*, I, xxiv, part 1, 373–75. On Feb. 24, Wilson wrote to Rawlins that Yazoo Pass was open for navigation. *Ibid.*, pp. 376, 378. On Feb. 27, USG forwarded this report to Maj. Gen. Henry W. Halleck. DNA, RG 108, Register of Letters Received.

To Act. Rear Admiral David D. Porter

Feb.y 16th 1863

ADMIRAL D. D. PORTER,
COMD.G MISS SQUADRON,
ADMIRAL,

The bearer of this, Mr. Carlisle, is a man of known loyalty and has been a refugee from his southern home whilst the country was in possession of the rebels. Out of everything he has nothing left but a few bales of cotton on his plantation about twelve miles above the mouth of White river. It would be an act of charity, worthily bestowed, to permit one of the gunboats to protect a steamer whilst taking this cotton on board. I have given him permission to ship his cotton to Memphis if the boat taking it can receive this protection.

Mr. Carlisle is not a cotton speculator but only desirous of geting his own to market.

I am Admiral
your obt. svt.
U. S. GRANT
Maj. Gen

ALS, MdAN. On Feb. 16, 1863, Act. Rear Admiral David D. Porter wrote to USG. "I gave Mr. Carlisle an order for a gun boat to protect him &c   I send you a letter I received this morning from Captain Selfridge—I am going to send another gun boat." LS, DNA, RG 393, Dept. of the Tenn., Letters Received. Porter enclosed a letter of Feb. 14 from Lt. Commander Thomas O. Selfridge, Jr., *Conestoga*, reporting the activities of C.S.A. batteries on the Arkansas River. ALS, *ibid.*

To Lt. Col. Charles A. Reynolds

Before Vicksburgh
Feby 16th 1863

Lt Col C A Reynolds
Chief Quartermaster

On your arrival at Memphis seize all transports coming into port for the use of the Army here except such as are absolutely necessary for carrying Government supplies from above. When it becomes praticable to release any boats again give those boats the preferance that have been constantly in Goverment employ Two boats may be continued in the trade between Memphis and Cairo subject to seizure any time Goverment may require their services   I would suggest however that the boats now running in that trade be taken and others substituted. Boats will be required here to transport a large army and nearly all at one time This must occupy your particular attention

U S Grant Maj Gen

Copies, DLC-USG, V, 18, 30; DNA, RG 393, Dept. of the Tenn., Letters Sent. On Feb. 19, 1863, Capt. John V. Lewis, Memphis, wrote to Lt. Col. Charles A. Reynolds. "A copy of General Grants letter to you dated 16th Inst has been referred to me, and in reply to the same I have the honor to report that in my opinion it is neccessary to have not less than eight steamers of large size run regularly between this point and St Louis, Mo, and not less than three between this point and Cincinnati Ohio that the Army of the Tennessee may exist; and that they may be allowed to run on their own account, as from my experience I have learned that many unneccessary delays arise when Steamers are employed by the day. As far as I can ascertain all are ~~both~~ willing to carry both troops and freight at the contract rates, made not long since with the sanction of Col. Robt. Allen Chief Q. M. at St Louis, Mo." ALS, Parsons Papers, IHi. This letter, favorably endorsed by Reynolds and by Capt. Asher R. Eddy, was also endorsed by USG. "Refered to Col. Parsons. The number of boats asked may be released on condition that they will carry Govt. freight and troops when called on to do so at the rates agreed upon heretofore and to the exclusion of every thing els." AES, *ibid*.

To Maj. Gen. Henry W. Halleck

———

Head Quarters, Dept. of the Ten.
Before Vicksburg, Feb.y 18th 1863.

MAJ. GEN. H. W. HALLECK,
GEN. IN CHIEF, WASHINGTON D. C.
GEN.

The work upon the canal here is progressing as well as possible with the excessively bad weather and high water we have had to contend against. Most of the time that troops could be out atall has been expended in keeping the water out of our camps. Five good working days would enable the force here to complete the canal sixty feet wide and of sufficient depth to admit any vessel here. Judging from the past it is fare to calculate that it will take ten or twelve days in which to get these five working days. Three more perhaps should be allowed from the fact that the work is being done by soldiers the most of whom under the most favorable circumstances could not come up to the calculations of the Engineer officers. McPherson's Army Corps is at Lake Providence prossecuting the work there. They could not be of any service in helping on the work here because there are already as many men as can be employed on it, and then he would have to go five or six miles above to find land above water to encamp on. I am using a few hundred contrabands on the work here, but have been compelled to prohibit any more coming in.[1] Humanity dictates this policy. Planters have mostly deserted their plantations taking with them all their able bodied negroes and leaving the old and very young. Here they could not have shelter nor assurances of transportation when we leave.

I have sent one Division of troops from Helena to join the

Yazoo expedition under Lt. Col. Wilson. Col. Wilson's last report was sent you a few days ago.[2] If successful they will destroy the rail-road bridges at Grenada and capture or destroy all the transports in the Yazoo and tributaries.[3]

The health of this command is not what is represented in the public press.[4] It is as good as any previous calculation could have prognosticated. I believe too there is the best of feeling and greatest confidance of success among them. The greatest draw back to the spirits of the troops has been the great delay in paying them.[5] Many of them have families at home who are no doubt in a suffering condition for want of the amounts due those bound for their support.

> I am Gen. very respectfully
> your obt. svt.
> U. S. Grant
> Maj. Gen. Com

ALS, NHi. *O.R.*, I, xxiv, part 1, 18.

1. On Feb. 12, 1863, Lt. Col. John A. Rawlins issued Special Field Orders No. 2. "The nature of the service the army is now called on to perform making it impracticable to transport or provide for persons unemployed by Government, the enticing of negroes to leave their homes to come within the lines of the army is positively forbidden. They should be permitted to remain at their homes, and, in pursuance of the recommendation of the President, in all cases where allowed to labor faithfully for reasonable wages. Those at present within the lines will not be turned out, but in future in the field no persons, white or black, who are not duly authorized to pass the lines of sentinels will be permitted to enter or leave camp. Whenever the services of negroes are required, details will be made by army corps commanders for the purpose of collecting them, and they will be registered, provided for, and employed in accordance with law and existing orders." *Ibid.*, I, xxiv, part 3, 46–47. These orders also forbade the arrest of citizens without charges and regulated the receipt of messages under flag of truce. *Ibid.*

On Feb. 16, Chaplain John Eaton, Jr., superintendent of contrabands, wrote to Rawlins asking numerous questions about the management of contrabands. ALS, DNA, RG 108, Letters Received. On Feb. 16, USG endorsed this letter. "Respectfully refered to Hd Qrs. of the Army with the request that ~~orders be published~~ instructions be sent covering such of these enquiries as are not already provided for by law or Gen. orders. If it is the design of the Government to cultivate Southern fields with the numerous contrabands coming into the Federal lines I would suggest Lake Providence as a most suitable place for a colony. The plantations are in a high state of cultivation, well improved as to quarters, and the place easily protected." AES, *ibid.*

2. See endorsement to Maj. Gen. Henry W. Halleck, Feb. 16, 1863.

3. On Feb. 18, Brig. Gen. Benjamin M. Prentiss, Helena, wrote to USG. "I have the honor herewith to hand to you two autograph letters from Brig. Genl. Washburne in command of the enterprise at the 'Yazoo Pass,' which I think will be the best report I can make to you of the progress of that enterprise—I have no doubt that the plan upon which we are there working will be successful, and will prove of great advantage to us—I will issue such a dispatch as is suggested by Gen. Washburne in enclosure No '2.'—" ALS, DNA, RG 94, War Records Office, Dept. of the Tenn. *O.R.*, I, xxiv, part 1, 401. The two reports of Brig. Gen. Cadwallader C. Washburn are printed *ibid.*, pp. 401–2. In the second, Washburn suggested giving the newspapers an erroneous story that the Yazoo Pass expedition had failed.

4. See letter to Col. Robert C. Wood, March 6, 1863.

5. See letter to Paymaster Edwin D. Judd, Feb. 19, 1863.

To Maj. Gen. John A. McClernand

Head Quarters, Dept. of the Ten.
Before Vicksburg, Feb. 18th 1863.

Maj. Gen. J. A. McClernand
Comd.g. 13th Army Corps,
Gen.

In answer to your note of this date suggesting an attack on Pine Bluff, Ark. after reflection I see but one objection to it. The objection is that all the forces now here, to operate with, are assigned to duties looking to the one great object, that of opening the Miss. and to take off the number of men suggested would retard progress.

I know the President is looking forward with great anxiety to the completion of the canal across the point so as to admit steamers through it. This work requires all the forces here. One Division is already taken from Helena for the Yazoo expedition and Gen. McPherson's Army Corps is employed on a work which may prove of vast importance.

On the return of Gen. Ross to Helena and the Brigade sent by you to clear out rebel forces in the neighborhood of Greenville[1] and Syprus bend[2] it may be practicable to fit out the requisite force by reducing Helena for the time to a minimum and using one Division from here.

The Yazoo expedition, if not successful, will return about as soon as the Brigade sent from here.

> I am Gen. very respectfully
> your obt. svt.
> U. S. GRANT
> Maj. Gen. Com

ALS, McClernand Papers, IHi. Misdated Feb. 15, 1863, in *O.R.*, I, xxiv, part 3, 57. On Feb. 15, Maj. Gen. John A. McClernand wrote to USG. "As connected with the subject of my communication of the 1st inst. relative to an expedition into Arkansas, I have the honor to add upon the authority of Genl Gorman that, on the 11th inst, there was a rebel force at Pine Bluff consisting of ten or fifteen thousand men, of all arms. If not inconsistent with your plans, I would ask that you would permit me with a force of 20,000 Infantry, including those of that arm here and at Helena, together with proper complements of Artillery and Cavalry, to move against the enemy at Pine Bluff and capture or disperse him. Of the aggregate force of 20,000 Infantry 8,230 could be drawn from that portion of the 13th Army Corps here, and 9,541 from that portion of it at Helena; while 3,808 Cavalry, or such portion of the same, as you might think proper to order, might be drawn from the same places; as also a proper complement of Artillery. The success of the expedition would virtually clear the west bank of the Mississippi River of the enemy and open the way to the extension of the Federal jurisdiction co-extensive with its rightful limits; and would doubtless meet with the approbation of both the President and Genl Curtis; who are well pleased with the issue of the late expedition against the Post Arkansas." LS, DNA, RG 94, War Records Office, Dept. of the Tenn. *O.R.*, I, xxiv, part 3, 56–57. See letter to Maj. Gen. John A. McClernand, Jan. 31, 1863.

On Feb. 18, McClernand wrote to USG. "I would respectfully recommend that the Island formed by the cut off between the White and Arkansas rivers be substituted for Helena as the site of the principal Garrison, on the west bank of the Mississippi river, between Memphis and this camp. 1st Because it is about equi-distant between Memphis and this place; and because Helena is so near to Memphis as to add but little to the security and convenience afforded by the Garrison at the latter place. 2nd Because any one of the five steamers on the Arkansas river and now in possession of the enemy might, with an armament of one or two guns, be used to interrupt the navigation of the Mississippi river and to destroy our transports near the mouth of the White and Arkansas rivers. 3rd Because the Island being isolated might be rendered more secure against successful attack than Helena. A squad of cavalry posted at each end of the cut off could easily bring information of any hostile approach. 4th Because a garrison on the Island would effectually command the mouths of the White and Arkansas rivers, and be a continual menace to any hostile Garrison on either of those rivers; and at the same time serve to facilitate any expedition up either of them that might be projected. It will be hardly possible for the Enemy to convey any other than light pieces of Artillery to the vicinity of Helena for the next three months; and these could avail nothing either against the works there or passing Steamers as long as a few heavy pieces of cannon are retained there. Again: if the enemy should attempt an expedition against Helena, while a strong Garrison was kept upon the Island, a force might be detached from the latter, which, marching upon the line of his advance, could cut him off. I think a Garrison at Helena consisting of an efficient brigade of Infantry, with 500 Cavalry, a battery of light Artillery and a few heavy guns in position, the whole properly entrenched, would suffice to secure that place. And, I think, a Garrison of one Division of Infantry, 1500 Cavalry and 3 Batteries of light Artillery on the Island, with a Gunboat to patrol the Mississippi, White and Arkansas rivers in that vicinity, would serve to secure that place. To guard against overflow on the Island a levee might be soon thrown up around the immediate camp by the Garrison, or by negroes found in the vicinity." DfS, McClernand Papers, IHi. On Feb. 27, USG forwarded this letter to Maj. Gen. Henry W. Halleck. DNA, RG 108, Register of Letters Received.

On Feb. 28, McClernand wrote to USG. "Still keeping in view the proposed Expedition to clear Arkansas and the west bank of the Miss. river of an organized hostile force, I have continued to avail myself all means of obtaining useful information in that respect. It appears that the force of the enemy on the Arkansas river is disposed somewhat differently from that it was according to my last communication upon this subject. Genl. Prentiss informs me under date of the 24th inst. that there is rebel force of 2000 at Pine Bluff; 10.000 at Little Rock, of which 4000 are sick; and I learn, otherwise, that there is a force of some 1500 at Post Arkansas. Genl. Prentiss' informant informs him that these troops are very scant of wholesome food, are much dissatisfied and demoralized, and are apprehensive of an attack coming from the Mississippi river. The force I suggested in my previous communication, suddenly thrown upon them, ought to capture or disperse the whole of them. If in your judgment the time has arrived for the movement I would be glad to lead it. In that event, I would like to confer with you in regard to the proportions of Infantry, Cavalry and Artillery which the movement ~~out~~ should to combine." ALS, *ibid.*, RG 94, War Records Office, Dept. of the Tenn. *O.R.*, I, xxiv, part 3, 73.

1. Greenville, Miss., about one hundred miles upriver from Vicksburg. See letter to Brig. Gen. Stephen G. Burbridge, Feb. 24, 1863.
2. Cypress Bend on the Mississippi River about thirty miles upriver from Greenville.

To Abraham Lincoln

Before Vicksburg, Miss.
February 19th 1863.

HIS EXCELLENCY A. LINCOLN, PRESIDENT,
SIR:

Mrs. Hoge of Illinois has shown me a letter from yourself expressing a willingness to commission her son, Holmes Hoge a member of the Chicago Mercantile Battery on the recommendation of some Maj. Gen. who could give him employment.

If Hoge were appointed Asst. Quartermaster with the rank of Captain and ordered to report to this Department he could be placed on duty.

My personal Staff is already provided or names sent in of those recommended to fill vacancies.

> With great respect
> your obt. svt.
> U. S. GRANT
> Maj. Gen.

ALS, DNA, RG 94, ACP, H166 CB 1863. On March 9, 1863, President Abraham Lincoln endorsed this letter. "I wish to have this appointment made at once." AES, *ibid*. On March 11, Secretary of War Edwin M. Stanton endorsed this letter. "Appoint Holmes Hoge Brig Qr Master" AES, *ibid*. On March 13, the U.S. Senate confirmed Private Holmes Hoge, Chicago Mercantile Battery, as capt., asst. q. m.

Mrs. Abraham H. Hoge, Jane Currie (Blaikie) Hoge, associate manager of the North-western Branch of the U.S. Sanitary Commission, was indefatigable in efforts to obtain military advancement for her sons. See Lincoln, *Works*, V, 512; VI, 40–41, 96; Mrs. A. H. Hoge, *The Boys in Blue* . . . (New York, 1867), pp. 201–3.

To Paymaster Edwin D. Judd

> Before Vicksburgh
> Feby 19th 1863

MAJOR E D JUDD
PAYMASTER U S A

It is a matter of vast importance to the troops here that they receive their pay promptly   I wrote to you some days ago requesting that a part of your force be sent here immediately to pay off the troops in the Field. So important do I regard this matter that if you are not under special orders already I wish you to regard this as an order to pay these troops first and to the exclusion of all others if necessary. This should be attended to immediately because a delay may find the troops actively engaged so that it will become impractable

U S GRANT
Maj Gen

Copies, DLC-USG, V, 18, 30; DNA, RG 393, Dept. of the Tenn., Letters Sent. Edwin D. Judd of Conn. was appointed additional paymaster of vols. as of June 1, 1861. On March 1, 1863, Judd, Memphis, wrote to USG. "Acting under orders from the Chief Paymaster I returned to St Louis, and Louisville on the 8th Febry. to render my accounts to the Department, which had been unsettled for a long time, owing to my having been constantly on duty. We were unable to obtain money to pay your troops at Vicksburg until the 23 Febry, when I left St Louis with some, intending to proceed immediately to your headquarters: on arriving here on the 27th ult, I found your two letters of the 8th & 19th Ultimo, and determined to start immediately down the river, but before I could secure safe transportation for my funds, Major Gen. Hurlbut received unfavorable news from below, and sent me a written communication, advising me, 'on no account to proceed down the river at present with funds,' but to await further advices from below. I have funds for the payment of the five unpaid divisions below, to Oct. 31, 1862 and will take it down as soon as I can with Safety, it was impossible for me to go before, and we had not the funds; from first to last, since the resolution of Congress ordering the troops paid up to date, we have received only $4,000,000, and it has been coming along in little lots of $250,000 at a time. I therefore hope you will have patience with me, as every effort is being made to secure more funds. I should have replied to your communications promptly, had I received them before. Majors Jordon & Osgood will proceed down the river by first boat, to prepare the way for the payment. I will follow with the funds as soon as I can with safety." LS, *ibid.*, Letters Received.

On March 30, Judd, Memphis, wrote to Lt. Col. John A. Rawlins. "I have advices that funds are on the way from Washington to pay your army up to Febry 28. 1863, that is *not* including the divisions lately come into your army from Eastern Arkansas & Missouri, those will have to be paid by the Missouri Pay District, Major N. W. Brown Chief Paymaster St Louis. The muster-pay rolls should be made out from date of last payment (instead of last muster) to February 28, 1863, containing all the data affecting the pay for the whole four months, so that we can pay the whole on one set of rolls. As soon as the money arrives I will send a party of paymasters down, under charge of Major Hazleton, probably in about a week. There are no mustering officers appointed here yet, and it occasions much trouble to those who have been promoted from one office to another." LS, *ibid.*

On Jan. 12, Judd had written to USG announcing that Maj. George L. Febiger would henceforth pay troops in USG's dept. and discussing procedures. ALS, *ibid.* On Feb. 17, Maj. Gen. John A. McClernand wrote to USG. "I am informed that there are men, and probably officers in this command, who have received no pay for nine months. This failure is naturally exciting bad feeling, prejudicial to good order, dicipline, and the cause of the country. Another grievance is the existing deficiency of Surgeons, and consequent suffering of the sick. If, with every Hospital boat sent away, a regimental Surgeon is detailed, this evil must continue to increase; particularly, if the Surgeons remain away for some time, as is often true. Can any steps be taken by you, in the premises, promising speedy and favorable results?" LS, *ibid*. On the same day, Rawlins wrote to McClernand. "In reply to your Communication of this date in relation to Paymasters and Surgeons, Maj. Gen. Grant directs me to say, that the Paymasters of this Department have received funds and have Commenced paying troops up to and including October 31st. He has made application to Major Judd, Senior Paymaster to send forward immediately a sufficient number of Paymasters, with the necessary funds to pay the troops at this place, and is expecting their arrival daily. An order was some days since sent to Maj. Gen Hurlbut for a sufficient number of Surgeons to supply the deficiency you refer to." LS, McClernand Papers, IHi.

To Maj. Gen. William T. Sherman

Head Quarters, Dept. of the Ten.
Before Vicksburg, Feb.y 21st 1863.

MAJ. GEN. W. T. SHERMAN
COMD.G 15TH ARMY CORPS,
GEN.

The enemy having captured one of our rams, with all her armament, and having several other armed vessels below here makes it necessary for our security to have a battery of Parrot guns below Vicksburg.

If practicable I would like to have this battery placed below Warrenten. In this case the battery should be supported by a Brigade of Infantry.[1] There would necessarily be some difficulty in supplying troops there, but as the country will afford forage and a plank road will be made across the point, on the canal embankment, I think it can be done.

Respectfully yrs.
U. S. GRANT
Maj. Gen

P. S. Capt. Prime is directed to located and build the battery required, and roads leading to it.

U. S. G.

ALS, deCoppet Collection, NjP. *O.R.*, I, xxiv, part 3, 61–62. On Feb. 21, 1863, Act. Rear Admiral David D. Porter wrote to USG. "I enclose a copy of a [—]

from Colonel Ellett.—The letter is rather unsatisfactory. I do not really understand the state of affairs. I am anxiously looking for a more minute report." LS, DNA, RG 45, Correspondence of David D. Porter, Mississippi Squadron, Letters Sent. Porter probably enclosed a copy of the note of the same date he had received from Col. Charles R. Ellet which referred to the loss of the *Queen of the West*. *O.R.* (Navy), I, xxiv, 382. Ellet submitted a full report to Porter later the same day. *Ibid.*, pp. 383–86. The *Queen of the West* later returned to Vicksburg flying C.S.A. colors. See letter to Act. Rear Admiral David D. Porter, Feb. 24, and telegram to Maj. Gen. Henry W. Halleck, Feb. 25, 1863.

Also on Feb. 21, Maj. Gen. William T. Sherman wrote to USG. "My engineer Capt Pitzman is just back from the reconnaissance to Johnsons plantation below our Pickets in front of Warrenton. To pass troops below Warrenton will require about one mile of corduroy Road, and a bridge about one hundred yards long. Capt Pitzman saw Col Ellet and received from him a more inteligible account of matters below. The Ram Queen of the West with the little Ferry Boat Desoto ascended Red River he says about 100 miles (to Barbins Landing I think) ~~and there~~ and there engaged a Battry of four heavy Guns. After considerable firings the Boat received a shot into her Boilers which filled her with steam and compelled all hands to escape by jumping overboard and to land. Col Ellet had time to leave his Boat but he had not the heart to burn her up with several wounded officers & men on board who could not escape or be removed. I should state her pilot had run the Ram aground at the time of the attack. She was therefore left and afterward taken by the Gun boat Webb,—getting on board the ferry boat desoto & the Prize Era No 5 they returned to the Mouth of Red River when the Desoto becoming disabled was burned. All hands were transfered to the Era No 5 which proceeded up the River pursued by the Gunboat Webb till they met the iron clad Indianola at Ellis Bluff. The Indianola at once engaged the Webb, and the Era came up without awaiting the result.—She is a poor boat, nearly worn out, could only make 3 miles against the Current and escaped the Warrenton Batteries by pure accident. He Col Ellet reports 22 guns at Warrenton, and that they fired 100 shots at him which missed his boat. He complains of the treachery of his Pilot, who ran his Boat aground repeatedly and he has the Pilot of the Queen of the West in arrest—Col Ellet is sick unable to ride over, but will come over tomorrow. Wants Admiral Porter to know that he will come tomorrow. This account varies so much from Col Abbotts letter of this mornig that I think it would be well to send this letter to the admiral. I cannot learn if the Ram Queen was badly grounded, whether she was seen afterward by the Colonel (Ellet), whether Ellet communicated these facts to Capt Brown of the Indianola, or indeed any material facts but those related above." ALS, MdAN.

On Feb. 12, Porter had written to USG. "I shall send the Indianola down to-night to run the batteries at Vicksburg. She will show two red lights when she gets near your pickets below. If you would let your people at the canal show a light, I would be much obliged. I want Captain Brown to send me a report. Will you please order it sent over?" *O.R.*, I, xxiv, part 3, 45; *O.R.* (Navy), I, xxiv, 375. On the same day, USG endorsed this letter. "I am just starting up the river. Will Gen. Sherman attend to the within." Parke-Bernet Sale No. 1190, Oct. 30–Nov. 1, 1950, p. 236. The *Indianola* successfully passed the Vicksburg batteries the following night.

1. On Feb. 25, USG wrote to Sherman. "The order to move one Brigade to

the support of the Battery below Vicksburgh was on the supprosition that the Battery would be located below Warrenton   As the Battery is located only a short distance below the canal however such a force will not be required. In fact I do not think any force will be required more than the guards you will have on that side of the point." Copies, DLC-USG, V, 18, 30; DNA, RG 393, Dept. of the Tenn., Letters Sent.

To Brig. Gen. Benjamin M. Prentiss

Before Vicksburg
Feby 21st 1863

BRIG GEN B M PRENTISS
COMM'DG DISTRICT OF EASTERN ARK

If Genl Gorman is not at Helena order him back at once and place him in arrest. Copy of charges preferred against him will be forwarded in a few days. Genl Gorman has been guilty of the indiscretion of diverting one of the gunboats intended for the Yazoo Expedition to protect a transport whilst gathering cotton south of Helena his son in charge of the said cotton. At least such is officialy reported. If there is any cotton at Helena, go collect it, seize it at once and hold it for the benefit of the Government. All cotton seized in the Department is shipped to Capt Eddy A Q M at Memphis Tenn to sell

U S GRANT
Maj Gen

Copies, DLC-USG, V, 18, 30; DNA, RG 393, Dept. of the Tenn., Letters Sent. See letter to Act. Rear Admiral David D. Porter, Feb. 15, 1863.

To Maj. Gen. Stephen A. Hurlbut

———

Head Quarters, Dept. of the Ten.
Before Vicksburg, Feb.y 22d 1863.

MAJ. GEN. HURLBUT,
COMD.G 16TH ARMY CORPS
GEN.

So soon as all the rolling stock of the rail-road is got away from Columbus the road North from Jackson may be abandoned, disposing of the troops guarding it as your judgement may dictate.

I directed Gen. Hamilton to have all workshops, Depots of stores, and every thing not required by the troops, removed from all posts between Grand Junction and Corinth, via Jackson, removed to points intended to be perminantly occupied, so that in case of necessity this part of the road may be abandoned and the troops removed to wherever their services may be required. I do not want Jackson abandoned however except in case of absolutely necessity.

If Col. Lee is perfectly satisfied that some of his men are being punished as described in his report, by rebel authority, he may serve in the same manner an equal number of the enemy and open a correspondence with Gen. Tilghman as he proposes.[1]

I will want one Division of troops brought forward and held in readiness to be join this expedition when called for.

I sent orders some time ago for the 2d Ill. Cavalry to be forwarded here without delay. As they have not come I presume my order never reached you. They may now be held for further orders.

If the six 8 in. howitzers at Memphis have not yet been sent here they need not be sent but forward them to Corinth, with all the ammunition belonging to them. The 1st Inf.y will come here as per orders.[2]

Gen. McClernand's Army Corps is deficient in Artillery.[3] I have not the returns before me to designate any particular battery to be sent but I want one with heavy guns, Parrots if possible, forwarded as soon as possible.

Vigerous measures will have to be adopted to prevent the smuggling going on from Memphis but I do not know what to suggest. This I leave to your own judgement.

> I am Gen. Very respectfully
> your obt. svt.
> U. S. GRANT
> Maj. Gen. Com

ALS, DNA, RG 393, 16th Army Corps, Letters Received. *O.R.*, I, xxiv, part 3, 63. On Feb. 20, 1863, Maj. Gen. Stephen A. Hurlbut, Memphis, wrote to Lt. Col. John A. Rawlins. "Three days since the rebel Guerillas at Hopefield surprised the Tow Steamer Hercules which had gone in to the Arkansas Shore in a dense fog—killed one of the crew & burned the Boat & a Barge of Coal. It having been ascertained that Hopeffeld is a mere shelter for Guerillas, I ordered the place burned—which was done on yesterday—Sixteen or 17 Horses were captured which no parties there would own, quite a number of Cavalry Saddles & other evidences of the haunts of the Guerillas—one Barn in burning blew up with a quantity of concealed powder   I have stopped all communication with Arkansas for the present   I have consulted with Genl Veatch as to the possibility of barricading the Streets & roads leading into Memphis & we unite that it can only be effectually done by cutting the bridges across Gayoso Bayou on such roads as may be selected—This however will leave outside of barricades a large portion of the suburbs of Memphis. With the immense depôts & Hospitals here both for the Army & Navy & the certainty that this point is to be a base of supplies it will require in my judgment an entire Division to cover this city so as to prevent the terrible smuggling which is now going on. The Effects of it are perfectly demoralizing. Bribery & corruption seem to go into every branch of service and the actual cases of which proof can be made are only, I am afraid, symptoms of a wide spread disease. I have sure information that Richardson's Guerillas have been supplied with Revolvers from this City. I propose to day to forbid any arms whatever being exposed or kept for sale in the command. Major Mudd supported by 2 Regts of Genl Quimby's command made a dash on Blythe captured twelve & ran the rest off to Coldwater, but they come back as fast as our troops are withdrawn. As soon as the Roads become decent I think of putting a Brigade in near Horn Lake in the country infested by the Guerillas & let them eat them out. The Country is rich in forage & provisions. Col: Webster informs me that the R. Road will be completed to day or tomorrow. It will soon be broken up again somewhere in the O'Bion country I think. The cavalry *Expedition* south starts to day or to morrow. I have heard nothing of importance from Dodge or from the Tennessee." ALS, DNA, RG 94, War Records Office, Dept. of the Mo.

1. On Feb. 20, Col. Albert L. Lee, Germantown, Tenn., wrote to Capt. Henry Binmore, adjt. for Hurlbut. "Yesterday arriving here, a private of the 4th Ills Cavalry who was captured by the rebels some three weeks since, and on Friday the 13th inst was released by them on parole, at Jackson Miss. he states that there

are few troops at Grenada, and very few along the line of Miss Central Rail Road. at Jackson Genl Adams of Tenn is in command, but at the Post was only about one or two Regts of men. Rebel gossip at Jackson puts their forces at Port Hudson and Vicksburg at 60 000. He was sent back by way of Meridian and over the Mobile and Ohio R. R. at a point between Jackson and Meridian are being erected large Machine Shops. Vast quantities of Cotton marked 'Confederate States' are piled along the Road. Recently great amounts of Sugar has been shipped from Vicksburg and vicinity to Jackson and other points, near. at Jackson five large Cotton houses are filled with the hogsheads. Along the Mobile & Ohio Rd hardly any troops are stationed. a single train of two or three cars, runs over the road each day for local accomodations about 10 miles north of Okolona are two Regiments of Cavalry Three miles north of Okolona a bridge is destroyed and trains stop at the Town. At Jackson are about 20 Federal officers kept in close confinement, and on hard fare also about 700 Federal Soldiers. The authorities parole and send North by rail 12 men each day. I desire to call your attention to one fact There are among these prisoners 3 men of the 7th Kansas Cav Genl Tilghman has ordered them in irons and they are now chained to gether hand and foot by heavy Irons this only because they are connected with that Regt. Is there any method of wrighting this wrong or of retalliation. If our policy will permit it, I will capture three Confederate officers within a fortnight and put them in irons in camp of 7 Kansas and then open a correspondence with Genl Tilghman. Along this road all is quiet. The Newspaper rumors of any considerable force south of it are entirely without foundation. The roads are almost impassible" Copy, *ibid.* *O.R.*, I, xxiv, part 3, 61. On the same day, Hurlbut endorsed this letter to Rawlins. AES, DNA, RG 94, War Records Office, Dept. of the Mo.

2. On Feb. 13, Rawlins wrote to Hurlbut. "Send forward immediately to this place the 1st U S Inf'try with the six 8 inch Howitzers placed in their charge by Special Orders No 39 from these Head quarters a copy of which is herewith enclosed. They will bring with them all the 8-inch Howitzer ammunition they have on hand" Copies, DLC-USG, V, 18, 30; DNA, RG 393, Dept. of the Tenn., Letters Sent.

3. On Feb. 24, Maj. Gen. John A. McClernand wrote to USG. "I am informed that there is one 32 and six 24 pdr. pieces at Helena but no 8. in. Howitzers, as I understood you to suppose." ADfS, McClernand Papers, IHi. On Feb. 17, McClernand had written to USG. "Having previously called your attention, to the comparatively small artillery force, in the two Divisions, of the 13th Army Corps, here; I write now to add a suggestion, as to the mode in which the deficiency may be remedied, probably, satisfactorily to all. Capt L. Hoffman of the 4th Ohio Battery, has, I understand been with Genl. Osterhaus, for a considerable period, and until lately. I am assured it is desired, by both of these officers, that the battery be attached, to the Genl's. Command, (9th Div 13th A.C.) If it be agreeable to you, and others concerned, I pray you may order it to be done" ALS, DNA, RG 393, Dept. of the Tenn., Letters Received. On the same day, Rawlins wrote to McClernand. "I am directed by Maj. Gen. U. S. Grant to acknowledge the receipt of your communication of this date and to say in reply that 6 8-inch Howitzers in charge of 1st U. S. Infantry, Maj. Mahoney, Com'd'g. has been added to Ross' Division of your Army Corps, and are now on the way here.—See enclosed order. The transfer of the 4th Ohio Battery will be made if practicable." LS, McClernand Papers, IHi.

To Maj. Isaac S. Stewart

Headq'rs Dep't of Tennessee,
Lake Providence, Feb. 23, 1863.

MAJOR I. S. STEWART PAYMASTER U. S. A.:

MAJOR:

In answer to yours of this date desiring to know the order in which I wish the troops of my command paid, I would state that as many of the soldiers in the army have families dependent on their pay for a support, and as those now in the field may be called on soon for such active service as to preclude the possibility of paying them for some time, they should be paid first and at once. Three paymasters will be sufficient to pay off the one division at Lake Providence, (McArthur's,) and twelve to pay off those of McClernand's and Sherman's army corps in front of Vicksburg. The remainder of the corps can pay off the troops in General Hurlburt's command in any order they may deem proper, on consultation with him, (Hurlburt.)

Very respectfully, your obedient servant,
U. S. GRANT, Major Gen.

Unidentified newspaper clipping, Grant Family Papers, USGA. The clipping states that the letter appeared earlier in the *San Antonio Express* in 1868. Isaac S. Stewart of Ind. was appointed additional paymaster with the rank of maj. as of Nov. 26, 1862. For a reminiscent interview in which Stewart mentioned spending the evening of Feb. 23, 1863, with USG on the *Magnolia*, see *New York World*, Aug. 7, 1885.

To Salmon P. Chase

Head Quarters, Dept. of the Ten.
Before Vicksburg, Feb.y 23d 1863.

HON. S. P. CHASE
SEC. OF THE TREASURY
WASHINGTON D. C.
SIR:

Enclosed herewith please find evidence of ownership adduced for cotton seized and sold for the benefit of Government, by my order, whilst the Army under my command occupied Northern Miss. I send these to you to show the difficulties a commander of troops in the field has to contend against whilst trade is allowed to follow the flag.

Whilst at Abberville and Oxford Miss. I authorized the seizure of cotton marked C. S. A. and also that owned by persons known to hold place in the so called Southern Confederacy. Besides the cotton marked C. S. A. that was seized there was something over four hundred bales belonging to Jacob Thompson,[1] Avent & Bowls three prominant men in the Southern Army and for which no claim has been set up. Notwithstanding this claims have come in for more than the amount received by Government, and in all cases unprincipled cotton speculators are the representatives of the parties loosing their cotton.

No doubt cotton has been seized where it should not have been, under the policy that has been pursued by Government. In all such cases I was ready to hear the claims of owners and return their cotton when they were entitled to it. In this way I caused several hundred bales to be returned to owners and I regret to say some of my juniors, without my knowledge, caused several hundred bales more to be returned.

The whole amount of cotton seized was near eighteen hundred (1800) bales and the amount that reached Capt. Eddy, A. Q. M. Memphis was but little over seven hundred (700). This claim is now to come out of that.

In directing the Quarter master to sell this cotton I ordered that he should keep an account of the marks and weight of all he sold and hold 25 cts. pr. pound, the amount agreed to be paid by speculators, subject to adjudication.

At the time this cotton was seized trade was not open to the points where it was taken from and therefore contracts made by speculators was in violation of orders. To say the least they should not have advantage of the proffits. If therefore anything is returned to them I would recommend that it be the 25 cts. per pound and there in addition to the evidence accompanying this they should prove the marks upon the cotton and Capt. Eddy determine whether such cotton was sold by him.

There is but little doubt in my mind but that there was much cotton seized by speculators themselves, and much obtained under false pretenses, all of which goes to the discredit of the Government in the minds of the Southern people.

I am, with much respect,

your obt. svt.

U. S. GRANT

Maj. Gen. Com

P. S. I send copies of the original evidence adduced and return the latter to the parties claiming.

U. S. G.

ALS, DNA, RG 56, Cotton and Captured and Abandoned Property Records, Case 21045.

On Feb. 23, 1863, Act. Rear Admiral David D. Porter wrote to USG. "I enclose you a copy of Treasury Regulations which were sent me from the Navy Department, with orders to have them enforced. It appears that these boards of trade have been exceeding their authority throughout this war, and so the Government is now waking up to the importance of protecting itself. I have sent a copy of these instructions to all Naval Commanders." LS, *ibid.*, RG 393, Dept. of the Tenn., Letters Received. The regulations enclosed by Porter formed the basis for an agreement dated Feb. 24 signed by both Porter and USG. "For the purpose of more effectually preventing all commercial intercourse between insurrectionary, and loyal states and of securing consistent, uniform, and efficient action in conducting trade with any places or sections in insurrectionary states opened to trade, pursuant to law, the following rules shall be observed throughout the States of Arkansas, Louisiana, Mississippi and Alabama. 1st No place or section in the said States shall be regarded as possessed and controlled by the forces of the United States until after the General commanding the Department in which such place or section is situated, and the Naval Officer Commanding the Mississippi Squadron concurring, shall so declare it in writing to the Secretary of the Treasury. 2nd No goods, wares, or merchandise (except Sutler's supplies, and other supplies for the exclusive use of the Army and Navy) shall be permitted by any Military, Naval or Civil officer, to go to any place or section in the states above named, until after such place or section shall be in manner aforesaid declared as possessed and controlled by the forces of the United States. 3rd No cotton or other production of the States aforesaid shall be permitted by any Military, Naval, or Civil Officer to go from any place or section in the States above named, until after such place or section shall be declared in manner aforesaid as possessed and controlled by the forces of the United States. 4th After declaration as aforesaid, all commercial intercourse with any place or section so declared as possessed and controlled by the forces of the United States, shall be conducted exclusively under the regulations of the Secretary of the Treasury, and no Military or Naval Officer shall permit or prohibit any trade with or transportation to or from any such place or section except when requested to aid in preventing 'violations of the conditions of any clearance or permit granted under said regulations, and in cases of unlawful traffic' or 'unless absolutely necessary to the successful exucution of Military or Naval plans or movements' in such place or section. 5th No place or section in the States aforesaid south of Helena, shall be regarded as possessed and controlled by the forces of the United States, until after declaration made as aforesaid. Places and Sections in said states north of Helena and within the Military lines of the United States Army shall be so regarded, and trade there with shall be conducted under regulations of the Secretary of the Treasury. 6th All Military and Naval Orders heretofore issued, and conflicting herewith, shall be revoked. I hereby approve the within rules and recommend their adoption so far as regards the Department of the Tennessee   Dated near Vicksburg February 24 1863" Copies, *ibid.*, RG 45, Area 5; Miss. Dept. of Archives and History, Jackson, Miss. *O.R.* (Navy), I, xxiv, 435–36.

1. See letter to Edwin M. Stanton, Dec. 6, 1862.

To Act. Rear Admiral David D. Porter

Feb.y 24th 1863.

ADMIRAL,

I will have a lookout at all times on the opposite side of the point. I have no rockets however to signal with but if you can furnish them I will have them sent to the Pickets with instructions to send one up as a signal that the Ram is passing up and two close together should she start up and turn back again. One Rocket will indicate a movement up stream and two down.

I think however she will not be here to-night though I will have a close watch kept. The enemy fired a number of shots at the dummy whilst she was in the eddy opposite the canal and afterwards it was loosened in the current and floated down and the Ram left Warrenton, probably on being signaled that a gunboat was after her. At Warrenton the dummy was hit and sunk. So it has been reported to me.

The point from which rockets will be sent up will be about Johnsons plantation say one mile below the mouth of the canal.

Very respectfully
your obt. svt.
U. S. GRANT
Maj. Gen.

P. S. Should you wish any change in this signal inform me and your suggestions will be conformed to.

U. S. G.

ALS, MdAN.

After the capture of *Queen of the West* by C.S.A. forces (see letter to Maj. Gen. William T. Sherman, Feb. 21, 1863), U.S. authorities feared the capture of the *Indianola*, the other U.S. ram below the batteries. Although taken on Feb. 24, 1863, the *Indianola* was blown up by her captors two nights later on the approach of a dummy gunboat constructed on a flat boat. *O.R.* (Navy), I, xxiv, 379–81, 410. See letter to Col. Lewis Parsons, March 4, 1863.

On Feb. 24, USG wrote two additional letters to Act. Rear Admiral David D. Porter. "I have men on the levee below the point observing every movement of the enemy, with orders to report to me immediately any thing of importance that may take place. I will communicate without delay anything reported. As no word has come of the cause of the last firing heard I conclude the enemy have been practicing on the Gunboat that run the blockade this morning, or els have discovered the battery we are building and are trying to stop the work." ALS, MdAN. "Report from opposite side of the point says the Queen has gone down the river, also that heavy guns have been heard far down the river. . . . The firing this afternoon was at the dummy. So far as heard no damage was done." ALS, MoSHi. On Feb. 25, Porter wrote to USG. "I have made all necessary arrangements to meet the Ram if she should attempt to come up, with the exception of establishing signals to know when she leaves the anchorage below. I would suggest that good look outs be placed at the best points, and signalize with rockets if she moves. We are having moon light nights now and she may not like to try it, and would be seen in time. I will direct my vessels to be ready to answer with rockets. If you will tell me where the rockets are fired from, I will have them watched; by tomorrow night I hope to have three Rams down, unless the run of bad luck keeps on. I will have a tug on the lookout below, tonight. They may attempt to deceive us by lights; having perhaps gotten hold of our signals, for the people left that Ram Queen of the West, in a most remarkable hurry: they were better at running blockades than fighting when under difficulty." LS, DNA, RG 393, Dept. of the Tenn., Letters Received.

Also on Feb. 25, USG wrote to Maj. Gen. William T. Sherman. "I have sent to Admiral Porter for some rockets and notified him that one rocket will be the signal indicating a movement up stream by the rebel ram, and two close together down stream. Also that the rockets will be set off some distance below the mouth of the canal. When these rockets arrive I will send them to your Hd Qrs. to be forwarded to the pickets with instructions how they are to be used." ALS, DLC-Stern Collection. On the same day, Sherman wrote to USG. "Yrs of today, giving the Rocket signals is this moment received. I sent you word by Capt Dayton that the Ram *had gone down stream*, and was out of sight. I was over this afternoon and the Ram *is gone*. She was anchored but got up anchor as the 'Sham boat' was drifted out into the Current and floated down, evidently mistaking the 'Sham' for a real Boat—Of course the signals shall be attended to, but the Ram not being there we ought to have another signal for her approach from below—. If not too late I suggest—1 Rocket. A Rebel boat is seen—. 1 Gun, & 3 rockets in succession—'she is passing above Warrenton.' Rapid firing   she is passing our Battery. 2 Rockets   a Rebel boat is seen but turns down stream." ALS, DNA, RG 393, Dept. of the Tenn., Letters Received.

To Maj. Gen. Stephen A. Hurlbut

Before Vicksburgh
Feby 24th 1863

Maj Gen S A Hurlbut
Comm'dg 16th Army Corps,

I sustain your cause in not permitting Bayfield to be tried before a disloyal court and jury and will also sustain you in forcing outside of our lines every disloyal person of whatever age or sex. I will also approve of closing all business with persons living outside of the city. In other words if you deem it proper to prohibit intercourse between the city and country do so. The District is in your command and you can make use of the means in your hands to enforce order. I would suggest Col Howe[1] 3 U S Cavalry as a good selection to place in command of the town, to bring it to order and enforce any new and stringent orders you may find it necessary to publish. Have Bayfield tried as you pro-

pose and prohibit all action of the civil authorities unless they
the officers give satisfactory evidence of their loyalty

U S GRANT
Maj Gen

Copies, DLC-USG, V, 18, 30; DNA, RG 393, Dept. of the Tenn., Letters Sent.
O.R., I, xxiv, part 3, 65–66. On Feb. 21, 1863, Maj. Gen. Stephen A. Hurlbut
had written to Lt. Col. John A. Rawlins. "Some time since one George Rayfield
killed a man of the name of Foley in Memphis. He was arrested by the Military
police and is held under heavy bonds. Lately the 'Criminal Court' of this place
presided over by Judge Swayne—found a 'True Bill' for Murder against him—
& ordered his arrest. No person connected with this Court that I can learn either
Judge, Attorney or Jury is loyal. I have declined to allow him to be arrested &
tried & propose to try him before a Military Commission.—I have requested
Judge Swayne to furnish me with evidence of his loyalty—which he has not done.
I do not think it wise to permit this Court to continue its Session unless all parties
in it take the oath of allegiance to the United States. I refer the question to the
Major Genl. before making any order and await reply. I strongly recommend as
sound policy and lawful war that every man woman & child in Memphis not loyal
be removed outside our lines & thrown upon those with whom they sympathize"
ALS, DNA, RG 109, Union Provost Marshals' File of Papers Relating to Individual Civilians.

1. Marshall Saxe Howe of Me. attended USMA 1823–27 without graduat-
ing; received appointment as 1st lt., 2nd Dragoons on June 11, 1836; advanced
to col., 3rd Cav., as of Sept. 28, 1861.

To Brig. Gen. Stephen G. Burbridge

Lake Providence
Feby. 24th 1863

BRIG GEN S G BURBRIDGE
COMM'DG EXPEDITION AGAINST GREENVILLE TENN [*Miss.*]

Information is just received that you have had a fight with
the enemy back of Greenville eight miles captured a Battery and
subsequently lost five of them   at last accounts you were twelve
miles off &c. This all looks favorable and I presume you require
no assistance but the men and boats are here and I send two
Regiments to your relief should they be required. I can give no

special directions from here what you should do, but trust you
will inflict the heaviest blow upon the enemy you can and follow
him as long as prudence will justify   If there is any large force
assembling on the Mississippi shore, (which they can nearly
approach by water from Vicksburgh) let me know it and I will
send you everything required in the shortest possible time   I
shall return to Vicksburgh (vicinity) this evening. Should therefore require anything address Gen McPherson here

U S GRANT
Maj Gen

Copies, DLC-USG, V, 18, 30; DNA, RG 393, Dept. of the Tenn., Letters Sent.
Stephen G. Burbridge, born in Ky., educated at Georgetown College and Ky.
Military Institute, was a farmer in Logan County, Ky., when the Civil War began.
Commissioned col., 26th Ky., as of Aug. 27, 1861, he was confirmed as brig. gen.
on June 9, 1862. For his assignment to USG, see *Calendar*, Aug. 8, 1862. On
Feb. 28, 1863, Maj. Gen. John A. McClernand wrote a letter addressed to Lt.
Col. John A. Rawlins at the head and to USG at the foot. "I have the honor to
inclose, herewith, the report of Brigadier Genl. S. G. Burbridge, Comd'g 1st
Brigde of the 10th Div, of the 13th Army Corps. It contains an account of the
operations of his brigade from the 4th, to the 26th, inst, upon the Mississippi.
During that time he met and drove, inland, a detachment of Cavalry and Artillery,
near Cypress Bend, in Arkansas—taking one 12 pdr, Howitzer, capturing ~~from~~ a
number of ~~200~~ mules, ~~100~~ horses, and ~~25~~ cattle; and killing and wounding about
30 of the enemy; our loss was one killed and two taken prisoner. The report of
Genl. Burbridge will furnish a more particular account of their operations, to
which reference is made for fuller information respecting the same." Copies (2),
McClernand Papers, IHi; DNA, RG 393, 13th Army Corps, Letters Sent. For the
report of Burbridge of his expedition to Greenville, Miss., Feb. 14–26, see *O.R.*,
I, xxiv, part 1, 349–52. On March 1, USG sent this report to Washington. DNA,
RG 94, Register of Letters Received.

To Maj. Gen. Henry W. Halleck

———

Before Vicksburg 12 30 A M
Feb 25-[*1863*]

MAJ GEN H W HALLECK
GENL IN CHIEF

The "Queen of the West" is now at Warrenton with the
rebel flag flying   Distant firing was heard lasting from four P M

yesterday until one this morning   It is supposed to have been between the Queen and "Indianola"   Apprehension is felt for the safety of the "Indianola"

U S GRANT

Telegram received, DNA, RG 107, Telegrams Collected (Bound); copies, *ibid.*, Telegrams Received in Cipher; *ibid.*, RG 393, Dept. of the Tenn., Hd. Qrs. Correspondence; DLC-USG, V, 5, 8, 24, 94. *O.R.*, I, xxiv, part 1, 18; *O.R.* (Navy), I, xxiv, 396–97. On Feb. 27, 1863, 2:30 P.M., USG telegraphed to Maj. Gen. Henry W. Halleck. "News just received that the Queen of the West and Webb attacked the Indianola about thirty five miles below Vicksburg the night of the twenty fourth and after a engagement of about forty minutes captured her ~~and~~ with most of her crew. It is said the Indianola afterward sunk"   Telegram received, DNA, RG 107, Telegrams Collected (Bound); *ibid.*, Telegrams Collected (Unbound); copies, *ibid.*, Telegrams Received in Cipher; *ibid.*, RG 393, Dept. of the Tenn., Hd. Qrs. Correspondence; DLC-USG, V, 5, 8, 24, 94. *O.R.*, I, xxiv, part 1, 18–19; *O.R.* (Navy), I, xxiv, 397.

On March 2, Maj. Gen. William T. Sherman endorsed a report concerning the loss of the *Indianola*. "Col Rawlins—read this to the General tonight. I think it is full and reliable. I cannot otherwise reconcile all the facts we know viz., the appearance of the *Queen* and the explosion." Kenneth W. Rendell, Inc., Catalogue 96 [*1974*], No. 118. USG also endorsed this report. "Respectfully forwarded to Admiral Porter." *Ibid.*

On March 3, Halleck telegraphed to USG. "Send any reliable information you may recieve in regard to the steamer 'Indianola.' Was she sunk or not?" ALS (telegram sent), DNA, RG 107, Telegrams Collected (Bound); telegram received, *ibid.*, RG 393, Dept. of the Tenn., Telegrams Received. On March 13, USG telegraphed to Halleck. "The 'Indianola' was sunk and is a total loss." Telegram received, *ibid.*, RG 107, Telegrams Collected (Bound).

To Maj. Gen. Stephen A. Hurlbut

Before Vicksburgh
Feby 25 1863

MAJ GEN S A HURLBUT
COMM'DG 16TH ARMY CORPS

I understand C M Willard late Major 1st Illinois Artillery is in Memphis. If this is the case notify him to leave the Department by the first boat going north and that if he does not avail himself of the first boat he will be arrested and confined in the Memphis

Military Prison. I have no doubt that many other Northern men
should receive similar notification. You however have a better
opportunity of judging of the matter than I have

U S GRANT
Maj Gen

Copies, DLC-USG, V, 18, 30; DNA, RG 393, Dept. of the Tenn., Letters Sent.
Charles M. Willard, born in 1825 in Livingston County, N. Y., moved to Ill. to
practice law in 1853, settling in Chicago in 1858. Mustered in as 1st lt., Chicago
Light Art., on July 16, 1861, he was promoted to capt. on Sept. 27 and to maj.,
1st Ill. Light Art. on March 1, 1862. On Jan. 16, 1863, he resigned because of
poor health. Charles B. Kimbell, *History of Battery "A" First Illinois Light
Artillery Volunteers* (Chicago, 1899), p. 245.

To *Act. Rear Admiral David D. Porter*

Feb.y 26th 1863.

ADMIRAL,

I have changed the signal to the following. One rocket will
denote the presence, in sight, of a rebel boat; two guns the presence of more than one. The same signals with the addition of a
single gun that they are passing up stream above Warrenton and
rapid firing that they are passing the batteries. Three rockets
will indicate tha[t] rebel boats have turned back and followed by
a single gun afterwards that. they have come to anchor below.
Entire silence after three rockets will indicate that they have
passed out of sight.

Very respectfully
U. S. GRANT
Maj. Gen.

ALS, MdAN. *O.R.* (Navy), I, xxiv, 438. A copy of this letter was endorsed by
Act. Rear Admiral David D. Porter on March 3, 1863. "A Tug will be on Picket
some mile and a half below the Canal on the left bank of the River.—Her signal
on the discovery of a vessel coming up the River is three Whistles and then three
more. A Red light to be displayed by all our vessels—and should the enemy dis-
play a red light also to deceive us, our countersign is 'Red light'—that is, a vessel
on being hailed, if a friend will answer 'Red light' " ES, Mrs. Walter Love,

Flint, Mich. *O.R.* (Navy), I, xxiv, 438. On Feb. 26, Porter wrote to USG. "Yours of this morning just received. I will notify the officers of the change, in reference to the signals. I have no idea that they will attempt to come up the river." LS, DNA, RG 393, Dept. of the Tenn., Letters Received.

Also on Feb. 26, 1st Lt. Charles P. Dennis, 47th Ohio, wrote to 1st Lt. P. B. Stanberry, adjt. for Brig. Gen. Hugh Ewing. "A Steamer has made its appearance and is running along the Meiss Shore near Warrenton, supposed to be the Ram. Must be a rebel boat or she would be fired at more. One gun was fired before she came in sight." Copy, MH. Maj. Gen. William T. Sherman endorsed this letter. "respectfully sent to General Grant" AES, *ibid.* USG also endorsed this letter. "Forwarded for the information of Admiral Porter." AES, *ibid.*

To Maj. Gen. Stephen A. Hurlbut

Before Vicksburg Feby 27th 1863.

MAJ GENL S. A HURLBUT
COMMD.G 16TH ARMY CORPS

Your Dispatch sent by special Messenger is just received   It may be that some of the force is leaving Vicksburg (Miss) but I have no evidence of the fact   It is impossible to get information from there. Even deserters who come can tell nothing except of their own regiments or Brigade at furthest   It will be well to hold the Division previously orderd in readiness to be moved as in that case if the report should prove true that the enemy are evacuating Vicksburg they could be readily sent by Steamer to Nashville. I also have a force of about two Divisions to come from St Louis which Genl Halleck can change the designation if it [*of if*] he becomes satisfied that they are more needed with Rosecrans than with me.

If you have not already done so telegraph Genl Halleck the substance of your dispatch to me. It would be well to telegraph Genl Halleck direct all information you receive effecting the safety of other commands

U S GRANT
Maj Genl

P. S. It is my desire that the Division to be held in readiness to be brought here should be brought to Memphis without any delay   I presume you so understood me but I mention it know because I may not have been distinct on this point before

U. S. G.

Copies, DLC-USG, V, 18, 30; DNA, RG 393, Dept. of the Tenn., Letters Sent. *O.R.*, I, xxiv, part 3, 71. On Feb. 25, 1863, Maj. Gen. Charles S. Hamilton, Corinth, telegraphed to Maj. Gen. Stephen A. Hurlbut. "The Cavalry of Gen. Dodge, under command of Col. Cornyne attacked Tuscumbia, and rear of Van Dorns' column, on Sunday 22d inst. at 4 a. m.   captured one piece artillery, 100 prisoners, 200 horses, a large amount of stores including a train of cars and 100 bales C.S.A. cotton, considerable money & a large number of mules. Col. Cornyn and his command have swam creeks and rivers, have operated during all these terrible storms and are now following enemy into the mountains   Officers & men behaved splendidly and all are entitled to warmest praise for perseverance and daring gallantry. Scouts have arrived from the interior of Mississippi during the last 24 hours and all report enemy rapidly evacuating Vicksburg. He is moving everything to the Eastward, and the talk is that all are going to reinforce the army opposed to Rosecrans now commanded by Jo. Johnson, Bragg having been removed. Prices' forces are on East side of Black river." Copy (incomplete), DNA, RG 94, War Records Office, Dept. of the Tenn. *O.R.*, I, xxiii, part 1, 63–64. At the foot, Hurlbut added an undated note to Lt. Col. John A. Rawlins. "I inclose you the above   Genl. Grant must judge of the necessities of the case by combining it with his information. I have no doubt that a considerable movement East is going on—I question whether it means abandonment of Vicksburgh except by their main force. It would be high strategy to draw our Army so far down and then sweep over their inland lines to attack Rosecrans—& the movement of Van Dorn intimates some thing of the kind. The Confederate authorities work for successful blows in war and are no respecters of persons or places—They would undoubtedly abandon Vicksburgh if thereby they should conquer & crush Rosecrans. I deem this of consequence enough to send by Special Messenger"   ALS, DNA, RG 94, War Records Office, Dept. of the Tenn. *O.R.*, I, xxiii, part 2, 87.

On Feb. 23, Brig. Gen. Grenville M. Dodge, Corinth, wrote to USG. "There are Some matters South of this, that may be of interest to you, and perhaps I may be excused for communicating them direct. They have been sent, part of them to my immediate Commanders   The Scouts posted at Mobile—Meridian and Jackson have sent in long reports, and the substance of those that can be relied upon are about as follows. 1st No Troops have come to Pemberton's Army since Smiths 10.000 joined him about Christmas. 2nd All Troops from Mobile, up the Road, and from Grenada, have gone to Vicksburg and Port Hudson, leaving a few thousand at Mobile—some six hundred at Meridian, and two Regiments at Jackson, and about three Regiments of militia at Grenada—A portion that left Grenada are posted on Black River—Everything in the shape of Cavalry, even to the Partisan Rangers, as low down as Port Hudson, joined Van Dorn in his move to Tennessee, leaving, perhaps, a Regiment or two, North of Grenada—a few at Okalona, and a few Companies just South of me. Everything in the shape of Government property, has been taken away from the Country bordering the Yazoo and adjacent Streams, and all prominent points, such as Jackson, Grenada, Columbus &c. At Jackson the Founderies are running, and a Cotton Mill or two—and perhaps a Government Shoe and Clothing Shop, but every preparation is being made to take them away—West Missisppi is being entirely stripped of Stock, provisions Forage &c and every thing indicates that they are gettin ready for a quick move. In the last ten days, some three thousand negroes have been pressed and put to work at Columbus Miss., and one or two points near Meridian while the great Stock of cars and Engines. at Meridian are being taken East and South—It appears to be the opinion of the Scouts that the enemy are making preparations to take up the Line of the Tombigbee for the next position, and say that it is openly talked there, that Gun boats will go up Big Black, when their Army will have to take position to save Selma, and Mobile.—The trains go loaded from Vicksburg daily with sick and discharged soldiers. They say that they average twelve cars a day. Last week two heavy Steamboat Engines, and the Prow to a Ram, went up the Road to Jackson, said, to be placed in some boat in the Yazoo. Deserters and Conscripts are flocking into my lines daily: and so far as the above statements are concerned they corroberate them. The raking of the entire State of Missisppi for stock & provisions, is as vigorously carried on as it was in Tennessee By Bragg —Van Dorn took about 8.000 mounted men and two Batteries away with him, he is now at Columbia Tenn. with Wheeler and Forrest, and Bragg has taken every thing that is moveable that that his Army does not really need South of the Tennessee. He has put the R. R. in order from Decatur to Tuscumbia. Bought up all the Corn in the valley, and got ready to move it by cars to Decatur and by boat to Bridgeport just as I struck Tuscumbia. My forces are on their way to Decatur now.   which will stop that game. I still have men in Meridian, Columbus Mobile & Jackson, while one has gone on to Vicksburg. and will try to get to you. Every one sends up the same report, & you have got the substance of them in this— These little items may all be known to you but as they came so direct to me I believe it is my duty to send them." LS, DNA, RG 94, War Records Office, Dept. of the Mo. *O.R.*, I, xxiv, part 3, 64–65.

On Feb. 25, Hurlbut wrote to Rawlins. "Notwithstanding my urgent application to Fleet Captain Pennock to push GunBoats rapidly up the Tennessee to intercept Van Dorn in crossing—the Boats for some cause did not arrive until after his column had crossed. On the 20th sixty men of 3d Michigan Cavalry crossed at Clifton captured Col Newsome & 61 officers & men—40 horses with Equipments & arms—losing none on our side   The town with considerable commissary stores & the ferries were destroyed—Dodge's Cavalry is out in North Alabama where he is materially assisted by the residents of that mountain district & is constantly picking up prisoners. Van Dorn is reported at Columbia. I keep Rosecrans informed of all movements. We are again in the midst of a heavy storm of rain and all movements on both sides are suspended—Neither cavalry nor infantry can make any progress in any direction—Genl. McClernand sent up here a few days since 200 women & children who were dropped upon the levee   It is not in my judgment humane nor advisable to send these contrabands here but if done I request that some communication may come with them so that the authorities here may be notified that they are here by proper authority. Night before last the Steamer Belle Memphis bound up—landed in defiance of orders at Island 37 to take on cotton as they supposed being hailed for that purpose—The Boat was seized by *five* men who compelled the Pilot to make a Landing at Cottonwood Point in Arkansas   They then went on shore guarding three prisoners one the pilot. The Engineer backed his boat out & went up the River with a Lieut of the force on board wounded by one of his own men. This Bands is commanded by Barton—As soon as the weather will permit I shall send an expedition to destroy his House near Bradley's Bend & to sweep all the male inhabitants they can find down to Memphis for the purpose of identification as members of the Band. If they are identified I shall probably not trouble your Head Quarters with any report. As soon as our roads are passable for teams the several changes necessary to reduce the number of Guards &c on the Road will be made   I regret to say that the Rail Road from Columbus down is not yet repaired—The delay seems inexcusable. It is promised to be finished by this week. I am informed by the officer commanding the 'Cricket' that he expects to leave soon. I consider it of vital importance that there should be one Gunboat on duty at Memphis all the time & request that Major Genl Grant may press this matter on the attention of the Admiral. Hospital accommodation is being prepared but our force of Carpenters is so light that the work moves slowly. Richardsons Guerillas near Covington & Blythe's below are still in motion but do not do us any harm—I have heard indirectly that Genl. Grant ordered Hamilton to investigate the misconduct of the 7th Kansas at Summerville. Genl H. says he has received no such order.—If such has been issued I request duplicates"   ALS, DNA, RG 94, War Records Office, Dept. of the Tenn. *O.R.*, I, xxiv, part 3, 67–68. On March 9, Act. Rear Admiral David D. Porter wrote to USG. "In answer to General Hurlburt's request for a gun boat at Memphis, I beg leave to inform you that the Cricket, commanded by a very active officer, is at that place and will remain there." LS, DNA, RG 45, Correspondence of David D. Porter, Mississippi Squadron, General Letters (Press). *O.R.*, I, xxiv, part 3, 95; *O.R.* (Navy), I, xxiv, 51.

To Maj. Gen. Stephen A. Hurlbut

Before Vicksburg Febry 27th 1863.

MAJ GENL S. A HURLBUT
COMMD.G 16TH ARMY. CORPS.

I was a good deal disappointed that Genl Hamilton should have countermanded the order of the expedition which you had fitted out for the purpose of cutting the road east from Vicksburg particularly on such flimsey grounds. We do not expect the Miss Central and Mobile and Ohio road to be left entirely unprotected and the number of troops shown to be there by Genl Dodge. dispatch is as few as could be expected at any time.

The way you had the expedition fitted out I think it must have succeeded. I wish you would try it again unless your information is such that you would deem it an act of folly to send them

U. S. GRANT.
Maj Genl

Copies, DLC-USG, V, 18, 30; DNA, RG 393, Dept. of the Tenn., Letters Sent. On Feb. 21, 1863, Maj. Gen. Stephen A. Hurlbut wrote to Lt. Col. John A. Rawlins. "Having just received the Dispatch (Copy Enclosed) I forward it for information of Maj Gen Grant   I have considered it prudent under this information to withhold the Cavalry dash on Jackson. I very respectfully suggest to the Major Genl that it will be necessary in order to maintain our troops in provisions & forage that at least Eight good boats be kept running between this point & St Louis. The army horses are perishing for want of long forage. I also call attention to the copy of a letter from Parsons at St Louis herewith which indicates the necessity at that point of a considerable amount of River Transportation which I take it are forces expected by Genl Grant from Missouri. We are again afloat with a heavy rain. Nothing has been heard here of the Gunboats ordered up the Tennessee. We are examining the lists of Regimental Surgeons & will send down such as can safely be spared. Dr Wirtz & Dr Irwin his successor in charge of Hospitals affirm that none can be spared from Genl Hospital here. The progress of rebuilding R. Road from Columbus is very slow but Col. Webster assures me it will be completed tomorrow"   ALS, *ibid.*, RG 94, War Records Office, Dept. of the Tenn. *O.R.*, I, xxiv, part 3, 62–63. Enclosed was a copy of a telegram of Feb. 21 from Maj. Gen. Charles S. Hamilton, Corinth, to Hurlbut. "A scout came in from Jackson last night, reports two regiments of Infantry at Jackson and a large portion of the rebel army encamped on East side of Black river, near the bridge. A force of eight hundred men, only, at Meridian, but all the surplus rolling stock of rail road centred there. One brigade of rebel cavalry north of Grenada and Bartons' regiment 800 at Okalona. Dodge says this is entirely reliable. I have therefore suspended movement of Hatch for the present." Copy, DNA, RG 94, War Records Office, Dept. of the Tenn. *O.R.*, I, xxiv, part 3, 63. Hurlbut also enclosed a copy of a letter of Feb. 16 from Capt. Charles Parsons, St. Louis, to Capt. John V. Lewis, Memphis, urgently requesting the return of three steamboats to St. Louis. Copy, DNA, RG 94, War Records Office, Dept. of the Tenn.

On March 1, Hurlbut wrote to Rawlins. "I have sure information that cars do not run beyond: the Yockna. The Lafayette passed Columbus yesterday at 12. M & is now due—She will be hurried forward with all dispatch   Quimby is now embarking on his Boats. for Lake Providence. I beg leave to state that officers from the army below are in the constant habit of publishing all that they know or imagine as to the condition of the Expedition its probable movements and the health of the men. If officers who stop at Memphis were required to report they might be checked. I also request that official dispatches when sent by a messenger may be ordered to be delivered at my Head Quarters by such messenger and not thrown into the Post office"   ALS, *ibid.*, RG 393, Dept. of the Tenn., Letters Received.

To Maj. Gen. James B. McPherson

Before Vicksburg Feby 27th 1863
MAJ GENL J. B. McPHERSON
COMMD'G 17TH ARMY CORPS.

There are two more dredge boats comeing down the river   I have instructions to Genl Prentiss to stop one of them and instruct them to report to Col Wilson to work in Yazoo pass, the other to report to you at Lake Providence[1]   The instructions however may reach Prentiss after the boats have passed   If so stop them and turn one back to Delta or Helena to report as indicated above, and keep the other

The ram captured from us by the rebels and the "Webb" came out of Red River and attacked the Indinola and succeeding in capturing her[2]   A rebel Flag of Truce is just up from Baton Rouge with exchanged prisoners abroad and report the Indianola sunk

U. S. GRANT
Maj Genl.

Copies, DLC-USG, V, 18, 30; DNA, RG 393, Dept. of the Tenn., Letters Sent.

1. On Feb. 27, 1863, Col. George P. Ihrie wrote to Brig. Gen. Benjamin M. Prentiss, Helena. "I am directed by the Major Gen Commanding this Department to inform you that you will direct one Dredge boat to proceed to Yazoo Pass and report to Lieut Col. Wilson in charge of Yazoo Expedition and one other to proceed to Lake Providence and report to Maj Genl McPherson   When the services of these two dredge boats are no longer required, they will be instructed to report at these Head Quarters, to Capt. F. E. Prime chief U S Engineer of this Department. There are three dredges en route" Copies, *ibid.* On Feb. 13, Maj. Gen. Henry W. Halleck telegraphed to USG. "Cannot dredge-boats be used with advantage on the cannal? There are four lying idle at Louisville bel belonging to Borton Robinson & co, canal contractors." ALS (telegram sent), *ibid.*, RG 107, Telegrams Collected (Bound); telegram received, *ibid.*, RG 393, Dept. of the Tenn., Telegrams Received. *O.R.*, I, xxiv, part 1, 17. On Feb. 17, USG telegraphed to Halleck. "We have one Dredging Machine here and another ordered More than two could not be used advantageously" Telegram received, DNA, RG 107, Telegrams Collected (Bound); *ibid.*, Telegrams Collected (Unbound); copies, *ibid.*, Telegrams Received in Cipher; *ibid.*, RG 393, Dept. of the Tenn., Hd. Qrs. Correspondence; DLC-USG, V, 5, 8, 24, 94. On Feb. 16, George G. Pride telegraphed to USG. "Have succeeded in getting two efficient Dredge Boats that will dig twenty feet—One of the above is purchased and is on the way down,

the second will be ready in three days, and is hired by the day—I can get a third and advise it by all means—Shall start down to Memphis to-morrow myself—answer there if you will have the three—" ALS (telegram sent), DNA, RG 107, Telegrams Collected (Unbound); telegram received, *ibid.* See letter to Maj. Gen. Henry W. Halleck, March 7, 1863.

2. See telegram to Maj. Gen. Henry W. Halleck, Feb. 25, 1863.

To Maj. Gen. William T. Sherman

Before Vicksburg Feby 27th, 1863.

MAJ GENL W T SHERMAN
COMMD.G 15TH ARMY CORPS,

Admiral Porter has just sent a request that instructions be sent in the morning to the Officer who belonged to the "Queen" now on the "Era" to go down near enough Warrenton to ascertain what there is there   will you be kind enough to send this message over   The Admiral also sends word that a tug is placed down the river on Pickett duty. Three whistles an interval, and three whistles will indicate a boat comeing up. Six whistles that it is an enemy and nine whistles, interval, and Nine whistles that she shows our light

U. S. GRANT
Maj Genl

Copies, DLC-USG, V, 18, 30; DNA, RG 393, Dept. of the Tenn., Letters Sent. Dated Feb. 26, 1863, in Stan. V. Henkels Sale No. 1201, Nov. 2, 1917, p. 4.

To Col. William S. Hillyer

Feb.y 27th 1863.

DEAR HILLYER,

Your letter giving an account of things generally was duly received and I would have answered but expected you down. I wish you would come down by first boat.

Now that I am out of the Dist. of West Ten. I want to relieve myself as far as possible from the responsibility of administration of affairs there. To that end I have directed Hurlbut to relieve all officers who are on special duty in the city whilst their regiment are elswhere, back to their regiments and appoint their successors himself. I have also modified previous orders so that Army Corps commanders will appoint their own Provost Marshals and Agts for executing their orders.[1] There has been much complaint at the liberality with which Col. Anthony issues permits for goods to go to the country. I have also published an order requiring all resigned officers and discharged soldiers to quit the Department.[2] Some certificates of disability seem to indicate a disease that might be called *Cotton on the brain*. This order is intended to remove as far as practicable all contageous tendencies of the disease. I purposly leave the order a little ambiguous as to whether it applies to officers who have heretofore resigned, wishing in reality to get all the trading ones out and at the same time not desiring to make an order ex post facto in its application.

Commanders and Provost Marshals can so interpret it as to make it apply to those who out to be expelled.

The everlasting rains set us back here wonderfully in our work. It is impossible for us to get done more than one days work in three.

Has Mrs. Grant left yet?

My regards to Mrs. Hillyer and children.

Yours Truly

U. S. GRANT

ALS, CtY.

1. By General Orders No. 16, Dept. of the Tenn., Feb. 16, 1863. Copies, DLC-USG, V, 13, 14, 95, (printed) 101; (2) DNA, RG 393, Dept. of the Tenn., General and Special Orders.

2. See letter to Maj. Gen. Stephen A. Hurlbut, March 2, 1863.

To Brig. Gen. Benjamin M. Prentiss

Before Vicksburg Feby 28 1863

Brig Genl B. M. Prentiss
Commd.g Dist. of Eastern Ark

I send you the smallest stern wheel steamer we have here. I want you to keep up communication with the Yazoo Expedition, and report progress to me from time to time, supply them with rations and everything required by them so far as it is in your power.

Inform Genl Ross that by the last information I have had from that country the rebel, force is small all the way north from Haines Bluff at Grenada there is not over two thousands men and I doubt if that many

The Advance boats should be cautious in approaching Grenada and also Yazoo City looking out for torpedoes. In approaching a town they should notify the inhabitants to surrender and give them but a very short time, say thirty minutes at the outside to make up their minds and not permit them to move their women and children Being near where all vessels from Genl Ross expedition strike the river, act on your own Judgement in all matters requiring prompt action

U. S. Grant
Maj Genl.

Copies, DLC-USG, V, 18, 30; DNA, RG 393, Dept. of the Tenn., Letters Sent. On Feb. 26, 1863, Brig. Gen. Benjamin M. Prentiss, Helena, wrote to USG. "Genl Ross.s Division is by this time on ColdWater I went nearly through the Pass Yesterday with the Gunboats Chillicothe & Dekalb. they had no trouble up to time I left. more than one half of the Fleet got through yesterday unless some accident all are certainly through at this hour. 12 Oclock (M) I need one of those Tugs. with it I can communicate for a time with Genl Ross. Water rising rapidly we shall have to move evrything to the Bluff I have stopped all supplies going to the Country from this Point The occupation of Helena has been a God send to the Rebels. in the way of getting supplies heretofore. It is raining incessantly I fear you will suffer from high water this time. Genl Washburne Genl Ross & Myself are of the opinion that Yazoo Pass is the route to Vicksburg or in other words we will be compelled to take that route Genl Hurlbut. request me to send this Steamer down with his Despatches please have her return immediately we need her much" ALS, *ibid.*, Letters Received.

To Lt. Gen. John C. Pemberton

—————

Head Quarters, Dept. of the Ten.
Before Vicksburg, March 2d 1863.

LT. GEN. J. C. PEMBERTON,
COMD.G DEPT. OF MISS. & E. LA.
GEN.

Maj. Gen. C. L. Stevenson's letter of the 24th Ult.[1] written at your dictation, was received last evening. This letter enclosed what purports to be a copy of an order issued by Admiral D. D. Porter to his Squadron[2] and make inquiry if it is authentic.

I will state that Admiral Porters command over the Miss. Squadron is as complete as mine over the Army in this Department, and that he alone is responsible for any orders he may issue. One thing however I can guarantee. Admiral Porter has never departed from the rules of civilized Warfare and never will unless driven to do so in retalliation for offences committed by persons who by their acts cease to be entitled to the treatment due soldiers captured in legitimate Warfare.

There has been much done by citizens of the Southern states that is not in accordance with any known rules of civilized warfare and for which they individually are responsible and can call for protection in their acts upon no people or Government. These are persons who are always in the guise of citizens and on the approach of an armed force remain at their homes professing to be in no way connected with the army, but entitled to all the indulgences allowed non-combattants in a country visited by an opposing army. These same persons, many of them, are ever ready to fire upon unarmed vessels, or to capture, and sometimes murder, small parties of Federal soldiers who may be passing. I do not here instance an isolated case but a rule that seems to have been adopted particularly in Mississippi and Arkansas.

In the absence of any standard authority on this subject I believe all persons engaged in War must have about them some insignia by which they may be known, at all times, as an enemy to entitle them to the treatment of prisoners of War. Then their hostilities must be carried on in accordance with the rules of civilized warfare.

In the absence of these two conditions being fulfilled they who violate them become responsible for their own acts.

I have never threatened retaliation upon those recognized as engaged in warfare against the government for these illegal acts, and until the southern authorities formally recognize them as their own do not propose to do so. It is not my intention, nor do I believe it to be the intention of Admiral Porter to hold the innocent responsible for the acts of the guilty.

I regret that Gen. Stevenson's letter, whilst making enquiries should contain a threat. I have yet to hear, for the first time, of such a course securing any alleviation from the hardships necessarily produced by a state of War.

All prisoners that have fallen into my hands have been kindly and humanely treated. Unprincipled and overzealous persons many times may exagerate unavoidable suffering but a sensible commander will always know how to receive such reports.

I will refer Gen. Stevenson's letter to Admiral Porter who alone can answer the queries.

> I am Gen. very respectfully
> your obt. svt.
> U. S. GRANT
> Maj. Gen. Com

ALS, CSmH. *O.R.*, II, v, 308–9. See following letter.

1. Carter L. Stevenson of Va., USMA 1838, held the rank of capt. when he was dismissed on June 25, 1861, his commanding officer having neglected to forward his resignation. Appointed C.S.A. brig. gen. as of Feb. 27, 1862, he advanced to maj. gen. as of Oct. 10. On Feb. 24, 1863, Stevenson wrote to USG. "I am instructed by the Lt. Gen'l Com'dg this Dept, to transmit to you the enclosed copy of a notice purporting to have been issued by Admiral David D. Porter, U.S. Navy. I request that you will inform me whether this document is authentic, and if it be, whether the operations of any part of the forces under you are to be conducted in accordance with the principles announced by Admiral Porter, or with those of civilized warfare. While the troops of this Confederacy, whom I have the honor to Command, will actively repel the invasion of our territory by the forces of the United States, it is my desire that their operations shall be in accordance with the

usages of war, of humanity, and of civilization. I shall deplore the necessity for any departure from them. Therefore I hope this notice of Admiral Porter is not authentic, or that it will be re-considered, and that in no case will its threats be executed, because, I am instructed to say, if they are. the fullest retaliation will be inflicted upon the Federal prisoners now in our hands, or whom we may capture, and no quarter will be given to any officer, soldier, or citizen of the United States, taken in the act of burning houses, laying waste the plantations, or otherwise wantonly destroying the property of the citizens of this Confederacy; and that all such persons suspected of having been guilty of such acts, will not, if taken, be treated as prisoners of war, but will be kept in close confinement. Relying upon your disposition to co-operate with me in averting the necessity for a resort to such measures, . . ." LS, DNA, RG 94, War Records Office, Dept. of the Tenn. *O.R.*, I, xxiv, part 3, 66; *ibid.*, II, v, 293–94; *O.R.* (Navy), I, xxiv, 364–65.

2. Stevenson enclosed a copy of an undated order of Act. Rear Admiral David D. Porter. "Persons taken in the act of firing on unarmed vessels from the banks, will be treated as highwaymen and assassins and no quarter will be shown them. Persons strongly suspected of firing on unarmed vessels will not receive the usual treatment of prisoners of war, but will be kept in close confinement. If this savage and barbarous Confederate custom cannot be put a stop to, we will try what virtue there is in hanging. All persons no matter who they are, who are caught in the act of pillaging the houses of the inhabitants along the River, levying contributions, or burning cotton, will receive no quarter if caught in the act, or if it is proved upon them." Copy, DNA, RG 94, War Records Office, Dept. of the Tenn. *O.R.*, I, xxiv, part 3, 66–67; *ibid.*, II, v, 294; *O.R.* (Navy), I, xxiv, 365.

To Act. Rear Admiral David D. Porter

March 2d 1863.

ADMIRAL D. D. PORTER
COMD.G MISS. SQUADRON.
ADMIRAL,

I send you my reply[1] to the letter brought by "Flag of Truce" yesterday from which you will see that I have left the queries to be answered by you.

I would like to send my letter this afternoon the day being a very clear one to observe all that can be seen. Will you be kind enough to let me have a tug for the purpose at any hour you may designate.

Very respectfully
U. S. GRANT
Maj. Gen.

ALS, MoSHi. On March 2, 1863, Act. Rear Admiral David D. Porter wrote to USG. "On consideration I thought it best to write the enclosed letter (a copy of which I send you) in answer to General Pemberton. I don't think he will gain any great consolation from it, and it may enlighten him on the subject of Civilized warfare." LS, DNA, RG 94, War Records Office, Dept. of the Tenn. *O.R.*, II, v, 309. Porter enclosed a copy of his lengthy letter of March 2 to Maj. Gen. Carter L. Stevenson justifying harsh treatment for those who fired on unarmed vessels. LS, DNA, RG 94, War Records Office, Dept. of the Tenn. *O.R.*, I, xxiv, part 3, 77–78; *ibid.*, II, v, 309–10; *O.R.* (Navy), I, xxiv, 365–67.

1. See preceding letter.

To Maj. Gen. Stephen A. Hurlbut

Head Quarters, Dept. of the Ten.
Before Vicksburg, March 2d 1863.

MAJ. GEN. S. A. HURLBUT
COMD.G 16TH ARMY CORPS,
GEN.

I am now sending transports to bring down the Division of troops which you received notice some days ago to hold in readiness.[1] I hope Gen. you will push them forward with all possible dispatch.

These troops should bring with them two hundred rounds of ammunition, ten days rations, all their camp & Garrison equipage and four teams and two ambulances per regiment. Any poor mules they may have might just as well be turned over to the Quartermaster in Memphis as this country abounds in such stock and of a good quality.

I am Gen. very respectfully
your obt. svt.
U. S. GRANT
Maj. Gen. Com

ALS, DNA, RG 393, 16th Army Corps, Letters Received. *O.R.*, I, xxiv, part 3, 80.

1. See letters to Maj. Gen. Stephen A. Hurlbut, Feb. 22, 27, 1863.

To Maj. Gen. Stephen A. Hurlbut

Head Quarters, Dept. of the Ten.
Before Vicksburg, March 2d 1863.

MAJ. GEN. S. A. HURLBUT
COMD.G 16TH ARMY CORPS,
GEN.

Break up all your garrisons North of Jackson as soon as possible and hold all your surplus forces in the vicinity of Germantown, or nearer Memphis if you think proper, in readiness to be ordered here should they be required.[1] Do not weaken Corinth however and only abandon Jackson Bolivar & Bethel when you are satisfied that these forces will be required to hold your East & West line.

The rolling stock should be got over South of the break before abandoning the Northern parts if there is any immediate prospect of geting the road completed.

I am Gen. Very respectfully
your obt. svt.
U. S. GRANT
Maj. Gen. Com

ALS, DNA, RG 393, 16th Army Corps, Letters Received. *O.R.*, I, xxiv, part 3, 80.
On March 2, 1863, Maj. Gen. Stephen A. Hurlbut wrote to Lt. Col. John A. Rawlins. "Scouts just arrived from below at LaGrange report that part of the Rebel forces have already left Vicksburgh—Some have gone South. Tilghman's command to Granada, 31st Mississippi Col. Orr to Yazoo City—Some troops have also gone from Vicksburgh to Jackson on line of Pearl River—Several Regiments have gone by way of Selma to fortify the crossing of Tombigbee River. 80 mounted Infantry and two Hundred Infantry from Corinth went to the Gun-Boats on Tennessee. Have destroyed all flats & ferries for many miles on the River—Captured one Captain one Lieut. twenty men—forty horses and a large number of arms & broken up a dangerous gang. The Tennessee is as high as ever known. The delays about the Rail Road are very annoying. Col Webster now reports that he will not be able to run trains before the 7th. As soon as this is done I will execute the orders in relation to abandoning the Road as far as Jackson. This will require where done a force of Cavalry at Columbus & I am waiting for the Regiment of Cavalry which was promised by the Major General. No news of any moment here—" ALS, DNA, RG 94, War Records Office, Dept. of the Tenn. *O.R.*, I, xxiv, part 3, 81.

1. On March 4, USG wrote to Hurlbut. "If the Columbus road cannot be repaired within forty-eight hours from the receipt of this break up the garrisons North of Jackson and bring the rolling stock of the road to Memphis on transports. You need not send the Parrott guns from Corinth nor any other battery for the present, except what belongs with the troops you are sending." ALS, DNA, RG 393, 16th Army Corps, Letters Received. *O.R.*, I, xxiv, part 3, 82–83. On Feb. 28, Hurlbut had written to Rawlins. "Col. Webster reports to me that his Rail Road repairs will not be completed until some time next week, owing to the high water. The Streams are higher than ever before known.—Wolf River in front of LaGrange is impassable. Genl Hamilton from LaGrange reports a Brigade of Rebel Cavalry at Holly Springs & states a rumor that Cars are running there— As soon as we can cross the Wolf an Expedition is ordered to push down there and destroy the works on the R Road. The Tallahatchie is and has been so high that the Rail Road Bridge cannot be burned. As soon as possible after getting the Rolling Stock down over the Road I shall call in all forces above Jackson and post them below keeping Sullivan's Head Quarters there & recall from above Union City to Columbus. Strengthen the garrison at Fort Pillow & Hickman & send a Regiment of Cavalry to Asboth at Columbus. The General informed me some time since that he would send up another Cavalry Regiment it has not yet reported. I was requested by Genl Grant in the last communication recd to forward to Genl McClernand a Battery of Parrotts I have none within my command except at Corinth & would not recommend that they be withdrawn. If such however be the order of Genl Grant I will send a 20 lb Parrott Battery from Corinth. My other guns are light. Can send one of the light Batteries if desired. There is nothing new here I expect to hear further from Holly Springs to day but not in time for this Boat. Rosecrans telegraphs that he is prepared for any movement. It is reported to me that a strong naval force of the Rebels is in Yazoo River & that one or more of their Boats is heavily iron clad. I doubt the full truth as the last reliable intelligence was in January that their proposed iron clad had not her machinery in & was considered a failure There is no special news here—I am trying to get this region into shape but the amount of rascality here is beyond all estimate" ALS, DNA, RG 393, Dept. of the Tenn., Letters Received. *O.R.*, I, xxiv, part 3, 73–74.

On March 9, Hurlbut wrote to Rawlins. "All the movements required by orders are in progress, but as they involve a change of position from Columbus throughout to Memphis it is rather slow process. The garrisons belonging to Columbus are being drawn in to that point, all troops below Union City to Jackson —this will leave a stretch of about 70 miles between outposts of Columbus & Jackson which can only be explored by Cavalry. Sullivan is directed to keep his Cavalry moving East & North & I shall send Asboth the 3d Ills from this place 6 companies, which with two now at Columbus he is directed to keep out My only apprehension is of the crossing by mounted men being made over the Tennessee and a dash through this open space on Hickman or Fort Pillow. Grierson with 3 Battalions of Cavalry left LaGrange yesterday to break up Richardson's gang near Covington. Lee with four hundred moved this morning direct from Germantown—The 3d Michigan or a portion of that Regt from Jackson to watch the crossing of the Hatchie—and 3 companies from Ft. Pillow to break up a ferry above Covington. The Hatchie is so high that I do not think they can escape that way & my orders are to make the work thorough but spare all peaceable people. If the 2d Ills. Cavalry is not needed below, it would be of great use around

Memphis   I consider the 2d & 6th Ills. worth all the rest for duty in this neighbor-hood. Lauman will be ready to embark as soon as transports arrive, and no delay shall occur which I can possibly prevent. We will lose telegraph communications from Jackson to Columbus I think to night as I have no doubt the people along the line or some of them will destroy the wires. Orders have been published & will be enforced as to Resigned officers, which will specially affect the prospects in business of Col. Van Arman & Capt. Silversparre. Van Arman two weeks since applied for leave to go to Cairo while waiting his resignation. I allowed him four days   He has not returned & is I hear at Springfield. He has therefore not yet received his papers." ALS, DNA, RG 94, War Records Office, Dept. of the Tenn. Misdated March 3 in *O.R.*, I, xxiv, part 3, 82. See letter to Maj. Gen. Stephen A. Hurlbut, Feb. 25, 1863.

On Jan. 18, Capt. John H. Lowe, 127th Ill., wrote a letter in which he com-plained that he had paid Col. John Van Arman, 127th Ill., thirty dollars for nine recruits who were mustered into another co. but were carried on his morning reports as present for duty. DLC-USG, V, 21; DNA, RG 393, Dept. of the Tenn., Register of Letters Received. Van Arman resigned on Feb. 23.

On March 16, Van Arman wrote a letter asking that the orders compelling resigned officers to leave the dept. be waived in his case. In an endorsement, Rawlins asked Hurlbut to modify the orders to apply only to those dishonorably discharged. DLC-USG, V, 25; DNA, RG 393, Dept. of the Tenn., Endorsements. On Feb. 22, Maj. Gen. William T. Sherman endorsed to USG the resignation of Capt. Axel Silfversparre, 1st Ill. Light Art. "Captain Silversparre is an officer of prominent endowments & the motives which led him services to our country at the time and in the manner he did entitles him to the thanks and gratitude of our people   He has for many months had the charge of the heavy guns at Memphis & as all are now well mounted & in position his services can well be spared. His battery H. 1st Ills Arty. were composed of 4 heavy 20 pdr. Parrott Rifles, so heavy that they broke down the horses & compelled me to divide them between two companies, or sections, one of which is comd'g by Lt Hart & the other by Lt Putnam. I recommend the resignation of Capt Silversparre with the thank of the Government for the good services he has thus far rendered"   Copy, *ibid.*, 15th Army Corps, Endorsements. On March 21, C. A. Partridge, Washington, who had resigned on Jan. 22 as 1st lt., 48th Ohio, wrote to Maj. Gen. Henry W. Halleck protesting Hurlbut's implementation of USG's orders expelling resigned officers, mentioning that the War Dept. had revoked USG's orders expelling Jews. ALS, *ibid.*, RG 108, Letters Received.

To Brig. Gen. Benjamin M. Prentiss

Head Quarters, Dept. of the Ten.
Before Vicksburg, March 2d 1863.

BRIG. GEN. B. M. PRENTISS,
COMD.G DIST. OF E. ARK.
GEN.

Hold Gorman's Division in readiness to move under the command of Gen. Hovey the moment Ross returns from his Yazoo expedition. I want you to hold the country ~~from~~ from the Mississippi river to Coldwater, by way of the Pass, as long as we are likely to use it. For this purpose you can use such of your troops as you may deem proper.

Transfer one of the best old regiments from Ross to Hovey and send Col. McGinnis back to his regiment, or the Brigade in which it is.[1]

With a few days such weather as we are now having I hope to be ready for prompt action and want Hovey with his old Division with me. Gen. Gorman will receive orders assigning him to the command of the post, and Hovey to the command of the 12th Division (his present Div.) 13th Army Corps.[2]

These troops when they move will bring with them their camp & Garrison equipage, ammunition to the amount of two hundred rounds per man and ten days rations. Four teams and two ambulances will be all the transportation required.

I am Gen. very respectfully
your obt. svt.
U. S. GRANT
Maj. Gen. Com

ALS, DNA, RG 94, War Records Office, Union Battle Reports. *O.R.*, I, xxiv, part 3, 80.

1. George Francis McGinnis, born in Boston in 1826, served in the Mexican War as capt., 2nd Ohio, and manufactured hats in Indianapolis before the Civil War. Enlisting as private, 11th Ind., on April 15, 1861, he rose to col. as of

Sept. 3. On Feb. 24, 1863, Lt. Col. Walter B. Scates, adjt. for Maj. Gen. John A. McClernand, wrote to Lt. Col. John A. Rawlins. "Colonel G. F. McGinnis 11th Ind Vol Infty requests to be releived from the command of the 2nd Brigade 12th Division 13th Army Corps, under Special orders No 39 paragraph 15 Dept of the Tennessee. His reasons stated are—that he has not been confirmed as a Brig. Genl, and that he had rather be returned to his Regiment, than command a Brigade which does not include his old Regiment   The Major General Commanding is constrained to ask that Col McGinnis's request be granted"   Copy, DNA, RG 393, 13th Army Corps, Letters Sent. The nomination of McGinnis as brig. gen. as of Nov. 29, 1862, though returned to the President on Feb. 12, 1863, was resubmitted and confirmed on March 9.

2. Special Orders No. 63, Dept. of the Tenn., March 4. DS, McClernand Papers, IHi; copies, DLC-USG, V, 26, 27; DNA, RG 393, Dept. of the Tenn., Special Orders.

To Maj. Gen. Stephen A. Hurlbut

Head Quarters, Dept. of the Ten.
Before Vicksburg, March 4th 1863.

MAJ. GEN. S. A. HURLBUT,
COMD.G 16TH ARMY CORPS.
GEN.

Seeing your last returns I am satisfied that another Division can be spared from your command. In the Dist of Columbus and the Dist. of Jackson there are more troops than are necessary, particularly after giving up the eighty-seven miles of road North of Jackson. I would direct therefore that such troops as you deem advisable be brought to the front to relieve Lauman's Division from rail-road duty and bring that Division to Memphis, or vicinity, and hold it in readiness to be moved here.

Make these changes with all promptness. I want to loose no time from this forward. I will send transportation for Laumans Division in a few days. The same directions as givin for the troops now enroute, as to what shall be brought along, will be applicable to them.

Direct all the troops coming from Memphis to debark at Greenville Miss unless otherwise directed.

> Very respectfully
> your obt. svt.
> U. S. GRANT
> Maj. Gen Com

ALS, DNA, RG 393, 16th Army Corps, Letters Received. *O.R.*, I, xxiv, part 3, 83. On March 7, 1863, Maj. Gen. Stephen A. Hurlbut wrote to Lt. Col. John A. Rawlins. "Brig. Genl John E Smiths Division is about to embark for Greenville Miss. Great delay has taken place from the necessity of moving the entire line of troops down from LaGrange to this place—Lauman's Division is moving in to day two Brigades will camp on the right & left of the R. R. Depot the other covers the Rail Road to Germantown. On Monday morning the Rail Road from Jackson to Columbus will be abandoned & the garrisons ordered down. The most inconvenience that I apprehend from that will be the loss of Telegraphic communication. Genl. Asboth is in constant apprehension of attack but I think with little reason but as he had no light artillery I have sent him the 9th Inda. Battery. I propose to bring in Denvers division to cover the whole Rail Road when Lauman moves below. I received the 131st Regiment from below & am preparing a Regiment to go with Smiths Division to report to Genl McClernand, this Regiment will be taken from the Garrison and will still further reduce a force insufficient now to cover the City. If it is expected that smuggling be repressed & the immense stores here protected from the thieves of both sides I renew my statement that an entire Division is necessary. I shall call down two Regiments from Columbus in a day or two as soon as it is certain that Van Dorn will not recross the Tennessee, and bring in Grierson's Cavalry from LaGrange to patrol the neighborhood of Memphis for which service they are worth all the rest since the 2d Illinois went below. Cornyn has done splendidly with the 10th Mo. Cavalry and has got back safe to Corinth. I have directed Hamilton to garrison LaGrange & its neighborhood with troops from Jackson & Corinth as I think 5000 effective men enough in Corinth. I believe that with a good pile driver the road from LaGrange to Corinth could be repaired in three weeks if it is worth while so to do this however is not a matter of necessity as long as we hold Jackson which I see no occasion for abandoning. The amount of plunder & bribery that is going on in and about the City of Memphis is beyond all calculation. I have one or two tolerably honest detectives at work but am afraid they will be bought up. Is it utterly impossible to devise some way by which cotton & cotton dealers can be abolished. As the U. States cannot be expected to hire all the cardinal virtues for $13 a month—soldiers on picket are bribed—officers are bribed—& the accursed system is distroying the army. Men are looking for opportunities to make money & the whole course of the Treasury Department is tending to corrupt & degrade every body connected with the administration of affairs. I am heartily sick tired & disgusted. Honesty is the exception & peculation the rule wherever the army is brought into contact with trade" ALS, DNA, RG 94, War Records Office, Dept. of the Tenn. *O.R.*, I, xxiv, part 3, 91–92.

On Jan. 16, Rawlins issued Special Orders No. 16 appointing Col. William H. H. Taylor, 5th Ohio Cav., Lt. Col. Charles H. Adams, 1st Ill. Light Art., and

Lt. Col. Francis M. Smith, 17th Ill., to serve as a military commission at Memphis. Copies, DLC-USG, V, 26, 27; DNA, RG 393, Dept. of the Tenn., Special Orders; (printed) *ibid.*, RG 109, Union Provost Marshals' File of Papers Relating to Individual Civilians. *O.R.*, I, xxiv, part 3, 1067. On Feb. 13, the members wrote to USG denouncing the detective dept. at Memphis for accepting bribes to release prisoners and recommending "that this whole detective department be superseded by honest, upright men, . . ." *Ibid.*, pp. 50–51. On the same day, Taylor wrote to Hurlbut denouncing Henry L. Cleveland, chief of U.S. detectives at Memphis. *Ibid.*, p. 51. On Feb. 16, USG endorsed the report of Taylor, Adams, and Smith. "Respectfully referred to Maj. Gen. Hurlbut Comd.g Dist of West Tenn who will please see that the reform recommended is made." Copies, DLC-USG, V, 25; DNA, RG 393, Dept. of the Tenn., Endorsements.

Later, Cleveland addressed an undated petition to USG. "The petition of H. L Cleveland, would state that on the 18th Feby 1863 he was arrested at Memphis-Tenn. and carried before the Military commission of which W W H Taylor was President, there he was charged with *Robbery, bribery* and *extortion* He entered his plea of 'not guilty' to the *charges* and *specifications* and the case continued until the second day of March—during the meantime your petitioner made application by petition to Col Hillyer, Provost Marshal Genl. to have a new commission appointed to try his case, as he believed that commission had imbibed prejudices against him with a further request that the finding of the new commission should be refered to you. On the 9th day of March his case was taken up by the new commission of which Col. Matheny was presdent. Some four or five days were spent in examining the case. Some 20 or 30 witnesses being summoned and examined on the part of the Government. The case was then closed   the court was satisfied it was a malicious prosecution gotten up by the Jews whom I had detected in smuggling and forthwith found in my favor, and sent the papers to Genl. Hurlbut who has them yet, and will not or has not acted on them, and I am still under arrest.—This petition therefore prays that you will order said papers sent to your *Head quarters* allowing the petitioner to accompany the same, where the case may be further examined and your petitioner discharged that he may return to service &c" DS, *ibid.*, RG 109, Union Provost Marshals' File of Papers Relating to Individual Civilians. On April 22, USG endorsed this petition. "Refered to Maj. Gen. Hurlbut. I do not wish to see the prisoner in person but if the case is as stated he is entitled to a decission at once or the papers refered." AES, *ibid.*

On April 6, Lt. J. C. Harley, special detective, Memphis, wrote to USG. "I ask your indulgence for a few moments in order to lay before you an honest, frank, and truthful statement, of what has come to my personal knowledge while acting in the capacity of detective in this department. By unceasing vigilance I have made myself thoroughly acquainted with every channel of trade, vice, bribery & corruption, and I find that in high quarters as well as low, the most scandalous and disgraceful corruption holds high carnival, and villainy runs riot on every side. In my official character, I called on one Capt Franks, who acts as chief of the detective force here, and informed him, that three miles from the city a lot of revolvers and six hundred dollars worth of Goods were secreted,   my authority was the owner himself, the second evidence ocular proof, Franks paid no attention to it,   Another party who had taken out 90 ounces of quinine and a large lot of pistols, I arrested, brought him to Franks, and in an hour or so he was turned loose, J. B. Wasson, a druggist, whose clerks had by a continuous series of allurements extending over a period of three months sold a small quantity of goods to one of Franks detectives, was arrested, bailed out, and the second day informed through a third party that he would be released and his store given up if he would pay Capt Franks $15000, The same scandalous and traitorous course is pursued on the Memphis and Charleston R. R. in the way of smuggling, My Nephew was offered one Thousand dollars per month, by a Rail Road employee, to aid in smuggling, the truth is, It is a gigantic scheme to smuggle goods out, the employees being the parties engaged in it. How is it that (the (Confed) Col Richardson, Guerilla chief, has such an abundant supply of new repeaters, and even the new Burnside Carbine,? . . ." ALS, *ibid.*, RG 393, Dept. of the Tenn., Letters Received.

To Maj. Gen. Stephen A. Hurlbut

March 4th 1863.

MAJ. GEN. HURLBUT,
COMD.G 16TH ARMY CORPS,
GEN.

Admiral Porter has, at my request sent a gun boat to bring down, or convoy the Paymasters with their funds. I wish you would hasten them off with all dispatch. The absenc[e] of the Paymasters has a very depressing effect upon the men many of whom have families at home suffering for the means of subsistence. Then too I hope to be able to make a move very soon which may delay payments for some time.—I was excessively put out at the nonarrival of Paymasters with funds.

Respectfully &c.
U. S. GRANT
Maj. Gen. Com

ALS, DNA, RG 94, War Records Office, Military Div. of the Miss. *O.R.*, I, xxiv, part 3, 83–84. On March 4, 1863, Lt. Col. John A. Rawlins wrote to Maj. Gen. Stephen A. Hurlbut. "You will send the Twenty-five Paymasters that were ordered here from Memphis, for the purpose of paying the troops at this place, with their funds, at once, as prisoners, under a sufficient guard, in charge of a reliable Commissioned officer, for the protection of them and their funds. This disobedience of orders and trifling with the payment of troops, will not be tolerated." LS, DNA, RG 393, 16th Army Corps, Letters Received. *O.R.*, I, xxiv, part 3, 83. On March 7, Hurlbut wrote to Rawlins. "Col Webster will have his rolling stock over tomorrow. I have issued orders to call in garrisons to Jackson

& Columbus. I received this morning orders to arrest and send down under guard twenty five paymasters & their funds. Major Judd with a corps of Pay Masters started on Tuesday with Genl Quimby's Division to Lake Providence with orders to take convoy from that point below. I enclose report of Senior Pay Master here. As I never received any orders as to the movements of Pay Masters referred to I suggest that any orders of the kind be forwarded through these & I will see them promptly obeyed. I have never exercised any control over this branch of the service. Col Roddy with Cavalry & one Regiment Infantry are at Tuscumbia. No other troops moving within my limits. Van Dorn has threatened Donelson & occasionally is reported about to cross the Tennessee, but has not done so. It is reported by Spies that a Division of the enemy has gone to Yazoo City, it is probably true. There is but little stirring here except the ordinary routine of speculation and thievery" ALS, DNA, RG 94, War Records Office, Dept. of the Tenn. *O.R.*, I, xxiv, part 3, 91.

To Maj. Gen. Stephen A. Hurlbut

Head Quarters, Dept. of the Ten.
Before Vicksburg, March 4th 1863.

MAJ. GEN. S. A. HURLBUT,
COMD.G 16TH ARMY CORPS,
GEN.

There is a man by the name of *John P. Fairley* living in Memphis who has been engaged in enticing our soldiers to desert, and in one instance that can be proven enticed a sergeant of an Ia regiment to take a ride with him in his buggy for the purpose of having him captured and paroled. The man was captured and paroled whilst Fairley was left unmolested and allowed to return to the city with his horse and buggy.

Fairley is an Indiana man but married south. I presume he passes for a Union man but the above are no doubt facts against him. As the evidence would have to be got from Ia it might satisfy the ends of justice to expel this man from our lines, family and all, and take possession of his property, real estate, by the Quartermaster.

Very respectfully
U. S. GRANT
Maj. Gen. Com

ALS, DNA, RG 109, Union Provost Marshals' File of Papers Relating to Individual Civilians. *O.R.*, I, xxiv, part 3, 84. In May, 1863, John P. Fairly, who had left Memphis to avoid arrest, was apprehended in St. Louis and returned to Memphis where he spent at least six months in prison. Papers in DNA, RG 109, Union Provost Marshals' File of Papers Relating to Individual Civilians.

To Maj. Gen. James B. McPherson

Before Vicksburg, March 4. 1863.

MAJ. GEN. J. B. MCPHERSON.
COM'D'G. 17TH ARMY CORPS.

The Dredging machine which has been doing excellent service here, gave out this afternoon. This compels me to send to Lake Providence for the boat ordered to be left there. I wish you would have it forwarded at once if it has reached you. If not send forward on arrival.

U. S. GRANT.
Maj. Gen.

Copies, DLC-USG, V, 19, 30; DNA, RG 393, Dept. of the Tenn., Letters Sent. On March 4, 1863, Col. George P. Ihrie wrote to Maj. Gen. James B. McPherson. "The Major General commanding this Department directs to write you and say: you will send all the cotton now in your possession, and as much more as you can obtain, to this point, to be used in fitting out and protecting 'Rams' Also, you will send one of two Dredge boats up in your vicinity, if not with you, down to this place to report to Capt. Prime." Copies, *ibid.* On the same day, Lt. Col. John A. Rawlins wrote to Brig. Gen. Benjamin M. Prentiss. "The Dredge-boat directed to be retained at Helena to be used in the clearing out and deepening the entrance into Yazoo Pass, you will send forward to this place at once, for work in the canal opposite Vicksburg." Copies, *ibid.* On March 6, Prentiss wrote to Rawlins. "I have the honor to acknowledge the receipt of your communication of the 4th inst., relative to the Dredge Boat directed to be retained at this point for use at the Yazoo Pass—and to report that the Boat has as yet never reported to me—I learn that the Boats passed here before I was notified.—" LS, *ibid.*, Unregistered Letters Received.

To Col. Lewis B. Parsons

Head Quarters, Dept. of the Ten.
Before Vicksburg, March 4th 1863.

Col. L. B. Parsons,
A. Q. M. & Supt. of Transptn,
Col.

The few fine days we have had has enabled the work to progress so rapidly on the Canal that before this reaches you it will be navigable for boats. Or at least I hope so. I want to loose as little time as possible now and send to you therefore for transportation.

In addition to all the transportation retained here I shall want steamers sufficient for 20 000 men; in addition too to the transportation required for any additional forces I may receive from St. Louis. I have ordered two Divisions from the District of Memphis in addition to all that were under orders when you was here.

As drawing this amount of transportation from regular trade may prevent the shipment of supplies as fast as required by the Army I would suggest that boats coming down be partially loaded with subsistence stores and forage. All the freight brought should be placed below deck so as to leave all the the upper part of the boats for troops.

I shall be glad to see you down here if your services can be spared from St. Louis.

It is tolerably well settled that the Indianolia was not only sunk but that before giving up she so disabled two of the enemies boats that they sunk also.

Very respectfully
your obt. svt.
U. S. Grant
Maj. Gen.

ALS, Parsons Papers, IHi. On March 1, 1863, Col. Lewis B. Parsons, Memphis, wrote to USG. "I found letters from Saint Louis here directing me to bring up boats to move Gen. Davidson's Division (10,000 men) to Vicksburg. I have written Capt. Reno requesting he would at once send the boats, provided you approved of the same.—Genl. Quimby's Division is not yet loaded and he does not expect to be able to leave before Tuesday or Wednesday.—I found the most exaggerated reports already in circulation here in regard to the 'Indianola' derived from rebel sources. According to their reports the 'Indianola' was all in good order in the hands of the rebels, and had already in company with the 'Queen of the West' and several other boats come up to Vicksburg and threatened an attack which had driven all our Army and flotilla up the river.—In fact the d'l was to pay generally. Similar false reports also went forth from our boat. In reply to many anxious inquiries I gave the facts—that of the loss of the boat there was no doubt, but that there was such evidence as to render it at least probable she was sunk and that notwithstanding this 'all was quiet along the lines' except on the *line of Capt. Primes' canal*!! As was to be expected the loyal men heard the news with pain and the traitors with malignant joy.—I have been thinking that if you determine to make a decided demonstration by the Yazoo Pass you are like to want more small boats. Would it not be well to settle this matter so I can send them instead of larger? ~~ones~~ you may send up for Genl. Davidson; otherwise you may be delayed. I think Col. Williams' report said 'stern wheel boats of not over 185 feet length could only be used.' ' ALS, DNA, RG 393, Dept. of the Tenn., Letters Received.

On March 4, USG telegraphed to Parsons. "I have sent Messenger to St Louis to get transports Have them ready to send as soon as possible" Telegram received, Parsons Papers, IHi; copies, DLC-USG, V, 19, 30; DNA, RG 393, Dept. of the Tenn., Letters Sent. On March 8, Parsons telegraphed to USG. "Your dispatch of the 4th just received. Have ordered transports to be ready at once. Several large boats have gone to Memphis and Helena the last week, which will be ordered by telegraph to report to you.—" ALS (telegram sent), *ibid.*, RG 107, Telegrams Collected (Unbound); telegram received, *ibid.*

On March 5, USG telegraphed to Parsons. "Among the transports you have been directed to send forward here, I will require as many as thirty (30) of less than two hundred feet in length. These I understand can be procured at Cincinnati and Louisville. They should be here at the earliest possible moment. Use any exertion to procure them." LS (telegram sent), *ibid.*; telegram received, Parsons Papers, IHi.

On March 9, Parsons twice wrote to USG. "I recd your T. D. of the 4th (to wit 'I have sent Messenger to St Louis to get transports. Have them ready to send as soon as possible,') last evening, and at once notified every Boat in the Harbor to be ready to leave as soon as possible. Your T. D. of the 5, (to wit 'Among the transports you have been directed to send forward here I will require as many as thirty of less than two hundred feet in length, these I understand can be procured at Cincinnati and Louisville, they should be here at earliest possible moment, use every to procure them') is just received, and I would start to Louisville & Cincinnati to night if your Messenger was here so I could get particulars. There has been quite a number of Boats sent below Memphis in the last week, mostly of a large class. I fear however that those and most we have here will not answer your present purpose as they are large. I will seize every suitable boat here and every where as soon as possible after I get the orders per your Messenger. I anticipate some difficulty, as we have but few small Boats except what you have already, and I understand Genl Rosencrans has taken most all the small Boats on the Ohio, but every thing shall be done, that can be to comply with your orders. I hope Capt Reno will send back such large Boats as you can consistently spare if it be but for 2 or 3 weeks at a time, as you can scarcely conceive how short we are of transportation even for necessary Army stores and Troops. I hope Maj Primes Canal is still doing well and that my stock in it is not fancy stock." "I wrote you at length this forenoon as to you T. D. for boats—Several will start tomorrow—There are not over 5 or 6 now here not over 200 feet in length   I am anxiously waiting the arrival of your Messenger in order to get more definite orders before going to Louisville and Cincinnati—You do not say whether *side* wheel boats if less than 200 feet long will do—It was supposed they would not when I was with you— but I have notified one or two to be ready—If I conjecture right—you want these boats about Delta.—If so would it not be well to send up troops on your larger boats and stop the small ones there, as the latter will go but slowly up stream— It will take some days to gather up all the small boats but I will push them off as fast as possible—I shall order them to report at Memphis and then to you unless they get other orders at Memphis or Helena   I shall be much obliged if you can do as you send about advising me about what time to come down to see something done   I am very sorry to say that there seems to be a very strong effort making to break down Gen Halleck   If you can open the Miss—it will strengthen him, as it is complained that nothing has been done since he went to W—All eyes are centered on your army and there is no mistaking the fact that the anxiety is intense —Many almost feeling that the fate of the Republic now rests on your success or failure   I am glad to say, with the papers of today that your 'stock is good and rising—'   It is reported in the papers that the rebels blew up the Indianola, when they saw the Admirals *bogus* monitor coming after them—a splendid joke if true— Please keep them advised at Memphis and Helena of any changes in your orders for the boats I send if any changes there are"   ALS and LS, DNA, RG 393, Dept. of the Tenn., Letters Received.

On March 10, Parsons, Cincinnati, wrote to USG. "After waiting two days for the arrival of the messenger mentioned in your dispatch I started for this place last night without him. Fortunately I meet Col Blood at Odin with you letter of the 4th inst—I find Gen Wright & Col Swords quite unwilling to allow boats to leave this Dept as they say Gen Rosecrans has ordered *10.000.000* rations to Nashville—and boats are very scarce—I have endeavoured to show your want was the most pressing.—and have sent Gen Wright a letter—a copy of which I enclose—and will advise you in the morning of the result—If the boats are refused. I am at a loss what to do, but think I shall venture to telegraph Gen Rosecrans and Gen Halleck—but I hope I shall not be refused, though I know boats are greatly wanted here—"   ALS, *ibid.*

On March 12, Parsons wrote to USG. "I sent you last night a copy of my letter to Gen Wright, though I think dated wrongly as the 10th—I have only been able to get a reply today—a copy of which I enclose. The progress is most unsatisfactory, but I can do no more here—I have however ordered every boat that comes from this or any place to be siezed at Cairo—I feel annoyed and surprised that Gen Wright will not act at once under such pressing circumstances, but perhaps I do not see both sides—I hope for a reply to his T. D. to Gen Rosecrans by morning—"   ALS, *ibid.*, RG 94, War Records Office, Dept. of the Tenn. *O.R.*, I, xxiv, part 3, 103. A copy of the letter of March 10 from Parsons to Maj. Gen. Horatio G. Wright is in the Parsons Papers, IHi. Wright's reply is *ibid.* and in *O.R.*, I, xxiv, part 3, 102–3.

On March 13, Parsons wrote to USG. "I inclose copy of letter to Gen. Rosecrans which contains copy of his telegraph in reply to mine. Genl. Wright sent another urgent telegraph to day to Gen. Rosecrans—I have got to day by hook or crook three boats, less than two hundred (200) feet, which leave at once. I feel confident General Rosecrans as soon as he gets my letter will let us have more; but I am tired of this delay and go to Louisville to night and St Louis to morrow night, leaving Capt. Turner here to push up boats here. Excuse haste" Copies, Parsons Papers, IHi; DNA, RG 94, War Records Office, Dept. of the Tenn.

On March 16, Parsons wrote to USG. "I arrived here from Cincinnati yesterday. I inclose copies of telegrams from Gen. Rosecrans to General Wright with indorsement of Gen. Wright & also copy of dispatch by me to Gen. Rosecrans with his answer of his Quartermaster & also of telegram and letter to Colonel Reynolds.—It will be extremely difficult to replace any boats from the Ohio. Everybody is complaining of me here for want of boats. The Forage Quartermaster says we are interfering with his contracts up the upper rivers, and demands we do not take boats engaged bringing down Forage, to which Col. Allen, Chf Quartermaster, assents. The Commissary wants his Stores forwarded very promptly. Genl. McNeil is said to be in a tight place, and we are required to send him three boats instanter: Genl. Pope demands that we send three (3) more boats up the Missouri, to chase up those poor devils—the Indians &c. &c. The fact is Gen. Rosecrans or Gen. Wright have nearly all the *small boats* engaged on the Tennessee & Cumberland, and it seems they absolutely require them there, while we have already at or below Memphis the great bulk of our boats, and consequently it is *extremely difficult* doing our *necessary* business here. As you are aware I sent you three (3) small boats from the Ohio and could only get permission to take eight more under any circumstances. We have sent you five more from here and suppose several more have been sent from Cairo and Memphis. We have two (2) or three (3) more here repairing which I hope to send in two (2) or three (3) days. I have also sent above the rapids for two or three I hear are running there and will send them as soon as I can get them. There are also two (2) on the Illinois, but Col. Allen says they must not be taken unless I can supply their places with larger ones; which I cannot do. These are all the boats less than two hundred (200) feet long I can control, except such as we may seize at Cairo or when they come into port here. There have gone to you in addition, of large boats, since your orders, as follows : . . . The following boats leave here to night or to morrow : SouthWestern (capacity 1000 men) City of Alton (capacity 1500 men) making in all a capacity for 25,200 men. On these boats however I have sent about 2,500 men, which leaves transportation for a little over the number of men required by you though not by any means so many small boats as you desire. I think in addition there will be, within a few days, as many as six to ten more small boats. I regret my inability to comply with your wishes almost as much as you can, but I have done my best. Our wants for transportation here I have stated *without exaggeration* and *earnestly request* for the good of the whole service that you will instruct the Quartermaster of Transportation to send back such boats as you can best spare as soon as can be safely done. I deeply regret that I can not be permitted to accompany these boats and share the labors and good fortune which I trust await you. . . . P. S. If any changes are desirable please telegraph me." LS (press), Parsons Papers, IHi. *O.R.*, I, xxiv, part 3, 115–16. Also on March 16, Parsons wrote to USG. "I have written you fully by Steamship today. But send duplicates by Mail herewith" Copy, Parsons Papers, IHi.

On March 20, Parsons wrote to USG. "I received some days since a letter from Mr James Robb who was for many years a very extensive Broker and Railroad proprietor in New Orleans. Mr Robb is well acquainted with the country and makes some suggestions which I believe you are pretty well advised as to already but thinking his views might strengthen your own I enclose a copy. We have sent you from here and the Ohio at least twenty three or twenty four boats less than two hundred feet long and will send two or three others by tomorrow. I sent up to Galena for six but my agent telegraphs me they are at Lacrosse River and cannot get through the Ice as yet. We sent you several large boats but some how or other several of them got the privelidge of turning back from Memphis or Helena—I donot understand how. We have sent Genl. Rosecrans four large boats and shall send others as soon as possible to supply the place of the smaller boats we are getting from him for you. I confess to a good deal of anxiety about the Yazoo Pass Expedition and wish I could send you fifty boats of right size if an army is sent there, and then go along myself. I am crowded with *drudgery* accumulated in my absence and can't see out. . . . P. S. What Mr Robb says as to opening of Canal arises from a lack of knowledge of the matter and our situation there which those at a distance do not fully comprehend." LS, DNA, RG 393, Dept. of the Tenn., Letters Received. Parsons enclosed a copy of a letter he had received from James Robb, Chicago, Feb. 22, commenting on efforts to approach Vicksburg. Copy, *ibid.*

To Maj. Gen. James B. McPherson

Head Quarters, Dep't of the Tennessee,
Before Vicksburgh, March 5th 1863.
Maj. General J. B. Mc.Pherson,
Comm'dg 17th Army Corps.
General.—

Stop Quinby from debarking any more troops where he now is. All transports, no matter what their size, can run into the Pass to Moon Lake, which is about half way from the river to Coldwater. I want your Corps to get in there as rapidly as possible, and effect a lodgement at Yazoo City, or the most eligable point on Yazoo river from which to operate.

Send Quinby in advance with a good supply of provisions and coal. All transports he may have of over One hundred and eighty feet in length, direct him to unload at Moon Lake and order back to this place.

I will send immediately from here all boats that will answer to go through the Pass, and should they arrive in time, Quinby can transfer to them where he is, and send such boats as he leaves immediately down here.

Quinby will have general directions in the Pass until you arrive. He may detain Ross' Division, now there, until there are sufficient forces to defend his position.

Then I want Ross sent back to Helena, to form the garrison of that place, and take Hovey's, which is composed of old and tried troops, whilst the others are raw, and with rather indifferent Brigade Commanders, I fear.

If you think there is a reasonable prospect of the river making a channel through by either of the routes you are now working upon, you may prosecute it with the force you have left. At all events clear out the channel of the timber in it, and let the water in to see what it will do. I will send orders to have Denver's Division stop at Moon Lake, and go in by the same route.

This will give you five Divisions to operate with, which, with the Gunboats, I hope will enable you to carry out one end of the proposed programme.

Send all boats you may have at Lake Providence under 180 feet in length to Quinby.

> Very Respectfully
> Your Obed't Serv't
> U. S. GRANT
> Major General.

LS, DNA, RG 94, War Records Office, 17th Army Corps. *O.R.*, I, xxiv, part 3, 86–87.

On March 1, 1863, Maj. Gen. James B. McPherson had written to USG. "I have just returned from an examination of 'Bayou Baxter' from its source down about seven miles. The work of clearing it out is much greater than I was led to believe from the Engineers Report. The recent heavy rains have raised the water in the Lake and Bayou from two to three feet, overflowing a considerable portion of the low country and making it extremely difficult for the working parties to get along. They are however doing very well, and the men seem to be in fine Spirits. About five miles have been cleared out—I am going tomorrow morning up to Ashton near the Arkansas Line where Bayou Macon approaches within three miles of the Miss' River, and if there is a probability that by cutting the Levee at this point Boats can be floated into Bayou Macon I shall have it done immediately, and unless the water in Bayou Baxter falls very soon, I shall cut the levee here and let in the water to fill the Lake and Bayou in order to get in Boats so that we can make use of a Steam Captsan to haul out logs, snags &c. The trees will of course have to be sawed off under water in this case, but I am a little apprehensive that, in cutting them off at the surface of the water now, the water when the levee is cut *will not rise high enough* to float the Boats clear of the stumps. I have had numerous applications here from parties owning cotton (or *claiming* to own it) to ship it to Memphis and sell it on their own account. If I once open the door to this sort of thing I presume nearly every Bale of Cotton in this vicinity would be claimed by some one who would come forward and say that he had never done anything to encourage the Rebellion, and had always been opposed to secession— My plan is to send it all to Memphis and let it be sold by Capt. Eddy, and if any of these people can establish a good, *lawful* and *loyal claim* let them receive the nett proceeds of what belongs to them. In some instances where the facts came under my own observation & I know the families have been stripped of almost everything, and are really in destitute circumstances I will grant a permit for them to sell or ship a small proportion on their own account to purchase necessaries—I have granted the permission asked for in the enclosed letter—*Mrs. Sparrow* (wife of Mr. Sparrow Senator in the Rebel Congress) with her Family consisting of three or Four Daughters at present residing here on the Lake wishes permission to pass into the Rebel Lines *to remain* at Vicksburg—and to take two or three of her female house servants, Can it be granted ?" ALS, DNA, RG 393, Dept. of the Tenn., Unregistered Letters Received. *O.R.*, I, xxiv, part 3, 76.

On March 2, McPherson wrote to USG. "I have just returned from making explorations between Ashton and Grand-Lake with a view of determining the practicability of getting into 'Bayou Macon' from the River at that point. There is now a difference of *Eight feet* between the surface of the water in the River, and the general level of the country behind the *levee*, and there is an open route across the fields and following a road to the Bayou. So that, the only question is, whether the country between the River and the Bayou will fill up with water after the *levee* is cut, deep enough to float Steam Boats. If so, the route is perfectly feasible and can be opened in four or five days. I have given Col: Bissell directions to try it, and he goes up in the morning with his Regiment to commence the work. The 'Rocket' I have sent down to the Fleet to obtain the powder for blasting out the *levee*. The point where the *levee* will be cut is a very short distance below the Arkansas line. No portion of Genl. Quinby's Division has yet arrived, though I am expecting him hourly—I shall unless otherwise directed, have his command disembark at 'Grand Lake' and push rapidly across to Bayou Macon and thence down on the high ground on the Western side, to some good point to the *W.* or *N. West* of this place, where he can guard the Bayou, to prevent the Rebels from obstructing it by felling trees &c, and probably secure a large amount of Rebel property, cotton, horses cattle mules &c which have been moved over there for safety. The road from the River to 'Bayou Macon' at Grand Lake is very good, and will require only two bridges, which Col: Bissell can readily construct out of his Pontoon Train. The work of clearing out Bayou Baxter is progressing as rapidly as the circumstances will admit—" ALS, DNA, RG 94, War Records Office, Union Battle Reports. *O.R.*, I, xxiv, part 3, 78–79.

On March 5, McPherson wrote to USG. "The Steam Dredging Boat 'Hercules' has just this moment arrived here & in accordance with your instructions I have ordered the Captain of the Steam Boat 'Niagara' to tow it down to Youngs Point—Genl. Quinby's Division has arrived and is now disembarking at 'Grand Lake,' Col: Bissell is at work cutting the Levee near the Arkansas Line & I will know in two or three days whether we can get boats through to Bayou Macon at that Point—The River is rising here slowly—The work of opening Bayou Baxter progresses more slowly than I wish, on account of the great difficulty of getting at it, the low ground being all overflowed—The little Propeller '*Rawlins*' is in the Lake and works well. I can send down Several Hundred Bales of cotton in a few days, and have just sent up to Quinby to send me a good Boat for the purpose, as I have none here. I have just received a *Verbal Order* from Comr Graham, coming from a man I don't know directing me to send down *all the Steam Boats* which brought down Genl. Quinby's Division. I do not like to act upon it, for the reason that there may be some mistake, and your written orders to me were to keep these Boats. Then again if it should be necessary to send troops to Genl. Quinby's assistance or move his Division, I would have no means of doing it. I am glad to hear the 'Indianola' went down 'game.' The old Flag is not dishonored under such circumstances—I can let the water in here at any time, but think I will wait and see the result above. I shall do everything in my power to hasten things forward, and Col: Leggett is pushing matters in the '*Bayou*' as rapidly as he can. The troops are well and in fine spirits . . . P. S. This is written on the Boat and in great haste" ALS, DNA, RG 94, War Records Office, Union Battle Reports. *O.R.*, I, xxiv, part 3, 85–86.

To Col. Robert C. Wood

Head Quarters, Dept. of the Ten.
Before Vicksburg, March 6th 1863.

ASST. SURG. GEN. R. C. WOOD
ST. LOUIS MO.

DEAR SIR:

Your letter showing the efforts you have been making to supply everything necessary pertaining to the Medical Department, in this Army, is received. I can assure you nothing has been left undo[ne] here to secure the health of the men. No Army ever went into the field better provided with medical stores and medical attendents than is furnished the Army now in front of Vicksburg.

There was a deficiency in Volunteer surgeons but now that deficiency is fully supplied.[1] The hospital boats are supplied with their own surgeons, nurses and every thing for the comfort of the sick.[2] The Purveyors department not only has every thing usually furnished the sick but more than I ever dreamed was ever furnished an Army, more than the great majority of men could have at home. Then too there is not that amount of sickness that persons would be led to believe from the statements in the public prints. I question whether the health of the St. Louis forces is better to-day than that of this command.

On arrival here the men had been pent up so long a time on steamers then camping on low ground and in the most terrible weather ever experienced there was for a time, necessarily a great number of sick   Surgeon Laub[3] has been sick ever since he arrived here and entirely unfit to attend to any of his duties. The Dr. is not willing, or at least has never intimated a willingness, to give up. I have however found it necessary, for my own relief, to order him away. The duties would be sufficient for the Dr. if in good health   As he is he is entirely incapable of them and his desire to perform his duties would prevent his recovery if he should be kept here.

I have assigned Surgeon McMillan[4] ast act. Med. Director for the present, but leave the place for you to fill. McMillan is the senior surgeon in my Dept. but belongs to the Volunteer service. He is well qualified for the position but Surgeon Sutherland[5] of the regular service, is here, unassigned, and holding a commission of the same date with Surg. Wirts who was assigned to the position of Medical Director over these same Volunteer surgeons he may feel himself entitled to the position.

I leave this assignment entirely to you. Either of these officers I believe to be well qualified for the position. I have no choice. All I want is some one qualified and willing to perform the duties and will willingly take either of these two or such other as you may designate.[6]

> Very respectfully
> your obt. svt.
> U. S. GRANT
> Maj. Gen.

ALS, Mrs. Walter Love, Flint, Mich.

On Feb. 22, 1863, Col. Robert C. Wood wrote to USG. "I have advised you officially of certain changes in the Medical Officers in your Department. Every effort has been made by me to furnish you efficient Medical aid and accommodations for the Sick. Yesterday I directed Surgeon Hammond U. S. A. now at Helena to proceed to your Head Quarters, also Asst. Surgeon Wright now at Jackson to proceed to Memphis to relieve Surgeon Sutherland in the duties of Medical Purveyor. Dr Sutherland to proceed to your Head Quarters for duty, this will give you two efficient Medical Officers of the Medical Staff. Surgeon Irwin has been ordered some time since to relieve Surgeon Wirtz whom I would recommend should be ordered forthwith to obey his Orders from the Secretary of War dated January 31st 1863 to repair to General Pope's Head Quarters, who has no Medical Director. Surgeons of Volunteers, Quider, Darrach, Churchman and Bobbs have also been ordered to your Head Quarters—Bobbs has been at Memphis three weeks, as Dr Wirtz reports, doing nothing. I am thus particular General that you may have the necessary orders given for their prompt execution, as some of them will tarry at or be detained at Memphis. There are now accommodations at this City, and vicinity for two thousand sick, so that the necessary orders can be given for their transportation without crowding the Hospitals with you & at Memphis. There are now three SteamBoats fully equipped for Hospital purposes in addition to the 'Nashville' now at Helena—the 'D. A January' the 'City of Memphis,' & the 'City of Alton.' I regret the great sickness and mortality in your Army and believe it is dependent in a great degree on locality, the latter dependent on Military necessity. Abundant supplies are on hand at Memphis—if they are deficient in your Army it is the fault of the proper Officers not making timely requisitions. When I give any orders changing the positions of Medical Officers in your Department, in advance of your sanction, I beg to assure you that it is done for expedition, and from no other motive, feeling a great solicitude for your personal success, and the accomplishment of your designs,—I trust therefore that they will be sustained by you in every case." LS, DNA, RG 393, Dept. of the Tenn., Letters Received.

On Feb. 23, Surgeon W. D. Turner, *City of Memphis*, wrote to Wood. "I have the honor to acknowledge the receipt of a letter from your office referring to a communication in the Missouri Democrat of the 23d February as to the condition of the Boats Ohio Belle, Pembina, & Fanny Bullitt. The article referrd to was not authorized by me and my name was improperly appended—'Still the facts stated are true. The cause of the filth of the Boats, in my opinion was mainly due to the Surgeon in charge, though they mentioned they had no Brooms, or anything else to work with nor could they get them. On the Pembina I saw one Camp Kettle   the surgeon in charge informed me he had nothing else as a cooking utensil: The Surgeon did not obtain from the Boat (Pembina) any cooking or other vessels for his sick, who were lying on the floor without bedding, an inch deep in filth of every Description   He complained much of bad treatment from the crew of the Boat, who refused him all assistance   In regard to the sick on the Fanny Bullitt not having food or medical attendance from the 23d of January (on which day they were transfered from the J. C. Swan & other Boats) till the 25th January I refer to Surgeon Gerrish 67th Indiana who was Surgeon in charge from the 25th January at which time there was no Surgeon on the Boat or any one who had authority to draw Rations or Medicines were drawn on the Fanny Bullitt previous to Dr Gerrishs arrival"   ALS, *ibid.* On Feb. 24, Wood referred this letter to USG. ES, *ibid.*

On March 14, Wood wrote to USG. "Complaints of a grave character through official and other sources have reached me, respecting the inefficiency of the Medical Staff connected with the Army now operating before Vicksburg— also of the want of the proper Medical Supplies in sufficient quantity, and of the deficiency of Hospital accommodations. I have the honor to inquire whether these allegations are founded on facts, and if the Army has not been provided with a proper number of Medical Officers, and with sufficient Medical Supplies as far as the nature of the service will permit. Every effort has been made to keep the Army provided with efficient Medical aid and Medical Supplies, and ample and additional Hospital accommodati[ons] have been prepared for the sick at St. Louis. (three thousand (3000) vacant beds at St. Louis—also large Hospitals at Memphis). Five Hospital Boats are also available near Vicksburg. Any additional suggestions are asked for, and all available means will be provided by the Medical Department to improve the sanitary condition, and add to the efficiency of the Army now before Vicksburg." LS, *ibid.* See letter to Brig. Gen. William A. Hammond, March 12, 1863.

On Feb. 17, U.S. Representative George H. Pendleton of Ohio introduced a resolution "That the Military Committee be instructed to inquire into the efficiency of the medical department of the army under General Grant . . ." *CG*, 37-3, 1029. Pendleton later explained that he based his resolution on reports in the *Cincinnati Times*. Pendleton to Wood, Feb. 24, copy, DLC-Robert T. Lincoln. Wood then made a personal inspection of the camps at Vicksburg. Wood to Montgomery Blair, March 5, ALS, *ibid.*; *O.R.*, I, xxiv, part 3, 109–10.

1. On Feb. 15, Lt. Col. John A. Rawlins wrote to Maj. Gen. Stephen A. Hurlbut, Memphis. "You will please detach and send forward for service in the field all the Surgeons and assistant Surgeons that can be spared from Regiments left behind. Also such competent Surgeons as are not absolutely needed in Hospitals. The scarcity of Medical Officers here and the sickness among them make this a necessity   The Medical Director Dr Laub has been sick ever since his arrival   Orders were issued about 22nd Jany 1863 to the Medical Department at Memphis to provide Hospital accomodations for at least five thousand (5000) additional sick but little has been done towards the compliance with the order. You will please take the matter in hand and have it pushed with all possible dispatch. Releive Surgeon Wardner in charge of Mound City Hospital from duty in same and order him to report in person to these Head Quarters"   Copies, DLC-USG, V, 18, 30; DNA, RG 393, Dept. of the Tenn., Letters Sent. On Feb. 21, Wood wrote to USG. "Surgeons Chas. Sutherland and George Hammond U. S. A. & Surgeons J. E. Quidor, Barton Darrach, H. J. Churchman U. S. V. are now under orders to report to the Maj. General Commanding, for duty with the Army of the Tennessee before Vicksburg. Officers, of rank and experience will be sent as fast as they become available. Letters have been addressed to the Governors of states within the Medical Department of the West, calling their attention to the deficiency in the required numbers of Regimental Medical Officers on duty in the field, and urgently requesting that immediate appointments be made to supply the want. I would respectfully suggest that the General Commanding, with a view to the more prompt supply of this scarcity of Medical Officers, direct Colonels of Regiments to report at once to the Governors of their respective states all vacancies in the Medical Staff of their Regiments, and all absences either authorized or unauthorized, which impair the effeciency of the Medical Department of their

Commands." LS, *ibid.*, Letters Received. A copy of Wood's letter to the governors, sent by him to USG, is *ibid.*

2. On Feb. 19, Surgeon Alexander H. Hoff wrote to USG. "I have the honor to respectfully report that the present arrangements for the transportation of the sick and wounded consist of the U. S. Hospital Steamer D. A. January, Steamers City of Memphis, City of Alton and the Floating Hospital Nashville. The January is owned by the Government having been purchased in April last, since which time she has carried six thousand six hundred and twenty seven to the different General Hospitals from the several battle fields. Out of this number one hundred and sixty five died on board the boat. Some forty capital operations have been performed   This boat with a few exceptions has been provided with a full corps of Surgeons & Nurses so that it has not been necessary to interfere with Regimental Medical corps for Surgeons or draw from the ranks the necessary quota of nurses. The Nashville is fitted up very much after the plan of the January and also has a full corps of Surgeons and nurses. The City of Alton has a full corps of Surgeons but not of nurses. The City of Memphis, I believe, depends entirely upon detail for both. The Nashville cannot be towed by one boat with any safety and the arrangement I desire to make was to have two boats independant of her owned and fitted up by Government expressly for the transportation of the sick. One of these boats should be very fast so that in a case of emergency her trips could be made with great rapidity, she running to the most remote points while the January filled up the Hospitals nearer by. With such an arrangement, I am quite satisfied, ten thousand sick and wounded could be transported from any battle field by the time they could be gathered together for transportation. It ~~would~~ would give you in the absence of both the Steamers in an emergency twelve hundred beds in the immediate vicinity of the army with a thousand more ~~arriving~~ moving between her and the General Hospitals. Should the plan meet with your views, you, knowing the necessities in anticipation, I would respectfully request that another boat be purchased enabling me to complete this plan. I am quite satisfied that it would not only save life but prevent hundreds from leaving their posts unnecessarily and the boat would pay for herself twice over as against the amount of transportation that would necessarily have to be paid for and that of the most uncomfortable character and which, in some instances cannot be obtained without seriously interfering with the necessities of the Army." ALS, *ibid.* On the same day, Hoff wrote again to USG criticizing the practice of transporting military stores on hospital steamers, thus making them military targets. ALS, *ibid.*

3. Charles H. Laub of D. C. entered the U.S. Army as asst. surgeon in 1836 and was promoted to surgeon in 1854. On Jan. 21, Rawlins issued General Orders No. 8. "Surgeon C. H. Laub, U. S. A., having reported for duty, and being the Senior Surgeon in the Department, is hereby announced as the Chief of the Medical Department, and will relieve Surgeon H. R. Wirtz, in the duties of the Same." Copies, DLC-USG, V, 13, 14, 95; DNA, RG 393, Dept. of the Tenn., General and Special Orders. *O.R.*, I, xxiv, part 3, 5. On the same day, Rawlins issued Special Orders No. 21 assigning Surgeon Horace R. Wirtz as superintendent of hospitals, Memphis. Copies, DLC-USG, V, 26, 27; DNA, RG 393, Dept. of the Tenn., Special Orders.

4. Charles McMillan of N. Y., appointed surgeon as of Aug. 3, 1861, served as medical director, Dept. of the Tenn., March 5–7, 1862.

5. Charles Sutherland of Pa., appointed asst. surgeon in 1852 and promoted to surgeon as of April 16, 1862.

6. On March 7, by Special Orders No. *66*, Dept. of the Tenn., Surgeon Henry S. Hewit relieved McMillan as chief of the medical dept. Surgeon Horace Wardner was assigned as asst. to Hewit and "inspector of Camps, Hospitals, and Transports." DS, McClernand Papers, IHi; copies, DLC-USG, V, *26, 27*; DNA, RG *393*, Dept. of the Tenn., Special Orders. On March 17, Maj. Gen. Robert C. Schenck, Baltimore, Md., wrote to USG. "I have the honor herewith to enclose to you copies of papers in the case Surgeon H. S. Hewitt U. S. Vols, who it appears has been ordered to report to you for duty, for your information, and action. I trust you will have this matter fully investigated & have Surgeon Hewitt brought to punishment." Copy, *ibid.*, Middle Dept. and 8th Army Corps, Letters Sent. No action resulted. On March 22, Rawlins issued General Orders No. 18. "Surgeon Madison Mills, U. S. A., having reported for duty, is hereby as Medical Director for the Department. All reports and returns required by existing orders and Army Regulations will be made to him at these Head Quarters." Copies, DLC-USG, V, *13, 14, 95*; (2) DNA, RG *393*, Dept. of the Tenn., General and Special Orders. *O.R.*, I, xxiv, part 3, 128. On March 28, Rawlins wrote to Lt. Col. Edward P. Vollum, medical inspector, listing the surgeons who had held the post of medical director under USG since Sept., 1861. Copies, DLC-USG, V, *19, 30*; DNA, RG *393*, Dept. of the Tenn., Letters Sent.

To Julia Dent Grant

March 6th 1863.

DEAR JULIA,

I wrote you a letter the other day that I know made you feel badly.[1] It was hard for me to do because I love you but then I thought it would bring you to reflect. I have written another to father which I send for you to read and mail. I do not want you to exercise any judgement about whether it should be sent but I want you to send it immediately.

I am well, better than I have been for years. Every body remarks how well I look. I never set down to my meals without an appetite no go to bed without being able to sleep.

You will see from my letter that I want Fred. to come and stay with me. Keep the balance of the children with you until you can join me. If after the battle of Vicksburg I can have the Head Quarters of my Dept. where you can all be with me I will have it so and get a private teacher for the children if no other way. If they cannot come you can put them at a good school and be with me yourself as much as circumstances will admit of and spend the balance of your time with the children. If we had acquaintances in Jacksonville Ill. it would be the best place for you and them to stay. Ottoway Ill. would also be a good place. That is where Mrs. Wallace lives, and Col. Dickey who will resign and go home soon.[2]

I will be sending Col. Hillyer back in a few days. I did not order him here to keep him but to talk with him about affairs in Memphis and to devise ways of correcting some of the abuses about Memphis. Kisses for yourself and children dear Julia. I send this to Memphis thinking you may not yet be gone from there. But you had better start soon. I have drawn my pay and have $1100 00 besides enough to keep me until more is due. I will not send it however until I hear from Mr. Douglas.

Remember me to Mrs. Hillyer and children. Get Jess a suit of soldier clothes for his pa with stripes on his pants and eagle shoulder straps on his jacket. I think Jess would make a good Colonel.

ULYS.

P. S. put my letter to father in the mail to go and dont carry it yourself.

U.

ALS, DLC-USG.

1. This letter has not been found.
2. Ann Dickey Wallace, widow of Brig. Gen. William H. L. Wallace, was the daughter of Col. T. Lyle Dickey. On Jan. 29, 1863, Dickey wrote to USG's hd. qrs. "Tenders his resignation on acc't. of advanced age, is unable to stand the hardships consequent upon his position. Private business and domestic affairs require his personal attention. Believes owing to the peculiar condition of politics in the State of Ills. he can be of more use and service to the Genl. Gov't. as a private citizen than as an officer of the army. . . ." *Ibid.*, V, 21; DNA, RG 393, Dept. of the Tenn., Register of Letters Received. Dickey's resignation was accepted as of Feb. 16.

To Brig. Gen. Lorenzo Thomas

Head Quarters, Dept. of the Tennessee
Youngs Point La. March 7th, 1863.

BRIG. GENL. L. THOMAS
ADJUTANT GENERAL OF THE ARMY,
WASHINGTON. D. C.
GENERAL,

I have the honor to acknowledge the receipt of your communication of February 17th, 1863, and to say in reply, that the Tri-Monthly Returns for January 10th, 20th and 31st. and for February 10th. have been forwarded to your office.

The returns received have been so incomplete that it has been impossible to make the returns on the blanks required, by the printed notes.

I have been unable to obtain correct Monthly Returns for the month of January, but hope to be able to forward this report in a short time.

> I am, General Very Respectfully,
> Your obt. Servt.
> U. S. GRANT
> Major General, Comdg.

Copies, DLC-USG, V, 5, 8, 24, 94; DNA, RG 393, Dept. of the Tenn., Hd. Qrs. Correspondence.
   On Feb. 23, 1863, Col. John C. Kelton wrote to USG. "The General-in-Chief calls for a Return of the troops in your Dept. for the months of November and December, to be forwarded to the Adjutant Generals Office, no Returns having yet been received for those months." LS, *ibid.*, RG 108, Letters Sent (Press). On March 19, USG wrote to Brig. Gen. Lorenzo Thomas. "I have the honor to transmit herewith, duplicate copy of Tri-monthly Return for the forces under my command for November 10, 1862. All other returns received for the month of November were destroyed at Holly Springs to prevent their falling into the hands of the enemy. I shall forward a duplicate return of Dec. 1862, at the earliest practicable moment." Copies, DLC-USG, V, 5, 8, 24, 94; DNA, RG 393, Dept. of the Tenn., Hd. Qrs. Correspondence. USG regularly sent his tri-monthly returns to Thomas with a routine cover letter which is omitted from these volumes.
   On Feb. 13, Maj. Robert Williams, AGO, wrote to USG. "I am directed to request you to furnish this Office, Special Orders, in all cases of acceptance of the resignations of officers, in the Volunteer service, as soon as practicable after their

occurrence, that the Governors of the different States may receive early informa-
tion of the same, and have their places supplied in their Regiments promptly."
LS, *ibid.*, Letters Received. On March 27, USG endorsed a copy of this letter.
"Respectfully returned to Head Quarters of the Army Washington, D. C., A copy
of all Special Orders, as well as an abstract of Resignations are forwarded to the
Adjutant General of the Army on the 10th, 20th and 30th of each month." Copies,
DLC-USG, V, 25; DNA, RG 393, Dept. of the Tenn., Endorsements. Numerous
cover letters from USG to Thomas transmitting general and special orders are
also omitted from these volumes, as are letters transmitting lists of staff officers
and proceedings of courts-martial.

To Maj. Gen. Henry W. Halleck

Head Quarters, Dept. of the Ten.
Before Vicksburg, March 7th 1863.

MAJ. GEN. H. W. HALLECK
~~Com'g Dept~~ GEN. IN CHIEF
WASHINGTON D. C.
GEN.

I telegraphed you yesterday the near approach to completion
of the canal.[1] The water is extremely high, several feet above
the highest ground inside of the levee. Last night one of the dams
across the upper end of the canal gave way filling up where men
were at work geting out stumps and thus seting back the work
for several days. I hope yet however to have this work completed
as early as I could possibly take advantage of it if it was already
done.

The troops expected from St. Louis are not yet heard from,[2]
and all that I am bringing from West Tennessee are not yet
down.

The work of geting through Lake Providence and Bayou
Macon there is but little possibility of proving successful. If the
work had been commenced in time however there is but little
question of the success of the enterprise. The land from Lake
Providence, and also from Bayou Macon, receedes until the low-

est interval between the two widens out into a Cyprus swamp where Bayou Baxter, which connects the two, is lost. This flat is now filled to the depth of several feet with water making the work of cleaning out the timber exceedingly slow and rendering it impracticable to make an artificial channel. The Yazoo Pass expedition is a much greater success. Admiral Porter sent in four gunboats and I sent a fleet of transports with about six thousand men. They were to clear the Yazoo and tributaries of all steamboats and embryo gunboats, and if possible destroy the rail-road bridges at Grenada.

The gunboats were to approach as near Haines Bluff as possible and fire signal guns to warn the Squadron in the mouth of the Yazoo of their presence. Last night about 12 oclock Admiral Porter sent me word that the signal agreed upon was heard.

I am now sending Gen. McPherson with his Army Corps, and enough other troops to make full twenty-five thousand effective men, to effect a lodgement on the high ground on the East bank of the Yazoo. Once there with his entire force he will move down on transports and by land to the vicinity of Hains Bluff. Before moving down however below Yazoo City Gen. McPherson will be made acquainted with the full plan of attack that may then be determined upon and time will be so arranged that there will be full co-operation of my entire force.

Our movements have evidently served to distract the enemy and make him scatter his heavy guns. His forces are also scattered but they, with the Light Artillery, can be got to any one point.

The health of this command is good and the greatest confidence felt by officers and men. The most ample provision that I ever saw has been made for the comfort of the sick.

The dredging machines brought here by Col. G. G. Pride work to a charm.[3] After the accident of last night all work would have to be suspended until there was a fall of at least three feet (the river is yet rising) but for these machines.

Much credit is due Col. Pride for his selection of these machines. But for his personal attention to the selection of them old and worn out ones would have been sent and the result probably would have been that they would have given out before their work was half done.

> I am Gen Very respectfully
> your obt. svt.
> U. S. GRANT
> Maj. Gen. Com

ALS, IHi. *O.R.*, I, xxiv, part 1, 19–20. On March 20, 1863, Maj. Gen. Henry W. Halleck wrote to USG. "Your letter of March 7th is recieved. It is the first communication from you for some time which has reached here. It is very desirable that you keep us advised of your operations, in order that proper instructions may be sent to Genl Banks, Genl Rosecrans, &c. Send telegrams to Memphis by every opportunity. In operating by the Yazoo you have no doubt fully considered the advantages and dangers of the expedition. Our information here on that subject is very limited and unsatisfactory. There is one point, however, which has been discussed, and to which I would particularly call your attention: It is the danger, on the fall of the water in the Miss. of having your steamers cout in the upper Yazoo so as to be unable to extricate them. In the present scarcity of steamers on the western rivers, this would be a very serious loss. Another danger is that the enemy may concentrate a large force upon the isolated column of McPherson, without your being able to assist him. I mention these matters in order that you may give them your full attention. When the operations of an army are directed to one particular object, it is always dangerous to divide forces. All accessaries should be sacrificed for the sake of concentration. The great object on your line now is the opening of the Mississippi river, and every thing else must bend to that purpose. The eyes and hopes of the whole country are now directed to your army. In my opinion the opening of the Mississippi river will be to us of more advantage than the capture of forty Richmonds. We shall omit nothing which we can do to assist you. Permit me to repeat the importance of your frequently advising me by telegraph from Memphis." ALS, DNA, RG 108, Letters Sent (Press). *O.R.*, I, xxiv, part 1, 22. See letter to Maj. Gen. Henry W. Halleck, March 29, 1863.

On March 1, Halleck wrote to USG. "There is a vacant Major-Generalcy in the Regular Army, and I am authorised to say that it will be given to the General in the field who first wins an important & decisive victory." ALS, DNA, RG 393, Dept. of the Tenn., Letters Received. *O.R.*, I, xxiv, part 1, 19; *ibid.*, part 3, 75. Identical letters went to Maj. Gens. (of Vols.) Joseph Hooker and William S. Rosecrans. USG apparently did not respond to Halleck's letter.

1. On March 6, USG telegraphed to Halleck. "The canal is near completion. Troops expected from Saint Louis not yet heard from. I will have Vicksburg this month or fail in the attempt" Telegram received, DNA, RG 107, Telegrams Collected (Bound); *ibid.*, Telegrams Collected (Unbound); copies, *ibid.*, Telegrams Received in Cipher; DLC-USG, V, 94. *O.R.*, I, xxiv, part 1, 19.

2. On March 2, USG had telegraphed to Halleck. "I have received no forces from the Department of the Mo. except those at Helena. Are any more to come?"

Copies, DLC-USG, V, 5, 8, 24, 94; DNA, RG 393, Dept. of the Tenn., Hd. Qrs.
Correspondence. On the same day, USG telegraphed to Maj. Gen. Samuel R.
Curtis. "Are any troops coming from St. Louis for me. I have understood so but
hear nothing of them.—answer." ALS (telegram sent), *ibid.*, RG 107, Telegrams
Collected (Bound); telegram received, *ibid.*, Telegrams Collected (Unbound).
On March 4, Curtis drafted his reply at the foot of the telegram received. "A regi-
ment embarked to day   The marine Brigade leaves Thursday—Other troops as
fast as transportation can be furnished"   ALS, *ibid.*; telegram received, *ibid.*,
RG 393, Dept. of the Tenn., Telegrams Received.

    3. On March 7, 6:00 A.M., USG telegraphed to Halleck. "Three Dredge
boats are here. They work to a charm doing the work of three hundred men ~~each
hour~~ per day each hour"   Telegram received, *ibid.*, RG 107, Telegrams Collected (Bound); copies (dated March 6), *ibid.*, RG 393, Dept. of the Tenn., Hd.
Qrs. Correspondence; DLC-USG, V, 5, 8, 24, 94. On March 10, USG wrote to
Act. Rear Admiral David D. Porter. "Will you be kind enough to furnish our
Dredging Machines with one barrel of lubricating oil to last until some already
sent for can be brought from Memphis? I would also request the use of a man,
whos name I do not know, but he is rated as an ordinary seaman on board the
'Mound City.' This is thoroughly acquainted with the working of Dredge boats."
ALS, New York State Library, Albany, N. Y. See letter to George G. Pride,
April 23, 1863.

To Maj. Gen. John A. McClernand

Head Quarters, Dept. of the Ten.
Before Vicksburg, March 7th 1863.

MAJ. GEN. J. A. MCCLERNAND
COMD.G 13TH ARMY CORPS.
GEN.

    The dam across the upper end of the canal gave way lastnight
and from the rush of water through where the levee is cut by the
canal may wear it away so as to fill up our camps and drive the
troops to the levee and on board transports.

    Have your Engineer officer, supported by all the details he
may requir, look to preventing as far as possible the influx of
water from the rear and left of your camps.

    The troops nearest the canal will attend to the work in that
direction.

Respectfully &c.
U. S. GRANT
Maj. Gen. Com

ALS, McClernand Papers, IHi.

On March 7, 1863, Col. George P. Ihrie twice wrote to Maj. Gen. John A. McClernand. "The General commanding this Department directs me to say to you, that you will immediately have all the empty gunny bags to be found in your Corps immediately gathered together, and sent to the canal, *with the utmost dispatch*. To facilitate this, you will cause details to be made, to visit each and every Regiment in your Corps. At the canal, they will be delivered to the Chief Engineer —Capt. Prime." "I am directed by the General Commanding this Department to write you as follows: Having gathered together, and sent down to the canal, all the empty gunny bags in your Corps, you will move your Command to Miliken's Bend, occupying the highest ground. For this purpose, you will use the *unloaded* transports at your camp. Additional transports will be sent you, without delay." ALS, *ibid*. On the same day, McClernand wrote to USG. "Please place a Steamer at my disposal. I wish to send her immediately up as far as Millikens Bend. Lt. Col Schwartz of my Staff will go on her to ascertain whether there is anything to prevent the Cavalry and loose animals from going up there by land. If there is not I can much hasten my movements and shorten the time of the use of transports. The Capitola is near here and if she is a government boat could be made immediately available. The Argyle which has just left the landing with steam up, would do better. I can return the boat to-morow morning." Copies, *ibid*.; DNA, RG 393, 13th Army Corps, Letters Sent. On March 12, McClernand, Milliken's Bend, wrote to USG. "That portion of my command lately at Youngs Point will all have been transferred to this place by night. Maj Mudd bears this on the Steamer Fanny Ogden to bring up a Paymaster promised by Major Judd. If the 'Ogden' can be left with me until greater urgency calls her elsewhere it will be a great accommodation." DfS, McClernand Papers, IHi; copies, *ibid*.; DNA, RG 393, 13th Army Corps, Letters Sent.

To Lt. Col. George T. Allen

Head Quarters, Dept. of the Ten.
Before Vicksburg, March 8th/63

LT. COL. G. T. ALLEN,
MEDICAL INSPECTOR,
COL.

I would respectfully call your attention to Gen. Orders No 61 & 100 series 1862 on the subject of leaves of absence.

A number of leaves have come to this office for approval where the certificates have been for a period beyond the time authorized which should not be. In discharging soldiers the "Act of Congress" approved May 14th 1862 and embraced in Gen.

Orders from the War Department dated May 16th 1862 and Numbered 53 should be closely observed.

Officers who are remote from the proper Military authority to grant them leaves of absence should have some means of visiting their homes without delay, but they should not be granted except in extreme cases and then for a period not exceeding twenty days. Officers who have a certificate for sixty days, or a period longer than that authorized, may deem themselves authorized to remain absent for the full period and thus subject themselves to being reported "absent without leave" and recommended to be mustered out of service.

Very respectfully

U. S. GRANT

Maj. Gen. Com

ALS, Rosenberg Library, Galveston, Tex. George T. Allen, born in New York City in 1812, brought to Ill. in 1817, graduated from the College of Physicians and Surgeons in 1838, served as an Anti-Nebraska Democrat representative of Madison County in the Ill. General Assembly (1855–56). Mustered in as surgeon, 14th Ill., on May 25, 1861, he was appointed U.S. surgeon as of April 4, 1862, medical inspector with the rank of lt. col. as of June 4, and assigned to USG's dept. on Jan. 1, 1863. *The United States Biographical Dictionary . . . Illinois Volume* (Chicago, Cincinnati, and New York, 1876), 578–79. Allen commented on USG in letters to U.S. Senator Lyman Trumbull of Ill., April 25, May 11, 1862, Jan. 20, 1863. ALS, DLC-Lyman Trumbull. Allen reported to USG on the hospital at Helena, May 6, and on the hospital steamer *City of Memphis*, May 7. ADS, DNA, RG 393, Dept. of the Tenn., Letters Received.

To Brig. Gen. Benjamin M. Prentiss

Head Quarters, Dept. of the Ten.

Before Vicksburg, March 8th 1863.

BRIG. GEN. B. M. PRENTISS,

COMD.G DIST. OF E. ARK.

GEN.

Direct the first Div. of troops coming from Memphis, probably the one commanded by Brig. Gen. J. E. Smith, to pass in to Moon Lake and there await orders and transports from Maj. Gen. McPherson. They will keep with them all boats of less dimentions than fifty feet beam and one hundred and ninety feet in length. All other transports they will send here.

There are also troops coming from St Louis. Direct them to land at Lake Providence unless they receive other directions from these Head Quarters. They will retain all their large class boats but release for the Yazoo their small ones. They will probably find at Lake Providence some of Gen. McPhersons command awaiting transportation, but if they have gone they will send these boats into Moon Lake to transport such troops as may be there.

Direct Gen. C. C. Washburn to hold such a force of cavalry as you can spare, not less than twelve hundred men, in readiness to obey the summons of Gen. McPherson.

Gen. McPherson, to avoid the delay of sending through these Head Quarters, is directed to call directly upon you for this Cavalry as soon as he can use them and can send the transports. It would be well to send Gen. Washburn to Moon Lake as soon as the weather and roads will permit of him doing service ther and have him that much nearer where he will be wanted.

> I am Gen. very respectfully
> your obt. svt.
> U. S. GRANT
> Maj. Gen. Com

ALS, DNA, RG 94, War Records Office, Union Battle Reports. *O.R.*, I, xxiv, part 3, 93–94. On March 9, 1863, Lt. Col. John A. Rawlins sent a copy of this letter to Maj. Gen. Stephen A. Hurlbut. LS, DNA, RG 94, War Records Office, Union Battle Reports. *O.R.*, I, xxiv, part 3, 95.

On March 8, Brig. Gen. Benjamin M. Prentiss, Helena, wrote to USG. "This day Genl Quinby arrived with his Division and will go into Moon Lake in the morning   I have made arrangements to keep up communication with advancing Forces—I find that Genl Quinby will take charge on the Pass untill McPherson arrives. I presume it is your intention that I should render assistance in way of keeping open communication Guarding Pass—in short do all I can to assist forward the Expedition   I shall do this untill otherwise ordered and have assured Genl Quinby of my hearty cooperation. We should have one of those *small Steam Tugs*—as—Steamboats are compelled to run slow the streams being narrow. I trust Genl you will let me hear from you on rect of this and any thing I can do here shall be done at once   Helena will soon become a respectable place   Troops improving in Discipline   Cotton Buyers getting scarce; and Trade without our lines cut off—"   ALS, DNA, RG 393, Dept. of the Tenn., Letters Received.

To Act. Rear Admiral David D. Porter

March 9th 1863.

ADMIRAL D. D. PORTER,
COMD.G MISS SQUADRON,
ADMIRAL,

Three men from Vicksburg are just in and brought with them Vicksburg papers of the 6th & 7th. The former of these dates I have but the officer of the Day retained the latter. It contains I understand a full account of the capture and total destruction of the "Indianola."

I have sent for this paper and when received will send it to you.

Very respectfully
U. S. GRANT
Maj. Gen.

ALS, MdAN.

On March 7, 1863, Act. Rear Admiral David D. Porter wrote to USG. "Will you be kind enough to have the enclosed telegraph to the Hon. Secretary of the Navy, put into cipher, and forwarded. By so doing you would oblige." LS, DNA, RG 45, Correspondence of David D. Porter, Mississippi Squadron, General Letters (Press). On the same day, Porter telegraphed to Secretary of the Navy Gideon Welles. "We know pretty positively that the Indianola was too much damaged to be used offensively at once, but they might in the course of a month be able to operate against the fleet below. Any vessel with a ram could easily destroy her if she is not already blown up. She is a weak vessel. If she exists, I hope to have her before a month is over." *O.R.*, I, xxiv, part 3, 89; *O.R.* (Navy), I, xxiv, 392.

To Maj. Gen. Stephen A. Hurlbut

Before Vicksburg, March 9, 1863

MAJ. GEN. S. A. HURLBUT
COM'D'G 16TH ARMY CORPS.

I send Col. Dickey commanding Cavalry Division, to report to you. I have explained to Col. Dickey, verbally, that I want the available in the next few weeks for heavy service.

My plan is to have the cavalry force you command cooperate with the cavalry it is in contemplation to start from some point on the Yazoo, either Yazoo City or Liverpool.[1]

The object will be to have your Cavalry move Southward from La Grange, in as large a force as possible, destroying the bridge over the Tallahatchie, thence move East of South so as to head Black River, or strike it where it can be crossed. The larger portion of the Cavalry to move from about Yallobusha river Eastward as if to threaten the Mobile road, but in reality to cover a move of a select portion of the Cavalry which will go South, and attempt to cut the Railroad east of Jackson. Washburn will move Eastward, and cut the Miss. Central road where it crosses the Big Black.

It is hoped by these moves of large forces of cavalry, to cover the smaller party sufficiently to insure their succes in reaching the road east of Jackson, and to do what they are sent for and return to the main body.

No vehicles should be taken along except ambulances, and they should have an extra pair of horses each. The troops should be instructed to keep well together, and let marauding alone for once and thereby better secure success.

I regret that the expedition you had fitted out was not permitted to go. The weather, however, has been intolerably bad ever since that it might have failed.

I look upon Grierson as being much better qualified to command this expedition than either Lee or Mizner. I do not dictate, however, who shall be sent.

The date when the expedition should start will depend on movements here. You will be informed of the exact time for them to start.

U. S. GRANT
Maj. Gen.

Copies, DLC-USG, V, 19, 30; DNA, RG 393, Dept. of the Tenn., Letters Sent. *O.R.*, I, xxiv, part 3, 95. On March 14, 1863, Maj. Gen. Stephen A. Hurlbut wrote to Lt. Col. John A. Rawlins. "Col Dougherty at Paducah having telegraphed that Fort Heiman was occupied by rebel forces I ordered Genl Asboth

with two Regiments & a Battery to disperse any force there before they obtained
a Lodgment. I have heard from him at Paducah, on his way up—I am informed by
Genl Rosecrans that he does not think any serious movement is intended there,
but that our Expedition will answer a good purpose. Col Hatch with 2d Iowa
Cavy destroyed the bridge across the Tallahatchie thoroughly—in the face of a
considerable force of Rebel Cavalry without loss. Grierson started from LaGrange
and by forced march surprised Richardson's camp near Covington killing 25 &
capturing 68—the remainder took to the bushes. His camp & camp Equipage were
burned. Lt Col Wallace moving from Germantown for the same purpose, captured Col. Looney 38th Tenn. three officers & several men. Among this number
is the notorious Cushman who is wounded in the arm. I have telegraphed to St
Louis for fifteen Hundred horses to remount the Cavalry and get them into condition for hard service. Lauman's Division (4th) is now camped along the City lines
about 2 miles from CourtHouse. No special news of interest in this vicinity. I
enclose copies of Telegrams from Hamilton which strongly indicates the abandonment of Vicksburgh. I submit them for what they are worth. It has been my
opinion for some days that they will not risk a large army about Vicksburgh and
that you may expect as soon as foothold for any large force is obtained on the
East side of Yazoo that they will retire. Fifty desperate men with small boats it
appears to me might drop unperceived past Vicksburgh to the mouth of the Big
Black and pulling up that stream through the swamps now overflowed could
destroy the Bridge over it. I do not think they dread any thing in that shape or
from that direction & suggest it at this distance to the consideration of those who
can judge better on the spot"   ALS, DNA, RG 393, Dept. of the Tenn., Letters
Received. *O.R.*, I, xxiv, part 3, 106–7.

On March 22, Hurlbut wrote to Rawlins. "I enclose herewith copy of Report
of scouts from Corinth which contains much information. Genl. Asboth has returned to Columbus having been up the Tennessee as far as Perryville and
destroyed or brought off all flats and skiffs on the river. He has left a garrison at
Heiman, which I consider improper and have ordered him to bring them to
Paducah   I have no official report yet from him. It is reported from various
sources that Chalmers has taken command in North Miss & was to rendezvous
at Senatobia   His probable force it is difficult to state. The 'Grape vine' reports
it 15,000 and on the march for Memphis—It is to be hoped they may try it, my
men are in good trim & I will answer for the result. It may be that they will attack
the road. Orders are out to exercise the most rigid caution & to be constantly in a
state of preparation. Thirty Guerillas yesterday broke the track three miles above
G. Junction capturing the conductor negroes & train men of the Wood train and
escaped. Cavalry are out after them   A portion of Carrs Division are here & will
go forward. I find great difficulty in getting horses for Cavalry and Artillery—
I need a remount of 1500 for Cavalry alone. If the Surgeons hitherto detailed from
this corps are not absolutely required below, I hope they will be returned as heavy
drafts are made from necessity on this Corps for Hospitals"   ALS, DNA, RG 393,
Dept. of the Tenn., Letters Received. *O.R.*, I, xxiv, part 3, 129.

1. Liverpool, Miss., about thirty-three miles northeast of Vicksburg.

To Elihu B. Washburne

———

March 10th 1863.

HON. E. B. WASHBURN, M. C.

DEAR SIR:

Now that Congress has adjourned I have thought possible you might want to make a visit to this part of the country. I need not assure you that I would be most glad to see you here and have you stay during the contest which will take place in the next thirty days from this writing. You will have time to join me if Mails are prompt. The canal through would have been a success by to-day but for the great rise of water. The river is now several feet above the whole country herabouts and our canal was dependentent for its success upon keeping the water out of it. The upper dam has broken and submerged things generally. To stop this off will take a number of days, but we will do it. In the mean time, so far as I now know, and have official reports, the Yazoo Pass expedition is going to prove a perfect success. This is highly important if for no other purpose than to destroy the transportation, and embryo Gunboats, the enemy had there. They have been working for one year on one boat, of gigantic proportions, up that stream.

Lieut. Col. Wilson, a young man of great merit, who has been put on Gen. Hunter's staff, but who was on mine as a Lieutenant and I objected to relieving until the present campaign is over, writes to Rawlins in a private letter that our success in geting into Yazoo Pass is due to the energy of C. C. Washburn. He felt an interest in the enterprise and took hold with a will, and with men, worthy of the object to be accomplished. I have ordered the Army Corps of McPherson through that way with additional forces making him effective men to the number of about 28,000. McPherson is one of my best men and is fully to be trusted. Sherman stands in the same catigory. In these two men I have a host. They are worth more than a full Brigade each.

McPherson will effect a lodgement on the high lands on the Yazoo river, East bank, and will co-opperate with the troops from here. The class of transports adapted to the Pass being so limited some delay will necessary take place in geting them to their destination. I have sent up the river for all the small class of boats that can be got.

We are going through a campaign here such as has not been heard of on this continant before. The soldiers see the ~~places~~ position of the enemy in front of them but I presume do not see how they are to attack. Their camp ground is several feet below water held in its place by the levees, ~~and~~ Constant rains falling ~~which~~ keep the roads almost impassable.—With all this the men are in good spirits and feel confidant of ultimate success.

The health of this command is a subject that has been very much exagerated by the press. I will venture the assertion that there is no Army now in the field showing so large a proportion of those present with their commands being for duty. Really our troops are more healthy than could possibly have been ~~be~~ expected with all their trials. Although I have told you but little of plans here it is more than I am in the habit of writing on this subject. You will excuse me therefore from saying how I expect to co-operate with McPherson, at least until you ~~should~~ come down. Gen. Washburn will have command of a very important Cavalry expedition from the Yazoo river if all other plans succeed.

Hoping that you will be with us (and bring Jones[1] if you can)
I remain yours
U. S. GRANT

ALS, IHi.

1. J. Russell Jones, born at Conneaut, Ohio, on Feb. 17, 1823, moved to Ill. in 1838, settling at Galena in 1840. After prospering as officer of a steamboat co., Jones entered Republican politics and was elected to the Ill. House of Representatives in 1860, resigning after President Abraham Lincoln appointed him marshal for the northern district of Ill. In letters of Jan. 6, 17, 1863, to U.S. Representative Elihu B. Washburne, Jones wrote of his cotton-buying expedition to USG's command from which he expected to clear $6,000. ALS, DLC-Elihu B. Washburne. Later the same month, Jones returned to USG's hd. qrs. in search of additional

opportunities to buy cotton, and his letters to Washburne indicate a growing friendship with USG. Letters of Jan. 28 (2), 29, Feb. 5, 15. ALS, *ibid*. See George R. Jones, *Joseph Russell Jones* (Chicago, 1964), chap. 6.

To Maj. Gen. James B. McPherson

Before Vicksburg, March 11 1863

MAJ GEN. J. B. MCPHERSON
COMM'DG 17TH ARMY CORPS.

Order Mr Hood's cotton restored to him, and also give him authority to ship it to Memphis, and sell, there on his own account. He cannot be authorized to sell this side of Memphis.[1]

I think it highly probable a force has been sent up the Yazoo to meet our coming down, but do not think it can amount to anything like the number indicated in your letter. I am anxious, however, to see you in the Yazoo in person, and with all the force you can take in   I have sent North for boats, of a class to navigate there and they ought to be in Moon Lake as soon as you are ready to use them.

I do not much think of using by Bayou Macon even if it can be used at this time. It would too much seperate my forces. I told you when your forces were in the Yazoo river to send for Gen Washburne and the Cavalry   I have given the order for them to be ready, and to obey your summons without further notice from here. They will probably be on the Coldwater, or at least in Moon Lake when you call for them.

I send you an extract from the Vicksburg Whig of the 5th, which shows that the "Indianola" was destroyed. I also got Vicksburg papers of the 6th and 9th, the latter of which speaks of the total loss of the "Indianola"

There is no doubt of her destruction.

U. S. GRANT
Maj Gen

Copies, DLC-USG, V, 19, 30; DNA, RG 393, Dept. of the Tenn., Letters Sent.

On March 9, 1863, Maj. Gen. James B. McPherson, Lake Providence, wrote to USG. "A couple of my scouts have just returned from the west side of Bayou Macon having crossed the swamps and Bayou in a canoe, They report a force of three or Four hundred Rebel Cavalry on the 'Macon Hills' nearly west from Bunch's Bend, & a Force of three thousand Infantry mostly conscripts near Floyd, I would send out an expedition after them, but it is impossible to get across the country on account of the high water—They also report as current among the secessionists, who are in weekly communication with Vicksburg by a route which strikes the Missippi River nearly opposite Warrenton, that the 'Indianola' was not sunk, and in fact very little injured; that she was captured by boarding and nearly all the officers and crew taken prisoners, That she immediately started with the Ram 'Queen of the West' for Port Hudson and arrived in time to participate in the attack against Genl. Banks, and succeeded in capturing the 'Essex,' That Genl. Banks has met with a serious repulse, That the Rebels have four Steam Boats up the Red River converted into Gun Boats ready to come down as soon as our transports make their appearance. I give you these reports for what they are worth, simply stating that the Rebels on the West side of Bayou Macon believe them to be true—Genl. Quinby's Division left Grand Lake day before yesterday (the 7th) at 12 M. We have here now about twenty four hundred negroes men, women and children, What is to be done with them when the command leaves? I shall go up to Moon Lake with Genl. Logans Division, probably the last of this week—" ALS, *ibid.*, RG 94, War Records Office, Union Battle Reports. *O.R.*, I, xxiv, part 3, 96.

On March 10, McPherson wrote to USG. "Col: Bissell came down last night and reported that he could now take boats in from the Miss' River to 'Bayou Macon,' I accordingly went up to see, and do not think the route practicable as yet though there is no doubt that in five or six days when the back country becomes filled with water it can be done, The water is now rushing like a torrent through several of the crevasses he has made, & the back country is filling up so fast that a strong current sets from Bayou Baxter into Lake Providence. In consequence of the water incomoding you so much opposite Vicksburg do you want any of the Boats ~~released~~ sent by Genl. Quinby from Moon Lake and ordered to stop here to take up Genl. Logan's Division, sent down to you? None of them have arrived yet, though I shall expect some by day after tomorrow." ALS, DNA, RG 94, War Records Office, Union Battle Reports. *O.R.*, I, xxiv, part 3, 98.

1. On March 9, Govy Hood, Lake Providence, wrote to Col. George W. Deitzler that he had suffered property losses at the hands of U.S. troops although he was a loyal citizen. ALS, DNA, RG 109, Union Provost Marshals' File of Papers Relating to Individual Civilians. On the same day, Deitzler endorsed the letter. "Respectfully forwarded, I believe the statements contained in the within communication to be true. The soldiers who extorted the money—$30,000—from Mr Hood, belonged to my Brigade, 15 to the 17th Ill Vols and 5 to the 95th Ill vols—when they discovered that they were about to be arrested for the robbery they all deserted and have not yet returned, I have no doubt that the losses sustained by Mr Hood, since the Federal troops came to this place, by this robbery and the unauthorized taking and destruction of property, amount to not less than $40.000. All who know Mr Hood testify that he is a quiet and peacible Citizen and that he has never been in arms against our Government nor given aid or

encouragement to the enemies of the same. Under these circumstances, and under the impression that it is not the policy of the Government to seize and confiscate the cotton or other private property of such citizens in the confederate states, I respectfully recommend that the prayer of Mr Hood be granted." AES, *ibid*. On the same day, McPherson endorsed the statement. "Respectfully forwarded. Mr. Hood's money was taken & property destroyed about a week before my arrival—" AES, *ibid*. On March 14, Q. M. Capt. John G. Klinck authorized Hood to ship 291 bales of cotton to Memphis. Copy, *ibid*., RG 92, Letters Received by Capt. Asher R. Eddy. Because the steamboat arrived at Memphis with 304 bales consigned by Hood, Brig. Gen. Lorenzo Thomas questioned the transaction. Thomas to Secretary of War Edwin M. Stanton, June 23, 1863, LS, *ibid*., RG 94, Letters Received, 815A 1863. See letter to Col. William S. Hillyer, March 23, 1863.

To Brig. Gen. William A. Hammond

Head Qrs Dep't of the Tenn:
Before Vicksburg, March 12, 1863

BRIG: GEN'L W. A. HAMMOND
SURGEON GENERAL U. S. A.
SIR,

Surg: J. R. Smiths letter of the 20th of February, is just received inquiring into the Sanitary condition of this command, and asking for suggestions for its improvement.[1] I know a great deal has been said to impress the public generally, and all officials particularly, with the idea that this Army was in a suffering condition, and mostly from neglect. This is most erroneous. The health of this command will compare favorably with that of any Army in the field, I venture to say, and every preparation is made for the sick that could be desired.

I venture the assertion that no Army ever went into the field with better arranged preparations for receiving sick and wounded soldiers than this. We have Hospital Boats expressly fitted up, and with the Government and Volunteer Sanitary supplies, it is a great question whether one person in ten can be so well taken care of at their homes as the Army here can.

I will refer Surgeon Smiths letter to my Medical Director for a fuller report of the condition of the Medical Department here.

I am Sir, Very Respectfully
Your Obt Servt
U. S. GRANT
Major General

Copies, DNA, RG 112, Letters Received; *ibid.*, RG 393, Dept. of the Tenn., Hd. Qrs. Correspondence; DLC-USG, V, 5, 8, 24, 94. William A. Hammond, born in Annapolis, Md., in 1828, a medical graduate of the University of the City of New York in 1848, entered the U.S. Army as asst. surgeon in 1849, resigning in 1860 for a professorship at the University of Maryland at Baltimore. When he entered the U.S. Army in 1861, he had lost his prewar seniority, but the need for leadership in the Medical Dept. led to his appointment as surgeon-gen. on April 25, 1862. On March 23, 1863, Hammond wrote to USG. "I have been much gratified by the reception of your letter of the 12th inst. I was satisfied that in no event could things be as bad as represented—and I knew that you have always shown yourself solicitous for the welfare of the army under your command   I must thank you for the constant support you have given to the officers of the Medical Department under your command"   ALS, DNA, RG 393, Dept. of the Tenn., Letters Received.

1. Joseph R. Smith of N. Y., who entered the U.S. Army in 1854 as asst. surgeon, was promoted to surgeon as of June 11, 1862. On Feb. 20, Smith wrote to USG. "The Surgeon General directs me to address you, stating that very many complaints have reached this Office in reference to the management of the Medical Department of your Army—The Surgeon General has twice during the winter made formal application for permission to visit the Armies of the West for the purpose of learning their exact condition, and of taking in concert with Commanding Generals such steps as might be found necessary to promote the efficiency of the Medical Department; the permission desired was not granted—I am instructed to ask you for any suggestion you may be disposed to make tending to promote an effective hospital service, whether relating to increase of supplies or a change in the personnel of the Medical Staff in your Department." LS, *ibid.*

To Maj. Gen. Stephen A. Hurlbut

[*March 13, 1863*]

. . . whilst you can retain your present command I would . . . beg you to hold on . . . I have never failed to give you a good name and especially have I done this to Halleck who you can

count on as a fast friend . . . Anything I can do for you or any
testamonials that I can give in your behalf will be most freely
given and in a way too to assure any reader that they are not
merely idle and given because asked but that they are felt and
earnest.

The Collector, March, 1947, A360; *ibid.*, June, 1951, W971. The nomination of
Stephen A. Hurlbut to serve as maj. gen. from Sept. 17, 1862, had been returned
with others by the U.S. Senate to President Abraham Lincoln since appointments
were dated during a recess of Congress. Hurlbut's nomination, resubmitted by
Lincoln, was confirmed on March 13, 1863.

To *Maj. Gen. James B. McPherson*

Before Vicksburg March 13th 1863

MAJ GEN J. B. MCPHERSON
COMM'DG 17TH ARMY CORPS

Lagow has just returned and called my attention to several
points that you want instructions on. As regards Quinby: going
into the pass with his present transports, he is the best judge of
the practibility. Let him use a proper discretion. I have sent
North for small class Steamers, which should be expected to
commence arriving soon. In regard to the contrabands the question is a troublesome one. I am not permitted to send them out
of the Department, and such numbers as we have it is hard to
keep them in. You have received my order with regard to the
Pioneer Corps: This will enable you to use three hundred men
to each Division[1]   The balance will be left at Lake Providence
as being as it is a Military Post. When it is broken up they will
have to be sent to Memphis, or some other prominent Post.
Memphis will be the place in the absence of other instructions

Exercise your own judgement about when the the levee
should be cut at Lake Providence.

The object of having cotton brought in is to make some of
our transports into rams. I will send up for what you have col-

lected which with what we have, I think will be sufficient for the purpose.

The Yazoo Expedition seems to move slow. Wilson thinks the ranking Naval Officer is somewhat to blame.[2] I am anxious to see Quinby in with his force. I have a great deal of confidence in his judgement and still more in the increased force there will be in the Yazoo when he gets there.

My instructions may not have been plain in one point, but I want Quinby to move until he joins Ross, as rapidly as possible and not wait for transports to take his whole Division. Have him go in just as rapidly as transports can take him.

U. S. GRANT
Maj Genl.

Copies, DLC-USG, V, 19, 30; DNA, RG 393, Dept. of the Tenn., Letters Sent. *O.R.*, I, xxiv, part 3, 105.

On March 13, 1863, Maj. Gen. James B. McPherson, Lake Providence, wrote to USG. "Enclosed please find copies of Dispatches just received from Gens. Quinby & Ross which will give you an idea of the difficulties they have to contend with, The whole country on the East side of the Miss' in the Vicinity of 'Yazoo Pass' and in 'Moon Lake' is overflowed and Genl. Quinby was obliged to disembark his Troops on the Western Bank of the Miss, not far from the Pass on the only dry ground he could find, As Genl. Quinby was obliged to discharge some Boats for Repairs only six have returned and I cannot learn that any more are coming down, These will carry about two thirds of Logan's Division, unless I can obtain more Boats, it will take over two weeks to get the command here to the entrance to 'Moon Lake' I am extremely anxious to get into the 'Yazoo' as soon as possible with reinforcements, for I am apprehensive that Quinby will meet with a stronger force than he can attend to General Logan's Division will commence embarking tomorrow and will probably be off the day after, or at least as much of it as the Boats can carry Col. Lagow has I presume given you all the points in relation, to cotton, contrabands, cutting the Levee, &c," ALS, DNA, RG 94, War Records Office, Union Battle Reports. *O.R.*, I, xxiv, part 1, 403. The report of Brig. Gen. Isaac F. Quinby is *ibid.*, p. 404; reports of Brig. Gen. Leonard F. Ross addressed to Brig. Gen. Benjamin M. Prentiss are *ibid.*, pp. 393–94.

On March 15, McPherson wrote to USG. "Your dispatch by Lt. Gile was received last evening, The instructions to Genl. Quinby were to push forward to the support of Genl. Ross as rapidly as possible which I am confident he will do, as he is fully awake as to the importance of the matter, The 1st & 2nd Brigades of Genl. Logan's Division are embarking this morning & will in all probability get off this afternoon, There are not boats enough here to take the whole Division, Since the water has risen so that the country between here and 'Bayou Macon' can be explored by in small Boats I have had out several exploring parties, and Capt. Hickenlooper has just returned having discovered a thoroughly practicable route indicated by the *red line* on the enclosed sketch,—With the exception of one point where you leave *Bayou Baxter* at "A"—the water is from seven to Eight feet deep along an open wash sixty feet wide, At the point "A" it is between 2½' & 3' feet deep and still rising at the rate of from ten to twelve inches in 24 hours, When the Levee is cut here, which I propose to have done—as soon as I can get the Troops & public property on ground which will be overflowed removed—it will rise very much higher & faster—Genl. Logan goes up with his two Brigades under instructions to disembark them near or at the Yazoo Pass if the ground will admit and send the Boats back here for the balance of his command and a portion of Genl. McArthurs, He is also instructed to embark on small Boats, suitable to run the 'Pass' and push on to the support of Genl. Quinby as rapidly as possible, I shall go up on the next trip of the Boats—" ALS, DNA, RG 393, Dept. of the Tenn., Letters Received. *O.R.*, I, xxiv, part 3, 110. See letter to Maj. Gen. James B. McPherson, March 14, 1863.

1. On March 7, Lt. Col. John A. Rawlins issued Special Orders No. 66. "There will be added by Division Commanders to the Pioneer Corps of each Division, required to be organized by Special Field Orders No. 22 of date December 13th 1862, three hundred contrabands to be taken from those now within our lines, and such as may hereafter be collected They will be organized into Squads of thirty in charge of enlisted men under the directions of the officers of the respective Pioneer Corps They will be mustered monthly on company muster rolls and their names will also be borne on the Quartermasters report of the respective Divisions of 'Persons and things employed and hired' three dollars of which monthly pay may be in clothing. Rations and clothing will be issued to them on proper requisitions the same as to enlisted men, the issue of rations being governed by the regulations established by the Chief Commissary in the issue of rations to contrabands These contrabands will be used for fatigue duty as far as practicable, for the purpose of saving every soldier possible to the ranks" Copies, DLC-USG, V, 27, 28; DNA, RG 393, Dept. of the Tenn., General and Special Orders; *ibid.*, Special Orders. On Feb. 24, Rawlins had written to Maj. Gen. Stephen A. Hurlbut. "Please send to this place with as little delay as possible as many able-bodied Negro laborers as can be had or spared from Memphis and other portions of your command. They are much needed here for work on the Canal." LS, *ibid.*, 16th Army Corps, Letters Received. *O.R.*, I, xxiv, part 3, 65.

2. Lt. Commander Watson Smith. See letter to Maj. Gen. Benjamin M. Prentiss, March 17, 1863. On March 12, Act. Rear Admiral David D. Porter wrote to USG. "Lieut Comdr Watson Smith informs me that he has but a month's supply of provisions. I am anxious to supply him but have no vessel. Can you furnish me with a small steamer that will go, without fail, through the pass and join the vessels and troops you have sent up ? He will also want ammunition which I will send him by same conveyance." LS, DNA, RG 94, War Records Office, Dept. of the Tenn. *O.R.*, I, xxiv, part 1, 409; *O.R.* (Navy), I, xxiv, 267–68. Porter enclosed reports of March 3 and 7 from Smith, U.S.S. *Rattler*, describing his advance on the Tallahatchie and Coldwater rivers. LS, DNA, RG 94, War Records Office, Dept. of the Tenn. *O.R.*, I, xxiv, part 1, 409–11; *O.R.* (Navy), I, xxiv, 262–64.

To Maj. Gen. Benjamin M. Prentiss

Head Quarters, Dept. of the Ten
Before Vicksburg, March 13th 1863

Gen. B. M. Prentiss
Comd.g Dist. E. Ark.
Gen

You are doing perfectly right, and are carrying out previous instructions, by holding the pass from the Mississippi into Cold-water. Being near the entrance I want you to supply everything to the command they require. Rations and coal may be required soon. If so send them without delay.

Give me all the news you receive from the Yazoo expedition promptly and direct without sending through the Army Corps Commander.

Very respectfully
your obt. svt.
U. S. Grant
Maj. G[en]

ALS, Mrs. Leah G. Carter, Bethany, Mo. *O.R.*, I, xxiv, part 3, 105. On March 10, 1863, Maj. Gen. Benjamin M. Prentiss, Helena, wrote to USG. "I have the honor to enclose to you herewith copies of the despatches received by me last night from Brig. Gen. Ross commanding the Yazoo Expedition—I have furnished copies of the same to Brig. Gen. Quinby for his information and guidance, and have prof-fered him all the assistance in my power for the furtherance of his expedition—I send you copies of Gen. Ross' communications as the best report I can make of the progress of his movement—" LS, DNA, RG 393, Dept. of the Tenn., Letters Received. Prentiss enclosed letters of March 7 and 8 from Brig. Gen. Leonard F. Ross. Copies, *ibid. O.R.*, I, xxiv, part 1, 393–95. On March 11, Prentiss wrote to USG. "States sending out 500 men to break camp of Rebel reported between Big & sick Rivers and that no considerable party are there." DLC-USG, V, 21; DNA, RG 393, Dept. of the Tenn., Register of Letters Received.

On March 2, Ross wrote to Lt. Col. John A. Rawlins requesting a leave of absence for sixty days to attend to private business. ALS, *ibid.*, RG 94, ACP, R154 CB 1863. On March 14, USG endorsed this letter. "Approved and respect-fully forwarded to Headquarters of the Army, Washington, D. C." ES, *ibid.* On March 30, Col. Edward D. Townsend, AGO, wrote to USG. "The Application for a leave of absence for Brigadeir General Leonard F. Ross has been submitted to the General in Chief and in reply he directs me to say that it cannot, at this time, be granted." Copies, *ibid.*, Letters Sent; *ibid.*, RG 393, Military Div. of the Miss., Letters Received from the War Dept.; DLC-USG, V, 93.

To Capt. Asher R. Eddy

Before Vicksburg March 13th 1863

CAPT A. R. EDDY. A. Q. M.

MEMPHIS, TENN.

My attention has been called to the fact unofficially, that monies received in this Department from rents of rebel property confiscated cotton &c are not used within the Department. Col Reynolds has never mentioned this to me, and I do not know that such are the facts. If they are however I want them corrected, and will give an order that the funds collected from all sources be turned over to the cheif Quartermaster for distribution among the various Quartermasters

This will not of course prevent your keeping so much of such funds as are required to run your end of the machine.

U. S. GRANT

Maj Genl.

Copies, DLC-USG, V, 19, 30; DNA, RG 393, Dept. of the Tenn., Letters Sent.

To Maj. Gen. James B. McPherson

Head Quarters Dept of the Tenn
Before Vicksburg Miss
March 14th 1863

MAJ GEN J B MCPHERSON

COMM'DG 17TH ARMY CORPS

GENERAL.

I send a steamer for the purpose of bulk heading two or more steamers to be used as rams in case of necessity

Do not move up the river with the remainder of your forces until you receive further notice from me. Admiral Porter has made a reconnoisance which demonstrated the practicability of getting all the smaller class of Gun-boats and Rams through Steele's Bayou and across Bayou at the Yazoo river above the raft[1]   This if so will enable me to land my forces on Johnson's plantation[2] and fully arrange them whilst holding a footing in the Yazoo river and keep them to-gether. Gun-boats will be able to move up the river and meet Quinby coming down and convoy him directly to the balace of your Army Corps

Instruct Quinby to move down with great caution, but as if no force was to be expected but what is already in his own Division and Smith's from Memphis

Keep this move an entire secret as it is not suspected by the enemy and there is no telling, sometimes, how they are enabled to get information

Very Respectfully
U S GRANT
Maj Gen

Copies, DLC-USG, V, 19, 30; DNA, RG 393, Dept. of the Tenn., Letters Sent. On March 15, 1863, Maj. Gen. James B. McPherson, Lake Providence, wrote to USG. "Dispatch just recd. Genl. Logan's 1st & 2nd Brigades were on board and just ready to move, have stopped them, and shall let them remain on board until further orders— . . . P. S No Boats here to take another soldier—" ALS, *ibid.*, RG 94, War Records Office, Dept. of the Tenn. *O.R.*, I, xxiv, part 3, 110.

1. The route through Steele's Bayou, which involved leaving the Yazoo River near the mouth and returning to it above C.S.A. fortifications, was more fully described in USG's letter to Maj. Gen. Henry W. Halleck, March 17, 1863. Act. Rear Admiral David D. Porter reconnoitered Steele's Bayou on March 13. Log Book of U.S.S. *Carondelet*, DNA, RG 24. An error concerning the date of this reconnaissance in *O.R.* (Navy), I, xxiv, 687, and USG's *Memoirs*, I, 453, is corrected in Myron J. Smith, Jr., "Gunboats in a Ditch: The Steele's Bayou Expedition, 1863," *Journal of Mississippi History*, XXXVII, 2 (May, 1975), 167*n*.

2. Johnson's Plantation at the mouth of Steele's Bayou.

To Act. Rear Admiral David D. Porter

Before Vicksburg March 16 1863

Admiral D D. Porter
Comm'dg Miss Squadron

I sent to day one boat with soldiers and send to-morrow two more, all I have suited to that navigation.

I will send in the morning troops to the Bayou where it approaches the Mississippi the nearest which will have to be ferried up with the boats there. This will give you seven or eight hundred troops on arrivals of the boats, and all you ask as fast as they can be taken up from the point designated

All the cooking utensils and rations for the command will be taken on the boat that goes directly through so that there will be nothing but men to embark at the midway point

U. S. Grant
Maj Gen.

Copies, DLC-USG, V, 19, 30; DNA, RG 393, Dept. of the Tenn., Letters Sent. On March 16, 1863, Act. Rear Admiral David D. Porter, Steele's Bayou, wrote to USG. "The boats ahead, got up before me, and improvidently went in before the Bayou was clear. The work has not been very hard, and we are within a quarter of a mile of 'Deer Creek,' but it is ~~impossible~~ indispensible that we should have at least *three thousand* troops *at once* to hold our present position. If the enemy were to throw in troops, they could stop our work, and put us in a very tight place. I want to see the Soldiers! Please send them at once, if with only one day's rations. The work is quite practicable, tho' it looks bad before the boats go through. Yours in haste.—At present the head boats are stuck between the trees. The Champion got up here without the Mortars. The Benten cannot come through unless the place is cleared more than it is at present" LS, *ibid.*, Letters Received. *O.R.* (Navy), I, xxiv, 480–81.

Also on March 16, USG wrote a note addressed to "Gen.," probably intended for Maj. Gen. William T. Sherman. "Read the enclosed note to Admiral Porter and enclose it in another envelope for him. It is in answer to the enclosed just received. . . . P. S. I am sending the balance of Stuarts Div." ANS, Winterthur Mss., Eleutherian Mills Historical Library, Greenville, Del.

To Maj. Gen. James B. McPherson

Before Vicksburg March 16, 1863

MAJ GEN J. B. MCPHERSON
COMMDG 17TH ARMY CORPS.

I returned this morning from a reconnoisance some thirty miles up Steele's Bayou   Admiral Porter and myself went in in a large Gunboat preceeded by four of the old "Turtles"[1]

These boats are pushing on with all dispatch to get into the Yazoo. It is important that a force should get in there with all dispatch   I have information direct from Vicksburg and the Yazoo river both from persons who have been there and from late papers that our Gunboats had been down to Greenwood and exchanged a few shots with the fort at that place.[2] The enemy have sent up reinforcements from Vicksburg and some more guns. If we can get our boats in the rear of them in time, it will so confuse the enemy as to save Ross' force. If they do not I shall feel restless for his fate until I know that Quinby has reached him. Quinby will have the most abundant force for that route with his Division and that of John E Smith. I am now almost sorry that I directed the latter to join him

I seems impossible to get Steamers of the class we want   I sent long enough since for them to have received them from Pittsburg if necessary.

The route through Bayou Macon may prove a good thing for us yet in some operation. But this one to get all our forces in one place and that where it will be in striking distance of the enemy's lines of communications North is the most important until a firm foothold is secured on the side with the enemy.

It may be several days before I will move Logan   His freight had better be kept aboard, but the men might stay on shore as much as possible.

U. S. GRANT
Maj Genl

Copies, DLC-USG, V, 19, 30; DNA, RG 393, Dept. of the Tenn., Letters Sent. *O.R.*, I, xxiv, part 3, 112; *O.R.* (Navy), I, xxiv, 480.

On March 18, 1863, Maj. Gen. James B. McPherson, Lake Providence, wrote to USG. "The Levee was cut here yesterday afternoon and the water is flowing in at a tremendous rate filling up the Lake and Bayous. We will soon be able to take a good sized Steamer in. I have directed Genl. Logan to go up about 5 miles where there is comparatively high ground, and disembark and send the boats back for the remainder of his Division. If the country about the Lake is likely to be *overflowed* I shall move Genl. McArthur's Division up to the same point—" ALS, DNA, RG 94, War Records Office, Dept. of the Tenn. *O.R.*, I, xxiv, part 3, 120.

1. The seven ironclad gunboats built by James B. Eads early in the Civil War had been nicknamed "turtles." The *Louisville, Cincinnati, Carondelet, Mound City,* and *Pittsburg,* with four mortarboats and four tugs, comprised the Steele's Bayou expedition. *O.R.* (Navy), I, xxiv, 474.

2. Greenwood, Miss., on the Yazoo River, about three miles below Fort Pemberton, where C.S.A. forces halted the Yazoo Pass expedition.

To Maj. Gen. William T. Sherman

Millikins Bend
March 16th 1863

GEN. SHERMAN,
DEAR SIR:

I have just returned from a reconnoisance up Steele's Bayou with the Admiral and five of his gun boats. With some labor in cuting tree tops out of the way it will be navigable for any class of steamers.

I want you to have either your Pioneer corps or one regiment of good men for such work detailed and at the landing as soon as possible.

The party will want to take with them their rations & arms and sufficient camp & garrison equipage for a few days.

I will have a boat at any point you may designate as early as the men can be there. The 8th Mo. being many of them boatmen would be excellent men for this purpose.

As soon as you give directions for these men to be in readiness come up and see me and I will explain fully. The Tug that takes this is instructed to wait for you.

A full supply of axes will be required.

Very respectfully

U. S. GRANT

Maj. Gen.

ALS, DLC-William T. Sherman. Maj. Gen. William T. Sherman endorsed this letter at 8:00 A.M. on March 16, 1863. "Col Giles H Smith will have the 8th Mo. at the Landing steamer Depot as quick as possible armed & with axes Capt Terry Engrs will supply as many axes as they want—and will send along some Pioneers." AES, *ibid.* Col. Giles A. Smith acknowledged receipt at 9:15 A.M. AES, *ibid.* After receiving USG's letter at Young's Point, Sherman conferred with USG at Milliken's Bend; the conference led to the following letter. *Memoirs of Gen. W. T. Sherman* (4th ed., New York, 1891), I, 334.

To Maj. Gen. William T. Sherman

Head Quarters, Dept. of the Ten.

Before Vicksburg, March 16th 1863,

MAJ. GEN. W. T. SHERMAN,

COMD.G 15TH ARMY CORPS,

GEN.

You will proceed as early as practicable up Steele's Bayou and through Black Bayou to Deer Creek and thence with the Gunboats now there by any route they may take to get into the Yazoo river for the purpose of ~~making a~~ determining the feasability of geting an Army through that route to the East bank of that river and at a point from which they can act advantageously against Vicksburg.

Make such details from your Army Corps as may be required to clear out the channel of the various bayous through which transports would have to run, and to hold such points as, in your judgement, should be occupied.

I place at your disposal to-day the steamers Silver Wave & Diligent, the only two suitable for the present navigation of this route. Others will be supplied you as fast as required and they can be got.

I have given directions, and you may repeat them, that the party going on board the steamer Diligent push on until they reach Black Bayou only stopping sufficiently long at any point before reaching there to remove such obstructions as prevent their own progress. Capt. Kossack will go with this party. The other boat load will commence their work in Steeles Bayou and make the navigation as free as possible all the way through.

There is but little work to be done in Steeles bayou except for about five miles about Midway of the bayou. In this portion many overhanging trees will have to be removed and should be draged out of the channel.

Very respectfully

U. S. GRANT

Maj. Gen. Com

ALS, DLC-William T. Sherman. *O.R.*, I, xxiv, part 3, 112–13; *O.R.* (Navy), I, xxiv, 481. See preceding letter.

On March 16, 1863, Maj. Gen. William T. Sherman, Deer Creek, wrote to USG. "I came up Steeles Bayou and overtook the fleet of Iron Clads just before they reached Deer Creek. Four of them have gone up Deer Creek to Rolling Fork cut off, then into Sun-flour, thence into Yazoo just below Yazoo City. The Louisville remains here, but goes up the moment I can get a guard through to this point. Deer Creek is not as large, nor has it as much current as I expected, but the water is deep & narrow.   the iron clads push their way along, unharmed, but the trees and overhanging limbs tear the wooden boats all to pieces. I found the Diligent nearly up to the Fleet, and they have been at work today, but most of the time was engaged in collecting rafts whereon to stand whilst cutting trees. I dont think any boat can as yet come through this, Black Bayou. We will push the work. There is no high land here, nor is the route practicable for troops, unless the admiral cleans out the Yazoo and secures the mouth of Deer Creek, when I might use Deer Creek as the route for a diverting force.   the main attack on Haines Bluff must be in larger boats directly up the main Yasoo. None but my small boats can navigate Deer Creek. I dont think we can make a lodgemt on high land by this route on account of the difficulty of navigation. The admiral wants me to hold this place secure for him whilst he operates above and I will undertake it. We are only 25 miles by land from Haines Bluff, but I dont apprehend they will do more than land a party up to ascertain our strength & purposes. One Brigade, Giles A Smith is as much as should be sent here till the trees are cut away. The plantation here is not more than 3 feet above water, and is the same kind of ground we have on the Mississippi. I send the Diligent back having landed the 8th Missouri here, a arranged for bringing it through the Bayou in a Coal barge towed by a tug. Col Ihrie will describe the topographical features of this locality." ALS,

DNA, RG 94, War Records Office, Dept. of the Mo. *O.R.*, I, xxiv, part 1, 431;
O.R. (Navy), I, xxiv, 483–84.

Also on March 16, Lt. Col. John A. Rawlins wrote to Col. Giles A. Smith.
"You will please hold in readiness one Regiment of your Command, with their
transportation camp and garrison equippage complete and four days rations for
embarkation to morrow morning 17th inst. at the lower landing where a Steamer
has been ordered to be in waiting for them. Hold the remainder of your Brigade
in readiness to move on receipt of orders   You will report in person at these
Head Quarters to morrow morning for detailed instructions"   Copies, DLC-
USG, V, 19, 30; DNA, RG 393, Dept. of the Tenn., Letters Sent. On the same
day, Rawlins wrote to Brig. Gen. David Stuart. "You will hold the entire Infantry
force of your Division, with one day's rations in haversacks, their arms, ammunition and accoutrements in readiness for embarkation by 8 o'clock A. M. to-morrow
morning, the 17th inst., at the upper landing, where Steamboats have been ordered
to be in waiting for them. Five days rations, and the ammunition not required to
be carried by the men by existing orders, together with their axes, will be put on
board the Steamer Silver Wave at the lower landing early to-morrow morning,
in charge of a non-commissioned officer and three men from each Regiment, to
look after that which belongs to their respective Regiments, and all to be under
Command of a Field Officer. The transportation, Camp and garrison equippage
and the sick will be left in charge of convalescents and suitable medical and commissioned officers. For detailed instructions as to place of debarkation, you will
report in person to these Headqrs." LS, *ibid.*, 15th Army Corps, 2nd Div., Letters
Received.

On March 17, USG wrote to Capt. William Le Baron Jenney. "Send Capt.
Ashmeads Pioneer Company on board the Empress to-night and direct them to
proceed immediately up the river to where Gen. Stuart landed to-day. I go up
to-night and will direct them there what they are to do." ALS, Berg Collection,
NN. On the reverse, Jenney described his response. "Received at 11. PM. At
3 AM. Capt Ashmeads Company, were on their way up Steeles Bayou. Were
landed at a point opposite Eagle's Bend on the Mississippi River. Where they
built a road and bridge across the neck, (distance about 2½ miles,). to enable
troops and supplies to pass from the Mississippi to Steeles Bayou, thus saving
considerable distance of Bayou navigation." ADS, *ibid.*

To Maj. Gen. Henry W. Halleck

Head Quarters, Dept. of the Ten.
Before Vicksburg, March 17th 1863.

MAJ. GEN. H. W. HALLECK,
GEN. IN CHIEF, WASHINGTON D. C.
GEN

Since the giving way of the dam at the upper end of the canal
work with the dredges has progressed favorably, but all attempts

to stop the rush of water into the canal have proven abortive. If required however the canal can be made to pass boats of ordinary size in a few days.

The enemy were busily engaged firing from the opposite hights yesterday and last night at the dredge boat nearest the lower end of the canal. Their their shots done no damage though many of the larger ones reached half way across the point.

Ordinary Ohio river boats can now pass from Lake Providence into Bayou Macon and from thence by easy navigation to the mouth of Red River. I make no calculation upon using this route for the present but it may be turned to practical use after effecting present plans. The same may be said of the canal across the point.

I learn from Jackson Miss. papers of the 14th that one of our gunboats had run down to Greenwood and exchanged a few shots with the fort at that point. Further information from the enemy shows that several thousand troops have gone from Vicksburg up the Yazoo. Besides four gunboats, one of them Iron clad, I have a Division of troops there now and Quinby's Division in the pass on their way down. One Division from Memphis should also be on their way now.

The great difficulty of geting small class steamers adapted to this service has retarded movements by the way of Yazoo Pass materially.

To hem in the enemy on the Yazoo Admiral Porter has gone into Deer Creek by the way of Steeles Bayou and Little Black Bayou. From there he can get into the Yazoo either by runing up Deer Creek to Rolling Fork, thence through the Fork and down the Big Sunflower, all of which is navigable, or down Deer Creek to the Yazoo.

Admiral Porter and myself went up Steeles Bayou to Little Black Bayou on the 15th. With the exception of over hanging trees in some places the navigation was good for the gunboat Gen. Price. I am having those obstructions removed. We were preceded by four of the old Iron clads that found no difficulty in the navigation.

I returned in the evening for the purpose of hurrying up men and means for clearing the channel. I also sent sherman to make a reconnoisance, in company of the gunboats, with the view of affecting a landing with troops on high ground on the East bank of the Yazoo, from which we may act against Hains Bluff.

Last night I received a dispatch from Admiral Porter saying that the Iron clads had pushed into Black Bayou and had reached to within a fourth of a mile of Deer creek where they had become entangled in the timber and could not move until it was cut out, and asking me for a force of 3000 men to act with him.[1] Fortunately I had already sent all the boats at hand suitable for that navigation, and immediately available, could carry. I am now sending the remainder of Sherman's old Division, and will push troops through, if Sherman reports favorably, as fast as our means will admit. These troops go up the Miss. river, in large transports, about thirty miles and to where Steeles Bayou comes within one mile of the Miss. The small class boats can ferry them from that point and thus save the distance from the Mouth of the Yazoo to it ~~that point~~ and also the most difficult part of the navigation in Steeles Bayou.

There is evident indication of considerable excitement in Vicksburg. I think they are removing many of their troops but cannot satisfy myself to what point. Some we know have gone up the Yazoo and it may be others are going to Port Hudson. I have no means of learning anything from below except what is occationally learned through Southern papers.

> I am Gen. Very respectfully
> your obt. svt.
> U. S. GRANT
> Maj. Gen.

ALS, DNA, RG 94, War Records Office, Union Battle Reports. *O.R.*, I, xxiv, part 1, 20–21; (incomplete) *O.R.* (Navy), I, xxiv, 484–85. In DLC-USG, V, 24, and DNA, RG 393, Dept. of the Tenn., Hd. Qrs. Correspondence, this letter is entered as addressed to Brig. Gen. Lorenzo Thomas.

On April 2, 1863, Maj. Gen. Henry W. Halleck wrote to USG. "Your despatch of March 17th, and also your telegrams of March 24th & 25th, were recieved yesterday. While working upon the canal, the division of your forces into

several excentric operations may have been very proper, for the purpose of reconnoitering the country; but it is very important that, when you strike any blow,
you should have your troops sufficiently concentrated to make that blow effective.
The division of your army into small expeditions destroys your strength, and,
when in the presence of an enemy, is very dangerous. What is most desired, and
your attention is again called to this object, is that your forces and those of Genl
Banks should be brought into cooperation as early as possible. If he cannot get up
to cooperate with you on Vicksburg, cannot you get troops down to help him on
Port Hudson? Or, at least can you not destroy Grand Gulf before it becomes too
strong? I know that you can judge of these matters there much better than I can
here; but, as the Prest., who seems to be rather impatient about matters on the
Miss., has several times asked me these questions, I repeat them to you. As the
season when we can do very little on the lower Miss., is rapidly advancing, I hope
you will push matters with all possible despatch." ALS, *ibid.*, RG 108, Letters
Sent (Press). *O.R.*, I, xxiv, part 1, 25.

1. See letter to Act. Rear Admiral David D. Porter, March 16, 1863.

To Maj. Gen. Benjamin M. Prentiss

———————

Head Quarters, Dept. of the Ten.
Before Vicksburg, March 17th 1863.

BRIG. GEN. B. M. PRENTISS,
COMD.G DIST. E. ARK.
GEN.

Your course in in doing everything in aid of the Yazoo expedition is fully sustained and what I wanted and expected. I sent
to Col. Parsons A. Q. M. over two weeks ago for the class of
boats required, and sent a Quartermaster from here on Friday
week to attend to the same thing. As you were not aware of this
however you done right to send an agent to look after them.[1]

It is too late now to send a greater force through the Pass
than has already gone and will be made up with Smith's Division.

My intention was, and is, that Ross shall return to Helena
and Hovey take the field with his Division. Such instructions
have been given Gen. McPherson who I intended should command that expedition.[2]

Now that I have been so much disappointed in geting transports of the right class no more troops will go by that route than what is indicated above. I will make the transfer of Ross' and Hoveys forces as soon as practicable.

The necessity of a large force descending the Yazoo I think has ended by the discovery of a route into the Yazoo from here by the way of Steeles Bayou and other cross Bayous. Five gunboats are now on their way, four of them Iron clads, by this route. If successful this will entirely hem in at least the transports of the enemy and force them to surrender or retreat Eastward. My orders in regard to trade prohibits it below Helena. Trade having been opened by the Treasury Department, to Helena, I did not interfere with it further than to prohibit the landing of boats at any point on the Miss. river other than at places occupied by troops or under protection of a Gunboat. As a corrollary to this all freight assending the river is contraband unless it has a Provost Marshals permit from some point not lower down than Helena, and if taken on where no forces are stationed then Treasurers permits and the statement of the commander of the gunboat affording protection whilst such freight was being loaded, that he had afforded such protection.

You may make such local restrictions to trade as you may think healthful, and keep out and restrict passing through your lines as much as you want. Also, expell all citizens, both from the North and the South, that are troublesome or exercise an unhealthful influance upon the troops. I regard a mersinary ~~Northern~~ pretended Union trader within the lines of an Army as more dangerous than the shrewdest Spy.

> Very respectfully
> U. S. GRANT
> Maj. Gen. Com

ALS, DNA, RG 94, War Records Office, Union Battle Reports. *O.R.*, I, xxiv, part 3, 118–19.

On March 14, 1863, Maj. Gen. Benjamin M. Prentiss, Helena, wrote to USG. "The expedition to the Yazoo River having been very seriously delayed on account of lack of the proper transportation, I have, after mature consultation with Generals Washburne and Hovey, decided to send immediately for all boats of the dimensions mentioned by you, that may be found on the river above here. Gen. Hovey leaves today on this errand, with instructions to proceed forthwith to Memphis, Cairo, St. Louis, Louisville & Cincinnatti, and hurry forward all boats of that class." ALS, DNA, RG 393, Dept. of the Tenn., Letters Received.

On March 16, Prentiss wrote to USG. "Genl Smith with his Division arrived here last night, and was stopped as directed by you. Genl Quinby with a portion of his Division was to be through the Pass into Cold Water yesterday. There are no light Boats arriving, and none here. Fearing that the entire Expedition would be delayed I consulted with Genls Wasburne & Genl. Hovey, and came to the conclusion to send the latter on a flying Trip for Boats for this Expedition and learn that he procured 4 or 5 at Memphis which I expect to arrive to-night   I have not heard from Genl McPherson yet. On yesterday I learned that Genl Ross was getting on without meeting resistance   this information was recd. by a Gentleman who received a letter from an intimate friend of his residing on Yazoo. Stating that Genl Ross had passed his place. 120 miles from here,   One week ago I started two small Steamers to Genl Ross with Subsistence. They have not returned   I think Ross is so far advanced that it will be difficult for me to communicate but he will get a Message either to me or you shortly   I am fully impressed with the necessity of getting McPherson forward promptly and assure you that evry thing shall be done here to that end and trust you will endorse the course taken to hasten forward Transports   Genl I may be too confident but I am of the Opinion that Ross' Expedition ere this have taken Yazoo, City. Genl Hovey will return with Boats in time to go with his Division.   let me ask now do you wish his Division to leave here before Ross' return. I ask this Question from the fact that the order to Hovey was based upon the expected return of Ross. My opinion is that if Ross does not come back—one Brigade of Hovey' should remain here—or that some of the Troops from above should be ordered to this Point. I shall forward all information I receive, and have this day sent to Genl McClernand report of a success on St Francois river   Having several Dispatches I send with them Mr I W Caldwell, who will return with any you have for me. He will ask for some instructions concerning Shippments from here to Memphis please advise me concerning" ALS, *ibid. O.R.*, I, xxiv, part 3, 114–15. A postscript to this letter (*ibid.*, p. 115), copied in Prentiss's letterbook (DNA, RG 393, District of Eastern Ark., Letters Sent), does not appear in the letter received by USG.

On March 18, Maj. Gen. John A. McClernand wrote to USG. "Genl. Prentiss Comd'g Districts of Eastern Arkansas reports under date of the 15. inst: that an expedition sent out by him to reconnoiter up the St Francis river for about 150 or 200 miles has returned. Col. Clayton of the 5th Kansas Cavalry commanded the expedition consisting of 75 men, and one section of Artillery; on board of a small transport. The General seems to think that there is a rebel force in that direction. He says Col Clayton, met, and drove, several detachments of them killing 15 or 20 of their number, and taking 37 prisoners; 27 horses 35 stand of Arms, 15 hhds sugar and 87 bottles of Quinine; besides a quantity of Pork and Bacon. He sustained no loss, excepting two men slightly wounded. Genl. Prentiss is desirous of sending an expedition up the White river, believing that it would be attended with valuable results." Copies (2), McClernand Papers, IHi; DNA, RG 393, 13th Army Corps, Letters Sent.

On March 17, Prentiss wrote to Lt. Col. John A. Rawlins. "I have the honor to enclose with this, for the information of the General comdg. Dept., a copy of a dispatch this day received by me from Brig. Gen. Ross on the Yazoo, giving an account of his meeting with the enemy at Greenwood—also, copy of a plan of the enemy's works at that point, which accompanied the despatch.—These despatches came by the small steamer "Carl," which left Greenwood at 9 a. m. on Saturday last, up to which time the firing had not been re-commenced.—The Carl arrived here this P. M.—having consumed a little over 3 days in the trip—Tomorrow morning I send the "Hamilton Beele" a small boat, with 50.000 rations to Gen. Ross—I enclose also copy of a letter received from Gen. Hovey, whom I have sent on a flying trip to secure small boats—He notes some of the difficulties in the way of obtaining boats suitable to go into the Pass—" LS, *ibid.*, RG 94, War Records Office, Dept. of the Miss. *O.R.*, I, xxiv, part 1, 391–92. For the enclosed letter of Brig. Gen. Leonard F. Ross, March 13, see *ibid.*, p. 395. Prentiss also enclosed a letter of March 15 from Brig. Gen. Alvin P. Hovey, Memphis, listing eleven suitable steamboats. Also enclosed was a letter of March 13, 9:00 P.M., from Lt. Col. James H. Wilson, "Dr. Curtiss' Plantation, near Greenwood, Miss.," to USG. "The land and naval forces constituting the Yazoo Expedition, after many provoking delays arrived at this point on the morning of the 11th, and after a reconnoissance of the fort, and a slight engagement between the "Chilicothe" and one of its heavy guns the troops were landed. The "Chilicothe" on the afternoon of the 11th from a position, near the one indicated on the enclosed sketch, opened her batteries upon the enemy—but in a very short time, received a rifle shot in her left port, killing and wounding fourteen of her crew. On the night of the 11th a cotton bale battery was erected, at the point marked, about 700 yds. from the large gun, with a view to dismounting it if possible. Having no seige guns, a naval 30 pdr. battery was placed in it. On the 12th the naval forces not being ready to attack, nothing was done—but on that night (last) another 30 pdr. was added to the battery; And this morning at 10, it and the "Chilicothe," Baron DeKalb, and the Mortar boat began the attack; but tonight we are not able to perceive any advantage gained. Last night the enemy erected heavy traverses against our Parrott battery, so that it could do him no serious damage today. The rebel position is a strong one—by virtue of the difficulties of approach; though it is defended by only two guns of any weight—one a powerful rifle 6.4, inch bore. Genl. Tilghman is in command—Genl. Loring was there, but recently releived—how many troops he has we cannot ascertain. The "Chilicothe" has not stood the work well; that too at 1100 yards—what may be the result at close range must depend entirely upon chance—I understand, Comd. Smith intends to go close up tomorrow—though I don't think he or his commanders are very sanguine." ALS, DNA, RG 94, War Records Office, Dept. of the Miss. *O.R.*, I, xxiv, part 1, 378–79; *O.R.* (Navy), I, xxiv, 280.

On March 15, 9:00 P.M., Wilson wrote to Rawlins. "We are no nearer Greenwood than when I wrote you night before last. We didn't attack yesterday because the gunboats had not finished their repairs; and put it off to day out of respect for the Sabbath; but tomorrow it is arranged to try it again, though I am not over-sanguine of success since I can see a disposition on the part of the navy to keep from a close and desperate engagement. I've talked with them all & tried to give them backbone but they are not confident. Smith, you doubtless have understood by this time, I don't regard as the equal of Lord Nelson. Walker & Foster of the DeKalb and "Chilicothe," are good men and will cheerfully do what they are ordered; but both think of Comd. Smith just as I do. I don't hesitate to say, that although the rebels got ahead of us in obstructing the Pass, and thereby kept us back ten days, and although we were furnished with miserable old transports and a new element of delay introduced, Comodore Smith is entirely responsible for the detention at this point and the consequent failure of the expedition—and responsible for no other reason than his timid and slow movements. When the iron clads started into the pass, I urged with all the for[c]e I could the absolute necessity of sending them the rams and two mosquitos' forward with all possible despatch; both Foster & Walker and Gen'l. Ross, agreed with this plan; had this been done they could have reached the mouth of the Tallahatchie in four days I think, and even less; I'll bet my life I could have brought them to this point in 3 days—but grant that it would have required five days, that would have brought them to this place on the 1st of March; two whole weeks ago—at which time no heavy guns were here; the rifle did not arrive till about ten days ago. This we have from reliable authority. I haven't time to tell you all the details of our operations here; but in the gunboat engagements, they have suffered pretty heavily, from the effect of the heavy rifle; at the distance of 1100 yds the shots from this gun ha[v]e battered and hammered the armored crafts, sadly; they haven't penetrated but come so near that there is no fun in it. The Chilicothe is an inglorious failure; the wooden backing to her armor is of only 9 inch pine, & shivers into pieces every time the plating is struck; her bolt work flies off at a terrible rate; If she is hit half as many times tomorrow at close range as she has been at long; she'll be in a sad condition; the deKalb stands it well, as long as she is square to the front—though her sides do not fare so well. Add to all this these gentlemen have ammunition for only two hours fighting. I have erected a battery on shore only 700 yds from the rebel fort, and have two 30 pdr. Parrott's and one 8 inch ship gun in position to assist the navy but have only an average of 50 or 60 rounds for them. In addition to this it is intended to embark one brigade in the light draught gunboats, and in case the rebel batteries are silenced they will be landed at the fort to assault it and attack the rebel infantry if it should stand. The latter part of the programme cannot be carried out unless the battery is completely disabled, so that we can run down and break up the raft that lies just above the fort. The old steamship Star of the West is sunk just below the raft across the stream, and they have the John Walsh close to the same place, either ready to sink or use as a boarding craft and ram. We have captured several prisoners but can learn nothing of the rebel force—nothing definite at least. Loring, Tilghman, Col. Wall, of the Texas Legion, The 2nd Texas, 46 & 20 Miss. are all the troops we'v[e] heard of. The 2nd Texas, left Vicksburg on the 15th of Feby. went to Jackson; marched thence to Yazoo City, and came from there by steamer. They are doubtless fortifying Yazoo City strongly.—If we should succeed tomorrow in capturing their fort, and all depends upon the determination and distance, we may succeed in capturing a large number of prisoners. The rebel Fort, called 'Greenwood' & 'Pemberton,' is constructed of cotton bales covered over with sand & earth, and in itself would be very valuable.—Colonel, I've written you freely upon all that concerns this expedition and wish you to preserve my letters; they are semi official—and I believe in no case will you find a misstatement of facts or an error in judgement stated in them. I should have directed them to the General perhaps but upon deliberation thought I could write with more fredom to you, and subserve the same purpose. There is yet one matter to which I wish to call your attention; and that is, notwithstanding, your wish that I should have been consulted, and the General's letter to Gen'l Prentiss, directing the same thing—in no case, and in no regard was my opinion solicited either explicitely or implicitly; directly or indirectly. With reference to the organization of the expedition; I knew as I told you, absolutely nothing of it, till I returned to Moon Lake. Since we have been on the Move Genl. Ross has consulted me freely upon all matters. From all this you will see I am solicitous for my reputation at Head Quarters. I would not have you or any one else imagine I have stood upon punctillio in matters that concern the public Welfare—but to the contrary, I have not hesitated to tender my opinion upon a single occasion, where I thought it worthy of attention—even to the Naval authorities. The only case in which I regret my own negligence, or want of foresight was in not advising Genl. Gorman to send a heavy detachment down the Pass to Coldwater, before we began operations at the levee in order to prevent interference with it. I was thrown off my guard by the appearance of the country giving confirmation to the report of the people that the whole country was flooded from back water and crevasses. Every appearance indicated this to be so—The fact is, it *was* so, nearly everywhere, and the trees had to be cut by men standing in boats. We might have prevented this; and might not: even if we had, the expedition would not have been expedited by it; for as it was it did not get ready to enter till a couple of days after we had returned to Helena. The transports were not ready till two or three days after. But suppose they had been and the trees had not been cut the rebels instead of depending upon the obstructions and difficulties of navigation, to detain us, would have begun at once to fortify at Greenwood,— As the thing stands now, without two or three good iron clads are sent very soon, together with a seige train, of 6 or 8, 8 in howitzers & 30 pd. rifles—Or unless fortune should favor us tomorrow, the game is blocked on us here, as well as below. Should it turn out this way Vicksburg becomes subordinate; Our department secondary & Rosecranz's army our hope in the West. Won't we in that event be required to furnish 50 or 60.000 men?—Before closing this letter, it may not be improper to mention the fact that the rebels are making Great calculations 'to bag us' entire; as long as we are here, that's out of the question and only becomes practicable when they have rammed our iron clads, or carried them by boarding. It is said that they have a battalion of Volunteers from the different Miss. regiments, commanded by Todd, selected for their prowess, and to be used as boarders. We can receive such gentlemen with bloody hands.—What has become of Casey and my horse? Remember me to Bowers, and Osband—say to the latter if he moves his horses from Memphis, to please make arrangements concerning my mare. I wrote you hastily a few evenings ago, and referred to my brother, of the 18th. I wish I could show you the testimonials and recommendations he has received since his court Martial, from Haynie, Sullivan, Brayman, Lawler & his Lt. Col. (who preferred the charges against him and has been at enmity with him) urging his promotion to the majority of the 18th. He has twice rec[ei]ved this promotion, and twice had it withdrawn in favor of political aspirants. He ought to have it now. And if you can do anything for him, I wish you would. Remember me kindly to the General, and say I will write again when the result of tomorrow's attack is known. I believe I explained the difficulty of land operations here arising from the high water. Nearly the whole country is under water; there is no way of our reaching the fort except by landing against it with our boats, after the guns are silent and the raft destroyed. Write me about affairs below and the prospect. Your letter of the latest date was very interesting. Accept my grateful acknowledgements of the kind sentiments manifested towards me & believe me Dear Rawlins. . . . I would write you more to night if I thought there was no probability of my writing again—I have learned since this expedition to think I bear a charmed life. God Bless John A. Logan; don't his letter ring splendidly? With such men we'll crush these rebels, at home a[n]d before us, certain; I hope to God they'll confirm him Major General. Remember me again to Jo. Bowers—and tell him I wish I had some of his good clothes; I'm getting down." ALS, DNA, RG 94, War Records Office, Union Battle Reports. Incomplete in *O.R.*, I, xxiv, part 1, 380–82.

On March 16, Wilson wrote to USG. "I wrote you hurriedly a few days ago, and to Col. Rawlins, quite fully last night. I am sorry to say we are no nearer the accomplishment of our object tonight than we were yesterday. In accordance with the arrangement between Genl. Ross and the Comodore, we had placed an eight inch shell gun in battery with our Parrott's last night, and were ready at daylight to make the final effort. Gen'l. Ross selected the three best regiments of his command and embarked them on three of the light clad gun boats, ready to throw them ashore at the battery provided the heavy guns of the enemy should be silenced and the raft broken so as to permit a landing. About noon, our battery opened and were vigorously replied to by some rifled field pieces, from two little batteries, erected on the bank of the Yazoo, 3 or 400 yards below the Fort, last night. Our eight inch gun was well handled but having only the muzzle of their heavy gun to fire at, could not have effected much without great good fortune. Then too the rebels were supplied with plenty of cotton bales, which they used judiciously in covering their piece; In a few minutes after the land battery opened, the Chilicothe followed by the DeKalb, moved out with the intention of 'going in' upon the well established principle of gunboat warfare, 'close quarters and quick work, but the Former had hardly reached her old position 1100 yards from the fort before she was struck with great violence, several times and in fifteen minutes, during which her two guns were fired only seven times, she was struck six times, with solid 8 *inch* shot and the rifled 6.4 inch gun, resulting in closing 'hermetically' both ports, so that neither could be opened, till they were lifted off and hammered out. The DeKalb for the reason that the "Chilicothe" was compelled to retire, was also drawn out.—The fire from our land battery was kept up till night, and with so much effect that, I am convinced the two boats assisting it, would have had a better chance than at any previous time—I urged that the DeKalb alone should try it at close quarters, but it was not done. Our sharp shooters, were pushed out through the overflow, to a point only 450 yards distant from the rebel batteries and succeeded in annoying their gunners very greatly. The rebel 8 inch gun was mounted and placed in position last night; and a few more days of such policy as we have been compelled to adopt by the tardy unreadiness of the naval Commander, will enable them to make Fort Greenwood entirely efficient against any force that can operate against it from this quarter. It has already shown considerable power in resisting gunboats and battering them. The Chilicothe has been under its fire *five* times, varying from 15 minutes to an hour and a quarter, during which she has been hit 52 times! And I don't hesitate to say is now almost incapable of further active service. In the first place, she is a great, cheat and swindle upon the government. Her plating is laid against abacking of only 9 inches of pine wood, and fastened on by spikes shaped thus (6 inches), instead of bolts with taps and screws. The framing which supports the plating, is broken short, nearly the middle of the two ports, and has settled down so that the grating over the top has to be propped up in order that the stearing wheel may be turned. Another 8 inch solid shot between the ports will bring the whole turrett down. If we had the guns, and materials, and a good supply of ammunition, with another division of troops, we might be able to erect counter batteries on this and the left bank of the Tallahatchie river, sufficiently strong to silence the rebel guns, every where else, but at the positions of the two pointing up the river; and by means of raft and boat bridges throw our troops upon the point in rear, or beyond the present line of rebel works. But with the troops now here, without siege materials of any kind, it's impossible to do any thing without the gun boats first silencing the large guns. Remember the enemy is in an isolated position, unapproachable by land, and no way for transports to reach him except by the river; directly in front of his heavy guns—We can get within about 450 yards of their works, or different parts of them on both banks of the Tallahatchie and at one place on the left bank, can approach nearly opposite their camps, but it seems to me without a direct approach to the fort, no serious damage can be done them, for they can traverse their guns from oblique fire easily, and still command the river. However, I am perfectly certain the place can be taken in time, by a *proper and prompt array* of Strength, and all the necessary materials for such an operation; I have no confidence in the snap or activity of the present naval Commander in this quarter and don't hesitate to say I regard him entirely responsible for the failure to take this place without a fight. His juniors, Capt.s Foster and Walker I believe will bear me out in this; they both agreed with me in the policy to be pursued and both attribute our failure to its neglect. There is no doubt but that with all the difficulties we encountered, the iron-clads could have been here by the 1st instant; there is just as lit- doubt that we would have found this point unprepared for resistance. Before adopting the policy of concentrating a heavy force here there are one or two points to be regarded. First: the confluence of the Yalobusha and the Tallahatchie, is a position of considerable importance, as being the key to a large area of rich country—at the head of a river capable of *easy* navigation for large steamers, while to approach it, we are compelled to thread several streams, with more or less difficulties of navigation to overcome. Without the gun boats sent, could of themselves, silence and destroy the rebel batteries at once; we should be compelled to adopt the slow and tedious process of a siege— under no very favorable circumstances—A siege, with the object of silencing and destroying their guns, in the first place and in the second, to cross the river in such force as expell the rebels from the point and hold it ourselves till the obstacles to navigation could be removed. I don't undertake to say how many days this would require but it is quite clear, that as the matter now stands, it would require several weeks. A fall of ten feet in the Mississippi would probably prevent the return of our transports and Naval vessels; there would then remain, the necessity of going out by the Yazoo, or of burning the boats. A contingency of this kind *could* be prevented by beginning the operation with the understanding that it should be abandoned, when the river had fallen a certain amount. There is yet one other point in the enemy's favor. He can move guns up the railroad to Panola, and float them down to the Mouth of Coldwater, and unless that point is vigilantly guarded, can erect a strong battery there. I have suggested that a regiment of troops and one 'tin' clad be left or sent to that point as soon as possible. There is also, a great chance yet for us. If the water rises four feet more here, it will flood almost the entire country—so much of it, at any rate, that the rebels cannot occupy their present position. To induce this rise, I have advised Gen'l. Ross to write to Genl. Prentiss, requesting him to put a strong force at work destroying the levee near the entrance to the Pass. The General's letter will go out by the naval despatch boat that leaves in the morning. If the river is still as high as it was at the last dates we had, an opening even a half mile wide, near the entrance will let in an immense volume of water, but whether enough to produce the desired effect is the problem to be solved. It's worth trying, I think.—We had one man wounded in the land battery today. A six pounder rifle shot came in at the embrasure, traversed a cotton bale from end to end, and took off his arm. Several of our men have been wounded in different skirmishes, and, have taken several prisoners.— You will please remember, General, that I am not responsible for the defects in the organization of this expedition, neither directly nor indirectly for although you were good enough to direct Gen'l. Prentiss to answer my suggestions and 'requisitions for troops and materials' as coming from yourself; I received no notice of this till furnished with a copy by Col. Rawlins, and in no way was I consulted by any one in authority. I don't mention this with a desire to convince you that the result would have been otherwise had I been consulted, but simply to assure you that the land forces would not have been entirely without seige materials—and guns suitable for any ordinary operations. In relation to the activity displayed by the expedition, I wish to be clearly understood. I have written Colonel Rawlins quite fully, from time to time concerning the causes of delay   I frequently from, the day the expedition left Moon Lake, urged that the rams, Iron-Clads, and two light clads, but certainly the rams & iron clads, should be pushed forward with the greatest possible speed; leaving the transports and balance of naval vessels to come forward as rapidly as they could. I went so far as to obtrude my opinions upon Actg. Comd. Smith—urging that for the main objects of the expedition, the troops were an incumbrance, and could only assist by occupying important points *after they* had been taken possession of. But, notwithstanding Gen'l. Ross, insisted on this in more than one interview, it was not assented to. It was with the greatest difficulty that we could persuade him to put his coal barges behind, and allow the expedition to steam a little faster than the stream would float them   I believe, I have given you, quite as full an account of matters here as I can in a letter. Our offensive operations are suspended, till more ammunition can be obtained; the gun boats wishing to hold some on hand for defense. I don't know what course Gen'l. Ross and Com.d Smith will now adopt, but it is the intention to wait on the defensive, till we can determine something better." ALS, DNA, RG 94, War Records Office, Union Battle Reports. *O.R.*, I, xxiv, part 1, 382–85.

On March 18, 10:00 P.M., Wilson wrote to Rawlins. "Military and naval operations here are about terminated for the present. His Excellency Acti.g. Rear Admiral, Comodore Smith, left today for a more salubrious climate, very sick; giving it as his opinion that the present force of iron clads, could not take the two rebel guns in our front. Capt. Foster, the next in rank has assumed command, and insists on withdrawing his force. Gen'l. Ross assented at first but has since determined to delay here till Genl. Quimby arrives to assume the responsibility, of attempting to reduce the rebel work, or of withdrawing the land forces. I am satisfied there is but one right way to take the fort and that is for the gunboats to go right at it and hammer it till they take it. A deserter came in this morning confirming in every particular the justice of my view. He says there were no heavy guns mounted here till the 10th or 12th of this month; that a heavy force is collecting at Yazoo City—and that they are building a tremendous raft there upon which they keep constantly employed a thousand men. They are also building one gunboat a mile below the city 300 ft. long, but for want of material it will require 24 months to finish—with this exception they have neither gunboat nor ram anywhere on these waters. Gen'l. Loring is in command in our front, don't know his force but heard some one say, over 3000 men. Capt's Brown and Shepherd of the rebel navy have charge of the two large guns over in the fort. And when we made our attack on Monday, they had but a very limited supply of ammunition —the rifle 6.4 pr was, in fact, silenced for want of projectiles. The "Chilicothe," drew out early, and Smith wouldn't let the DeKalb go down to press the matter. The deserter says there is no possibility of a doubt that we should have captured the battery had our gunboats continued in action. Night before last they received a small supply of rifle shot, and on Sunday night they received and mounted the 8 inch gun which threw solid shot at us on Monday.—We have thrown away a magnificent chance, to injure the enemy and all because of the culpable and inexcusable slowness of the Naval Commander in the first place, and his timidity and cautiousness in the Second. The matter rests just this way now; if Admiral Porter can send three good iron clads well supplied with ammunition say 400 rounds for each gun and a good man to fight them they can yet capture the place—if he can't do so, it's childish folly to keep the present force here, thereby causing the enemy to strengthen his position—and allowing him an opportunity to bag our entire force. 20.000 men, would be safe here, and supplied with a liberal allowance of siege materials might so damage the enemy as to require him to evacuate; but if the land forces are required to stop at every point of importance and reduce it by a siege how long do you think it will require them to reach Yazoo City? It's provoking beyond measure to think that everything we undertake must be marred by incompetency and stupidity. I am intensley disgusted to night!— In case of our withdrawal entirely or partially I shall avail myself of the first opportunity to return to Vicksburg or to Hd. Qrs. to see you and the General. It seems to me the principle advantages of this line have already been lost; and what remain derive their importance from the fact that the gun boats by being vigorously handled, ought to open us a rapid and safe line of communications at least to Yazoo City. If the Gunboats can't do this work the venture fails—at least so far as concerns its advantages. An army in time *can* go thro' unassisted, but I wouldn't like to be answerable for all the time consumed, nor for the success of the army afterwards. I have just finished dismantling our land battery and removing the guns to the landing. This was thought best, since we were nearly out of ammunition for them, and to save the labor of guarding the battery. I can't begin to give you an idea of my disgust. Write me soon, and in the meantime beleive me Dear Rawlins," ALS, DNA, RG 94, War Records Office, Union Battle Reports. *O.R.*, I, xxiv, part 1, 385–86.

On March 17, Maj. Gen. Cadwallader C. Washburn, Helena, wrote to USG. "When I left you eleven days ago, I supposed that by this time a large force would be in the Yazoo Pass or advanced beyond there. Instead of that, to all appearances, little or no progress has yet been made. It is now twenty three days since the first boat passed into the Cold Water, and demonstrated the practicability of that route, and it is three weeks tomorrow since, the fleet with Gen. Ross.' Command entered the pass. We have no information from the expedition since the 8th inst. except a report of Cannonading in the direction of the Yazoo; heard at Greenville, one week ago today. The importance of hurrying through forces to take and hold Yazoo City of course you fully understand. Yazoo City in our possession and Vicksburgh is at our mercy   I presume that you are, not aware of the extent of the delays up here, or the cause of them. No boats of the right size have been sent here, nor can I hear of any. I have made daily inquiry in regard to the prospect for boats, but as no satisfactory information could be had from any source, I consulted with Genl. Hovey, who volunteerd to go up the river & hurry the transportation along. Genl. Prentiss gave him a permit to go & he left three days ago, so that I hope in time we may have the means to do something. I cannot disguise my impatience at these delays which are so fatal to the success of this undertaking. Your order for a portion of my Cavalry to be ready was duly recd. They are ready, but unless more progress is made in procuring transportation in the future than in the past, I may wait here a long time. I cheerfully comply with any orders that may be made by my superior, and am content to be placed where in your judgement I can be of most service. With great labor Col. Wilson & myself opened the Yazoo Pass, in the face of every possible discouragement, and after it was pronounced an impracticable & foolish undertaking by nearly all prominent Army officers here. Having had the utmost faith in the undertaking from the outset, and believing then as now, that it was the way to take Vicksburgh, I should have been gratified to have had some command in connection with the advance expedition—that however is past, and to the future only that I care to look. The President has seen fit to appoint & the Senate to confirm me as a Maj Genl   I need not say that I should like a command on this Expedition such as my rank would properly entitle me to. . . . P. S. Since writing the above the Str. Carl has come up with despatches from the Yazoo. The necessity for immediate reinforcements is now renderd certain. The delays at Greenwood & above will enable them to fortify Yazoo City, so that by the time we reach it we shall have another Vicksburgh there." ALS, DNA, RG 393, Dept. of the Tenn., Letters Received; ADfS, Washburn Papers, WHi.

On March 19, Prentiss wrote to USG. "I have the honor to report that my latest advices from Gen. Ross are of the date of the 15th inst., when he was still confronting the rebel Fort Greenwood. He was still at work, cannonnading the enemy, but had made little or no impression on them, although he had added an 8 inch Howitzer to his land battery.—Gen. R. reported the Fort as being much stronger than was anticipated, and required more work for its reduction. He intended on Monday to resume firing, but could not sustain an action for over two hours, owing to scarcity of ammunition, for which he sent to me.—Col. Wilson also sent requisition for 4 8 in. Seige Howitzers and 4 30n Parrotts. I have today sent to Gen. Ross a supply of ammunition, all I had here—Last night I despatched a boat to Memphis to procure the Guns called for, and ammunition for the same. I expect they will arrive tonight, so that they can be sent to Gen. R. tomorrow.—I am sparing no pains to keep up communication with Gen. Ross, keep him supplied with rations &c—and do all in my power to help him, till General Quinby assumes command of the expedition—I do not doubt my ability to keep up communication with both Generals, but am sadly in want of transports at present. Fort Greenwood, Gen. Ross represents as inaccessible to infantry, so that he must depend upon artillery for its reduction—I look for further advices from there very soon— . . . P. S.—20th—8. A.M.—Two regiments from Gen. Carr's command at St. Genevieve are just in—I shall change them from small to large boats and send them immediately forward, retaining the small boats—" LS, DNA, RG 94, War Records Office, Union Battle Reports. *O.R.*, I, xxiv, part 1, 392.

On March 20, Prentiss wrote to USG. "I have the honor to transmit herewith copies of a communication just received (6.30 P. M.) from Gen. Ross—and a communication from Col. Wilson to Gen. Ross—I have made the copies in haste, to detain the Gun Boat as brief a time as possible— . . . P. S.—I shall follow the suggestions of Gen. Ross, and cut the levee and let the water in. It will do us no harm, and can do the enemy no good—" ALS, DNA, RG 94, War Records Office, Dept. of the Tenn. *O.R.,* I, xxiv, part 1, 392–93. The enclosures are printed *ibid.,* p. 396.

On March 21, Prentiss wrote to USG. "I have the honor to acknowledge the receipt this morning of your communication of the 17th concerning the new aspect of affairs on the Yazoo. Deeming it important for the furtherance of your designs as therein explained, that Gen. Smith should not be longer delayed at this end of Yazoo Pass, I have issued orders to him to join Gen. Quinby as soon as possible after securing a sufficient number of suitable transports. I enclose a copy of the order. I have issued no detailed orders or instructions, not considering it my duty to interfere with either your plans or Gen. Quinby's, but merely to extend all the aid in my power, whenever and wherever possible, without such interference." LS, DNA, RG 393, Dept. of the Tenn., Letters Received. *O.R.,* I, xxiv, part 3, 123–24.

1. On March 22, Maj. Gen. Stephen A. Hurlbut, Memphis, wrote to USG. "Four days since Genl Prentiss sent his Q. Master & Chief of Artillery here to obtain Boats—Heavy guns and heavy ammunition for the troops at Greenwood in the Yazoo. I considered his statement so pressing that I sent him from the Fort four twenty four pound si[e]ge guns & filled the requisition for ammunition. I also sent down the Boats (list enclosed). Brig Genl. A. P. Hovey had passed up the River to St Louis & Cincinnati to look up transportation under orders from Genl Prentiss—I should have stopped but he assured me the orders were by your direction. Capt Lyman A. Q. M—has orders to seize & send forward every available boat. No exertions will be spared here to push this matter forward   I have telegraphed your message to Col. Parsons." ALS, DNA, RG 393, Dept. of the Tenn., Letters Received. *O.R.,* I, xxiv, part 3, 129.

2. See letter to Maj. Gen. James B. McPherson, March 5, 1863.

To Maj. Gen. John A. McClernand

Head Quarters, Dept of the Ten
Head of Millikins Bend La.
March 18th 1863.

Maj. Gen. J. A. McClernand,
Comd.g 13th Army Corps.
Gen.

It was my intention to have stoped at the Bend to-day to have explained fully to you the nature of the present movements. But being delayed so late compells me to pass on to Youngs Point.

I have had information both from my own means of knowing, and from Southern papers, that Ross has penetrated to Greenwood on the Yazoo river; further that the rebels have sent a number of steamers loaded with troops, up to resist him.—My efforts to get down steamers to carry troops to the support of Ross, in time, have proven somewhat abortive. It is necessary therefore to give him aid from here. Admiral Porter, who was equally interested, and much more familiar with the country intervening between the Miss. river and the Yazoo, caused a partial exploration of the Passes through by the way of Steele's Bayou to Deer Creek, and thence to the Yazoo, for the purpose of geting in the rear of any force that may have been sent up.— I went with the Admiral on his second excursion, and so far as explored, *know* it to be perfectly practicable. I am therefore sending an Infantry Division to their support, on Admiral Porter's request, and hope such favorable reports will be received as to justify me in sending all available forces through by that route.— I would thus have all my forces concentrated on a given point, and save the necessity of dividing them, which I wish to avoid, if possible.

I have countermanded the order for Gen. McPherson to go through Yazoo Pass on account of the difficulty of procuring the right kind of transportation, and because it is now too late, and will bring him with this end of the expedition.[1]

Two Divisions however, Gens. J. E. Smith's and Quinby's are going that route, and, I hope, Quinby is already with Ross.

These are the facts which I wished to communicate, principally, and to notify you that you would hold your Corps in readiness to move when called on.

> Very respectfully
> your obt. svt.
> U. S. GRANT
> Maj. Gen. [Com.]

ALS, McClernand Papers, IHi. *O.R.*, I, xxiv, part 3, 119.

1. See letter to Maj. Gen. James B. McPherson, March 14, 1863.

To Maj. Gen. Stephen A. Hurlbut

Before Vicksburg March 19th 1863

MAJ GENL S. A. HURLBURT
COMDG 16TH ARMY CORPS.

I sent orders to Col Parsons A. Q. M. for small steamers suitable for the navigation of the Bayous and small streams through this country[1] and sent Captain Reno to expedite the procurement   It seems that Col Parsons has conceived the idea that stern wheel boats alone are wanted. I told Captain Reno especially that this was not the case. Side wheel boats are preferable if they are of the right size. If any of these boats have reported at Memphis order them directly down with instructions to report at Helena to bring any troops that may be there not yet removed and to take them wherever their orders may direct. At last accounts General [*John E.*] Smith who was destined for Yazoo Pass had not yet got off. If he is off on the arrival of these boats I want them to report here. Such of them as are not required for Smith's command will come immediately down.

U S. GRANT
Maj Genl.

P. S. Telegraph Col Parsons that Side Wheel steamers are even better than stern wheel boats

U S. G.

Copies, DLC-USG, V, 19, 30; DNA, RG 393, Dept. of the Tenn., Letters Sent.
    On March 20, 1863, Lt. Col. John A. Rawlins wrote to Capt. Asher R. Eddy, Memphis. "I am directed by the General commanding the Department to request you to send immediately to this place all the small boats lying at your place that belong to the 'cotton speculators   There are a number there that will not answer to carry troops on account of their extremely small size but are just what are wanted here at this moment for dispatches in the different bayous. Please send all of them at once no matter how small. Also send the dredge forward as soon as it arrives." Copies, *ibid.*

    1. See letter to Col. Lewis B. Parsons, March 4, 1863.

To Rear Admiral David G. Farragut

March 21st 1863.

ADMIRAL FARRIGUT,
U. S. NAVY,
ADMIRAL

Hearing nothing from Admiral Porter I have determined to send you a barge of coal from here. The barge will be cast adrift from the upper end of the Canal at 10 O'clock to-night   Troops on the opposite side of the point will be on the lookout and should the barge run into the eddy will start it adrift again.

Admiral Porter is now in Deer Creek, or possibly in the Yazoo, below Yazoo city. I hope to hear from him this evening. As soon as I do I will prepare dispatches for Gen. Banks and forward them to you.

I have sent a force into the Yazoo river by the way of Yazoo Pass. Hearing of this force at Greenwood Miss. and learning that the enemy were detaching a large force from Vicksburg to go and meet them determined Admiral Porter to attempt to get gunboats in the rear of the enemy. I hope to hear of the success of this enterpris soon.

I am Admiral
Very respectfully
Your obt. svt.
U. S. GRANT.
Maj. Gen.

ALS, DNA, RG 45, Area 5. *O.R.*, I, xxiv, part 3, 123; *O.R.* (Navy), I, xx, 7. An undated letter from Rear Admiral David G. Farragut to USG was received on March 20, 1863. "I herewith transmit to you, by the hand of my Secretary, a despatch from Maj: Gen'l N. P. Banks; it was sent up to me the evening I was to pass the Batteries at Port Hudson. Having learnt that the Enemy had the Red River trade open to Vicksburg and Port Hudson, and that two of the Gun Boats of the upper Fleet had been captured, I determined to pass up, and if possible, recapture the boats and stop the Red River trade, and this I can do most effectually, if I can obtain from Rear Admiral Porter or yourself, *coal* for my vessels;—by my trip up the River I have become perfectly acquainted with the Enemy's forces on the Banks and his boats in the adjacent waters. I shall be most happy to avail myself of the earliest moment, to have a consultation with yourself and Rear Admiral Porter, as to the assistance I can render you at this place, and if none then I will return to the mouth of Red River and carry out my original design." LS, DNA, RG 94, War Records Office, Miscellaneous War Records. *O.R.*, I, xxiv, part 3, 104–5; *ibid.*, I, xv, 693; *O.R.* (Navy), I, xx, 5.

On March 21, Lt. Col. John A. Rawlins wrote to Col. Charles H. Abbott, 30th Iowa. "A barge of coal will be let loose at the point above Vicksburgh at 10. P. M. to-day to float down with current to Admiral Farragut's fleet   The master of transportation thinks it will reach the mouth of the canal in two hours from the time it is turned loose above   you will therefore please be on the lookout and give it safe conduct to its place of destination. You will also please give timely notice to Admiral Farragut that he may know what to expect   It was thought that the communication of Lt Commanding Breese of yesterday to Admiral Farragut was in reference to furnishing him coal as the matter had been referred to him. Commodore Graham says that a yaul with a line attached to the coal barge can keep it in the current. A line will therefore be placed on the barge for the purpose of ennabling your men to guide it   You will please forward the enclosed communication to Admiral Farragut without delay." Copies, DLC-USG, V, 19, 30; DNA, RG 393, Dept. of the Tenn., Letters Sent. See letter to Rear Admiral David G. Farragut, March 23, 1863.

To Rear Admiral David G. Farragut

Head Quarters, Dept. of the T[en.]
Before Vicksburg, March 22d/63

ADMIRAL FARRAGUT
COMD.G GULF SQUADRON,
ADMIRAL;

I regret that Admiral Porter has not been here to answer your communications. On the subject of your communication in regard to furnishing coal it can always be supplied either by the Admiral or myself, supposing that it can be successfully floated past the batteries at Vicksburg.

It is a matter of the utmost importance to cut off trade with the Red River country. I do not know what Admiral Porter would suggest if he was here, but I think he might possibly spare one or more of his rams.

I have not heard whether the barge of coal started to you last

night reached its destination or not. Hoping that this coal reached
you all right

> I remain, Very respectfully
> your obt. svt.
> U. S. Grant
> Maj. Gen.

ALS, DNA, RG 45, Area 5. *O.R.*, I, xxiv, part 3, 126. On March 22, 1863, Rear
Admiral David G. Farragut wrote to USG. "I have just received your several
communications, & one for Genl. Banks, which I hope to be able to convey to him
in the course of a few days—as I will probably leave here tomorrow or the next
day at furthest—I regret that I did not see Admiral Porter as he no doubt would
have sent down at least 2 of Genl. Ellet's Rams. The two Rams & one Iron Clad
would make the Blockade of Red River complete—there are only two Boats fitted
as Rams—the Queen of the West & Webb—there are also the Beaty & another
River Boat fitted with Cotton Bales for the purpose of Boarding our Gun Boats
but carry no guns—The Webb is at Alexandria repairing & the Queen of the
West is now in the atchaphalia—the moment we have the mouth of the River they
transport all their provisions for Vicksburg & Port Hudson across the River to
Angola place & then they travel up to this place by land—I had hoped to have
sufficient force, not to disturb the admiral, but as my vessels failed to get past
Port Hudson in fact I know one was hurt & I find it reported that another was
sunk, but this loss I do not believe—My services are so important below that I
shall be compelled to return to New Orleans & the coast very soon—I still cherish
the hope that I will find some one of my Gallant fellows at the mouth of Red River,
which will enable me to leave soon—I know that Genl Banks does not think he
has sufficient force to attack Port Hudson with any chance of success. Wishing
you every success in your difficult opperations I again tender you my thanks,"
ALS, DNA, RG 393, Dept. of the Tenn., Letters Received. *O.R.*, I, xxiv, part 3,
125; *O.R.* (Navy), I, xx, 9–10.

To Maj. Gen. Nathaniel P. Banks

> Head Quarters, Dept. of the Ten.
> Before Vicksburg, March 23d [*22*]/63

Maj. Gen. N. P. Banks,
Comd.g Dept. of the Gulf,
Port Hudson La,
Gen.

Your communication of the 13th inst. per Admiral Farragut
was duly received.

The continuous high water and the nature of the country almost precluding the possibility to land a force on the East bank of the Miss. any where above Vicksburg has induced the hope that you would be able to take Port Hudson and move up to Black river. By the use of your transports I could send you all the force you would require.

Finding the canal commenced here last Summer by Gen. Williams[1] I have prossecuted that work and would, before this, had it completed to the width of sixty feet but for the heavy rise in the river breaking in the dam a cross the upper end. It is exceedingly doubtful if this canal can be made of any practical use even if completed. The enemy have established a battery of heavy guns opposite the mouth of the canal completely commanding it for one half its length.

Soon after taking command here I concieved the idea of geting possession of the Yazoo river by the way of Moon Lake & Yazoo Pass. Five gunboats were furnished for this expedition and I sent in addition a Division of troops, to which has since been added conciderable reinforcement. This enterprise promised most farely, but for some cause our troops and boats delayed so as to give the enemy time to fortify.

My last information from this command was to the 17th. They were at Greenwood on the Yazoo, a fortified place, and had abandoned all idea of geting past until they could receive additional Ordnance stores. By a prompt movement Yazoo City could have been captured without opposition.

Admiral Porter with five Gunboats, and Gen. Sherman with a Division of troops are now attempting to get into the Yazoo by the way of Steeles Bayou, Black Bayou, Deer Creek, Rolling Fork and the Sunflower. They got in as far as Deer Creek without any great difficulty but I fear a failure of geting further.

This experiment failing there is nothing left for me but to collect all my strength and attack Hains Bluff. This will necessarily be attended with much loss but I think it can be done.

The best aid you can give me, if you cannot Pass Port Hudson, will be to hold as many of the enemy there as possible. If they could be sent I could well spare one Army Corps to enable you to get up the river. My effective force, including all arms, will be between sixty & seventy thousand, if I bring all from Memphis that can be spared in an imergency. An attack on Hains Bluff cannot possibly take place under two weeks if so soon. My forces are now scattered and the difficulty of geting transportation is very great.

> I am Gen. Very respectfully
> your obt. svt.
> U. S. GRANT
> Maj. Gen.

ALS, CSmH. *O.R.*, I, xv, 300–1. This letter was copied with the date March 22, 1863, in DLC-USG, V, 19, 30; DNA, RG 393, Dept. of the Tenn., Letters Sent. *O.R.*, I, xxiv, part 3, 125–26; *O.R.* (Navy), I, xx, 8–9. Since Rear Admiral David G. Farragut mentioned receipt of this letter on March 22, USG probably misdated the original. On March 13, Maj. Gen. Nathaniel P. Banks, Baton Rouge, had written to USG. "Anticipating the success of Admiral Farragut's proposed attempt to run the enemys batteries at Port Hudson and to open communication with you, I avail myself of the opportunity to give you a statement of our position, force and intentions. We have now at Baton Rouge a force of about 17,000 effective Infantry and one negro regiment, one regiment of Heavy Artillery with six light batteries, one 20 pounder battery, a dismounted company of Artillery and ten companys of Cavalry, of which, eight are newly raised and hardly to be counted on. Of this three regiments of Infantry, the Heavy Artillery manning the siege train, the 20 pounder Parrot battery, the dismounted artillery and one company of Cavalry, will remain at Baton Rouge   Leaving this force to hold the position of Baton Rouge, we march to day upon Port Hudson by the Bayou Sara road to make a demonstration upon that work for the purpose of cooperating in the movement of the fleet. The best information that we have of the enemys force places it at 25,000 or 30,000. This and his position preclude the idea of an assault upon our part, and accordingly the main object of the present movement is a diversion in favor of the Navy, but we shall of course avail ourselves of any advantage which occasion may offer. Should the Admiral succeed in his attempt, I shall try to open communication with him on the other side of the river, and, in that event, trust I shall hear from you as to your position and movements and especially as to your views of the most efficient mode of coöperation upon the part of the forces we respectively command"   Copy, DNA, RG 393, Dept. of the Gulf, Letters Sent. *O.R.*, I, xv, 692–93; *ibid.*, I, xxiv, part 3, 104; *O.R.* (Navy), I, xx, 5–6.

On April 6, Farragut wrote to Banks that he was sending USG's letter. *Ibid.*, p. 45. On April 10, Banks wrote to USG. "The secretary of Admiral Farragut, Mr. Gabaudan, called upon me at Brashea city this morning and gave me the substance of your despatch. We have fifteen thousand men, that can be moved with facility. The artillery is strong, the cavalry weak, but we hope to strengthen the cavalry without delay, as one of the results of the Expedition—We shall move up the Bayou Teche tomorrow: probably encounter the enemy, at Pattersonville,

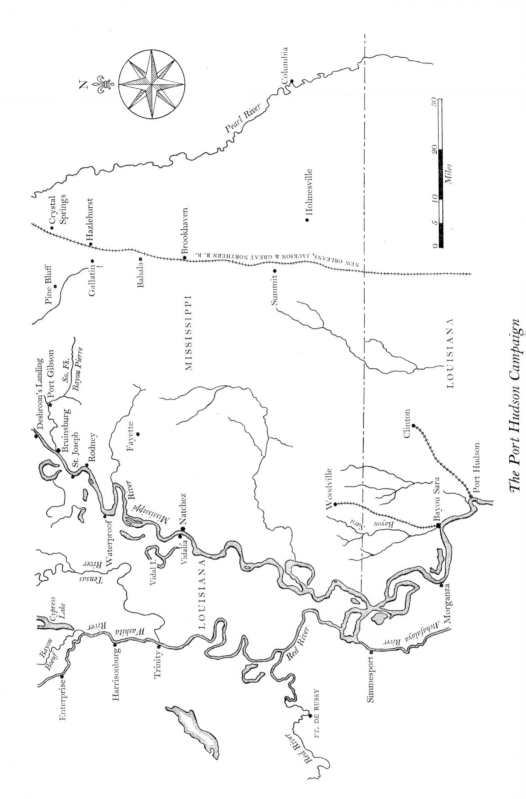

The Port Hudson Campaign

and hope to move without delay, upon Iberia to destroy the salt works, and then upon Opelousas. This is the limit proposed. We do not intend to hold any portion of this country as it weakens our force but will at once return to Baton Rouge to cooperate with you against Port Hudson. I can be there easily by the 10th May. There are now ~~there~~ 4,500. ~~men~~ Infantry at Baton Rouge, with three Regiments colored troops, & two companies of cavalry, three Batteries of artillery with several heavy guns in position, and five Gun Boats, and six mortars   The land force is under commd of Major Genl. Augur.—The fleet under Captain Alden of the Richmond—we shall endeavor to establish commcation with Admiral Farragut, near Bayou Sara, but the opening of the Levee opposite Port Hudson may make it impossible. If so we will commcate with you freely by the way of New York as to our progress. I should be very glad if you will commcate with us, in the same manner. To avoid delays, by mail, I will send my despatches by an officer." LS, DNA, RG 94, War Records Office, Dept. of the Tenn. *O.R.*, I, xv, 296; *ibid.*, I, xxiv, part 3, 182–83; *O.R.* (Navy), I, xx, 50.

On May 1, Farragut wrote to USG. "I herewith enclose to you a communication brought from General Banks by my Secretary, who went down past Port Hudson in a skiff, carrying my despatches to General Banks and the Fleet below —its soiled condition is owing to the Secretary being compelled to carry it in his mouth when pursued by the enemy's pickets on his return to the ship, across the Peninsula—General Banks has defeated Gen. Taylor at Pattersonville on the Teche, capturing two thousand prisoners—Our Gun Boats captured the 'Queen of the West,' 'Diana' and one other—the 'Queen' was burnt but we got her guns. The enemy was flying before General Banks, who when last heard from was at Holmesville, within thirty miles of Alexandria. Kirby Smith has gone up to Arkansas for reinforcements for Taylor and if I had one or two of Admiral Porter's vessels to send up to the mouth of Black River I could capture Kirby Smith's whole Fleet—by remaining here I prevent them from sending reinforcements from Port Hudson to Alexandria—General Banks, learning that the Gun Boats of Admiral Porter had past Vicksburg, calculated on my being able to meet him at Alexandria and so I will, if the boats come down to me—I have written a most imploring appeal to the Admiral for them, otherwise, my time and fuel being nearly expended I shall soon have to abandon my post and return to New Orleans—The enemy have sent every man that they can spare to Johnson in anticipation of the coming battle between him and Rosecranz   If I had obtained the two Iron clads I asked for I would have been I think, this day with General Banks in Alexandria, how it will be now I can not say—The enemy has removed the guns of the 'Indianola' from Fort DeRussy on Red River (where the 'Queen of the West' was captured ~~by~~ from us) to Alexandria, to defend that city—There are no guns between this and Alexandria, but this ship draws too much water and the two small boats would be captured by the enemy's Fleet of Gun Boats and Transports, by boarding. I can get no news of Gen. Banks since Monday last. We learn, through rebel sources, that your cavalry has made a most successful raid on the Jackson R. R— I sincerely hope it is true." LS, DNA, RG 94, War Records Office, Dept. of the Tenn. *O.R.*, I, xv, 308; *ibid.*, I, xxiv, part 3, 259–60; *O.R.* (Navy), I, xx, 71–72.

On April 23, Banks wrote to USG. "I have the honor to acknowledge the receipt of your dispatches dated at Head Quarters before Vicksburg, March 23rd 1863, on the 21st by the hand of Lieut Tenney of Gen Augurs Division at Baton Rouge. On the 10th April Mr Gabadan, the private Secretary of Admiral Farragut, Commanding the Hartford at the mouth of Red River, reported at my Head

Quarters at Brashear and gave verbally the substance of your dispatches, Which he said he had read but did not bring with him, in the dangerous passage, which he was compelled to make of the Batteries at Port Hudson. The information received from Mr Gabadan differs somewhat from your dispatches. I understood from him that it was your intention to send a force by the way of Lake Providence and the Black River, passing through the intermedeate Bayous to the mouth of Black River on the Red River and that this force would probably reach, the Red River by the 1st of May. proximo, to co-operate with my command against Port Hudson Stimulated by this Report and cheering prospect of assistance, we pushed with vigor the expedition upon which we were then engaged Our success has been complete, We have utterly destroyed the Army and Navy of this part of the Confederacy and made it impossible for the enemy to re-organize his forces for some months to come. We occupy Opelousas and my advance is about thirty miles in front of this place on the Road to Alexandria. The Forces of the enemy are divided, a portion of Sibley's Brigade—Cavalry—being on the Plaguemine Bayou on the road to Texas, with Gen Morton and the Artillery and some Cavalry on the road to Alexandria. The Infantry is completely dispersed. We have captured two thousand prisoners, a thousand Stand of Arms, Ammunition, Ordnance Stores, etc; twenty (20) heavy guns, demolished his founderies at Franklin and New Iberia and the Salt works below Iberia. We have captured two Steamers and several boats and compelled the the destruction of ten or twelve transport Steamers, some of them laden with flour, Ammunition and Arms. The Gun Boats 'Diana,' Hart' and Queen of the West have been destroyed and their armament captured by our forces. We have among our prisoners the most important Officers of all arms. Captain Fuller the Commander of their Fleet and captured from the 'Queen of the West,' known here as the 'King of the Swamp' long in the Legislature and the head of the fillibustre or fighting element of the State whose Candidate he was for the office of Governor. We have also Captain Semmes, the first Officer of their Artillery and Colonel Vincent the Chief of their Cavalry. They can make no stand this side Alexandria. The capture of the fortifications at Butte-a-la-Rose by the Army and Navy which occurred on the morning of the 20th April opens to us completely the Atchafalaya to the Red River. Several days since I addressed to the Admiral an inquiry whether he could navigate the Red River to Alexandria and to yourself a request to communicate the time when your co-operative force could reach Red River Our communication with the Admiral is open only on Thursdays, when he comes down to Port Hudson. It will be communicated to him as I am informed by dispatches from Gen Augur to day. It must be some time before it reaches you. I was disappointed in learning from the perusal of your dispatches, that at their date it was undetermined whether you can send a force to the Red River or not on account of the deficiency of your transportation. It is a grief on my part that I cannot aid you in this respect. Our transportation is lamentably deficient. I had but one Steamer with which to pass two divisions of my corps over Berwick Bay in this campaign. The route is open but I can reach Red River only by forced marches. It is Six day's march to Alexandria, and four or five to Semmesport at the mouth of the Atchafalaya, but until we can hear from you shall make Washington on the Courtablea my base of operations. We can co-operate with you in any manner you suggest, by a junction on the Red River or by an attack from Baton Rouge, joining your forces on the Bayou Sara in the rear of Port Hudson. My belief is that this is the best method, as the passage of the mississippi from the Red River is very difficult with our short transportation and will require a landing, and places our forces between the Armies of Vicksburg and Port Hudson. But we shall not hesitate   I wait anxiously to hear from you upon these points. Viz: 1st When can you be at the mouth of Black or Red Rivers? 2nd In what manner shall my forces co-operate with you?   3rd Can you furnish transportation for your passage to Port Hudson or do you rely upon us?   4th Can you supply your troops or will you rely upon us?   5th Is it not practicable for your force to join us by the Atchafalaya? It is doubtful if we can supply your forces from New Orleans in operations above Port Hudson, on account of our deficient transportation. My belief is that the best junction is by the Atchafalaya. We can reach Baton Rouge by the Grand River and the Plaguemine without trans-Shipment and our forces united make the reduction of Port Hudson certain, my own command is insufficient. Waiting anxiously your response and with full confidence in your judgement and earnest co-operation"   Copies, DNA, RG 94, War Records Office, Union Battle Reports; *ibid.*, RG 393, Dept. of the Tenn., Unregistered Letters Received; *ibid.*, Dept. of the Gulf, Letters Sent. *O.R.*, I, xv, 303–4; *ibid.*, I, xxiv, part 3, 223–25; *O.R.* (Navy), I, xx, 65–66. Although Banks repeatedly referred to more than one communication from USG dated March 23, the second was a copy of USG's letter of that date to Farragut. *O.R.*, I, xv, 299, 301.

On April 23, Banks again wrote to USG. "Further reflection upon the subject of my letter of this date and additional information as to the condition of the country on this line leads me to urge more strongly the point of junction indicated at its close, Viz: by the Atchafalaya, Grand River and Plaquemine Bayous to Baton Rouge, we are now one hundred and Eighty miles from New Orleans. It is with great difficulty that we obtain supplies now. Corn and Beef are our chief support. To extend this line a hundred miles further, as it will be on the Red River increases the difficulty and to push it further Still to the opposite side of the Mississippi at Bayou Sara will render supplies very insecure if not impossible. I commend this subject to your earnest consideration. By the Atchafalaya all difficulties of this kind are obviated, supplies of provisions and ammunition are secured. A perfect field of operations is in our possession, and the United forces make the result we wish certain. There are insuperable difficulties to encounter on the other line from the extent of the operations and the deficiency of transportation. They cannot be too carefully weighed, nor too much consideration given to the advantages presented by the more Southerly route. Let me say that all my ideas upon this subject have been changed by my experience in this campaign. Enclosed I send a Map, indicating the route proposed for co-operation and also our line of march in this campaign." Copies, DNA, RG 94, War Records Office, Union Battle Reports; *ibid.*, RG 393, Dept. of the Tenn., Unregistered Letters Received; *ibid.*, Dept. of the Gulf, Letters Sent. *O.R.*, I, xv, 304–5; *ibid.*, I, xxiv, part 3, 225. In his *Memoirs* (I, 491) USG states that Banks's letter of April 10 reached him on May 3. See letter to Maj. Gen. Henry W. Halleck, April 19, 1863, note 1.

1. See telegram to Maj. Gen. Henry W. Halleck, June 28, 1862.

To Maj. Gen. John A. McClernand

———

Head Quarters, Dept. of the Ten
Before Vicksburg, March 22d 1863,

MAJ. GEN. J. A. MCCLERNAND,
COMD.G 13TH ARMY CORPS,
GEN.

Your communication of the 19th in regard to the assignment of Gen. Hamilton is just received. I found it necessary to relieve Gen. Hamilton from duty with the 16th Army Corps and in looking around could see but two Divisions where he could properly be placed. These were the cases of Gens. Morgan & Morgan L. Smith both of whom are absent from their Divisions. I look upon Gen. Morgan as the most likely to remain absent and made my order accordingly.[1]

I readily perceive your embarassment however and will releive you from it either by assigning direct to some specific duties within your Army Corps or by placing him elswhere on duty.

In regard to taking all the command to myself of your Corps, with the exception of the two small Divisions immediately with you I think you are mistaken. It is true that I have given the general instructions to the Yazoo expedition, composed of troops from the 13th & 17th Army Corps, and have instructed Gen. Prentiss to supply all their wants without waiting instructions. This I regarded as necessary.

Feeling anxious to get news from there promptly I directed Gen. Prentiss to forward me all reports direct, but did not mean this should preclude the same reports from ~~should~~ being sent to you also.

I am Gen. very respectfully
your obt. svt.
U. S. GRANT
Maj. Gen. Com

ALS, McClernand Papers, IHi. On March 19, 1863, Maj. Gen. John A. McClernand, Milliken's Bend, wrote to USG. "Your notification to me that Genl. Hamilton had been ordered by you to report to me for duty places me in a dilemma. Where can I assign him? What can I assign him to? True, nominally, I have the immediate command of all the forces operating on the Miss. river, but in fact you exercise immediate as well as general command over all except the two small and imperfectly organized divisions here. The commanders of these divisions having proved their merit and gained the confidence of their men I could not in my judgement on the eve of active operations in the face of the enemy, supercede them, or either of them, without jeopardising the public interest. I say this without intending any disparagement of Genl. H.—whom I understand to be a good officer. Hence, if after receiving this dispatch, you leave it to me to assign the Genl. I will send him to Helena if his rank will entitle him to assume command there— or if you intend that he should supercede either Genl. Smith or Genl. Osterhaus, here, please so order." ADfS, *ibid.*

1. On March 17, Lt. Col. John A. Rawlins issued Special Orders No. 76. "Brig. Genl. C. S. Hamilton, U. S. V. is hereby relieved from duty in the 16th Army Corps. and will report without delay to Major Genl. John A. McClernand, Commanding 13th Army Corps for duty." DS, *ibid.*; copies, DLC-USG, V, 26, 27; DNA, RG 393, Dept. of the Tenn., Special Orders.

To Maj. Gen. James B. McPherson

Before Vicksburgh March 22nd 1863

MAJ GENL J B McPHERSON
COMM'DG 17TH ARMY CORPS

It is now clearly demonstrated that a further force in by the way of Yazoo Pass can be of no service. The party that first went in have so delayed as to give the enemy time to fortify, I see nothing for it now but to have that force return the way they went in. I will let them try Greenwood a short time longer however and see too if Admiral Porter succeeds in reaching the Yazoo on his present route. In the meantime I want concentrated as near here as possible all the troops now scattered from Youngs Point to S̶t̶ Helena You may take immediate steps to collect you forces. The Division of Gen J E Smith will belong to your Army Corps[1]

U S GRANT
Maj Genl.

Copies, DLC-USG, V, 19, 30; DNA, RG 393, Dept. of the Tenn., Letters Sent. *O.R.*, I, xxiv, part 3, 127. On March 22, 1863, 4:00 P.M., Maj. Gen. James B. McPherson, Lake Providence, wrote to USG. "One Brigade of Genl. Logan's Division and part of another are on Board of Transports ready to start for 'Eagle Bend' and will reach that point Early tomorrow. I shall leave General McArthur here, and go down with Genl. Logan's Division   I enclose you a copy of Genl. Quinbys Dispatch just received from which you will understand the difficulties he has had to contend with. I have just received a letter from Col. Boomer dated the 20th stating that Boats enough had arrived to take the balance of Genl. Quinbys' Division & that he would be off '*double quick*'   He also stated that he thought Boats enough would be down yesterday to take Genl. Smith's Division—Since cutting the *Levee* at this point the water has risen steadily in the Lake until the shore is all overflowed, except in a few high points. I have been obliged to move the whole of Logan's Division and all but one Brigade of McArthur's up the River about five miles, in order to get camping ground—Genl. Ransom is still up the River at 'American Bend' with two Regts from here and the force that came up from the Fleet. I am expecting him down to night or tomorrow"   ALS, DNA, RG 94, War Records Office, Dept. of the Tenn. *O.R.*, I, xxiv, part 1, 403–4. The enclosed letter from Brig. Gen. Isaac F. Quinby is printed *ibid.*, p. 406. On March 21, Lt. Col. John A. Rawlins had written to McPherson. "You will please move one division of your corps to Eagle Bend on the east bank of the Mississipi river where Stuarts division landed with a view to reinforcing Maj Genl. Sherman from that point. Let there be no delay. Send them by brigades as rapidly as they can be embarked"   Copies, DLC-USG, V, 19, 30; DNA, RG 393, Dept. of the Tenn., Letters Sent. On March 25, Rawlins issued Special Orders No. 84. "Brig General M D Leggett will move with his Brigade from Eagle Bend to Lake Providence and there rejoin his Division   The Q M will furnish the necessary transportation"   Copies, DLC-USG, V, 26, 27; DNA, RG 393, Dept. of the Tenn., Special Orders. *O.R.*, I, xxiv, part 3, 146.

1. On March 22, Rawlins issued Special Orders No. 81 assigning the div. of Brig. Gen. John E. Smith to McPherson. Copies, DLC-USG, V, 26, 27; DNA, RG 393, Dept. of the Tenn., Special Orders. *O.R.*, I, xxiv, part 3, 130–31.

To Maj. Gen. Benjamin M. Prentiss

Head Quarters, Dept. of the Ten
Before Vicksburg, March 22d/63

BRIG. GEN. B. M. PRENTISS,
COMD.G DIST. E. ARK.
HELENA ARK.
GEN.

I am sending up to-day per steamer Continental some Ordnance stores for the gunboats now near Greenwood. Please have these stores forwarded as soon as possible. Also send twenty thousand rations from your stores for the use of the Navy. They will either be replaced or returns made for the Infantry sharp shooters who are aboard these gunboats to cover the issue. If there are troops still at Moon Lake or in the vicinity of Helena to come down here you can turn the Continental back to aid in bringing them down. If there are no troops to bring down she can go up to Memphis and bring the Mails and a load from there.

Very respectfully
U. S. GRANT
Maj. Gen. Com

ALS, DNA, RG 94, War Records Office, Union Battle Reports. *O.R.*, I, xxiv, part 3, 128.

Also on March 22, 1863, Lt. Col. John A. Rawlins wrote to Maj. Gen. John A. McClernand. "You will please send forward at once to the Yazoo Pass Expedition four of your thirty pound Parrott guns and a sufficient force (not less than 80 men) from the 1st U. S. Infantry to man them, under command of Capt. G. A. Williams, of said 1st U. S. Inft. They will take with them thirty days rations. The Steamer 'Dacotah' has been ordered to transport them, and will be in readiness at Milikens Bend, early to-morrow morning, the 23d inst. for their embarkation." LS, McClernand Papers, IHi. *O.R.*, I, xxiv, part 3, 127.

To Maj. Gen. William T. Sherman

Head Quarters, Dept. of the [*Tenn.*]
Before Vicksburg, March 22/63

MAJ. GEN. W. T. SHERMAN,
COMD.G 15TH ARMY CORPS,

Your report,[1] and also Admiral Porters, were received yesterday. As the Admiral called for more troops to protect him I immediately ordered McPherson to send down one Division of his command.[2]

I regret that the chances look so gloomy for geting through to the Yazoo by that route. I had made so much calculation upon the expedition down Yazoo Pass, and now again by the route proposed by Admiral Porter, that I have made really but little calculation u[p]on reaching Vicksburg by any other than Hains Bluff[.]

As soon as the Admiral can get his gunboats back for service I wil[l] concentrate all my forc[e]s and make a strike.

Finding that we fail in reaching the East bank of the Yazoo upon the route you have gone there is nothing further to do with troops where you are than to guard the gunboats and return when they do.

What difficulty is in the way of reaching the Yazoo by going down ~~the~~ Deer Creek?

> Very respectfully
> U. S. GRANT
> Maj. Gen. Com

ALS, DLC-William T. Sherman. *O.R.*, I, xxiv, part 3, 127; *O.R.* (Navy), I, xxiv, 489.

1. On March 21 and 29, 1863, Maj. Gen. William T. Sherman addressed to Lt. Col. John A. Rawlins lengthy reports of the Steele's Bayou expedition. ALS and LS, DNA, RG 94, War Records Office, Union Battle Reports. *O.R.*, I, xxiv, part 1, 432–36. Part of the second report is in *O.R.* (Navy), I, xxiv, 490–92. On March 21, Brig. Gen. Hugh Ewing, Steele's Bayou, reported to Rawlins the movements of his brigade. LS, DNA, RG 94, War Records Office, Dept. of the Tenn. *O.R.*, I, xxiv, part 3, 123.
2. See letter to Maj. Gen. James B. McPherson, March 22, 1863.

To Rear Admiral David G. Farragut

> Head Quarters, Dept. of the Ten
> Before Vicksburg, March 23d/63

ADMIRAL,

As you kindly offered me the co-operation of your vessels, and the use of them to transport troops to Warrenton, should I want to send an expedition to destroy their batteries I have determined to take advantage of the offer.

I have directed Gen. Steele to select two Regts. from his command and get them to the opposite side of the peninsula today ready to embark as soon as in your judgement you think it should be done.

I send no special instructions for this expeditions further than to destroy effectually the batteries at Warrenton and return to their Camp here.

They will be glad to receive any suggestion or direction from you. This is a bad day for troops to be out, but in that particular may be favorable to us.

Thanking you admiral for your offer of the services of your vessels I remain

> your obt. svt.
> U. S. GRANT
> Maj. Gen

P. S. Capt. Walke, who is the Senior Naval Officer here in the absence of Admiral Porter, asked me yesterday for cotton bales with which to pack two of the Rams for the purpose of sending them to join you. I promised him anything in the world the Army has for the acomplishment of this purpose and presume the vessels will be sent. I look up[on] it as of vast importance that we should hold the river, securely, between Vic[ks]burg & Port Hudson.

> U. S. G.

To Admiral Farragut
Comd.g Squadron of the G[ulf.]

ALS, James S. Schoff, New York, N. Y. *O.R.*, I, xxiv, part 3, 131; *O.R.* (Navy), I, xx, 15. On March 22, 1863, Rear Admiral David G. Farragut wrote to USG. "I am most happy to inform you that the coal barge arrived safely and we are now coaling from her. She is much larger than our necessities required but it is a good fault and we will carry her down with us. I see the enemy is building a very formidable casemated work at Warrenton. I fired at it yesterday coming up but I think did it little or no injury. I see they are at work on it again and shall interrupt them today with an occasional shot or shell to prevent their annoying me on my way down, but if you think proper to make a little expedition over that way to destroy it my two vessels will be at your service so long as I am here. On my way down I shall pass close to it and do my best to destroy it, but I suppose that will not amount to much as they will soon be able to repair the damages. They do not appear to have any amount of armed force there but quite an extensive working force, which I have just ordered a gunboat down to break up. I will be happy to receive your dispatch for Genl Banks. There are no other batteries between this

place and Red River except Grand Gulf, where they have 4 20 & 30 pounder
Parrot guns & they annoyed us very much coming up. There are no steamers on
the Miss. River between here & Red River or were not when I came up & if they
have come out since I will have them below me when I go down, so that if Admiral
Porter wishes to send down any of his boats he will know what they will have to
contend with. I am greatly obliged to you for your politeness & remain . . . If
you wish to send over a force to break up Warrington, these vessels will be at
your service while we remain here." Copy (undated), DNA, RG 45, Letterbook
of David G. Farragut. Dated March 22 in Loyall Farragut, *The Life of David
Glasgow Farragut* (New York, 1879), pp. 340–41. *O.R.* (Navy), I, xx, 7–8.

On March 23, Farragut wrote to USG. "I have just received your communication of this date and am most happy to find that you concur in opinion with me
as to the necessity for destroying the casemated Battery now near completion at
Warrenton—I gave it a good shelling today and will be ready to act in concert
with your troops and afford any facility in my power whenever they are ready—
I will cover the landing, and in case the Ram Switzerland comes down in time,
that as she will be best suited to land the troops, but in case the Ram does not get
down in time, the Albatross will do it. I beg to assure you in conclusion that it
will always afford me great pleasure to cooperate with you in any undertaking for
the common good of our common country." ALS, DNA, RG 94, War Records
Office, Dept. of the Mo. *O.R.*, I, xxiv, part 3, 132; *O.R.* (Navy), I, xx, 16.

To Rear Admiral David G. Farragut

March 23d 1863,

ADMIRAL,

In the various notes I have written, including the dispatch for
Gen. Banks, I have not mentioned that soon after taking command here, in person, I collected my suplus troops at Lake
Providence and directed the Commanding officer to effect a passage through from the Miss river to Bayou Macon.[1] This will
give navigable water through by that route to the Red river.

This is now reported practicable for ordinary Ohio river
steamers.

I sent several weeks ago for this class of steamers and expected them before this. Should they arrive and Admiral Porter
gets his boats out of the Yazoo so as to accompany the expedition
I can send a force of say 20,000 effective men to co-operate with
Gen. Banks on Port Hudson.

This force certainly would easily reduce Port Hudson and enable them to come on up the river and maintain a position on high land near enough to Vicksburg ~~to~~ until they could be reinforced from here sufficiently to opperate against the city.

Please inform the Gen. of the contents of this and much oblige

your obt. svt.
U. S. GRANT
Maj. Gen.

To Admiral Farragut
Comd.g Gulf Squadron

ALS, CSmH. *O.R.*, I, xv, 301; *ibid.*, I, xxiv, part 3, 131; *O.R.* (Navy), I, xx, 14.

1. See letters to Act. Rear Admiral David D. Porter and to Maj. Gen. John A. McClernand, Jan. 30, 1863.

To Act. Rear Admiral David D. Porter

Head Quarters, Dept. of the Ten.
Before Vicksburg, March 23d 1863

ADMIRAL D. D. PORTER
COMD.G MISS. SQUADRON,
ADMIRAL,

Troops were promptly sent to Eagle Bend on the Miss. river, just where the bayou makes from the river to Steeles Bayou,[1] and have made a good road across. It is not practicable to keep a large force on the land there, but there will be constantly as many as the boats suitable for navigating Steeles Bayou can ferry. I have no more boats of the class required, here, to send.

The expedition by the way of Yazoo Pass seems to have come to a dead lock at Greenwood. More forces are on the way to them. But I doubt their being of any service. Col. Wilson, in whos judgement I place great reliance, writes that land forces cannot act until the batteries are silenced. He thinks too that there has been unnecessary delay in reaching that point.[2]

By Admiral Farragut I received dispatches from Gen. Banks. The Gen. writes that he has advanced to near Port Hudson with all the force he could spare for the expedition, about 20,000 of all arms. But as the enemy have 30,000, or over, and are fortified, he cannot expect to take the place.[3]

I have written back by Admiral Farragut, who will leave to-morrow, and reported the position of our Naval and Military forces at this time, and the practicability of sending an Army Corps by the way of Lake Providence to co-operate with him but that we had not at present the transports, or the gunboats, suitable for this enterprise.

I have sent instructions to Gen. Quinby, who now commands the Yazoo Pass expedition, to push down the river and destroy the enemy's fleet, if possible, but to return immediately if he does not deem this practicable. He will confer with the Naval commander in this matter. It is now perfectly practicable for such vessels as we have in the Yazoo to get into Bayou Macon. The latter has always been reported as a navigable stream. With the return of either of the expeditions now in, or near, the Yazoo I could send such a force as to insure the fall of Port Hudson. With the fall of that place Banks could move up with say 15,000 men, besides all I would send him, and take every point to Warrenton without detention. I submit this to you Admiral for your views whether it would not be advisable to get out all the forces we have attempting to gain possession of the Yazoo river and use them in the way here indicated.

I will heartily co-operate with you in the present enterprise so long as you deem it advisable to push it. Troops may have seemed slow in reaching you after your call. But all was due to the natural obsticals in the way of their reaching you earlyer. I sent them promptly to Eagle Bend, having no more transports suitable to the navigation of the bayous, but the land from the Miss. to Steels Bayou was found covered with water and had to be bridged. This is now done and no difficulty is found in geting them up there.

Please let me hear from you by Maj. Bowers of my staff who bears this.

> I am Admiral, Very respectfully
> your obt. svt
> U. S. Grant
> Maj. Gen.

ALS, MdAN. *O.R.*, I, xxiv, part 3, 132–33; (incomplete) *O.R.* (Navy), I, xxiv, 489–90.

1. At Eagle Bend, approximately twenty miles upriver from Vicksburg, Muddy Bayou connected the Mississippi River and Steele's Bayou.
2. See letter to Maj. Gen. Benjamin M. Prentiss, March 17, 1863.
3. See letter to Maj. Gen. Nathaniel P. Banks, March 22, 1863.

To Maj. Gen. Benjamin M. Prentiss

> Head Quarters, Dept. of the Ten.
> Before Vicksburg, March 23d/63

Maj. Gen. B. M. Prentiss,
Comd.g Dist. of E. Ark.
Gen.

Not hearing of the arrival of small boats so long expected I directed Gen. McPherson to collect all of his forces in the vicinity of Helena and bring them down to where he is.[1]

I to-day learn of the arrival of a number of these boats and the probability that Gen. Smith has alread embarked for the Pass. If this is so let him go. Understand, if Gen. Smith is already in Yazoo pass send him down to Quinby. If not then send him to McPherson.

I send instructions to Quinby by the same conveyance that takes this. I tell him that he will be informed by you exactly what forces have gone and that no more can be expected.

> Very respectfully
> U. S. Grant
> Maj. Gen. Com

ALS, DNA, RG 94, War Records Office, Union Battle Reports. *O.R.*, I, xxiv, part 3, 133.

1. See letter to Maj. Gen. James B. McPherson, March 22, 1863.

To Maj. Gen. Frederick Steele

Before Vicksburgh March 23 1863

MAJ GEN F. STEELE
COMM'DG 1ST DIVISION 15TH ARMY CORPS

This is bad day for troops to be out but may be the more propitious for the plan of yesterday for all that. I have no special instructions to send further than to effectualy destroy the enemy's batteries at Warrenton and return to camp. I have written to Admiral Farragut informing him that this expedition might be looked for if possible for them to reach the other side of the point. I told him furthur the limited instructions from me and that suggestions from him would be gladly received by the commanding Officer. If not already prepared for starting these troops should be got ready as soon as possible

U S GRANT
Maj Genl

Copies, DLC-USG, V, 19, 30; DNA, RG 393, Dept. of the Tenn., Letters Sent. *O.R.*, I, xxiv, part 3, 133.

To Brig. Gen. Isaac F. Quinby

Before Vicksburgh March 23d 1863

BRIG GEN J. F. QUINBY
COMM'DG. YAZOO EXPEDITION

Learning of the slow progress in getting small steamers suitable for your expedition, I wrote to Gen McPherson to collect all of his forces not already in the Yazoo Pass and bring them to where he is.

Since sending this order I have learned of the arrival of a number of small boats at Helena and the probability that Smith's Division had started. As he may have made a start but not got so far but what orders could readily be sent for his return I hasten to change this and will instruct Gen Prentiss if Smith has gone to let him go. You will understand from Prentiss at the same time you receive this what force you are to expect. It is highly desirable that your expedition should clear out the Yazoo river and if possible effect a a lodgment from which we could act against Haines Bluff. You will be the best judge whether this can be done. You will also have to be governed by the disposition of the Navy to co-operate. We cannot order them but only ask their co-operation. I leave to you judgment to say whether the expedition with you should return from Greenwood or prosecute the attack further   It may be necessary for you to take more or less supplies from the citizens along the route but in doing so prevent all the plundering and destruction of property you can and only permit such things to be taken as are actually required for the use of the Army. Admiral Porter started about one week ago to try and reach the Yazoo river below Yazoo City with five Gunboats. His route was by way of Yazoo river to Steele's Bayou up the latter to Black Bayou through that to Deer Creek and up it to Rolling Fork thence across to Big Sunflower and down the Sunflower to the Yazoo. I sent Sherman with an army force of about equal to yours to co-operate. If successful they will come in below the enemy you contending against and between the two forces you would find no further difficulty before reaching the ground I so much desire. I have not heard from this expedition for several days. At last accounts they had got up Deer Creek but had not got through Rolling Fork   I cannot promise success to this expedition but it is possible that if it does get through such consternation will be created among the inhabitants and the troops on the Yazoo that you will hear of it. Feeling great anxiety for your success or speedy return if the object of the expedition shall prove impraticable

U S GRANT

Maj Genl

P. S. If not sanguine of success return immediately with your entire force and fleet. Banks is at Port Hudson but he writes with a force inadequate to the task. If I now had the forces in the Yazoo river upper and lower and I could send an army corps to co-operate with Banks and the two to-gether would easily take the place and every thing on the river from there to Warrenton just below Vicksburgh. The Lake Providence route through to Red river has proven a success and it is by this route I would send them   I have neither transports or Gunboats suitable for this expedition all of them being in the Yazoo

U. S. G   .

Copies, DLC-USG, V, 19, 30; DNA, RG 393, Dept. of the Tenn., Letters Sent.
On March 25, 1863, Brig. Gen. Clinton B. Fisk wrote to Brig. Gen. Leonard F. Ross protesting the recall of steamboats from the Yazoo Pass expedition. Endorsed by Ross, Brig. Gen. Isaac F. Quinby, and Maj. Gen. James B. McPherson, the letter reached USG's hd. qrs. ALS, *ibid.*, RG 94, War Records Office, Dept. of the Tenn. *O.R.*, I, xxiv, part 3, 144–45.
On April 18, Ross wrote to Lt. Col. John A. Rawlins a lengthy report of the causes of the failure of the Yazoo Pass expedition. *Ibid.*, I, xxiv, part 1, 398–400; *O.R.* (Navy), I, xxiv, 291–93. On June 18, Lt. Col. James Harrison Wilson wrote to USG. "The report of Brig. Gen. L. F. Ross, commanding the Yazoo expedition, having failed to reach you, I have the honor to make the following statement, for your information: On the 23d day of February, 1863, the Yazoo Pass was opened for navigation. On the 24th, the expedition left Moon Lake, and on the 10th day of March arrived at or near Fort Pemberton. The distance traversed was about 225 miles. The difficulties of navigation, as described in my letters to you, were great, and some of the transports were old and unseaworthy, yet all of these things are insufficient to account for all of the delay. Such other causes as may have existed should be known, and out of justice to both branches of the public service involved in the expedition I deem it my duty to state them. To the timidity, over cautious-ness, and lack of interest displayed by Lieut. Commander Watson Smith, com-manding the gunboats, and the delays growing out of them, is attributable the failure of the entire expedition. Lieutenant-Commander Smith was frequently urged by General Ross, myself, and Captains Walker and Foster, of the Navy, to move with more rapidity, or, at least, allow the iron-clads and rams to proceed with all practicable dispatch to the mouth of the Tallahatchee. I have no hesitation in saying that, had these suggestions been followed, the entire expedition could have reached Fort Pemberton from three to five days sooner than it did, and that

the iron-clads, the only ones depended upon in attacking land batteries, could have arrived there by the 2d of March at furthest. It is not necessary at this time to urge the importance of the lost days, or what might have been the result had more activity been displayed by Lieutenant-Commander Smith. With the highest admiration for the gallantry and intelligence displayed by Captains [James P.] Foster and [John G.] Walker, of the Chillicothe and De Kalb, and the earnest conviction that they would have cheerfully obeyed any order from their superior officer, I am constrained to state that in the attack upon Fort Pemberton Lieutenant-Commander Smith again failed to exhibit the decision and intelligence necessary under such circumstances to secure the advantage of a victory. After the Chillicothe and De Kalb had silenced the fort, he failed to push the latter close enough to it to ascertain the cause of its not replying to her fire. I requested General Ross at the time to urge upon him the importance of this step and the probability of our success, and have reason to believe he followed my suggestion. At all events, it was ascertained a few days afterward, from reliable sources, that had the De Kalb been advanced she would have met with no further resistance, because the rebel ammunition was exhausted. The truth of this is now beyond peradventure. It was simply impossible for General Ross to assault the works at this or any other time, with or without re-enforcements. Hoping that this matter may be investigated, and the responsibility fixed where it belongs, . . ." *O.R.*, I, xxiv, part 1, 390–91.

To Col. William S. Hillyer

Before Vicksburg March 23, 1863

COL W. S. HILLYER
PROVOST. MARSHAL. GENERAL

In the case of Mr Hood, whose Cotton is retained at Memphis, the following are the circumstances of its release. Mr Hood was represented as a good citizen of Kentucky, and a man in every way reliable. These representations were made by influential men in Kentucky, among whom General. Boyle. is one endorsing him.—Hood is the owner of a plantation near Lake Providence from which he has lost everything except a portion of his cotton. Of that which was concealed in different places in the woods he did not know what quantity there was left. But a count being made, by parties sent by Mr. Hood for the purpose, placed the number at 291 Bales, and for this application was made and the permit given by me.—In addition to Mr Hood's hardships in the loss of his other property, he was waylaid by some of our soldiers and robbed of $20.000 in money, the soldiers immediately deserting. How a portion of this cotton came to be marked C. S. A. I do not know but suppose it may have occurred by every planter being compelled to subscribe a portion of his cotton to the so called confederacy. This should justly go to the Goverment. As Mr Hood has been so severely looser however already, I would direct that all not marked C. S. A be turned over immediately to him or his agent M J. Keene & co. at once, and the other (the C. S. A. cotton) to Mr Yeatman of the Treasury Department,[1] to be disposed of by him

U. S. GRANT

Maj. Genl.

Copies, DLC-USG, V, 19, 30; DNA, RG 393, Dept. of the Tenn., Letters Sent. See letter to Maj. Gen. James B. McPherson, March 11, 1863.

1. On April 15, 1863, Thomas H. Yeatman, Memphis, wrote to USG. "I have recieved and accepted the appointment of Special Agent of the U. S. Treasury Department in addition to my former duties: 'To receive and collect abandoned or captured property including all cotton, Tobacco, and other merchandize, and property seized under Military or Naval orders, or abandoned by the owners, In the States of Tennessee, Arkansas, Louisiana, Mississippi and Alabama, excepting army ordnance, ships, Steam Boats, or other water craft, and their furniture, Forage muitions of war and military supplies necessary in Military and Naval operations.' and respectfully ask for your cooperation and the turning over to me as such agent all property of the aforesaid character under your Command." LS, DNA, RG 109, Union Provost Marshals' File of Papers Relating to Individual Civilians. On April 26, Lt. Col. John A. Rawlins issued General Orders No. 26 directing that captured property be turned over to Yeatman. Copies, DLC-USG, V, 13, 14, 95; (2) *ibid.*, RG 393, Dept. of the Tenn., General and Special Orders. On May 7, Yeatman wrote to USG. "Being the authorized agent appointed by the Honl Secretary of the U. S. Treasury, under the act of Congress approved March 12, 1863. I have contracted with Richard M. Robinson, for the Parish of Madison and Thomas Conner for the Parish of Carroll in the State of Louisiana, (and will from time to time appoint others for different places) 'to gather Gin and Bale, and transport to Memphis Tenn. all the abandoned ungined Cotton in said Parishes. All of which is to be done free of Expense to the United States. And for so doing the United States agree to give said parties *one fourth* ¼ of Said Cotton.' 'Said parties are also to Gather and bale all abandoned Ginned Cotton in said Parish' (which is not baled) and deliver it at Memphis Tenn. For which the United States is to allow them a reasonable Compensation.' And with a view to facilitate their operations: I beg leave to ask that you give them such aid and protection as may be consistent with your Judgment." LS, *ibid.*, Letters Received.

To Maj. Gen. Henry W. Halleck

———

Near Vicksburg
Mch 24th [*1863*]

MAJ GEN H W HALLECK
GEN IN CHIEF

At last accounts Yazoo Pass Expedition were yet at Greenwood   Admiral Porter and Sherman are attempting to get in to
the Yazoo below Yazoo City   No news from them for several
days   Farragut holds the River above Port Hudson

U S GRANT
Maj Genl

Telegram received, DNA, RG 107, Telegrams Collected (Bound); *ibid.*, Telegrams Collected (Unbound); copies, *ibid.*, Telegrams Received in Cipher; *ibid.*,
RG 393, Dept. of the Tenn., Hd. Qrs. Correspondence; DLC-USG, V, 5, 8, 24,
94. *O.R.*, I, xxiv, part 1, 22.

To Maj. Gen. Henry W. Halleck

———

Head Quarters, Dept. of the Ten
Before Vicksburg, March 24th/63

MAJ. GEN. H. W. HALLECK,
GEN. IN CHIEF WASHINGTON
GEN.

I am led to believe, and think there is no doubt of the fact,
that Maj. Gen. C. S. Hamilton is making indirect efforts to get
Gen. McPherson removed from the command of his Army Corps,
and to get the command himself. If this is so I wish to enter my
solemn protest. There is no comparison between the two as to
their fitness for such a command.

McPherson from his activity, good sense, winning maners
and effort to harmonize all parts of his command towards each
other, and to preserve the same harmony towards all parts of this

army has made him the favorite with his men and officers and one of the most suitable Corps Commanders probably in any service. Gen. Hamilton lacks these qualifications. As a soldier I have no fault to find with him further than his natural jealous disposition which influances his Military Conduct and acts prejudically upon the service.

I enclose with this some correspondence between Gens. Hurlbut and Hamilton and which forms part of the ground upon which I have felt it a duty to order the latter to the front and shows partially the justness of what I here say of him.

I would respectfully ask to have this laid before the President.

> I am Gen. Very respectfully
> your obt. svt.
> U. S. GRANT
> Maj. Gen

ALS, IHi. *O.R.*, I, xxiv, part 3, 137. For the enclosures, see *ibid.*, pp. 137–43. Among the many documents enclosed was a letter of March 11, 1863, from Maj. Gen. Stephen A. Hurlbut to Lt. Col. John A. Rawlins. "I transmit to you the enclosed copies of Telegrams recieved and their answers. Maj Genl Hamilton seems disposed to provoke my good nature to which there are limits. I have treated him with exceeding kindness but meanfully to vindicate myself and the authority vested in me by the President & the Maj Genl Comg' Dept. I shall probably have to arrest Genl Hamilton, not only on this account but because of his neglect to comply with the order in relation to the 7th Kansas. I have directed him to report on this subject whi he has not yet done. I am unofficially informed that he recieved the order and stated that it was one that should not be issued which he would not execute. I have sent for the proof & if it be so I shall arrest him & forward him to Vicksburg for trial. I have trouble enough without torturing my soul on questions of Rank on telegraphic information of outside people, until I learn by authority that I am superceded I shall act under orders already recieved & known to be valid." Copy, DNA, RG 393, 16th Army Corps, Letters Sent. *O.R.*, I, xxiv, part 3, 137–38.

Also enclosed was a letter of March 15 from Maj. Gen. Charles S. Hamilton, La Grange, to USG. "I do not know whether Hurlbut has furnished you with the information received from time to time through Dodge's and my own spies from the south. I have furnished it fully to him, and I send you herewith the last intelligence from Dodge; also my own. All the transportation in the shape of rolling stock along the Jackson road from Meridian and elsewhere had gone west to Vicksburg a week since. The inclosed letter from Dodge shows where it is. One of my spies brought me word from [Sol. G.] Street's guerrilla headquarters that the heavy guns were being dismounted in Vicksburg and being transferred east as rapidly as possible. All sources of information point to the belief that the rebels contemplate an evacuation the moment their rear is threatened. The road from

Jackson, Tenn., to Columbus having been abandoned, I have drawn four regiments from Sullivan and added them to Denver's division, which now stretches from Davis' Mills to Memphis. The force is sufficient to protect the road from the guerrillas now in the country, but, should any considerable portion of Van Dorn's forces return, it will be necessary to increase the road guard or else concentrate it at the most important points. Bethel is now garrisoned from Dodge's forces, and the two regiments that were stationed there are now guarding the road near Memphis. Everything is perfectly quiet in the whole district. During the past week I organized and planned an expedition to clean out [R. V.] Richardson, embracing a column from here, under Grierson, one from Lee, at Germantown, and a watching force from Fort Pillow. You have been made aware of the results of the expedition, which, though considerable, did not meet my expectations. I have also destroyed, during the week, the Tallahatchee Bridge. I have been planning an expedition with Dodge from Corinth, by which Cornyn, supported by a brigade of infantry, should try and reach Meridian, breaking up the gangs of conscripts known to be scattered at various points along the Mobile and Ohio road. To do it I should have to increase Cornyn's cavalry force by another regiment, and when he moves from Corinth I should send another strong cavalry force from here to Pontotoc, breaking up Falkner, who is reorganizing his regiment at the latter place. Hurlbut says you have ordered the cavalry put in condition for heavy service, and thinks it will be hardly possible for the expedition to go. I think it would be productive of good results. Hurlbut is at last confirmed, from September 17, myself from September 19; action on McPherson's case not known. If I am to remain in the District of West Tennessee, on duty, let me ask that the district be divided, and that I report direct to you. If you deem it necessary for me to remain in my present position, I request the Districts of Jackson and Corinth, and as far west as Moscow, be assigned me as a separate command, reporting direct to department headquarters. It is altogether probable that my rank is senior to McPherson, and that I am entitled to the command of the Seventeenth Corps, but it will be some time before this can be officially known. Buford is left out of the confirmed list of major-generals. I am anxious to come down to see you. Everything is so quiet that I can well be spared from my position. I send this by one of my aides, Lieutenant [Edward F.] Pierce, and trust that he will bring back an affirmative reply." *Ibid.*, pp. 138–39. For Hamilton's resignation, see letter to Brig. Gen. Lorenzo Thomas, March 28, 1863.

To Brig. Gen. Alfred W. Ellet

Before Vicksburg March 24th 1863.

BRIG GENL ELLIT

COMMDG MARINE BRIGADE

I am just informed that to insure the success of the enterprise against Warrenton, ten or twelve small boats will be required. May I request that you furnish that number. If it is intended to send a Ram past Vicksburg to night they could be sent by her, if not by sending them down the canal. to night to the lower end. Col Wood, who will command the expedition, and who is now there, will get them[1]   I will see that these boats are returned

U S GRANT

Maj Genl.

Copies, DLC-USG, V, 19, 30; DNA, RG 393, Dept. of the Tenn., Letters Sent. *O.R.*, I, xxiv, part 3, 136; *O.R.* (Navy), I, xx, 18. Alfred W. Ellet, born in Pa. in 1820, left a farm at Bunker Hill, Ill., to enter the Civil War as capt., 59th Ill. When his older brother Charles organized the ram fleet, Alfred joined him as lt. col. and second-in-command. Charles died of wounds received at Memphis in June, 1862, and Alfred succeeded to command, holding the rank of brig. gen. as of Nov. 1, 1862.

On March 24, 1863, Capt. Warren D. Crandall, U.S.S. *Autocrat*, wrote to USG. "I am directed by General Ellet to inform you that he has arranged with Admiral Farragut to send two Rams down to his assistance to night. These Vessels when safely below will, with the Albatross, according to an arrangement already made, with the officer commanding the troops opposite Warrenton convey the troops accross to attack the Batteries while the Flagship Hartford silences their Guns. No small boats will therefore be needed for the purpose contemplated to day." ALS, DNA, RG 94, War Records Office, Dept. of the Tenn. *O.R.*, I, xxiv, part 3, 136–37; *O.R.* (Navy), I, xx, 17. For the passage of Vicksburg on March 24 by the rams *Switzerland* and *Lancaster*, see Warren D. Crandall and Isaac D. Newell, *History of the Ram Fleet and the Mississippi Marine Brigade . . .* (St. Louis, 1907), pp. 193–217.

1. Charles R. Woods of Ohio, USMA 1852, held the rank of 1st lt. when he commanded the troops sent to Fort Sumter on the *Star of the West* in Jan., 1861. Appointed col., 76th Ohio, as of Oct. 13, 1861, he joined USG's command with his regt. in time for the battle of Fort Donelson. On March 24, Woods, "Briggs Plantation La," wrote to Capt. Joseph W. Paddock, adjt. for Maj. Gen. Frederick Steele. "I have the honor to inform you that I arrived at this place last evening about 8 Oclock with my two Regts & found that Admiral Farragut with the Hartford had dropped down below Warrington. I was in consequence unable to communicate with him. I suppose he will be up again this morning. I learn that the Admiral is very poorly supplied with boats, & it will be necessary to have ten or twelve more in order to land the troops Rapidly. I would suggest that that number of boats might be sent down to night, with the *Ram*, which I suppose Genl. Ellet is going to send around to night. If no Ram comes, If they can be sent to the mouth of the Canal near the battery I can send up & get them.   it is of the utmost importance that I should have the boats to insure success in the enterprise as the Gun Boats will not probably go nearer the shore than one or two hundred yards . . . P. S. Genl. Ellet is expected down here this morning to see the Admiral. should any different arrangements be made I will advise you." ALS, DNA, RG 393, Dept. of the Tenn., Letters Received. On the same day, Steele endorsed this letter. "Respectfully referred to Maj. Gen. Grant. I have no yawls at my command." ES, *ibid.* Also on March 24, USG wrote to Steele. "Please inform

Col Wood that I will have him furnished with as many of the boats required as can be got. They will be sent by one of the ways suggested by the Colonel" Copies, DLC-USG, V, 19, 30; DNA, RG 393, Dept. of the Tenn., Letters Sent.

On March 25, Woods wrote to Paddock. "I have the honor to inform you, that the Ram Lancaster was totaly destroyed this morning in passing the Vicksburg batteries & that the Monarch recieved an eighty four pound shot in her boiler & had one of her steam pipes cut.   the extent of the damage cannot yet be assertained on account of the heat. I think it will take three or four days at least if not ten days to repair her. Admiral Farragut seems to think that the troops can be landed from the Gun Boats & the place destroyed. I do not feel so sanguin on the subject, as landing troops in small boats under the most favorable circumstances, is necessarily slow work, & the enemy would have time to reinforce the place to any extent   I send Maj Warner with this dispatch in order to receive orders.   if it is determined to push this matter it will be necessary to have Rations as our Rations run out to day after dinner. Please indicate to Maj Warner what is to be done & if additi[on]al rations are required he will attend to having them got down to the canal   Owing to the disaster to the Rams I was obliged to keep my men under the Levy near the crevasse until near ten Oclock, & in removing them to the shelter of the wood above this place it was impossible to keep them entirely concealed from the enemy, & I think it more than likely that they are aware of our intended movement." ALS, *ibid.*, Letters Received. On the same day, Steele referred this letter to USG. ES, *ibid.* Also on March 25, Col. Charles H. Abbott, 30th Iowa, "Briggs plantation," wrote to Steele reporting the damage to the two rams. ALS, *ibid.* On the same day, Steele forwarded this letter to USG. AES, *ibid.*

To Lt. Col. Charles A. Reynolds

Head Quarters, Dept. of the Ten.
Before Vicksburg, March 25th 1863.

COL. C. A. REYNOLDS,
CHIEF QUARTER MASTER,
COL.

You will retain in the service of the Government sufficient river transportation for the carriage of fifty thousand (50.000) men, including the proper proportion of Artillery & two regiments of Cavalry, Quartermaster Store & forage, Commissary Stores, Ordnance Stores, Camp & Garrison equipages, &c.

Get an exact account of all boats now here and on the way, and their exact capacity, and direct the quartermaster in Memphis to supply any deficiency.

Boats longest out of Govt. Service should be first taken but there must be no delay for the purpose of doing justice to any parties.

Boats left to keep the Depot at Memphis supplied must not come below. Those retained for the transportation of troops will do the carrying trade between the fleet & Memphis.

Very Respectfully,

U. S. GRANT

Maj. Gen'l.

P. S. Instruct the Quartermaster in Memphis that all boats from below Memphis hereafter, are to be immediately returned, with such stores as may be for shipment at the time.

U. S. G.

Copy, DNA, RG 94, ACP, 1172 ACP 1875. On March 25, 1863, USG again wrote to Lt. Col. Charles A. Reynolds. "Detail the steamer of 'Silver Moon' now loaded with ordnance stores in good shape for issueing, and another steamer of the capacity of about six hundred, (600) tons for the Ordnance Department." Copies, DLC-USG, V, 19, 30; DNA, RG 393, Dept. of the Tenn., Letters Sent.

To Rear Admiral David G. Farragut

———

March 26th 1863,

DEAR ADMIRAL,

Your note of yesterday is just received. In regard to attacking Warrenton I do not know what now to say.

When I first learned that twelve to fifteen Yawls would be required I called on Gen. Ellet for them. The Gen. being over to see you no reply was received (except from his Adjt. Gen. that he thought they had that number) until the Generals return in the evening when he informed me that it was arranged for the Rams & Hartford to transport the troops. No small boats would be required.

After learning again that smal boats would be required I again called on G[en]. Ellet for them and only learned after dark that after his losses of these vessels with the Rams he could not furnish them. I then sent for the boats belonging to the transport fleet and found that not more than two could be got. By this time so much of the night was consumed that I could not call upon the Navy with any prospect of geting them through in time to be used this morning. About 9 O'clock last night I learned that a force of apparently about 1500 men left Vicksburg in the direction of Warrenton. I communicated this fact to Col. Wood[s] and left it for you and himself, who would probably have better means of knowing the destination of these troops, to judge what course was best to pursue.

With a little lower stage of water I would endeavor to occupy New Carthage. This occupied and one gunboat from this fleet below the city the enemy could be kept out of Warrenton, and also from taking supplies from a rich country that can be reached through Bayous with flat boats on this side of the river.

I see by southern papers received yesterday[1] that Vicksburg must depend upon Louisiana, or West of the Miss. for supplies. Holding Red River from them is a great step in the direction of preventing this. But it will not entirely accomplish the object. New Carthage should be held and it seems to me that in addition we should have vessels sufficient below to patroll the whole river from Warrenton to the Red River. I will have a consultation with Admiral Porter on this subject. I am happy to say the Admiral and myself [hav]e never yet disagreed upon any policy.

I am looking for a Mail in to-day, and should one arrive with later dates of papers than you have already been furnished I will send them over.

I am Admiral, very truly yours
U. S. GRANT
Maj. Gen.

To Admiral D. G. Farragut
Comd.g Western G. B. Squadron.

ALS, DNA, RG 45, Area 5. *O.R.*, I, xxiv, part 3, 147–48; *O.R.* (Navy), I, xx, 26–27. On March 25, 1863, Rear Admiral David G. Farragut wrote to USG. "I have this moment received your kind note, and like yourself deeply regret the failur of the Rams to reach me in order. I blame myself very much for not insisting on Gen'l Ellets waiting for a dark night   I was so much afraid of their impetuosity that it deprived me of sleep all night but I never for a moment supposed that he would come down in the day time. The 'Switzerland' is not much injured. My Engineers inform me her boilers can be repaired in four days but unless she goes below Warrenton to make her repairs she will be blockaded so as to have to run it in the night—As the Enemy is working very industriously to mount heavy Guns, I have shelled them three or four times very heavily but with very slight effect as they lie down until we are finished and then get up and work industriously again   My isolated position renders it necessary that I should be very careful of my ship and hence I will drop down below the town until I know the result of your determination on the subject of attacking it. My idea was to have landed your men in the Switzerland and covered the landing with my ship. I understand they have reenforced their Garrison some 200 men to day. I do not know the difficulties of our carring the Rifle Pits as well as those who have carried them. I regret exceedingly 'General' that the only time I have felt the time at my disposal I was too unwell to take the trip up to see you but I would have been delighted to have seen you on board at any time, and hope yet to have the pleasure of meeting you in this part of the world. I feel however that even now that I am absent from Red River is a serious loss to our country and our cause. Permit me to repeat my sincere thanks for your kindness in affording me every facility in your power since my arrival here   Wishing you every success in all your undertaking"   LS, DNA, RG 94, War Records Office, Dept. of the Mo. *O.R.*, I, xxiv, part 3, 143; *O.R.* (Navy), I, xx, 25–26.

1. On March 25, Col. Charles H. Abbott, 30th Iowa, wrote to Lt. Col. John A. Rawlins. "I hand you late Rebel papers which I obtd. via underground R. R. Important news in them. I also have direct information from Vicksburg, that the Rebels have bursted the heavy Gun with which they were fireing upon the Dredge Boats in the Canal and were yesterday drawing her into Vicksburg to cut her off & make a Morter gun of her. Genl. Bartlett is in Command at Warrenton. Hd. Qrs. one & one half mile from town where they have three Rgts between Warrenton & Vicksburg. Genl. Taylor is 2d in Command. The Confederates themselves burned the Steamer Natches up the Yazoo River to prevent her falling into the hands of our forces. They also blowed up the ~~Star~~ Confederate Gun Boat Star of the West for the same reasons. I should like that Maj Genl. Steele should have access to these papers." ALS, DNA, RG 94, War Records Office, Dept. of the Tenn. *O.R.*, I, xxiv, part 3, 145–46. On March 26, Abbott wrote to Rawlins. "I send you Seven Contrabands who came over from Vicksburg last night. The men are bright and inteligent and can give you a great deal of information in regard to the condition of affairs at Vicksburg. One of them has been in the Artilery service since the war and can tell you the possition & numbers of almost every gun from Vicksburg down to Warrenton. They seem to be well posted and brought yesterdays Vicksburg & Jackson papers which I have already handed over to Genl Grant [.] They desire to go North, have money to pay their way   I hope that Genl. Grants permission may be obtained for them to do so   You will of course examine them closely as to what they know about matters at Vicksburg, & if approved of by Genl. Grant, I hope you will aid them in leaving for the North . . . *P. S.* Genl. Grand desires that you keep them until he returns" ALS, DNA, RG 393, Dept. of the Tenn., Letters Received.

To Act. Rear Admiral David D. Porter

March 26th 1863

DEAR ADMIRAL,

Should twelve to fifteen small boats be required at the foot of the Canal to-night, to be taken below to be used in landing troops at Warrenton, can they be got from you? I expected to get them from Gen. Ellet and only found out after dark that they could not. I then tried the transport fleet and found their yawls had all been taken for Army purposes.

Thus not knowing that small boats would be required the expedition failed one day. The Rams failing to get through, safely, and obviating the necessity of small boats, another day was lost and now a third by relying upon Gen. Ellet and the transport fleet for these boats.

It may all be providential however and I shall expect a change of apparent luck soon.

Very Truly yours
U. S. GRANT
Maj. Gen.

To Admiral D. D. Porter
Comd.g Miss. Squadron

ALS, MoSHi. On March 26, 1863, Act. Rear Admiral David D. Porter, Yazoo River, wrote to USG. "We have the boats you desire, but I should not have a boat left for the vessels—the boats of the fleet above were all smashed up. You can have what there is if you really desire it, but my advice is not to use a boat, the soldiers cannot manage them in the stream, and it will give the timid a chance to keep out of fire. I would advise that all the troops be carried over in the steamers and that the Hartford engage the batteries lying close to the bank and silence them, which she can easily do. I think this a risky affair, for if anything should occur to the Hartford, the landing party will be captured—still I am ready to send the boats if you wish them." ALS, USG 3.

To Col. Robert Allen

Before Vicksburg March 26th 1863.

COL ROBERT ALLEN
CHIEF QR MASTER ST LOUI MO.

It is now necessary for our movements, that we have further means of transportations, and of different kind than we have now   There is required with the greatest dispatch 30 yawl of 6 to 10 oar each and a number of flat boats, and scow that can be towed upon which I can place troops and Artillery. I must have not less than 25 flat boats and more if possible and also get me if possible from chicago through the canal for or five of their tugs for towing. If it should cripple the business at chicago, they can be replaced from Detroit, Cleveland and Buffalo. Please give this your urgent attention. This will releive me of the necessity of keeping so many Steamboats on hand and will answer, purposes, that are of the highest importance, that cannot be accomplished by Steamboats.

U. S. GRANT.
Maj Genl.

P. S. Please telegraph me to Memphis and write me upon reciept of this the probabilities of getting the above and when I may dipend upon them

U. S. G.

Copies, DLC-USG, V, 19, 30; DNA, RG 393, Dept. of the Tenn., Letters Sent; (2) Parsons Papers, IHi; Alcorn Collection, University of Wyoming, Laramie, Wyo. See letter to Col. Robert Allen, March 31, 1863.

On April 4, 1863, Col. Lewis B. Parsons telegraphed to USG. "Your letter of the 26th is received   Cant fill your requisition here   have sent to Chicago Louisville and Cincinnati. I think most if not all the articles can be on the way South within 8 to 10 days" ADfS, Parsons Papers, IHi. On the same day, Parsons sent to Col. Robert Allen a detailed report of his efforts to comply with USG's request; Allen added an undated endorsement to USG. LS, DNA, RG 94, War Records Office, Dept. of the Tenn. *O.R.*, I, xxiv, part 3, 172–73.

On April 11, Parsons wrote to USG. "In accordance with your requisition on Col Allen chief Quarter Master I have secured 30 flat boats, Coal boats and Scows. In filling your order we have seized every thing *at all* suitable. I have also secured the required number of Yawls. Also 4 Tugs from Chicago—One of which is already here and starts at once. The flats will also start to day. I expect the other Tugs were through the canal this morning if no bad luck has happened, and if so they should leave here tomorrow (Sunday)   They went through the first lock in the Canal all right. You said nothing in your letter to Col Allen about any alterations, or how you desired the boats fitted up, but I have ventured to put on board some 80,000 feet of lumber with a large quantity of Nails Spikes Oakum &c &c to make floors, And have advised Mr Jameson (Col Reynolds Master Mechanic whom I judge Col Reynolds has sent for this purpose) to put Carpenters on and have boats all ready for service on arrival at Youngs Point. I have also sent a special agent to see that the flats Tugs &c go forward with the greatest possible dispatch. I regret to see by your letter to Col Allen that you were disappointed in the time of arrival of the small boats for the Yazoo expedition. Certainly not a moment was lost after getting your dispatch, not even to await your Messenger with instructions. Every boat suitable any where in this Department was seized, Agents dispatched to Galena and I went personally to Cincinnati. That Genl Meigs or Genl Rosecrans did not feel willing or deem it safe to let boats go, was something we could not help. But I am sure you will bear in mind that so great is the demand for all kinds of boats in various directions that it is not so easy as usual to meet demands. I think you will find the 'Little Giant' a good boat for a dispatch boat for your head quarters. I only got four Tugs; as you said *four* or *five*—and there were but four that it was believed would go through the Canal. Wishing you the most complete success, . . . P. S— I could not get so large Yawls as I desired but got the largest and all I could find in Chicago or St Louis   Col Swords telegraphed me there were none to be had in Cincinnati"   LS, DNA, RG 393, Dept. of the Tenn., Letters Received. On April 12, Parsons telegraphed to USG. "All the boats on the way South.   one (1) Tug here ready to start.   the others are on the Ills   Will send as soon as they arrive. Have written fully." ALS (telegram sent), *ibid.*, RG 107, Telegrams Collected (Unbound); telegram received, *ibid.*; *ibid.*, RG 393, Dept. of the Tenn., Telegrams Received.

To Maj. Gen. Henry W. Halleck

———

Head Quarters, Dept. of the Ten.
Before Vicksburg, March 27th 1863.

MAJ. GEN. H. W. HALLECK,
GEN. IN CHIEF, WASHINGTON,
GEN.

All work, except repairing the crevasse in the Canal levee, has been suspended for several days, the enemy having driven the Dredges entirely out. The canal may be useful in passing boats through at night to be used below, but nothing further.

Admiral Porter has returned from his attempt to reach the Yazoo River below Yazoo City. The difficult navigation of the bayous from the Yazoo river, through Black bayou & Deer Creek, caused so much time to be consumed that the enemy got wind of the movement in time to blockade the creek just where the boats would leave it.

As the enemy occupied the ground in considerable force where they could prevent the clearing out of these obstructions the Admiral was forced to desist from further efforts to proceed when within a few hundred yards of clear sailing to the Yazoo. Rolling Fork and the Sunflower are navigable, steamers having come by this route to within sight of our gunboats whilst they were in Deer Creek.

The moment I heard that Admiral Porter had started on his return I sent orders for the return of the Yazoo Pass expedition from Fort Greenwood. From information I have other and greater difficulties would be found in navigating the Yazoo below Greenwood. Considerable preparation has been made to receive our forces coming by that route.

I get papers and deserters frequently from Vicksburg but am not able to arrive at any definite conclution as to their numbers. I do not anticipate any trouble however if a landing can be effected.

On the morning of the 25th Gen. Ellet sent two Rams, the Switzerland and the Lancaster, to join Admiral Farragut. The latter received a shot in the boiler long before reaching the front of the city. She floated down however receiving many more shots but without materially further disabling her. She will be ready for service before to-morrow night and is a fine vessel.

The Lancaster received a shot and immediately went to pieces. One part, with the Machinery, tipped over and spilt it out in the river. The wreck floated down and lodged at our lower pickets, bottom up. She was very rotten and worthless. The shot received would not have seriously damaged a sound vessel. This is what Admiral Farragut, and Army officers who have examined the wreck, report to me.—As no casualties occurred to life or limb on this vessel it is fortunate she was lost so. Had she been saved it might occur some time that more valuable vessels would have been risked relying on this one for assistance. It is almost certain that had she ever made one *ram* at another vessel she would have *closed up* like a *spy-glass* encompassing all on board.

I have just learned from a contraband (reliable) that most of the forces from Vicksburg are now up the Yazoo leaving not to exceed 10,000 in the city to-day. The batteries are the same however and would cause the same difficulty in landing that would be experianced against a heavy force. Besides the very cause of the absence of so many troops from Vicksburg, our Gunboats & troops in and towards the Yazoo, prevents taking advantage of this circumstance. I have no doubt of the truth of this assertion of the contrabands because it is substantiated by Southern papers and deserters, so far as to large forces being sent up the Yazoo.

> I am Gen. Very respectfully
> Your obt. svt.
> U. S. GRANT
> Maj. Gen.

ALS, ICHi. *O.R.*, I, xxiv, part 1, 23–24. On March 25, 1863, USG had telegraphed to Maj. Gen. Henry W. Halleck. "Two (2) Rams attempted to run the blockade this morning. One succeeded in damaged condition. They were intended to strengthen Farragut. Porter is returning, did not succeed in reaching the Yazoo." Telegram received, DNA, RG 107, Telegrams Collected (Bound); *ibid.*, Telegrams Collected (Unbound); copies, *ibid.*, Telegrams Received in Cipher; *ibid.*, RG 393, Dept. of the Tenn., Hd. Qrs. Correspondence; DLC-USG, V, 5, 8, 24, 94. *O.R.*, I, xxiv, part 1, 23; *O.R.* (Navy), I, xx, 18.

To Julia Dent Grant

March 27th 1863.

DEAR JULIA,

I do not know where a letter will reach you but will venture to send it to the care of Col. Hillyer at Memphis.

I am very well but much perplexed. Heretofore I have had

nothing to do but fight the enemy. This time I have to overcome obsticles to reach him. Foot once upon dry land on the other side of the river I think the balance would be of but short duration. I am now looking for Fred home. Was your visit to Cincinnati disagreeable? I have had no letter from you since you left Memphis but heard of you at Cincinnati.

It would be a great holiday for me to have one month to myself.

Just here Dr. Holston come in with a message from you. I am glad you and the children all look so well.

Did you keep my black coat? I looked for it last night and find it is not in there.

The health of the troops is good here.

Rawlins & Staff generally are well. Lagow is in Memphis. I am afraid it will be a long time before he gets strong again.

Remember me to Col. & Mrs. Hillyer.

Kisses for yourself and children. Good buy Dear Julia.

ULYS.

ALS, DLC-USG.

To Brig. Gen. Lorenzo Thomas

Head Quarters, Dept. of the Ten.
Before Vicksburg, March 28th/63

BRIG. GEN. L. THOMAS,
ADJ. GEN. OF THE ARMY,
GEN.

Enclosed with this I send you the resignation of Maj. Gen. C. S. Hamilton, out of form not giving the reasons for tendering it.

It is due that I should state that I have approved this resignation for the following reasons. I saw from the correspondence between the two Generals that Gen. Hamilton and Gen. Hurlbut could not get along to-gether. For this reason I relieved the former from duty in the Dist. of West Tennessee and ordered him here. Commanders having been assigned to Corps by the President I had nothing larger, in the field, to give Gen. Hamilton than a Division. This he refused to accept.

Gen. Hamilton being a capable officer I gave him the choice between taking his old position under Gen. Hurlbut, a Division in the field, the command of the Dist. of Eastern Arkansas or to be relieved from duty in this Dept. and ordered to report to Washington for orders. He accepted the latter with the request that his resignation be forwarded.

I think in justice to the service his resignation should be accepted. The officer who shows that he expects a command to be fixed up for his express benefit, in my opinion becomes a beneficiary instead of what he should be, a support to the Govt.

The proposition which Gen. Hamilton said he could accept were first, a division of Gen. Hurlbuts Command, in a certain way, and him to be independent of the latter; the other that I take two Divisions of the Army in the field and give him independent of Army Corps Commanders. This I could not do without manifest injury to the service.

I am Gen. very respectfully
your obt. svt.
U. S. GRANT
Maj. Gen.

ALS, DNA, RG 94, ACP, H556 CB 1864. O.R., I, xxiv, part 3, 151. On March 23, 1863, Maj. Gen. Charles S. Hamilton wrote to Secretary of War Edwin M. Stanton. "I tender my resignation as Major General of Volunteers. to take immediate effect. I have no indebtedness to the Government either in money or property." ALS, DNA, RG 94, ACP, H556 CB 1864. On March 27, USG endorsed this letter. "Respectfully forwarded to Headquarters of the Army, Washington, D. C. and recommended." ES, *ibid*. Hamilton was relieved of duty by Special Orders No. 86, Dept. of the Tenn., March 27. Copies, DLC-USG, V, 26, 27; DNA, RG 393, Dept. of the Tenn., Special Orders. On March 31, Hamilton drafted a letter to Stanton explaining his resignation. After briefly mentioning his private business and wife's health, Hamilton wrote at length about his claim to command a corps in place of Maj. Gen. James B. McPherson. ADf, Hamilton Papers, Illinois Historical Survey, University of Illinois, Urbana, Ill.

On April 1, Lt. Col. John A. Rawlins issued Special Orders No. 91. "Major General Richard J. Oglesby, U. S. Vols. will report in person to Major General S. A. Hurlbut, Commanding 16th Army Corps, for assignment to the Command vacated by Major General C. S. Hamilton." Copies, DLC-USG, V, 26, 27; DNA, RG 393, Dept. of the Tenn., Special Orders. *O.R.*, I, xxiv, part 3, 165.

To Maj. Gen. Benjamin M. Prentiss

————

Head Quarters, Dept. of the Ten.
Before Vicksburg, March 28th/63

MAJ. GEN. B. M. PRENTISS,
COMD.G DIST. E. ARK.
GEN.

The troops that have gone down Yazoo Pass are now ordered back. On their return to Helena debark them and send Hovey's Division immediately down to join Gen. McClernand at Millikins Bend. You will please add to Hovey's Div. two, or three if you think they can be safely spared from Helena, of the oldest regiments from Ross'.

I do not much like taking troops that have been so long on board steamers as Gen. Ross' command has immediately into the field, but it is a necessity.

I am Gen. very respectfully
your obt. svt.
U. S. GRANT
Maj. Gen. Com

P. S. Send Quinby's and Smith's Divisions directly forward, the former to Lake Providence, and the latter to this point. Let there be no delay.

U. S. GRANT
Maj. Genl.

ALS, DNA, RG 94, War Records Office, Union Battle Reports. *O.R.*, I, xxiv, part 3, 151. On April 1, 1863, Maj. Gen. Benjamin M. Prentiss, Helena, wrote to USG. "I have the honor to report that your directions in relation to the changes of the troops here, on the return of the Yazoo Expedition, have been attended to, so far as my co-operation was ordered. I am holding Gen. Hovey's division in

readiness to embark at any time—and as soon as Gen. Quinby's fleet begins to
arrive, I shall embark Hovey's men, that they may move down the river the
moment Ross arrives.—" ALS, DNA, RG 393, Dept. of the Tenn., Letters
Received. On the same day, Maj. Gen. John A. McClernand, Milliken's Bend,
wrote to USG. "My guards report this morning, that a number of boats, passed
down last night supposed to have, *Genl Hovey's* Division from Helena, Arkansas,
on board. I desire to know whether I shall order them back or whether you will
do so. I have to report, that I have found other small boats in this vicinity, and
will send them to Richmond to day. Another Regiment of infantry: with a section
of Artillery has gone forward to Richmond." Copies, *ibid.*, 13th Army Corps,
Letters Sent; McClernand Papers, IHi.

To H. J. Loring & Co.

Before Vicksburg March 28th 1863.
MESSER. H J. LORING & CO.
STATIONERS &c. ST LOUIS MO.

Please manufacture and forward by Express, to this point
with as little delay as possible, one Book of "Letters Received"
for the use of "Department of the Tennessee" to be of the same
size and style as the one put up by you for this Department in
October last. Mark "B" the pages to be lettered in the proportion that the figures opposite the several letters of the alphabet,
on the enclosed slip bear to each other in order to avoid as much
as possible the transfer of entries under one alphabetical letter,
to the pages of another   se[e] last paragraph on page Eleven of
circular from Adjutants Generals Office War Department   send
bill for book direct to these Head Quarters, and the amount of
same will be promptly remitted to you

U. S. GRANT,
Maj. Genl

Copies, DLC-USG, V, 19, 30; DNA, RG 393, Dept. of the Tenn., Letters Sent.
    On April 18, 1863, Lt. Col. John A. Rawlins wrote to H. J. Loring & Co.
"Please manufacture and send by express to this place with as little delay as possible one 'Letter Book' and One 'Book of Special Orders' with two indexes for
each for use of 'Department of the Tennessee.' The books will be marked "B"
and be of same size and style as those put by you for this Department in October
last. The indexes to be six times as large as the one recently received and the

number of pages to each letter to be in proportion with the number in the book of 'Letters Received' Send bill direct to these Head Quarters and the amount will be promptly remitted to you." Copies, *ibid.*

To Maj. Gen. Henry W. Halleck

> Head Quarters, Dept. of the Ten.
> Before Vicksburg, March 29th 1863

MAJ. GEN. H. W. HALLECK,
GEN. IN CHIEF, WASHINGTON D. C.
GEN.

A dispatch to release boats,[1] and letter on the subject of the Yazoo expedition[2] are both just received, the letter also enjoining me to keep you informed of the *situation* constantly by telegraph.

I have been very particular to write and telegraph often even when there was nothing important to say knowing that you would feel anxious to be constantly posted. The letters I presume reach but the dispatches must in many instances have failed.

In regard to sending back boats from here ~~that was an order~~ I gave and reiterated the order to Gen. McClernand to do so before leaving Memphis. On my arrival however I found the river rising so rapidly that there was no telling what moment all hands might be driven to the boats. As soon as this danger was passed so many boats were released that I could have moved but a small force at one time.

I wrote you fully on the subject of the Yazoo expedition a few days ago.

If you do not receive at least one letter and two dispatches per week from me Gen. be assured that some of them miscarry. In addition I will telegraph as often as anything may occur of any importance.

> I am Gen. very respectfully
> your obt. svt.
> U. S. GRANT
> Maj. Gen. Com

ALS, MH. *O.R.*, I, xxiv, part 1, 24. On April 9, 1863, Maj. Gen. Henry W. Halleck wrote to USG. "Yours of March 29th is just received. Your explanation in regard to sending back steamers is satisfactory. I hope you will keep in mind the great importance of not unnecessarily detaining them, on account of the great embarrassment it causes the Quartermaster Dept in supplying our western armies. In regard to your despatches, it is very probable that many fail to reach here in time. It is exceedingly important that Genl Banks should be kept advised of everything that is done in your vicinity, and the only way he can get this information is through these Head Quarters. You are too well advised of the anxiety of the government for your success & its disappointment at the delay, to render it necessary to urge upon you the importance of early action. I am confident that you will do everything possible to open the Mississippi river. In my opinion this is the most important operation of the war, and nothing must be neglected to ensure success. Genl Hamilton's resignation has been received, but has not yet been acted on, the President & Secretary being absent. No doubt he resigns to get a higher command. This game sometimes succeeds, but it also sometimes fails." ALS, DNA, RG 108, Letters Sent by Gen. Halleck (Press). *O.R.*, I, xxiv, part 1, 27–28.

1. On March 24, Halleck telegraphed to USG. "I must again call your attention to the importance of your not retaining so many steamers in the Miss. It is absolutely necessary that a part of these boats be returned. We cannot otherwise supply our armies in Tennessee & Kentucky. This matter *must* be attended to without delay." ALS (telegram sent), DNA, RG 107, Telegrams Collected (Bound); telegram received, *ibid.*, RG 393, Dept. of the Tenn., Telegrams Received. *O.R.*, I, xxiv, part 1, 22. On March 31, USG telegraphed to Halleck. "I have ordered the release of all boats that can be spared for General Rosecrans." Telegram received, DNA, RG 107, Telegrams Collected (Bound); *ibid.*, Telegrams Collected (Unbound); copies, *ibid.*, RG 393, Dept. of the Tenn., Hd. Qrs. Correspondence; DLC-USG, V, 5, 8, 24, 94. On March 5, Halleck had telegraphed to USG. "It is of great importance that transports be returned from your command, so far as possible, otherwise you will be short of supplies. Steam vessels on the upper rivers are very scarce. Vessels on the river between Memphis and Vicksburg should go in fleets, under convoy. Make requisitions on Admiral Porter for convoys. The unnecessary detention of transports down the Miss. River is a matter of the most serious importance & requires your immediate attention." ALS (telegram sent), DNA, RG 107, Telegrams Collected (Bound); telegram received, *ibid.*, RG 393, Dept. of the Tenn., Telegrams Received. *O.R.*, I, xxiv, part 1, 19.

2. See letter to Maj. Gen. Henry W. Halleck, March 7, 1863.

To Act. Rear Admiral David D. Porter

Head Quarters, Dept. of the Ten.
Before Vicksburg, March 29th 1863.
ADMIRAL D. D. PORTER,
COMD.G MISS. SQUADRON,
ADMIRAL,

I am about occupying New Carthage with troops, and opening the Bayous from here to that place sufficiently for the passage
of flats, a number of which I have ordered from St. Louis. With
this passage open I can run the blockade with steamers sufficient
to land troops, with the aid of flats, either at Grand Gulf or
Warrenton which ever seemed most promising. Under these
circumstances is it not absolutely essential that Warrenton &
Grand Gulf should be so controlled by gunboats as to prevent
further fortifications?

It looks to me Admiral as a matter of vast importance that
one or two vessels should be put below Vicksburg both to cut off
the enemies intercourse with the West bank of the river entirely,
and to ensure a landing on the East bank for our forces if wanted.

Will you be good enough Admiral to give this your early
consideration and let me know your determination. Without the
aid of gunboats it will hardly be worth while to send troops to
New Carthage or to open the passage from here there: as
Preparitory surveys for doing this are now being made.

I am Admiral, very respectfully
your obt. svt.
U. S. GRANT
Maj. Gen.

ALS, DNA, RG 45, Correspondence of David D. Porter. *O.R.*, I, xxiv, part 3,
151–52; *O.R.* (Navy), I, xxiv, 517. On March 29, 1863, Act. Rear Admiral
David D. Porter, "Yazoo River," wrote to USG. "I am ready to cooperate with
you in the matter of landing troops on the other side, but you must recollect that
when these gun-boats once go below we give up all hopes of ever getting them
up again. If it is your intention to occupy Grand Gulf in force, it will be necessary
to have vessels there to protect the troops, or quiet the fortifications now there.

If I do send vessels below it will be the best vessels. I have, and there will be nothing left to attack Hayne's Bluff in case it should be deemed necessary to try it. It will require some little preparation to send these vessels below. Coal & provisions are wanted—they cannot well do without. With the force Farragut now has he can easily dispense with one vessel to patrol the Coast as far as Grand Gulf, while we are preparing this thing. I will come over and see you. I have been quite unwell all night, and not able to move about much. Before making a gunboat move I should like to get the vessels back from the Yazoo Pass Expedition." LS, DNA, RG 94, War Records Office, Dept. of the Tenn. *O.R.*, I, xxiv, part 3, 152; *O.R.* (Navy), I, xxiv, 518.

To Maj. Gen. Stephen A. Hurlbut

Head Quarters, Dept. of the Ten.
Before Vicksburg, March 29th 1863.

MAJ. GEN. S. A. HURLBUT,
COMD.G 16TH ARMY CORPS,
GEN.

You may direct Gen. Webster, Supt. of Military R. Roads, to commence immediately the reconstruction of the rail-road between La Grange and Corinth. To facilitate this work I will send you six companies of the Engineer regiment.[1] You are authorized to detail a regiment of Infantry also for this duty and employ contrabands to any extent.[2]

Detail a suitable officer for collecting any guns that may still be left on the line of the river and not in use. Have them brought to Memphis and mounted in the fort. Such as Gen. Davies has practiced his skill upon will have probably to have a new vent reamed out.

Gen. McClernand has made application for the 18th Ill. regiment.[3] If you can send it as well as not you may do so. As they are mounted however, and no more mounted men are required here, it may not be advisable to send it. Felling every desire to gratify Gen. McClernand in every possible, consistently with the good of the service, I leave this with you, with the understanding that McClernand can send you a very poor new regiment in place of the 18th.

I may not want Lauman's Division atal, but if I do send for it it will be in an imergency and will want it to move with the greatest promptness, leaving baggage in charge of details from each regiment to follow.[4]

Very respectfully
U. S. Grant
Maj. Gen. Com

ALS, ICHi. *O.R.*, I, xxiv, part 3, 152–53.

1. On April 3, 1863, USG wrote to Col. Josiah W. Bissell. "You will proceed immediately on board the Steamer herewith sent, to Memphis, Tenn., and report to Major General S. A. *Hurlbut*, for railroad duty. You will send back without delay, the Steamer 'Crescent City,' together with all small boats you may have collected, and everything belonging to the regiment except such tools as you will require in the duty you are going at. You need not wait to cut a single tree after the reception of this order." Copies, DLC-USG, V, 19 (2), 30; DNA, RG 393, Dept. of the Tenn., Letters Sent.

2. On March 26, Maj. Gen. Stephen A. Hurlbut had written to Lt. Col. John A. Rawlins. "I forward with this communication all papers due upt to this time. I ask the consideration of the Maj Genl comdg to this question now of pressing importance. It is spring. Planters & farmers should be at work, but negroes, horses, and mules are gone, fences destroyed & everything necessary to carry on business is delapidated   What am I to do with the vast number of worthless negroes, now running at large in this city, they are now running at large in this city, they are not enrolled do no work & live by stealing & vice. Is it competent to hire them out putting the hirers under bond to treat them kindly and pay a reasonable sum. The contraband Camps are a tremendous failure and a mere excuse for misplaced charity. I propose if permitted to enroll every negro who can be employed in Govt service, and attach him to that branch where he is best qualified and to seize the hord of pilferers about the city and hire them out. I do not know that I have any right to do it, & desire before action to have the opinion of the Maj Genl or to be allowed to communicate directly with Washington. The Elephant is decidedly to heavy a prize." Copy, *ibid.*, 16th Army Corps, Letters Sent.

3. On March 28, Maj. Gen. John A. McClernand, Milliken's Bend, wrote to USG. "The officers and men of the 18th Ill. Infy. are known to both of us heroes of many a hard fought field. They are now languishing in a camp near Jackson Tenn, and are depressed by the prospect of continued in-action. They wish to join me. I would be pleased to have them as a leaven for the new troops in my command. They could take the place of the 131st Ill. sent back, or the 108th Ill. which I have asked to be sent back. Although, seemingly, ignored as to promotion Col. Lawler is one of the *bravest and most valuable officers in action* that has commanded a regiment or brigade in this department. I know he feels deeply. I would do what I can to relieve his mortification." ADfS, McClernand Papers, IHi.

4. On March 25, USG wrote to Hurlbut. "If Laumans Div. is not already enroute for this place hold them in readiness to move at short notice but await orders from here. They need not be turned back if started." ALS, DNA, RG 94, War Records Office, Military Div. of the Miss. *O.R.*, I, xxiv, part 3, 146.

To Maj. Gen. James B. McPherson

Before Vicksburg March 30th 1863.

MAJOR GENL. J. B. MCPHERSON
COMMANDG. 17TH ARMY CORPS.

As it is probable that Laumans, Divisions will not be brought down here, I have attached Genl. J. E. Smith Divisions to the 15th Army Corps. send them down to report to Sherman. Has Quinbys two Divisions come down yet. they should be got down as early as possible please send me your report on Wallaces case[1] at Pittsburg landing on the 6th of April 1862. as early as you can. Have you investigated the case yet of the practicability of getting into Bayou Macon? I do not expect to use that route but want to know if it can be used in case of necessity

U. S. GRANT
Major Genl.

Copies, DLC-USG, V, 19, 30; DNA, RG 393, Dept. of the Tenn., Letters Sent. Maj. Gen. James B. McPherson quoted USG's letter in a letter of March 31, 1863, to Brig. Gen. Isaac F. Quinby. Copy, *ibid.*, 17th Army Corps, Letters Sent. *O.R.*, I, xxiv, part 3, 159; *O.R.* (Navy), I, xxiv, 290–91. McPherson quoted two sentences from USG's letter; when printed, four additional sentences written by McPherson were attributed to USG. On March 31, McPherson, Lake Providence, wrote to USG. "I have the honor to acknowledge receipt of dispatches per Steam boat Emperor. Genl Smith's Division reached here last night and to day. It will be ordered down immediately. I enclose the last dispatch which I have received from Gen'l. Quinby—will send a messenger up to Genl Quinby by the first opportunity, directing him to come down as rapidly as possible. I have within the last few days had the passage from here to Bayou Macon thoroughly reconnoitered. Following the route indicated on a sketch recently sent you the shallowest water is 3½ feet, this at the point where you leave 'Bayou Baxter,' and just before reaching 'Bayou Macon,' a distance from 250 to 300 yards, which could be dredged out in a short time. There are also twelve or fifteen trees to be cut off under water, for which I have been waiting for the *Sawing Machine* to come from Memphis, while Col Pride told me ought to have been five days ago. After this work is done, the class of Boats which navigated 'Yazoo Pass' can go through this route. My report with a copy of the Map in my possession with regard to Wallace's movements on the 6th of April, was sent to you by the Steam Boat Emperor, three days ago. If it does not come to hand I can send you a Copy." Copies (2), DNA, RG 393, 17th Army Corps, Letters Sent. *O.R.*, I, xxiv, part 3, 159.

On April 1, McPherson wrote to USG. "From information just received from a man by the name of 'Hawkins' a northern man by birth I learn the following. Gen. Price and Hindman were in Munroe one week ago last Sunday, Hindman on his way to Vicksburg to attend a court martial for the trial of Lovell for the surrender of New Orleans, Price on his way to Little Rock to organize his forces for the invasion of Mo, determined to do it or perish in the attempt. Rebels nearly starved out at Vicksburg & Port Hudson, only two weeks supply on hand— Expectation pretty general that they will have to evacuate. The 'Indianola' was raised Guns taken off and sent to Alexandria on Red River, Boat taken up the Big Black about a day before Admiral Farraguts Arrival—Hull comparatively un-injured, upper works having been blown off by explosion—Ram 'Queen of the West' up Red River with the Webb. A Battery of 2-11″ guns at the junction of the Washita & Big Boeuf Rivers—General depression among the people. Gov. Moore of La. issued an order calling out all the Militia of the State. Many of them object on the ground that the Law authorizing it is unconstitutional, having been passed when there was not a quorum in the Senate—Mr Hawkins has some additional information which he wishes to communicate to you personally—shall I permit him to come down—" ALS, DNA, RG 94, War Records Office, Dept. of the Tenn. *O.R.*, I, xxiv, part 3, 164–65.

1. See letter to Col. John C. Kelton, April 13, 1863.

To Julia Dent Grant

March 30th 1863.

DEAR JULIA,

Col. Hillyer, Fred. & Willie[1] arrived here all safe last night having had a tedious trip on account of the storm. They were obliged to lay up at Lake Providence. Fred. is looking well and seems as happy as can be at the idea of being here. I have not had an opportunity of talking to him alone yet. You can stay at Memphis as well as any other place tha until the fate of Vicksburg is settled. There has been some delay in the attack unavoidable on my part. I hope to be ready soon however. Once landed on the other side of the river I expect but little trouble.

I never enjoyed better health or felt better in my life than since here. The weather however will soon begin to grow warm and unpleasant.

I have but little to write about that would interest you. Fred. is also writing and says he will write twice each week. I will require Fred. to read and study his arithmetic. I will not be able to hear lesson his lessons much however. I am sorry Buck did not come down to stay as long as Col. Hillyer does!—I sent Jess. a Silver dollar by Orly.[2] He must keep that as that kind of money is scarce. Tell Jess that as soon as he gets on his Maj. Gen. shoulderstraps he can order Col. Hillyer in Irvin Block.[3] Col. Hillyer will be afraid of him. He must not scare "Old Blowhard" though.

Tell Col. Lagow to go home if it will benefit him. I would like to see him back here well as soon as possible but he can go wherever his health would be the most improved in the mean time.

Kisses for yourself and children dear Julia.

ULYS.

ALS, DLC-USG.

1. See commission for William S. Hillyer, Nov. 1, 1861.
2. For Capt. Orlando H. Ross, see letter to Edwin M. Stanton, Nov. 27, 1862, note 2.
3. Irving Block Military Prison at Memphis.

To Col. Robert Allen

Head Quarters, Dept. of the Ten.
Before Vicksburg, March 31st 1863.

Col. R. Allen,
Chief Q. M.
Col.

I wrote you a few days ago for tugs and barges for the transportation of this Army! With these I could spare a corresponding proportion of steamers and use them when the steamers cannot be used.

Quite a number of coal barges can be prepared here so that the tugs are of the greatest importance. I hope you will give this early attention.

I have ordered the release of a number of boats sent from the Ohio river and will keep no more than are absolutely necessary.

Very respectfully
U. S. Grant
Maj. Gen

ALS, Parsons Papers, IHi. See letter to Col. Robert Allen, March 26, 1863.

Calendar

———

1862, DEC. 9.   To Capt. Theodore S. Bowers. "Detail Lieut. J. W. Barnes as requested by Gen. Dodge."—Copies, DLC-USG, V, 18, 30, 91; DNA, RG 393, Dept. of the Tenn., Letters Sent; Dodge Papers, IaHA.

1862, DEC. 9.   Maj. Thomas M. Vincent, AGO, Washington, to USG. "By direction of the Secretary of War you will discharge Private Alexander Diven, of Captain Cooley's Chicago Mercantile battery and let him come home for promotion."—LS (telegram sent), DNA, RG 107, Telegrams Collected (Bound); copies, *ibid.*, RG 94, Vol. Service Division, Letters Sent; *ibid.*, RG 393, Dept. of the Tenn., Letters Sent; DLC-USG, V, 18, 30, (2) 91; (misdated Nov. 9) *ibid.*, V, 5, 8, 24, 88; DNA, RG 393, Dept. of the Tenn., Hd. Qrs. Correspondence. Private Alexander Diven, Chicago Mercantile Battery, was discharged Dec. 11 to accept promotion; he was appointed paymaster to rank from Nov. 26.

1862, DEC. 10.   USG endorsement. "Respectfully refered to the Gen. in Chief. I would be pleased to have Gen. Davidsen and troops but am not able to judge of the necessity of retaining him where he is."—AES, DNA, RG 108, Letters Received. Written on an informal letter of Nov. 19 from Brig. Gen. John W. Davidson, Pilot Knob, Mo., to Maj. Gen. William T. Sherman requesting a transfer to the Dept. of the Tenn. because his health was not up to a winter campaign in Mo., which would involve "plodding thro' the swamps . . . in search of an enemy that does not exist."—ALS, *ibid.* On Nov. 25, Sherman wrote a favorable endorsement.—AES, *ibid.* Davidson, however, remained west of the Mississippi River through the war.

1862, DEC. 10.   To Maj. Gen. William S. Rosecrans. "Capt. Dickson was relieved from duty in the field not being able to ride on horseback. He is now at Paducah recruiting his health."—Telegram, copies, DLC-USG, V, 18, 30, 91; DNA, RG 393, Dept. of the Tenn., Letters Sent. On Dec. 10, Rosecrans had telegraphed to USG. "Capt Dickson A. A. G. formerly with Genl McArthur has been ordered to report to me—Please ask Genl McArthur to telegraph him to report at once as I need him very much"—Copies, *ibid.*, Dept. of the Cumberland, Telegrams Sent; *ibid.*, RG 107, Telegrams Collected (Unbound).

1862, DEC. 10.   Maj. Gen. Henry W. Halleck to USG. "Company K, 18th regt Ill. volunteers will report to Brig. Genl A. W. Ellett for duty on the Ram fleet. Genl Ellett is at Cairo, but probably the company can best join the fleet at Memphis."—ALS (telegram sent), DNA, RG 107, Telegrams Collected (Bound); telegram received, *ibid.*, RG 393, Dept. of the Tenn., Telegrams Received. This telegram was entered in USG's records correctly dated in DLC-USG, V, 91, but misdated Nov. 10, *ibid.*, V, 5, 8, 24, 88; DNA, RG 393, Dept. of the Tenn., Letters Sent. On Dec. 10, Lt. Col. John A. Rawlins issued Special Field Orders No. 19 transferring this co.—DS, *ibid.*, RG 94, Dept. of the Tenn., Special Orders; DLC-USG, V, 26, 27, 91. See also *O.R.*, I, xvii, part 2, 398. On Dec. 11, Brig. Gen. Jeremiah C. Sullivan, Jackson, telegraphed to Rawlins. "Replying to Special field order No 19 Co K Eighteenth 18 Regt Ills infy volunteers has been brought in from duty on Railroad & is now at Depot to go forward on first train" —Telegram received, DNA, RG 393, Dept. of the Tenn., Telegrams Received.

1862, DEC. 10.   John W. Resor, Holly Springs, to Capt. Theodore S. Bowers. "As an act of justice allow me to relate to you the particulars of an affair which occurred near Hudsonville Station, a few days since. A party of seven men from the 26th Ills Regt, having been out in the country some two or three miles from their Camp were fired on by a Band of Guerillas under command of a man named Mitchell, by which one was killed, two or three wounded, and the rest taken Prisoners. The facts as near as I can learn them are these. The men were on their return to Camp, and had stopped at the House of a Mr Thompson, while there they were overtaken by Mitchell, when the above events occurred. Mr Thompson was sitting in his House at the time, and was first made aware of their presence by hearing the shots fired, when on going out in the yard he found the three men lying there. As soon as possible he had them taken care of, and then fearing that he would be blamed by our Troops, (as it had happened on his place) he was induced by his Family to leave. His Wife then packed up a few clothes and started with their children to this place, but meeting with some accident they were obliged to leave everything, and finally managed to reach here in safety. Since then our Troops have burned the House, and destroyed nearly everything on the place, with the exception of four Bales of Cotton, which was seized by the 26th Regt, and taken to the Depot. The most of the Clothes belonging to Mrs Thompson and her children were taken by a Major, (supposed to be the Major of the 26th Ills Regt.) who said he intended sending them to his Wife in Illinois. As far as the Loyalty of Mr Thompson is concerned, I can only say this much, (which I have learned from his neighbors and those who were well acquainted with him,) that he has never taken up arms against the Federal Government, and was by some considered a union man, and had always treated the Federals as well as was in his power to do, and previous to this time has never had any trouble with them. I believe what I have stated to be the facts in regard to the case, and in my opinion it would be an act of *justice* to restore to Mrs Thompson such of her Goods as can be recovered. Hoping you may inquire into the matter and do justice to the parties concerned"—ALS, DNA, RG 109, Union Provost Marshals' File of Papers Relating to Individual Civilians. On Dec. 14, Lt. Col. John A. Rawlins referred this letter to Col. John M. Loomis, 26th Ill.—ES, *ibid.* On Dec. 17, Loomis wrote to Rawlins that M. H. Thompson had arranged the ambush and exulted in the death of U.S. troops.—ALS, *ibid.*, RG 94, War Records Office, Union Battle Reports. *O.R.*, I, xvii, part 1, 507–8.

1862, DEC. 11. To Governor Edward Salomon of Wis. "In an enemy's country to preserve order and protect our lines of communication it is necessary in many instances to detail companies from Reg'ts to garrison posts and stations. These companies cannot be relieved without the detaching of companies from other regiments which will be subject to similar objections from others"—Copies, DLC-USG, V, 25; DNA, RG 393, Dept. of the Tenn., Endorsements. Written on a letter of Nov. 27 of Salomon requesting that two cos. of the 15th Wis., then at Island No. 10, be ordered to rejoin the regt. at Nashville.—*Ibid.*

1862, DEC. 11. Maj. Thomas M. Vincent, AGO, to USG. "Respectfully returned to Major General Grant The men mentioned herein as being detailed on Ram Fleet cannot at present be returned. If Lt Col McCown will make a report in each of the other cases their return will be ordered—"—Copy, DNA, RG 393, 17th Army Corps, Endorsements; *ibid.*, Dept. of the Tenn., Endorsements; DLC-USG, V, 25. Written on a letter of Nov. 16 of Lt. Col. Joseph B. McCown, 63rd Ill., La Grange, asking that troops of his regt. on detached service be returned.—*Ibid.*, V, 21.

1862, DEC. 11.   Maj. Gen. William S. Rosecrans, Nashville, to USG. "Ten miles from Grenada on Mississipi Central Rail Road, under charge of George W. Peel, is a ~~cotton~~ plantation with two cotton crops belonging to Widow of the late President James K. Polk—Let me request you to protect her property—"—Telegram, copies, DNA, RG 107, Telegrams Collected (Unbound); *ibid.*, RG 393, Dept. of the Cumberland, Telegrams Sent.

1862, DEC. 11.   Brig. Gen. Grenville M. Dodge, Corinth, to USG. "On the examination of Champion & Colb I find that they had taken the advice of the Provost Marshal before issuing the shinplasters Who ~~in m~~ innocently told them he saw no ~~more~~ wrong in useing it for change   they have but Eighty dollars & have promptly redeemed it they are represented to me as reliable men   under the Circumstances shall I send them out of the Dept"—Telegram received, DNA, RG 393, Dept. of the Tenn., Telegrams Received.

1862, DEC. 12.   Col. DeWitt C. Anthony, 66th Ind., Columbus, Ky., to USG. "I am disembarked at Columbus with my Reg 66 Ind under you last order   am I to proceed to Memphis with it ~~to~~ as directed by Gen Sherman when I left Memphis   my Reg is unfut for the field & my official affairs at Mmphis entirely unsettled"—Telegram received, DNA, RG 393, Dept. of the Tenn., Telegrams Received. On the same day, Lt. Col. John A. Rawlins telegraphed to Anthony. "You will proceed with your Regt. to Corinth, and there report to Gen Dodge."—Copies, DLC-USG, V, 18, 30, 91; DNA, RG 393, Dept. of the Tenn., Letters Sent.

1862, DEC. 13.   USG endorsement. "Respectfully recommended and forwarded. Col. Deitzler is universally acknowledged to be an officer of merit."—AES, DNA, RG 94, ACP, D213 CB 1863. Written on a petition of Dec. 12 from officers of the 1st Kans. to President Abraham Lincoln recommending Col. George W. Deitzler, 1st Kans., for promotion to brig. gen., later favorably endorsed by other officers and Kans. politicians.—DS, *ibid.* On March 4, 1863, Lincoln nominated Deitzler as brig. gen. to rank from Nov. 29, 1862, and the appointment was confirmed on March 9, 1863. On Aug. 29, USG endorsed a certificate of Aug. 12 of Dr. S. B. Prentiss, Lawrence, Kans., stating that Deitzler was unfit for service due to chronic diarrhea. "Respectfully

forwarded to Headquarters of the Army Washington, D. C. By inclosed Special Order No. 112. Brig. Genl. Deitzler was relieved from
duty in this Department and ordered to report to Major General
McDowell, President of the Military Court of Inquiry then in session
at Saint Louis, Mo. Sometime after he reported to Major General
McDowell he was ordered by him, to report in person at these Headquarters: Immediately thereupon he made application for leave of
absence, based on surgeons certificate, which was granted him June 10,
1863, by the inclosed Special Order No. 156. He has not been on duty
since he was relieved April 22, 1863 and from this certificate it would
appear that he is not only unfit for duty but will so remain for sometime
to come. I would therefore most respectfully request that he be mustered out of the service under G. O. No. 196. A. G. O. C. S."—ES,
ibid. Deitzler's resignation was accepted as of Aug. 27.

1862, DEC. 14.   USG endorsement. "Respectfully forwarded to Head-
quarters of the Army, Washington, D. C. and recommendation of Gen.
McKean approved."—Copies, DLC-USG, V, 25; DNA, RG 393,
Dept. of the Tenn., Endorsements. Written on a letter of Dec. 6 of
Capt. John W. Meacham, 14th Ill., endorsed by Brig. Gen. Thomas J.
McKean explaining that after Meacham was discharged for absence
without leave, he then returned and was continued on duty and ought
to be paid for the latter period.—*Ibid.*

1862, DEC. 14.   USG endorsement. "Respectfully returned to Head
Quarters of the Army, Washington, D. C. calling attention to the
enclosed communication from Col. Noble, Comm'g Post at Paducah,
Ky."—ES, DNA, RG 107, Irregular Series, Letters Received. Written
on a statement of Aug. 5 of Clothilde Cecilie Colinet, Paducah, Ky., a
French citizen, claiming damages of $5,000 to her property, resulting
from the occupation of Paducah in Sept., 1861, when U.S. troops cut
down trees in order to erect fortifications.—Copy, *ibid.* On Dec. 2,
1862, Col. Silas Noble, Paducah, wrote to USG that the property was
really owned by Etienne Girard, a disloyal U.S. citizen, son-in-law of
Mme. Colinet.—ALS, *ibid.*

1862, DEC. 14.   USG endorsement. "Respectfully forwarded to Head
Quarters of the Army, Washington D. C. and for report attention is
called to the enclosed statement of Col Dollins."—Copies, DLC-USG,

V, 25; DNA, RG 393, Dept. of the Tenn., Endorsements. Written on a letter of Nov. 29 from Maj. Thomas M. Vincent, AGO, to USG requesting information concerning the addresses of the enlisting officer and examining surgeon in the case of Private Larkin Cantrell, 4th Ill. Cav., discharged because he had lost his right arm before enlistment. —Copy, *ibid.*, RG 94, Vol. Service Division, Letters Sent. USG enclosed a statement of Col. James J. Dollins, 81st Ill., that Cantrell was enlisted by order of Maj. Gen. John A. McClernand.—DLC-USG, V, 25; DNA, RG 393, Dept. of the Tenn., Endorsements.

1862, Dec. 15.   USG endorsement. "Respectfully referred to Head Quarters of the Army. Col Mather of the 2d Ill Arty has never been in the field in command of his regiment, but for a few weeks and then left without authority from these Hd Quarters   His time has been spent almost exclusively in Ill. where he has been of no service to his Regiment. I would respectfully recommend that he be mustered out of service"—Copies, DLC-USG, V, 25; DNA, RG 393, Dept. of the Tenn., Endorsements. Written on a letter of Dec. 1 of Col. Thomas S. Mather replacing 2nd Lt. Horatio N. Towner as adjt. with 1st Lt. Frank B. Smith.—*Ibid.*

1862, Dec. 16.   Col. Edward D. Townsend, AGO, Washington, to USG. "You will furnish to this office with the least possible delay by mail the following information in answer to a call of Congress. How many commissioned officer of the troops under your command are now absent from their respective commands, specifying the number of each grade and whether absent on leave, without leave, or by detail."—LS, DNA, RG 393, Dept. of the Tenn., Letters Received; telegram received, *ibid.*, Telegrams Received. An LS (telegram sent, dated Dec. 15), *ibid.*, RG 107, Telegrams Collected (Bound), indicates that an identical telegram was sent to half a dozen other officers.

1862, Dec. 16.   Brig. Gen. Thomas A. Davies, Columbus, Ky., to Lt. Col. John A. Rawlins. "Three (3) car loads of negroes have just arrived here from Bolivar without orders for their disposition from you   there is no place for their accommodation here & to turn them out of the cars into mud is inhuman   they are still unloaded   what shall be done with them"—Telegram received, DNA, RG 393, Dept. of the Tenn., Telegrams Received; copy, *ibid.*, Hd. Qrs. District of

Columbus, Telegrams Sent. On Dec. 16, Rawlins telegraphed to Davies. "Make the best disposition of the Negroes you can in tents and vacant houses, and issue to them rations. Let them be employed in the Quartermaster's Department and on the levee and hired to Steamboats for works on the river reporting in the mean time to the Secty of War asking as to what final disposition shall be made of them. They were sent there without the order of the Genl. Commdg."—Copies, DLC-USG, V, 18, 30, 91; DNA, RG 393, Dept. of the Tenn., Letters Sent.

1862, Dec. 16. Col. Silas Noble, Paducah, to USG. "Shall civil officers be Sworn into office who express disloyal Sentiments"—Telegram received, DNA, RG 393, Dept. of the Tenn., Telegrams Received.

1862, Dec. 17. USG endorsement. "Respectfully forwarded to Head Quarters of the Army Washington, D. C. The order accepting resignation was received immediately after the granting of leave of absence and entered of record. By my direction the order was forwarded to the colonel of of the regiment with request that he indicate his approval in writing thereon for for its revocation. But from some cause, probably the movement of troops on the expedition made about that time in Kentucky, never reached him. Capt Roberts returned from his leave in due time and took command of his Company, and continued in command of the same until he was taken prisoner at the battle of Shiloh. No one has been commissioned to fill the vacancy. He is a brave and competent officer. It is therefore respectfully requested that the order accepting his resignation, a copy of which is herewith enclosed, be revoked."—Copies, DLC-USG, V, 25; DNA, RG 393, Dept. of the Tenn., Endorsements. Written on a letter of Dec. 8 of Ill. AG Allen C. Fuller concerning the resignation of Capt. William R. Roberts, 28th Ill.—*Ibid.* Roberts was honorably discharged as of Oct. 20, 1863.— *Ill. AG Report,* 2, 438.

1862, Dec. 17. USG endorsement. "Respectfully forwarded to Head Quarters of the army and recommended"—Copy, DLC-USG, V, 25; DNA, RG 393, Dept. of the Tenn., Endorsements. Written on a letter of Dec. 3 of Brig. Gen. John Cook, Sioux City, Iowa, requesting the assignment of 2nd Lt. Paul J. B. Marion, 7th Ill., to his staff.—*Ibid.*

1862, DEC. 17.   USG endorsement. "Respectfully forwarded to the Adjutant of the Army Washington D. C in Compliance with Genl Order No 100 par 3rd War Department"—Copies, DLC-USG, V, 25; DNA, RG 393, Dept. of the Tenn., Endorsements. Written on a letter of Dec. 12 of Col. Hugh T. Reid, 15th Iowa, concerning the application of a private for discharge because of permanent disability.—*Ibid.*; DLC-USG, V, 21; DNA, RG 393, Dept. of the Tenn., Register of Letters Received.

1862, DEC. 17.   USG endorsement. "Respectfully referred to Head Quarters Army Washington, D. C. for decision of the President."— Copies, DLC-USG, V, 25; DNA, RG 393, Dept. of the Tenn., Endorsements. Written on the proceedings of a court of inquiry concerning 1st Lt. Ferdinand E. Peebles, 1st Minn. Battery.—*Ibid.*

1862, DEC. 17.   USG endorsement. "Respectfully referred to Maj Gen'l Wright, Comdg Dept. of the Ohio, with the request that this man be relieved and ordered to his regiment if practicable."—Copies, DLC-USG, V, 25; DNA, RG 393, Dept. of the Tenn., Endorsements. Written on a letter of Dec. 11 of Lt. Col. John Shane, 13th Iowa, requesting the return to his regt. of a private detailed to the provost guard in Cincinnati.—*Ibid.*

1862, DEC. 17.   To Col. Joseph D. Webster, Jackson. "There is a Conductor by name of Parsons said to be of doubtful loyalty and who was seen to take the mark off of a package for me saying there was no such person in this country as Major Genl. U. S. Grant and appropriated the Articles for his own use. Discharge him and send him North of the Dept."—Telegram, copies, DLC-USG, V, 18, 30, 91; DNA, RG 393, Dept. of the Tenn., Letters Sent.

1862, DEC. 17.   Col. John K. Mizner, Water Valley, Miss., to USG. "A Recent order prohibits the sale of Comsy stores to officers Except by Division Comsys   Cannot the Cavalry be relieved from the operation of this Order   The officers of this Command are without supplies & there is no one at hand from whom they Can purchase   the ~~rations~~ nature of the duty performed by the Cavalry is such as to keep much of it detached from any Hd Qrs & the present Order applying to the cavalry causes much inconvenience   Cannot brigade Comsys of Cavalry be authorized to sell to Cavalry officers   Supplies for officers are very much needed here"—Telegram received, DNA, RG 393, Dept. of the Tenn., Telegrams Received.

1862, Dec. 18.   USG endorsement. "Respectfully referred to Maj Genl S. R. Curtis Com'd'g Dept. of the Missouri, in whose command the 21st Mo. Infy Vols now is"—Copy, DLC-USG, V, 25; DNA, RG 393, Dept. of the Tenn., Endorsements. Written on a letter of Dec. 5 of Private Henry G. Smith, 21st Mo., stating that he had been in the hospital at Jackson since April, and had received no pay for a year because he lacked proper papers.—*Ibid.*

1862, Dec. 18.   Mr. Johnson, express agent, Jackson, Tenn., to USG. "Have got a car load of freight for you   what shall I do with it"— Telegram received, DNA, RG 393, Dept. of the Tenn., Telegrams Received. On Dec. 18, Lt. Col. John A. Rawlins telegraphed to Johnson. "Send the Car load of freight for Maj Gen U. S. Grant to Holly Springs Miss. and deliver the same to Major T. S. Bowers in charge of Head Quarters Office at latter place"—Copies, DLC-USG, V, 18, 30, 91; DNA, RG 393, Dept. of the Tenn., Letters Sent.

1862, Dec. 19.   John C. Dent, St. Louis, to USG. "Permit me to introduce Colonel Madison Miller of the Army who has been lately actively employed in service in your section and previous to that in the field with Genl Lyon   The Col served in the war with Mexico   I have been acquainted with him for forty years and during that time have always found the Col to be a perfect gentleman, he is the brother of Mrs John Willson & Mrs Stine of this place   I hope you will receive & treat the Colonel with every consideration and do as much for the Colonel and his Regiment as will be satisfactory to him & congenial to your wishes and much Oblige"—ALS, Miller Papers, MoSHi.

1862, Dec. 24.   USG endorsement. "Approved and respectfully forwarded to Headquarters of the Army. Washington D C"—Copies, DLC-USG, V, 25; DNA, RG 393, Dept. of the Tenn., Endorsements. Written on a letter of Col. Rodney Mason, 71st Ohio, concerning two lts. reported absent without leave.—*Ibid.*

1862, Dec. 25. USG endorsement. "Respectfully referred to Maj Gen. S. R. Curtis Comdg Dept of the Mo. with the request that Lieut Sumner be relieved from duty in Missouri and ordered to rejoin his Regt at this place"—Copies, DLC-USG, V, 25; DNA, RG 393, Dept. of the Tenn., Endorsements. Written on a letter of Col. Josiah W. Bissell stating that 2nd Lt. Heywood M. Sumner, detailed as ordnance officer in Mo., had been serving as adjt. for a gen. officer of Mo. militia.—*Ibid.*

1862, Dec. 26. To 2nd Lt. Stephen C. Lyford, chief of ordnance. "Have you any arms better than the Austrian Musket? The 90th Illinois at Coldwater are badly armed and want to exchange."—Telegram, copies, DLC-USG, V, 18, 30; DNA, RG 393, Dept. of the Tenn., Letters Sent. On the same day, Lyford telegraphed to USG. "Can only furnish Austrian or Prussian plenty of them on hand"—Telegram received, *ibid.*, Telegrams Received.

1862, Dec. 27. Col. Ebenezer S. Sibley, deputy q. m. gen., to USG. "I have the honor to inform you, that on an examination of Lt. E. V. Cherry's Property Returns in this office, it is found they are in good condition, and that he has been prompt in their rendition. The Quarter Master General has, therefore, recommended his appointment as Assistant Quarter Master of Volunteers—Lt. Alonzo Eaton having been reported to the Secretary of War for the non rendition of his accounts for the Second quarter of 1862, the Quarter Master General cannot recommend his appointment as Assistant Quarter Master of Volunteers."—LS, DNA, RG 92, Letters Sent (Press); copies, *ibid.*; *ibid.*, RG 393, Dept. of the Tenn., Hd. Qrs. Correspondence; DLC-USG, V, 5, 8, 24, 88.

1862, Dec. 28. USG endorsement. "Respectfully forwarded to Headquarters of the Army Washington D. C. with the recommendation that the order dismissing Lieut Harlow from the service be revoked"—Copies, DLC-USG, V, 25; DNA, RG 393, Dept. of the Tenn., Endorsements. Written on the proceedings of a court of inquiry concerning 1st Lt. Edward G. Harlow, 12th Wis. Battery.—*Ibid.* On Nov. 27, Harlow had written a letter demanding a court of inquiry, and on Dec. 1, Brig. Gen. Charles S. Hamilton endorsed this letter to USG. "This subject is respectfully referred to Dept. Hd. Qrs. for a decision, as to whether Lieut. Harlow is entitled to a Court of Inquiry. He was charged at Iuka, with leaving his section in action and going to the rear—and at Corinth, with being drunk. He had not been mustered into service at Iuka or Corinth, but was mustered in at La Grange, previous to receipt of order dismissing him from service. He acknowledges leaving his section at Iuka—but pleads ignorance of his duties; and at Corinth drank some whiskey when much exhauste[d.] He is a temperate man, and desires to exculpate himself before a Court, to save himself from disgrace. If exculpated, he will ask for a remission of the order dismissing him, and will resign."—Copy, *ibid.*, Army of the Miss., Endorsements. Harlow, however, continued in service.

1862, Dec. 29.   USG endorsement. "Approved and respectfully forwarded to the Headquarters of the Army at Washington D. C."— Copies, DLC-USG, V, 25; DNA, RG 393, Dept. of the Tenn., Endorsements. Written on a letter of Dec. 20 of Lt. Col. John S. Snook, 68th Ohio, requesting leave of absence to attend to private business.—*Ibid.*

1862, Dec. 29.   To Brig. Gen. Jeremiah C. Sullivan. "Mr. Lea has already suffered more according to his means than any other Citizen. of Jackson   You may therefore spare his sugar unless it becomes absolutely necessary for the use of the army"—Telegram received, DNA, RG 109, Union Provost Marshals' File of Papers Relating to Individual Civilians; copies, *ibid.*, RG 393, Dept. of the Tenn., Letters Sent; DLC-USG, V, 18, 30. On the same day, Col. Joseph D. Webster, Jackson, had telegraphed to USG. "Dr Lea wishes permission to retain his Sugar which you know about   under the circumstances it seems to me proper to allow him to do so   do you remember giving him a safe guard"—Telegram received, DNA, RG 393, Dept. of the Tenn., Telegrams Received.

1862, Dec. 29.   Brig. Gen. Lorenzo Thomas to USG. "From the records of this office many General and Staff officers appear absent without leave, and, therefore, liable to be dismissed and many unemployed. It is supposed that this may, in some cases, be on account of the neglect of the proper officers to make the reports required to this office. The Secretary of War, therefore, directs that you furnish with the least possible delay to this office the names of all General and Staff officers serving under your command showing, if a General Officer his

command, whether a Brigade, Division, &c., if a Staff Officer the name of the General on whose Staff he is serving and how he is employed."
—LS, DNA, RG 393, Dept. of the Tenn., Letters Received.

1862, Dec. 30. To commanding officer, Lumpkin's Mill, Miss. "Mr. Balfour a known Union man living in the neighborhood. of your forces is entitled to protection from our army. I wish you whilst remaining there to see that he is no further molested."—ALS, NjP. On Jan. 24, 1863, USG wrote two passes. "Mr Balfour & family, loyal citizens of the State of Mississippi are permitted to pass North through the lines of the Federal Army." "Pass Mr Balfour and son through the lines with bill of goods, authorized by Treasury Dept"—Copies, DNA, RG 109, Union Provost Marshals' File of Papers Relating to Individual Civilians. John Balfour, a blind citizen of Holly Springs, Miss., was described as loyal in accompanying papers.—*Ibid.*

1862, Dec. 30. Brig. Gen. John A. Logan to Lt. Col. John A. Rawlins. "I desire a military Commission appointed to try Benj F Dougherty of Co K 31 Ill Ify for shooting a negro boy"—Telegram received, DNA, RG 393, Dept. of the Mo., Telegrams Received. On the same day, Rawlins telegraphed to Logan. "Please telegraph names of three Officers available for duty on Military Commission and name of negro boy shot"—Copies, DLC-USG, V, 18, 30; DNA, RG 393, Dept. of the Tenn., Letters Sent. On the same day, Logan telegraphed to Rawlins. "Detail on Commission Lt Col Maltby of 45th Ills Lieut Col F M Campbell of 81st Ill infy & Maj Herman Leib of 8th Ill infy   the name of negro boy unknown"—Telegram received, *ibid.*, Dept. of the Mo., Telegrams Received.

1862, Dec. 30. Col. John A. Rogers, Humboldt, Tenn., to USG. "Has a recruit the right to leave any command that he has received clothing & Subsistence from for 2 months & join another without a regular transfer from the troops that he last served in or not   the reason I ask the question is I was commissioned by the War Dept to raise a Regt & swear the men into the service as enrolled which was done.   some have left this Regt & have been mustered into the Cavalry service   is it my duty to arrest & bring them back into the command   answer—"—Telegram received, DNA, RG 393, Dept. of the Tenn., Telegrams Received.

1862, DEC. 31. USG endorsement. "Respectfully forwarded to Headquarters of the Army Washington D. C. with the request that Lieut. Nott Smith be ordered to join his Battery"—Copies, DLC-USG, V, 25; DNA, RG 393, Dept. of the Tenn., Endorsements. Written on a letter of Dec. 30 of Capt. Frederick Sparrestrom, 2nd Ill. Light Art., asking the return to his co. of 2nd Lt. Mott Smith, detached as post q. m., Camp Butler, Springfield, Ill.—*Ibid.*

1862, DEC. 31. USG endorsement. "Approved and Respectfully forwarded to Hd Qrs of the Army Washington D. C."—Copies, DLC-USG, V, 25; DNA, RG 393, Dept. of the Tenn., Endorsements. Written on a letter of Dec. 25 of 2nd Lt. George L. Godfrey, 2nd Iowa, requesting leave "to attend to private business"—*Ibid.*

1862, DEC. 31. USG endorsement. "Respectfully forwarded to Washington D. C. with Special Orders No. with the request that the same be approved by the Secy of War"—Copies, DLC-USG, V, 25; DNA, RG 393, Dept. of the Tenn., Endorsements. Written on a letter of Dec. 18 of Private Edward St. Clair, 7th Mo., requesting a transfer to the 4th U.S. Cav.—*Ibid.* On Dec. 18, Col. John D. Stevenson endorsed this letter. "Private St. Clair was formerly in U. S. Cavalry service is an excellent soldier, was mustered into service of the U. S. in my Regt (7th Mo Vols), but his relations with the officers of his Co. are such in my opinion without cause, as to render his service in 7th Mo. Vols of little value to Govt. I therefore recommend the transfer asked, beleiving it to be for the good of the service—"—Copy, *ibid.*, 17th Army Corps, Endorsements.

1862, DEC. 31. USG endorsement. "Approved and respectfully forwarded to his Excellency the Governor of the State of Missouri"—Copies, DLC-USG, V, 25; DNA, RG 393, Dept. of the Tenn., Endorsements. Written on a letter of Dec. 25 of Capt. Michael M. Piggott, 14th Mo., requesting the appointment of 1st Sgt. William H. Saunders as 1st lt. of his co.—*Ibid.*

1862, DEC. 31. USG endorsement. "Respectfully referred to his Excellency Gov Yates of the State of Ill. and Lt Col. Duffs. Chief of Arty—endorsement approved"—Copies, DLC-USG, V, 25; DNA, RG 393, Dept. of the Tenn., Endorsements. Written on a letter of

Dec. 29 of Capt. George C. Gumbart, 2nd Ill. Light Art., regarding
the condition of his battery.—*Ibid.* Gumbart's letter was endorsed by
Lt. Col. William L. Duff. "would respectfully suggest that the Governor of Illinois be urgently requested to fill up this Battery, which is
not singular amongst Ill Batteries, in being much reduced, Capt. Gumbart is one of the most valuable Artillery Officers in the Dept and could
ill be spared"—Copies, *ibid.*

1862, Dec. 31. S. R. Chapin, Jackson, Tenn., to USG. "The undersigned would respectfully make known to your Honour. that his store
in Lexington Tenn Was broken into by a part of Forrest Confederate
Cavelry on their late raid, and that they were robed of goods to the
Amount of Twentyfive Hundred Dollars, (2500$) and that the same
was instigated and justified by Wm P. Collins and Others Citizens of
Lexington and that the said Collins has or had some of the goods in
his house   the said Collins is a Notorious rebel that he has furnished
boots and money to the said Confederates since he took the Oathe and
that he has declared that he would spend the last dollar in their cause
and that the said Collins with Others procured the arrest of the undersigned and his imprisonment in New Orleans   These and Other
Wrongs have bin done the Undersigned solely because he has bin ever
Faithfull to the Union   The undersigned would therefore pray your
Honour that you cause the arrest of said Collins if to be found, and if
not found that his Property may be held liable for any damage that may
be Awarded—And the undersigned would further pray your Honour
that you would cause an investigation be had as to the conduct of
John F Clark R. B. Jones C. W. Jones John Smith John West & others
as to the treatment of Union men of Henderson County—The above
is respectfully submitted."—ALS, DNA, RG 109, Union Provost
Marshals' File of Papers Relating to Individual Civilians.

[1862, Dec.?]   Col. Joseph D. Webster, Jackson, Tenn., to USG.
"We have not cars or engines enough   am obliged to tax them to the
utmost   an Engine broke down today—"—Telegram received, DNA,
RG 393, Dept. of the Tenn., Telegrams Received.

1863, Jan. 1.   USG authorization. "Mrs. M. J. Brown has authority
to retain one pair of mules and team complete. Government authorities

are prohibited from taking them without authority from these Head Quarters."—AES (misdated Jan. 1, 1862), DLC-USG.

1863, Jan. 2. USG endorsement. "Respectfully forwarded to Headquarters of the Army Washington D C This Officer Capt. Alexander T Somerville of the 31st Regt of Ill Infy Vols was dismissed the service for cowardice, by Special Orders. No 212 from Headquarters. Department of the Missouri of date March 7. 1862. and there is nothing in the proceedings to show that the same should be revoked and said Officer, returned to duty, but on the contrary that the order was just, and should remain in force, Of this Capt. Somerville has been notified"—Copies, DLC-USG, V, 25; DNA, RG 393, Dept. of the Tenn., Endorsements. Written on the proceedings of a court of inquiry.—*Ibid.* See *Calendar*, March 7, 1862.

1863, Jan. 2. Maj. Gen. Henry W. Halleck to USG. "Respectfully referred to Major Genl Grant."—AES, DNA, RG 393, Dept. of the Tenn., Miscellaneous Letters Received. Written on a letter of Dec. 30 from Commodore William D. Porter to Halleck recommending a staff appointment for Act. 4th Master J. Harry Wyatt, gunboat *Essex*, and efforts to obtain the release by exchange of 4th Master Spencer Kellogg, *Essex*, captured Aug. 15, 1862.—ALS, *ibid.* See *O.R.*, II, iv, 503.

1863, Jan. 3. To Col. Joseph D. Webster, Jackson. "Please inquire at the Express Office if there is a package for me or Mrs Grant and if so send it by first opportunity"—Telegram, copies, DLC-USG, V, 18, 30; DNA, RG 393, Dept. of the Tenn., Letters Sent. On the same day, Webster telegraphed to USG. "There is nothing in the Express for your self or Mrs Grant I want all of the Engr Regt which can be sent me with tools for railroad repairs & stockades."—Telegram received, *ibid.*, Telegrams Received.

1863, Jan. 3. Brig. Gen. Thomas A. Davies, Columbus, Ky., to Lt. Col. John A. Rawlins. "Col Lowe reports that a train going from ft Donelson to ft Henry was attacked by Spauldings band of Guerrillas a fight ensued Spaulding was killed & several others with some prisoners & routing the remainder our loss three 3 killed & three 3 taken prisoners"—Telegram received, DNA, RG 393, Dept. of the Tenn., Telegrams Received; copy, *ibid.*, Hd. Qrs. District of Columbus, Letters Sent. *O.R.*, I, xvii, part 1, 698.

1863, JAN. 3.   Brig. Gen. John A. Logan to Lt. Col. John A. Rawlins. "I have a Genl Court Martial in session who have ordered the reduction of one months pay for sleeping on post I have disapproved the sentence give the Court martial the devil & now want an order sending the man to Alton at Hard labor during his enlistment   the name of soldier is Wm H Pond priv. Co E 23 Reg Ind. Vols"—Telegram received, DNA, RG 393, Dept. of the Tenn., Telegrams Received. On the same day, Rawlins wrote to Logan. "You served the court right   Publish the order to your command reprimanding the court and ordering the prisoners to be confined in military prison at Alton Illinois for the balance of his term of enlistment with forfeiture of pay and allowance and disgraceful dismissal at the expiration of his sentance and send Orders to these Hedd Quarters for approval"—Copies, DLC-USG, V, 18, 30; DNA, RG 393, Dept. of the Tenn., Letters Sent.

1863, JAN. 4.   To Commanding officer, Grenada, Miss. "Captain J M Brook A. Q. M. C. S A a paroled prisoner of war on this day passed through the Federal lines with authority to apply to southern authorities to effect an exchange for Captain R. E. Bryant, C. S. U S A who is now at Holly Springs a prisoner on parole. Capt Brooks is at liberty to regard his exchange as fully effected immediately on notice being sent to me of the release of Captain Bryant."—Copies, DLC-USG, V, 18, 30; DNA, RG 393, Dept. of the Tenn., Letters Sent.

1863, JAN. 4.   USG order. "Mr. James Sims, living 8 miles southwest of Holly Springs, is authorized to retain four mules and the remainder of stock, grain, and provisions on hand. All United States troops are prohibited from further molesting or taking from Mr. Sims, he having already contributed largely to the support of the Federal Army."—*HRC*, 50-1-3128, 52-1-418, 53-2-540; *SRC*, 55-1-40, 55-2-544. USG's order was submitted by James Sims as evidence of his loyalty during the war to support a claim for $6,338 for supplies taken for U.S. Army use, a claim finally paid in 1898.—*U. S. Statutes at Large*, XXX, 1209.

1863, JAN. 5.   1st Lt. Alonzo Eaton, 2nd Iowa, act. asst. q. m., Cairo, to USG. "can the parold Machanicks and Laborers of my department be employed again untill they have been exchange" "can General Tuttle appoint an inspector to go to Mattoon to inspect stock there   I have three hundred caveraly & artilary horses ready to ship   shall I ship them by way of Memphis or or waitt untill the R R is open   Shall I make arrangements for starting Another shop at Holly Springs. I shall leave here on the first boat for Memphis unless there is something I can do here"—ALS (telegrams sent), DNA, RG 107, Telegrams Collected (Unbound); telegrams received, *ibid.*, RG 393, Dept. of the Tenn., Telegrams Received. On Jan. 5, Lt. Col. John A. Rawlins telegraphed to Eaton. "Ship the Cavalry horses you have to this place, via Memphis. Brig Genl' Tuttle is hereby authorized to appoint an inspector, to inspect the public animals belonging to Government at Mattoon, Ill. You need make no arrangements for starting another shop at this place. What news from Washington, or Rosecrans"—Copies, DLC-USG, V, 18, 30; DNA, RG 393, Dept. of the Tenn., Letters Sent.

On Jan. 25, Eaton wrote a letter probably intended for Brig. Gen. Montgomery C. Meigs. "I have learned from Lt. Col. Rawlins Asst. Adgt. Genl. that the application of Lt Col Reynolds and Maj Gen Grant for my promotion to Captain and assistant Quarter Master, has been rejected on account of the failure on my part to transmit Reports of my duty in the Quartermasters Department for 2d Quarter, 1862 with sufficient promptitude . . ."—LS, *ibid.*, RG 94, ACP, E116 CB 1864. On Jan. 26, Lt. Col. Charles A. Reynolds endorsed this letter favorably, and on the same day USG added his endorsement. "I take great pleasure in recommending Lieut. Eaton for the position of Assistant Q. M. and in stating that I think the reasons assigned satisfactory for the lack of promptness in not forwarding his Acts. Mr. Eaton has been one of the most active and efficient Quartermasters in this Dept." —AES, *ibid.* See *Calendar*, Dec. 27, 1862. Eaton was not confirmed as capt. and q. m. until June 30, 1864.

1863, JAN. 7. USG endorsement. "Respectfully refered to the Sec. of War. The goods were taken or destroyed on the reoccupation of Holly Springs by the Federal troops. I do not feel authorized to order the payment and if such claims are to be paid would recommend that the amount be collected from disloyal citizens of the town and vicinity."— AES, DNA, RG 94, Letters Received. Written on papers presenting the claim of Henry Charnock, Holly Springs, a British subject, for reimbursement for goods taken from his store by U.S. troops.—*Ibid.*

1863, JAN. 7.   Brig. Gen. Charles S. Hamilton, La Grange, to USG. "There are some thirty Confed. prisoners here captured at Davis Mill & picked up at diffnt times   what shall be done with them"—Telegram received, DNA, RG 393, Dept. of the Tenn., Telegrams Received.

1863, JAN. 7.   Brig. Gen. John E. Smith, Grand Junction, to USG. "Co. F 2d Iowa Cavalry consists of 30 men for duty   were assigned to my comd.   but sent with Gen Ross   Order recd for them to report to Love   Can I retain them   have no Cavalry"—Telegram received, DNA, RG 94, War Records Office, Dept. of the Tenn. On the same day, Lt. Col. John A. Rawlins telegraphed to Smith. "There are a number of Independent companies of Cavalry at Corinth from which you can procure an escort. It is desirable to have the company now with you rejoin their Regiment"—Copies, DLC-USG, V, 18, 30; DNA, RG 393, Dept. of the Tenn., Letters Sent.

1863, JAN. 7.   Capt. William H. Ross, 2nd Mich. Battery, Grand Junction, to USG. "I arrived here from Detroit Mich with sixty five men & two officers this Eve—I ł await furthers orders   No Equipments"—Telegram received, DNA, RG 393, Dept. of the Tenn., Telegrams Received. On the same day, Lt. Col. John A. Rawlins telegraphed to Brig. Gen. Grenville M. Dodge. "Is the detachment of the 2nd Michigan Battery at Corinth? It was attached to Major Cavender's Battalion of First Missouri Light Artillery, at Pittsburgh Landing last Spring   Please answer"—Copies, DLC-USG, V, 18, 30; DNA, RG 393, Dept. of the Tenn., Letters Sent. On Jan. 8, Dodge telegraphed to Rawlins. "There are some thirteen (13) enlisted men of that Battry in Co D 1st Mo Lt. Artillry   no officers are there   any news from Vicksburg that is not contraband   am anxious   all my old troops are"—Telegram received, *ibid.*, Telegrams Received. On the same day, Rawlins telegraphed to Ross. "You will proceed with your men to Corinth Miss, and report to Brig Genl G M Dodge, where the detachment of your Battery now is, make requisition for equipments on Chief Ordnance Officer of the Dept and they will be furnished as soon as possible"—Copies, DLC-USG, V, 18, 30; DNA, RG 393, Dept. of the Tenn., Letters Sent.

1863, JAN. 7.   U.S. Treasury Special Agent William P. Mellen, Cincinnati, to USG. "I beg leave to introduce for your favorable consideration, the bearer hereof Mr. I. A. Donnelly. He has been driven from his home for being an honest and true man, faithful to his country, and now wishes to return there and to purchase cotton. So many of those engaged in this trafic are bad men, disregardful of all things, except making money, that I am disposed to be very considerate of any man I find engaging in it whom I believe to faithful in his observance of all regulations and orders Mr. Donnally has complied fully with the regulations of the Treasury Department and obtained permits to purchase and ship Cotton. He has been fully informed as to his duties under these permits, and is anxious to conduct his business under them in such manner as in no way to offend against any military orders necessary to the safety of your army or the success of its operations. May I ask from you such written directions for him as will protect him from unnecessary interference while in your Department so long as he transacts his business in pursuance of the terms of his permits and faithfully observes all orders as aforesaid."—Copy, DNA, RG *366*, First Special Agency, Letters Sent.

1863, Jan. 8.   To Secretary of War Edwin M. Stanton. "The following referred to Secty of War from Paducah Maj Genl Grant, Can the sheriff of this Co. be permitted to enter the fort at this place to execute a civil process from our circuit court to obtain possession of fugitive slaves belonging to citizens of this &. the adjoining Counties. The process is issuing in conformation with our laws. The Commander of Post makes no objection but the Commander in fact resists & refuses to turn slave out. Signed P D Zeigler Judge Dist"—Telegram received, DNA, RG 107, Telegrams Collected (Bound).

1863, Jan. 10.   USG pass. "The sanitary boat in charge of Dr. McLain will pass Messrs. H. J. Cox, and J. B. Harper to Gen. Shermans Command, and return, free."—ANS, MoSHi. On the same day, Dr. R. G. McLean, U.S. Sanitary Commission, Memphis, wrote to USG. "When I saw you in person, to day, I expected again to call in person, but fearing that I may be prevented, I wish to say that I have on board, 1000 packages, San Stores for Gen Shermans fleet. I am prepared should the wants of his Army require it to take on board & carry back to hospitals his sick and wounded. I will await your order as per your suggestion."—Copy, DNA, RG *393*, 13th Army Corps, Letters Received.

1863, JAN. 12. USG endorsement. "Respectfully referred to Maj. Gen S. R. Curtis, who will please relieve this officer and order him to rejoin his Regiment in this Department"—ES, DNA, RG 393, Dept. of the Mo., Letters Received. Written on a letter of Jan. 3 from Col. William S. Oliver, 7th Mo., to Lt. Col. John A. Rawlins. "Lieut Neville Quarter Master 7th Regt Mo Vols has been detached as A. A. C. S. at Lexington Mo. (Spec = Orders No 215 Hd. Qrs. Dept. Missi a copy of which I enclose) since June 2d/62—We have had an 'Acting Quarter Master' in the mean time who is doing the work of the Regular Quarter Master without receiving compensation. I most respectfully request an order ordering him to rejoin his Regiment."— ALS, *ibid.* On Feb. 11, Brig. Gen. Benjamin F. Loan, Jefferson City, Mo., wrote to Maj. Henry Z. Curtis, adjt. for Maj. Gen. Samuel R. Curtis, recommending that Lt. John F. Neville be relieved from duty at Lexington, Mo., by orders from hd. qrs., Dept. of the Mo.—ALS, *ibid.*

1863, JAN. 12. Maj. Thomas M. Vincent, AGO, to USG. "By direction of the Secretary of War, I have the honor to invite your attention to Par. 1647, Revised Army Regulations, which authorizes the acceptance of resignations by Commanders of Army Corps. Many officers, absent from their Regiments, tender their resignations directly to the War Department: these are invariably referred to the Head Quarters of the Corps in which the Regiment is serving, not with a view to their being '*returned approved*' but that, if proper, they should be accepted, in compliance with the Regulations quoted. It is therefore: respectfully requested that all such papers be hereafter acted on as suggested, and if accepted, the *Special Order*, forwarded as usual to this office, and, also, the tender of resignation with the *action noted thereon.* The reason for thus referring to the Corps Commander, is, that, in many instances, the rolls have not been filed in this office, regularly, and the officer's status with his command is not known for a period of two, and sometimes four months prior to his application for discharge."—LS, DNA, RG 393, Dept. of the Tenn., Letters Received. See telegram to Brig. Gen. Lorenzo Thomas, Aug. 20, 1862, and *Calendar*, Oct. 31, 1862.

1863, JAN. 12. Dr. W. T. Belisle, Jackson, Tenn., to USG. "I. take the privilege of your honor to to ask of you a favor which I would be glad that you would confer to me I. am the man who on was Guide for your detachment ~~last~~ last march in capturing All that Bulk Pork on the Tennessee River. I. have since that time Been in the Recruiting Service By order of Andrew Johnson Millitary Gov of this state. I. have raised a great many recruits But at the present time the Recruiting Bussiness is verry dull. I desire of you if it is consistent with you: to give me a permit to Scout in this Part of the country   I. think I could do a great deal of good to the Government in keeping down the midnight Marauders of this country. And save the Rail Road in Many instances No Doubt. I am tolerably well acquainted in this country and know most of the Rebbel leaders: and know to be the cause of a great deal of Devilment done in this country and if They ware stoped in thier Career thear would be no one to haul out inducements to The Rebbell Cavalry: I know many who have taken the oat of Allegiance to the United States and have Violated it: and are standing in open Rebellion against our Government Regardless of consequences   I have not the Power to arrest those Rebbels though I have arrested many by order of the Provo Martials   I have done a great deal of Bussiness for the Government By order of Col. Haynie commander of the Post at Bethel Station   I. captured 2,000 dollars worth of salt at time from the Secesh and hauld it to Bethel   If you will give me a permission to arrest those Rebbell Villains and to capture such Property as is considered contraband I. can proffit Uncle Sam one hudred Thousand dollars a year, if so be the war should last that long. I have the authority given to me by Gov. Johnson to recruit any where in the state of Tennessee. Now if you will arm me withe the arm I wish you to I will Make those Rebbels who are cutting up so big walk a chalk line and will obey Every precept given me, by you or those under your Controle   I have been a faithful Servent for my country evir since the 5th day of last March and have not been Idle two weeks during the time up to this date and Pray you therefore to arm me with this wepon. that I may be more proffitable to This Glorious Government"—ALS, DNA, RG 393, Dept. of the Tenn., Letters Received. On Jan. 6, Belisle had written to Brig. Gen. Jeremiah C. Sullivan. "When Tennessee ceceded I opposed it and the Rebels chased me from home   I was forced to go to Illinois   I left my wife and one child to Suffer behind me   I was forced to travel in the night, and lay up in the day   it was in Feb. when natur was Shooting her icy darts but I reched Mound City safe. I continued in Illinois where I was raised until the fleet came up Tennessee River   Being acquainted in my neighbourhood I soon found out where the rebels had two large pork houses full of Bulk pork which they had hauld about 2 miles from the Tenssee River and had deposited it in a Camp ground. I informed U. S Grant concerning it   he sent a detachment after it. Viz Col Smith of Ills. Reg of Infantry and Capt A Husburn of the Chicauga dragoons his boddy guard & we Boared the John Raine   I went as guide and we captured the whole of it and braught it to Pittsburgh Landing   I. then Remained with Gen Grants Boddy guards and was at the Battle of Shilo the in which I. participated and fought the Rebels the most part of two days. I Then assisted in making up a company of volunteers at Savannah Tenn Known as Governors Guards by order of Governor Andrew Johnson of Nashville Tenn. I went with D company to Nashvill and acted as sargeant of the 1st Tennessee Regiment for considerable time. And being desireous to see my little family once more; Gov. Johnson gave me a commission to Recruit in the state of Tennessee known as governors guards   I Recruited for Col Hursts Reg. And have been in the Recruiting Service ever sin since 5th day of last June"—ALS, *ibid.*, RG 109, Union Provost Marshals' File of Papers Relating to Individual Civilians.

1863, JAN. 12.   Sworn statement of Emily E. Brown, Madison County, Tenn., addressed to USG, asking the release of her husband, C.S.A. Capt. William H. Brown, then in poor health at Alton Prison and willing to take an oath of allegiance.—Copy, DNA, RG 109, Military Prison at Alton, Ill., Letters Sent and Received. On Jan. 20, Col. William S. Hillyer, provost marshal, endorsed the petition favorably.—Copy, *ibid.* See *O.R.*, II, v, 342.

1863, JAN. 13.   USG endorsement to Maj. Daniel M. Emerson, 6th Tenn. Cav., ordering him to proceed to Jackson, Columbus, or Memphis to procure "equipment and military supplies . . . necessary to the full preparation of this regiment for Service . . ."—Charles Hamilton Auction 28, July 25, 1968, No. 72.

1863, JAN. 14.   To Brig. Gen. James M. Tuttle, Cairo. "Capt Kinzie of the 89th Indiana Vols left here at 3 P M yesterday whilst member of a court martial not yet through with their business. If he can be stopped send him back to finish up his business."—Telegram, copies, DLC-USG, V, 18, 30, 98; DNA, RG 393, Dept. of the Tenn., Letters Sent.

1863, JAN. 14. To Col. Joseph D. Webster, Jackson, Tenn. "You will please designate the cars on the Railroad in which the mail is to be carried, that there may be no fuss between the Conductors and Mail Agents, The Caboose Car is the one in which it has previously been carried but the Conductors object to its being so carried saying 'the car is for their own convenience"—Telegram, copies, DLC-USG, V, 18, 30, 98; DNA, RG 393, Dept. of the Tenn., Letters Sent.

1863, JAN. 14. Maj. Thomas M. Vincent, AGO, to USG. "I have the honor to inform you that a copy of Special Orders No 37, Head Quarters, 13th Army Corps, discharging Sergeant Charles C. Wood, Company G, 32nd Wisconsin Volunteers for promotion, has been received at this office. In connection therewith, I have respectfully to invite your attention to Par. 163. Revised Army Regulations, giving authority to the Commanders of Army Corps to discharge enlisted men *only* on *certificate* of *disability*, or by sentence of *Court Martial*. It is therefore respectfully requested that all applications for discharge not covered by the Paragraph quoted, be referred for the action of the War Department."—LS, DNA, RG 393, Dept. of the Tenn., Unentered Letters Received.

1863, JAN. 17. USG endorsement. "Respectfully forwarded to Head Quarters of the Army at Washington D. C. and the discharge of this man recommended."—Copies, DLC-USG, V, 25; DNA, RG 393, Dept. of the Tenn., Endorsements. Written on a letter of Jan. 15 from Col. Risdon M. Moore, 117th Ill., requesting the discharge of Dr. Charles H. Hitchcock, Co. K, 117th Ill., so that he could be commissioned as surgeon.—*Ibid.* On March 19, USG endorsed a letter of Surgeon Henry S. Hewit, medical director, Dept. of the Tenn., recommending the same thing. "Respectfully returned to Head Quarters of the Army Washington D. C. and attention invited to endorsements." —Copies, *ibid.* On April 3, Maj. Samuel Breck, AGO, wrote to USG. "In reply to the application of Private C. H Hitchcock, Co "K" 117th Ill Vols to be discharge that he may be appointed a surgeon of Vols, forwarded with your approval to this Office, I am directed by the General-in-chief to instruct you to discharge him from the Military Service of the United States upon receipt of this communication."— Copies, *ibid.*, Military Div. of the Miss., Special Orders Received; *ibid.*, RG 94, Enlisted Branch, Letters Sent; DLC-USG, V, 103. Hitchcock was discharged on April 15.

1863, JAN. 21. Brig. Gen. Lorenzo Thomas to USG. "Please direct maj Gen sherman Hurlbut & McPherson to report to this Office the names of the Officers they deem best suited for the Position of adjt Genl & inspector General of the army Corps comded by them respectively section ten *10* Act of July seventeenth 17"—Telegrams received (2), DNA, RG 107, Telegrams Collected (Unbound); *ibid.*, RG 393, Dept. of the Tenn., Telegrams Received.

1863, JAN. 21. Brig. Gen. Alexander Asboth, Columbus, Ky., to Lt. Col. John A. Rawlins. "Rumers having been spread that the Rebel Genl Forrest was again approaching Union City Tenn with his forces, I took all precautions and ordered cavalry scouting parties from here and from Union City who just report all quiet and no enemy in force." —Copy, DNA, RG 393, Hd. Qrs. District of Columbus, Letters Sent. *O.R.*, I, xxiii, part 2, 3. On Jan. 23, Asboth telegraphed to Rawlins. "Colde D Moore from Union city telegraphs this morning as follows there is a rumor here that large bodies of Rebels cavalry are crossing the Tennessee river"—Telegram received, DNA, RG 393, Dept. of the Tenn., Telegrams Received; copy, *ibid.*, Hd. Qrs. District of Columbus, Letters Sent. On the same day, Brig. Gen. Jeremiah C. Sullivan, Jackson, Tenn., telegraphed to USG. "As soon as I recd. Col. Moores report, I ordered out detachments to river—and am prepared to meet them—My orders from Genl. Hamilton were positive as soon as stores were received to call in my troops and be prepared to move—I have not done so, deeming it very imprudent at present—The orders have been kept secret by me, and I have made no movements that look like evacuating—I requested Genl. Ashboth to send an infantry force under protection of a Gun boat up the river and destroy the ferries—I will promise to destroy any rebel force that crosses—" —ALS (telegram sent), *ibid.*, RG 107, Telegrams Collected (Unbound); telegram received, *ibid.*, RG 94, War Records Office, Dept. of the Tenn. Also on Jan. 23, Brig. Gen. Grenville M. Dodge, Corinth, telegraphed to USG. "I am going to load the transports with troops & send them up the Tennessee with the two Gunboats & during their attack by River I will try & get my cavalry into albama"—Telegram received, *ibid.*, RG 393, Dept. of the Tenn., Telegrams Received. On Jan. 24, Asboth telegraphed to Rawlins. "The scouting parties sent out to ascertain the truth of rumors in regard to bodies of rebel cavalry crossing the Tennessee have returned from sixteen 16 miles beyond union city & report all quiet"—Telegram received, *ibid.*; copy, *ibid.*, Hd. Qrs. District of Columbus, Letters Sent.

1863, JAN. 23. U.S. Treasury Special Agent William P. Mellen, Cincinnati, to USG. "The bearer hereof, Mr. John J. Hooker, of this City, has permits under the Regulations of the Treasury Department to purchase and ship Cotton from Northern Alabama and other points on the Tennessee River. He is a very worthy, loyal and honorable man, and served in the army until the illness of his family required his personal care. Relieved from this, he now desires to trade in Cotton. He has a son now serving in the army.—*Such* men I am anxious to give every facility proper to be given, to trade in Cotton, instead of the hundreds of unpatriotic and unreliable sharpers *infesting* the army. Mr. Hooker wishes such instructions from you as to what your orders may require of him as will enable him strictly to comply with them By giving him such written permission and directions as will enable him act in conformity with all rules you will oblige a man entitled to your confidence and consideration. I would also suggest that if you desire the service of any body in the section where he is going in furnishing you any information, you can *depend* upon the judgment, faithfulness and discreetness of Mr. Hooker. Hoping you may be able to serve Mr. Hooker without interfering with your ideas of propriety"—ALS, DNA, RG 366, First Special Agency, Letters Sent (Press).

1863, JAN. 25. USG endorsement. "Respectfully forwarded to Head-quarters of the Army. Late Lieut. Col. John Olney of the 6th Ills. Cavalry was dismissed the service for being absent without leave and being captured by the enemy during such absence. Col. Olney, though a man of talent and of good habits and good moral character is one of the most inefficient officers I ever saw. If he should be reinstated it would be better for his Regiment and this service that he should have a perpetual leave of absence. The 6th Ills. Cavalry under its present officers is one of the best, is not the best Cavalry Regt. in this Department, and I would respectfully urge that nothing be done to diminish its usefulness."—Copies, DLC-USG, V, 25; DNA, RG 393, Dept. of the Tenn., Endorsements. Written on a letter of Jan. 21 of Col. Benjamin H. Grierson, La Grange, requesting that Lt. Col. John Olney, 6th Ill. Cav., not be reinstated.—*Ibid.*

1863, JAN. 25. Brig. Gen. Grenville M. Dodge, Corinth, to USG. "Capt Harper ordnanc officer informs me he cannot issue Carbins except upon your order I need two hundred will you direct him to issue them"—Telegram received, DNA, RG 393, Dept. of the Tenn., Telegrams Received.

1863, JAN. 25. Brig. Gen. Jeremiah C. Sullivan, Jackson, to USG. "A Son of Mr. Williams, has just arrived from Mobile, He reports the City as being strongly fortified and General Buckner in command with Twenty Thousan[d] troops. The M. & O R R. is run no farther North than Okalona where there are 2000 Cavalry—Mobile is protected on north side by a triple line of works a distance of three miles from the City—The harbor is driven full of spiles leaving a winding channel command by heavy guns—This channel is so narrow that a heavy steamer which run the blockade was unable to reach the City— Vicksburg has been re-inforced to what extent he does not know—He understands that no cars run as regular train higher than Jackson—The boy is about 14 years old—"—ALS (telegram sent), DNA, RG 107, Telegrams Collected (Unbound); telegram received, *ibid.*, RG 94, War Records Office, Dept. of the Tenn. *O.R.*, I, xxiv, part 3, 12.

1863, JAN. 25. Col. George P. Ihrie, Cairo, to USG. "Fitz-John Porter is dismissed the service. No battle on the Rappahannock."— ALS (telegram sent), DNA, RG 107, Telegrams Collected (Unbound); telegram received, *ibid.*, RG 393, Dept. of the Tenn., Telegrams Received.

1863, JAN. 26. USG General Orders No. 10. "*I.*—It being a violation of the provisions of the Dix-Hill Cartel to parole prisoners at any other points than those designated in said Cartel, except by agreement between the Generals commanding the opposing forces, no paroles, hereafter given to Federal Soldiers, in violation of such provisions of said cartel, will be respected. *II.*—Officers or soldiers, who, by straggling from their commands, are captured and paroled, will at once be arrested and brought to trial before a Court Martial. *III.*—Guerillas or Southern Soldiers caught in the Uniforms of Federal Soldiers will not be treated as organized bodies of the enemy, but will be closely confined and held for the action of the War Department. Those caught within the lines of the Federal Army in such uniforms, or in citizen's dress, will be treated as spies.   *IV.*—Officers, Soldiers and citizens are prohibited from purchasing horses, mules or military clothing from any one connected with the Army, without special authority. In order that improper and dishonest appropriations of captured property may be prevented, commanding officers will exercise vigilance in enforcing this order, and report every violation of it, to the end that offenders may be summarily punished.   *V.*—Steamboats are prohibited from carrying stock of any description North, without permits granted by Division or Army Corps Commanders, or the Provost Marshal General, and violations of this restriction will be punished at the discretion of a Military Commission."—Copies, DLC-USG, V, 13, 14, 95; DNA, RG 393, Dept. of the Tenn., General Orders; *ibid.*, General and Special Orders. *O.R.*, I, xxiv, part 3, 14–15. On the same day, Lt. Col. John A. Rawlins issued Special Orders No. 26. "I. . . The Bars on all boats in Government service in this Department will be closed, and no spirituous vinous or malt liquors will be allowed to be sold on the boats or in the camps   Card playing and gaming is strictly prohibited. It is made the special duty of all Provost Marshals and of Commissioned Officers Guards and patrols to see that this order is enforced and to arrest all parties violating the same, and deliver them over to the nearest Commanding Officer by whom they will be held in confinement and reported to these Headquarters."—Copies, DLC-USG, V, 26 (2), 27; DNA, RG 393, Dept. of the Tenn., Special Orders; *ibid.*, General and Special Orders. Variant text in *O.R.*, I, xxiv, part 3, 15.

1863, JAN. 26.   USG endorsement. "Approved and respectfully forwarded, to Headquarters Army, Washington, D. C."—ES, DNA, RG 94, ACP, 149Q CB 1864. Written on a letter of the same date from Capt. Henry S. Fitch, Memphis, to USG resigning his commission as q. m. with the expectation of receiving an appointment as judge advocate.—ALS, *ibid.* On April 16, Lt. Col. James A. Hardie, AGO, wrote to USG. "As Capt. Henry S. Fitch, Asst. Qr. Mr. of Vols., has tendered his resignation, and it appears that he is in debt to the Government to the amount of $6.897.02, will you please appoint a proper officer to inspect his accounts, and report the result to this office."—Copy, *ibid.*, Commissions and Returns, Letters Sent. Fitch's resignation was not accepted, but he did serve in 1863–64 as judge advocate on the staff of Maj. Gen. William T. Sherman.

1863, JAN. 26.   Brig. Gen. Jeremiah C. Sullivan, Jackson, to Lt. Col. John A. Rawlins. "Brig. Genl. M. Brayman, Bolivar Tenn reports John C. Cumming a clergyman, just escaped from a years imprisonment at Carrolton Miss., says Pemberton and Price are at Grenada well fortified, that they were proposing to aid Bragg, that Van Dorn has been largely reinforced and intends as soon as Genl. Grant moves below to fall upon Jackson or Bolivar with (15 000) fifteen thousand cavalry, that he learned this while in prison and on his way through the country. Cumming was on his way to his relations near Trenton, appears candid, loyal and truthful, and Genl. Brayman thinks the information worthy serious notice and enquiry."—ALS (telegram sent), DNA, RG 107, Telegrams Collected (Unbound); telegram received, *ibid.*, RG 94, War Records Office, Dept. of the Tenn. *O.R.*, I, xxiv, part 3, 17.

1863, JAN. 28.   To Maj. Gen. Samuel R. Curtis. "If consistent with the interests of the service I would be pleased if you could order the 25 Mo. Vols. Col. Harding Comdg. to report to me at this place. This regiment has served in this Dept. and was sent back to Missouri to recruit up and with the expectation that it would return as soon as possible."—Copies, IaHA; DLC-USG, V, 18, 30; DNA, RG 393, Dept. of the Tenn., Letters Sent. On Feb. 8, Curtis wrote to USG. "Yours of the 28th ulto. requesting me to send Col. Hardings regt. 25th Missouri to your command is duly received. The regiment is far down near Batesville Ark. or near the border of Missouri at West Plains. It would require a long march to reach the river and weaken my advance, which I hope to unite with a move up White River as soon as you can spare gunboats and other forces for such a move. It is, therefore quite impossible at present to comply with your request, but I will try to do so when an opportunity offers."—Copy, *ibid.*, Dept. of the Mo., Letters Sent.

1863, JAN. 30.   USG endorsement. "Respectfully forwarded to Headquarters of the Army with the recommendation that Colonel Cavender be mustered out of service."—Copies, DLC-USG, V, 25; DNA, RG 393, Dept. of the Tenn., Endorsements. Written on a letter of Jan. 28 of Brig. Gen. Francis P. Blair, Jr., stating that Col. John S. Cavender, 29th Mo., had left for St. Louis after applying for leave, assuming that leave would be granted.—*Ibid* Blair asked that Cavender's offense be overlooked, but on Jan. 30, Maj. Gen. William T. Sherman endorsed this letter to USG. "I regret that I cannot agree with Genl's Blair & Steele in this matter. Col Cavender is a most intelligent officer, & has set an example that would destroy any army. Doubtless his private interests are as important as can be possible imagined but he has against orders, against well known military rules gone away without leave or authority—This in a soldier is Desertion, Death, & the Laws draws no distinction in favor of Officers—I refer this case to the commander of the Dept."—Copy, *ibid.,* Army of the Tenn., 5th Div., Endorsements. Cavender resigned as of Feb. 19, 1863.

1863, JAN. 30. Brig. Gen. Grenville M. Dodge, Corinth, to Lt. Col. John A. Rawlins. "I respectfully request that the funds raised here from the sale of contraband cotton and from the funds collected by the Provost Marshal General for this district under existing orders, be turned over to me to be used as a secret service fund. The General is aware, that I cannot procure funds from the Q. M. of the District, or Department for that purpose, and he must also be aware, that it is impossible to obtain competent men, for such service unless, they are well paid in cash. By personal attention to this matter I have collected a corps of rather efficient men, and unless I can have funds to use I cannot hold them together. These men work for money, most of them and run great risks. I consider it for the benefit of the service, that they be retained, and that such authority be given me, that my use of this money may not be a cause of trouble hereafter. I desire that the General's Commanding the Department, attention be called to this matter."—ALS, DNA, RG 393, Dept. of the Tenn., Letters Received. On Feb. 26, Rawlins wrote to Dodge. "I am directed by the Major General Commanding to acknowledge the receipt of your communication of the 30th ultimo and to say in reply that the Provost Marshall in your District will turn over to you all monies collected by them under existing orders taking your receipts therefor which they will forward to the Provost Marshall General in settlements of their accounts in lieu of the money, and which you will account for as secret service fund any additional funds you may require can be obtained by requisition on the Provost Marshall General. All sales of cotton confiscated should be made by Captain Eddy, at Memphis Tenn and properly accounted for by him"—Copies, DLC-USG, V, 18, 30; DNA, RG 393, Dept. of the Tenn., Letters Sent.

1863, JAN. 30.   C. B. Conant, New York City, to USG. "A lady who
arrived here not long since, from Vicksburgh (having a son in the
Rebel service) & well known to me, informs me, that the Rebels have
very cunningly covered certain ravines near the city, & planted trees
over them—the more effectually to deceive—& have stored gun
powder & combustibles, intending to blow up the whole concern, if
they can entice the 'Yankees' over them. I felt it my duty to communicate this for what it is worth. At all times you can't be too careful in
your approaches to these devils. God save the Nation!"—ALS, DNA,
RG 393, Dept. of the Tenn., Letters Received.

1863, JAN. 31.   USG endorsement to Act. Rear Admiral David D.
Porter referring the claims of a young man in the Mississippi Squadron.
—Anderson Sale No. 4345, 1937.

1863, JAN. 31.   Maj. Gen. Henry W. Halleck to USG. "The Comsr
Genl of prisoners has referred to me a list of exchanges effected by
Genl Dodge on the 19th of December. Genl Dodge was not authorised
by the Cartel to make exchanges, and such assumption of authority
necessarily leads to difficulty and trouble."—ALS (telegram sent),
DNA, RG 107, Telegrams Collected (Bound); telegram received,
ibid., RG 393, Dept. of the Tenn., Telegrams Received.

1863, JAN. 31.   Lt. Col. Walter S. Scates, adjt. for Maj. Gen. John A.
McClernand, to Lt. Col. John A. Rawlins principally concerning the
appointment of Col. Addison S. Norton, 17th Ill., as provost marshal.
—Copy, DNA, RG 393, 13th Army Corps, Letters Sent. On the same
day, USG added a twelve-line endorsement to a letter of Scates, most
likely concerning Norton.—Stan. V. Henkels Catalogue No. 1021,
Dec. 20, 1910, p. 99. See letter to Julia Dent Grant, June 15, 1863,
note 2.

1863, JAN. 31.   Governor Richard Yates of Ill. to USG. "I desire to
Commend to your favorable Consideration Judge Kellogg, who was
about visiting Washington, but at my request has Concluded to visit
the army under your Command.   he expects soon to return & accompany me to Washington. *Communicate freely* with him, and if I can be
of any Service to you there, or elsewhere, advise me through him, &
I shall be pleased to Serve you to the best of my ability."—ALS, DNA,

RG 109, Union Provost Marshals' File of Papers Relating to Individual Civilians. On Feb. 15, USG issued a pass. "Col. Kellogg is permitted to pass through all parts of this Department, stopping at such military posts as he may desire, traveling free on chartered steamers and on military railroads. Good until countermanded."—Paul M. Angle, ed., "The Recollections of William Pitt Kellogg," *The Abraham Lincoln Quarterly*, III, 7 (Sept., 1945), 331.

1863, FEB. 1. Maj. Gen. John A. McClernand to USG. "B. F. Livingston an old and experienced detective, recommended to me by Genl Burbridge, has been employed by me in his profession since the 13th ulto. He has rendered valuable service in divers respects; particularly in searching transports about leaving for unauthorized persons & property. I think you could make him eminently useful not only now, but when we move against the enemy"—Copies (2), McClernand Papers, IHi; DNA, RG 393, 13th Army Corps, Letters Sent.

1863, FEB. 2. R. G. Baldwin, steamboat *St. Louis*, to USG. "I have been here at this place for ten days, and have been trying to see you ever since your arrival. But have in every attempt found your boat besieged with Speculators and other vexasious persons to such an extent. as to prevent my being admitteded. to your presence. But having the assurance of that Patriot and Lawyer. Joseph Holt of my States that whenever the right time arrived you would give me every protection and facility I needed, my case is this My Brother who I was in copartnership with for five years. was left in the brakeing out of this rebellion with a large debt due in this country. for cotton Gin machinery and saw mill engines the loss of which debt will prove our utter distruction those creditors have now fallen within your lines and I have seen some of them. who tell me that all are willing to pay their debt in cotton and are glad to do so for fear of it being burned by the rebels or, captured by us, or lossed by high water Now, General, in the name of humanity and justice to a man who has faced the Storm of Battle as much as any other man in this country I ask you, if it is in accordance with the laws of our country, to allow me to collect this debt in cotton, and to guard me in the execution of it, before it is loste forever . . . Be kind enough, General to answer."—ALS, DNA, RG 393, Dept. of the Tenn., Letters Received.

1863, [*Feb.* ?] 4.   George G. Pride, St. Louis, to USG. "I am troubled to find the men I want   may not get down for 2 or 5 days   shall I be needed before the first of the week"—Telegram received, DNA, RG 393, Dept. of the Tenn., Telegrams Received.

1863, FEB. 5.   USG endorsement. "Respectfully forwarded to Headquarters of the Army, Washington, D. C., with the recommendation, that he be discharged from the Army, to enable him to accept the position tendered him by the Navy."—ES, DNA, RG 94, Letters Received, 139B 1863. Written on a statement of Feb. 1 of Lt. Commander K. Randolph Breese, U.S.S. *Black Hawk.* "David Chillis having passed a satisfactory examination as an acting 2d asst. Engineer on temporary service in the Mississippi Squadron Admiral Porter will appoint him to that position *providing he can get his discharge from the Army"*— DS, *ibid.* Attached was a petition addressed to USG by officers of the 83rd Ind. requesting the discharge of Private David Chillis.—DS, *ibid.* Chillis was appointed act. 2nd asst. engineer as of Feb. 3, 1863.

1863, FEB. 6.   USG endorsement. "Respectfully forwarded to His Excellency Andrew Johnson Governor of the State of Tennessee."— ES, DLC-Andrew Johnson. Written on an undated petition from citizens of Hardeman County, Tenn., to USG asking that the sheriff be allowed to collect debts as before the war.—DS, *ibid.* Also on Feb. 6, a military commission headed by Col. William H. H. Taylor, 5th Ohio Cav., Memphis, wrote to USG asking that the commission be allowed to issue letters of administration and guardianship to protect the property of widows and orphans.—DS, *ibid.* On Feb. 14, Lt. Col. John A. Rawlins endorsed this letter. "The application should be made to Gov. Johnson, Nashville, Tenn. The Com'd'g General cannot properly exercise jurisdiction in the premises."—ES, *ibid.*

1863, FEB. 7.   Maj. Gen. Samuel R. Curtis, St. Louis, to USG. "Allow me to introduce Lt Col H. C. Nutt A. D. C to Gov Kirkwood who goes to Vicksburgh under orders of his chief to look after the interests of Iowa soldiers. Any assistance given him will be duly appreciated"—LS, DNA, RG 109, Union Provost Marshals' File of Papers Relating to Individual Civilians.

1863, FEB. [8 ?].   USG endorsement. "Approved"—AES, DNA, RG 393, Dept. of the Tenn., Letters Received. Written on a letter of

Feb. 8 from Brig. Gen. Stephen G. Burbridge and Col. William J. Landram, 19th Ky., Young's Point, to Brig. Gen. Andrew J. Smith asking that an officer be sent to Ky. to "gather up and forward" sick troops left behind.—LS, *ibid.* On Feb. 8, Maj. Gen. John A. McClernand endorsed this letter. "Not only for the strong reasons herein assigned, but also because Col. Landrum's failing health caused by long and hard service in the field requires it, he is ordered, subject to the approval hereof by the Genl. Comg. the Dept. of the Tenn, to proceed to Ky. and reclaim and send back the absentees referred to."—AES, *ibid.*

1863, Feb. 9. To Col. Lewis B. Parsons. "If Capt. Prime, who is now out of the office, decides that he does not require the services of the propeller Lelia she may be released."—ALS, Parsons Papers, IHi.

1863, Feb. 9. To Lt. Col. Charles A. Reynolds. "Send everything called for independent of the Engineer Regiment's outfit except the wheelbarrows. You need not duplicate them without further orders" —Copies, DLC-USG, V, 18, 30; DNA, RG 393, Dept. of the Tenn., Letters Sent.

1863, Feb. 9. Lt. Col. Walter B. Scates, adjt. for Maj. Gen. John A. McClernand, to Lt. Col. John A. Rawlins. "I have the honor to send you enclosed papaers with one prisoner. There is strong reason to believe that the prisoner has been engaged by others in hunting up cotton hid back in the swamps—claiming it as his own, and under pretense of shipping it to Memphis he will sell and deliver it on board Steamer. Negroes at these Head Quarters, know where 25 bales are hidden. They lived near Millikan's Bend—know the settlers from here to 8 miles above the Bend—and yet they know of no inhabitant of this prisoner's name yet he claims to have raised this cotton on his mothers farm. I do not beleive the cotton is his. There may be also ground to watch him as a spy—passing through the lines of both parties under pretense of bringing in his cotton. I have the honor to submit these papers with these suggestions, that a further investigation may be made."—Copy, DNA, RG 393, 13th Army Corps, Letters Sent.

1863, Feb. 9. "Unconditional Union," Louisville, to USG. "In conversing with a friend about the canal at Vicksburgh I think his views are valuable. It is Capt Lewis Dunham last of the Steamer Autocrat of long experience on the Mississippi and a campanion of *Capt Shreve* who long at an early day had charge on the western waters, after whom Shrevesport was named, who opened the Red river raft & made numerous of the existing cutoffs on the Mississippi & other rivers, which was effectually done with small force & simple means & when there were more trees & stumps in the way than there is at Vicksburgh. The plan was to cut a ditch of very moderate width part of the way down to the quicksand—leaving the upper & lower ends closed—then say every Thirty or Forty Feet sink holes into the quicksand & place in each a keg of powder (well protected by coal tar &c from moisture with fuse &c) tamping them in well, but not so as to break the kegs, & then blowing up the kegs & shattering the 'hard pan' above the quick sand. (Leaving some elbows in the canal allows it to 'undermine' better). Then open the ends & let it go. He says it would be easier to dig a new ditch than to deepen the old one with the water in it, and that the whole thing can be done in 24 hours   If you will remember that this is the result of experience under Capt Shreve in many cases you will doubtless consider the sugestions valuable. The Capt knows nothing about this communication and the writer send it because he thinks it valuable *experiance*, & thinks the capt would put it through if allowed to do so untrammeled by intermediate authority. The capt is here now & if not detained long would no doubt answer your call to Memphis at least. Wishing you all success in your plans . . . If you wish to communicate to him please do so through some of the military Authorities in a sealed envelope as it would be more sure to reach him"—AL, DNA, RG 393, Dept. of the Tenn., Letters Received.

1863, Feb. 10.   Brig. Gen. Lorenzo Thomas, AGO, to USG and other commanders. "The Gen orders authorizing enlisted men of Vols into regular Service are recinded by the secy of war—"—ALS (telegram sent), DNA, RG 107, Telegrams Collected (Unbound); telegram received, *ibid.*, RG 393, Dept. of the Tenn., Telegrams Received.

1863, Feb. 11.   USG endorsement. "Respectfully forwarded to Headquarters of the Army, Washington, D. C. (see enclosed report)"—ES, DNA, RG 94, Vol. Service Branch, C1384 VS 1862. Written on a letter of Dec. 10, 1862, from Private Thomas M. Crews, Co. H, 108th Ill., to Secretary of War Edwin M. Stanton accusing Col. John Warner of crediting the same men to different cos. in order to create a false impression that the regt. was adequately filled.—ALS, *ibid.* The report of the brigade commander, Col. William J. Landram, 19th Ky., supported the charges, and Warner was dismissed on March 13.

On Feb. 27, Maj. Thomas M. Vincent, AGO, endorsed to USG a letter of Feb. 10 from Governor Richard Yates of Ill. to Stanton. "I desire to call your attention to the enclosed letter in relation to the condition of 108th Ill Regt'. I think that the removal of this Regt'. to an Ills. Camp to recruit would be beneficial, and recommend that the same be done."—Copy, McClernand Papers, IHi. On March 20, USG endorsed this letter. "Respectfully forwarded to Head Quarters of the Army Washington D. C. Attention is invited to the enclosed report of Major General John A. McClernand. I have directed the the officers be cited before a Board of Examiners, and respectfully recommend that this Regiment be consoldiated with one of the old regiments from the same state."—Copies, DLC-USG, V, 25; DNA, RG 393, Dept. of the Tenn., Endorsements.

On March 7, O. Sackett, Peoria, wrote that Warner's wife "expresses disloyal sentiments and alleges that her husband entertains the same views with herself and will resign his position if negroes are enlisted in the service."—DLC-USG, V, 105. On June 9, USG endorsed this letter. "Respectfully returned to Headqrs. of the Army, Washington, D. C. and attention invited to endorsement hereon of Col Landram, Com'd'g Brigade."—ES, DNA, RG 94, Records and Pensions W 1168 VS 1863. Landram's endorsement pointed out that Warner had already been dismissed.—ES, *ibid.*

1863, FEB. 12. Secretary of War Edwin M. Stanton to USG. "General Grant is authorized ilto enroll, enst, organize and muster into the service of the United States, one or more cavalry regiments, one regiment of mounted rifle-men one artillery Battery and any number of infantry to the number of three regiments. The said force to be armed, equipped and organized according to the rules and regulations of the service, and such regulations as, at the instance of General Grant, may be prescribed by the President, and to be employed as rangers and in such other service as may be prescribed, their term of service to be for three years or during the war and to be officered by persons appointed by the President upon the recommendation of General Grant."— Copies, DNA, RG 107, Orders Sent Concerning Vols.; *ibid.*, RG 110,

Letters Sent to State Officials; *ibid.*, RG 393, Dept. of the Tenn., Hd. Qrs. Correspondence; DLC-USG, V, 5, 8, 24, 94. *O.R.*, III, 3, 46. On Feb. 25, Lt. Col. John A. Rawlins issued Special Orders No. 56. "Maj Genl S. A. Hurlbut Commanding 16th Army Corps and and the Districts of Memphis and Corinth will receive, ration and muster into the service such able bodied troops as may offer their services, at any of the Posts of his command, and when there is sufficient number to conform to the law for organizing military Companies they may be so organizing either as Infantry Cavalry or mounted Rifles, and into Regiments when sufficient Companies are formed to the number authorized by authority from the War Department of February 12th 1863, a copy of which is here with accompaning"—Copies, DLC-USG, V, 26, 27 (misdated Feb. 23); DNA, RG 393, Dept. of the Tenn., Special Orders.

1863, FEB. 14.   USG endorsement forwarding report of Brig. Gen. Grenville M. Dodge concerning "outrages committed on the citizens of Alabama by the Confederate forces."—DNA, RG 94, Register of Letters Received; *ibid.*, RG 108, Register of Letters Received. See *O.R.*, I, xxiii, part 2, 11.

1863, FEB. 14.   USG permit. "Mr. A. C. Babcock and N. B. Taylor having all the authority Civil and Military to purchase and ship Cotton are at liberty to do so from all points on the Mississippi River north of Helena and South of it as rapidly as limits of trade are extended, by getting any Gunboat to protect them while loading such freight at other than Military Points, . . ."—Anderson Auction Co., Sale No. 1119, Jan. 8, 1915, p. 21. For Amos C. Babcock of Canton, Ill., former Whig member of the Ill. General Assembly, political associate of U.S. Representative William Kellogg, appointed by President Abraham Lincoln as assessor, ninth district of Ill., see Newton Bateman and Paul Selby, eds., *Historical Encyclopedia of Illinois and Biographical Memoirs* (Chicago, 1917), I, 30; Lincoln, *Works*, VI, 307, VIII, 334–35.

1863, FEB. 14.   Lt. Col. John A. Rawlins to Maj. Gen. John A. McClernand. "The order was duly authorized by the General Commanding and will be respected."—ES, McClernand Papers, IHi. Written on a letter of the same day from McClernand to USG. "I beg to call your attention to the inclosed paper and to inquire, inasmuch as you were probably absent at its date, whether it shall stand as it is, or the application for the leave be required to be made through the regular channel?"—ALS, *ibid.*

1863, FEB. 15. USG endorsement. "Respectfully forwarded to Headquarters of the army Washington, D. C In going from my Headquarters, at Oxford Miss. to Genl. Shermans at College Hill to review his command on the 7th day of December, 1862, I discovered three men of the 63rd Ills Vols. about three miles from their Regiment without authority in positive violation of orders prohibiting straggling. They were all dressed as Privates and I ordered them sent back to the Provost Marshal at Oxford to be bucked. On my return I received this communication informing me that one of the men was 2nd Lieut James Huntzleman of said Regiment and I therefore published the enclosed Special Field Order, No. 16, dismissing the said 2nd Lieut. James Huntzleman from the service, which I respectfully ask may be approved. The order was forwarded to Headquarters of the army immediately upon its promulgation."—Copies, DLC-USG, V, 25; DNA, RG 393, Dept. of the Tenn., Endorsements. Written on a letter of Dec. 7, 1862, of Lt. Col. Evan Richards, 20th Ill., provost marshal, Oxford, discussing the case of 2nd Lt. James Houselman, 63rd Ill.—*Ibid.*

1863, FEB. 17. Maj. Thomas M. Vincent, AGO, to USG. "The Secretary of War directs that Private W. J. Bostwick, Company B. 30th Ohio Volunteers in Hospital opposite Vicksburg be discharged."—ALS (telegram sent), DNA, RG 107, Telegrams Collected (Bound); copies, *ibid.*, RG 393, Dept. of the Tenn., Hd. Qrs. Correspondence; DLC-USG, V, 5, 8, 24, 94.

1863, FEB. 18. To Col. Josiah W. Bissell about tools for fortifications.—Charles Hamilton Catalogue 53, Oct. 21, 1971, p. 34.

1863, FEB. 18. Military Secretary W. H. Watson of Wis. to USG. "I am directed by the Governor to request that copies of dismissals, discharges, and acceptances of resignations of officers of Wisconsin Regiments in your Department may be forwarded to this office, in order that proper record of their dates may be preserved."—ALS, DNA, RG 393, Dept. of the Tenn., Letters Received.

1863, FEB. 19.   USG endorsement. "I do not feel authorized to adjust this claim in the way proposed and know of no method by which it can be done except by special act of Congress. As however, officers are frequently subjected to losses in the Gov't Service in a manner entirely beyond their control, it would seem as if some provision should be made to cover such cases. Respectfully referred to Hd. Qrs of the army" —Copies, DLC-USG, V, 25; DNA, RG 393, Dept. of the Tenn., Endorsements. Written on a letter of Feb. 18 from Col. George P. Ihrie asking that the Mobile and Ohio Railroad be ordered to pay him $400 for baggage destroyed by the enemy.—*Ibid.*; DLC-USG, V, 21; DNA, RG 94, Register of Letters Received. On March 17, Brig. Gen. Lorenzo Thomas endorsed this letter. "Respectfully returned to Major General Grant. There is no way in which remuneration can be obtained except by Special Act of Congress. There is a special law under which horses lost in battle are paid for."—Copy, *ibid.*, Endorsements.

1863, FEB. 20.   USG endorsement. "I heartily concur in the recommendations of Gens. Stuart & Sherman for the promotion of Capt. McDonald A. A. G."—AES, DNA, RG 94, ACP, 166A CB 1863. Written on a letter of Feb. 18 from Brig. Gen. David Stuart to Brig. Gen. Lorenzo Thomas, favorably endorsed by Maj. Gen. William T. Sherman, recommending the promotion of Capt. Charles McDonald. —ALS, *ibid.* McDonald received no promotion and resigned as of Aug. 18, 1863.

1863, FEB. 21.   Act. Rear Admiral David D. Porter to USG. "Allow me to introduce to you Fleet Surgeon Ninian Pinkney who will take this opportunity to express to you my views and wishes in regard to establishing a hospital at Memphis for our sick and wounded. It is necessary that we should be nearer to our main Depot than we now are, and I intend gradually to move every thing from Cairo to Memphis. The first thing to be thought of is the sick and wounded—I cannot provide for them as I would desire without your assistance, and the exercise of your authority. You will I am sure be convinced on the moment, by what Surgeon Pinkney will tell you."—LS, DNA, RG 45, Correspondence of David D. Porter, Mississippi Squadron, General Letters (Press). On the same day, Lt. Col. John A. Rawlins issued Special Orders No. 52 instructing Capt. Asher R. Eddy, q. m. at Memphis, to permit the naval surgeon to seize buildings owned by rebel sympathizers for a naval hospital suitable for five hundred patients.—Copies, DLC-USG, V, 26, 27; DNA, RG 393, Dept. of the Tenn., Special Orders.

1863, FEB. 21. Act. Rear Admiral David D. Porter to USG. "I enclose herewith a letter received from Pilot I. F. Morton who went up to Yazoo Pass."—LS, DNA, RG 45, Correspondence of David D. Porter, Mississippi Squadron, General Letters (Press).

1863, FEB. 22. Maj. Gen. John A. McClernand to USG. "I have the honor to report that a detachments of the 1st Ind. Cavalry, under, Lieut Col. H. D. Wood, engaged. a detachment of some 200. of Forest, Rebel, Cavalry, on the 19th Inst near Yazoo Pass,—killing 6. wounding. 3. and captureing, 15 of the enemy, and completely putting him to rout. No loss on our side. He also reports that the prospect of opening the pass is encourageing and that Genl. Washburn, expected to reach the Coldwater, with his transports tomorrow."—Copies (2), McClernand Papers, IHi; DNA, RG 393, 13th Army Corps, Letters Sent. *O.R.*, I, xxiv, part 1, 360–61.

1863, FEB. 22. Maj. Gen. John A. McClernand to USG. "According to the weekly report, of General. Gorman. ending Feby 14th 1863, thirty two men were discharged   The rapid drain upon the strength of the Army through this vent makes it important that all proper precautions should be practiced to restrain it within legitimate limits"—DfS, McClernand Papers, IHi; copies, *ibid.*; DNA, RG 393, 13th Army Corps, Letters Sent.

1863, FEB. 23. Maj. Gen. John A. McClernand to USG. "The resignations of Captain Cooley and Lieut's Willson and Bickford of the Illinois Mercantile Battery, having been accepted, the company is left without any Commissioned Officers. In view of these facts I would recommend that Lieut Patrick White of Co. B, 1st Regt Ill's Light Artillery be placed immediately in command of the company as acting Captain."—DfS, McClernand Papers, IHi; copies, *ibid.*; DNA, RG 393, 13th Army Corps, Letters Sent.

1863, FEB. 24. Maj. Gen. John A. McClernand to USG. "For the reasons stated in my last interview with you, I would urgently recom-

mend that the 3rd Ky. of the 2nd Brigade of the 9th. Division, and the
108th and 131st Ills of the 2nd Brigade, of the 10th, Division of this
Corps be sent to some healthy Garrison for duty, and three others in
better condition be sent to take their places. The fatal diseases to which
new troops are subject here make it important that old troops should
be assigned to this portion of the general field, as far as possible. The
impendency of active and important operations commends these suggestions to early and favorable consideration"—DfS, McClernand
Papers, IHi; copies, *ibid.*; DNA, RG 393, 13th Army Corps, Letters
Sent.

1863, FEB. 26. To Governor Richard Yates of Ill. "Respectfully
returned. The proceedings in this case were forwarded to Head
Quarters of the Army on the 21st inst. in pursuance of the 5th Section
of the act approved July 17. 1862. for the decision of the President"—
Copies (misdated Feb. 25), DLC-USG, V, 25; (dated Feb. 26) DNA,
RG 393, Dept. of the Tenn., Endorsements. Written on a letter of
Yates of Jan. 29 enclosing a letter of Sgt. John Meyer, Meyers, or
Myers, Co. G, 7th Ill., asking clemency.—*Ibid.* On Feb. 21, USG had
endorsed the court-martial record of Meyers. "Approved and respect-
fully forwarded to the Adjutant General of the Army, Washington,
D. C., for the decision of the President."—ES, *ibid.*, RG 153, MM 929.
On March 18, Judge Advocate Gen. Joseph Holt wrote to USG that
Congress had recently repealed the provision requiring the approval
of the president to sentences of this sort, but that commanding officers
might suspend such sentences, referring the cases to the president.—
LS, *ibid.*, RG 94, Compiled Service Records, 7th Ill. On June 1, USG
again endorsed the court-martial record. "The proceedings findings
and sentence in the foregoing case are confirmed, but as the law at the
time of the trial and conviction in this case was had prohibited the
carrying into execution of the sentence of death, until the same should
be approved by the President, the execution of the sentence in this case
is suspended in pursuance of the authority conferred by the 89th Article
of War, until the pleasure of the President of the United States, to
whom these proceedings are respectfully forwarded can be known"—
Copies, DLC-USG, V, 25; DNA, RG 393, Dept. of the Tenn., Endorsements. On Dec. 3, 1862, Meyers had shot and killed Capt. Henry W.
Allen, Co. G, 7th Ill., during an argument which followed the arrest of
another soldier for striking an elderly Negro. Meyers asked mercy

because he had been drunk. "Rum has been the cause of my ruin." *Ibid.*, RG 153, MM 929. On Feb. 10, 1864, President Abraham Lincoln endorsed the proceedings, "Sentence approved"—ES, *ibid.* Meyers was hanged on April 28. See *Diary of E. P. Burton, Surgeon 7th Reg. Ill., 3rd Brig., 2nd Div., 16 A. C.* (Des Moines, 1939), pp. 10–11.

1863, FEB. 26.   Maj. Robert Williams, AGO, to USG. "I am directed to request, that you will order Company "C" 2d U. S. Cavalry, to join the rest of the Regiment, now serving in the Army of the Potomac, so soon as you can dispense with their services. Efforts, are being made, to have all detached Companies sent to their Regiments as soon as possible."—LS, DNA, RG 393, Dept. of the Tenn., Unregistered Letters Received.

1863, FEB. 26.   Maj. Robert Williams, AGO, to USG. "Relieve 2nd Lieut Edgar M. Cullen Co "C" 1st U S. Infantry from duty with that company, to enable him to avail himself of a leave of absence granted him until further orders to command a regiment of Volunteers. If he is not with your command please inform this office if you know anything of his whereabouts."—ALS (telegram sent), DNA, RG 107, Telegrams Collected (Unbound); copy, *ibid.*, RG 94, Letters Sent. On March 1, Williams again telegraphed to USG. "Please acknowledge receipt of telegram from this office of the 26th ultimo, directing you to relieve 2nd Lieut Edgar M. Cullen Co "C" 1st U S. Infantry from duty with his Company to enable him to accept command of a regiment of Volunteers."—ALS (telegram sent), *ibid.*, RG 107, Telegrams Collected (Unbound); telegram received, *ibid.*

1863, FEB. 26.   Maj. John J. Mudd, 2nd Ill. Cav., Young's Point, to Lt. Col. John A. Rawlins. "On 14th inst I notified Brig Gen Veitch of my readiness to embark for this point under your order of   There being no suitable transports ready I was ordered to unite with Gen Quinby in an expedition against Majr Blythes command near Hernando, from which I returned without loss on the night of the 17th. On the 19th we embarked and were ready to move at 5 oclock P. M. but for want of orders from Q. M. Deptmt. remained there until 10½ oclock next day. Soon after starting the David Tatum (one of my transports) was forced to return to repair some damaged machinery. Having freight for Helena we were then delayed 48 hours for want of

action on part of the receiving Q. M. During this time the David
Tatum with two companies passed us without reporting   At Greenville Miss on morning of 23rd under orders of Gen Burbridge I
debarked and reported to Col Wright 6th Mo for a combined movement against Col Furgerson the particulars of which will be furnished
you by the officers commanding. I lost two men ~~captured to~~ supposed
to have been captured by the enemy   I arrived here on the 25th at
noon & reported to you in person."—ALS, DNA, RG 393, Dept. of
the Tenn., Letters Received.

1863, FEB. 26.   Nathaniel B. Baker, Iowa AG, to USG. "I have the
honor to request, that you cause copies of the orders of your department, accepting the resignation or discharging officers in Iowa Reg'ts
or Batteries from U. S. service, to be forwarded to me at the date of
their issue. Promotions are delayed, and the efficiency of Iowa Regiments consequently, much impaired by the nonreceipt of such orders."
—ALS, DNA, RG 393, Dept. of the Tenn., Letters Received. On
March 11, Lt. Col. John A. Rawlins wrote to Baker that his request
would be granted.—Copies, DLC-USG, V, 19, 30; DNA, RG 393,
Dept. of the Tenn., Letters Sent. On March 17, USG wrote to Governor Oliver P. Morton of Ind. "I have the honor herewith to transmit
list of resignations accepted of officers of Indiana troops in this Department from the 1st to and including the 15th day of March 1863"—
Copies, *ibid.* On the same date, USG sent similar letters to governors
of other states supplying troops to his army.—*Ibid.*

1863, FEB. 28.   USG endorsement. "Respectfully forwarded to Head
Quarters of the Army, Washington D. C. with the recommendation
that this officer be dishonorably dismissed the service."—Copies,
DLC-USG, V, 25; DNA, RG 393, Dept. of the Tenn., Endorsements.
Written on a letter of 1st Lt. James McDaniel, 31st Mo., resigning
because he opposed a war for the abolition of slavery.—*Ibid.* On Feb.
27, Maj. Gen. William T. Sherman had endorsed this letter. "The
whole theory of Army Discipline would be destroyed if subordinate
officers 'sworn to obey the orders of the President of the U. S. & officers
appointed over him' be permitted to reflect on the policy of the General
Government   This officer should be permitted to explain the terms of
this paper & if he adheres to the expressions used & is found engaged

in spreading them among his associates he merits condign punishment. This paper is referred to Gen. Grant that some rule may be adopted in such cases, with my entire disapproval of the application for resignation, or that he be mustered out or reduced to the ranks, for which we have no lawful authority—He merits severe punishment & I refer this paper that such punishment may be ordered as will be exemplary"— Copy, *ibid.*, 15th Army Corps, Endorsements.

1863, [*March* ?]. Surgeon Thomas F. Azpell, *City of Alton*, to USG requesting the assignment of two privates as nurses aboard the hospital boat.—ALS, DNA, RG 393, Dept. of the Tenn., Miscellaneous Letters Received. This undated letter was received by USG on March 6.— DLC-USG, V, 21; DNA, RG 393, Dept. of the Tenn., Register of Letters Received.

1863, March 2. Act. Rear Admiral David D. Porter to USG. "Will you oblige me by detailing 150 men, to report themselves to me here, for duty"—LS, DNA, RG 45, Correspondence of David D. Porter, Mississippi Squadron, General Letters (Press).

1863, March 4. USG endorsement. "Steamers leave here on alternate days regularly commencing on Mondays and omitting Sundays which Gen. McClernand can avail himself of. In addition to this there are trancient steamers leaving almost daily. It is not practicable to assign a steamer exclusively for the purpose indicated."—AE (signed by Lt. Col. John A. Rawlins), McClernand Papers, IHi. Written on a letter of March 3 from Lt. Col. Walter B. Scates to Rawlins. "I am directed by the Genl Commanding the 13th Army Corps to represent the necessity of a Steamer being placed at his control to enable him to communicate readily, from time to time, with that portion of his command at Helena, and, therefore, he requests that a small, swift, steamer may be assigned to him for that purpose."—ALS, *ibid.*

1863, March 4. Act. Rear Admiral David D. Porter to USG. "I enclose you letters just received from Lieut Comdr Le Roy Fitch giving some account of his doings on the Tennessee—also containing other news that may interest you."—LS, DNA, RG 94, War Records Office, Dept. of the Tenn. Porter enclosed copies of a letter of Feb. 9 from C.S.A. Col. B. F. Parker to Maj. Gen. Sterling Price reporting C.S.A.

sentiment in Mo., and letters of Feb. 24, 25 from Lt. Commander Le Roy Fitch to Capt. Alexander M. Pennock reporting operations of his five gunboats on the Tennessee River.—Copies, *ibid*. For the Fitch reports, see *O.R.* (Navy), I, xxiv, 44–46. The Parker letter (*ibid*., pp. 418–20), although filed with the Fitch reports, may have been transmitted separately in another letter of Porter to USG of the same date. "I enclose herewith copy of a letter found in a Rebel mail, which was seized on one of the boats up river, thinking it may be of interest to you."—LS, DNA, RG 45, Correspondence of David D. Porter, Mississippi Squadron, General Letters (Press).

1863, MARCH 5.   Col. William Hoffman to USG. "This paper is supposed to have come from Gen'l Grants command, and it is therefore respectfully returned to him with the request the list be made more complete. Besides giving a definite locality, it should show where the captures were made and what became of the prisoners, whether they were delivered to a responsible officer of the rebel Army or whether they were sent beyond our lines. Without this information such lists can be of no use in effecting exchanges"—Copy, DNA, RG 249, Letters Sent.

1863, MARCH 5.   Act. Rear Admiral David D. Porter to USG. "I send you a letter recd from Lieut Comdr Selfridge of the U. S. S. 'Conestoga' which may prove interesting to you."—LS, DNA, RG 94, War Records Office, Dept. of the Tenn. *O.R.*, I, xxiv, part 3, 85. The enclosed letter, discussing information from deserters that C.S.A. forces in Ark. might cross the Mississippi River, is printed *ibid*.; *O.R.* (Navy), I, xxiv, 446.

1863, MARCH 7.   USG endorsement. "Respectfully referred to Head Quarters of the Army, Washington, D. C."—ES, DNA, RG 94, ACP, 164H CB 1863. Written on a letter of March 3 from Brig. Gen. Isham N. Haynie to Lt. Col. John A. Rawlins submitting his resignation because of illness in his family.—ALS, *ibid*.

1863, MARCH 7.   Maj. Gen. Samuel R. Curtis to USG. "Lt. Col. Wm. H. Coyl has been badly wounded and is on sick leave. He belongs to 9th Iowa. He is not fit for field duty and would like to be on detached duty; he is a friend and I would like to have orders to report to me. He needs cheering up and recruiting. I am sending you all available troops. If Price rallies in Arkansas, I want them all back to pursue him."— Copy, DNA, RG 393, Dept. of the Mo., Letters Sent.

1863, March 8.   To Maj. Gen. John A. McClernand. "Mrs. Groves whose circumstances you probably know more about than I do, having been here, whilst she was yet living on her plantation at this point, has called on me for some of our abandoned horses or mules, having been stripped entirely of all stock. If it was practicable to send them from here I would give the order without any hesitation, and request that you will do so from the surplus, or disabled stock in your Corps."— Copy, DNA, RG 393, 13th Army Corps, Letters Received. See *O.R.*, I, xxiv, part 3, 10.

1863, March 9.   Maj. Ezra P. Jackson, 58th Ohio, to USG requesting that four men of his regt. be sent to Ohio on recruiting service.— Copy, DNA, RG 94, 58th Ohio, Letters Sent.

1863, March 10.   USG endorsement. "Respectfully forwarded to Head Quarters of the Army Washington D. C. and recommend that the Surgeon be dismissed the service."—Copies, DLC-USG, V, 25; DNA, RG 393, Dept. of the Tenn., Endorsements. Written on a letter of Capt. Thomas Hightower, 81st Ill., discussing the discharge of Private John K. Hightower, 81st Ill., by Surgeon Lewis Dyer.—*Ibid.* Dyer was dismissed for accepting money to discharge soldiers on certificates of disability by War Dept. Special Orders No. 158, April 6.— Copy, DLC-USG, V, 105. On April 18, USG endorsed another letter concerning Dyer. "Respectfully forwarded to Head Quarters of the Army, A recommendation for the discharge of Surgeon Dyer, was forwarded through these Head Quarters on the 10th day of March, 1863, and approved. I have ordered a Court of Inquiry in his case and would respectfully ask that no action be taken until the result of the Court may be received."—Copies, *ibid.*, V, 25; DNA, RG 393, Dept. of the Tenn., Endorsements. On April 14, Lt. Col. John A. Rawlins wrote to Maj. Gen. James B. McPherson. "You will immediately convene a Court of Inquiry, consisting of three officers of proper rank to examine into and investigate the charges against Surgeon L Dyer of the 81st Regiment, Illinois Infantry Volunteers of having received money

for procuring the discharge of a soldier belonging to said Regiment."
—Copies, DLC-USG, V, 19, 30; DNA, RG 393, Dept. of the Tenn.,
Letters Sent. On April 23, McPherson endorsed the proceedings of the
Court of Inquiry. "Respectfully forwarded for the consideration of
Brig Gen'l L. Thomas. Adjt Gen'l U. S. A. with the statement of
Surgeon Dyer enclosed. The order dismissing from the service Surgeon
Dyer has been issued, but the investigation by the court shows no moral
turpitude on the part of the Surgeon and I am pursuaded both from his
own statement and from information derived from reliable sources, that
while the Surgeon committed a very grave error, he really intended no
wrong and his whole conduct has otherwise been so exemplary and he
has discharged his duties so faithfully that I fully recommend that the
order dismissing him be revoked, and that he be reinstated."—Copy,
ibid., 17th Army Corps, Endorsements Sent. On May 1, Maj. Thomas
M. Vincent, AGO, wrote to USG. "I have respectfully to inform you
that previous to the receipt of your endorsement on papers of Surgeon
Dyer, 81st Ill. Vols. asking for suspension of action in his case until the
action of the Court should be received, he had been dismissed by Special
Orders. 158, current series, from this office."—Copies, DLC-USG, V,
105; DNA, RG 393, Dept. of the Tenn., Letters Received; *ibid.*, Military Div. of the Miss., War Dept. Correspondence Received. On May
27, Col. Edward D. Townsend, AGO, issued Special Orders No. 235
reinstating Dyer on McPherson's recommendation.—Copy, DLC-USG, V, 105.

1863, MARCH 11. Mary L. Smith, Madison Parish, La., to USG. "I
wrote to you a few days ago and also to Genl. Burbridge (who can
inform you who I am), but fearing the letters may not have reached
you, I now write again to renew my request for a passport to Versailles
Ky. I have two small children and one servant. I am entirely isolated
from all my relations, and ~~without~~ my little girl who is afflicted with
diseased spine, is now in such impaired health from continued chills
that I fear she will not live through the coming Season unless I can take
her to a healthier latitude. I am anxious to reach my father, Catesby
Barnes of Woodford Co. Ky. If you will grant a passport for me, my
two children and one servant, you will confer a great favor upon me
and a benefit upon my suffering child. Grant me also a separate passport for the safe return of the drivers and conveyances, ~~otherwise~~ to
be used in conveying me and my baggage to the River, otherwise I

shall not be able to procure them upon any terms. If convenient, let me have these passports immediately, as I am anxious to get out of the Country, before the high-water renders the roads impassable. . . . P. S. Direct my passports to Mrs Mary L. Smith on Mrs A. R. Hymes' plantation near Richmond."—ALS, McClernand Papers, IHi.

1863, MARCH 12. USG endorsement. "Respectfully forwarded to Head Quarters of the Army Washington D. C."—Copies, DLC-USG, V, 25; DNA, RG 393, Dept. of the Tenn., Endorsements. Written on a letter of Col. Warren L. Lothrop, 1st Mo. Light Art., concerning lts. for the 2nd battalion.—*Ibid.* Secretary of War Edwin M. Stanton later endorsed this letter. "Respectfully returned to Maj. Genl. Grant, Comdg Dept of the Tennessee, with authority to have mustered into service the extra commissioned and non com'd Officers, for 6 Gun Batteries. In the case of 4 gun Batteries the extra officers and non com'd. officers cannot be allowed. It seems strange that Genl Orders No. 126, of 1862 has been so long reaching the regiment."—Copies, *ibid.*

1863, MARCH 13. USG endorsement. "Respectfully forwarded to Head Quarters of the Army with the request that some solution be made to the difficult question, 'When is an officer entitled to pay?' Paymasters generally decides that they must be mustered in by an officer of the Regular Army after each promotion, and cannot under any circumstances receive pay before formally accepting their new positions. This decision works great hardships upon many officers, who are promoted, and do not know that they have anything to do but assume their new duties. I would suggest that an order be published dating an officers pay from the time he can show that he assumed the duties of his office."—Copies, DLC-USG, V, 25; DNA, RG 393, Dept. of the Tenn., Endorsements. Written on a letter of Maj. Gen. William T. Sherman inquiring about pay for officers.—*Ibid.* On Feb. 23, Brig. Gen. Isaac F. Quinby wrote to Lt. Col. John A. Rawlins about the same matter.—Copy, *ibid.*, 15th Army Corps, District of Corinth, Letters Sent. USG added an undated endorsement to this letter. "Respectfully forwarded to Head Quarters of the Army, with the request that an early decision be made on the matter of complaint. Almost every regiment has officers who have been promoted from the ranks and never dreamed of the necessity of a muster out, and again in being necessary. By the decision of some Army Paymasters they are deprived of their

Pay. This seems wrong."—Copies, DLC-USG, V, 25; DNA, RG 393, Dept. of the Tenn., Endorsements. AGO General Orders No. 48, Feb. 25, required all soldiers to be "mustered in by the proper officer" before receiving pay.

1863, March 13. Col. George P. Ihrie to Maj. Gen. John A. McClernand. "I am directed by the Major Genrl. commanding this Department to write you the following:—If, on inquiry into, and examinations of, the statements of Charles Warfield, (a colored man) who represents he 'has from twenty-five to thirty bales of cotton, which he wishes to sell,' you find them to be facts, you are authorized to give him a permit to sell, on the condition, that they are sold to no cotton speculator this side of Memphis."—ALS, McClernand Papers, IHi. On March 14, McClernand wrote to Lt. Col. John A. Rawlins. "Having caused the claim of the negro Charles Warfield to a quantity of cotton in this vicinity to be investigated, and finding that it does not belong to him, but is 'abandoned' by its owners, I have ordered it to be searched for and if found, seized and turned over to the Q. M. as forfeited to the U. S."—DfS, *ibid.*; copy, DNA, RG 393, 13th Army Corps, Letters Sent.

1863, March [13]. Brig. Gen. Francis P. Blair, Jr., to USG. "Respectfully forwarded to Genl. Grant. I have already made the representations regarding this regiment and request that it be ordered to join my command."—ES, DNA, RG 393, Dept. of the Tenn., Letters Received. Written on a letter of March 12 from Lt. Col. John H. Hammond to Blair warning that the 27th Mo. might be assigned to Maj. Gen. John A. McClernand.—ALS, *ibid.* On March 13, Lt. Col. John A. Rawlins issued Special Orders No. 72 assigning the 27th Mo. to Blair's brigade.—ADf, *ibid.*; copies, *ibid.*, Special Orders; DLC-USG, V, 26, 27.

1863, March 14. Thomas L. Van Fossen, Erin Plantation, Lake Providence, La., to USG. "I have on my Plantation between three & four Hundred bales of Cotton most of it not yet Ginned which I wish to Send to Memphis for Sale & respectfuly request your permission for doing So—my intention being in after doing so to go north with my family to live untill this Cruel war is ended   I am from New York Genl & Every blood relation I. have on Earth save one live north—

I have never done one act against the union nor have I in any way contribution to aid the southern Confederacy. I have lost nearly all my negros (some 85) 40 head of Cattle, 33 mules & I have been robbed by some soldiers of the 11th Ill & 10th Ohio Battery of nearly all my clothing as well as my wife   in short we have been nearly ruined & the proceeds of my cotton is all I have to depend upon for the Support of my family during the war. For the truth of the above I will refer you to any of the respectable Planters living here who I think will Substantiate all I have said. Should you have the Kindness to grant my request please Send the permit care of Maj Genl McPherson at this Place & receive in advance the grateful thanks of"—Copy, DNA, RG 217, Third Auditor, Southern Claims Commission, Carroll Parish, La. On the same day, Maj. Gen. James B. McPherson favorably endorsed this letter to USG.—Copy, *ibid*. USG added an undated endorsement. "Left to the discretion of Gen McPherson"—Copy, *ibid*. On April 24, McPherson again endorsed this letter. "Mr Van Forsen has permission to go to Memphis Tenn with his Cotton & Establish his claim before the proper Authority at that place"—Copy, *ibid*. See Frank W. Klingberg, *The Southern Claims Commission* (Berkeley and Los Angeles, 1955), pp. 94–95.

1863, March 15.   Maj. Thomas M. Vincent, AGO, to USG. "I have the honor to acknowledge receipt of the letter of Lieut James Oates Co "K" 9th Illinois Vols, forwarded thro' your Head Quarters February 26, 1863, asking leave of absence   In reply I am directed to inform you that the case has been submitted to the General in Chief and returned by him 'not approved' "—Copies, DLC-USG, V, 93; DNA, RG 393, Military Div. of the Miss., War Dept. Correspondence.

1863, March 17.   Lt. Col. John A. Rawlins to A. R. Whitney, St. Louis. "Your letter of date March 8th 1863 has been received. The enclosure it contained and which is herewith returned to you shows that you are an improper person to be within the lines of the army. I am therefore directed by the Major General Commanding the Department to notify you that if at any time hereafter you are found within the limits of this Department you will be arrested and confined in the Military prison at Alton, Ill, during the war"—Copies, DLC-USG, V, 19, 30; DNA, RG 393, Dept. of the Tenn., Letters Sent.

1863, MARCH 18. Brig. Gen. Lorenzo Thomas to USG. "The secy of war directs that you give orders requiring the Comdr of each Regiment Battery Independent Battalion & Company to prepare immediately duplicate lists of desertions now absent from their commands & send both to the Provost Marshal Genl War Department Washington one direct the other through usual Military Channels here here after similar reports will be made the first day of each Month"—Telegram received, DNA, RG 393, Dept. of the Tenn., Telegrams Received; copies (dated March 19), *ibid.*, Hd. Qrs. Correspondence; (dated March 18) *ibid.*, RG 94, Letters Sent; (dated March 19) DLC-USG, V, 5, 8, 24, (dated March 18) 94. On March 23, Lt. Col. John A. Rawlins issued General Orders No. 20 implementing these orders from Washington.—Copies, *ibid.*, V, 13, 14, 95; DNA, RG 393, Dept. of the Tenn., General and Special Orders.

1863, MARCH 18. Maj. Gen. James B. McPherson to USG. "Respectfully ford to Maj Gen U. S. Grant and approved on condition that Mr. J J Shermard takes the oath of allegiance to the United States and remove North with his family to pursue a true and loyal course during this present war"—Copy, DNA, RG 92, Letters Received by Capt. Asher R. Eddy Relating to Cotton. Written on a letter of March 17 from J. J. Shermard, Lake Providence, to McPherson. "I have been informed that I must apply to you for permission to go to Memphis with my family and property. I own 312 bales Cotton—I have never aided nor abetted the Confederats Except in sofar . . . I was obliged to countenance there doings to save my neck."—Copy, *ibid.* USG added an undated endorsement. "Genl McPherson is authori[zed] to give Permits in all cases when he deems them meritorious within his Command"—Copy, *ibid.* Shermard subsequently shipped 229 bales of cotton to Memphis.—*Ibid.*, First Special Agency, Book Records.

1863, MARCH 19. To George W. Graham, master of transportation. "Col R. V. Montague is authorized to bring in his crop of cotton, six hundred bales, including 225 bales on the plantation of Mr Parham, to the River, and ship the same to Memphis on his own account"—Copies (3), McClernand Papers, IHi; DNA, RG 393, 13th Army Corps, Letters Received. On March 26, Maj. Gen. John A. McClernand endorsed a report affirming the loyalty of both W. I. Parham and

Robert V. Montague. "Respectfully referred to Dept. Hd. Qrs. as a report of facts : with the explanation, that having had the cotton hauled to the landing, in ignorance of Mr Montague's claim, as property abandoned and lawfully forfeited to the U. S., I was unwilling that he should appropriate it except upon proofs."—AES, McClernand Papers, IHi. On March 29, Lt. Col. John A. Rawlins endorsed this report. "Respectfully returned.—The action of Maj. Gen'l McClernand, in this matter, is approved by the Maj. Gen. Commanding"—ES, *ibid.* On March 22, USG recommended Montague as "a Southern man of known loyalty."—Copy, DNA, RG 366, Box 369.

1863, March 20. Maj. Thomas M. Vincent, AGO, to USG. "Respectfully referred to the Comdg General, Troops in front of Vicksburgh—"—ES, McClernand Papers, IHi. Written on a letter of Feb. 8 from Col. George W. Neely, 131st Ill., Young's Point, to President Abraham Lincoln. "Excuse me for troubling you with things of so little importance whilest you have the interest of the destressed condition of our Government to look after at a time when you are greatly annoyed to no doubt but hear my short statement of my case Last August I went to work in southern Ills to raise a regiment of *Infry Vols* & soon succeeded and was ordred to report to *Gen Mc*Clernard at Memphis Tenn and did so but before I left I was threatened by Wm H Green to a friend that I had to report to J A *Mc*Clernard & I should be superseeded for the active part I had taken in the Election & found out that he had been in communication with *Gen Mc*Clenard   I was not treated wright about my guns but I shal not speak of it hear   I went to vicksburgh & Arcansa Post without any chance to get accoutrements for my guns but on our landing at this point oposit Vicksburgh I was accosted by one of *Gen. Mc*s friend (*Gen* Smith) on the subject of polatics but I declined an argument from caution but he finally bursted out in stranes like this   first I wish to god that every D—d Republican was in Hell yes in the deepest lavy of Hell and continued in like stranes for some time & the nex day I was put under arrest by the order of *Gen Mc.* as the charges stated for one of my men having fired his peace in my presents which was partly trew   the peace was not fired in my presents but was fired & I had punished the offender & the same thing was being done hourly from one end of the lines to the other but I have been confined to the narrow limits of my quarters for

2 weeks & have no hope of a hearing and as I am well satisfied for no other reason than my polatics not suiting them   I say from all that I have seen and learned this part of the army is is fighting for Political glory and some of the *Gens* like W H Green would save the Democratic party if it sunk the Government in that lavy spoken of by *Gen* Smith And if you can save me from this Political Hell by putting me any where elce commanding a Post fight Gurrillas or Judge Advocate & if nothin elce a Discharge, I am in for the war under the Administration but not under a Democratic political Tyrant"—ALS, *ibid*. On April 2, Lt. Col. John A. Rawlins endorsed this letter to Maj. Gen. John A. McClernand. —ES, *ibid*.

1863, M ARCH 21.   Brig. Gen. Lorenzo Thomas to USG. "I have respectfully to call your attention to paragraph 16. S. O. 121. Current series War Department directing the enlisted men of the 3 Cavalry, 4th Artillery, and General Service, now serving with the 1st Missouri Light Artillery, to be transferred to the regular troops serving in the Department of the Tennessee, and to inform you that in the execution of that order you will be guided by your own judgement in view of the interests of the service—"—LS, DNA, RG 393, Dept. of the Tenn., Miscellaneous Letters Received.

1863, M ARCH 23.   President Abraham Lincoln to USG. "This is to introduce an old acquaintance and friend, Thomas Lewis, of Springfield, Illinois. He will make his business known, which, in fact, is not known to me. Any kindness shown him, not inconsistent with the regulations under which you are acting, will be appreciated by me."—*St. Louis Daily Globe*, Dec. 19, 1873. On March 21, Lincoln had written to Secretary of the Treasury Salmon P. Chase. "Please see and hear my old acquaintance and friend, Thomas Lewis."—*Ibid*. Thomas Lewis, of Springfield, Ill., at various times shoemaker, merchant, banker, lawyer, and newspaperman, published these letters in answer to William H. Herndon's charge that Lewis's testimony regarding Lincoln's commitment to Christianity was untrustworthy: "Mr. Lincoln detested this man, I know."—*Ibid*., Dec. 14, 1873.

1863, M ARCH 25.   USG endorsement. "Respectfully referred to Maj. Gen. McPherson, who, if the facts are found as stated, may restore the amount of cotton lost and grant authority for the cotton and family to go to Memphis but not to be sold until it reaches there."—Stan. V. Henkels, Catalogue No. 1439, Jan. 31, 1930, No. 49; American Art Association, Jan. 21–22, 1926, No. 85. On April 5, Maj. Gen. James B. McPherson endorsed this letter. "I have investigated this case and as far as I can learn the facts are as stated."—*Ibid.* Probably written on a letter of March 24 from Mrs. C. A. Blackburn, Lake Providence, La., to USG. "Permit me to claim your attention for *one* moment. I shall be brief—I have been deprived of *all* means of support, by the Federal Army—My gin house, containing seventy (70) bales of cotton has been burned—And *now* I am inundated by the cut in the Levee at Lake Providence—I am anxious to go up to Memphis, but have no means of *living* after I get there—My object in addressing you, is to ask that you will restore to me the same amount of cotton as that which was burned, or any *portion* of it, you may think proper.—I have proof positive that it was burned by a Federal in revenge for some *fancied* injury —I think you can conscientiously, without determent to your honor, bravery or humanity, replace this cotton out of the abundance which has been taken from this immediate neighborhood—Neither yourself nor the Federal government could miss this small lot of cotton—Yet it would bring bread to myself and children—When I say that I am a widow with seven children, it is *all* that need be said to a man of your known generosity, and kindness of heart—You are a husband and a father   God grant your wife and little ones may never be placed in a similar situation—I spoke to Genl. McPherson upon this subject   he thought you would without hesitancy replace the cotton—Nothing but dire necessity could induce me to make this appeal, therefore I beg you will give it your earliest attention—"—ALS, ICarbS.

1863, MARCH 26. USG endorsement. "Respectfully forwarded to Head Quarters of the Army, Washington, D. C., for the decision of the President."—ES, DNA, RG 153, MM 189. Written on the proceedings of the court-martial of Sgt. Thomas M. Griffith, 11th Ill. On March 24–26, USG similarly endorsed courts-martial proceedings of seven other non-commissioned officers of Co. G, 11th Ill.—Copies, DLC-USG, V, 25; DNA, RG 393, Dept. of the Tenn., Endorsements. These men had refused to serve under 2nd Lt. Louis C. Blake because they believed themselves entitled to elect their officers. On April 20, USG endorsed a petition of April 4 of John B. Carpenter and other citizens of Effingham, Ill., to President Abraham Lincoln for the pardon of Griffith and Sgt. William Wilcox, 11th Ill. "Respectfully forwarded to Head Quarters, of the Army, Washington, D, C., The proceedings of the Court Martial in the cases, of Thomas M. Griffith, and William Wilcox, sergt's, Co. G. 11th. Ills. Vols. were forwarded to the Head Quarters of the Army, Washington, D. C., on the 26th day of March, 1863, for the decision of the President."—Copies, *ibid.* Later, seven officers who had served on the court-martial prepared a petition for clemency for Griffith, which USG endorsed on Oct. 7. "Proceedings Findings and Sentence confirmed, but the Court having recommended the accused to the clemency of His Excellency the President of the United States, and the Major General Commanding the Army Corps to which said Man belongs also having recommended a mitigation of said sentence which recommendations are approved, the execution of said sentence is hereby suspended under the authority conferred by the 89th Article of War until the pleasure of the President, to whom these proceedings are respectfully forwarded, is known"—ES, *ibid.*, RG 153, MM 189. Identical petitions for the other convicted men received identical endorsements on the same day.—ES, *ibid.* On Feb. 15, 1864, Lincoln endorsed with the word "Pardon" a report of the case prepared on Oct. 26, 1863, by Judge Advocate Gen. Joseph Holt.—AES, *ibid.*

1863, MARCH 26. USG endorsement. "Lieut Dickey entered the service at the breaking out of the rebellion : served as Sergeant Major in the 11th Ill. Vols. during the three months enlistment, and at the experation of that time was appointed Adjutant of the Regiment : was in the Battle of Fort Donnelson, and upon Col. W. H. L Wallaces promotion to a Brigadier General, he was promoted to an Actg Asst. Adjut. General on his staff, and served in this capacity at Shiloh (Battle of) where Gen. Wallace fell mortally wounded. Upon Brig. Gen Judahs being assigned to the command of the 1st. Division of the Army of the Tennessee he was detailed for duty as Acting Asst. Gen. Adjt on his Staff and was by Gen. Judah recommended for appointment as A. A. G. and since Gen Judah was relieved from command in this Army, Lt Dickey has served in the capacity of Asst Adjt Gen and Regimental Adjutant as the necessities of the service required, and has ever given satisfaction. He is well acquainted with the duties of an Asst Adjt. Genl. in the Field : is a brave, intelligent, and accomplished officer, energetic and honest in the support of his country in arms. I therefore earnestly recommend, and urge his appointment as applied for. There are no A. A. G's in this Department unassigned."—Copies, DLC-USG, V, 25; DNA, RG 393, Dept. of the Tenn., Endorsements. Written on a letter of March 20 of Brig. Gen. Thomas E. G. Ransom asking that 1st Lt. Cyrus E. Dickey, 11th Ill., be appointed capt. and asst. adjt. gen.—*Ibid.* Dickey was so appointed to rank from May 1.

1863, MARCH 26. John Gager, Memphis, to USG offering large rafts of white pine for use in the Vicksburg campaign.—ALS, DNA, RG 393, Dept. of the Tenn., Letters Received.

1863, MARCH 27. USG endorsement. "Respectfully forwarded to Head Quarters of the Army, Washington D. C., and recommend that chaplain Peterson of the 103. Ill. Vols. be dismissed the service for misrepresentation and falsehood and absence without leave, see enclosed papers."—Copies, DLC-USG, V, 25; DNA, RG 393, Dept. of the Tenn., Endorsements. Written on communications forwarded by Maj. Gen. Stephen A. Hurlbut vindicating Thomas Robb of Ill. against charges preferred by Chaplain William S. Peterson, 103rd Ill.—*Ibid.* Peterson was dismissed as of April 17, 1863. On July 9, USG endorsed letters and petitions asking the reinstatement of Peterson with a reaffirmation of his earlier recommendation based upon the papers forwarded earlier.—Copies, *ibid.*

1863, MARCH 28. To Col. Addison S. Norton, provost marshal. "Dr. Wm J. Brown, is hereby released from arrest and suspicion for anything past. I am entirely satisfied not only of the Drs. loyalty but of his patriotism."—ALS, Kay Collection, NjP. On March 11, Lt. Col. John A. Rawlins prepared a pass for Dr. William J. Brown.—Julia Sweet Newman, List No. 229 [*1968*].

1863, MARCH 28. Maj. Gen. John A. McClernand, Milliken's Bend, to USG. "The writer of the within note is represented to be a young man of education and parts. He has been the subject of numerous letters to me expressing great solicitude for his welfare. His father I knew. I have, with others, reccommanded him for a place in the Navy, for which he has a preferance, but so far without result. If you could in any way promote him, I would be pleased, or if you choose to send him to me under a detail, I will try to apply his capabilities, to the best advantage."—DfS, McClernand Papers, IHi; copies, *ibid.*; DNA, RG 393, 13th Army Corps, Letters Sent. The enclosed letter was written by Private P. C. Koscialowski, 106th Ill., who remained at that rank through the war.—Copies, *ibid.*

1863, March 28. Col. Lewis B. Parsons to USG. "I have been absent for a few days and on my return I learn an urgent request has been made for the Tow boat 'Eagle' and I understand Col. Allen has telegraphed she must be released. . . . Can you not order the 'Eagle' at once discharged and also all other Tow boats required on the Ohio or Miss for towing? I wish the 'Eagle' and other tow boats would bring *up all the barges they possibly can* and transfer them to Capt Woolfolk at Cairo as it is getting extremely difficult to get coal owing to failure to return barges"—ALS (press), Parsons Papers, IHi. On April 6, Lt. Col. John A. Rawlins endorsed this letter. "Respectfully referred to Lt Col C. A. Reynolds chief Quartermaster, who will release all the tow boats that can be possibly dispensed with, in compliance with the within request."—Copies, DLC-USG, V, 25; DNA, RG 393, Dept. of the Tenn., Endorsements.

1863, March 30. To President Abraham Lincoln requesting permission for Col. George P. Ihrie to raise a brigade in Mo. and Ill. "for duty in the Territories of Utah & New Mexico & Arizona for the purpose of squelching out Polygamy, quieting hostile Indians and watching the French in Mexico and to return home through Texas."—DNA, RG 108, Register of Letters Received. On May 1, Maj. Thomas M. Vincent, AGO, wrote to USG. "I have the honor to acknowledge the receipt of your letter of the 30th ult., recommending that Colonel George P. Ihrie, A. D. C. be permitted to raise a Brigade, for duty on the frontier, in Utah, New Mexico & Arizona. In reply I am directed to inform you that the same has been submitted to the General-in-Chief, & returned by him, endorsed, 'Not Approved' "—Copies, *ibid.*, RG 94, Staff Papers, Ihrie; *ibid.*, RG 393, Military Div. of the Miss., Special Orders Received; DLC-USG, V, 105.

1863, March. USG endorsement. "There has been no order or direction given, that would change the authority granted Genl McClernand, to bring from Helena the Cavalry mentioned herein."—Copy, McClernand Papers, IHi. Written on a letter of March 12 from Lt. Col. Walter B. Scates to Lt. Col. John A. Rawlins. "In pursuance of Genl. Grant's order, the 6th Mo. Cavalry were ordered from Helena to this place. But for want of sufficient transportation, a small part of the command, with a portion of transportation were left. Genl. Prentiss now refuses to send it forward, I am informed, on the ground that the regiment will soon return. If this is not in accordance with the plans of Genl. Grant, the Major Genl. Commanding desires that transportation be given to the remainder, so that it may rejoin the Regiment." —Copies (3), *ibid.*; DNA, RG 393, 13th Army Corps, Letters Sent.

1863, [*March*].   Maj. Gen. William T. Sherman to USG. "I know that Col Cockrell is a man of the best character, heart, and influence. He is a good friend of our cause and to remove him from his Hotel would be *very harsh*—I beg of you to make an order that the Gayoso House be not taken for any purpose. It is absolutely needed, and will be for years as a hotel. If you will make such an order, please send it to me that I may have the pleasure to transmit it."—AES, DNA, RG 393, Dept. of the Tenn., Letters Received. Written on a letter of March 3 from D. Cockrill, Gayoso House, Memphis, to Sherman stating "there has been much talk here lately of taking the Gayoso House for Hospital purposes. . . ."—ALS, *ibid.*

1863, [March–April].   To Maj. Gen. John A. McClernand. On Oct. 29, McClernand wrote to Col. Dick Robinson. "Failing to find Genl. Grant's letter to me relative to you; at your request, I undertake, substantially, to reproduce its contents, as far as I am able at this distance of time. ~~The~~ Gen Grant's letter was delivered to me about the last of March or the first of April of the present year. ~~It~~ and stated that you had suffered ~~considerably~~ severely at the hands of rebels, and that he desired me to facilitate you in securing some indemnity therefor. Learning from you or from the letter, that you had a number of promissory notes executed by debtors living in La, for property sold by you to them which you wished to use in purchasing cotton or other property, I directed that the notes should be identified by being scheduled, and that you should not be prevented from converting them into Cotton, or other personal property, by fair negociation with persons residing within the limits of my military lines. Whether ~~the latter~~

branch of my instructions in these particulars was carried into effect out, I am unable to state, as I left for the Mississippi Campaign resulting in the fall of Vicksburg about the same time; but my impression is that they were at least verbally communicated to Ca you. The promissory notes, of course, were left in your hands. I was at Milliken's Bend when you handed me Genl. Grant's letter; also, another letter from Genl. Burbridge & Col Landrum of Ky. commending you to me as a loyal man & worthy citizen . . . P. S. I was at Milliken's Bend La. when Genl. Grant's letter was handed to me."—ADfS, McClernand Papers, IHi.

Index

All letters written by USG of which the text was available for use in this volume are indexed under the names of the recipients. The dates of these letters are included in the index as an indication of the existence of text. Abbreviations used in the index are explained on pp. xvi–xx. Individual regts. are indexed under the names of the states in which they originated.